2003-2004

EVANGELICAL SUNDAY SCHOOL LESSON COMMENTARY

FIFTY-SECOND ANNUAL VOLUME
Based on the
Evangelical Bible Lesson Series

Editorial Staff

Lance Colkmire — Editor
Tammy Hatfield — Editorial Assistant
Bill George — Editor in Chief
Daniel F. Boling — General Director of Publications

Lesson Exposition Writers

Jerald Daffe	Homer G. Rhea
Carl R. Hobbs	R.B. Thomas
Rodney Hodge	Richard Keith Whitt

Published by

PATHWAY PRESS   Cleveland, Tennessee

* To contact the editor, call 423-478-7597.
* To place an order, call 1-800-553-8506.

Lesson treatments in the *Evangelical Sunday School Lesson Commentary* for 2003-2004 are based upon the outlines of the Pentecostal-Charismatic Bible Lesson Series prepared by the Pentecostal-Charismatic Curriculum Commission.

Copyright 2003

PATHWAY PRESS, Cleveland, Tennessee
ISBN: 0-87148-225-8

Printed in the United States of America

TABLE OF CONTENTS

Introduction to the 2003-2004 Commentary 7
Using the 2003-2004 Commentary 8
Golden Text Homily Writers 9
Scripture Texts Used in Lesson Exposition 10
Scripture Texts Used in Golden Text Homilies 12
Acknowledgments 13
Lesson Cycle (1999-2006) 14

FALL QUARTER LESSONS
Introduction to Fall Quarter Lessons 16

UNIT ONE THEME—JUDGMENT AND COMFORT (ISAIAH)
September 7, God's Remedy for Rebellion 17
September 14, Judgment and the Savior 27
September 21, Way of Redemption 36
September 28, God Comforts His People 45
October 5, The Servant Savior 54
October 12, The Sin-Bearing Savior 63
October 19, True Fasting Brings Restoration 72
October 26, A Glorious Future 81

UNIT TWO THEME—VALUES AND PRIORITIES
November 2, Devotion to God 90
November 9, Foundation for Family Living 101
November 16, Responsibility to the Church 110
November 23, Our Responsibility to the World 119
November 30, Invest in Eternal Treasure 128

WINTER QUARTER LESSONS
Introduction to Winter Quarter Lessons 136

UNIT ONE THEME—1 AND 2 CORINTHIANS
December 7, Promote Unity in the Church 137
December 14, Dealing With Moral Problems 146
December 21, God With Us (Christmas) 156
December 28, Living Right in a Wrong World 165
January 4, Spiritual Gifts, Unity and Love 175
January 11, Ministry Principles 185
January 18, Christian Authority 194

UNIT TWO THEME—LESSER-KNOWN PEOPLE OF THE BIBLE
January 25, Nathan, Reprover and Couselor 203
February 1, Micaiah, Devoted to Truthfulness 214
February 8, Jehoiada, Righteous Statesman 224

February 15, Huldah, Prophetess of Encouragement 234
February 22, Three Notable Disciples 244
February 29, Ministry Colleagues of Paul 255

SPRING QUARTER LESSONS
Introduction to Spring Quarter Lessons 266

UNIT ONE THEME—STUDIES FROM JEREMIAH AND LAMENTATIONS
March 7, Called to Serve 267
March 14, The One True God 275
March 21, Messages From the Potter's House 284
March 28, The New Covenant 293
April 4, Hope in God 302
April 11, Resurrection Hope (Easter) 311

UNIT TWO THEME—OUT OF EXILE (EZRA AND NEHEMIAH)
April 18, Return From Exile 320
April 25, Overcoming Opposition 329
May 2, Returning to God's Way 339
May 9, Knowing and Doing God's Will 348
May 16, Leadership During Crises 357
May 23, Repentance Brings Spiritual Renewal 366
May 30, Promise of the Spirit (Pentecost) 375

SUMMER QUARTER LESSONS
Introduction to Summer Quarter Lessons 384

UNIT ONE THEME—PRISON EPISTLES (EPHESIANS, PHILIPPIANS,
COLOSSIANS, PHILEMON)
June 6, Spiritual Blessings in Christ 385
June 13, Transforming Power of Grace 396
June 20, Unity and Edification 405
June 27, Advancement of the Gospel 414
July 4, Imitating Christ 423
July 11, The Preeminence of Christ 432
July 18, Practical Instructions for Living 442
July 25, Christian Character 452

UNIT TWO THEME—REVIVAL AND RENEWAL
August 1, Confession and Repentance 461
August 8, Hearing and Obeying 472
August 15, Renewal Through Spiritual Disciplines 482
August 22, Renewal Through Praise 492
August 29, Passion for Christ 501

INTRODUCTION TO THE 2003-2004 COMMENTARY

The *Evangelical Sunday School Lesson Commentary* contains in a single volume a full study of the Sunday school lessons for the months beginning with September 2003 and running through August 2004. The 12 months of lessons draw from both the Old Testament and the New Testament in an effort to provide balance and establish relationship between these distinct but inspired writings. The lessons in this 2003-2004 volume are drawn from the fifth year of a seven-year cycle, which will be completed in August 2006. (The cycle is printed in full on page 14 of this volume.)

The lessons for the *Evangelical Commentary* are based on the Evangelical Bible Lesson Series Outlines, prepared by the Pentecostal-Charismatic Curriculum Commission. (The Pentecostal-Charismatic Curriculum Commission is a member of the National Association of Evangelicals.) The lessons in this volume are drawn from the Old and New Testaments; and taken together with the other annual volumes of lessons in the cycle, they provide a valuable commentary on a wide range of Biblical subjects. Each quarter is divided into two units of study.

The 2003-2004 commentary is the work of a team of Christian scholars and writers who have developed the volume under the supervision of Pathway Press. All the major writers, introduced on the following pages, represent a team of ministers committed to a strictly Evangelical interpretation of the Scriptures. The guiding theological principles of this commentary are expressed in the following statement of faith:

1. WE BELIEVE the Bible to be the inspired, the only infallible, authoritative Word of God.

2. WE BELIEVE that there is one God, eternally existing in three persons: Father, Son, and Holy Spirit.

3. WE BELIEVE in the deity of our Lord Jesus Christ, in His virgin birth, in His sinless life, in His miracles, in His vicarious and atoning death through His shed blood, in His bodily resurrection, in His ascension to the right hand of the Father, and in His personal return in power and glory.

4. WE BELIEVE that for the salvation of lost and sinful men, personal reception of the Lord Jesus Christ and regeneration by the Holy Spirit are absolutely essential.

5. WE BELIEVE in the present ministry of the Holy Spirit by whose cleansing and indwelling the Christian is enabled to live a godly life.

6. WE BELIEVE in the personal return of the Lord Jesus Christ.

7. WE BELIEVE in the resurrection of both the saved and the lost— they that are saved, unto the resurrection of life; and they that are lost, unto the resurrection of damnation.

8. WE BELIEVE in the spiritual unity of believers in our Lord Jesus Christ.

USING THE COMMENTARY

The *Evangelical Sunday School Lesson Commentary* for 2003-2004 is presented to the reader with the hope that it will become his or her weekly companion through the months ahead.

The fall quarter 2003 continues a seven-year cycle of lessons which will be completed with the summer quarter 2006. The 28 quarters of studies, divided into two or more units each, are drawn from both the Old and New Testaments. Also a number of studies will be topical in nature as attention is focused on contemporary issues. A complete listing of the themes that will be included in the seven-year cycle is printed on page 14 of this volume.

Quarterly unit themes for the 2003-2004 volume are as follows:

• Fall Quarter—Unit One: "Judgment and Comfort (Isaiah)"; Unit Two: "Values and Priorities"

• Winter Quarter—Unit One: "1 and 2 Corinthians"; Unit Two: "Lesser-Known People of the Bible"

• Spring Quarter—Unit One: "Studies From Jeremiah and Lamentations"; Unit Two: "Out of Exile (Ezra and Nehemiah)"

• Summer Quarter—Unit One: "Prison Epistles (Ephesians, Philippians, Colossians, Philemon)"; Unit Two: "Revival and Renewal"

The lesson sequence used in this volume is prepared by the Pentecostal-Charismatic Curriculum Commission.

The specific material used in developing each lesson is written and edited under the guidance of the editorial staff of Pathway Press.

STUDY TEXT: At the opening of each week's lesson, you will see printed the study text. These references point out passages of Scripture that are directly related to the lesson, and it is advisable for you to read each one carefully before beginning the lesson study.

TIME and PLACE: A time and place is given for most lessons. Where there is a wide range of opinions regarding the exact time or place, the printed New Testament works of Merrill C. Tenney and Old Testament works of Samuel J. Schultz are used to provide the information.

PRINTED TEXT and CENTRAL TRUTH: The printed text is the body of Scripture designated each week for verse-by-verse study in the classroom. Drawing on the study text the teacher delves into this printed text, exploring its content with the students. Although the printed text contains different insights for each teacher, the central truth states the single unifying principle that the expositors attempted to clarify in each lesson.

DICTIONARY: A dictionary, which attempts to bring pronunciation and clarification to difficult words or phrases, is included with many lessons. Pronunciations are based on the phonetic system used by Field Enterprises Educational Corporation of Chicago and New York in *The World Book Encyclopedia*. Definitions are generally based on *The Pictorial Bible Dictionary*, published by Zondervan Publishing Company, Grand Rapids, Michigan.

EXPOSITION and LESSON OUTLINE: The heart of this commentary—and probably the heart of the teacher's instruction each week—is the exposition of the printed text. This exposition material is preceded by a lesson outline, which indicates how the material is to be divided for study. These lesson outlines are not exhaustive but, rather, provide a skeleton for the teacher to build upon.

GOLDEN TEXT HOMILY: The golden text homily for each week is a brief reflection on that single verse. As the word *homily* implies, it is a discourse or sermon on a particular point. The homily may often be used effectively to help apply the lesson to life.

SENTENCE SERMONS: Two or more sentence sermons—popular and pithy single-line thoughts on the central truth of the lesson—are included each week.

EVANGELISM APPLICATION: The evangelism application relates the general theme of the week's lesson to the ongoing task of evangelism. The theme of the lesson (but not necessarily of the lesson text) is used to make this application. At times the emphasis of the section bears on direct evangelism of class members who may not be Christians; at other times the emphasis bears upon exhorting the class members to become more involved in evangelizing others.

ILLUMINATING THE LESSON: In this section, illustrative material is provided for the teacher to use to support the lesson at whatever point seems most appropriate.

DAILY BIBLE READINGS: The daily Bible readings are included for the teacher to use in his own devotions throughout the week, as well as to share with members of his class.

TRUTH SEARCH: This is a tool offered in each lesson for teachers who want to take a more interactive approach to teaching. Each Truth Search provides a series of questions and one other teaching method.

GOLDEN TEXT HOMILY WRITERS

Wilma Amison, Managing Editor
Church of God Evangel
Pathway Press
Cleveland, Tennessee

French L. Arrington, Ph.D.
Professor of New Testament Greek and Exegesis
Church of God Theological Seminary
Cleveland, Tennessee

Greg Baird, M.Div.
Church of God State Youth and Christian Education Director
Roanoke, VA 24019

Terry A. Beaver (Retired)
Former Pastor, Church of God
Sea Grove, North Carolina

Clyne Buxton, Minister
End-Time Events
Cleveland, Tennessee

Lance Colkmire, Editor
Evangelical Sunday School Lesson Commentary
Pathway Press
Cleveland, Tennessee

Paul Duncan, Superintendent
Smoky Mountain Children's Home
Sevierville, Tennessee

Calvin Eastham, Chaplain (LTC)
1st Engineering Brigade
Fort Leonard Wood, Missouri

Richard Fowler
Pastor, Church of God
Corbin, Kentucky

The Reverend Ted Gray
Pastor, Church of God
Weatherford, Texas

Bill Helmstetter
Carson City, Nevada

James E. Humbertson, D.Min. (Retired)
Former Administrative Editor
Church School Literature
Pathway Press
Cleveland, Tennessee

Gerald Johnson
Evangelist, Church of God
O'Brien, Florida

Lee Roy Martin
Pastor, Church of God
Ocoee, Tennessee

F.J. May, D.Min. (Retired)
Former Professor
Church of God School of Theology
Cleveland, Tennessee

The Reverend Grant McClung
Field Director, World Missions
Cleveland, Tennessee

Christopher C. Moree (Retired)
Former Administrative Assistant
World Missions
Church of God International Offices
Cleveland, Tennessee

Benjamin Perez, Chaplain (Col.)
Chairman of External Studies
Lee University
Cleveland, Tennessee

O.W. Polen, D.D. (Retired)
Former Editor in Chief
Pathway Press
Cleveland, Tennessee

Jerry Puckett
Director of Printing
Pathway Press
Cleveland, Tennessee

Richard D. Raines
Christian Education Director
Church of God
Valdosta, Georgia

Kathy Sanders
Women's Ministries Speaker and Writer
Cleveland, Tennessee

Douglas W. Slocumb, M.Ed., M.A., D.Min.
Director of Ministerial Development
Church of God Theological Seminary
Cleveland, Tennessee

Ann Steely, Secretary
Young Adult Curriculum
Pathway Press
Cleveland, Tennessee

J. David Stephens
State Overseer
Lexington, Kentucky

Fred G. Swank (Retired)
Former Pastor
Monroe, Michigan

Eugene Wigelsworth, M.Div.
Director of Religious Programs
Mississippi Department of Corrections
Jackson, Mississippi

SCRIPTURE TEXTS USED IN LESSON EXPOSITION

Deuteronomy
6:4-9, 20-25   November 9

2 Samuel
12:7, 9-15   January 25

1 Kings
22:7-9, 14, 19-23,   February 1
26-29, 34, 37

2 Kings
11:4, 11, 12, 17-21   February 8

1 Chronicles
17:2-4, 11, 12, 14, 15 January 25

2 Chronicles
24:1, 2, 15, 16   February 8
34:1, 2, 14, 15,   February 15
19-23, 27, 28
36:19-21   April 18

Ezra
1:1-3, 5   April 18

Ezra (Cont.)
3:1-3   April 18
4:1-4   April 25
5:1, 5   April 25
6:3, 7, 14-16   April 25
9:1-3, 5, 6, 14, 15   May 2
10:1-3   May 2

Nehemiah
1:1-4, 11   May 9
2:1, 2, 4, 5, 11,   May 9
17, 18
4:1,14-16   May 16
5:1, 6, 7, 9, 11   May 16
6:2, 3, 15, 16   May 16
8:2, 3, 5, 6   May 23
9:1, 5, 6, 19   May 23
10:28, 29   May 23

Psalm
30:2-5, 10-12   August 1
51:1-14   August 1
78:1, 4-7   November 9

Psalm (Cont.)

92:1-5	August 22
100:1-5	August 22
107:1, 2, 31, 32	August 22
119:1-16	November 2
134:1-3	August 22

Isaiah

1:2-7, 16-19	September 7
2:2-5	September 7
10:1-4	September 14
11:1-5	September 14
12:1-6	September 14
33:17, 22-24	September 21
35:1-10	September 21
40:1-5, 10-14, 28-31	September 28
42:1, 6-13	October 5
49:1, 3, 5, 6	October 5
53:3-7, 10-12	October 12
55:1, 3, 6, 7	October 12
58:3-12, 14	October 19
61:1-8	October 26
65:17, 18, 24, 25	October 26

Jeremiah

1:4-14, 16-19	March 7
10:1-7, 10-16	March 14
18:3-6, 15-17	March 21
19:1, 10, 11	March 21
30:18, 19, 21, 22	March 21
31:31-34	March 28

Lamentations

1:3, 4, 8, 9	April 4
2:11, 15-17	April 4
3:18-25	April 4

Joel

2:28-32	May 30

Matthew

1:1, 16-25	December 21
6:7-13	August 15
6:19-34	November 30
14:22, 23	August 15
26:28	March 28

Mark

1:35	August 15
16:15-18	November 23

Luke

6:12, 13	August 15
22:39-41	August 15

John

1:35-46, 47-49	February 22
10:4, 5, 27-30	August 8
12:20-22	February 22

Acts

2:14-18, 37-39	May 30
18:1-3	February 29

Romans

6:16-23	August 8
13:1-10	November 23
15:4	August 15
16:1, 2-6, 12	February 29

1 Corinthians

1:10-13	December 7
3:1-13	December 7
5:1-5	December 14
8:4, 7-11	December 28
9:24-27	December 28
10:13, 27, 28, 31-33	December 28
12:4-12, 18-20, 27, 28	January 4
13:4-8, 13	January 4
15:3-8, 12-20, 24-26, 52, 53	April 11

2 Corinthians

2:4-8	December 14
3:5-8	January 11
3:7-9	March 28
3:17, 18	January 11
4:1, 2, 5, 7, 15, 16	January 11
5:14, 15, 18, 19	January 11
6:14-18	December 14
7:1	December 14
10:3-5, 17, 18	January 18
11:2, 3	January 18
12:14-19	January 18
13:2, 8-10	January 18

Galatians

6:1-18	November 16

Ephesians

1:3-7, 13-23	June 6
2:1-16	June 13
4:1-8, 11-16	June 20

Philippians

1:12-28	June 27
2:1-18	July 4
2:25, 29, 30	February 29
3:1-14, 20, 21	August 29

Colossians

1:15-29	July 11
3:1-14, 18-24	July 18

2 Timothy

1:16-18	February 29
2:15	August 15
3:16, 17	August 15

Philemon		**Hebrews (cont.)**	
1-19	July 25	13:15, 16	August 22
Hebrews		**James**	
10:1-4, 12-14	March 28	1:22-25	August 8

SCRIPTURE TEXTS USED IN GOLDEN TEXT HOMILIES

Deuteronomy
6:7 — November 9

1 Kings
22:14 — February 1

2 Chronicles
7:14 — May 23

Nehemiah
2:18 — May 16

Psalm
51:1 — August 1
59:1 — April 25
119:10 — November 2

Proverbs
15:32 — January 25
29:2 — February 8

Isaiah
1:18 — September 7
12:2 — September 14
35:8 — September 21
40:31 — September 28
42:1 — October 5
53:5 — October 12
58:6 — October 19
65:17 — October 26

Jeremiah
10:6 — March 14
18:6 — March 21
29:13 — April 18

Lamentations
3:21, 22 — April 4

Matthew
1:23 — December 21
6:33 — November 30
14:23 — August 15
26:28 — March 28

Mark
16:15 — November 23

John
1:47 — February 22

Acts
2:39 — May 30
3:19 — May 2

Romans
12:1 — March 7

1 Corinthians
1:10 — December 7
10:31 — December 28
14:26 — January 4
15:22 — April 11

2 Corinthians
7:1 — December 14
3:5 — January 11
10:4 — January 18

Galatians
6:10 — November 16

Ephesians
1:3 — June 6
2:8 — June 13
4:2, 3 — June 20

Philippians
1:3, 5 — February 29
1:20 — June 27
2:5 — July 4
3:8 — August 29

Colossians
1:18 — July 11
3:17 — July 18

Philemon
21 — July 25

Hebrews
10:24 — February 15
13:15, 16 — August 22

James
1:22 — August 8

1 John
3:17 — May 9

ACKNOWLEDGMENTS

Many books, magazines and newspapers have been used in the research that has gone into the 2003-2004 *Evangelical Commentary*. The major books that have been used are listed below.

Bibles

King James Version, Oxford University Press, Oxford, England
Life Application Study Bible, Zondervan Publishing House, Grand Rapids
New American Standard Bible (NASB), Holman Publishers, Nashville
New International Version (NIV), Zondervan Publishing House, Grand Rapids
New King James Version (NKJV), Thomas Nelson Publishers, Nashville
The Nelson Study Bible, Thomas Nelson Publishers, Nashville
Word in Life Study Bible, Thomas Nelson Publishers, Nashville

Commentaries

Adam Clarke's Commentary, Abingdon-Cokesbury, Nashville
Barnes' Notes, BibleSoft.com
Be Joyful, Warren Wiersbe, Victor Books, Colorado Springs
Be Rich, Warren Wiersbe, Victor Books, Colorado Springs
Commentaries on the Old Testament (Keil & Delitzsch), Eerdmans Publishing Co., Grand Rapids
Ellicott's Bible Commentary, Zondervan Publishing House, Grand Rapids
Ephesians, The Mystery of the Body of Christ, R. Kent Hughes, Crossway Books, Wheaton, IL
Expositions of Holy Scriptures, Alexander MacLaren, Eerdmans Publishing Co., Grand Rapids
Expository Thoughts on the Gospels, J.C. Ryle, Baker Books, Grand Rapids
Jamieson, Fausset and Brown Commentary, BibleSoft.com
Life Application Commentary, Tyndale House, Carol Stream, IL
The Broadman Bible Commentary, Volumes 10 and 11, Broadman Press, Nashville
The Expositor's Greek Testament, Eerdmans Publishing Co., Grand Rapids
The Interpreter's Bible, Abingdon Press, Nashville
The Letters to the Corinthians, William Barclay, Westminster Press, Philadelphia
The Pulpit Commentary, Eerdmans Publishing Co., Grand Rapids
The Wesleyan Commentary, Eerdmans Publishing Co., Grand Rapids
The Wycliffe Bible Commentary, Moody Press, Chicago
Zondervan NIV Bible Commentary, Zondervan Publishing House, Grand Rapids

Illustrations

A-Z Sparkling Illustrations, Stephen Gaukroger and Nick Mercer, Baker Books, Grand Rapids
Knight's Master Book of New Illustrations, Eerdmans Publishing Co., Grand Rapids
Notes and Quotes, The Warner Press, Anderson, IN
1,000 New Illustrations, Al Bryant, Zondervan Publishing Co., Grand Rapids
Quotable Quotations, Scripture Press Publications, Wheaton
The Encyclopedia of Religious Quotations, Fleming H. Revell Co., Old Tappan, NJ
The Speaker's Sourcebook, Zondervan Publishing House, Grand Rapids
3,000 Illustrations for Christian Service, Eerdmans Publishing Co., Grand Rapids
Who Said That?, George Sweeting, Moody Press, Chicago

General Reference Books

Biblical Characters From the Old and New Testament, Alexander Whyte, Kregel Publications, Grand Rapids
Harper's Bible Dictionary, Harper and Brothers Publishers, New York
Pictorial Dictionary of the Bible, Zondervan Publishing House, Grand Rapids
Pronouncing Biblical Names, Broadman and Holman Publishers, Nashville
The Interpreter's Dictionary of the Bible, Abingdon Press, Nashville

Evangelical Bible Lesson Series (1999-2006)

	Fall Quarter (September, October, November)	Winter Quarter (December, January, February)	Spring Quarter (March, April, May)	Summer Quarter (June, July, August)
1999	Unit One—Beginnings (Genesis) Unit Two—Personal Ethics			
1999-2000		Unit One—Gospel of the King (Matthew) Unit Two—Growing Spiritually		
2000	Unit One—Providence (Exodus) Unit Two—Spiritual Warfare Unit Three—Worship		Unit One—Ruth & Esther Unit Two—Divine Healing Unit Three—Great Prayers of the Bible	Unit One—Acts (Part 1) Unit Two—Family Relationships
2000-2001		Unit One—Faith for the 21st Century Unit Two—Jesus the Servant (Mark)		
2001	Unit One—Christian Living (Romans & Galatians) Unit Two—Christian Discipleship		Unit One—The Kingdom of God Unit Two—Law & Gospel (Leviticus-Deuteronomy)	Unit One—Acts (Part 2) Unit Two—Evangelism
2001-2002		Unit One—The Gospel According to Luke Unit Two—Message of the Early Church		
2002	Unit One—Wisdom From Job, Proverbs, & Ecclesiastes Unit Two—God's Great Promises		Unit One—Leadership (Joshua & Judges) Unit Two—The Church	Unit One—Psalms (Part 1) Unit Two—Learning From Samuel, Elijah & Elisha
2002-2003		Unit One—Jesus the Son of God (John) Unit Two—Gifts of the Spirit		
2003	Unit One—Judgment & Comfort (Isaiah) Unit Two—Values & Priorities		Unit One—Kings of Israel (Samuel, Kings, Chronicles) Unit Two—Second Coming	Unit One—Heaven & Hell Unit Two—Psalms (Part 2)
2003-2004		Unit One—1 & 2 Corinthians Unit Two—Lesser-Known People of the Bible		
2004	Unit One—God's Sovereignty (Ezekiel) Unit Two—James		Unit One—Jeremiah & Lamentations Unit Two—Out of Exile (Ezra & Nehemiah)	Unit One—Prison Epistles Unit Two—Revival & Renewal
2004-2005		Unit One—1 & 2 Thessalonians Unit Two—Pastoral Epistles		
2005	Unit One—Minor Prophets II (Nahum-Malachi) Unit Two—Parables of Jesus		Unit One—Minor Prophets I (Hosea-Micah) Unit Two—Redemption	Unit One—Faith (Hebrews) Unit Two—Daniel
2005-2006		Unit One—Peter & Jude Unit Two—Numbers		
2006			Unit One—People Who Met Jesus Unit Two—Christian Formation (inc. Fruit of the Spirit)	Unit One—1, 2, 3 John Unit Two—Studies in Revelation

Real Life

Sunday School for Young Adults

When young adults come to Sunday school, they want to think for themselves . . . enter into dialogue with each other . . . and discover how God's Word applies to their daily lives'

With Pathway's new *Real Life* curriculum, Sunday school becomes a place young adults want to be.

Real Life's lessons correlate with the *Evangelical Sunday School Commentary,* which serves as a great resource for young adult teachers.

Real Life

**To receive a free sample of *Real Life* curriculum,
call 1-800-553-8506.**

INTRODUCTION TO FALL QUARTER

W ritings of the prophet Isaiah—addressing themes of rebellion, redemption, judgment, restoration and the future—are the focus of the first unit. Expositions for this unit (lessons 1-8) were written by the Reverend Dr. Homer G. Rhea (L.H.D.).

Homer Rhea is editorial director at the Church of God School of Ministry. He formerly served as editor in chief of Church of God Publications, with the responsibility of editing the *Church of God Evangel.* Reverend Rhea was reared and educated in Mississippi, where he served in the pastoral ministry for 18 years. He is author of *A Call to Excellence; A New Creation: A Study of Salvation;* and *Come, Worship With Us.*

Unit Two (lessons 9-13) focuses on Christ's values and priorities: devotion to God, the family, the church and ministry. Various Scripture passages are covered.

The Reverend Dr. R.B. Thomas (D.Litt., M.S., B.A., Th.B.), writer of lessons 9 and 10, is headmaster of Tennessee Christian Academy. He is founder and president of Master Ministry in Cleveland, Tennessee. Master Ministry is a service agency providing assistance to pastors and congregations in key areas of ministry effectiveness.

Dr. Thomas earned his bachelor of arts degree at Northwest Bible College, a master of science degree at Northern State University, a doctor of theology degree at American Divinity School, and his doctorate of literature degree at Northwest Bible College.

The Reverend Dr. Carl R. Hobbs (Ed.D.), who wrote lessons 11-13, is associate pastor of South Cleveland Church of God. He has served the Church of God as pastor, district overseer, member of the state council, and Bible college teacher and administrator.

Dr. Hobbs is author of *Games Church Bosses Play.* He holds degrees from Lee University, Tennessee Wesleyan College and the University of Tennessee.

God's Remedy for Rebellion

Study Text: Isaiah 1:1 through 2:5

Objective: To recognize the painful consequences of rebellion and accept God's prescription for restoration.

Time: Between 742 and 687 B.C.

Place: Judah, perhaps Jerusalem

Golden Text: "Come now, and let us reason together, saith the Lord: though your sins be as scarlet, they shall be as white as snow; though they be red like crimson, they shall be as wool" (Isaiah 1:18).

Central Truth: God provides the cure for rebellious hearts.

Evangelism Emphasis: God provides salvation for contrite hearts.

PRINTED TEXT

Isaiah 1:2. Hear, O heavens, and give ear, O earth: for the Lord hath spoken, I have nourished and brought up children, and they have rebelled against me.

3. The ox knoweth his owner, and the ass his master's crib: but Israel doth not know, my people doth not consider.

4. Ah sinful nation, a people laden with iniquity, a seed of evildoers, children that are corrupters: they have forsaken the Lord, they have provoked the Holy One of Israel unto anger, they are gone away backward.

5. Why should ye be stricken any more? ye will revolt more and more: the whole head is sick, and the whole heart faint.

6. From the sole of the foot even unto the head there is no soundness in it; but wounds, and bruises, and putrifying sores: they have not been closed, neither bound up, neither mollified with ointment.

7. Your country is desolate, your cities are burned with fire: your land, strangers devour it in your presence, and it is desolate, as overthrown by strangers.

16. Wash you, make you clean; put away the evil of your doings from before mine eyes; cease to do evil;

17. Learn to do well; seek judgment, relieve the oppressed, judge the fatherless, plead for the widow.

18. Come now, and let us reason together, saith the Lord: though your sins be as scarlet, they shall be as white as snow; though they be red like crimson, they shall be as wool.

19. If ye be willing and obedient, ye shall eat the good of the land.

2:2. And it shall come to pass in the last days, that the mountain of the Lord's house shall be established in the top of the mountains, and shall be exalted above the hills; and all nations shall flow unto it.

3. And many people shall go and say, Come ye, and let us go up to the mountain of the Lord, to the house of the God of Jacob; and he will teach us of his ways, and we will walk in his paths: for out of Zion shall go forth the law, and the word of the Lord from Jerusalem.

4. And he shall judge among the nations, and shall rebuke many people: and they shall beat their swords into plowshares, and their spears into pruninghooks: nation shall not lift up sword against nation, neither shall they learn war any more.

5. O house of Jacob, come ye, and let us walk in the light of the Lord.

LESSON OUTLINE

I. DIAGNOSIS: REBELLION AGAINST GOD
   A. The Depth of Rebellion
   B. The Fruit of Rebellion
   C. A Remnant in the Midst of Rebellion
II. TREATMENT: WILLINGLY OBEY GOD
   A. Rebellion in Worship
   B. Repentance in Worship
   C. Obedience in Worship
III. RESTORATION: GOD GIVES PEACE
   A. Pain in Restoration
   B. Justice in Restoration
   C. Peace in Restoration

LESSON EXPOSITION

INTRODUCTION

Isaiah was called of God to proclaim prophetic utterances that would test the spine of any messenger of God, then or now. The messenger bearing bad news is seldom received with warmth, and Isaiah's bad news was offensive to almost all who heard it. Through him God indicted all of Judah and Jerusalem—from the throne to the Temple to the throngs—all were called to account.

Isaiah prophesied in Judah during the reigns of four kings—Uzziah, Jotham, Ahaz and Hezekiah. Uzziah was a good king at first, but he eventually died from leprosy brought on by prideful rebellion. Jotham and Hezekiah feared the Lord, but Ahaz's kingdom was one of complete debauchery and rebellion against God.

Isaiah's prophecies of judgment began during the era of King Uzziah, and the indictment was not only for idolatry but for corruption within the Hebrew faith itself. Judah and Jerusalem had replaced devotion with ritual, and had become complacent, apathetic and alien to their God-given role as His chosen people. The heart and mind of the people had deserted their worship. All that remained was empty ritual performed without thought or emotion.

I. DIAGNOSIS: REBELLION AGAINST GOD (Isaiah 1:2-9)

As the Great Physician, God is able to see through all the excuses we contrive to somehow add validity to our actions. He is not swayed by the "spin" we give to our situation because He not only knows what we do, but He also knows exactly why we do it. Therefore, God's diagnosis of our situation never needs a second opinion.

God's diagnosis of Judah and Jerusalem was one of blatant and chronic rebellion.

A. The Depth of Rebellion (vv. 2-4)

2. Hear, O heavens, and give ear, O earth: for the Lord hath spoken, I have nourished and brought up children, and they have rebelled against me.
3. The ox knoweth his owner, and the ass his master's crib: but Israel doth not know, my people doth not consider.
4. Ah sinful nation, a people laden with iniquity, a seed of evildoers, children that are corrupters: they have forsaken the Lord, they have provoked the Holy One of Israel unto anger, they are gone away backward.

God's characterization of Judah and Jerusalem as His children was not metaphorical. He had indeed reared them and nurtured them throughout their history. They had come to this juncture by His grace and selection from the nations of the world. From the first words whispered to Abraham, to the laws and commands recited to Moses, to the profound wisdom of government imparted to Solomon—God had been Father, protector and provider.

How frustrating and painful it must have been then for God to look upon their rebelliousness—children who held little respect for their Father and attended His house with mere cursory appreciation. Their approach to visiting their Father was one of burdensome obligation rather than joyous renewal of relationships.

When grown children return home for a visit with their parents, it is usually a refreshing of family ties—a time of remembering all the wonderful things that family relationships engender. Sometimes, however, because of our own imperfections, we have difficult or painful relationships with loved ones. Under those circumstances, visits may be strained.

For Judah, there was no reason to feel strained or burdened by time spent in God's house. He had been nothing but righteous, just and good in His dealings with His children. He had nourished and brought them up with the kindness and favor only God could bless them with. Therein lay the problem.

The ignorant ox knows to whom he belongs and responds to his master's voice; the ignorant donkey knows where his nourishment lies and obligingly follows his master's commands. Although these animals were far inferior to Judah in every way other than mere brawn, God seemed to hold the animals in higher esteem because they recognized and acknowledged by action their reliance upon and submission to their masters. Israel, however, "does not know, my people do not understand" (v. 3, *NIV*).

This condemnation was twofold in that their lack of knowledge was due to a failure to consider the reasons for their standing in the world. Most children arise to their place in the world by standing on the shoulders of their parents. Israel was like a turtle on a fence post who had come to believe that the climb was accomplished without assistance. Simple consideration of their abilities opposed to their position would have resulted in the acknowledgment that God had done great things for them. But they did not know because they did not understand.

This lack of knowledge or consideration had been the seed of their rebellion. The evidence of rebellion lay in the deterioration of the moral fiber of their society. The city of faith had given itself to harlotry; murders resided in the home of judgment and righteousness. Nobility had become indistinguishable from common thieves. Bribery was common. Justice for the poor, orphans and widows was nonexistent (see vv. 21-23).

The Israelites had become evildoers, corrupters and a sinful nation "laden with iniquity." They had forsaken God and provoked Him to anger by "turning away backward" (see v. 4).

When rebellion takes place among God's people, when faith and religious practice are denigrated to a burdensome drudgery, society will begin to experience moral decay. God's people, then and now, serve as guardians holding Satan in restraint by their acts of worship performed in faith, knowledge and joy. When the faith, knowledge and joy of such worship are gone, so also is its power to retard the work of Satan.

B. The Fruit of Rebellion (vv. 5-8)

(Isaiah 1:8 is not included in the printed text.)

5. Why should ye be stricken any more? ye will revolt more and more: the whole head is sick, and the whole heart faint.

6. From the sole of the foot even unto the head there is no soundness in it; but wounds, and bruises, and putrifying sores: they have not been closed, neither bound up, neither mollified with ointment.

7. Your country is desolate, your cities are burned with fire:

your land, strangers devour it in your presence, and it is desolate, as overthrown by strangers.

A careful reading of verses 5-8 reveals that God's judgment had already begun upon the rebellious people. The question, "Why should you be stricken again?" (v. 5, *NKJV*) indicates they had already experienced God's anger. *Adam Clarke's Commentary* suggests that God was actually asking, "Upon what limb shall you be smitten?" The whole of Judah and Israel had been punished to the point that God said, "From the sole of your foot to the top of your head there is no soundness" (v. 6, *NIV*). Further, none of the wounds that had been afflicted upon them had been tended. It is as though they did not know—did not understand—God was punishing them. why

The image of the wounds, bruises and putrefying sores is made clear in verses 7 and 8. Judah was in ruins. The country was desolate, its cities had been burned, and strangers had devoured the good of the land while the people helplessly looked on.

To be compared to a "cottage in a vineyard" (v. 8) may present a beautiful mental image, but the meaning indicates something very different. The walls of a vineyard enclose the valuable crop and a lodging for someone responsible for its protection. But suppose an enemy overtook the vineyard. The enemy would control the walls and reap the harvest while the caretaker huddled within the cottage (shelter) in fear. Such was the state of Judah. They were as a besieged city. The land and the fruit had been taken, leaving them without freedom, nourishment or peace. Heve

C. A Remnant in the Midst of Rebellion (v. 9)

(Isaiah 1:9 is not included in the printed text.)

God is always preserving a remnant. Noah and his family were a remnant preserved in the time of the great flood. Israel itself was a rem-

nant taken through Abraham from a rebellious world that had forgotten God. Judah was left as a remnant after the northern kingdom, Israel, left the worship of Jehovah to serve other gods.

It is not surprising, then, that at Judah's rebellion God would retain a remnant from among them—a few who had neither lost their awe in worship nor forgotten their role in God's creation.

This reflection upon God's continual preservation of a remnant amid mass rebellion offers an important caution for the believer today. When the majority—no matter how strong and compelling—is intent on following one path, the Christian should be wary and prayerfully consider God's will in the matter. The small minority of objectors may very well be God's remnant chosen from among the rebellious.

II. TREATMENT: WILLINGLY OBEY GOD (Isaiah 1:10-20)

The primary cause of the rebellion of Judah was the decay of their worship. They had not failed in carrying out the rituals of the law of Moses concerning worship, but they had miserably failed in achieving the spirit of the Law. God's rebuke of Judah leaves no doubt that going through the motions of obedience is as distasteful to Him as disobedience.

A. Worship in Rebellion (vv. 10-15)

(Isaiah 1:10-15 is not included in the printed text.)

The activity of their worship is made clear as God recounts His displeasure in it all. He acknowledges the "multitude" of their sacrifices and their frequent gatherings before Him. The intent of this acknowledgment, however, was to ask them the purpose of these things.

In one question God cut through all of their pretense and ritual. He asked the question that few of them could answer—Why? The majority would have answered, "Because the Law requires it," or "It is what we are supposed to do—isn't it?"

These responses are as untrue as they are true. The people were indeed required by the Law to bring sacrifices, burnt offerings, oblations and incense to be offered up to God in worship. They were indeed required by the Law to appear before God on regular occasions for feasts, solemn assemblies and worship. Sadly, all of these things had become as dried flowers.

When painstakingly dried, a flower can retain much of its loveliness and color. At a distance it may even seem to be fresh and alive. On closer inspection, however, a dried flower has lost its beautiful aroma; its texture is no longer silky and soft but dry and brittle; its beauty dims greatly when inspected in intimacy. It is lifeless.

Worship is always an intimate experience. If it is lacking in intimacy, it is not worship. It has become routine. Judah had retained the acts but had lost the purpose. In the intimacy of worship they were miserable failures. Therefore, as they spread their hands in worship, God looked away; as they prayed, He refused to listen (v. 15).

B. Worship in Repentance (vv. 16, 17)

16. Wash you, make you clean; put away the evil of your doings from before mine eyes; cease to do evil;

17. Learn to do well; seek judgment, relieve the oppressed, judge the fatherless, plead for the widow.

It must have been extraordinarily difficult for people so focused on ritual and routine to understand that all they were doing was correct yet incorrect. However, a simple reflection upon their lives outside of the Temple would certainly have suggested that all was not right in Jerusalem and Judah. They needed only to look around at the ungodliness and corruption prevalent among them to know that repentance was mandated.

If their worship was ever to mean anything again, if their rebellion was ever to be brought into submission, they had to repent and physically, forcefully change the status quo. Not only did their attitudes in worship have to change, but the community had to change to reflect the renewed attitudes.

The first order of the day was to "wash"; not to physically enter into water with soap and towels, but to cleanse their hearts through mournful repentance. Repentance is an active experience requiring effort on the part of the repenter. It must be motivated by a heartfelt sorrow for previous actions, accompanied by a determination to live differently, and pursued through sincere and expressed prayers for forgiveness. In short, their worship had to become something it had never been before—real.

The new life God expected to spring from the repentance of Judah and Jerusalem was relatively the same as He expects from a repentant sinner today. Life in repentance focuses on two bold and demanding goals. First, the repentant person must "cease to do evil" (v. 16). When considering that most of a person's life is made up of habitual actions, thoughts and words, it is easy to see the difficulty involved in simply stopping wrong actions, thoughts and words from manifesting themselves. But this is the first requirement of repentance. To attempt to enter into repentance without first resolving to live a life free from the sins of the past is to fail before one starts.

Second, repentance is a learning process. God told Jerusalem and Judah, "Learn to do good" (v. 17,

NKJV). Again, reflection must be made on the normal standards of the previous life. If it was customary for an individual to lie, he or she had to learn to tell the truth. If a person had a habit of an impure nature, that person had to learn to live in wholesomeness and purity. If the person was given to thievery or deceptive and fraudulent business practice, he must learn honesty in all of his affairs. Repentance was not, and is not, a momentary emotional catharsis; it must be a life-changing transformation.

Specifically, God told His people to practice justice, stand up against the oppressors and for the oppressed, and minister to widows and orphans. How well is the church today carrying out these commands?

C. Worship in Obedience (vv. 18-20)

(Isaiah 1:20 is not included in the printed text.)

18. Come now, and let us reason together, saith the Lord: though your sins be as scarlet, they shall be as white as snow; though they be red like crimson, they shall be as wool.

19. If ye be willing and obedient, ye shall eat the good of the land.

The treatment prescribed for Judah and Jerusalem offered a cure that was nothing less than miraculous. If they would come and "reason together" with God, they would see the error of their ways, repent and find mercy.

They had come to the place where their worship was repulsive to God, yet He told them that their scarlet sins could become white as snow. It was not going to take a lifetime to regain the favor of God; it would be restored in an instant when they repented and began to live in righteousness. Crimson stains would be erased from the whitest wool in a

moment's time with the repentance of Judah and Jerusalem. They would spread their hands and no longer embrace only air; they would pray and God would once again listen.

The two requirements for such transformation were willingness and obedience. If these were present in their repentance, the land would remain in their hands and they would enjoy its fruit. However, if they remained stiff and rebellious, an enemy would devour them with the sword (v. 20). The grace offered by God always has a curse lurking in the shadows—a curse that is rightfully the fate of the sinner. We should view the mercy offered to us by God with awe because He did not have to offer it. Without His grace, however, we would know nothing but the curse of our sins.

III. RESTORATION: GOD GIVES
    PEACE (Isaiah 1:24-31; 2:2-5)

In this time period, Judah had developed a great fear of the Assyrian Empire because it had recently destroyed the northern kingdom of Israel. In attempts to avoid the same fate, Judah tried to forge alliances first with Assyria, then with Egypt. Rather than trusting God for their safety and peace, they looked for political solutions. In doing so, they had estranged themselves even further from God.

Isaiah's prophecy redirected their attention to the One that the unrighteous should truly fear and the just should look to for peace.

A. Pain in Restoration
    (1:24, 25, 28-31)

(Isaiah 1:24, 25, 28-31 is not included in the printed text.)

In the process of restoring something—an old home, an antique piece of furniture, and so forth—there must first be the painful work of tearing away the parts that have decayed or will otherwise weaken the restoration process. In the worst scenario, the superstructure may have to be gutted and rebuilt. This was the case with Judah.

History has witnessed time and time again the decay of morality in nations whose leaders have become corrupt. When those in authority have little respect for ethics and moral principle, the general public assumes the same posture and the entire society becomes corrupt and lawless.

Thus, God's judgment on Judah would begin with the judges and counselors. God determined to turn His hand against them and all those who loved the way of unrighteousness. His intent was to "purely purge away" (v. 25) the wickedness of Judah from the top down.

It should come as no surprise that God would hold the leaders of His people to a high standard and require accountability of them for the state of the people. Jesus said, "For unto whomsoever much is given, of him shall be much required: and to whom men have committed much, of him they will ask the more" (Luke 12:48). Peter said, "For the time is come that judgment must begin at the house of God: and if it first begin at us, what shall the end be of them that obey not the gospel of God?" (1 Peter 4:17). God looks first to the leaders of His people in accountability and in restoration.

Judgment, however, is not the fate of leaders only; all unrighteousness will be judged as well, whether great or small. The "destruction of the transgressors and of the sinners" (Isaiah 1:28) was to be wide and sweeping. None who fit such a profile would escape. Even the strongest would be consumed and "none shall quench them" (v. 31). God's remedy for rebellion was to destroy the rebellious so the righteous might once again flourish.

B. Justice in Restoration (vv. 26, 27)

(Isaiah 1:26, 27 is not included in the printed text.)

If the leaders were first to be judged, they should also be first in restoration. To begin this process, however, God refused contemporary models for His judges and counselors. He had given the best model to Moses in the beginning and that model would be used in Judah's restoration. God would restore "judges as at the first" and "counsellors as at the beginning" (v. 26).

When justice was restored to the city of Jerusalem, it would once again be called "the city of righteousness, the faithful city" (v. 26). This characterization stands in stark contrast to Jerusalem's description in verse 21, stating that the "faithful city" had become a "harlot"; the vivid contrast reveals the differences between the fallen and the redeemed.

The importance of the restoration of justice as a first step to the restoration of Jerusalem cannot be overemphasized. Judgment would be the key to her redemption and all who were converted to her would be redeemed by righteousness (see v. 27). Once God's righteous judges and counselors had reestablished in the community the justice prescribed by God's law, the tenor of the whole society would change. Peace would replace lawlessness, and fear of enemies would be replaced by faith in God.

C. Peace in Restoration (2:2-5)

2. And it shall come to pass in the last days, that the mountain of the Lord's house shall be established in the top of the mountains, and shall be exalted above the hills; and all nations shall flow unto it.

3. And many people shall go and say, Come ye, and let us go up to the mountain of the Lord, to the house of the God of Jacob; and he

will teach us of his ways, and we will walk in his paths: for out of Zion shall go forth the law, and the word of the Lord from Jerusalem.

4. And he shall judge among the nations, and shall rebuke many people: and they shall beat their swords into plowshares, and their spears into pruninghooks: nation shall not lift up sword against nation, neither shall they learn war any more.

5. O house of Jacob, come ye, and let us walk in the light of the Lord.

Almost as a soothing balm applied to a painful sore, God's words to Isaiah turn to a time of ultimate peace and restoration. After a scathing rebuke and warnings of impending judgment, God gave the faithful something to hold on to in hope. A time is coming when the "mountain of the Lord's house" will be exalted and the nations will be drawn to it. In that time, all will want to study the just ways of God. Under the rebuke of the Lord, arms will be transformed into utensils for honest labor, and war will be a thing of the past.

This prophecy of Isaiah has served to bolster the efforts of the righteous as they have struggled throughout the centuries. Whenever rebellion is faced and the painful process of restoration takes place, God's people have always found strength and comfort in the fact that an ultimate restoration will one day occur. A lasting and transcendent peace will come, and God will reign supreme.

GOLDEN TEXT HOMILY

"COME NOW, AND LET US REASON TOGETHER, SAITH THE LORD: THOUGH YOUR SINS BE AS SCARLET, THEY SHALL BE AS WHITE AS SNOW; THOUGH THEY BE RED LIKE CRIMSON, THEY SHALL BE AS WOOL" (Isaiah 1:18).

The courtroom scene is set.

Jehovah God presides majestically behind the bench. Before the bar, Isaiah, the prosecutor, paces back and forth, eager for the proceedings to begin. Judah, the accused, sits in the dock, head lowered, staring intently at the floor.

Deliberately, Jehovah raps the gavel and calls the court to order. With a sweep of His hand, He beckons to Isaiah to read the accusations against Judah.

One by one Isaiah intones the damaging charges:

• Judah has rebelled against God.
• They have forsaken the Lord.
• They have provoked the Holy One of Israel.
• They have failed to heed Jehovah's warnings.

Isaiah finishes and slowly bows to the Judge as if to say, "The decision is now Yours." Jehovah scans the courtroom looking for someone who can stand to defend Judah. But who can mount a defense against such serious charges?

The Judge pauses, His brow creased in serious thought. All eyes are fixed on Him as a deathly stillness settles over the court. Surely the verdict must be, "Guilty!"

Jehovah stares at Judah causing him to cringe in fear. Amazingly, when Jehovah finally does speak, He speaks softly, with compassion, "Come now, and let us reason together . . . though your sins be as scarlet, they shall be as white as snow; though they be red like crimson, they shall be as wool." And this is only a part of the good news. The Judge continues, "If ye be willing and obedient, ye shall eat the good of the land." He concludes with a solemn warning, "But if ye refuse and rebel, ye shall be devoured with the sword" (vv. 18-20).

This golden text, containing many truths, has occupied the attention of countless scholars. And all of those precious promises are made possible by this fact: in spite of Judah's terrible sins, God initiates the action of reconciliation.

How like God this is: He, the One grieved, the One sinned against, seeks sinful man and calls him to repentance and reconciliation. And this has been true from the beginning. When Adam sinned in the Garden, God sought him, calling, "Adam . . . where art thou?" (Genesis 3:9).

And God's call is to reason, not to judgment. He appeals to man's intellect as well as his emotions. Man is not asked simply to put his brains into neutral when dealing with God.—**Christopher Moree**

SENTENCE SERMONS

GOD PROVIDES the cure for rebellious hearts.

—Selected

BETTER TO BE PRUNED to grow than cut up to burn.

—John Trapp

HE WHO PROMISED PARDON on our repentance has not promised life till we repent.

—Francis Quarles

EVANGELISM APPLICATION

GOD PROVIDES SALVATION FOR CONTRITE HEARTS.

How do we avoid the pain of a broken heart? No one wants to feel such hurt, so we keep our hearts under guard, building walls to protect them. But the heart is precisely the aim of God's redemptive call. It must be broken before God's grace can be applied.

It is in the contrite heart that the grace of God shines the brightest. In the broken heart His love is the sweetest. When our hearts become broken, God's grace becomes the balm that heals the hurts and soothes the soul with mercy.

ILLUMINATING THE LESSON

In Matthew 21, Jesus told the story of a father who asked his two sons to work in his vineyard. The first son refused, then recanted and went to work in the vineyard. The second immediately said he would go; yet he did not. Jesus asked the question of the chief priests and elders, "Whether of them twain did the will of his father?" (Matthew 21:31).

What a powerful illustration of obedience and rebellion. We have all heard the expression, "Words are cheap." Words are important and our words should speak the truth that is in our life. But in reality, words are cheap. Words that are not followed by corresponding actions cost the speaker nothing.

The first son spoke rebellious words yet repented of them and obeyed his father. The second son spoke words of obedience yet never demonstrated the obedience his words implied. Rebellion is not a matter of words but a matter of action.

DAILY BIBLE READINGS

M. A Bad Choice Brings Calamity. Genesis 4:6-12
T. Result of Disobedience. Joshua 7:19-26
W. Tragedy of Rebellion. 1 Chronicles 10:1-14
T. Choices and Consequences. Matthew 7:21-27
F. Rebuke and Repentance. Acts 8:18-24
S. Caring Confrontation. Revelation 3:14-19

TRUTH SEARCH
Creatively Teaching the Word

DISCUSSION QUESTIONS

Isaiah 1:2-9
- Who is doing the speaking in this passage, and to whom is He talking?
- How did God rear these people as children and bring them up? Give specific examples.
- What accusation is made against Judah in verse 2?
- Discuss the meaning and implications of God's illustration in verse 3.
- How would you describe a sinful nation? How does God describe one in verse 4?
- What did God mean by saying, "Why should you be stricken again" (v. 5)?
- What do you suppose God meant when He spoke of "wounds and welts and open sores" (v. 6, *NIV*)?
- According to verses 7-9, what separated the people of Judah from ancient Sodom and Gomorrah?

Isaiah 1:11-20
- How did God view Judah's religious activities (vv. 11-14)?
- Why wouldn't God answer their prayers (v. 15)?

- What did God command that they quit doing (v. 16)?
- What five deeds did God command them to do (v. 17)?
- What did God promise to do (v. 18)?

RESPONSE TO THE WORD

Before the Bible study, hand out an index card to each student and have them write the following incomplete phrase: "I have been rebellious against God by . . ." At this point they should only *think* about ways they might respond.

After considering Judah's rebellion in the Bible study, students should complete the cards. Perhaps they have been practicing disobedience to God in a way the people of Judah did, or maybe in another way. Possible answers could include pride, being religious without being spiritual, being self-indulgent, ignoring the needy, neglecting family time, and so on.

Challenge students to confess their rebellion to God and receive His forgiveness and help for the future.

Judgment and the Savior

Study Text: Isaiah 10:1 through 12:6
Objective: To understand that sin brings judgment and celebrate Christ as Savior.
Time: About 740 B.C.
Place: Judah, possibly Jerusalem
Golden Text: "God is my salvation; I will trust, and not be afraid: for the Lord JEHOVAH is my strength and my song; he also is become my salvation" (Isaiah 12:2).
Central Truth: Christians celebrate Christ as Emancipator and Savior.
Evangelism Emphasis: The lost are drawn to Christ as Christians proclaim the freedom He gives.

PRINTED TEXT

Isaiah 10:1. Woe unto them that decree unrighteous decrees, and that write grievousness which they have prescribed;

2. To turn aside the needy from judgment, and to take away the right from the poor of my people, that widows may be their prey, and that they may rob the fatherless!

3. And what will ye do in the day of visitation, and in the desolation which shall come from far? to whom will ye flee for help? and where will ye leave your glory?

4. Without me they shall bow down under the prisoners, and they shall fall under the slain. For all this his anger is not turned away, but his hand is stretched out still.

11:1. And there shall come forth a rod out of the stem of Jesse, and a Branch shall grow out of his roots:

2. And the spirit of the Lord shall rest upon him, the spirit of wisdom and understanding, the spirit of counsel and might, the spirit of knowledge and of the fear of the Lord;

3. And shall make him of quick understanding in the fear of the Lord: and he shall not judge after the sight of his eyes, neither reprove after the hearing of his ears:

4. But with righteousness shall he judge the poor, and reprove with equity for the meek of the earth: and he shall smite the earth with the rod of his mouth, and with the breath of his lips shall he slay the wicked.

5. And righteousness shall be the girdle of his loins, and faithfulness the girdle of his reins.

12:1. And in that day thou shalt say, O Lord, I will praise thee: though thou wast angry with me, thine anger is turned away, and thou comfortedst me.

2. Behold, God is my salvation; I will trust, and not be afraid: for the Lord JEHOVAH is my strength and my song; he also is become my salvation.

3. Therefore with joy shall ye draw water out of the wells of salvation.

4. And in that day shall ye say, Praise the Lord, call upon his name, declare his doings among the people, make mention that his name is exalted.

5. Sing unto the Lord; for he hath done excellent things: this is known in all the earth.

6. Cry out and shout, thou inhabitant of Zion: for great is the Holy One of Israel in the midst of thee.

DICTIONARY

grievousness—Isaiah 10:1—oppression, injustice
quick understanding—Isaiah 11:3—to delight in
the girdle of his reins—Isaiah 11:5—the sash around his waist

LESSON OUTLINE

I. SOCIAL INJUSTICE JUDGED
  A. The Certainty of Judgment
  B. The Tools of Judgment
  C. Hope in Judgment

II. THE SAVIOR PROMISED
  A. A Savior Shall Come
  B. The Peace He Will Bring
  C. The Unity He Will Bring

III. THE SAVIOR CELEBRATED
  A. Celebrate His Mercy
  B. Celebrate His Glory

LESSON EXPOSITION

INTRODUCTION

Injustice is abhorrent to God. Whether committed by individuals or by governments, by impersonal systems or by personal prejudice, by intent or by negligence, someone is responsible and God holds him or her accountable. Not only the perpetrators are indicted, but also the society—the people—that stand idly by allowing the injustice to take place without objection.

Social injustice cannot be excused by saying, "That's just the way things are." When a tornado strikes, or when a drought takes place, that's just the way things are. But when someone is injured and hurting because of the deeds or decisions of another, it did not have to be that way. Someone will give an account to God.

It was to the poor, the hurting and those deprived of justice that God sent His Son. Jesus has a promise to those suffering injustice (see Isaiah 11:4). Those who delight in privilege and bask in social elevation, those

who give an occasional cursory nod to the deprived and wounded, they should fear His coming. He comes to judge them for perpetrating injustice or allowing it to be perpetrated on others who also bear His image.

I. SOCIAL INJUSTICE JUDGED
(Isaiah 10:1-27)

The corruption of Judah had become so pervasive that to be poor, orphaned or widowed was to be left without opportunity for justice and subject to the greed of any with a little power or authority. How ironic that a people brought from slavery by a merciful and just God would themselves come to a place where such injustice and cruelty ruled their society. If God would find such injustice repugnant in the world, how much more so would He find it to be among His own people?

A. The Certainty of Judgment
(vv. 1-4, 11, 12, 16-19)

(Isaiah 10:11, 12, 16-19 is not included in the printed text.)

1. Woe unto them that decree unrighteous decrees, and that write grievousness which they have prescribed;
2. To turn aside the needy from judgment, and to take away the right from the poor of my people, that widows may be their prey, and that they may rob the fatherless!
3. And what will ye do in the day of visitation, and in the desolation which shall come from far? to whom will ye flee for help? and where will ye leave your glory?
4. Without me they shall bow down under the prisoners, and they

shall fall under the slain. For all this his anger is not turned away, but his hand is stretched out still.

When Isaiah pronounced woe upon Judah, he was simply stating a divine message that is repeatedly voiced throughout Scripture. God will undoubtedly and unavoidably bring injustice to judgment. The requirement of proper treatment of the deprived was one of the founding tenets of Moses' law (see Exodus 23:1-9; Leviticus 19:15; Deuteronomy 16:19, 20; 24:17, 18). The person who would dare to ignore this requirement of the Law was sentenced to a curse from God (Deuteronomy 27:19). Injustice is sin, and "the soul who sins shall die" (Ezekiel 18:4, *NKJV*).

In essence, the acts of injustice Isaiah observed were in direct violation of the basic tenets of Mosaic Law, and by all appearances, new laws were being enacted to condone such corruption. The "unjust laws [and] oppressive decrees" (Isaiah 10:1, *NIV*) were evidently giving license to the unjust to do exactly what was disallowed in the Ten Commandments. They were specifically told, "You shall not bear false witness against your neighbor. You shall not covet your neighbor's house; you shall not covet your neighbor's wife, nor his male servant, nor his female servant, nor his ox, nor his donkey, nor anything that is your neighbor's" (Exodus 20:16, 17, *NKJV*).

This presents us with a priceless lesson in society: legal does not mean right. Every person will give an account to God not of how they obeyed the laws of man, but of how he or she obeyed the laws of God, conscience and justice.

God's rhetorical question, "What will you do in the day of punishment?" and His pronouncement of "desolation which will come from afar" (Isaiah 10:3, *NKJV*) were a prelude to His planned judgment upon the unjust. They would not have anywhere to flee for help and their glory would be taken. Those who inflicted injustice would "bow down [among] the prisoners" and "fall [among] the slain" (v. 4). Even then, God's anger toward them would not be quenched. Hell awaited them.

As God had done to Samaria, He was about to do to Mount Zion, the "Holy City" (see vv. 11, 12). He would bring leanness—a fire of destruction—that would waste away the glory of Judah and Jerusalem (see vv. 16-19).

B. The Tools of Judgment (vv. 5-10, 13-15)

(Isaiah 10:5-10, 13-15 is not included in the printed text.)

Judgment will ultimately take place in the courts of heaven where everyone will stand before God having their lives exposed. However, God does also bring about judgment upon men, women and nations here in this life. God warns us clearly, "Do not be deceived, God is not mocked; for whatever a man sows, that he will also reap" (Galatians 6:7, *NKJV*).

Assyria, the nation that conquered Israel and caused great fear to fall upon Judah, was God's chosen tool of justice in Isaiah's time. A nation of idolatry and heathenism would become the "staff" of God's "indignation" (vv. 5, 6). God's way of bringing justice and calling His people to repentance is often cloaked in irony. Even in circumstances where an attack from an enemy of God is directed toward us, we should reflect upon the possibility that God has allowed it to happen to correct some shortcoming on our part.

The Assyrians, however, did not know they were being used of God to do His bidding. They prided themselves in their own power and reaped all the glory along with the spoils of Judah. To them, Judah and Jerusalem would be conquered as they had conquered other nations. Assyria's haughtiness, however, would be short-lived. Even the tool must give reverence to the hand that wields it (see vv. 12-15).

C. Hope in Judgment (vv. 20-27)

(Isaiah 10:20-27 is not included in the printed text.)

God's capacity and desire to extend mercy is revealed in the Bible almost every time He is shown rendering judgment. At the sin of Adam and Eve, He pronounced a curse upon them laced with the first promise of a redeeming Savior (Genesis 3:15). Here, in Isaiah 10, on the heels of a dramatic and devastating pronouncement of impending judgment, God declared that a remnant of Israel would escape the judgment and would no longer be dependent upon the mercy of a conqueror, but would depend solely upon Him.

God determined He would bring righteousness out of the destruction He had decreed upon Judah. God's promise to the remnant was that He would bring to a quick end the heavy hand of Assyrian domination. So, the righteous among His people should not fear them, but patiently wait for God's deliverance (vv. 24, 25).

God made clear His reasons for the destruction of both the unrighteousness in Israel and the conquering Assyrians. Israel was His chosen people. Their kings, priests and prophets were anointed by God to serve Him and the people in righteousness. They had failed in this and would be judged. Assyria, though victorious in battle against the unjust leaders of God's people, was not anointed of God and would also be judged. The remnant of Israel would become the heirs of the anointing oil (v. 27)—the righteous people of God. ᵉ ℕ ᵟ ᵗ

II. THE SAVIOR PROMISED
(Isaiah 11:1-16)

Whenever God used an Old Testament prophet to condemn and judge His people, He also often took the opportunity to renew or give greater insight into His recurring promise of the Messiah. Speaking through Isaiah, God bolstered the courage and

endurance of the remnant for the present (10:20-34), but He also gave them a reason to hold on to His promises far into the future.

A. A Savior Shall Come (vv. 1-5)

1. And there shall come forth a rod out of the stem of Jesse, and a Branch shall grow out of his roots:

2. And the spirit of the Lord shall rest upon him, the spirit of wisdom and understanding, the spirit of counsel and might, the spirit of knowledge and of the fear of the Lord;

3. And shall make him of quick understanding in the fear of the Lord: and he shall not judge after the sight of his eyes, neither reprove after the hearing of his ears:

4. But with righteousness shall he judge the poor, and reprove with equity for the meek of the earth: and he shall smite the earth with the rod of his mouth, and with the breath of his lips shall he slay the wicked.

5. And righteousness shall be the girdle of his loins, and faithfulness the girdle of his reins.

Royalty is the first insight given into the person who will be the Savior. He will come from the house of Jesse, the father of David. As a rod or branch springs up from the root of a felled tree, so would this royal Savior come from the house of David. Most importantly, the Spirit of the Lord would "rest upon Him." Through the Spirit, the Messiah would have wisdom, understanding, counsel, might and knowledge, and He would delight in God.

Considering the injustice that the people had suffered at the hands of their leaders and judges, the most important statement to them was the vantage point from which this Messiah would rule and judge. Whereas their former judges could be swayed by the wealthy appearance of some who came before them, or by words of promise or flattery uttered in their ears, the Messiah would not judge by sight nor by hearing but solely by righteousness. The poor would no longer be at great disadvantage. The widow and orphan would stand on equal ground with the wealthy and powerful. Wickedness would be vanquished and righteousness and faithfulness would be the norm.

B. The Peace He Will Bring (vv. 6-9)

(Isaiah 11:6-9 is not included in the printed text.)

The coming of the Messiah would bring unimaginable peace. To a people living in an era where war far too often touched their lives, the peace promised in Isaiah's message must have been thought by many to be the ravings of a madman. The wolf dwelling peacefully with the lamb—how absurd.

However, to those who believed, the message was clear. The Messiah would bring such a peace that conflict between peoples need not be mentioned. His peace would be so pervasive and complete that the mighty lion would become a vegetarian rather than disturb the peace of God. Not only would peace reign between animal and animal, but also between animal and humanity. Even the weakest child would have nothing to fear from the deadliest of snakes.

This peace would not be the product of a powerful enforcer or the result of a dreadful threat if one would break the peace. It would be the unavoidable result of a clear and universal knowledge of the Lord. To know God is to live in absolute peace.

C. The Unity He Will Bring (vv. 10-16)

(Isaiah 11:10-16 is not included in the printed text.)

The Messiah, the "Root of Jesse," will bring about a grand unity of nations and peoples according to those who put their trust in Him. It is obvious from the latter portion of chapter 11 that not all will come to Him, but the indication is that all who do will find unity. As a "banner to the people" (v. 10, *NKJV*), He will draw to Himself a multitude of Gentiles as well as the remnant of His people from the nations of the world. The Gentiles will seek Him out so that they may follow Him. The tribes of Israel will come together without past rivalries and follow as one.

The reference in the text to a second restoration (v. 11) of the remnant is a wonderful prophecy for today. It passes over the first restoration that would take place under Zerubbabel in 537 B.C. and portends a final great restoration in a latter day. The first restoration had not yet taken place and yet Isaiah was looking farther ahead to a second. On May 18, 1948, God began the process of that restoration by allowing Israel to become a nation once again after centuries of being scattered over the world. With the foundation for that second restoration now well established, we can excitedly anticipate the fulfillment of this prophecy—possibly even in our own lifetime.

As a united people under Christ, they will confront the unrepentant and unconverted nations, and will be victorious over them in a miraculous manner reminiscent of the victory God gave Israel at the Red Sea.

III. THE SAVIOR CELEBRATED
(Isaiah 12:1-6)

For the remnant of Israel then, the prophecies of Isaiah surely gave plenty of reasons for rejoicing. The injustice they had suffered was about to be judged and, though defeat was imminent, victory would soon follow. They would have reason to give God praise.

From our vantage point, we have even more reason to praise God. We not only see what God did in Isaiah's day, we can also transpose the promises God gave through the prophet to our time as we foresee wonderful victories ahead for God's church. If worship is indeed celebration, then every moment we spend in worship should reflect our joy in the mercy and salvation granted to us as we approach the fulfillment of these prophecies.

A. Celebrate His Mercy (vv. 1-3)

1. And in that day thou shalt say, O Lord, I will praise thee: though thou wast angry with me, thine anger is turned away, and thou comfortedst me.
2. Behold, God is my salvation; I will trust, and not be afraid: for the Lord JEHOVAH is my strength and my song; he also is become my salvation.
3. Therefore with joy shall ye draw water out of the wells of salvation.

The foundation for our praise and celebration of the Savior is, of course, our salvation. Paul stated the condition of all humanity when he said, "For all have sinned, and come short of the glory of God" (Romans 3:23). At some point in our conversion, we sensed the same kind of emotion expressed by Isaiah: "Though You were angry with me, Your anger is turned away, and You comfort me" (v. 1, NKJV). When the sinner experiences the conviction of the Holy Spirit, he or she senses the anger of the Lord at the sin in his or her life. When that conviction is acted upon and repentance takes place, suddenly the sense of anger is replaced with a sense of comfort—the heart once condemned receives comfort from the same source.

Sounding as poetic as a psalmist, Isaiah said he would "trust and not be afraid; for Yah, the Lord, is my strength and song" (v. 2, NKJV). It is wonderful to feel the strength of the Lord as He upholds us in times of trouble, but how much more wonderful when His presence is the cause of

our heart bursting forth in song. Singing is not simply intended as a pleasure for the hearer; it is intended to be a joyful release for the singer. For the children of God, He is the source of our strength and the fountain of our joy, often bubbling forth in joyful song.

The same God who is judge to the unrighteous is Savior to the just. With joy—wonderful, refreshing exuberance—the righteous will drink of the "wells of salvation" (v. 3). Anyone who has tasted water drawn with a bucket and rope from a deep well can attest to the sweetness of that water. Though this metaphorical image well illustrates the refreshing nature of the experience of salvation, it doesn't come close to expressing the joy of the forgiven heart. God's mercy is sweeter than cool water to a parched tongue and more joyful than any other experience of the human condition.

B. Celebrate His Glory (vv. 4-6)

4. And in that day shall ye say, Praise the Lord, call upon his name, declare his doings among the people, make mention that his name is exalted.
5. Sing unto the Lord; for he hath done excellent things: this is known in all the earth.
6. Cry out and shout, thou inhabitant of Zion: for great is the Holy One of Israel in the midst of thee.

Revelation 4 depicts an awesome scene in heaven in which God receives praise and worship as He sits upon His glorious throne. In John's vision, 24 elders clothed in white and wearing crowns of gold fall prostrate and cast their crowns at the feet of God, crying, "You are worthy, O Lord, to receive glory and honor and power; for You created all things, and by Your will they exist and were created" (v. 11, NKJV).

If the inhabitants of heaven give God such worship and celebrate His glory, how much more so will those whom He has redeemed from the corruption of the world?

Isaiah identifies several ways God's people will exalt Him in that day of glory. First, the people will simply "praise the Lord"—such a simple term with such an important function. It does not matter if the one praising God is rich or poor, wise or simple—praise delights Him.

Then Isaiah says they will *declare* His deeds and *exalt* His name. God's name always reflects His actions, so in exalting His name they are also declaring His deeds and vice versa.

God's people will glorify Him in *song*, singing of His excellence for all to hear. They will also *cry out* and *shout*, "For great is the Holy One of Israel in [your] midst" (v. 6).

With the injustice of those in authority condemned and the Savior promised, the voice of Isaiah no doubt brought cause for celebration among the oppressed in that day. God had recognized their plight and sent a prophet to tell them of a coming judgment against the unjust and a coming Savior. This alone was reason for them to have hope and rejoice.

The same is true today. Injustice is still alive and well in this world, and we too still look for the Savior. Now, however, we know who He is and we can expect His return soon. We have all the more reason to rejoice as Isaiah's prophecy is being fulfilled in our day.

GOLDEN TEXT HOMILY

"GOD IS MY SALVATION; I WILL TRUST, AND NOT BE AFRAID: FOR THE LORD JEHOVAH IS MY STRENGTH AND MY SONG; HE ALSO IS BECOME MY SALVATION" (Isaiah 12:2).

Words are inadequate when we try to describe the greatness of God's goodness. He has been wonderfully gracious to us in bestowal: the gifts of our being, our spiritual nature, our physical nature, our human relationships, our material needs. His greatest kindness to us is deliverance through salvation—redemption from sin and the hope of a higher and endless life in another world.

One response of our hearts to the divine love is a confidence that excludes anxiety—"I will trust, and not be afraid."

Many are the occasions of human fear and anxiety: the maintenance of the family, the preservation of our personal integrity, our passage through the gateway of death, and so on. We are insufficient in ourselves to meet fear and anxiety. But if our confidence is in God, we can have the assurance of His divine help.

The continuance of His greatest gift is imparting spiritual strength. Having redeemed us from the power and condemnation of sin, and lifted us up to the state of adoption and heirship, He sustains us in our new and blessed life.

In response to the divine love, we should be filled with gratitude that finds utterance in sacred song. We should always be ready to break forth into praise. Our life should be a song of gratitude for the salvation of the Lord.

God is great! How fortunate and blessed we are to be His children. —**O.W. Polen**

SENTENCE SERMONS

CHRISTIANS CELEBRATE Christ as Emancipator and Savior.

—Selected

WHEN GOD MEASURES a man or a nation, He puts the tape around the heart instead of the head.

—*Encyclopedia of Religious Quotations*

HEAVEN is above all yet; there sits a judge that no king can corrupt.

—**William Shakespeare**

EVANGELISM APPLICATION

THE LOST ARE DRAWN TO CHRIST AS CHRISTIANS PROCLAIM THE FREEDOM HE GIVES.

The judgment of God against sin and injustice is not given to us in Scripture so that we may gloat over those who will be condemned. Although we can't help but have a sense of justice about their condemnation, the intent of God is to convict the unjust and the sinner of their errors, and induce a state of repentance in their hearts.

To suffer injustice does not entitle a person to seek delight in the punishment of the one that inflicted the injustice upon him. Rather, prayers should be made in behalf of the offender by the sufferer. Jesus said: "You have heard that it was said, 'You shall love your neighbor and hate your enemy.' But I say to you, love your enemies, bless those who curse you, do good to those who hate you, and pray for those who spitefully use you and persecute you, that you may be sons of your Father in heaven; for He makes His sun rise on the evil and on the good, and sends rain on the just and on the unjust" (Matthew 5:43-45, NKJV).

ILLUMINATING THE LESSON

Our American judicial system is fraught with so many rules and limitations that often criminals who are undoubtedly guilty of the crime for which they are charged suffer no consequence—instead, they freely walk away.

In God's judicial system, however, the One serving as the Judge in each case is also the prosecution's eyewitness. This Judge sees all things, knows all things and judges all things. Only the accused that repentantly request the defense services of the Judge's Son will escape punishment.

DAILY BIBLE READINGS

M. God's Judgment Declared.
   Isaiah 19:1-4
T. God's Judgment Deferred.
   Jonah 3:3-10
W. God's Judgment Questioned.
   Malachi 3:5-10
T. God's Judgment Determined.
   John 16:5-11
F. God's Judgment Averted.
   Colossians 2:13-17
S. God's Judgment Includes Mercy.
   Revelation 6:1-6

TRUTH SEARCH
Creatively Teaching the Word

DISCUSSION QUESTIONS

Isaiah 10:1-4
• What do you suppose makes a law *unrighteous* and *grievous* ("oppressive") in God's eyes (v. 1)?
• Describe the different groups that were being treated unjustly and the unjust acts being carried out (v. 2).
• According to verse 3, was a "day of reckoning" (*NIV*) imminent or merely threatened by God?
• What would be the purpose of this day of reckoning?
• What does verse 4 say to people who think they can get away with unjust practices?

Isaiah 11:1-5
• Explain the description of the Savior as a "rod" and a "Branch" (v. 1).
• What does verse 2 say about the abilities and character of the Savior?
• What kind of Judge would the Savior *not* be (v. 3)?
• Who would look forward to His works of justice, and who would dread His coming (v. 4)?
• What is the Savior's hallmark (v. 5), and why is this important?

VIDEO ILLUSTRATION

Use a video camera to film areas around your community that depict social problems. For instance, you might film dilapidated public housing, public schools in need of repair, streets that aren't safe at night, areas where children or the elderly live in poverty, areas where the homeless hang out, and so on.

You also can clip pictures and articles from newspapers that highlight social injustices in your community.

Show the video and newspaper clips to highlight local problems. Ask how Jesus would address the injustices if He were living on earth. Then discuss how He expects the church to act.

Way of Redemption

Study Text: Isaiah 33:1 through 35:10
Objective: To acknowledge God's power to transform rebellious lives and walk in righteousness.
Time: Between 742 and 687 B.C.
Place: Judah, possibly in Jerusalem
Golden Text: "An highway shall be there, and a way, and it shall be called The way of holiness" (Isaiah 35:8).
Central Truth: Christians depend on God's transforming power for holiness in living.
Evangelism Emphasis: Sinners are attracted to Christ when believers reflect His character.

PRINTED TEXT

Isaiah 33:17. Thine eyes shall see the king in his beauty: they shall behold the land that is very far off.

22. For the Lord is our judge, the Lord is our lawgiver, the Lord is our king; he will save us.

23. Thy tacklings are loosed; they could not well strengthen their mast, they could not spread the sail: then is the prey of a great spoil divided; the lame take the prey.

24. And the inhabitant shall not say, I am sick: the people that dwell therein shall be forgiven their iniquity.

35:1. The wilderness and the solitary place shall be glad for them; and the desert shall rejoice, and blossom as the rose.

2. It shall blossom abundantly, and rejoice even with joy and singing: the glory of Lebanon shall be given unto it, the excellency of Carmel and Sharon, they shall see the glory of the Lord, and the excellency of our God.

3. Strengthen ye the weak hands, and confirm the feeble knees.

4. Say to them that are of a fearful heart, Be strong, fear not: behold, your God will come with vengeance, even God with a recompence; he will come and save you.

5. Then the eyes of the blind shall be opened, and the ears of the deaf shall be unstopped.

6. Then shall the lame man leap as an hart, and the tongue of the dumb sing: for in the wilderness shall waters break out, and streams in the desert.

7. And the parched ground shall become a pool, and the thirsty land springs of water: in the habitation of dragons, where each lay, shall be grass with reeds and rushes.

8. And an highway shall be there, and a way, and it shall be called The way of holiness; the unclean shall not pass over it; but it shall be for those: the wayfaring men, though fools, shall not err therein.

9. No lion shall be there, nor any ravenous beast shall go up thereon, it shall not be found there; but the redeemed shall walk there:

10. And the ransomed of the Lord shall return, and come to Zion with songs and everlasting joy upon their heads: they shall obtain joy and gladness, and sorrow and sighing shall flee away.

DICTIONARY
habitation of dragons—Isaiah 35:7—place of desolation

LESSON OUTLINE
I. SEEING THE REDEEMER
   A. A Visible Kingdom
   B. A Vanishing Terror
   C. A Victorious City

II. JOY OF TRANSFORMATION
   A. From Barrenness to Beauty
   B. From Fear to Faith
   C. From Weakness to Wholeness

III. PATH OF THE REDEEMED
   A. Highway of Holiness
   B. Highway of Rejoicing

LESSON EXPOSITION
INTRODUCTION

The prospect of judgment has always been one of God's beckoning calls for people to repent. It is this desire of God to bring us to repentance that causes Him to include such statements as Isaiah 33:14-16:

> Who among us shall dwell with the devouring fire? Who among us shall dwell with everlasting burnings? He who walks righteously and speaks uprightly, he who despises the gain of oppressions, who gestures with his hands, refusing bribes, who stops his ears from hearing of bloodshed, and shuts his eyes from seeing evil: he will dwell on high (Isaiah 33:14-16, NKJV).

Those who decry preaching messages of an eternal hell or of a vengeful God are either not students of the Bible or have come to believe that not all of the Bible is the Word of God. From Genesis to Revelation, the Bible contains numerous accounts of judgment both pronounced and executed by God, the most dreadful of which awaits us at the conclusion of time.

There are two sides to the prophecies of the Bible concerning this ultimate judgment. There is of course the horrible side of fear and dread of the punishment God intends to inflict upon the sinners and the unjust. The second side to such judgments is the vision of what God intends for His people—those who repent and find mercy.

While condemnation is being pronounced against unbelievers, rejoicing will be taking place in the congregation of the righteous. The saints will rejoice not because of the judgments against the unrighteous but because of the salvation bestowed upon them through Christ.

To those who do find salvation, those redeemed from the judgments ahead, God has given wonderful glimpses of the joys that await.

I. SEEING THE REDEEMER
(Isaiah 33:17-24)

"Faith is the substance of things hoped for, the evidence of things not seen" (Hebrews 11:1). The truth of this statement is most clearly seen concerning salvation. We are saved by our faith in the risen Lord. Having never looked upon the face of Jesus, Christians today long for the time when we will see Him face-to-face.

Because we live by faith and not by sight, there is a special blessing assigned to us. When Thomas was convinced of Jesus' resurrection by virtue of seeing Him alive, Jesus said, "Blessed are they that have not seen, and yet have believed" (John 20:29). This blessing, however, does not diminish the desire of the faithful follower of Christ to look upon Him in His glory.

A. A Visible Kingdom (v. 17)

17. Thine eyes shall see the king in his beauty: they shall behold the land that is very far off.

Jesus prayed a very revealing prayer in John 17 concerning His disciples and His approaching crucifixion. He prayed that the Father would sanctify those who followed Him; that He would keep them and protect them from the Evil One; that they would have unity, and that the joy of Christ would be fulfilled in them.

Jesus also asked, "Father, I desire that they also whom You gave Me may be with Me where I am, that they may behold My glory which You have given Me; for You loved Me before the foundation of the world" (John 17:24, *NKJV*). Isaiah's prophecy foresaw the answer to that prayer many years before Christ made the request.

"Your eyes will see the King in His beauty" (v. 17, *NKJV*). Isaiah did not elaborate on this statement. The most obvious reason is that the beauty of our King is incomparable to anything in the earth. At the fulfillment of this prophecy it will not be the beauty of His throne or His kingdom, but *His* beauty that will stand out in our vision—the beauty of our Redeemer.

Not only will the Redeemer be visible to us, but also the kingdom over which He rules will be seen. That land seems to be "very far off" (v. 17), and our eyes are troubled by the visions of the kingdoms of the earth as they are today. In every sense, we are like Abraham who sojourned in a land waiting and looking for a "city which hath foundations, whose builder and maker is God" (Hebrews 11:10). In the strength of our faith and the surety of the promises of God, we will one day see that city.

B. A Vanishing Terror (vv. 18, 19)

(Isaiah 33:18, 19 is not included in the printed text.)

As Christ and His coming kingdom become visible to the faithful, the visions of the present world become pale and less threatening. In hindsight, the fears of the world will be little more than moments to "meditate" upon.

The inhabitants of Jerusalem in the day of Isaiah's prophecy would one day ask, "Where is the scribe? Where is he who weighs? Where is he who counts the towers?" (v. 18, *NKJV*). Most commentaries indicate that the *scribe* was some important class of officer in the Assyrian army rather than the Hebrew scribe. Also, *he who weighs* and *he who counts towers* were probably Assyrian officers in charge of assessing monetary values and defensive strengths of Israel. These were a source of terror for the inhabitants of Jerusalem. In the future meditation of Jerusalem, these causes of fear would be noticeably absent.

In the Day of the Lord, noticeably absent will be the causes of terror for the believer. Gone will be the threats of wicked men who today rob and kill without regard for human life. Gone will be the threat of injustice through governments that have no regard for the welfare of their citizens.

A term Isaiah used in reference to the Assyrians—"a fierce people" (v. 19)—is an appropriate adjective for much of the world today. Jesus said that the last days would be vexed by wars and dangerous times (see Matthew 24:4-13). Paul called these days "perilous times" (2 Timothy 3:1). As these scriptures indicated, today we face "fierce people" wherever we turn, whether in the Middle East, South America, Africa, and even here at home—multitudes of people whose reasoning and ideas are to us "beyond perception" (Isaiah 33:19, *NKJV*).

At that final gathering of God's people, there will be no fierce people and no obscure speech, only the communication of the righteous and the fellowship of the saints. All causes of fear and trepidation in this world will have vanished in the light of Jesus sitting on His throne. E N d

C. A Victorious City (vv. 20-24)

(Isaiah 33:20, 21 is not included in the printed text.)

22. For the Lord is our judge, the Lord is our lawgiver, the Lord is our king; he will save us.

23. Thy tacklings are loosed; they could not well strengthen their mast, they could not spread the sail: then is the prey of a great spoil divided; the lame take the prey.

24. And the inhabitant shall not say, I am sick: the people that dwell therein shall be forgiven their iniquity.

Isaiah's exhortation to "look upon Zion" (v. 20) was intended to draw the reader's attention to the distressful state of the city where they had gathered for their feast of the Lord in generations past. He wanted them to look upon Jerusalem in her sorrow to tell them that one day that city would appear drastically different.

Even today, Jerusalem is a place of trouble and war. Though many leaders have tried to establish a lasting peace in Jerusalem, the battles still rage and people still die. The Jerusalem we see today is still not the one Isaiah prophesied about.

The Jerusalem Isaiah saw was "a quiet habitation" (v. 20) that will be eternally peaceful. That Jerusalem will reflect the Tabernacle in the wilderness in that it will be a meeting place for God and His people. Rather than camping around the Tabernacle as Moses and Israel did, however, the city itself will be the Tabernacle—our home. The prominent difference between the Tabernacle of Moses and the Tabernacle of Jerusalem will be that the new Tabernacle will be permanent. Not one stake will be pulled up and not one cord will be broken. That Jerusalem will be an eternal place of residence for God and His followers.

In an interesting twist of words, Isaiah says that in Jerusalem "the majestic Lord will be for us a place of broad rivers and streams" (v. 21, *NKJV*). This description indicates a major crossroads city where navigated rivers converge and merchants and travelers frequent. In other words, it refers to a major metropolitan area of great importance. However, the text says, "*The Lord will be for us a place of broad rivers and streams.*" It will not be the commerce, the night life or the vistas of the city that will make it a place of convergence of the masses; instead, the presence of the Lord will draw the multitudes.

Though Jerusalem will be a wonderful center of attraction, warships will never sail the city's waters (v. 21) and instead will be rendered harmless (v. 23). Jerusalem will be a city of peace. The obvious reason is that the One who will make that city a gathering place of the masses will also be Judge, Lawgiver and King (v. 22). He will draw the masses, govern and judge them, and rule over all. No one in His kingdom will suffer from sin-sickness, for all will be forgiven and redeemed (v. 24).

II. JOY OF TRANSFORMATION
   (Isaiah 35:1-7)

There is no doubt that God has set a time to judge the enemies of His people. There is also no doubt that He has also set a time to gather His people and complete the transformation begun in us at the beginning of our faith.

Isaiah 34 is compared by many to Revelation 19:17-21 and the gathering for the Battle of Armageddon. There is also a resemblance to Revelation 6:14 in the description of the sky being rolled up as a "scroll" (Isaiah 34:4). In similar fashion, the prophecies of Isaiah 35 are thought to refer to the millennial reign of Christ as mentioned in Revelation 20.

The terrible judgments in Isaiah 34 and Revelation 19 are set in stark contrast to the wonderful transformations God intends for His people and their habitation as seen in Isaiah 35. Fear of judgment may be an effective deterrent to sin, but the desire to experience the dramatic and wonderful transformation God has in store for His people offers an outlook of unspeakable joy.

A. From Barrenness to Beauty (vv. 1, 2)

1. The wilderness and the solitary place shall be glad for them; and the desert shall rejoice, and blossom as the rose.

2. It shall blossom abundantly, and rejoice even with joy and singing: the glory of Lebanon shall be given unto it, the excellency of Carmel and Sharon, they shall see the glory of the Lord, and the excellency of our God.

Isaiah prophesied that under the reign of the Messiah, the land itself will undergo a great transformation. For the benefit of the regathered people of God, the barren land will be blessed and is said to experience gladness and rejoicing for God's people because of that transformation (v. 1).

Wilderness places, deserts and wastelands will flourish and blossom abundantly. If color and lushness can be compared to joy and singing, then the land will be alive with rejoicing and songs. The glory of Lebanon was her cedars, and the excellence of Mount Carmel and the plains of Sharon were their beautiful flowers and lush plants. This glory and excellence will be made to flourish in Zion as God prepares her for His people.

With God's glorious presence in direct contact with the earth, how could it do anything else but flourish and rejoice?

B. From Fear to Faith (vv. 3, 4)

3. Strengthen ye the weak hands, and confirm the feeble knees.

4. Say to them that are of a fearful heart, Be strong, fear not: behold, your God will come with vengeance, even God with a recompence; he will come and save you.

Fear has no place in the kingdom of God. Fear denotes a lack of faith or a lack of self-confidence. Those who are weak in hand or feeble in the knee must find the courage to grip hard and stand tall. The means of finding this strength is obvious. The psalmist said of the Lord, "You have armed me with strength for the battle" (Psalm 18:39, *NKJV*) and "The Lord is my strength and my shield; my heart trusted in him, and I am helped" (28:7). It is the Lord himself who strengthens the fearful.

Isaiah's message to the fearful was that the Lord was coming with "vengeance" and with the "recompence" of God (v. 4) to carry out justice. He would not be coming to condemn the righteous, but to save them. Therefore, they had no need to fear Him. He would transform their fear to faith.

C. From Weakness to Wholeness (vv. 5-7)

5. Then the eyes of the blind shall be opened, and the ears of the deaf shall be unstopped.

6. Then shall the lame man leap as an hart, and the tongue of the dumb sing: for in the wilderness shall waters break out, and streams in the desert.

7. And the parched ground shall become a pool, and the thirsty land springs of water: in the habitation of dragons, where each lay, shall be grass with reeds and rushes.

In our time as throughout the centuries, God's people have not been immune to the tragedies and suffering that are common to humanity.

Although God has called us out of the world, the world is still very much with us. Many of those who follow the Lord struggle daily with maladies and ailments that cause constant suffering. It will always be so for everyone in this world—the just and the unjust alike.

When the Day of the Lord has come, however, the weaknesses of this flesh will give way to the renewing power of the Lord. Among all of the saints, there will be no illness, no maladies and a complete absence of suffering. The blind will see, the deaf will hear, the dumb will sing, and the lame will "leap like a deer" (vv. 5, 6, NKJV). Just as the arid land will spring forth with water, the physical being of the redeemed will spring forth with renewed wholeness of life.

How exciting it is to think of the transformation awaiting the earth and the saints in that day. The saints who long ago went to rest in the presence of the Lord will live again as spry as in their youth. The scarred and hurting world that has been ravaged by the neglect and mistreatment of mankind will be refreshed and renewed. Together, people and earth will exalt the name of God for His transforming power.

III. PATH OF THE REDEEMED
(Isaiah 35:8-10)

As the renewed city of Zion is established and the righteous saints are drawn to it, God will build a highway for the redeemed to travel upon. Believers will journey together toward the city of God, no doubt worshiping as they go.

We have heard the stories of the old saints who often walked to church services in small groups. As they would walk and talk of the goodness of God, the Holy Spirit would move among them and rejoicing and singing would begin to flow from the little groups as they journeyed together. Surely, travelers on the highway built by God will enjoy even greater rejoicing as they journey toward Zion.

A. Highway of Holiness (vv. 8, 9)

8. And an highway shall be there, and a way, and it shall be called The way of holiness; the unclean shall not pass over it; but it shall be for those: the wayfaring men, though fools, shall not err therein.

9. No lion shall be there, nor any ravenous beast shall go up thereon, it shall not be found there; but the redeemed shall walk there:

The highway built by God will be a limited-access highway. Rather than being limited by tolls or by locations of access, that highway will be limited by the contents of the traveler's heart. No one with an impure heart may traverse this road. No one who delights in sin or wickedness will find an access ramp. Only the holy may travel this road, for it will be the "Highway of Holiness."

Navigating the route to Zion will not require an expertise in map-reading or following directions. The righteous person, though limited in intellect, will easily be able to make his or her way to that city. The kingdom of God has always belonged to the simple and the pure. A childlike faith, simple acceptance and belief, is all that God requires.

No lions or ravenous beasts that can threaten a weary traveler will have access to this highway. There will never occur a single incident of "road rage" because all will be engrossed in the joys of "road praise." There will never be a collision, never a crash, never a fender bender, but travelers will always be joyful, always safe, and always worshiping.

B. Highway of Rejoicing (v. 10)

10. And the ransomed of the Lord shall return, and come to

Zion with songs and everlasting joy upon their heads: they shall obtain joy and gladness, and sorrow and sighing shall flee away.

The travelers on that highway will have one central quality in common—each will have been ransomed by the Lord. Every traveler on that road will have been held hostage at some point in his or her existence. The bondage of sin will have held each of them fast and left them without any possibility of purchasing their own freedom. But the Bible says, "There is one God, and one mediator between God and men, the man Christ Jesus; who gave himself a *ransom for all*, to be testified in due time" (1 Timothy 2:5, 6).

Each traveler then, knowing the One who ransomed him or her from certain death, will travel that road in wondrous delight and rejoicing. Singing will be heard from all who travel that road, songs borne from "everlasting joy" that will be poured upon their heads as they travel. All sorrow and sadness will "flee away."

If the trip to Zion on the Highway of Holiness is going to be so joyful, one can only wonder what joys will actually await within the walls of the city. As the multitudes of the redeemed converge upon Zion, the shouts of praise and the purity of the worship of God will surely ignite the most awesome demonstration of adoration for God that has ever been seen in this world.

GOLDEN TEXT HOMILY

"AN HIGHWAY SHALL BE THERE, AND A WAY, AND IT SHALL BE CALLED THE WAY OF HOLINESS" (Isaiah 35:8).

To those of us who look forward to the time when God himself will "make all things new" (Revelation 21:5) and our holy Lord "shall reign forever" (Psalm 146:10), the word *holiness* is full of beauty. It connotes a way of life that is pure—free from deceit, corruption, insecurity, sin and sadness. It speaks of a time of perfect harmony, an overwhelming love from God the Father, and protection from all evil.

If we then look forward to—even long for—that idyllic time when the loving rule of God will no longer be challenged by the evil influence of Satan, why do we so often fall prey to Satan's tricks in this world? He tempts us to express our anger when we perceive that we have been ill-treated, and sometimes we succumb with an indignant outburst. He tempts us to criticize when another person receives an honor or a promotion we deem should have been ours.

When we display the same behavior as those who do not know the redeeming love of Christ, they see nothing beautiful in our lives to draw them to the Savior. But when we surrender our lives completely to our holy Lord, He enables us to live a life of holiness in this present world that is a foretaste of an eternity with Him where holiness will reign. Such a lifestyle will advance His kingdom here and now.—**Wilma Amison**

SENTENCE SERMONS

CHRISTIANS DEPEND on God's transforming power for holiness in living.

—Selected

THE TRUE CHRISTIAN IDEAL is not to be happy but to be holy.

—Vance Havner

YOU CAN ALWAYS TELL when you are on the road to righteousness.

—Ernest Blevins

OUR RIGHTEOUS ACTS are like filthy rags.

—Isaiah 64:6

EVANGELISM APPLICATION

SINNERS ARE ATTRACTED TO CHRIST WHEN BELIEVERS REFLECT HIS CHARACTER.

A pure and wholesome life can have two drastically different effects upon others, both arising out of the same root cause. To many, someone living a holy life because of their faith is fair game for the butt of jokes, ridicule and antagonism. To others, the same person will be looked up to as an example of a lifestyle they would like to live, but feel too inadequate—too sinful—to achieve.

One person views the Christlike life of another and senses the condemnation of the Holy Spirit for his or her own sinful life. In response, he or she will lash out at the witness of the Christian with ridicule. Another person observes the same witness, also feels condemnation, and reasons within his or her heart, "That is the way I would live if I could."

In both circumstances, the testimony of a Christlike life has had an effect. A seed has been sown with the potential of germinating into an experience of repentance and salvation.

ILLUMINATING THE LESSON

All who will travel the Highway of Holiness were at one time anything but holy. Paul wrote, "For all have sinned, and come short of the glory of God" (Romans 3:23).

When someone wants to travel the highways of our nation, he or she must earn that privilege by proving he or she can operate a motor vehicle. The obligation is upon the person to prepare for the exam, acquire the license, purchase insurance and buy a vehicle. When these things are accomplished, one may enter the highway and travel among the other drivers.

To travel on the Highway of Holiness, God prepares the heart and mind, He provides the license, He provides the vehicle, and God himself is the insurance that one's trip will be successful. God's grace provides us all the opportunity to travel this road if we choose.

DAILY BIBLE READINGS

M. Redemption Previewed.
Genesis 3:14, 15, 21-24
T. Song of the Redeemed.
Exodus 15:11-18
W. A Personal Redeemer.
Job 19:25-27
T. Redemption Accomplished.
John 19:28-35
F. Redemption Applied.
Romans 8:1-4
S. Redemption Completed.
Revelation 21:22-27

TRUTH SEARCH
Creatively Teaching the Word

DISCUSSION QUESTIONS
Isaiah 33:17-24

• What roles will God play when His people dwell with Him (vv. 17, 21, 22)?
• Describe what life with God will be like (vv. 18-20, 23).
• What will God do for His people (v. 24)?

Isaiah 35:1-10

• How will the desert and the wilderness be transformed, and how will it happen (vv. 1, 2)?
• How could this desert miracle have a spiritual application?
• What message brings strength and steadiness (vv. 3, 4)?
• Describe the miraculous acts God will perform (vv. 5-7).
• What will be the name of the highway in the place God will bless (v. 8)?
• Who will be forbidden from traveling on this highway?
• What do you think Isaiah means by "unclean" in verse 8?
• Who will walk on this highway (v. 9)?
• Do you think Isaiah was speaking of literal lions and ferocious beasts (v. 9)? If not, what do they symbolize?
• What does it mean to be "ransomed" by God?

• Sometimes holiness is equated with dullness and misery. How are the holy ones seen in verse 10? Why?

GRAFITTI WALLS

To begin the session, write each letter of the word *HOLY* on a separate sheet of construction paper. Divide your class into four groups, giving each group one of the pieces of paper and a marker.

On the side of each paper on which you wrote a letter, have the students list words beginning with that letter which accurately describe what it means to be holy. On the opposite side, they should list words beginning with that letter which is contrary to holiness. Following are possible responses:

H: happy, healthy, honor, heaven, humility; *not* hardness, hatred, hardhearted, heavy

O: obedient, only, ordained, OK; *not* obsolete, old-fashioned, out-of-touch

L: loving, Lord's, lively; *not* lost, lustful, losing, lazy

Y: yes, Yours, yielded; *not* yucky, yesterday

Have the students present their work.

God Comforts His People

Study Text: Isaiah 40:1-31
Objective: To appreciate and rely on God's gentleness and strength.
Time: Between 742 and 687 B.C.
Place: Judah, possibly Jerusalem
Golden Text: "They that wait upon the Lord shall renew their strength; they shall mount up with wings as eagles; they shall run, and not be weary; and they shall walk, and not faint" (Isaiah 40:31).
Central Truth: In times of distress, we can rely on God's comfort and strength.
Evangelism Emphasis: Our waiting on God in stressful times can be a witness to those experiencing difficulty.

PRINTED TEXT

Isaiah 40:1. Comfort ye, comfort ye my people, saith your God.

2. Speak ye comfortably to Jerusalem, and cry unto her, that her warfare is accomplished, that her iniquity is pardoned: for she hath received of the Lord's hand double for all her sins.

3. The voice of him that crieth in the wilderness, Prepare ye the way of the Lord, make straight in the desert a highway for our God.

4. Every valley shall be exalted, and every mountain and hill shall be made low: and the crooked shall be made straight, and the rough places plain:

5. And the glory of the Lord shall be revealed, and all flesh shall see it together: for the mouth of the Lord hath spoken it.

10. Behold, the Lord God will come with strong hand, and his arm shall rule for him: behold, his reward is with him, and his work before him.

11. He shall feed his flock like a shepherd: he shall gather the lambs with his arm, and carry them in his bosom, and shall gently lead those that are with young.

12. Who hath measured the waters in the hollow of his hand, and meted out heaven with the span, and comprehended the dust of the earth in a measure, and weighed the mountains in scales, and the hills in a balance?

13. Who hath directed the Spirit of the Lord, or being his counsellor hath taught him?

14. With whom took he counsel, and who instructed him, and taught him in the path of judgment, and taught him knowledge, and shewed to him the way of understanding?

28. Hast thou not known? hast thou not heard, that the everlasting God, the Lord, the Creator of the ends of the earth, fainteth not, neither is weary? there is no searching of his understanding.

29. He giveth power to the faint; and to them that have no might he increaseth strength.

30. Even the youths shall faint and be weary, and the young men shall utterly fall:

31. But they that wait upon the Lord shall renew their strength; they shall mount up with wings as eagles; they shall run, and not be weary; and they shall walk, and not faint.

LESSON OUTLINE

I. GOD PROCLAIMS COMFORT
   A. God Comforts Through Peace
   B. God Comforts Through Hope
   C. God Comforts in Death
II. GOD IS GENTLE AND STRONG
   A. God Is Present
   B. God Is Strong and Compassionate
   C. God Is Powerful
III. GOD STRENGTHENS THE WEARY
   A. God Knows
   B. God Empowers
   C. God Renews

LESSON EXPOSITION

INTRODUCTION

Isaiah 40 represents a new direction in the prophetic ministry of Isaiah. Until this chapter, he had pronounced judgment upon the unrighteous and offered frequent vistas into a grand hope for the future. In this chapter he begins to pronounce the advent of comfort and restoration for the people of Judah and Israel. Such a drastic transition from the previous chapters has led some scholars to claim a second writer authored the remaining chapters of Isaiah. A careful study of the styles and events of the writings disallow a second writer and confirm Isaiah to be the author of the last part of the book as well as the first.

The message of this chapter is overtly positive and filled with encouragement. Jerusalem had suffered so tremendously that God would say she had been punished "double for all her sins" (v. 2). In His divine strength and shepherdly compassion, God was announcing that the time of punishment was coming quickly to an end and a time of renewal was ahead.

God's ancient message of comfort to the people of Jerusalem is easily transferable to those who suffer or are overpowered in our time. Christians today can read these words and easily place themselves in the sentiments expressed in the message: God truly is the Good Shepherd who brings comfort to all His people.

I. GOD PROCLAIMS COMFORT
   (Isaiah 40:1-8)

The message begins as though it were being shouted from a rooftop: "Comfort, yes, comfort My people!" (v. 1, *NKJV*). The intended audience of the message was obviously those in authority—people who could command the ears of the people. They were being given the task of bringing a message of comfort to suffering Israel.

The preaching of judgment and the preaching of comfort are not mutually exclusive. The person who delights in preaching the condemnation of God upon the world should also recognize that more Scripture is devoted to comfort than damnation. God punishes out of necessity, but He loves and comforts because it is His nature.

A. God Comforts Through Peace
   (vv. 1, 2)

1. Comfort ye, comfort ye my people, saith your God.

2. Speak ye comfortably to Jerusalem, and cry unto her, that her warfare is accomplished, that her iniquity is pardoned: for she hath received of the Lord's hand double for all her sins.

The message God gave to Isaiah for Jerusalem was that her wars had ended and her iniquity had been pardoned. In other words, Jerusalem was at peace with the world and at peace with God.

Peace is a dual concept. I might be at peace with those around me while inside I am fighting a battle that leaves me as ravaged and beaten as any physical battle. Or I may be at peace with myself but find my country at war and my loved ones at risk. Both of the aspects of peace are fragile and may be disrupted at a moment's notice.

The Old Testament frequently uses the analogy of a tent as representative of a home or family. The comparisons are especially revealing when it comes to the fragile nature of peace in the home. A severed cord or a broken stake will cause a tent to collapse. In the home, a tragic mistake or a fateful accident can shatter the peace of a home. Try as we will, peace is a commodity that we cannot store up for rainy days.

God is the source of our peace, whether it is peace with others or peace with ourselves. He gave comfort to His people by telling them their wars had ended. They could rest from their fighting—put away their swords. Most of all, He gave them comfort by forgiving their sins.

To have the comfort of peaceful relationships with those around us, we first must receive the peace that comes when our sins are forgiven and our iniquity is purged. When we are at peace with God and ourselves, peace with others comes much easier.

B. God Comforts Through Hope (vv. 3-5)

3. The voice of him that crieth in the wilderness, Prepare ye the way of the Lord, make straight in the desert a highway for our God.

4. Every valley shall be exalted, and every mountain and hill shall be made low: and the crooked shall be made straight, and the rough places plain:

5. And the glory of the Lord shall be revealed, and all flesh shall see it together: for the mouth of the Lord hath spoken it.

On the heels of the pronouncement of comfort through peace, Isaiah gave further comfort by announcing the preparation for the Lord's arrival. Today we recognize this passage as a prophecy of John the Baptist and his role as the one who would prepare the way for the ministry of Jesus. To those in Isaiah's day, the message meant that the Lord was coming to their wilderness to deliver them from captivity and preparations for His arrival must be made.

What wondrous hope that message must have brought to the captives of Jerusalem in a foreign land! What hope it gives to us as we look back and see the fulfillment of that message in the person of John. Most importantly, what hope it gives to us as we look forward to the coming of Jesus Christ at which time He will resurrect the dead and rapture His church away.

Hope is the message of the Bible from Genesis to Revelation. It is the foundation of our faith. We hope in Christ and therefore we can endure the wilderness. When He comes, every mountain will be brought low, every valley will be elevated, and every rough place will be made smooth. We might say that all things will become equal at His coming. There will be no great and small, no "haves and have-nots," but there will be equality among all who look for Him. If the adage that says, "The ground is level at the foot of the cross" is true, then the ground at the foot of the throne is also level.

Isaiah said, "The glory of the Lord will be revealed, and all mankind together will see it (v. 5, NIV). That is the hope of every Christian—to see the Lord with our own eyes and rejoice in His return.

C. God Comforts in Death (vv. 6-8)

(Isaiah 40:6-8 is not included in the printed text.)

Isaiah was commanded of God to "cry out" and acknowledge the frailty of the human condition: "All flesh is grass, and all its loveliness is like the flower of the field" (v. 6, *NKJV*). God reminds us that as grass withers, age causes the flesh to wither and lose its elasticity. The beauty of life also fades just like a flower that has seen too many sunny days.

God's reason for this reminder was not to cause pain or sorrow, but to provide comfort for those who had or would come to realize that the glory days of life were behind them. It can be hard to accept the fact that age is a transforming power. As age has overtaken all who have gone before us, it will overtake us as well. But God intends for us to know it is by His breath that we pass on just as it was by His breath that we came into being (v. 7). He intends for us no harm in this fact; it is simply the nature of things.

Although we will wither and fade as the grass and flowers, the Word of God that we have staked our life upon will never fade or wither—it will stand forever (v. 8). This means the promises of hope and peace are going to be just as valid after we die as they are today. The God who made these promises will never die, the promises will never go out of date, and, though we may die, we will one day see the fulfillment of every word.

Comfort is knowing there is Someone greater than the tragedies of this life. Comfort is knowing that Someone is in covenant with us—a covenant that continues on long after death.

II. GOD IS GENTLE AND STRONG
(Isaiah 40:9-26)

Every believer who comes to know the character of God and how He interacts and ministers to the needs of His children experiences a wonderful sense of comfort. Though the qualities of gentleness and strength are quite different from one another, they are not mutually exclusive. In fact, to be truly gentle a person also must be truly strong, and vice versa.

Every believer should find cause for comfort in the fact that God's character provides for both His strength to help us and correct us when needed, and His gentleness to comfort and encourage us when that is what we need.

A. God Is Present (v. 9)

(Isaiah 40:9 is not included in the printed text.)

God instructed the messengers, "those who bring good tidings," to arise to the highest points and with their strongest voices cry out to the cities of Judah, "Behold your God!" (v. 9). The message was clearly, "Look! Your God is present!"

God is "a very present help in trouble" (Psalm 46:1). And not just in times of trouble, for we know that God is omnipresent—that is, everywhere present at the same instant. He is present at all times with us and is more than able to assist us in whatever circumstance we face.

God is omnipresent simply because He is God, but He is present to help us because He is our Father and cares about our needs. What a wonderful concept! We are never without Someone who cares and is able to help.

B. God Is Strong and Compassionate (vv. 10, 11)

10. Behold, the Lord God will come with strong hand, and his arm shall rule for him: behold, his reward is with him, and his work before him.

11. He shall feed his flock like a shepherd: he shall gather the lambs with his arm, and carry them in his bosom, and shall gently lead those that are with young.

Two very different pictures of the presence of the Lord take shape in verses 10 and 11. First we see the Lord in strength with a strong hand and an arm that will rule His people. He is seen as focused upon giving rewards to those who deserve them.

This image of God is probably the one most people recognize. Many view God as a strong, somber Deity who will judge and punish. To a great degree that image is correct, but that side of God will not be fully observed until the end when final judgment takes place.

The strong hand of God reaches down to save, and His all-powerful arm rules with a compassion that only God could have. His work is to "feed His flock like a shepherd; He will gather the lambs with His arm, and carry them in His bosom, and gently lead those who are with young" (v. 11, NKJV).

It is the compassion of God that rules our world, not His judgment. If His judgment were predominant in His character, we would all have long ago perished. But because God loves us and desires that all repent and be saved, "His compassions fail not" (Lamentations 3:22).

C. God Is Powerful (vv. 12-26)

(Isaiah 40:15-26 is not included in the printed text.)

12. Who hath measured the waters in the hollow of his hand, and meted out heaven with the span, and comprehended the dust of the earth in a measure, and weighed the mountains in scales, and the hills in a balance?

13. Who hath directed the Spirit of the Lord, or being his counsellor hath taught him?

14. With whom took he counsel, and who instructed him, and taught him in the path of judgment, and taught him knowledge,

and shewed to him the way of understanding?

The vastness of His compassion can be realized only in reference to the vastness of His power. The litany of the majesty of God begins with a series of rhetorical questions concerning Creation. Answers to these questions are not necessary because of the obvious impossibility of any other answer but God.

"Who," He asks, "has measured out the waters in the hollow of His hand? Who has measured the heavens, calculated the dust, or weighed the mountains and hills?" (see v. 12). In these questions He announces Himself as the all-powerful Creator of the universe. No other could have possibly conceived of such things, much less carried them out.

In verses 13 and 14, Isaiah asks rhetorical questions regarding the unequaled wisdom of God. The prophet highlights the contrast between God and man.

Counsel indicates deliberating; forming a design or plan. Further, it refers to reciprocal consultation. Isaiah asks if any person could do this with God, or give God advice.

Instructed refers to explaining material needing to be understood. *Taught* refers to training with an emphasis upon acquiring information through intense and repetitive discipline. *Understanding* refers to perception and the ability to distinguish between issues. Isaiah asks what person could give God these capacities.

The answer is, God's wisdom is unequaled. Listing various disciplines required for wisdom, such as consultation, instruction, discipline, and perception, Isaiah affirms that no one can give these to God. God stands alone and unequaled in His wisdom.

In verses 18-24, Isaiah compares idols, princes and rulers who might challenge the incomparable God of Israel. No doubt the exiles had been tempted to think the rulers of Babylon were mighty in comparison to God. As a result, they could not see God's redemption and comfort.

Verse 25 is a climax to the rhetorical questions begun in verse 12. God personally asks the question, "To whom will you compare me? Or who is my equal?" (NIV).

To provide the answer, Isaiah uses the stars as a backdrop in verse 26. *Calleth* refers to God's calling forth stars. God created the stars by calling them forth. God named them and gave them their own distinct identity, no two stars being identical.

God's power is further demonstrated in the manner in which the stars subsist. Not one "fails" but is sustained by God. The stars are suspended and unattached from earth or earthly power. In the heavens they were created and remain by God's power alone. They stand as a demonstration of God's incomparable strength.

III. GOD STRENGTHENS THE WEARY (Isaiah 40:27-31)

The idea that such a powerful and majestic God actually cares for the weakest and smallest among His creation seems absurd to many. Such a concept even becomes hard for many believers to hold onto when they find themselves in dire straits. Nonetheless, God's Word is true and He has promised to be our strength in times of trouble. The Lord says, "Fear not, for I am with you; be not dismayed, for I am your God. I will strengthen you, yes, I will help you, I will uphold you with My righteous right hand" (Isaiah 41:10, NKJV).

A. God Knows (vv. 27, 28)

(Isaiah 40:27 is not included in the printed text.)

28. Hast thou not known? hast thou not heard, that the everlasting God, the Lord, the Creator of the

ends of the earth, fainteth not, neither is weary? there is no searching of his understanding.

"Does God know this is happening to me?" is a question that has probably crossed every believer's mind at some point while passing through suffering or distress. In verse 27, God's question was, "Why do you ask yourself such questions?" His people evidently thought that God did not know what had happened to them and that He was ignoring their "just claim" (NKJV).

God's response to them was, "Have you not known? Have you not heard?" (v. 28, NKJV). Irony is a wonderful literary tool for making a point. God was turning the tables on those who had thought to themselves that God didn't know their plight. If they, in their limited power and understanding, could know that God was the everlasting Creator of all things who never grew weary, surely they should also know that in His omniscience He knew their circumstances better than they did.

"Everlasting" and "Creator" (v. 28) highlight God's supremacy over both time and space. This supremacy is in stark contrast to the limited vision and circumstances of Israel. They who were nothing were doubting God who is everything.

Why would a faithful follower of Christ ever believe that He didn't care or that He had not noticed the crisis he or she was in? How could someone who knew God and knew the Word of God ever believe that He didn't care? This was God's question to Israel and His question to us today. God knows. God cares. God will intervene at the right time, every time.

B. God Empowers (v. 29)

29. He giveth power to the faint; and to them that have no might he increaseth strength.

The intervention of God into the affairs of His children reflects the ideal care and nurturing of an earthly father. When a child lacks enough strength to achieve a certain goal, the father of that child shouldn't step into the situation and take over for the child. A wise and caring father will allow the child to reach the limits of his ability and then will come to the child's assistance, supplying only the strength that was lacking. In doing this, the child will learn that he must continue to try to reach the goal for himself, and will also learn that the strength of the father can be relied upon when his strength reaches its end.

When one of God's children is completely without strength, God "gives power." It is a miraculous experience for a Christian to be lifted to a heavenly height from a point of greatest weakness, and it happens every day. When we have reached our limit, when we have exhausted every ounce of energy—whether in coping with life or fighting Satan—God will be there to lift us up.

When we face a challenging situation, God would not have us to back away because of feelings of inadequacy. The task may call for someone more mighty than we view ourselves to be, but the Bible says, "And to those who have no might He increases strength" (v. 29, *NKJV*). God has assured us that where our strength ends, His begins. When we have carried the load as far as our strength will take it, God will increase our strength so that we may finish the task.

C. God Renews (vv. 30, 31)

30. Even the youths shall faint and be weary, and the young men shall utterly fall:

31. But they that wait upon the Lord shall renew their strength; they shall mount up with wings as eagles; they shall run, and not be weary; and they shall walk, and not faint.

The strength of youth is not without limit. Even the strong and athletic person can reach the end of his or her endurance and become exhausted. No matter how strong the person, it is still the strength of the flesh—a fickle and vanishing strength.

In contrast to this fact, God presents us with one of the most recognized and cited passages of Scripture: "They that wait upon the Lord shall renew their strength" (v. 31). This reference is made not only to the young person who has become exhausted, but to any believer.

The word *wait* does not imply mere patience. It is more akin to the ideas of strength and unity. The word comes from a root word meaning "twist or bind." The emphasis in this context is to twist or bind oneself to God with a sense of anticipation. The renewed strength will bring greater vigor and stamina than the strength that was lost.

In the body we may have strength to climb, but never to fly. In the body we may have the strength to run, but weariness will invariably come. In the body we may have the strength to walk, but in the heat of the day we will surely faint. However, those who wait upon the renewing of the Lord will receive of His strength—the strength to fly, to run without weariness, and to walk without fainting.

GOLDEN TEXT HOMILY

"THEY THAT WAIT UPON THE LORD SHALL RENEW THEIR STRENGTH; THEY SHALL MOUNT UP WITH WINGS AS EAGLES; THEY SHALL RUN, AND NOT BE WEARY; AND THEY SHALL WALK, AND NOT FAINT" (Isaiah 40:31).

The Lord is keenly aware of our everyday trials and burdens. He is concerned with the irritations and setbacks causing us heartache and pain. Knowing we need an oasis to restore our faith and strength, He offers us spiritual renewal and refreshing.

To "wait upon the Lord" means to cast our life wholly upon Him. If we do this, He will supply a source of strength unknown to the world. This spiritual refreshing will empower us to overcome any obstacle or trial in our life.

Although we may sometimes feel we are an island, the Lord assures us this is not the case. Even the great prophet Elijah felt no one carried the burden he did. In 1 Kings 19:14, Elijah said, "Even I only, am left; and they seek my life, to take it away." But in verse 18 the Lord reminded Elijah there were 7,000 in Israel who had not bowed their knees to Baal.

No, we are not carrying our burdens alone; for we have a Savior who dwells within our very being. To serve Him is to know a strength and love that will sustain us in every situation.

In Christ there is strength for the weak, rest for the weary, guidance for those who are confused, and a refuge for all who have lost their way.— **Jerry Puckett**

SENTENCE SERMONS

IN TIMES OF DISTRESS, we can rely on God's comfort and strength.
—Selected

UNLESS THERE IS WITHIN US that which is above us, we will ever yield to that which is around us.
—Peter Forsythe

IN THE PRESENCE OF TROUBLE, some people grow wings; others buy crutches.
—Harold W. Ruopp

EVANGELISM APPLICATION

OUR WAITING ON GOD IN STRESSFUL TIMES CAN BE A WITNESS TO THOSE EXPERIENCING DIFFICULTY.

Being a witness for Christ is not a fair-weather activity. Christians are to let their light shine even in the darkness of personal hardship and suffering. In fact, the light of a witness for Christ shines brightest when others see our walk of faithfulness and patience, waiting upon the deliverance of the Lord. When God brings victory to our troubled life— and He will—the witness of our steady faith and confident patience will say more than all of our words.

ILLUMINATING THE LESSON

Some time ago there was a television commercial that pictured a large, muscular black man gently nestling his small baby in his arms. That image of massive arms cradling a newborn baby evoked in me a sense of wonder about the power, compassion and gentleness of God.

Though able to crush and discard the fragile life of His Creation, God instead cherishes and nurtures us even though we have fallen far short of His will. Have you ever observed the father of a newborn child as he caresses his baby in his arms? Place yourself in that image and you still won't even come close to understanding the love of God our Father.

DAILY BIBLE READINGS

M. Prayer for Comfort.
Psalm 77:2-11
T. Hope for the Future.
Jeremiah 32:8-15
W. Angelic Reassurance.
Zechariah 1:12-17
T. Encouraged by Healing.
Luke 8:40-48
F. Comfort From God's Word.
Romans 15:4-6
S. Comfort Each Other.
1 Thessalonians 4:13-18

TRUTH SEARCH
Creatively Teaching the Word

DISCUSSION QUESTIONS

Isaiah 40:1-8

• In what ways is the Lord's gentleness expressed in verses 1 and 2?
• In what ways is the Lord's strength expressed in verses 3-7?
• Why should the promise of verse 8 bring great comfort to God's people?

Isaiah 40:9-15

• *Sovereign* means someone or something above all else in rank or authority. It also means being independent of all others, such as a sovereign nation. In light of the term "Sovereign Lord" in verse 10 (*NIV*), how should Israel view their relationship with God? How should we view our relationship with Him?
• What does "his arm shall rule for him" (v. 10) mean?
• How did God reveal His mighty arm to the Israelites as they stood at the foot of Mount Sinai (Exodus 19:16-19)?
• Why does God not present Himself to the world in such a manner today?
• In Isaiah 40:11, who are the lambs? What is the significance of God gathering "the lambs with His arm"?
• Why does God "carry them in his bosom" and "gently lead" them (v. 11)?
• Make comparisons between Isaiah 40:11 and Psalm 23:1-4.

• Describe the incredible strength and wisdom of God as pictured in Isaiah 40:12-15.

Isaiah 40:27-31

• Why is the omnipotence of God (vv. 27, 28) so important to us (v. 29)?
• What is the key to receiving the Lord's strength (v. 31)? What does this mean?
• How does God promise to help those who wait on Him (v. 31)?

OBJECT LESSON

Items needed: Egg, marker, marker board, stuffed animal

Invite a strong man to class. Take a few moments to talk about the man's strength, or perhaps he can demonstrate his muscle by lifting something heavy or flexing a muscle.

Next, have the man complete the following tasks: tossing an egg in the air and catching it, writing his name on the marker board, tying his shoes, and cuddling the stuffed animal. Have the volunteer return to his seat.

Not only is this man strong; he could also perform acts that required him to control his strength and show gentleness. Today we are exploring two of God's attributes: His unlimited power and His loving gentleness.

The Servant Savior

Study Text: Isaiah 42:1-13; 49:1-7
Objective: To examine and appreciate Christ's role as the Servant Savior.
Place: Jerusalem
Golden Text: "Behold my servant, whom I uphold; mine elect, in whom my soul delighteth; I have put my spirit upon him" (Isaiah 42:1).
Central Truth: Jesus Christ, our Savior, exemplified servanthood.
Evangelism Emphasis: As Christians serve with the love of Christ, they draw others to Him.

PRINTED TEXT

Isaiah 42:1. Behold my servant, whom I uphold; mine elect, in whom my soul delighteth; I have put my spirit upon him: he shall bring forth judgment to the Gentiles.

6. I the Lord have called thee in righteousness, and will hold thine hand, and will keep thee, and give thee for a covenant of the people, for a light of the Gentiles;

7. To open the blind eyes, to bring out the prisoners from the prison, and them that sit in darkness out of the prison house.

8. I am the Lord: that is my name: and my glory will I not give to another, neither my praise to graven images.

9. Behold, the former things are come to pass, and new things do I declare: before they spring forth I tell you of them.

10. Sing unto the Lord a new song, and his praise from the end of the earth, ye that go down to the sea, and all that is therein; the isles, and the inhabitants thereof.

11. Let the wilderness and the cities thereof lift up their voice, the villages that Kedar doth inhabit: let the inhabitants of the rock sing, let them shout from the top of the mountains.

12. Let them give glory unto the Lord, and declare his praise in the islands.

13. The Lord shall go forth as a mighty man, he shall stir up jealousy like a man of war: he shall cry, yea, roar; he shall prevail against his enemies.

49:1. Listen, O isles, unto me; and hearken, ye people, from far; The Lord hath called me from the womb; from the bowels of my mother hath he made mention of my name.

3. And said unto me, Thou art my servant, O Israel, in whom I will be glorified.

5. And now, saith the Lord that formed me from the womb to be his servant, to bring Jacob again to him, Though Israel be not gathered, yet shall I be glorious in the eyes of the Lord, and my God shall be my strength.

6. And he said, It is a light thing that thou shouldest be my servant to raise up the tribes of Jacob, and to restore the preserved of Israel: I will also give thee for a light to the Gentiles, that thou mayest be my salvation unto the end of the earth.

DICTIONARY

Kedar (KEY-dur)—Isaiah 42:11—the tribe which descended from Kedar, one of Ishmael's 12 sons

the rock—Isaiah 42:11—a place in Edom known as Sela (*NKJV*) and later called Petra

LESSON OUTLINE

I. ANOINTED TO SERVE
   A. The Uniqueness of Christ's Servanthood
   B. The Power of Christ's Servanthood

II. EXALT THE LORD
   A. Exalt Him in Song
   B. Exalt Him Everywhere
   C. Exalt Him in Victory

III. SAVIOR FOR ALL PEOPLE
   A. The Foundation of His Mission
   B. The Scope of His Mission
   C. The Culmination of His Mission

LESSON EXPOSITION

INTRODUCTION

In the Book of Isaiah there are four passages known as "servant songs" that specifically cast the Messiah in the role of a servant. The text of this lesson contains two of the four. The third servant song is 50:4-11 and the fourth is 52:13—53:12. The messages of these servant songs illustrated and identified for Israel the ministry of the Messiah. Each song revealed the deity and humanity, the power and meekness, and the lordship and servanthood of the Savior who was to come.

This lesson explores the role of Christ as the Servant Savior and reveals the universality of His saving work. It must have been a problematic text for the scribes and strict Hebrews to deal with since it indicated that the Messiah would come not only for their benefit but also for the benefit of the Gentiles. To such an exclusive and closed society, it must have been vexing to think that the Messiah was not going to be their exclusive property.

Whatever interpretation Hebrew scholars have attempted to give to this text, it still must be acknowledged by all readers that the Messiah was coming to save not only the Jews but also the Gentiles. Jesus Christ—the Messiah—came to save the world from sin. He came as a servant to the Father and ultimately as a servant to humanity that through Him all might have access to salvation—Jew or Gentile.

I. ANOINTED TO SERVE
(Isaiah 42:1-9)

The extraordinary ministry of Jesus revealed to us in Scripture is made even more extraordinary by the frequent request He made of those whom He healed. After performing miraculous healings, He would ask the people not to broadcast the news of the miracles (e.g., Matthew 12:16). He did not want to be exposed as the Christ prematurely. He had an earthly ministry He wanted to complete and prophecies about Him that had to be fulfilled. His premature exposure as the Messiah would no doubt complicate these things.

A quotation from the text of this lesson (Isaiah 42:1-4) follows such a charge given by Jesus in Matthew 12:18-21. It was the intent of Jesus to do the servant's work as long as He could, and to avoid the controversy that would no doubt arise when He made Himself known. As we may easily observe in hindsight today, Jesus would not have had a chance to exemplify servanthood for us had He immediately revealed Himself as the Christ—and servanthood was at the core of the message He wanted to bring.

A. The Uniqueness of Christ's Servanthood (vv. 1-4)

(Isaiah 42:2-4 is not included in the printed text.)

1. Behold my servant, whom I uphold; mine elect, in whom my soul delighteth; I have put my spirit upon him: he shall bring forth judgment to the Gentiles.
The pattern of Jesus' ministry as servant set an example for every Christian to follow. Jesus' words to His disciples concerning His—and their—servanthood will always resound with expectation: "You know that those who are considered rulers over the Gentiles lord it over them, and their great ones exercise authority over them. Yet it shall not be so among you; but whoever desires to become great among you shall be your servant. And whoever of you desires to be first shall be slave of all. For even the Son of Man did not come to be served, but to serve, and to give His life a ransom for many" (Mark 10:42-45, *NKJV*).

Jesus came from heaven to serve people, and His servanthood was similar to that of any servant of God today yet with several inescapable and dramatic differences.

The similarities between Jesus' servanthood and ours rest mainly in the calling and its goal. God "upholds" those whom He has called into His service, He "delights" in their obedience to His call, and He puts His Spirit on and within them (Isaiah 42:1). From this calling the Christian servant preaches under the authority of the Holy Spirit, prays for the sick, cares for those in need, and leads people into a relationship with God. All of these things are observed in the ministry of Jesus, but there the similarities end.

Isaiah called Him the "Elect One" (v.

1, *NKJV*), meaning the One selected by God to fulfill the particulars of this prophecy. Both Jews and Christians agree that the person being spoken of is the Messiah. He is the Elect One because none other would have the power to "bring forth judgment [justice] to the Gentiles" (v. 1) and establish justice in the earth (v. 4).

In bringing justice to the earth, Isaiah anticipated He would not do it with the emphatic and fervent voice of a rebel stirring crowds in the street. He would not be a violent revolutionist. This Elect One would come with a soft voice, an easy step and a kind hand; so gentle in fact as to refuse to break a badly bent reed or quench the last sparks of a smoldering wick (see v. 3). In meekness, God's elect would come to establish truth and justice in the earth. But meekness is not weakness.

"He shall not fail," Isaiah said, "nor be discouraged" (v. 4). He was coming as the Elect One of God, one in whom God delighted, and in whom God had placed His Spirit. How could He fail? Why would He ever be discouraged?

Again, we compare the Messiah and the man or woman called to minister today. Ask any minister of God's Word if he or she has ever been discouraged or has ever failed. Of course you know the answer. Everyone faces discouragement, and no one ever achieves everything they set out to do—everyone fails once in a while. Just as we are human, so was Jesus. As a man, He succeeded where no other man could succeed. As a man, He never became discouraged as every other person occasionally becomes.

Sometimes, in our human condition, discouragements and failures cause us to experience "the blues." During those times (which can be quite lengthy) we are tempted to just give up and let someone else take over our God-given ministry. It is often the power of the memory of our calling that causes us to shake off the blues and continue on. Whatever discouragements Jesus faced—religious opposition, spiritual battles, struggles of earthly living, and so on—He knew who He was and what He must do. That calling inspired Him on, just as our calling inspires us on today. ⌐

B. The Power of Christ's Servanthood (vv. 5-9)

(Isaiah 42:5 is not included in the printed text.)

**6. I the Lord have called thee in righteousness, and will hold thine hand, and will keep thee, and give thee for a covenant of the people, for a light of the Gentiles;
7. To open the blind eyes, to bring out the prisoners from the prison, and them that sit in darkness out of the prison house.
8. I am the Lord: that is my name: and my glory will I not give to another, neither my praise to graven images.
9. Behold, the former things are come to pass, and new things do I declare: before they spring forth I tell you of them.**

For all things earthly, the creative power of God stands as the apex of His majesty. To have the power to speak all things out of nothing is so awesome that we cannot comprehend it. It was this power that God cited through Isaiah in proclaiming the calling, sustaining and ministry of the Messiah (v. 5).

With an assurance of divine care and keeping, Jesus was given "as a *covenant* to the people, as a light to the Gentiles" (v. 6, *NKJV*). God had intended from the beginning to bless the entire world through Abraham (see Genesis 18:18) and, in this prophesy of Isaiah, He demonstrates that fact again. Jesus came "to seek and to save that which was lost"

(Luke 19:10) regardless of nationality or background.

In the power of the Holy Spirit, Jesus fulfilled the charge of bringing justice to the Gentiles and established His law and justice in all the earth. His servanthood was fulfilled in bringing salvation to the entire world, and establishing a standard against which every individual will eventually be measured. As a servant, He became Savior. As servants, we minister to others in the Savior's name.

Both physical and spiritual evidences guaranteed Christ's ministry as "a covenant to the people and a light to the Gentiles." First, Jesus actually opened blinded eyes during His ministry on earth and continues to perform such miraculous restorations of sight through His servants today. This miracle, more than any other, seems to represent the Messiah's ministry in Scripture (Psalm 146:8; Isaiah 29:18; 35:5; 42:7, 16, 18, 19; Matthew 11:5; 15:31; Luke 4:18). But more than this, Christ brought light into a dark world—the light of God's ultimate plan for mankind. Imprisoned by the darkness of this world, all of humanity received an offer of divine pardon and release from that prison in Jesus (Isaiah 42:6, 7).

Because of God's mercy in sending Christ to deliver humanity, glory and honor are due to Him alone. God did away with the old means of coming to Him and established a new way—through Christ. In Jesus, God did a new thing—set a new standard for worship and means of repentance. The old ways passed on (v. 9).

II. EXALT THE LORD
(Isaiah 42:10-13)

If, then, in Christ a new way of worship was established, then a new song of worship is to be desired. This is not to say that a new song of musical composition is demanded, but a new hymn of God's mercy has dawned. Instead of singing of our deliverance from the hands of Pharaoh and out of the Red Sea, we are to sing of the deliverance of our souls from hell through Jesus Christ the Servant Savior. It is the same tune, but different lyrics.

A. Exalt Him in Song (v. 10)

10. Sing unto the Lord a new song, and his praise from the end of the earth, ye that go down to the sea, and all that is therein; the isles, and the inhabitants thereof.

Songs are one of our most important outlets for our emotions. When we are excited we may sing an up-tempo song or a lilt. If we are sad we may sing a slower, more subdued song of lament or even a dirge. Songs serve us in expressing ourselves; therefore, we are exhorted to worship God in song.

In the wilderness, God gave Israel water from the earth and Israel spontaneously worshiped in a song (Numbers 21:16-18). Besides being a spontaneous facet of worship, singing has been ordered of God to remind us of what He has done for us. Deuteronomy 31 and 32 tell of a song given to Moses by God which not only instructed Israel in remembrance of what God had done for them, but would also serve a judgment against them when they erred.

Music and singing then are tools of exaltation and instruction, leading followers in both spiritual and intellectual growth in Christ.

B. Exalt Him Everywhere (vv. 11, 12)

11. Let the wilderness and the cities thereof lift up their voice, the villages that Kedar doth inhabit: let the inhabitants of the rock sing, let them shout from the top of the mountains.

12. Let them give glory unto the Lord, and declare his praise in the islands.

We are exhorted to worship God by giving Him glory and declaring His praise (v. 12).

God wants people everywhere to praise Him. Those who lead a difficult existence in the wilderness, the inhabitants of cities, those who live outside Israel (represented by Kedar and "the rock [Sela]") should all glorify God (v. 11). He is to be praised to the farthest island and to the farthest extent of the coasts (v. 12). Wherever land exists and people reside, God is to be exalted.

C. Exalt Him in Victory (v. 13)

13. The Lord shall go forth as a mighty man, he shall stir up jealousy like a man of war: he shall cry, yea, roar; he shall prevail against his enemies.

The reason for this glorifying of God is made clear in verse 13: "The Lord will march out like a mighty man, like a warrior he will stir up his zeal; with a shout he will raise the battle cry and will triumph over his enemies" (*NIV*).

The battle is the Lord's. God will be victorious over all of Satan's plans to destroy His creation. Such a victory must be glorified and proclaimed abroad.

III. SAVIOR FOR ALL PEOPLE (Isaiah 49:1-7)

The expanse of the "islands" or "coastlands" again indicates the expanse of the Savior's reach. No one resides too far for His salvation to reach, and no one has ever built a hermitage that conceals him or her from the Savior's knowledge. God knows exactly where each of us lives—whether His salvation has reached us or not.

A. The Foundation of His Mission (vv. 1, 2)

(Isaiah 49:2 is not included in the printed text.)

1. Listen, O isles, unto me; and hearken, ye people, from far; The Lord hath called me from the womb; from the bowels of my mother hath he made mention of my name.

The impact of this passage points us to the Gospels concerning the birth and ministry of Jesus. While God knew us before we were born, the way in which Isaiah describes God's foreknowledge of the Servant Savior and His ministry describes something more dramatic.

Brought into the world by God the Father for a purpose that only the Son of God could fulfill, Jesus was called from His mother's womb in similar fashion to Jeremiah (v. 1; cf. Jeremiah 1:5). While Jeremiah's existence began in the womb of his calling, Jesus was preexistent in eternity past. If Jesus was to live as a man, however, God saw it fitting that He should receive the call of a man from His mother's womb.

The far reaches of the earth are challenged to heed the Servant Savior's voice. The limits of the earth are to take note that the Messiah is not sent of His own volition, but by the will of God the Father. God has called Him by name.

The authority given to Jesus is described as having a "mouth like a sharp sword" and being like a "polished shaft" of an arrow (Isaiah 49:2). This characterization brings to mind the many times Jesus rebuked the Pharisees, scribes and leaders of Israel. His words cut through their hypocrisy like a sword, piercing deeply their souls. No wonder the men sent to bring Jesus to the chief priests and Pharisees came back with the report, "No man ever spoke like this Man!" (John 7:46, *NKJV*).

B. The Scope of His Mission (vv. 3-6)

(Isaiah 49:4 is not included in the printed text.)

3. And said unto me, Thou art my servant, O Israel, in whom I will be glorified.
5. And now, saith the Lord that formed me from the womb to be his servant, to bring Jacob again to him, Though Israel be not gathered, yet shall I be glorious in the eyes of the Lord, and my God shall be my strength.
6. And he said, It is a light thing that thou shouldest be my servant to raise up the tribes of Jacob, and to restore the preserved of Israel: I will also give thee for a light to the Gentiles, that thou mayest be my salvation unto the end of the earth.

There is some disagreement as to whether verses 3 and 4 refer to Isaiah himself, the nation of Israel or to the Messiah. The most logical explanation is that the passage is a mixture of all three. Verse 6 is clearly a reference to the Messiah and His far-reaching ministry to the Gentiles. Verse 3, however, seems to be directed to Isaiah himself, but that reference may indeed be allegorical for the nation of Israel. It is on that premise that this lesson will continue.

Israel failed to fully accomplish the task of being a blessing to the nations of the earth, yet God received glory from them even in their failures. He restored them time and time again in order to bring about the birth of His Son, Jesus. Though Israel may have thought their labors were in vain, God was intent on being glorified in them.

With the advent of Christ, the fullness of God's intended blessing through Israel was fulfilled. Jesus was sent to first gather Israel to Himself (v. 5), but also to gather the Gentiles. Jesus was sent to be God's salvation to the ends of the earth, encompassing all nations, peoples and races. The umbrella of salvation would extend over "all that in every place call upon the name of Jesus Christ our Lord" (1 Corinthians 1:2).

C. The Culmination of His Mission (v. 7)

(Isaiah 49:7 is not included in the printed text.)

This study ends with a dramatic proclamation of the Lord to His Messiah. He begins with an affirmation of who He is and His authority to make such statements as He is about to make. God proclaims Himself to be "the Lord, the Redeemer of Israel, and [the] Holy One."

He also makes clear His knowledge of the hearts of those who would look upon the Messiah but not believe. God was saying to them, "Listen, this One that you despise—this One that the nations abhor—kings will stand in His honor and princes will worship Him" (see v. 7). Jesus is the Chosen One of God and the Holy One of Israel—the Servant Savior whom all shall one day worship.

As Paul said, "Therefore God also has highly exalted Him and given Him the name which is above every name, that at the name of Jesus every knee should bow, of those in heaven, and of those on earth, and of those under the earth, and that every tongue should confess that Jesus Christ is Lord, to the glory of God the Father" (Philippians 2:9-11, NKJV).

GOLDEN TEXT HOMILY

"BEHOLD MY SERVANT, WHOM I UPHOLD; MINE ELECT, IN WHOM MY SOUL DELIGHTETH; I HAVE PUT MY SPIRIT UPON HIM" (Isaiah 42:1).

The word *behold* is an emphatic declaration to "take notice and see." The word was not casually used in Scripture. It signified an important announcement, event or scene. Here the expression heralds the magnificent Servant.

"My" or "mine" is mentioned four times by God in reference to the Servant. These expressions convey the unity, oneness and love between God the Father and the Son.

There is a fourfold description of the Father's relationship to Christ in this verse. First, He upholds Christ. Second, Christ is the Father's elect. *Elect* in Hebrew is derived from a word meaning "to prove, try or examine." The word was used to represent the rubbing of a touchstone. A touchstone was a black stone used to test the purity of gold and silver. The metals were rubbed on the stone. The colors of the streaks produced on the metals revealed their quality. Here the concept represents the Servant as God's tested or proven One. Christ is the Father's genuine Servant.

Third, the Servant is the One in whom the soul of God delights. The depths of joy in the Father, because of Christ, are beyond measure.

The final description of the Servant is that God has put His Spirit upon Him. This signified the anointing and life of God the Father, carried in the Son. The sense of this relationship is carried even deeper in the expression used by Christ in the New Testament, "I and my Father are one" (John 10:30).

This fourfold description also applies to everyone who believes on Christ. The Father has *elected* us and will *uphold* us. He *delights* in our relationship with Him, and He *puts His Spirit upon us* to equip us for ministry.—**Selected**

SENTENCE SERMONS

JESUS CHRIST, our Savior, exemplified servanthood.

—**Selected**

THE SERVICE THAT COUNTS is the service that costs. It was that way with the Master.

—*Notes and Quotes*

THE CROSS is the greatest revelation of the love of God, and the manifestation of ultimate servant-hood.

—*Notes and Quotes*

CHRIST WAS FORSAKEN that none of His children might ever need to utter His cry of loneliness.

—**J.H. Vincient**

EVANGELISM APPLICATION

AS CHRISTIANS SERVE WITH THE LOVE OF CHRIST, THEY DRAW OTHERS TO HIM.

Servanthood is most appreciated when it comes without request or an anticipated reward. What personal benefit did Jesus anticipate from His ministry as the Servant Savior? Was there any necessity forced upon Him to become the incarnate Son of God? His servanthood was such that any reasonable person could and should wonder, *Why?*

The truth is that He came to earth as the Servant Savior simply out of love. If we, His children, were to serve our neighbors as Jesus served us, our witness of Him would become a beacon to the lost. Servanthood is what we are called to in Christ.

ILLUMINATING THE LESSON

The hardest part of servanthood is to put others first. A servant always considers the master's needs before his or her own. Translating that concept into Christianity, a sincere Christian is to put everyone before himself or herself, for we are servants of all.

Jesus said, "Whoever desires to become great among you shall be your servant. And whoever of you desires to be first shall be slave of all. For even the Son of Man did not come to be served, but to serve, and to give His life a ransom for many" (Mark 10:43-45, *NKJV*).

DAILY BIBLE READINGS

M. God Defends His Servant.
   Numbers 12:6-13
T. A Servant King.
   2 Samuel 7:4-11
W. Servant Witnesses.
   Isaiah 43:5-12
T. Servant and Judge.
   Matthew 12:18-21
F. From Servants to Heirs.
   Galatians 4:4-7
S. Perfect Example of Servanthood.
   Philippians 2:5-11

TRUTH SEARCH
Creatively Teaching the Word

DISCUSSION QUESTIONS

Isaiah 42:1-10

- What would the Savior come to do (vv. 1, 4, 7)?
- How widespread would His ministry be (vv. 1, 4, 6, 10)?
- What characteristics describe Him (vv. 2-4)?
- What "new things" (v. 9) would the Servant do?

Isaiah 49:1-7

- When did the Lord God establish His plan for His Son (v. 1)?
- How does verse 2 describe God's Son, and what does this description mean?
- Why is the Savior called a servant (v. 3)?
- Among whom did the Savior's work largely appear to be in vain (v. 4; also see John 1:11)?
- To whom did the Savior come to minister first (v. 5)?
- According to verse 6, how far does God's plan of salvation reach?
- What would be the result of the Savior's ministry (v. 7)?

ILLUSTRATION

On a marker board write the following descriptions of people:

- Muslim terrorist
- Columbian drug lord
- Serial murderer
- Filipino orphan
- Lesbian feminist
- Town drunk
- Crooked politician
- African dictator

Which of these people is most valuable in God's eyes?

Which of these people did Jesus Christ *not* die for?

The Sin-Bearing Savior

Study Text: Isaiah 53:1-12; 55:1-7
Objective: To acknowledge Christ as the sacrifice for sin and accept His invitation to abundant life.
Time: Between 742 and 687 B.C.
Place: Judah, probably Jerusalem
Golden Text: "He was wounded for our transgressions, he was bruised for our iniquities: the chastisement of our peace was upon him; and with his stripes we are healed" (Isaiah 53:5).
Central Truth: Christ's suffering and death provide for us a right relationship with God.
Evangelism Emphasis: Christ's suffering and death provide freedom from sin and an invitation to a relationship with God.

PRINTED TEXT

Isaiah 53:3. He is despised and rejected of men; a man of sorrows, and acquainted with grief: and we hid as it were our faces from him; he was despised, and we esteemed him not.

4. Surely he hath borne our griefs, and carried our sorrows: yet we did esteem him stricken, smitten of God, and afflicted.

5. But he was wounded for our transgressions, he was bruised for our iniquities: the chastisement of our peace was upon him; and with his stripes we are healed.

6. All we like sheep have gone astray; we have turned every one to his own way; and the Lord hath laid on him the iniquity of us all.

7. He was oppressed, and he was afflicted, yet he opened not his mouth: he is brought as a lamb to the slaughter, and as a sheep before her shearers is dumb, so he openeth not his mouth.

10. Yet it pleased the Lord to bruise him; he hath put him to grief: when thou shalt make his soul an offering for sin, he shall see his seed, he shall prolong his days, and the pleasure of the Lord shall prosper in his hand.

11. He shall see of the travail of his soul, and shall be satisfied: by his knowledge shall my righteous servant justify many; for he shall bear their iniquities.

12. Therefore will I divide him a portion with the great, and he shall divide the spoil with the strong; because he hath poured out his soul unto death: and he was numbered with the transgressors; and he bare the sin of many, and made intercession for the transgressors.

55:1. Ho, every one that thirsteth, come ye to the waters, and he that hath no money; come ye, buy, and eat; yea, come, buy wine and milk without money and without price.

3. Incline your ear, and come unto me: hear, and your soul shall live; and I will make an everlasting covenant with you, even the sure mercies of David.

6. Seek ye the Lord while he may be found, call ye upon him while he is near:

7. Let the wicked forsake his way, and the unrighteous man his thoughts: and let him return unto the Lord, and he will have mercy upon him; and to our God, for he will abundantly pardon.

LESSON OUTLINE

I. THE SUFFERING SAVIOR
   A. An Unlikely Source
   B. An Unlikely Sacrifice
   C. An Unlikely Savior
II. THE EXALTED SAVIOR
   A. Exalted on Earth
   B. Exalted in Victory
III. THE SAVIOR'S INVITATION
   A. An Invitation to Find Satisfaction
   B. An Invitation to Find Mercy

LESSON EXPOSITION

INTRODUCTION

This lesson deals with one of the most remarkable prophecies of the Old Testament, especially because of its relevance to the New Testament. Written between 600 and 700 years before Christ, the message is unmistakably that of one who had insight into the future. To any reader—believer or nonbeliever—Isaiah's uncanny predictions of the suffering of Jesus are a cause for further study.

Isaiah's name itself is evidence that his message would foretell of the coming Messiah and His saving work. *Isaiah* is translated from the traditional *Yeshaiah* or *Yeesha* (Isaiah 1:1), meaning "He (the Lord) shall save" (*Keil & Delitzsch Commentary on the Old Testament*). It is not surprising then that much of His prophecy was devoted to the coming Savior.

The text for this lesson stands at the center of all of Isaiah's prophetic messages concerning the Messiah as well as at the center of all Old Testament prophecies. If the Cross stands at the peak of all time and everything prior to the Cross was in preparation for it, and everything after drawing significance from it, then this text stands as an Old Testament billboard—a dramatic and unavoidable sign of God's plan for our salvation.

I. THE SUFFERING SAVIOR
   (Isaiah 53:1-9)

"Who has believed us?" Isaiah's cry in the first verse of chapter 53 was one of rejection. God had given a message of a coming Savior to the prophets, yet Israel did not believe. The report of the prophets had been ignored and Isaiah was not pleased. Thus, the second question, "To whom is the arm [or strength] of the Lord revealed?" (v. 1). Isaiah's prophecy of the coming Messiah had not been heeded and his second question seemed to ask, "Has God revealed another message, another strength, to someone else?"

The fact that God had indeed given such a message to Isaiah and in such detail surely must have distressed him when the people refused to believe his "report." Even in the day of Jesus, the messianic hope was for a delivering warrior to come and free the Jewish people from Roman rule. Isaiah's vision was something different than the people wanted him to see; therefore, they refused to believe what he saw.

A powerful truth lies in that complex contrast between the hope and the reality of Christ's coming. Things are not always what we would hope they would be—especially in God's design. Our hopes are often built upon earthly desires.

The peace we want is one that ends war and suffering. God's peace, however, may lead us to conflict with the society around us. The salvation we want may be one that destroys the temptations that stalk us. However, Christ's salvation is not *from* the temptations of this world but *within* the temptations of this world. His plans are frequently far different than our hopes.

A. An Unlikely Source (vv. 1-3)

(Isaiah 53:1, 2 is not included in the printed text.)

3. He is despised and rejected of men; a man of sorrows, and acquainted with grief: and we hid as it were our faces from him; he was despised, and we esteemed him not.

A tree severed at or near the ground is an unlikely source for the Tree of all trees, and the broken and captive house of Jesse was an unlikely source for the King of kings (see Isaiah 4:2; 11:1). Israel itself was an unlikely place for such a King. But the Messiah would spring from the root of Jesse out of the "dry ground" of Israel (53:2). As far as their faith and practice was concerned, the land of Israel in the day of Jesus was indeed a dry ground for Christianity to be born in.

The Christ would come not only out of an unlikely place and an unlikely lineage, but He would Himself be of ordinary appearance. Without "beauty" as people describe beauty, He was looked upon as an ordinary human being. Christ's appearance did not motivate people to follow Him. To them, He was just plain Jesus, the son of Joseph.

Then, the fullness of time came. This nondescript carpenter, the son of a carpenter, began a three-year ministry that propelled Him into the center of every life. He fulfilled His mission and took the reigns of the kingdom of God.

Rising from such an unlikely source almost assured Jesus of rejection. A person rising from poverty and meager surroundings who attempts to become someone of importance and stature is often a target for hatred from both the poverty-stricken that he rises from and also from the affluent that he aspires to join. Though Jesus had no such aspirations, we do know that when He began His ministry the residents of His hometown of Nazareth rejected Him, even attempting to kill Him (see Luke 4:16-30). The Pharisees and religious leaders were hostile toward Him. Isaiah said the Messiah

would be "despised and rejected [by] men" (53:3), and that prophecy was fulfilled as seen in the Gospels.

Jesus' sufferings and grief were excessive and no doubt exacerbated by His divine love for those who caused Him to suffer—those He came to save. As He neared the time of His crucifixion, even His own disciples deserted Him, "hiding their faces from Him" (see v. 3). Jesus entered the world with revelations from the Holy Spirit, acclamation of angels, an earthly mother and stepfather, shepherds and magi. But He had to face the cross alone. Even His Father had to turn away—hide His face—at His Son's death (see Matthew 27:46).

B. An Unlikely Sacrifice (vv. 4-6)

4. Surely he hath borne our griefs, and carried our sorrows: yet we did esteem him stricken, smitten of God, and afflicted.

5. But he was wounded for our transgressions, he was bruised for our iniquities: the chastisement of our peace was upon him; and with his stripes we are healed.

6. All we like sheep have gone astray; we have turned every one to his own way; and the Lord hath laid on him the iniquity of us all.

For centuries, the blood of bulls, lambs and goats had been shed upon the altars of Israel to remove the curse of sin from the people. By the time of Isaiah, God had become so repulsed by the meaningless rituality of the people's sacrifices that He declared, "To what purpose is the multitude of your sacrifices to Me? . . . I have had enough of burnt offerings" (1:11, *NKJV*). This message of God's displeasure with thoughtless sacrifices could easily be taken for a precursor of Isaiah's message about the suffering Savior.

Isaiah 53:4 prophesies that people would observe the sufferings of Jesus yet would not esteem His sufferings as intended for them—as a substitution for punishment rightfully due them as sinners. "Yes, we see His sufferings," the sinner might say, "but He has been smitten by God; afflicted and condemned by God for His own sins." To accept the idea that Christ's sufferings were rightfully ours is to admit our own guilt, and few people today believe they are guilty of the blood of Christ.

Isaiah, however, is very clear concerning the condition of every person. In this passage, he invokes the use of two words that inescapably link every man, woman or child to Isaiah himself. He said Jesus' sufferings would be "our" sufferings, and that "we" have all gone astray and therefore His sufferings were to bring us back to the fold. It was "our transgressions . . . our iniquities" that actually nailed Jesus to the cross (v. 5). It was "we" who were sick and in need of healing, "we" who had gone astray, "and the Lord hath laid on him the iniquity of us all" (v. 6). Just as the sins of the people were ceremonially laid upon the head of the animal of sacrifice, "all" of our iniquity was laid upon Jesus—the last and only true Sacrifice.

C. An Unlikely Savior (vv. 7-9)

(Isaiah 53:8, 9 is not included in the printed text.)

7. He was oppressed, and he was afflicted, yet he opened not his mouth: he is brought as a lamb to the slaughter, and as a sheep before her shearers is dumb, so he openeth not his mouth.

Jesus was an unlikely revolutionist. If death for Him had meant martyrdom for His cause, He miserably failed in taking advantage of the situation. Anyone seeking martyrdom will no doubt attempt a profound statement at death to assure that the cause will go on. Jesus was silent.

In the face of His oppressors and the afflictions forced upon Him, "Jesus kept silent" in fulfillment of Isaiah's words (Matthew 26:63, NKJV). Even on the cross, Jesus' communication was rare. He suffered in silence except for seven short utterances of necessity (see Matthew 27:46; Luke 23:34, 43, 46; John 19:26-30).

He endured His suffering in silence, knowing in His heart that this was not a *cause* to die for, but His death was the *cause* itself. This was the reason He had come into the world and that these prophecies of Isaiah must be fulfilled in silence. The day of proclamation would soon follow, but at that moment He remained mute.

The injustice of the foretold event also struck a note with Isaiah. The first phrase of 53:8 states, "By oppression and judgment he was taken away" (NIV). Jesus would be incarcerated and tried without following the due process of Hebrew or Roman law. Those responsible for His arrest and subsequent crucifixion were no more than the ancient equivalent of a lynch mob.

The fierceness of the punishment Isaiah foresaw, and which the Gospels relate as historical fact, is dramatically worsened when we know that Christ was completely spotless—without sin. Though He had done no wrong to others—neither by action nor words—yet He was given the maximum sentence. Who would have suspected that this One being so humiliated would lay claim to the title of *Savior*?

II. THE EXALTED SAVIOR
(Isaiah 53:10-12)

Treated as a common criminal, the Messiah was to die and to be numbered among the unjust. He was not a criminal, but Jesus was to lay down His life as one that He might fulfill the pleasure of God in bringing salvation to the world. When the sacrifice was over and the Atonement had been made, Jesus would see to it that the Father's pleasure of salvation to the lost would not go unfulfilled. Today He bears the "sin of many" and makes "intercession for the transgressors" (v. 12).

A. Exalted on Earth (vv. 10, 11)

10. Yet it pleased the Lord to bruise him; he hath put him to grief: when thou shalt make his soul an offering for sin, he shall see his seed, he shall prolong his days, and the pleasure of the Lord shall prosper in his hand.

11. He shall see of the travail of his soul, and shall be satisfied: by his knowledge shall my righteous servant justify many; for he shall bear their iniquities.

It was the Lord's "pleasure" to bring Christ to the point of such suffering because the end of that suffering was the building of the kingdom of God upon the earth. God made the life of Jesus a sin offering and gave a promise to Him that He would see "his seed"—a blessing of progeny (v. 10).

Of course we know that Jesus did not marry and have children, so the seed Isaiah prophesied of surely represents the church. All who believe on Jesus' name for salvation are the children of God—the seed of Christ. And Christ does indeed look down upon His children and walk with them. Jesus is therefore exalted on earth through the witness of His seed, who proclaim His praise in the earth.

A second blessing promised to the Messiah is that God would "prolong his days" (v. 10). This is considered by many to be a reference to the resurrection of Jesus on the first day of the week. When the stone rolled back and Jesus walked free from the grasp of death, His earthly days were prolonged. Jesus appeared to His disciples for 40 days after His resur-

rection before He ascended into heaven, leaving them a promise that He would return (Acts 1:3, 11).

Christ's exaltation in the earth springs from our salvation though His sacrifice, which resulted in His victory over sin, death and the grave, and His promise that He would come again. As Isaiah said about Him, "After the suffering of his soul . . . by his knowledge my righteous servant will justify many, and he will bear their iniquities" (53:11, *NIV*).

B. Exalted in Victory (v. 12)

12. Therefore will I divide him a portion with the great, and he shall divide the spoil with the strong; because he hath poured out his soul unto death: and he was numbered with the transgressors; and he bare the sin of many, and made intercession for the transgressors.

Christ is to be glorified, for He has "poured out his soul unto death." That death, however, is celebrated not as a death, but as a marvelous victory over death—a victory not only for Christ, but for those who follow Him as well. Jesus allowed Himself to be "numbered with the transgressors" that He might bear their sins and intercede for them.

Therefore, Jesus receives "a portion with the great, and he shall divide the spoil with the strong." The meek Lamb that "opened not His mouth" (v. 7) takes His place at the head of the great and the strong.

Who are these great and strong ones? Some believe they represent the church that He has redeemed. The very souls that He made intercession for have become strong and great in God's eyes, and Christ stands at their head in exaltation.

Others believe that "the great" are the mighty enemies—especially Satan—whom Christ defeated through His suffering and resurrection. Whoever "the great" are, we know that Christ's children will reap the fruit of His exaltation.

III. THE SAVIOR'S INVITATION (Isaiah 55:1-7)

Since Jesus suffered so horribly for the remission of sins; since He sacrificed Himself as a lamb for a sin offering; since He suffered the stripes on His back for our healing, the beckoning call goes out to "come." Come to this One who paid such a price that you might be redeemed. Come to this One who suffered in your stead that you might not suffer the pangs of hell.

God's message of salvation emphatically makes this call time and time again. He summons, "If anyone thirsts, let him come" (John 7:37, *NKJV*).

A. An Invitation to Find Satisfaction (vv. 1-5)

(Isaiah 55:2, 4, 5 is not included in the printed text.)

1. Ho, every one that thirsteth, come ye to the waters, and he that hath no money; come ye, buy, and eat; yea, come, buy wine and milk without money and without price.
3. Incline your ear, and come unto me: hear, and your soul shall live; and I will make an everlasting covenant with you, even the sure mercies of David.

Two remarkable facets about God's grace can be gleaned from this passage of Scripture. The first is the cost—it's free. Isaiah said, "And you who have no money, come, buy and eat. Yes, come, buy wine and milk without money and without price" (v. 1, *NKJV*).

Many people today still attempt to pacify the righteous requirements of their god (or gods) through self-flagellation. They will beat their backs until they bleed, they will impale portions of their body and attempt all kinds of painful exercise to appease their god. How sad that is, for the god they believe demands such painful offerings doesn't exist. Also, the real God does not want such painful repentance. His Son has already suffered the pain for our sins. God's grace is free to all who will only believe on the name of Jesus Christ. As the hymn says, "Jesus paid it all, / All to Him I owe; / Sin had left a crimson stain, / He washed it white as snow."

The second remarkable facet of God's grace observed here is that it is completely satisfying. Isaiah asks, "Why do you spend your hard-earned money on things that just don't satisfy you?" (see v. 2). Thirst is a driving force in every human being. The average person can survive only three days without water; therefore, we sense the need for water keenly. If someone is truly thirsty and dehydrated, the need for water grows from a simple desire to a driving need—a craving that must be heeded.

Nothing in this world can satisfy a thirsty soul. Only the salvation that comes through Jesus Christ can bring satisfaction—and that in abundance. The *New International Version* translates the latter part of verse 2, "Delight in the richest of fare." The most satisfying of meals has been set before us, and we are invited to partake to our satisfaction.

B. An Invitation to Find Mercy (vv. 6, 7)

6. Seek ye the Lord while he may be found, call ye upon him while he is near:
7. Let the wicked forsake his way, and the unrighteous man his thoughts: and let him return unto the Lord, and he will have mercy upon him; and to our God, for he will abundantly pardon.

Time is of the utmost importance. Not in terms of God's mercy, but in terms of our opportunity. Our opportunities are limited in time by our own lifespan. Life is short, especially if accident or illness intervenes. Therefore, God calls with urgency, "Seek . . . the Lord while he may be found, call . . . upon him while he is near" (v. 6).

There are two particular pleas made to us in the beginning of verse 7. We are urged to "forsake" wicked ways and unrighteous thoughts. These pleas indicate the depth to which God wants to change us. He wants to redeem not only our bodies, but our minds as well. To drink of the water He has for us is to be nourished in our bodies, minds and souls.

If we will forsake sinful ways and evil thoughts and return to God, He promises to "have mercy" on us and to "abundantly pardon."

GOLDEN TEXT HOMILY

"HE WAS WOUNDED FOR OUR TRANSGRESSIONS, HE WAS BRUISED FOR OUR INIQUITIES: THE CHASTISEMENT OF OUR PEACE WAS UPON HIM; AND WITH HIS STRIPES WE ARE HEALED" (Isaiah 53:5).

The most touching portrait of our Lord's vicarious sufferings is found in the prophetic poem of Isaiah 53 as the prophet reveals the person and passion of Jesus Christ and His provision for our salvation.

Verse 5 depicts Jesus as the Lamb of God. The prophet uses an accumulation of terms to describe the awful agony of our Savior at Calvary. He piles word upon word to enable us to grasp something of the intensity and extremity of our Lord's suffering.

With the use of the word *wounded*, the writer speaks of the piercing of Christ. The term *bruised* refers to the crushing weight of sin and woe upon the Lord, while *chastisement* tells us of the beating which left livid stripes in the flesh of Jesus.

Though we read the words which describe the sufferings of our Lord,

we can never begin to understand all that He endured when He was beaten, bruised, and bloodied at Calvary. We simply stand in amazement at such suffering.

But the great truth here is not the *revelation* of those sufferings, it is the *reason* for such sufferings. The prophet makes it clear that the Savior would not suffer for Himself, but for others. He was pierced, but it was for our transgressions. He was bruised, or crushed, but it was for our iniquities. He was beaten, but it was for our healing and peace. It was the innocent suffering for the guilty.

He took our place at Calvary and suffered the punishment we so clearly deserved, that we might be set free. Isaiah sums it up in verse 6: "The Lord hath laid on him the iniquity of us all." No wonder Paul called Jesus "the Son of God, who loved me, and gave himself for me" (Galatians 2:20).

Our Lord did not suffer and die in vain. Blessed are the results of His death. All who take His death to heart and accept Him as their sacrifice and substitute find their sins forgiven, their souls healed, and their minds resting in peace.—**Selected**

SENTENCE SERMONS

CHRIST'S SUFFERING AND DEATH provide for us a right relationship with God.

—Selected

CHRIST, AS FORETOLD BY PROPHETS, is the great central facet of history; to Him everything looks backward or forward.

—Charles Spurgeon

A RELIGION BORN ON A CROSS can't be a bed of roses.

—Notes and Quotes

EVANGELISM APPLICATION

CHRIST'S SUFFERING AND DEATH PROVIDE FREEDOM FROM

SIN AND AN INVITATION TO A RE-
LATIONSHIP WITH GOD.

Personally. That is how every person—man, woman or child—must
take Christ's sufferings. He suffered
not for the masses, but for every person. He laid down His life that I might
personally find His grace to be satisfying.

Salvation is not a communal blessing; it is accepted one soul at a time.
Every person must repent; every person must be forgiven; and every person must come to know Jesus as his
or her personal Savior. I must know
Jesus or I will not be saved.

ILLUMINATING THE LESSON

From the time of the first sin in the
Garden of Eden, bloody sacrifices
have been demanded to cover the nakedness of our errors. For Adam and
Eve, God killed animals and made
skins to cover them. From the time of
Moses, Israel used the blood of animals sacrificed on altars to avoid the

vengeance of God. Blood—always
blood—reminded us of our sinfulness.

When Jesus came and shed His
blood on Calvary, everything changed.
The shedding of His blood removed the
sins of everyone who would believe in
His sacrifice. Never again would blood
have to be shed. Instead, we can look
back at that single bloody sacrifice at
Calvary and be reminded not of our
sinfulness, but of God's infinite mercy
and grace. Thank God for the blood!

DAILY BIBLE READINGS

M. Sin's Curse.
    Genesis 3:9-13, 16-19
T. The Sin Offering.
    Leviticus 4:13-21
W. Prophecy Fulfilled.
    Matthew 1:20-23
T. Once-for-All Sacrifice.
    Hebrews 10:3-10
F. All Need the Savior.
    1 John 1:5-9
S. No More Curse.
    Revelation 22:1-5

TRUTH SEARCH
Creatively Teaching the Word

DISCUSSION QUESTIONS

Isaiah 53:2-9

1. According to verse 2, what role would physical beauty or majesty play in attracting people to the Savior?

2. According to verse 3, how far removed would Jesus be from suffering? From being hated or despised?

3. How would Jesus bear our grief and carry out sorrows (v. 4)?

4. How would the people of Israel look at Jesus when He walked on earth (v. 4)?

5. If Jesus had come to earth in our day, would most people have held Him in high esteem? Why? What types of people do you think would have been most likely to accept Him?

6. Who deserved to endure the punishment Christ would receive (v. 5)?

7. According to verse 5, what kind of healing can Christ give us?

8. What have we all done (v. 6)? What did Jesus do for us all?

9. According to verse 7, what defense would Jesus give for His innocence?

10. How were the prophecies of verses 8 and 9 fulfilled?

Isaiah 53:10-12

1. According to verses 10 and 11, what fruit would Christ see from His suffering?

2. What inheritance would Christ receive (v. 12)?

Isaiah 55:1-7

1. Why are people encouraged to "buy" yet to come "without money" (v. 1)?

2. How can one's "soul delight itself in abundance" (v. 2, *NKJV*)?

3. Why is the message of verse 6 so urgent?

4. What promise does God make (v. 7)? How can we receive the promise?

VIDEO ILLUSTRATION

Before class, cue the video *Snow White and the Seven Dwarfs* to the portion where the prince is freed from the witch's curse. Before the Bible study, play about six minutes of the video.

As the video is watched, ask the students to pay careful attention to the following:

1. Snow White's condition
2. The prince's physical appearance
3. What it takes for the prince to rescue her
4. Ways the prince identifies with Snow White

After the video, ask students to compare and contrast the saving work of the eternal Son of God with the heroic efforts of the imaginary prince.

True Fasting Brings Restoration

Study Text: Isaiah 58:1-14
Objective: To discover and practice the kind of fasting God accepts.
Time: Between 742 and 687 B.C.
Place: Judah, probably Jerusalem
Golden Text: "Is not this the fast that I have chosen? to loose the bands of wickedness, to undo the heavy burdens, and to let the oppressed go free, and that ye break every yoke?" (Isaiah 58:6).
Central Truth: True fasting focuses on emptying ourselves of worldly desires and being filled with God's love.
Evangelism Emphasis: Fasting that is acceptable to God can increase our compassion for the lost.

PRINTED TEXT

Isaiah 58:3. Wherefore have we fasted, say they, and thou seest not? wherefore have we afflicted our soul, and thou takest no knowledge? Behold, in the day of your fast ye find pleasure, and exact all your labours.

4. Behold, ye fast for strife and debate, and to smite with the fist of wickedness: ye shall not fast as ye do this day, to make your voice to be heard on high.

5. Is it such a fast that I have chosen? a day for a man to afflict his soul? is it to bow down his head as a bulrush, and to spread sackcloth and ashes under him? wilt thou call this a fast, and an acceptable day to the Lord?

6. Is not this the fast that I have chosen? to loose the bands of wickedness, to undo the heavy burdens, and to let the oppressed go free, and that ye break every yoke?

7. Is it not to deal thy bread to the hungry, and that thou bring the poor that are cast out to thy house? when thou seest the naked, that thou cover him; and that thou hide not thyself from thine own flesh?

8. Then shall thy light break forth as the morning, and thine health shall spring forth speedily: and thy righteousness shall go before thee; the glory of the Lord shall be thy rereward.

9. Then shalt thou call, and the Lord shall answer; thou shalt cry, and he shall say, Here I am. If thou take away from the midst of thee the yoke, the putting forth of the finger, and speaking vanity;

10. And if thou draw out thy soul to the hungry, and satisfy the afflicted soul; then shall thy light rise in obscurity, and thy darkness be as the noonday:

11. And the Lord shall guide thee continually, and satisfy thy soul in drought, and make fat thy bones: and thou shalt be like a watered garden, and like a spring of water, whose waters fail not.

12. And they that shall be of thee shall build the old waste places: thou shalt raise up the foundations of many generations; and thou shalt be called, The repairer of the breach, The restorer of paths to dwell in.

14. Then shalt thou delight thyself in the Lord; and I will cause thee to ride upon the high places of the earth, and feed thee with the heritage of Jacob thy father: for the mouth of the Lord hath spoken it.

LESSON OUTLINE

I. THE FAST GOD REJECTS
   A. Fasting in Ignorance
   B. Fasting in Offense
   C. Fasting in Pretense
II. THE FAST GOD ACCEPTS
   A. A Fast of Action
   B. A Fast of Reaction
III. THE FAST GOD REWARDS
   A. Rewards of Glory
   B. Rewards of Plenty
   C. Rewards of Joy

LESSON EXPOSITION

INTRODUCTION

Fasting can arguably be called the least practiced of the tenets of the Christian faith. The season of Lent— traditionally the 40 days from Ash Wednesday to Easter—is observed as a time for fasting for Catholic, Eastern and some Protestant faiths, but the practice of personal fasting is actually rare.

The reason for the rarity of fasting in today's world is twofold. First, we have developed a very selfish culture in most modern countries that emphasizes personal comfort and satisfaction. To be deprived of "creature comforts" actually places stress on the person being denied those comforts. The truth is that we fail to fast because we are too accustomed to satisfying our every whim, much less every need.

Second, we do not fast because we have forgotten the benefits derived from self-denial. The body as well as the soul can benefit from abstinence of food for a period of time. During an extended fast, the body is cleansed of impurities that build up in the digestive system and also in the bloodstream. While we feel hunger, our bodies experience a catharsis during a fast of three days or more.

The primary objective of fasting is to humble ourselves before God and heighten our sensitivity to His will for our lives. Fasting builds our faith by making us more sensitive to God's presence. As we sacrifice the delight and nourishment of our meals, we are to also spend the time in prayer that we would have otherwise spent eating.

Many people forget that fasting and prayer are two sides of the same sword. When Jesus cast out a demon that His disciples could not, He told them, "This kind can come fourth by nothing, but by prayer and fasting" (Mark 9:29). As we enter this lesson, we want to explore the act of fasting both in its misuse and in its perfect use.

I. THE FAST GOD REJECTS
(Isaiah 58:1-5)

Not all fasting is fasting. We may physically achieve the goal of skipping a meal or a day's meals or even several days' meals, but unless we have devoted that fast to God and have taken steps to make it meaningful to both God and ourselves, the fast will mean nothing. We would have been better off to eat our fill at every meal.

Just as God was the author of the sacrifices that were demanded in the Old Testament and were fulfilled in the sacrifice of Jesus on the cross, God authored fasting as well. If God has designed such a personal sacrament, then we are to follow His directions in participating in it. If we forget the fast that God approves of and follow our own plan, we are doomed to failure.

A. Fasting in Ignorance (vv. 1-3a)

(Isaiah 58:1, 2 is not included in the printed text.)

3a. Wherefore have we fasted, say they, and thou seest not? wherefore have we afflicted our soul, and thou takest no knowledge?

On several occasions in the Book of Isaiah, God exhorts the prophet to "cry out" or "cry aloud" in clear anger toward those who have not obeyed God's will—often those caught in a rebellion of ignorance. In our text, Isaiah is told, "Cry aloud, spare not; lift up your voice like a trumpet; tell My people their transgression, and the house of Jacob their sins" (v. 1, NKJV). As we delve deeper into the text, we will observe that the practice of fasting continued even as they were in obvious transgression of God's commands—as though Israel was ignorant of their sins.

The tone of God's message to Isaiah seems to be one of perplexity—if indeed God could be perplexed. Israel had transgressed God's commandments of social and moral obligation and still they came to Him with an air of respectability and holiness. How absurd it is for willful sinners to come to God without shame or repentance, especially in the form of fasting, and pretend that their real lives are unseen by God.

Israel had come to God in a manner of self-flagellation or self-deprivation reminiscent of some Eastern religions we can observe today. They enter a season of self-torture in order to appease their gods for the sins they have committed. For these people and for those Isaiah was to prophesy to, a few days of torture were substituted for a life of righteousness (v. 3a). Such substitution has no place in God's plan. A life of daily walking in faith and obedience is mandatory in God's economy; nothing else can be substituted.

The tragedy of all this is that Israel had full knowledge of the demands of righteous living. They sought God for "ordinances of justice" that they already possessed and took "delight in approaching . . . God" (v. 2). In their ignorance of God's Word and will for them, they fasted for naught.

B. Fasting in Offense (vv. 3b, 4)

3b. Behold, in the day of your fast ye find pleasure, and exact all your labours.

4. Behold, ye fast for strife and debate, and to smite with the fist of wickedness: ye shall not fast as ye do this day, to make your voice to be heard on high.

Seeing through their guise of self-denial, God focused on the truth of their fasts. They had not fasted to the affliction of their flesh, but made their fasts times of pleasure. Instead of denying the flesh, they catered to the wants and lusts of the flesh. The "pleasure" derived from their fasts was something obviously offensive to God. Whether it was the pleasure itself or simply their substitution of pleasure for self-abasement, it offended God. The people were consumed in the pursuit of the affairs of life in the midst of their fasting.

A second offense toward God was their harsh dealings with those in their employment. Rather than being allied with those in need through self-denial, their hearts were stirred to afflict their servants and laborers.

Fasting should always bring the believer into close harmony and empathy with those who suffer need. Depriving oneself purposely in a fast always offers escape through the decision to accept food. Those who are hungry because they have no food do not have that means of escape, and fasting should awaken the believer to their peril.

What seemed most offensive to God was the issue that had compelled them to fast. Out of a quarrelsome debate they had begun their fast—a fast against a neighbor or an enemy. They desired to use "the fist of wickedness" against others, and this led them to fast for God's approval. What could be more offensive to God than a sinful person fasting for authority to strike another?

God's reply was curt: "You cannot fast as you do today and expect your voice to be heard on high" (v. 4, *NIV*). Anyone entering a fast devoted toward God must enter in humility and in peace. God will not respond to selfish and ill-sponsored fasts.

C. Fasting in Pretense (v. 5)

5. Is it such a fast that I have chosen? a day for a man to afflict his soul? is it to bow down his head as a bulrush, and to spread sackcloth and ashes under him? wilt thou call this a fast, and an acceptable day to the Lord?

The fasts undertaken by these people were of their own design. They had not sought God's Word concerning the pattern or the duration of the fasts they held, and God could not and would not accept them.

Those participating in the fasts thought God should take notice of how much they had burdened themselves with their fasting (see v. 3). But God asked them, "Is this the kind of fast I have chosen, only a day for a man to humble himself?" (v. 5, *NIV*). A single day of fasting followed by mirth was not God's idea of humble fasting and repentance. The person fasting would bow his head "like a reed" (*NIV*), dress in sackcloth and pour ashes upon himself in a public display of sorrow and repentance—a public display not unlike that which Jesus chastised the Pharisees for (see Matthew 23:14; Mark 12:40; Luke 20:47).

God called upon their common sense to answer the question about the nature of their fasts. "Would you call this a fast, and an acceptable day to the Lord?" (Isaiah 58:5, *NKJV*). Common sense dictates that pretense is not acceptable to God in any form of worship. God demands sincerity in every aspect of our approach to Him.

II. THE FAST GOD ACCEPTS
(Isaiah 58:6, 7, 9, 10a)

The first truth that must be accepted regarding true fasting is the fact that God desires us to fast. The Bible is clear that fasting is a legitimate means of bringing our needs to God and also a means of repenting before God (see Nehemiah 1:4; 9:1; Psalm 35:13; Daniel 9:3; Joel 2:12; Acts 14:23; 1 Corinthians 7:5). Denying the body in order to strengthen the soul might seem strange to the earthly-minded person, but it is an act of spirituality that should be practiced often by every Christian.

Fasts, however, are not selfish attempts to gain greater access to and more favor with God. Fasts are a means to make the thoughts of God our thoughts and His concerns our concerns.

A. A Fast of Action (vv. 6, 7)

6. Is not this the fast that I have chosen? to loose the bands of wickedness, to undo the heavy burdens, and to let the oppressed go free, and that ye break every yoke?

7. Is it not to deal thy bread to the hungry, and that thou bring the poor that are cast out to thy house? when thou seest the naked, that thou cover him; and that thou hide not thyself from thine own flesh?

God interjects a facet to fasting that is not commonly viewed as connected to a customary fast—action. "This," He says, "is the fast that I have chosen."

All four actions mentioned is verse 6 bear the theme of liberation:
- To loose the bonds of wickedness
- To undo heavy burdens
- To free the oppressed
- To break every yoke

While verse 6 is a general overview of the fast of the Lord, emphasizing liberation, verse 7 is a specific application of the theme. These activities reveal the true actions of religion. There is a fourfold description applying the Lord's fast to action.

The first description is "to deal thy bread to the hungry." The emphasis of the Hebrew word for "hungry" is on the idea of emptiness. God calls the people to give of their resources to those who are empty of any resources.

The second application of God's fast is to "bring the poor that are cast out to [one's] house." The emphasis is upon those who are without material and social support.

The third application is to clothe the naked. *Naked* had a physical and social meaning in Hebrew. It meant to be without clothing or outer garments. It also meant to be stripped of the outer garments which designated social status or rank. The call was to assist those who were stripped and left destitute, either physically or socially.

The final application of God's fast was to "hide not thyself from thine own flesh." The phrase "thine own flesh" denotes the intimate way each individual is knit together with all persons. We are each other's own flesh. Note, the context regards the needy. Therefore, intimacy between individuals is especially important to God when it comes to ministering to those in need.

Obviously, God's idea of fasting is more complex than simply "pushing back the plate." Fasting is to be accompanied with acts of deliverance and kindness in order for the fast to be complete. During a fast, we must seek out needs of others and meet them as an equal sacrifice unto God. Then it will be marvelously apparent to God that our heart is anxious to know Him more and to feel the hurts that He feels as He looks upon the poor and deprived.

B. A Fast of Reaction (vv. 9, 10a)

9. Then shalt thou call, and the Lord shall answer; thou shalt cry, **and he shall say, Here I am. If thou take away from the midst of thee the yoke, the putting forth of the finger, and speaking vanity;**

10a. And if thou draw out thy soul to the hungry, and satisfy the afflicted soul.

Isaiah notes the power of this type of active fasting. When people not only pass up their meals but also actively pursue service to their neighbors, they open a clear channel directly into the throne room of God. They can call upon God with full confidence and He will hear and answer (v. 9). This is not to say God can be manipulated, but it is to affirm that He is true to His promises and He will react to our obedience in fasting and serving others.

The first part of verse 10 emphasizes the aspect of personal responsibility developed earlier in verse 7. "If thou draw out thy soul" is a phrase illustrating the action of investing oneself in the life of another. *Draw out* is from a Hebrew word meaning to "give out, furnish or supply." The first resource in ministering to others is not physical. This is important, but the first prerequisite for ministering to the needs of others is the drawing out of one's soul in order to meet the needs of someone in need.

The word *satisfy* comes from a Hebrew word which meant basically "to be filled in abundance." The people are directed to do this to the afflicted soul. *Afflicted* is the same word that was used earlier in verses 3 and 5. It means to be "labored, suffering, depressed, or oppressed." In verses 3 and 5, it was used to describe what the people were doing to themselves in order to please God. However, God's desire was that they bring abundance to those who were already afflicted. They did not need to afflict themselves; they needed to go to the afflicted.

III. THE FAST GOD REWARDS (Isaiah 58:8, 10b-14)

Rewards are promised throughout the Bible. God promises to reward the faithful believer both now and in the hereafter. Sincere fasting carries the promise of blessing in this life.

Fasting brings blessing to the soul and spirit of the believer. Anyone who has ever fasted for a period of time can attest to the wonderful and powerful presence of the Holy Spirit that surrounds the believer during and following the fast. God does indeed recognize our attempts to honor and seek Him in fasting.

A. Rewards of Glory (vv. 8, 10b)

8. Then shall thy light break forth as the morning, and thine health shall spring forth speedily: and thy righteousness shall go before thee; the glory of the Lord shall be thy rereward.

10b. Then shall thy light rise in obscurity, and thy darkness be as the noonday.

Scriptural and tangible promises abound for one willing to fast and pray. Twice in the text we are told that the "light" of the person fasting will "break forth" as "dawn in the darkness" (*NKJV*). This concept is a little difficult to explain since we have no light of our own but are simply reflective of the glory of God. This must be the specific meaning of the text. As we honor God and serve our neighbors as a part of our fast, God's light clings to us and shines through us to the point that we do "shine forth" as a dawn in darkest night, or as the sun breaking forth through heavy, dark storm clouds.

Isaiah paints a beautiful picture of the person who fasts the fast that God rewards. He indicates that righteousness will "go before" that person (v. 8). The report of the good name of a righteous person precedes him or her always. We all have heard reports of people who have had lives of renown—well known for their love of mankind and their compassion toward those who are hurting. Surely every believer would like to be in that company. To have people respect and admire you before they ever know you, simply because of a godly reputation, is something to be desired.

But Isaiah has a second part to this reputation. He states, "The glory of the Lord shall be thy rereward [your rear guard]" (v. 8). *Rereward* means a "gathering." The word was used in reference to the "gathering up of the scattered rear of an army, or the keeping it from straggling, and defending it from the attacks of an enemy" (William Wilson, *Old Testament Word Studies*).

The glory of God will maintain the good report of the righteous person after he or she has gone. No, God will not protect us from the critic's darts, but He will protect us in His own glory—and His report is the one that matters.

B. Rewards of Plenty (v. 11)

11. And the Lord shall guide thee continually, and satisfy thy soul in drought, and make fat thy bones: and thou shalt be like a watered garden, and like a spring of water, whose waters fail not.

We are faced every day with decisions that must be made in view of God's will. To know His will is of paramount importance.

The act of fasting, according to Isaiah, keeps a man or woman in touch with God's will and under His guidance. Even in the driest of times, God's Spirit will keep the soul satisfied when a person has committed himself or herself to a life of fasting and obedience. The soul of a person who fasts will be like a "well-watered garden." When the soul is thirsty, there is no satisfying it with the things of this world. When all the delights of this world are rejected and prayer is made to God, though the stomach may be empty, the soul will be lush and green from the wells of the Holy Spirit.

God's blessings are not only spiritual, however. His promise here extends to the "bones" as well. Healing of maladies will "spring forth speedily" (v. 8). This statement is possibly true because of the powerful faith derived in the person who has fasted and found God to be true to His promises and His Word.

C. Rewards of Joy (vv. 13, 14)

(Isaiah 58:13 is not included in the printed text.)

14. Then shalt thou delight thyself in the Lord; and I will cause thee to ride upon the high places of the earth, and feed thee with the heritage of Jacob thy father: for the mouth of the Lord hath spoken it.

In verse 13, God's people are urged to use the Sabbath as a day to set aside their own pleasure-seeking to focus on the Lord. Such obedience produces the three elements of joy given in verse 14.

The first element is joy in the Lord. The irony is that in denying the body that which pleases it (food which brings temporal happiness), fasting becomes the source of even greater joy—the joy of the Lord. The person who fasts will "delight . . . in the Lord." This joy in the Lord is not subject to the fullness of the stomach, but the fullness of the soul.

The second element of joy is that of honor bestowed by God upon the one who humbles himself in fasting. God will cause that person to "ride upon the high places of the earth." This of course must never be the purpose of the fast, for fasting with such a motive negates the fast itself. A fast in humility will elevate the believer. Jesus said, "And whoever exalts himself will be humbled, and he who humbles himself will be exalted" (Matthew 23:12, NKJV).

Finally, the promise of joy is everlasting. The devout Christian who fasts will be fed "on the inheritance of Jacob" (NIV). This might be construed to mean the Promised Land in the region of the world known as the Middle East. However, few Christians will ever own a parcel of land in that war-torn place. No, this passage of Scripture takes us to a greater inheritance.

A joyful inheritance awaits us at the end of our struggle here in this life. Believers who recognize this fact and are willing to deprive their body of the pleasures of this world through fasting will experience enhanced joy in their heavenly inheritance.

GOLDEN TEXT HOMILY

"IS NOT THIS THE FAST THAT I HAVE CHOSEN? TO LOOSE THE BANDS OF WICKEDNESS, TO UNDO THE HEAVY BURDENS, AND TO LET THE OPPRESSED GO FREE, AND THAT YE BREAK EVERY YOKE?" (Isaiah 58:6).

In our postmodern, pleasure-seeking culture, it is important that we examine ourselves as to why we do what we do. How much of our religious activities and duties, for example, are motivated by a genuine desire to obey and please God? Even our praise and worship, our preaching and teaching, and our benevolent works can be displeasing to God if they are not motivated by love of God and service to others.

The prophet Isaiah was directed by God to remind the people that even their fasting was not acceptable because their hearts were not turned toward righteousness. They fasted, but they did not follow after holiness in their devotion to God and in their compassion toward others.

God's chosen fast is one of self-denial and a genuine desire for a deeper walk with our heavenly Father. Such a fast will result in our seeking to alleviate human need and the sharing of our resources with the hungry, the loveless, the poor and the naked.

And, when we participate in His chosen fast, we are promised great reward and blessing. He will set us free from our self-centered, sinful nature. He will bring freedom from oppression, and His glory will be our protection and rear guard.

Our prayers will be answered, and God will give spiritual insight and influence. Our light will break forth like the dawn. He will guide us and fulfill our desires in the midst of difficult circumstances.

Moreover, when we choose God's chosen fast, He will give us the desire and the enablement to effectively help people in need; and, we will become restorers and rebuilders of right traditions and a godly heritage.—**Paul Duncan**

SENTENCE SERMONS

TRUE FASTING focuses on emptying ourselves of worldly desires and being filled with God's love.
—Selected

FASTING is feasting at God's banquet table.
—Selected

IT IS A GREAT DEAL EASIER to do that which God gives us to do than to face the responsibility of not doing it.
—J.R. Miller

TO OBEY GOD in some things and not in others shows an unsound heart.
—Thomas Watson

EVANGELISM APPLICATION

FASTING THAT IS ACCEPTABLE TO GOD CAN INCREASE OUR COMPASSION FOR THE LOST.

To fast is actually to awaken to the needs of others—especially the needs of the lost. As we deprive ourselves of food and spend time in quiet reflection with God, we are brought to a keen awareness of the distress awaiting the sinner who perishes without God. Heaven help us to fast meaningfully and pray sincerely for the lost in our own households as well as those around us.

ILLUMINATING THE LESSON

Eureka! That is the hallmark term for discovery. When something has been found that is worth a great deal, the finder might yell this word to the top of his or her lungs. That should be the cry of everyone hearing this lesson from the Bible today. We have found in this lesson a dramatic and powerful means of coming before God with our needs and cares.

Eureka! I know how to find blessings beyond imagination. Eureka! I know how to find healing for illnesses in my home, family or church. Eureka! I have found the perfect means of applying my heart's desire to help others. All I have to do is fast and pray—God will do the rest.

DAILY BIBLE READINGS

M. Fasting Used for Evil Purposes.
   1 Kings 21:7-16
T. Fasting and Prayer for Victory.
   2 Chronicles 20:1-12
W. Call to Lament.
   Joel 1:14-20
T. Fast in Secret.
   Matthew 6:16-18
F. Power Through Fasting and Prayer.
   Matthew 17:14-21
S. Rebuke for Not Fasting.
   Mark 2:16-20

TRUTH SEARCH
Creatively Teaching the Word

DISCUSSION QUESTIONS

Isaiah 58:1-5
• To what extent did God want the people to hear this message (v. 1)?
• What is the subject?
• Did the people appear eager to know God's ways and do what is right? Was this the reality?
• What were the people questioning God about (v. 3)?
• Describe how the people were acting during their fasts (vv. 3, 4).
• What could these people expect as a result of this type of fasting?
• What kind of attitude will accompany an acceptable fast (v. 5)?

Isaiah 58:6-9
• What is the theme of this passage?
• How could Judah "loose the chains of injustice" (v. 6, *NIV*)?
• What were the people to do with their food during the fast?
• What is meant by the command to "not hide yourself from your own flesh" (v. 7, *NKJV*)?
• Discuss what is meant by "Then shall thy light break forth as the morning" (v. 8).
• How could a correct fast effect healing (v. 8)?
• What will lead and what will follow those who sincerely seek God (v. 8)?
• How can we expect God to respond to a proper fast (v. 9)?

Isaiah 58:10-14
• What promises does God make to those who minister to the hungry and afflicted (vv. 10, 11)?
• What would God call those who arose to faithfully serve Him (v. 12)? What is the significance of those names?
• Who will find "delight" in the Lord and "ride upon the high places" (vv. 13, 14)?

CASE STUDY

A couple has a child who is in the hospital. Dad tells his wife, "I'm going to fast tomorrow and ask God to heal our child." Here's how the next day develops:
• Dad gets up late and does not pray.
• As he speeds to work, he drives aggressively and shouts at other drivers.
• His coworker asks about the man's long face, and he explains he is fasting.
• He drinks soft drinks during the day.
• He snaps at his wife in the evening.
• Staying up until 12:01 a.m., he then eats a sandwich.

A couple of days later, the man complains to his wife about God's lack of compassion. He says, "I fasted all day, but our daughter is no better."

Discuss what was right and wrong about this man's fasting.

A Glorious Future

Study Text: Isaiah 61:1-11; 65:17-25
Objective: To know the glorious future God has prepared for His people and serve Him joyfully.
Time: Between 742 and 687 B.C.
Place: Judah, probably Jerusalem
Golden Text: "For, behold, I create new heavens and a new earth: and the former shall not be remembered, nor come into mind" (Isaiah 65:17).
Central Truth: Christ is the center of God's plan for the future.
Evangelism Emphasis: Sinners can experience a glorious future by accepting Christ as their redeemer.

PRINTED TEXT

Isaiah 61:1. The Spirit of the Lord God is upon me; because the Lord hath anointed me to preach good tidings unto the meek; he hath sent me to bind up the brokenhearted, to proclaim liberty to the captives, and the opening of the prison to them that are bound;

2. To proclaim the acceptable year of the Lord, and the day of vengeance of our God; to comfort all that mourn;

3. To appoint unto them that mourn in Zion, to give unto them beauty for ashes, the oil of joy for mourning, the garment of praise for the spirit of heaviness; that they might be called trees of righteousness, the planting of the Lord, that he might be glorified.

4. And they shall build the old wastes, they shall raise up the former desolations, and they shall repair the waste cities, the desolations of many generations.

5. And strangers shall stand and feed your flocks, and the sons of the alien shall be your plowmen and your vinedressers.

6. But ye shall be named the Priests of the Lord: men shall call you the Ministers of our God: ye shall eat the riches of the Gentiles, and in their glory shall ye boast yourselves.

7. For your shame ye shall have double; and for confusion they shall rejoice in their portion: therefore in their land they shall possess the double: everlasting joy shall be unto them.

8. For I the Lord love judgment, I hate robbery for burnt-offering; and I will direct their work in truth, and I will make an everlasting covenant with them.

65:17. For, behold, I create new heavens and a new earth: and the former shall not be remembered, nor come into mind.

18. But be ye glad and rejoice for ever in that which I create: for, behold, I create Jerusalem a rejoicing, and her people a joy.

24. And it shall come to pass, that before they call, I will answer; and while they are yet speaking, I will hear.

25. The wolf and the lamb shall feed together, and the lion shall eat straw like the bullock: and dust shall be the serpent's meat. They shall not hurt nor destroy in all my holy mountain, saith the Lord.

LESSON OUTLINE

I. GOOD NEWS FOR THE
   OPPRESSED
   A. The Right Messenger
   B. The Right Time
   C. The Right Message
II. BLESSINGS OF REDEMPTION
   A. A Double Blessing
   B. A Covenant Blessing
   C. A Joyful Blessing
III. ALL THINGS NEW
   A. A New City
   B. A New Life
   C. New Relationships

LESSON EXPOSITION

INTRODUCTION

Perhaps the greatest joy of learning about prophecies of the Old Testament being fulfilled in the New Testament is discovering that there are many prophecies yet to be fulfilled. As the prophecies of the first advent of Christ were accurate in every detail, we can be assured that the fulfillment of the remaining prophecies will be just as accurate.

Today we await the rapture of the church and the subsequent thousand-year reign of Jesus just as the Hebrews awaited the coming of the Messiah in New Testament days. The shame of our day, as was the shame of the day of Jesus, is that so few are actually preparing for the coming of the Messiah.

The angels at Jesus' ascension said, "Men of Galilee, why do you stand gazing up into heaven? This same Jesus, who was taken up from you into heaven, will so come in like manner as you saw Him go into heaven" (Acts 1:11, NKJV). Even though Jesus left the earth with the promise to come again, many do not believe in and are not expecting His return.

Paul was very clear about the importance of being prepared for the second coming of Jesus: "For you yourselves know perfectly that the day of the Lord so comes as a thief in the night. For when they say, 'Peace and safety!' then sudden destruction comes upon them, as labor pains upon a pregnant woman. And they shall not escape. But you, brethren, are not in darkness, so that this Day should overtake you as a thief. You are all sons of light and sons of the day. We are not of the night nor of darkness. Therefore let us not sleep, as others do, but let us watch and be sober" (1 Thessalonians 5:2-6, NKJV).

I. GOOD NEWS FOR THE
   OPPRESSED (Isaiah 61:1-3)

When Jesus went home to His family and to the village of Nazareth, which He called home, He and His disciples went to the synagogue on the Sabbath Day. There Jesus read this passage from the scroll of Isaiah. After the reading, He closed the scroll and said, "Today this Scripture is fulfilled in your hearing" (Luke 4:21, NKJV). The villagers responded with outrage and attempted to cast Jesus over a cliff (see vv. 28-30).

That audience was privileged to hear an amazing and spectacular announcement of deliverance from the very lips of the Son of God, yet they responded with violent disbelief. For good news to be effective, it must be received with faith.

Jesus is coming again, and we who are looking for Him will need to be vastly more ready than those who lived in the presence of Jesus as He grew to be a man. Our hearts must be prepared to recognize Him, our ears must be ready to hear His call, and our lips must be ready to confess His name as Savior, or we too may miss an amazing and spectacular announcement of deliverance.

A. The Right Messenger (v. 1)

1. The Spirit of the Lord God is upon me; because the Lord hath anointed me to preach good tidings unto the meek; he hath sent me to bind up the brokenhearted, to proclaim liberty to the captives, and the opening of the prison to them that are bound.

The most important aspect of this scripture was not the ministries that were to take place; it was the person who would perform these ministries and the anointing that would empower Him. The Holy Spirit was to be upon this individual in such a way that His message could bring deliverance to everyone trapped in distress.

Notice the people who were to be recipients of His message: the poor ("meek"), the brokenhearted, captives and those bound in prison. The heart of God is always moved by afflictions and injustice perpetrated upon the oppressed. He is constantly seen in Scripture reacting to such needs and pronouncing judgment upon those who inflicted the oppression and upon those who did nothing about it.

It is significant that the quotation of this passage would be the first words of Jesus spoken to a gathering of people as recorded in the Book of Luke—significant in that it sets the tone of His ministry throughout the remainder of the book. Jesus' heart was moved by sorrow and pain, by poverty and oppression, and by the hopelessness of the multitudes who were lost in sin. His ministry was focused on needs that could not be met by anyone else.

First, He came to bind up the brokenhearted. *Bind up* means to wrap, as in wrapping a turban around the head. *Heart* refers to one's innermost being; thus the *brokenhearted* are those who have been completely shattered to the core of their existence.

Next, the Messiah came to proclaim liberty to the captives and the opening of prison doors to the bound. The declaration and fulfillment of this prophecy demonstrates the power of God. At God's declaration, things already began to be accomplished. It was Jesus—the Son of God—who preached the good news to the poor, who bound up the brokenhearted, who set captives free, and who set at liberty the oppressed. The power and the glory of this prophecy was, and is, in Jesus.

B. The Right Time (v. 2)

2. To proclaim the acceptable year of the Lord, and the day of vengeance of our God; to comfort all that mourn.

It was at the "fullness of time" that Jesus came into the world (see Galatians 4:4), and that fullness of time was twofold: "to proclaim the acceptable year of the Lord" and then to pronounce judgment upon transgressors.

At the start of the Jubilee year, the trumpet would sound and the people were to "proclaim liberty throughout all the land to all its inhabitants" (see Leviticus 25:8-17). This year of release from oppression and obligation was the ground for Isaiah's reference to the "acceptable year of the Lord." God's intent was that no one be permanently oppressed or obligated unjustly.

Revenge is not an acceptable motivation for actions in our society. No matter how harsh someone has been treated, society frowns upon vengeance. However, the Bible is clear that a time has been set when God himself will mete out vengeance upon those who have oppressed and harmed His children. Paul cautioned us about this when he said, "Beloved, do not avenge yourselves, but rather give place to wrath; for it is written, 'Vengeance is Mine, I will repay,' says the Lord" (Romans 12:19, *NKJV*).

As in verse 1, God's message through His Messiah was to be one of comfort—comfort to all who mourn. A year of acceptable release, combined with judgment against those who had unjustly afflicted them, would give great comfort to those who had endured such hardships.

C. The Right Message (v. 3)

3. To appoint unto them that mourn in Zion, to give unto them beauty for ashes, the oil of joy for mourning, the garment of praise for the spirit of heaviness; that they might be called trees of righteousness, the planting of the Lord, that he might be glorified.

God's message to His children has always been one of substitution. In the Old Testament, God allowed them to substitute the blood of animals in sacrifice for their sins. In the New Testament, the blood of Jesus was eternally substituted for the sins of all people. So it comes as no surprise that the message of the Messiah according to Isaiah was to be one of substitution. To bring comfort and to "console those who mourn in Zion" (NKJV), God planned to make some wonderful substitutions in their lives.

The Messiah was going to give those who would believe on Him, "beauty for ashes, the oil of joy for mourning, [and] the garment of praise for the spirit of heaviness." Jesus takes away the ashes of mourning and heaviness of heart and in its place He gives beauty, joy and garments of praise. The powerful message here is that all things positive will replace—be substituted for—all things negative. As Paul said, "Therefore, if anyone is in Christ, he is a new creation; old things have passed away; behold, all things have become new" (2 Corinthians 5:17, NKJV).

The purpose of this substitution, however, is not simply for the benefit of those who have been in mourning; it is ultimately for the glory of God. "That they might be called trees of righteousness, the planting of the Lord, that he might be glorified."

II. BLESSINGS OF REDEMPTION (Isaiah 61:4-11)

Redemption of lost people has been the ultimate passion of God throughout time. The Bible has been a message of God's plan of redemption for Jews and Gentiles alike for millennia. It was for the purpose of redeeming humanity that God sent Jesus Christ into the world. As Savior, He would rebuild the old patterns of faith upon the new foundation of His own blood.

A. A Double Blessing (vv. 4-7)

4. And they shall build the old wastes, they shall raise up the former desolations, and they shall repair the waste cities, the desolations of many generations.

5. And strangers shall stand and feed your flocks, and the sons of the alien shall be your plowmen and your vinedressers.

6. But ye shall be named the Priests of the Lord: men shall call you the Ministers of our God: ye shall eat the riches of the Gentiles, and in their glory shall ye boast yourselves.

7. For your shame ye shall have double; and for confusion they shall rejoice in their portion: therefore in their land they shall possess the double: everlasting joy shall be unto them.

Israel has always been a focal point of all of God's working in the earth. Simply because His purposes include the Gentile nations does not negate His favor of Israel. In His messianic kingdom, the nation and people of Israel will again play a major role. The old ruins and the desolations will be restored and the ruined cities will be repaired. Whatever symbolism might be found in this text, the truth still remains that God will restore Israel's glory as a part of His completed kingdom. They are indeed a chosen and blessed people.

The use of the terms "strangers," "sons of the alien," and "Gentiles" in verses 5 and 6 draws attention to the specific application of this passage to Israel. However, interpretation of these verses should not be limited to the contrast between Jews and non-Jews. The fuller context is of those who receive the work of the Anointed One described in verses 1-3. These are to be seen in contrast to those who do not receive this work.

"Strangers" and "sons of the alien" are those who do not accept the work of the anointed Redeemer. "Gentiles" comes from the same Hebrew word translated "nations" in verse 11. The understanding of the term should be of nations in general, emphasizing the people who choose not to accept the person and work of the Redeemer.

As "priests of the Lord" and as "ministers of our God," the followers of the Messiah will have access to an eternal blessing and a double portion. The idea expressed in verses 4-6 literally is that there will be no need to engage in business or agriculture. The world shall be tributary to the followers of the Messiah and we shall enjoy the products of all lands, devoting ourselves exclusively to the service of God.

Again, substitution will take place as God rewards those who have served Him. Instead of the shame that the world has cast upon the followers of God, we will receive a *double* honor and instead of confusion we will have a *double* possession (v. 7).

Most importantly, the blessing of God on the followers of the Messiah will be an everlasting joy. Whatever our reward might be and whatever privileges will be granted to us, joy will make all things equal. No one will be happier in his or her reward than any other. How important that message is to the ears of a hurting and poverty-stricken people in dire need of encouragement. "Yes," God says, "You will have plenty—a double portion—but most importantly, you will be joyful forever."

B. A Covenant Blessing (vv. 8, 9)

(Isaiah 61:9 is not included in the printed text.)

8. For I the Lord love judgment, I hate robbery for burnt-offering; and I will direct their work in truth, and I will make an everlasting covenant with them.

With God's close supervision, the work of the Kingdom will go on in the end time to the establishment of an everlasting covenant between God and those who have followed the Messiah. Generations of those who have followed Christ will be known "among the Gentiles, and their offspring among the people" (v. 9).

God has always been a covenant-making God and He has always upheld His covenants to the uttermost. God's covenant with the followers of Christ will stand throughout eternity.

So profound will this covenant blessing be that everyone who sees one of God's covenanted people will "acknowledge them, that they are the posterity whom the Lord has blessed" (v. 9, *NKJV*). This characterizes the covenanted people as being visibly different from others. Quite possibly, it will be the change of nature we know that will take place in the end time. John foresaw such a drastic difference: "Beloved, now we are children of God; and it has not yet been revealed what we shall be, but we know that when He is revealed, we shall be like Him, for we shall see Him as He is. And everyone who has this hope in Him purifies himself, just as He is pure" (1 John 3:2, 3, *NKJV*).

C. A Joyful Blessing (vv. 10, 11)

(Isaiah 61:10, 11 is not included in the printed text.)

There will be wonderful reasons for rejoicing when God calls His children together in the end times, and all of the rejoicing will be in humble appreciation toward the God who is our salvation. The blessings and joys will be none of our doing but will be entirely due to God's presence and His declaration. God will clothe us with the garment of salvation and cover us with robes of righteousness. To our great joy and gratitude, we will be adorned as a bridegroom or a bride just prior to a wedding.

Nothing is more refreshing than a garden that has been tended well and prepared with the best of seeds and the best of flowering plants. When that garden begins to bring forth its flowers and greenery, the fragrance and beauty are breathtaking. It is this illustration that Isaiah uses to relate how refreshing the righteousness of God's people will be in that day. "For as the earth bringeth forth her bud, and as the garden causeth the things that are sown in it to spring forth; so the Lord God will cause righteousness and praise to spring forth before all the nations" (v. 11).

III. ALL THINGS NEW (Isaiah 65:17-25)

In the Book of Revelation, John saw something similar to the prophecy given to Isaiah. "And I saw a new heaven and a new earth: for the first heaven and the first earth were passed away; and there was no more sea" (Revelation 21:1). The creative power of God will once again come to bear upon the earth, re-creating both heaven and earth in a more righteous and glorious fashion. This reflection in John's vision of what Isaiah had

prophesied hundreds of years before gives us both Old and New Testament proofs of what lies ahead.

A. A New City (vv. 17-19)

(Isaiah 65:19 is not included in the printed text.)

17. For, behold, I create new heavens and a new earth: and the former shall not be remembered, nor come into mind.

18. But be ye glad and rejoice for ever in that which I create: for, behold, I create Jerusalem a rejoicing, and her people a joy.

Create is from the Hebrew word *bara*. It can refer to the act of renovating something already existent into a totally new condition. This new creation of Jerusalem will be so wonderful that the old city of the past will not be remembered.

The new Jerusalem will be a city of rejoicing. There is little wonder that the people who inhabit that righteous city will rejoice because of the redemption that has brought them there. Jerusalem will be alive—teeming with the sound of rejoicing from the saints who have come to populate her streets. Singing will be heard from every street and avenue. Laughter will be her music.

Three times in verses 17 and 18, God says, "I create." This reminds us that the primary focus of Jerusalem residents will be on the Creator, not on His new creation. They will rejoice in the blessings while praising the One who blesses.

The joy of that city, however, will not simply be a joy of her inhabitants. God will rejoice with His people as well, for He says, "I will rejoice in Jerusalem, and joy in my people" (v. 19). In an extremely powerful fellowship, His children will be a joy to the Lord as He is a joy to them. His delight will be in the people He has redeemed and the redeemed of the Lord will delight in Him.

B. A New Life (vv. 20-23)

(Isaiah 65:20-23 is not included in the printed text.)

All of life will be transformed in God's new creation. Aging will be a thing of the past. Children will not die prematurely and the elderly will fulfill their days.

The way of life for the residents of that city will take on a sense of normalcy. Homes will be built, gardens and vineyards will be planted, and those who labor in building and planting will enjoy the fruits of their labors indefinitely. Children will be born, and their children's children will live as the "seed [descendants] of the blessed of the Lord" (v. 23). Everything about the life of the saints in that new city will bear resemblance to life today except for one dramatic difference: *righteousness* will reign supreme and God will rule over all!

C. New Relationships (vv. 24, 25)

24. And it shall come to pass, that before they call, I will answer; and while they are yet speaking, I will hear.

25. The wolf and the lamb shall feed together, and the lion shall eat straw like the bullock: and dust shall be the serpent's meat. They shall not hurt nor destroy in all my holy mountain, saith the Lord.

The relationship between God and the people in the new city of Jerusalem will be one of closeness and intimacy. Knowing the very thoughts of His people, God will answer before their prayer has been completed. Before the persons praying have a chance to say "Amen," God will have granted their request. It is interesting that prayer will still be an integral part of our lives in God's new economy as it is now. This thought alone should let us know the importance of being a praying person in this life.

Peace will be the rule of every day in that new city. Carnivorous animals will become vegetarians. The wolf and lion will dine on the same fare as the lamb and the ox—and that from the same trough. The serpent will not strike and the animal will not bite. All will be peace and love in God's Holy City.

It is this vision of what lies ahead that gives us the stamina to keep fighting the good fight in this life. Knowing that God has such wonderful things in store for us in the future can serve to bolster our resolve to live righteously in this life, "looking for the blessed hope and glorious appearing of our great God and Savior Jesus Christ" (Titus 2:13, 14, *NKJV*).

GOLDEN TEXT HOMILY

"FOR, BEHOLD, I CREATE NEW HEAVENS AND A NEW EARTH: AND THE FORMER SHALL NOT BE REMEMBERED, NOR COME INTO MIND" (Isaiah 65:17).

God has not finished His creative work. His coming masterpiece will be a new heaven and a new earth.

"Create" is from the Hebrew word *bara*, which can refer to the production of something new, rare and wonderful. *Bara* can also refer to the act of renovating—remaking something already in existence into a renewed form— which is the idea expressed in this verse. Through God's re-creative powers, there will be a totally new condition of things.

Believers will inherit this new world during Christ's millennial reign. The renewed creation will be so marvelous that life as we now know it will be forgotten—just a vague memory.

In this new order, God's children "will be priests of God and of Christ and will reign with him for a thousand years" (Revelation 20:6, *NIV*).—
Selected

SENTENCE SERMONS

CHRIST is the center of God's plan for the future.

—Selected

HAS THIS WORLD been so kind to you that you should leave with regret? There are better things ahead than any we leave behind.

—C.S. Lewis

IN ITS CONCERN with Left and Right, the world has forgotten there is an Above and Below.

—Glen Drake

EVANGELISM APPLICATION

SINNERS CAN EXPERIENCE A GLORIOUS FUTURE BY ACCEPTING CHRIST AS THEIR REDEEMER.

The glories of heaven should be as much or more of a witnessing point as the avoidance of hell. This is not to say the message of hell should be watered down or avoided, for hell is a real place with real torment. Heaven is also a real place with real pleasures and joys.

If happiness is all some seek in this world, they will always be left with failed expectations. If, however, they seek satisfaction in God now and in faith wait for the fulfillment of His joy in them, they will not be disappointed.

ILLUMINATING THE LESSON

"How can I believe there is a heaven when I have never seen it?" asked a man who had just accepted a tract from a witnessing student. The student thought for a moment and answered, "Sir, I have never seen heaven either, but I talk with the Architect every day and He assures me that it is ready for habitation. It is easy to question the things we have not seen, but we should never doubt the things God has promised."

DAILY BIBLE READINGS

M. Messiah Declared.
    Psalm 2:1-12
T. Contrasting Futures.
    Psalm 37:34-40
W. Repentance and Deliverance.
    Jeremiah 15:19-21
T. Restitution of All Things.
    Acts 3:12-21
F. Be Ready.
    2 Peter 3:10-14
S. New Heaven and New Earth.
    Revelation 21:1-7

TRUTH SEARCH
Creatively Teaching the Word

DISCUSSION QUESTIONS

Isaiah 61:1-3
• Whom would the Savior come to serve (v. 1)?
• Describe the different trades (exchanges) the Savior would offer (v. 3).
• What kind of trees does God want His children to become, and who is the gardener (v. 3)?
• How are the Savior's ministries (vv. 1-3) taking place now, and in what sense will they be completely fulfilled only in the eternal future?

Isaiah 65:17-25
• Who is the "I" in verse 17? What evidence do you have to support your answer?
• What "former" things "shall not be remembered" (v. 17) by believers about life on earth as we know it now? Why won't they be remembered?
• How will God and His people feel about life in the New Jerusalem (vv. 18, 19)?
• What will the infant mortality rate be in this new world?
• How will life spans be different?
• Given Israel's history of exile, why would verses 21-23 be especially comforting to them?
• Why do you suppose answers from God will come so suddenly in His new kingdom (v. 24)?
• Choose words to describe the new world pictured in verse 25.

Revelation 21:1-4
• Though written centuries apart, what is the similarity between Isaiah 65:17 and Revelation 21:1, 2?
• How will our relationship with God change in light of Revelation 21:3?
• What are some of the old things that will pass away (v. 4)?

OBJECT LESSON

Items needed: Toothbrush, map, bar of soap, pair of socks; each of the following words written on different pieces of paper: *Pain, Grief, Temptation, Sorrow, Fear, Loneliness, Bitterness, Bad Memories, Death.*

Have you ever gone on a trip and forgotten something you needed? If so, how did you feel? Use the toothbrush, map, soap and socks to encourage discussion and illustrate the point.

How many of you have ever gone on a trip and were happy about leaving some things behind for a few days? Encourage students to discuss their experiences.

When we go to heaven to be with Christ forever, consider some of the earthly realities we will leave behind. Display the words one at a time and let students comment about how easy it will be to leave each hardship behind.

Devotion to God

Study Text: Psalm 119:1-16
Objective: To realize that devotion to God is crucial and give it first priority in our lives.
Time: Perhaps during the reign of David
Golden Text: "With my whole heart have I sought thee: O let me not wander from thy commandments" (Psalm 119:10).
Central Truth: Devotion to God deserves highest priority in the believer's life.
Evangelism Emphasis: A Christian devoted to God will reach out to the unsaved.

PRINTED TEXT

Psalm 119:1. Blessed are the undefiled in the way, who walk in the law of the Lord.

2. Blessed are they that keep his testimonies, and that seek him with the whole heart.

3. They also do no iniquity: they walk in his ways.

4. Thou hast commanded us to keep thy precepts diligently.

5. O that my ways were directed to keep thy statutes!

6. Then shall I not be ashamed, when I have respect unto all thy commandments.

7. I will praise thee with uprightness of heart, when I shall have learned thy righteous judgments.

8. I will keep thy statutes: O forsake me not utterly.

9. Wherewithal shall a young man cleanse his way? by taking heed thereto according to thy word.

10. With my whole heart have I sought thee: O let me not wander from thy commandments.

11. Thy word have I hid in mine heart, that I might not sin against thee.

12. Blessed art thou, O Lord: teach me thy statutes.

13. With my lips have I declared all the judgments of thy mouth.

14. I have rejoiced in the way of thy testimonies, as much as in all riches.

15. I will meditate in thy precepts, and have respect unto thy ways.

16. I will delight myself in thy statutes: I will not forget thy word.

LESSON OUTLINE

I. WHOLEHEARTED DEVOTION TO GOD

    A. Freedom From Defilement

    B. Keepers of the Testimonies

    C. The Lifestyle of the Devout

II. LOVING OBEDIENCE TO GOD

    A. The Commandment to Obey

    B. A Prayer for Obedience

    C. Blessings of Obedience

III. DELIGHT IN GOD'S WORD

    A. A Significant Question

    B. A Responsible Answer

    C. A Workable Strategy

LESSON EXPOSITION

INTRODUCTION

God has always been concerned about the state and focus of the heart of those who would serve Him. This desire for a singular focus was revealed in the first commandment when He said, "Thou shalt have no other gods before me" (Exodus 20:3). This principle was affirmed by Jesus, who urged His followers, "Seek ye first the kingdom of God" (Matthew 6:33).

A banker friend in Minot, North Dakota, gave me an insight I shall never forget. He said, "I can scan the canceled checks of my customers and tell them what their values are." He was saying that what we spend our money for reflects our values and our priorities.

The Lord God does not need to see our canceled checks to know our values and priorities. He knows the focus of the heart, which determines our devotion to Him and shapes our behavior.

I. WHOLEHEARTED DEVOTION TO GOD (Psalm 119:1-3)

A. Freedom From Defilement (v. 1)

1. Blessed are the undefiled in the way, who walk in the law of the Lord.

The word *blessed* is often translated as "happy." This is true in the Beatitudes of Jesus given in the Sermon on the Mount. The psalmist says that the happy person is the one who walks in the ways of the Lord and keeps himself free from defilement.

Walk suggests moving toward a goal or objective. It is indicative of gradual progression as opposed to instant arrival. One step at a time, one day at a time, the happy person walks in the ways of the Lord.

In the secular world there are diverse ideas as to how to achieve happiness. Money is the key to happiness for some. Others see power and authority as their key. Still others think in turn to self-indulgences in sensual pleasures as the ultimate happiness.

That which we imagine will make us happy often has the opposite effect. For example, Jesus told the story of a rich man (Luke 16:19-31) who had all of the good things of this world. But in the end he begged for just one drop of water to soothe his burning tongue. On the other hand, Lazarus, who was deprived of most of the comforts of this life, was at peace in the presence of God.

The Prodigal Son left his father's house seeking happiness, but he squandered his inheritance in quest of it. Sadly, he became so destitute that he resorted to feeding the swine in order to survive (15:11-16).

Happiness, according to the psalmist, comes from living a life of integrity. The discipline of abstaining from potential defilements is the foundation to happiness. A clean heart and a clear conscience are always necessary if we are to have true happiness. Embracing God and walking in His ways require the abandonment of self-centered, sensual indulgences.

What most people need to do to be happy and what they actually are doing in an effort to achieve happiness are opposite each other.

B. Keepers of the Testimonies (v. 2)

2. Blessed are they that keep his testimonies, and that seek him with the whole heart.

Often the testimonies (laws) of the Lord are considered restrictive and inhibiting. Not so, says the psalmist. Instead, they bring blessings. The psalmist stated, "Your word I have hidden in my heart, that I might not sin against You" (v. 11, *NKJV*).

To keep His testimonies, one must know what they are. This means the testimonies must be read and reviewed. They must be studied and considered. Failure to read the Word of God makes it impossible to keep the Word.

To keep His testimonies requires understanding them. It is possible to know the words and not know the meaning. This does not mean we must have full and perfect understanding of all of His statutes. Understanding is a developmental process. We walk in the light as the light is shed upon us. Prayer and the influence of the Holy Spirit will reveal to us the meaning of His testimonies.

To keep the testimonies requires a love for them. Resentment, dread and fear will keep us from God's laws. When we understand that the testimonies are the revelation of a loving God to His people, we will come to love His ways. It is not possible to love God and reject His testimonies.

Keeping His testimonies means to obey them. His testimonies do more than educate the mind. They give direction and guidance to the heart. It is not enough to know them; we must *do* them. Values and behavior must be formed based on the testimonies of the Lord.

C. The Lifestyle of the Devout (v. 3)

3. They also do no iniquity: they walk in his ways.

We are known by what we do and by what we do not do. This chapter deals with both of these issues. This verse in particular states that a happy (blessed) person does no iniquity.

The word *iniquity* in the Old Testament carries the idea of moral impurity, acts of mischief, and evildoing. This kind of behavior has no place in the lifestyle of the believer.

Prohibitions are often considered negative. This is an incorrect concept. Any rule or mandate that serves the good of the individual and of others cannot rightly be called negative. Seven of the Ten Commandments begin with the phrase "you shall not." A close examination of each of them reveals that they are for the benefit of the individual and the protection of society.

The follower of God is not a thief, is not known for lying against his or her neighbor, does not commit adultery, nor desire his neighbor's wife. In the teachings of Jesus and of the apostle Paul, a contrast is clearly drawn between the morality and ethics of the believer and the sinner. What we do and what we refuse to do is a clear reflection of the kind of person we are.

It is possible to be successful and effective in most aspects of life only to have it all negated by an act (or acts) of iniquity. It is a tragic waste when gifted and talented men and women waste their lives and squander their skills because of iniquity. Being overcome by iniquity is not only a sin against God, it is a sin against others. We are told that it is possible to be the ruler of a strong city, yet be unable to rule our own selves (Proverbs 16:32). One Biblical character lamented, "They made me the keeper of the vineyards; but mine own vineyard have I not kept" (Song of Solomon 1:6).

A man I know was being enticed by others to do wrong. He said, "I cannot do such things; if I do, there is Someone inside of me who talks to me at night." It is wonderful to know that many are withheld from sin, folly and destruction by the Spirit's inner voice.

II. LOVING OBEDIENCE TO GOD (Psalm 119:4-8)

A. The Commandment to Obey (v. 4)

4. Thou hast commanded us to keep thy precepts diligently.

Psalm 119 follows the sequence of the Jewish alphabet. Each section contains eight verses. The first eight verses fall under the first letter *aleph.* It is no accident that the beginning point embraces the virtue of obedience. The poet is writing to young men, or a young man. He understands that the test of devotion is obedience.

Keeping the precepts of the Lord is not optional for the believer. God has commanded us to keep His statutes diligently. Many believers struggle with their spiritual life because they live in disobedience to God's law. All praying, fasting, churchgoing and Bible reading will not be effective if we refuse to obey the statutes of the Lord.

Numerous passages in both Testaments testify to the premium God places on obedience. In 1 Samuel 15:22 He said that obedience is better than sacrifice. Jesus challenged the value of calling Him "Lord, Lord," while refusing to do what He commands (Luke 6:46). We are told in 1 John 5:3 that the concepts of loving God and keeping his commandments are inseparable: "For this is the love of God, that we keep his commandments: and his commandments are not grievous." Obedience is not a burden for those who truly love the Lord.

A Sunday school teacher was teaching her young students about God's angels. She asked, "How do angels carry out God's will?" Many answers followed. One said, "They do it right away." Another, "They do it with all their hearts." A third, "They do it well." After a pause, a little girl said, "They do it without asking any questions." Of course all of these answers are correct. Just as the angels carry out the commands of the Lord, so should we.

B. A Prayer for Obedience (v. 5)

5. O that my ways were directed to keep thy statutes!

In verse 5 the psalmist offers a fervent request—that all the obstacles that would hinder obedience to the Lord would be removed from his path. The writer was aware that humans are not inclined to walk in the path of obedience. Since Adam, we have been more inclined to question and disobey than to follow. We do not seem to have it within us to obey the Lord. Aware of this, the psalmist prayed for assistance in the removal of all that would hinder obedience.

This is indeed a necessary and noble prayer. However, offering such a prayer does not exempt us from the disciplines of life. God's law must be obeyed in spite of difficulties, not in the absence of them. Was it easy for Abraham to offer up his own son on the altar of sacrifice? Obviously not!

While we may not have the strength within ourselves to obey, we must always have the will to do so. Only after we have exhausted all human possibilities can we expect God to clear the path so we can obey.

When Jesus came to earth, His orders were severe. He was to assume human form, subject Himself to human frailty, and to ultimately die on a cross. As He faced the ordeal of the cross with every intention of carrying out His Father's plan, He prayed for divine assistance, asking that the Father's will be accomplished. Jesus did not back away from the cross but instead relied on divine resources to enable Him to obey.

The commandments of the Lord are not always logical to the human mind. In fact, sometimes His commandments seem ridiculous. This was true when Abraham was commanded to offer his son as a sacrifice. The commands given by God to Noah regarding the ark and the Flood made no human sense. We can find many reasons why we should not do what the Lord commands. Obedience is a spiritual discipline we learn through practice and prayer.

C. Blessings of Obedience (vv. 6-8)

6. Then shall I not be ashamed, when I have respect unto all thy commandments.

7. I will praise thee with uprightness of heart, when I shall have learned thy righteous judgments.

8. I will keep thy statutes: O forsake me not utterly.

One of the blessings of obeying is that we have no reason to be ashamed when we stand before the Lord. We recall the reaction of Adam and Eve when they disobeyed the Lord. When they heard His voice calling them, the Bible says they were afraid and hid themselves (Genesis 3:1-10).

Disobedience breeds condemnation. Condemnation breeds shame and embarrassment. We do not want to face authority when we know we have transgressed.

We have both joy and peace when we are able to walk before the Lord without fear, guilt or condemnation. This ability comes from walking after the Spirit rather than walking after the flesh. The means of this walk and the results are described in Romans 8.

Another blessing of obeying is what we learn in the process. In the case of the psalmist, it was the righteousness of the Lord's judgments. When we first encounter the com-mandments of the Lord, they do not always look good to us. A thousand times we ask why. By following the commandments of God we learn that He is not playing games. He does not erect obstacle courses for us for the fun of watching us struggle through them. The commandments of God always have a redemptive purpose. He is a righteous God and therefore cannot issue unrighteous mandates.

Growing in the knowledge and wisdom of the Lord are developmental steps the Lord desires for all of His followers. To learn the ways of the Lord enhances the quality of life. To learn more about the Lord brings us closer to Him. The bonding between ourselves and God is made possible through growing in wisdom and knowledge. It has been well stated, "The better I know Him, the better I love Him; and the better I love Him, the better I serve Him."

The final blessing for obeying in this passage is the certainty of fellowship with God. In verse 8, the psalmist expressed a firm resolution to keep the statutes of the Lord, followed by a prayer for a continuing relationship with God. This was not an attempt to bargain with the Lord. The resolve to keep the statutes of the Lord is unconditional. Because God is God and because He is righteous are reasons enough to keep His commandments.

The most terrifying thing that could happen to the psalmist would be the loss of fellowship and communion with God. It is urgent that we realize that fellowship with God is contingent upon obedience. We cannot live in rebellion and expect Him to walk with us.

III. DELIGHT IN GOD'S WORD
     (Psalm 119:9-16)

A. A Significant Question (v. 9a)

9a. Wherewithal shall a young man cleanse his way?

The psalmist, apparently a young man, is contemplating his future. He is wisely giving consideration to the path he will take in life. Like everyone, he has choices. He can choose to follow the appetites of human nature or he can choose the high road of purity. In this case, the desire to follow the path of purity is evident. The question then is, how should he work out and walk out the chosen path?

The writer has been exposed to the temptations of youth and the desire to fulfill the flesh. He knows that walking in the pathway of purity calls for a resource outside himself.

No question can be more significant for a young person than the one asked here. The decisions we make in the early years of life often determine not only our path, but our destiny as well. We all stand at a crucial crossroad. According to Jesus there are only two ways. The broad way is popular and leads to destruction. The narrow way can be lonely and difficult, but it leads to life everlasting.

Other people, for generations to come, are affected by the path we take. Think of the positive impact of the path chosen by the psalmist. Consider the impact of the path taken by Saul of Tarsus, Martin Luther and Billy Graham. Consider the negative impact of the path taken by Adolph Hitler and Joseph Stalin. There is no way we can fully know the significance of the path we select.

B. A Responsible Answer (v. 9b)

9b. By taking heed thereto according to thy word.

As we read the Book of Psalms, we discover that the psalmist ponders and processes numerous questions and arrives at intelligent answers to his own inquiries. It pays to be thoughtful and deliberate when facing the significant issues of life.

In verse 9, the psalmist's answer is "By living according to your word" (*NIV*). The only reliable means to cleanse our way is to take heed to the Word of God.

Friends and family, even though they may have noble intentions, do not always give us the best advice. Their word is not the law; therefore it should be considered prayerfully and in the light of God's Word.

God has given us a conscience, but it is not infallible. It can be negatively programmed. The conscience can also be seared or numbed until it is not reliable.

The laws of society are necessary, and many of them are good. However, these laws are devised by people and may be corrupted. We need social rules and regulations, but they are not sufficient when it comes to cleansing our way.

The Word of God is the only reliable means whereby we may cleanse our ways. Jesus prayed for His followers, "Sanctify [cleanse] them through thy truth: thy word is truth" (John 17:17). The Word of God is a cleansing agent, but it does not work unless it is applied. The passage says that one's way can be cleansed by "taking heed" to God's Word.

Taking heed to the Word of God involves understanding it. God reveals understanding based on our effort, needs and desire to understand. His Spirit will give every earnest seeker sufficient understanding to assure that their way will be cleansed.

The Word of God also must be believed. Reading the Word with an unbelieving heart will not produce cleansing. The Word does not profit unless it is mixed with faith.

We also must love the Word of God. Jesus said that the test of loving Him is keeping His commandments (John 14:15). It is one thing to accept the Word of God, but quite another to have an affection for it.

The ultimate benefit belongs to those who love the Word. We demonstrate our love for the Word by reading it continuously, systematically and prayerfully. We demonstrate our love for the Word of God by meditating on it. To read Scripture and to think about it allows it to permeate every fiber of our being.

Believers sometimes feel their way through as though they were stumbling in the dark. This is usually not necessary. The answer to the dilemma of the disciples of Emmaus was in the Word of God. Jesus attributed their bewilderment to a lack of knowledge of the Word (Luke 24:25-27).

C. A Workable Strategy (vv. 10-16)

10. With my whole heart have I sought thee: O let me not wander from thy commandments.

11. Thy word have I hid in mine heart, that I might not sin against thee.

12. Blessed art thou, O Lord: teach me thy statutes.

13. With my lips have I declared all the judgments of thy mouth.

14. I have rejoiced in the way of thy testimonies, as much as in all riches.

15. I will meditate in thy precepts, and have respect unto thy ways.

16. I will delight myself in thy statutes: I will not forget thy word.

The psalmist outlined a strategy for not only selecting but continuing in the path of purity. This strategy worked for him then and it will work for us now. Let us focus on the steps of the workable strategy.

1. *"With my whole heart have I sought thee" (v. 10).* The King James Version puts this statement in the past tense. Other versions place it in the present tense, while others use the future tense. The true sense of this resolve is that we have sought

Him, we do seek Him, and we will continue to seek Him.

"Whole heart" means nothing is spared. With all the effort and energy possible, we should seek the Lord. A divided heart, like a divided kingdom, cannot stand. There is a vast difference between a routine prayer and seeking God with the whole heart. God, who sees the heart, knows when we seek Him halfheartedly or wholeheartedly.

The second part of verse 10 mentions the tendency to stray. This means that continuous effort must be expended to maintain the path of purity. Often the side roads are subtle and difficult to distinguish. Unless constant vigilance is maintained, we may get on the wrong road.

2. *"Thy word have I hid in mine heart, that I might not sin against thee" (v. 11).* It is possible to have the Word of God in our head but not in our heart. Scores of people can recite Scripture verses yet fail completely to live by their message. The devil himself frequently quotes from the Bible but only in a confusing, negative way. To have a head knowledge and not a heart knowledge of the Word is insufficient.

Having the Word in our heart means it becomes part of the fabric of our being. It is in us and with us and there is no way we can be separated from it. With the Word stored in our memory, the Holy Spirit can bring it to the forefront when we are under assault from the Enemy. When we need something to stand on, it is there!

When the Word is hid in our heart, we find guidance at the many crossroads of life. Many voices are more than ready to advise and direct. With the Word of God as a part of our identity, we may be certain that we are safe. Those who hide the Word in their heart can stay away from sin.

3. *"Blessed art thou, O Lord: teach me thy statutes" (v. 12).* A spirit of

praise and a teachable attitude are necessary components of a workable strategy. Devotion to God is perhaps best expressed in praise. True worship is more than a feeling. God should be worshiped regardless of how we feel. He is God and we should bless Him in all circumstances. Praising God secures us because it takes the focus off ourselves and embraces God.

A teachable attitude is as important as a worshipful spirit. If we truly adore God we will have a desire (obsession) to learn all we can about Him. The invitation from Jesus is to come to Him, find rest, and learn of Him (Matthew 11:28-30). Two of the best ways to learn of Him is worship and study.

True disciples realize how much they have to learn. Jesus himself is referred to often in the New Testament as Rabbi, or Teacher. One of the major functions of the Holy Spirit is to teach. It is a privilege and a joy to sit at Jesus' feet and learn of Him.

4. *"With my lips I have declared the judgments of thy mouth" (v. 13)*. This verse suggests another important expression of devotion—to talk about the laws of the Lord. Those who are truly devoted to Him not only know Him, they tell others about Him. This does not mean every believer becomes a preacher, priest or prophet. It does mean that all believers express to others the ways of the Lord. When we genuinely value a relationship, we are naturally inclined to talk about it.

The judgments of the Lord should be shared because they are the criteria by which God evaluates human action. Truth, duty, justice and even destiny are understood in the light of God's judgments.

It is our duty to witness about the ways of the Lord. God can speak through angels, and He often does. God is capable of thundering out His judgments by the force of His own actions. However, the primary way God has chosen to communicate His truths is through human instrumentality.

The contemporary world is bombarded daily with messages that are detrimental to the soul. Lies, deception and filth are in abundance. False doctrines abound. Should a truly devout believer in the judgments of God refrain the lips from the most meaningful message of all?

5. *"I have rejoiced in the way of thy testimonies, as much as in all riches" (v. 14)*. The psalmist now brings us to two very important principles. One has to do with the priority of God's testimonies, and the other has to do with the joy and delight derived from them. Without joy the statutes of the Lord can be burdensome. Attention to the Word of God is a dread and a bore to those who approach it from a sense of duty with no delight.

That which brings us joy and delight reveals much about our character. Why is it that some find it easy to sit through a three-hour movie or football game yet cannot tolerate a 30-minute sermon? If the comic strip and the sports page bring us more joy than the Word of God, we have lost our way.

The psalmist observed that many of his contemporaries derived their joy from riches and all that wealth represents. However, he declared that the testimonies of the Lord mean more to him than riches. While society may value people by the measure of the things they possess, God values people by the measure of the things that possess them.

6. *"I will meditate in thy precepts, and have respect unto thy ways" (v. 15)*. Meditation seems a lost art in contemporary society. *Run, rush* and *hurry* are modern watchwords. Meditation in a Biblical sense means listening to God's voice, reflecting on His goodness, remembering God's deeds, and rejoicing in His person. Meditation is more than detachment. It involves detachment from certain

things, but more importantly, it means attachment. It is a spiritual discipline that far too few modern-day believers practice. It does require intentional action. We need a time and a place. A simple plan followed on a regular basis will enhance our walk with the Lord.

The second part of this strategy is respect for the Lord's ways. We often prefer to advise God and expect Him to do things our way. A wholesome relationship with Him requires that we respect His ways. We may not always understand His ways, but we need to remember that He is God and does not need to explain nor does He need our approval. If we are devoted to Him we will respect His ways.

7. *"I will delight myself in thy statutes: I will not forget thy word" (v. 16).* We are to delight in Scripture because God is the author. The subject and the substance of the statutes are about Him. They are the expression of our Creator and our Benefactor, our Father and our deliverer. All of this being true, why should we not rejoice in His statutes?

We should delight in His statutes because of what they mean to us and what they do for us. They keep us from wandering and being lost. They keep us from worldliness and contamination. They enrich our lives day by day. Delighting in the statutes of the Lord will enable us to remember them. Once they are ingrained in our souls, and we are experiencing delight in them, we will remember them. And they will "remember" us by keeping our way blameless.

GOLDEN TEXT HOMILY

"WITH MY WHOLE HEART HAVE I SOUGHT THEE: O LET ME NOT WANDER FROM THY COMMANDMENTS" (Psalm 119:10).

This could be the summary statement of Psalm 119:1-16: The spiritual life is the life lived for God's glory only.

Throughout the meditation, the psalmist stresses his desire for personal holiness. For him it is the key to pleasing God. Sometimes we forget that God himself is at the center of His plan, and we sons and daughters of God bring Him glory as we live in simple devotion to Him.

Regarding the connection between true spirituality and the centrality of God in our life, the psalmist closely parallels Christ's statement in the disciples' prayer that His will be done as completely on earth as it is done in heaven (Matthew 6:10). Often we see ourselves at the center of God's plan, and that must be avoided.

The poet yearns for his life to be pure as he walks in God's law. Yet he knows he is capable of falling short of the standard for which he strives, and a note of pain can be heard in verses 5 and 8 as he grapples with the fear that he might fail.

Today's Golden Text message could be simply this: We lift up the Word of God; we serve Him as He directs; we yearn for His will to be done through us.—**Calvin Eastham**

SENTENCE SERMONS

DEVOTION TO GOD deserves highest priority in the believer's life.
                                          —Selected

TAKE MY LIFE, and let it be consecrated, Lord, to Thee.
                       —Frances Ridley Havergal

LOYALTY that will do anything, that will endure anything, that will make the whole being consecrated to Him, is what Christ wants. Anything else is not worthy of Him.
                              —Burdett Hart

EVANGELISM APPLICATION

A CHRISTIAN DEVOTED TO GOD WILL REACH OUT TO THE UNSAVED.

Each time your heart beats, at least one person leaves this world and goes out into eternity. According to the Bible there are only two places they can go—heaven or hell. What makes the difference in a person's final destiny? You and I could make that difference!

While it is true that each person is personally accountable to God, it is also true that the lost cannot find their way unless someone shows them. If I know the way and do not tell it to the lost, I bear some responsibility for the lost. I cannot bear to think that because of my silence, when my heart beats, a lost soul could fall into hell!

ILLUMINATING THE LESSON

Travelers among the Alps say they come to have a peculiar feeling, unlike any other, for their Alpine guide. Not so much a feeling of companionship, fellowship or friendship, but a combination of all of these. This feeling, they say, is produced by their obedience to the guide's commands. They realize that their safety and survival is contingent upon doing what the guide says.

Our Guide on the journey of life tells us, "If you keep My commandments, you will abide in My love" (John 15:10, *NKJV*). Obedience to Him will produce a bond of love and devotion. It builds confidence in Jesus, our guide. We are devoted to Him because we trust Him. This results in a sense of safety and security. He knows the way—He has been there before. When we disobey His commands or stray from His protective presence, we endanger ourselves.

DAILY BIBLE READINGS

M. Abraham Believed God.
   Genesis 15:1-6
T. Commitment to God.
   Ruth 1:6-18
W. Devoted to God.
   Deuteronomy 34:5-12
T. Faithful to God.
   Luke 2:25-38
F. Faith Displayed.
   Luke 7:1-10
S. Endure Hardship.
   2 Timothy 4:1-8

TRUTH SEARCH
Creatively Teaching the Word

DISCUSSION QUESTIONS

Psalm 119:1-8
• Who is a genuinely blessed person (vv. 1, 2)?
• How are we to walk (vv. 1, 3)?
• What kind of heart must we have (vv. 2, 7)?
• What does it take to "not be ashamed" before the Lord (vv. 4-6)?
• What does the psalmist vow in verse 8?
• What does the psalmist request in verse 8?

Psalm 119:9-16
• How can a young person live a clean life (v. 9)?
• Can the second part of verse 10 ("O let me not wander . . .") be a reality if a person does not live according to the first part ("With my whole heart . . .")?
• What does it mean to hide God's Word in one's heart (v. 11)? What is the purpose?

• What does it mean to declare God's judgments (v. 13)?
• How much should we value God's Word (v. 14)? Why?
• What four commitments did the psalmist make regarding God's Word (vv. 15, 16)?

PRAYER FOCUS

There are around 6,800 languages spoken around the world. An estimated 3,000 languages, representing at least 380 million people, have no published Scripture. There are Bible translation projects in progress in 1,500 other languages. It takes 10 to 20 years to translate the Bible into a language.

Pray for the current works in progress and for God to raise up translators to meet this great need. To learn more, contact Wycliffe Bible Translators (*www.wycliffe.org*).

Foundation for Family Living

Study Text: Deuteronomy 6:1-25; Psalm 78:1-8
Objective: To see God's plan for communicating truth through the family and choose to fulfill God's purpose.
Golden Text: "Thou shalt teach them [God's commands] diligently unto thy children, and shalt talk of them when thou sittest in thine house, and when thou walkest by the way, and when thou liest down, and when thou risest up" (Deuteronomy 6:7).
Central Truth: The Bible must be taught in the home.
Evangelism Emphasis: God uses Christian families to communicate His Word to succeeding generations.

PRINTED TEXT

Deuteronomy 6:4. Hear, O Israel: The Lord our God is one Lord:

5. And thou shalt love the Lord thy God with all thine heart, and with all thy soul, and with all thy might.

6. And these words, which I command thee this day, shall be in thine heart:

7. And thou shalt teach them diligently unto thy children, and shalt talk of them when thou sittest in thine house, and when thou walkest by the way, and when thou licst down, and when thou risest up.

8. And thou shalt bind them for a sign upon thine hand, and they shall be as frontlets between thine eyes.

9. And thou shalt write them upon the posts of thy house, and on thy gates.

20. And when thy son asketh thee in time to come, saying, What mean the testimonies, and the statutes, and the judgments, which the Lord our God hath commanded you?

21. Then thou shalt say unto thy son, We were Pharaoh's bondmen in Egypt; and the Lord brought us out of Egypt with a mighty hand:

22. And the Lord showed signs and wonders, great and sore, upon Egypt, upon Pharaoh, and upon all his household, before our eyes:

23. And he brought us out from thence, that he might bring us in, to give us the land which he sware unto our fathers.

24. And the Lord commanded us to do all these statutes, to fear the Lord our God, for our good always, that he might preserve us alive, as it is at this day.

25. And it shall be our righteousness, if we observe to do all these commandments before the Lord our God, as he hath commanded us.

Psalm 78:1. Give ear, O my people, to my law: incline your ears to the words of my mouth.

4. We will not hide them from their children, shewing to the generation to come the praises of the Lord, and his strength, and his wonderful works that he hath done.

5. For he established a testimony in Jacob, and appointed a law in Israel, which he commanded our fathers, that they should make them known to their children:

6. That the generation to come might know them, even the children which should be born; who should arise and declare them to their children:

7. That they might set their hope in God, and not forget the works of God, but keep his commandments.

DICTIONARY
frontlets [phylacteries]—Deuteronomy 6:8—parchment strips inscribed with scriptures and placed inside a leather case worn on the hand or forehead.

LESSON OUTLINE

I. TEACH GOD'S WORD
  A. Origin of the Word
  B. Purpose of the Word
  C. Teaching of the Word

II. KNOW YOUR SPIRITUAL HERITAGE
  A. Value of Heritage
  B. Substance of Heritage
  C. Responsibility Toward Heritage

III. TESTIFY OF YOUR FAITH
  A. Hearing God's Voice
  B. Communicating God's Law
  C. Walking in God's Way

LESSON EXPOSITION

INTRODUCTION

God was preparing His people to enter and dwell in a new land. Just as they had encountered numerous temptations in the wilderness wanderings, they would encounter temptations in this new land, which was inhabited by worshipers of idols and multiple versions of false gods. God yearned for His people to remain true to Him and execute a moral influence on their new neighbors. In fact, it was God's intention to give this new land to His people.

The starting place in preparing His people for their mission was indoctrination in His Word and the spiritual development of the family. This lesson deals with the fundamental issues upon which a strong family can be built. Family leaders need to teach God's Word, know and appreciate their spiritual heritage, and communicate their faith even though the environment may be hostile.

It is amazing how contemporary the ancient Scriptures can be. Believers of the 21st century face most of the same issues Israel faced. What was required for Israel to be strong is required today. In contemporary society, just as it was with Israel, the family is the basic unit of the social system. As the family goes, so goes the nation and the world. *Here*

This lesson examines three timeless principles essential to a strong faith, a strong family and a strong nation.

I. TEACH GOD'S WORD
  (Deuteronomy 6:1-9)

A. Origin of the Word (v. 1)

(Deuteronomy 6:1 is not included in the printed text.)

When we hear an edict or a command, our initial response usually is, "Who said so?" This is a reasonable question. The validity or authority of a statement always goes back to the source. When God called Moses to be the leader of Israel, Moses asked, "When I come unto the children of Israel, and shall say unto them, The God of your fathers hath sent me unto you; and they shall say to me, What is his name? what shall I say unto them?" (Exodus 3:13). God replied, "Say unto the children of Israel, I AM hath sent me unto you" (v. 14).

In Deuteronomy 6:1 we read, "Now these are the commandments, the statutes, and the judgments, which the Lord your God commanded to teach you, that ye might do them in the land whither ye go to possess" (v. 1).

The Word of God originates with God himself. We sometimes read and hear the phrase "the law of Moses" in reference to Old Testament statutes. Technically, this is incorrect. It is not the law of Moses; it is the law of God.

moral 1, character of behavior, 2 right are wrong, 3 conduct — capable of understanding

Moses was an instrument used of God to communicate *His* word. Moses did not originate the Law, he proclaimed it. Moses had an intimate, face-to-face relationship with God in which God did most of the talking. God commissioned Moses to transmit the message to the people.

The same principle is true in the New Testament. Technically there is no Gospel of Matthew, Mark, Luke or John. These instruments of the Holy Spirit never claimed to have a gospel. It has ever been and shall ever be "the Gospel of Jesus Christ" as written by the various servants of God. God is the authority behind the Word. This is why we must know it, teach it, and do it!

B. Purpose of the Word (vv. 2, 3)

(Deuteronomy 6:2, 3 is not included in the printed text.) *Here*

The first purpose of the commandments identified in our text is "that ye might do them" (v. 1). We are not to know God's laws for the mere sake of knowing them, teaching them, or debating them in the public square. We are to know them for the ultimate purpose of doing them.

The priority of doing the Word is powerfully reinforced in both the Old and the New Testament. Obedience being better than sacrifice is a concept expressed throughout the Old Testament. In the New Testament, Jesus underscored the priority of doing with the parable of the two builders (Matthew 7:24-29). The builder who hears *and* does is wise, and will endure. The builder who hears and does *not* is foolish and destined for failure. James wrote that if we hear and do, we shall be blessed in the doing (James 1:22-25).

Another purpose of the Word identified in Deuteronomy 6 is "that you may fear [reverence] the Lord your God" (v. 2, *NKJV*). Words of praise and mouthed expressions of devotion have their place in the worship of God, who takes pleasure in the praises of His people. However, words are never pleasing to God unless accompanied with obedience. The ultimate expression of devotion is obedience. True love for the Lawgiver dictates respect for the Lawgiver. When we love and respect God, we will obey Him.

A third purpose of the Word is to benefit the people of God. However, the words *commandment, statutes* and *judgments* usually conjure up negative connotations and we react defensively. There is a false yet prevailing notion that the laws of God are restrictive and detrimental. If this is what we really think and feel regarding God's law, it is no wonder why we have problems knowing and doing His commandments.

The purpose of God's commandments are for the benefit, welfare and happiness of God's people. When we know and understand this, we will relish the Word. Punishment and deprivation are consequences of not knowing and ignoring the Word.

One benefit from obeying the Word is prolonged life. Since humanity's survival instinct is so powerful, one wonders why the benefit of long life for obeying God's law is usually overlooked. What greater motivation do we need for obedience?

Another benefit of keeping His Word is "that it may be well with thee" (v. 3). *Wellness* embraces a wide variety of meanings, including physical health. God has always been concerned about the physical well-being of His people. Living as God prescribes is in the best interest of our health. One reason for physical breakdowns is self-abuse. God our Maker knows what is best for us.

Wellness can also concern relationships with family, friends and fellow citizens. It encompasses material prosperity and spiritual blessings. In short, all kinds of blessings will come to us if we obey Him.

God's intention to make a great nation of Israel was a specific benefit for their obeying Him. God said, "That you may multiply greatly as the Lord God of your fathers has promised" (v. 3, *NKJV*). Perhaps no other people in the world have stronger bonds of nationalism than Israel. This passion for national identity is best explained by looking at the promise God made to them. This was a personal word from God—He would be the One to make them great. It would not happen through their own genius or military might.

C. Teaching of the Word (vv. 4-9)

4. Hear, O Israel: The Lord our God is one Lord:

5. And thou shalt love the Lord thy God with all thine heart, and with all thy soul, and with all thy might.

6. And these words, which I command thee this day, shall be in thine heart:

7. And thou shalt teach them diligently unto thy children, and shalt talk of them when thou sittest in thine house, and when thou walkest by the way, and when thou liest down, and when thou risest up.

8. And thou shalt bind them for a sign upon thine hand, and they shall be as frontlets between thine eyes.

9. And thou shalt write them upon the posts of thy house, and on thy gates.

The Lord God is one! Because this is true, undivided loyalty must be given to Him. The heart, soul, mind and strength must be yielded to Him unconditionally (vv. 4, 5). Those who wholeheartedly love God are to teach His Word, especially to their children.

Providing a spiritual education for one's children is not a mere suggestion but is a holy command. The Word of God must be read and taught in the family.

Search - pursued

The most valuable heritage we can leave our children is a clear-cut understanding of God and His Word. A casual approach to teaching our children the Word of God is not sufficient. The mandate from God is, "Thou shalt teach them diligently" (v. 7). Diligent teaching is defined in verses 7-9.

While at home, believers should talk about the commandments and ways of the Lord. Children will never know the Lord's statutes unless someone teaches them. Teaching the Word of God must be intentional and methodical.

When walking in the park or on the way to the store, we have the opportunity to speak about the ways of the Lord. When retiring to bed, and when waking in the morning, teaching the Word should be given priority. *for th f...*

The Hebrews took Moses' command to bind God's Word on their person as literal. They prepared four pieces of inscribed parchment—the first with Exodus 13:2-10; the second with Exodus 13:11-16; the third with Deuteronomy 6:1-8; and the fourth with Deuteronomy 11:18-21. These four portions of Scripture, or phylacteries, were enclosed in a square case or box of tough skin, on the side of which was placed the Hebrew letter *shin* and bound around the forehead with a thong or ribbon. When designed for the arm, the four texts were written on a slip of parchment which, along with the ink, was carefully prepared for exposed use.

The ancient Egyptians had the lintels and doorposts of their doors and gates inscribed with sentences indicative of a favorable omen. Desiring to turn this custom to a better use, Moses ordered that the words of God be posted, enjoining the Israelites to hold God's Word in perpetual remembrance. *Here*

Symbols and reminders of God's law should be a part of the apparel worn today. This can include modesty in dress as well as clothes and jewelry depicting Christian symbols and messages. *Here*

Regarding the placing of portions of God's law on the doorposts of our homes, we could say to let our music, art, literature, recreation and entertainment reveal our commitment to teaching the commandments of the Lord.

The major issues that must be taught to the children, and practiced by the young and the old, are identified in 6:10-19:

- Do not forget the Lord after He prospers you.
- Reverence and serve God.
- Reject false gods.
- Do not tempt the Lord.
- Keep the commandments.
- Do what is right.
- Turn away from the Lord's enemies.

II. KNOW YOUR SPIRITUAL HERITAGE (Deuteronomy 6:20-25)

A. Value of Heritage (vv. 20, 21)

20. And when thy son asketh thee in time to come, saying, What mean the testimonies, and the statutes, and the judgments, which the Lord our God hath commanded you?

21. Then thou shalt say unto thy son, We were Pharaoh's bondmen in Egypt; and the Lord brought us out of Egypt with a mighty hand:

Israel's spiritual life was to be such an obvious and intregal part of their daily living that it would be normal for the sons and daughters of the younger generations to ask questions and seek to understand the sacred history of Israel's development as a nation. The setting presented here coincides with the command given in verses 6-9.

One distinguishing mark between mankind and the lower animal kingdom is the capacity to teach history to the succeeding generations. Lower animals know certain things instinc-

tively, but their ability to instruct is limited. Humanity is the centerpiece of the creative genius of God; we are the creative expression of God that is most like Him.

Heritage is of great value because it reveals the unfolding of God's master plan. Every person existing in the present has a connection with the past and with the future. We are participants in what God has done, what He is doing, and what He will do. Each generation in its own turn and time is responsible for passing a godly legacy along to the next. It only takes one generation to lose the legacy. Let us make sure we are not the generation that fails. *Here*

Heritage influences society and has implications for eternity. The development of the church in the world would be impeded if each generation had to reinvent the wheel. The maxim is true: "He who fails to learn from history is doomed to repeat it."

A primary value of heritage is its relation to faith and Christian formation. The text is implicit about what the answer should be when our children ask, "What does this mean?" God instructed Israel to tell their children about their bondage in Egypt and how God delivered them. They were to testify about miracles and other divine interventions. The effect of this was building the faith of their children. *Here*

B. Substance of Heritage (vv. 22, 23)

22. And the Lord showed signs and wonders, great and sore, upon Egypt, upon Pharaoh, and upon all his household, before our eyes:

23. And he brought us out from thence, that he might bring us in, to give us the land which he sware unto our fathers.

The inquiring mind of a child is a delightful thing, especially if his parents are able to give answers. Moses encouraged the Israelites to prepare for this occasion by reflecting on the past events.

The rescue from Egypt, where the Israelites served as bondservants under Pharaoh, always formed the grand background of Israel's history. This rescue disclosed the divine love and care of God for His people through miracles, patience and a covenant relationship. The great institution of sacrifice revealed provision for pardoning love; and the precepts for the individual, the family and the nation told what sort of people God would have them to be.   *Here*

Also the life histories of their fathers—Abraham, Isaac and Jacob—would tell the great joy of having Jehovah as their God. Such truths instilled in the hearts and minds of the youth, with the gentle love of parents, certainly would lead the young Israelites to want the God of their fathers to be their God also.

Here

C. Responsibility Toward Heritage (vv. 24, 25)

24. And the Lord commanded us to do all these statutes, to fear the Lord our God, for our good always, that he might preserve us alive, as it is at this day.

25. And it shall be our righteousness, if we observe to do all these commandments before the Lord our God, as he hath commanded us.

The purpose of knowing is to influence behavior. Verses 24 and 25 focus sharply on how God's people are to respond to Him and what He has done for them. Those who know the truth have a responsibility to respond to it obediently and to teach it.

First, we are to observe the commandments and the statutes of the Lord. Heritage teaches that He is God and we are to have no other gods but Him. If we believe the

story as it has been told by those who were eyewitnesses, we must acknowledge God and be careful to observe His commandments.

The second responsibility is to fear (reverence) God. If indeed He is the central focus of heritage and history, that reality must be acknowledged. We must know that God will not be ignored. We will voluntarily acknowledge Him as God or He will get our attention in ways that may not be pleasant for us or for those who follow us.   *Here*

III. TESTIFY OF YOUR FAITH
(Psalm 78:1-8)

A. Hearing God's Voice (vv. 1-3)

(Psalm 78:2, 3 is not included in the printed text.)

1. Give ear, O my people, to my law: incline your ears to the words of my mouth.

It would be shocking to know how often God speaks to us without us hearing or recognizing His voice. Examples are abundant in the Old Testament. Sometimes we do not hear His voice because of other voices vying for our attention. The tragedy of this is that we so desperately need to hear God's voice; He is speaking, but we are not listening.

God uses two terms in describing His efforts to get our attention: "Give ear" and "incline your ears" (v. 1). A significant principle in communication is this: No one can communicate with you without your permission. Listening is a voluntary, willing act on the part of the would-be hearer.

God is here announcing that He is ready to deliver a message to His people. Yet God knew the futility of this attempt if the people were not willing to listen. We must always open our ears to hear His voice and develop a sensitivity to it. Like the boy Samuel, our response to God should always be, "Speak, Lord, for your servant is listening" (1 Samuel 3:9, 10, *NIV*).

Here

B. Communicating God's Law (vv. 4-6)

4. We will not hide them from their children, shewing to the generation to come the praises of the Lord, and his strength, and his wonderful works that he hath done.

5. For he established a testimony in Jacob, and appointed a law in Israel, which he commanded our fathers, that they should make them known to their children:

6. That the generation to come might know them, even the children which should be born; who should arise and declare them to their children.

A resolve not to hide God's laws from one's children is expressed in verse 4. There arc many ways these truths can be hidden. The most obvious way is to keep silent. We can know God's law and keep it to ourselves. The Word can also be hidden by distortion—flawed emphasis or faulty interpretation.

Each recipient of God's law has a responsibility to communicate as God intended. It is God's message and the communicator does not have the authority to modify it. God's Word must be taught to our children in the purest form possible. *Here*

C. Walking in God's Way (vv. 7, 8)

(Psalm 78:8 is not included in the printed text.)

7. That they might set their hope in God, and not forget the works of God, but keep his commandments.

The purpose for hearing God's voice is that we might walk in His ways. Walking in God's ways is expressed behaviorally in verses 7 and 8. "That they might set their hope in God." His voice has a calming, reassuring effect. Hearing from Him, we understand the futility of hoping or trusting in any other.

Walking in God's way means reflecting upon His works. As impressive as God's works arc, it is easy to forget them. It is amazing how powerfully God reveals Himself in our circumstances, and how soon we forget. A major reason for testifying of the Lord's works is to overcome the compelling tendency to forget.

We may talk about God, sing about Him, write about Him, and preach about Him; but unless we keep His commandments, we are not pleasing Him. Unless we obey Him, everything else is vain. *Here*

GOLDEN TEXT HOMILY

"THOU SHALT TEACH THEM [GOD'S COMMANDS] DILIGENTLY UNTO THY CHILDREN, AND SHALT TALK OF THEM WHEN THOU SITTEST IN THINE HOUSE, AND WHEN THOU WALKEST BY THE WAY, AND WHEN THOU LIEST DOWN, AND WHEN THOU RISEST UP" (Deutcronomy 6:7).

God has given His "called-out ones" commandments to govern our lives. He has also instructed us how we are to hand down commandments to the next generation. He is explicit in His instructions. He promotes a pedagogy of saturation where God is at the center.

"Every community that wants to last beyond a single generation must concern itself with education," said Walter Brueggeman. Education has to do with the maintenance of a community from one generation to the next. We pass treasures, values and thoughts to our children. That which we have learned and seen is passed on through words and behavior.

God tells us how we are to educate our children and the next generation concerning His commandments. They should be able to repeat these commandments as freely as they can sing a popular song. We accomplish this by talking about God's laws with our children and applying them in everyday

Here

activities. We include them in our prayers as we lie down at night, and they should be on our minds when we rise in the morning.

His Word is the source of life for the Christian. We are to make it central to our lives, hiding it in our hearts and in our children's hearts.

One generation can lose what God has given us. If we do not pass on the teaching of God to our children, they will be led by others. If we fail to teach the Word to our children and grandchildren, they will not know the saving grace of Jesus Christ. What are we teaching the next generation?— **Douglas W. Slocumb**

SENTENCE SERMONS

THE BIBLE must be taught in the home.

—Selected

THE YOUNG, whether they know it or not, live on borrowed property.
—Richard Livingstone

IN A BROKEN NEST there are few whole eggs.
—Chinese Proverb

EVANGELISM APPLICATION

GOD USES CHRISTIAN FAMILIES TO COMMUNICATE HIS WORD TO SUCCEEDING GENERATIONS.

Most of us are familiar with the Great Commission, recorded in Matthew 28:19, 20. The followers of Jesus are commanded to go into all the world and preach the gospel to every person. The church is working to achieve this goal, although the task is not complete.

While we are fulfilling the Great Commission, we must not neglect the most obvious field of evangelism—the

family. The thrust of this lesson is creating a God-consciousness in our own children. We must be teaching them the Word, worshiping God with them, walking in His way in the presence of our children. What shall it profit us if we save the whole world and lose our own families?

ILLUMINATING THE LESSON

Guests at a wedding reception admire the beauty of the bride and the wedding cake. Eventually they will savor the flavor of the beautiful cake. Photographers will take pictures of the masterpiece, and of the bride and groom taking the first bites.

We all know that a beautiful wedding cake does not "just happen." All of the ingredients are carefully mixed and blended by the baker. Temperatures must be just right and the baking process carefully timed.

A successful marriage and subsequent family life is much like the wedding cake. A great variety of ingredients are required in a proper blend. It takes three to make a successful marriage: a bride, a groom, and God. Leave God out and failure will follow. God is the main ingredient for a blessed family.

DAILY BIBLE READINGS

M. Godly Family Leadership.
    Genesis 18:16-19
T. A Family Commitment.
    Joshua 24:14-24
W. God Blesses the Family.
    Psalm 128:1-6
T. Example of a Godly Family.
    Jeremiah 35:12-19
F. Solid Family Foundation.
    Matthew 7:24-27
S. Family Instruction.
    Ephesians 6:1-4

TRUTH SEARCH
Creatively Teaching the Word

DISCUSSION QUESTIONS

Deuteronomy 6:4-9

• What does "the Lord is one" mean (v. 4, *NKJV*)? Why is this truth important?

• Why did Jesus call the commandment in verse 5 the most important one (see Matthew 22:37, 38)?

• What does it mean to have God's Word "in your heart" (Deuteronomy 6:6, *NKJV*)?

• In what settings should children be taught God's ways (v. 7)?

• Why do you think God instructed His people to post and even wear His Word (vv. 8, 9)?

Deuteronomy 6:20-25

• How can parents ensure that their children will ask them about the meaning of God's laws (Deuteronomy 6:20)?

• In responding to their children, why would adults begin with their enslavement in Egypt?

• What are the purposes of the commandments (vv. 24, 25)?

Psalm 78:1-7

• What did the psalmist say he would declare to his children (vv. 1-4)?

• Why is it so important to lead the next generation in God's ways (vv. 5-7)?

CHALLENGE

Ask the adults to evaluate their home environment. If a stranger came into their house, would he or she recognize it as a Christian home? If there are children living at home, are parents making the most of the opportunity to influence them for Christ?

Ask students to evaluate their home by the following criteria:

• Is the home secure and generally peaceful?

• Are Christian art and scriptures displayed?

• Are Biblical entertainment guidelines being followed?

• Do parents pray with their children, read the Bible with them, and regularly talk about the things of God?

• Is the fruit of the Spirit (Galatians 5:22, 23) in evidence?

• At home, are Christian publications read and Christian music played?

Responsibility to the Church

Study Text: Galatians 6:1-18
Objective: To understand our God-given responsibility to the body of Christ and give loving service to others.
Time: Around A.D. 52
Place: Probably written from Corinth
Golden Text: "As we have therefore opportunity, let us do good unto all men, especially unto them who are of the household of faith" (Galatians 6:10).
Central Truth: Christians demonstrate the spirit of Christ through loving service to others.
Evangelism Emphasis: Christians should offer loving service to others as a witness to the world.

PRINTED TEXT

Galatians 6:1. Brethren, if a man be overtaken in a fault, ye which are spiritual, restore such an one in the spirit of meekness; considering thyself, lest thou also be tempted.

2. Bear ye one another's burdens, and so fulfil the law of Christ.

3. For if a man think himself to be something, when he is nothing, he deceiveth himself.

4. But let every man prove his own work, and then shall he have rejoicing in himself alone, and not in another.

5. For every man shall bear his own burden.

6. Let him that is taught in the word communicate unto him that teacheth in all good things.

7. Be not deceived; God is not mocked: for whatsoever a man soweth, that shall he also reap.

8. For he that soweth to his flesh shall of the flesh reap corruption; but he that soweth to the Spirit shall of the Spirit reap life everlasting.

9. And let us not be weary in well doing: for in due season we shall reap, if we faint not.

10. As we have therefore opportunity, let us do good unto all men, especially unto them who are of the household of faith.

11. Ye see how large a letter I have written unto you with mine own hand.

12. As many as desire to make a fair shew in the flesh, they constrain you to be circumcised; only lest they should suffer persecution for the cross of Christ.

13. For neither they themselves who are circumcised keep the law; but desire to have you circumcised, that they may glory in your flesh.

14. But God forbid that I should glory, save in the cross of our Lord Jesus Christ, by whom the world is crucified unto me, and I unto the world.

15. For in Christ Jesus neither circumcision availeth any thing, nor uncircumcision, but a new creature.

16. And as many as walk according to this rule, peace be on them, and mercy, and upon the Israel of God.

17. From henceforth let no man trouble me: for I bear in my body the marks of the Lord Jesus.

18. Brethren, the grace of our Lord Jesus Christ be with your spirit. Amen.

LESSON OUTLINE

I. CARE FOR FELLOW BELIEVERS
   A. Restoring the Weak and Fallen
   B. Considering Yourself
   C. Supporting the Ministry

II. DO GOOD TO OTHERS
   A. Sowing and Reaping
   B. The Household of Faith

III. LIVE AS A NEW CREATION
   A. Paul's Personal Salutation
   B. Salvation by Faith
   C. Conclusion

LESSON EXPOSITION

INTRODUCTION

In today's lesson, Paul is concluding his personal letter to the Galatians. In the previous chapters, he had done a masterful job in his argument against the Judaizers. These false teachers from Jerusalem had followed Paul around in his ministry and discouraged his new converts by teaching that Gentiles had to become Jewish proselytes through circumcision before they could become Christians. They had corrupted some of the believers in Galatia, and Paul's letter was written to help the church know how to deal with the situation.

In the first portion of the lesson, Paul instructs the church how to care for fellow believers (6:1-6). In the second part of the lesson, Paul explains how to do good to others both inside and outside the community of faith (vv. 7-10). And in the final portion of the lesson, the apostle tells the Galatians how to live as a new creation through faith and grace and not by works of the flesh (vv. 11-18).

I. CARE FOR FELLOW BELIEVERS (Galatians 6:1-6)

A. Restoring the Weak and Fallen (vv. 1, 2)

1. Brethren, if a man be overtak-
en in a fault, ye which are spiritual, restore such an one in the spirit of meekness; considering thyself, lest thou also be tempted.

2. Bear ye one another's burdens, and so fulfil the law of Christ.

Someone has said, "The Christian army is the only army that shoots its wounded." Sadly, there is some truth in this sarcasm. In verse 1 of our text, Paul admonishes those who have not fallen prey to the false teaching of the Judaizers to help restore their fallen comrades in a spirit of meekness rather than a spirit of spiritual superiority.

Dr. Warren Wiersbe said the word *restore* here is used in a medical sense as if one were setting a broken bone (*Expository Outlines of the New Testament*). Using this analogy, one might conclude that the initial confrontation, or setting of the bone, would be painful and the recovery period might take weeks or months. During the recovery period, the spiritual (or stronger) ones among the Galatians were to help bear the burdens of the weaker (or recovering) ones, thus fulfilling the "law of Christ" (v. 2).

What is this law of Christ to which Paul refers? It is the law of love and grace. Only as Christians have love for one another will they bear one another's burdens.

B. Considering Yourself (vv. 3-5)

3. For if a man think himself to be something, when he is nothing, he deceiveth himself.

4. But let every man prove his own work, and then shall he have rejoicing in himself alone, and not in another.

5. For every man shall bear his own burden.

In verse 3, the apostle returns to a theme he had begun in verse 1—the spiritually strong should not become haughty, or "high-minded," and therefore not help to restore the weak. Thinking of ourselves more highly than we ought will trap us in the sin of pride.

Proverbs 16:18 warns, "Pride goeth before destruction, and an haughty spirit before a fall."

Paul said that if the man who has such a high opinion of himself would look at the facts in his case, he would discover he is nothing, and is only deceiving himself. The apostle warned the Roman believer "not to think of himself more highly than he ought to think; but to think soberly, according as God hath dealt to every man the measure of faith" (Romans 12:3).

In Galatians 6:4, 5, the believer is first advised to test his own load limit and bear his own burdens before he attempts to help a weaker brother. Jesus taught the same lesson but used a different analogy. He said, "First cast out the beam out of thine own eye; and then shalt thou see clearly to cast out the mote [splinter] out of thy brother's eye" (Matthew 7:5).

J. Vernon McGee reported that when he was a boy, the town atheist used Galatians 6:2, 5 to attempt to show that the Scripture is contradictory. Verse 2 says to "bear . . . one another's burdens" and verse 5 instructs the believer to "bear his own burden." However, the apparent contradiction is clarified by verses 3 and 4. The Lord expects the stronger Christians to do both tasks, assist others and carry their own burdens as well (*McGee Thru-the-Bible Commentary*).

Actually, there are two different Greek words translated as "burdens" in these verses. In verse 5, *phortion* means "something carried" with no reference to weight. *Baros* (v. 2) denotes a weight that places a demand on one's resources, whether material or physical or spiritual. When something is too heavy for us to bear alone, fellow Christians are to help shoulder the load. But each person must carry his own cross of discipleship (burden), which Jesus called "light" (Matthew 11:30).

C. Supporting the Ministry (v. 6)

6. Let him that is taught in the word communicate unto him that teacheth in all good things.

Paul reminds the church to take care of their Bible teachers financially. The word *communicate* here means "to share with others." Evidently there were still faithful teachers and preachers among the Galatians who were preaching and teaching the true gospel that Paul had preached among them initially, and the apostle wanted the church to take care of their material needs. He had sent similar messages to other congregations (see Philippians 4:14; 1 Timothy 6:18; Hebrews 13:16).

The implication in Galatians 6:6 is that those who preach and teach the true gospel should be supported financially, but those who teach a false doctrine should not. It is the duty of the church to provide for its pastor. Ministers are the Lord's soldiers, captains and standard-bearers, and therefore are not to go to war at their own cost. In return the minister must diligently carry out his responsibility.

II. DO GOOD TO OTHERS
    (Galatians 6:7-10)

A. Sowing and Reaping (vv. 7-9)

7. Be not deceived; God is not mocked: for whatsoever a man soweth, that shall he also reap.

8. For he that soweth to his flesh shall of the flesh reap corruption; but he that soweth to the Spirit shall of the Spirit reap life everlasting.

9. And let us not be weary in well doing: for in due season we shall reap, if we faint not.

Verses 7-9 are not disconnected from the first six verses of chapter 6. Paul is still talking about giving to good causes and doing God's work. Believers supporting those who taught sound doctrine would be blessed, but those who supported the false doctrine of the Judaizers would not be blessed.

Even though Paul is talking about sharing material blessings with spiritual teachers, the principle of sowing and reaping applies to all areas of life. Young, old and middle-aged people need to understand this principle. Just as in agriculture it is impossible to plant corn and reap potatoes, spiritually it is impossible to live a wicked life and reap righteousness. King David committed adultery and lost his infant son. Queen Jezebel murdered the prophets and was murdered herself. Even the apostle Paul, who penned this letter to the Galatians, was not immune from this principle. As a young man he held the coats of the religious fanatics who stoned Stephen to death (Acts 7:58), and much later, as a seasoned evangelist and missionary, he was stoned and left for dead (14:19).

Keeping with his theme of sowing and reaping, Paul spoke words of encouragement to those who had stayed faithful in Galatia, urging them to "not be weary in well doing" (Galatians 6:9). The principle of sowing and reaping works for the righteous as well as the wicked. There is, however, a time factor involved. One does not reap a harvest in a day, week, or month after planting; but if the planter is patient, in time a bountiful harvest will be reaped. *Patient my*

B. The Household of Faith (v. 10)

10. As we have therefore opportunity, let us do good unto all men, especially unto them who are of the household of faith.

Paul instructed the church to keep on doing good for others whether they deserve it or not; but the needy Christians should be especially blessed by the prayers and generosity of those more fortunate. Paul did not collect offerings for all the poor people of Jerusalem but only for those in the community of faith (Romans 15:25, 26).

Sometimes individuals who never attend church will turn to the church for assistance during times of trouble or financial disaster. While screening for eligibility is Biblical (see 1 Timothy 5:9, 10), these situations do provide the church with opportunities to demonstrate Christian love and compassion and open doors for witnessing the gospel. *Blessed my Lord*

III. LIVE AS A NEW CREATION
(Galatians 6:11-18)

A. Paul's Personal Salutation (v. 11)

11. Ye see how large a letter I have written unto you with mine own hand.

Paul began the conclusion to his letter by pointing out that he had penned these words to the Galatians personally without the use of a secretary. This was no small task for a senior citizen with eye problems (see 4:15) writing from a dimly lit jail cell. No wonder he wrote "with large letters" (6:11, NKJV).

Some say Paul's "thorn in the flesh" was damaged eyes from his encounter with Jesus on the Damascus road. Others say his "thorn" was what he said it was, "the messenger of Satan to buffet me." In any case, God promised him sufficient grace to deal with the problem (2 Corinthians 12:7-9).

We are not told why Paul departed from his usual custom by penning his own letter on this occasion. But his statement was a pledge to the Galatians that the epistle was genuine, since it bore the marks of his own handwriting. It was also proof of special affection for them that he was willing to undergo this labor on their account.

Help me Lord to pray more

This special interest in those with whom he was communicating was characteristic of the apostle. Again and again he reminded the churches that they were on his prayer list. He wrote of how often his thoughts turned to them. He spoke of the personal sadness that being separated from them brought, and of the sheer delight he experienced when with them. Surely, those who received this letter felt the love and regard the apostle had for them.

B. Salvation by Faith (vv. 12-16)

12. As many as desire to make a fair shew in the flesh, they constrain you to be circumcised; only lest they should suffer persecution for the cross of Christ.

13. For neither they themselves who are circumcised keep the law; but desire to have you circumcised, that they may glory in your flesh.

14. But God forbid that I should glory, save in the cross of our Lord Jesus Christ, by whom the world is crucified unto me, and I unto the world.

15. For in Christ Jesus neither circumcision availeth any thing, nor uncircumcision, but a new creature.

16. And as many as walk according to this rule, peace be on them, and mercy, and upon the Israel of God.

Paul returned to the major theme of salvation by faith and not by works of the Law in the concluding verses. Remember, this letter was written primarily to combat the false doctrine of the Judaizers who were trying to mix grace and the law of Moses.

In these final verses Paul delivered some of his most stinging criticism toward the Judaizers. He accused them of preaching circumcision so they might bypass the persecution and humiliation connected with the cross

(v. 12). In modern times, the cross has become a shiny piece of jewelry that Christians and non-Christians wear around their necks; but in Paul's day, it was a cruel instrument of death and humiliation.

In verse 13, Paul indicted the Judaizers for not keeping the very law they preached while insisting the Gentile converts become Jewish proselytes through circumcision. Paul had made a similar accusation against the Jews in his letter to the Romans (2:17-23). Earlier, Jesus had accused the lawyers with laying on the people "burdens grievous to be borne" while not being willing to lift a finger to help (Luke 11:46).

Paul compared himself to the false teachers by indicating he was not ashamed to be associated with the cross of Jesus Christ. The Lord was crucified for Paul's salvation, and Paul was crucified with Christ for his own sanctification (separation from the world). Salvation by faith does not just give the repentant sinner a face-lift, but makes him a whole "new creature" (Galatians 6:15). This was something the Law could never do.

After the new birth, this new creature is to walk in the Spirit and not in the flesh (5:16). To those who followed this lifestyle, Paul pronounced a rabbinical blessing of *shalom*, or "peace . . . and mercy" (6:16). This blessing is reserved for spiritual Israel—the church. Individual children of Abraham may have this blessing by renouncing the old legalistic system and accepting salvation by faith alone in Jesus Christ.

C. Conclusion (vv. 17, 18)

17. From henceforth let no man trouble me: for I bear in my body the marks of the Lord Jesus.

18. Brethren, the grace of our Lord Jesus Christ be with your spirit. Amen.

Finally, Paul asked the church not to trouble him anymore with these matters. Among other things, the shadow of Nero's chopping block was looming across his path; and Paul's thoughts were becoming preoccupied with things he wished to say in his final days to his son in the Lord, Timothy.

Before closing, Paul took a parting shot at the Judaizers by reminding his readers that while he had suffered much for Christ, "bear[ing] in [his] body the marks of the Lord Jesus," these pampered, well-fed false teachers from Jerusalem had not suffered at all. The word *marks* here means "a mark incised or punched (for recognition of ownership), that is, a scar of service [much like branding]" (Strong). A slave owner in Paul's day might brand those who belonged to his household. Paul considered himself to be a love slave to Jesus.

When Paul thought of his physical marks, perhaps he was thinking of the fang marks from the snake bite (Acts 28:3), or maybe the 195 lashes with a cat-o'-nine-tails he received of the Jews in five separate beatings, or the calluses on the bottoms of his feet from the three times he was beaten with rods (2 Corinthians 11:24, 25), or his many scars from the time he was stoned and left for dead (Acts 14:19). In any case, it is not likely that the Judaizers had any such "badges of honor" to show since they preached a non-offensive message to the Jews.

Finally, Paul gave another rabbinical blessing to his readers, referring to them as "brethren" and pronouncing upon them "the grace [unmerited favor] of our Lord Jesus Christ" (v. 18). His central message to the Galatians was salvation by grace, so it was fitting that he closed with that very thought.

GOLDEN TEXT HOMILY

"AS WE HAVE THEREFORE OPPORTUNITY, LET US DO GOOD UNTO ALL MEN, ESPECIALLY UNTO THEM WHO ARE OF THE HOUSEHOLD OF FAITH" (Galatians 6:10).

This statement of the apostle Paul comes at the end of several specific imperatives which he included in his instructions to the Galatian Christians concerning practical ways to live the Christian life. Paul taught that fruits and good works will grow out of our salvation experience. These imperatives of verses 1-10 illustrate what good works really are.

• We are to restore anyone overtaken in a fault or a trespass (v. 1).

• We are to bear one another's burdens (v. 2).

• We are to prove our own work, not someone else's (vv. 3-5).

• We are to share good things with those who teach us the Word (v. 6).

• We are not to deceive ourselves but remember that we reap what we sow (vv. 7, 8).

• We are not to grow "weary in well doing" (v. 9).

• We are to do good to all people (v. 10).

This Golden Text gives us a summary statement concerning our good works. They are to be directed toward all people, and especially toward other members of the body of Christ.

In this chapter, Paul gave the law of the harvest—we reap what we sow. In verse 10, he tells us how and where to sow. We sow to the Spirit when we do good to all. When others see our good works, they will glorify our heavenly Father.

We are especially to do good works that bless other members of the body of Christ. We sow to the Spirit when we lift others up, share burdens, do not judge others, give financially, and when we sow joyfully and willingly. All our good works help to edify, or build up, the body of Christ. This makes the church healthy and appealing to others.

The end results of our living out a practical Christianity are that others are blessed, God is glorified, and we shall reap a rich harvest in due season.—**F.J. May**

SENTENCE SERMONS

CHRISTIANS DEMONSTRATE the spirit of Christ through loving service to others.

—Selected

BEARING ONE ANOTHER'S burdens is different from bearing down on them.

—Selected

THERE IS NO EXERCISE better for the heart than reaching down and lifting people up.

—John Andrew Holmer

BIBLICAL ORTHODOXY without compassion is surely the ugliest thing in the world.

—Francis Schaeffer

EVANGELISM APPLICATION

CHRISTIANS SHOULD OFFER LOVING SERVICE TO OTHERS AS A WITNESS TO THE WORLD.

While the gospel was never intended to be a social message nor the church merely a charitable organization, there is a place for reaching out to the lost through acts of benevolence. Christians should be involved in community volunteer organizations and church outreaches.

Can the church get so caught up in benevolence work that it begins to lose its focus on the central message of the gospel? Yes, the early church did so, but Peter met with the church and appointed Spirit-filled men to administer the benevolence program while he and the other apostles gave themselves to "prayer and the word" (see Acts 6:1-4).

ILLUMINATING THE LESSON

I once observed a father and his young daughter unloading their gear at a ski lodge. The father was middle-aged and looked strong and healthy. The daughter was thin and frail. Yet, the father insisted that the young girl carry her own skis, boots, and poles to the lodge—a load that probably equaled about one-fourth her body weight. I watched with a critical eye as the child struggled with the burden. It was only when her knees buckled beneath the load that the father offered a helping hand. Then I understood the father's strategy.

Knowing that shortly his little daughter would be facing even greater challenges on the mountain looming above them, he was trying to make her mentally and physically tough enough for those challenges. Only when it became obvious that the load was too great did the father offer a helping hand, while at the same time continuing to carry his own equipment.

Likewise, the heavenly Father has promised not to place on us more than we can bear (1 Corinthians 10:13). Also, as Christians we are to help bear each other's burdens (Galatians 6:2).

A student pastor and his youth group went out into the city to do random acts of kindness for others as the Lord would lead. They entered a restaurant and noticed a couple sitting at a table with their two young children. The youth leader called for the manager and quietly paid for the couple's dinner and then left the restaurant.

The next day the recipient of this random act of kindness was telling his coworker about the incident only to find out that the coworker was a member of the church where the young people attended. Besides being given an opportunity to witness to the young husband and father, the coworker got to hear the couple's side of the story. It had been the wife's birthday and family funds were very limited. The husband had taken his family to dinner, not knowing for sure how he would pay for the meal and make ends meet until the end of the week. This loving act opened his heart to hear the gospel message.

DAILY BIBLE READINGS

M. Love Your Neighbor.
Leviticus 19:11-18

T. Caring for the Less Fortunate.
Deuteronomy 15:7-11

W. Continue in Fellowship.
Acts 2:41-47

T. Serving God's People.
Acts 6:1-7

F. Submit to Godly Leaders.
Hebrews 13:7-17

S. Don't Show Favoritism.
James 2:1-9

TRUTH SEARCH
Creatively Teaching the Word

DISCUSSION QUESTIONS

Galatians 6:1-6
- What is the Christian's responsibility to a fellow believer who falters (v. 1)?
- Why must the ministering Christian be careful (v. 1)?
- What is the "law of Christ" mentioned in verse 2?
- What warning is given in verse 3?
- What instruction is given in verses 4 and 5?
- What is our responsibility to those who teach and preach the Word (v. 6)?

Galatians 6:7-10
- Why is it easy to be deceived about the law of sowing and reaping?
- Why does verse 7 say "God is not mocked"?
- How does a person sow "to his flesh" (v. 8), and what will the result be?
- How does a person sow "to the Spirit" (v. 8)? What will the result be?
- Why is it easy to become "weary in well doing" (v. 9)?
- Explain the practical commandment in verse 10.

Galatians 6:11-18
- Why do you think it was important for Paul to tell the Galatians he had written this letter with his own hand (v. 11)?
- What burden were some people trying to put on believers, and why (vv. 12, 13)?
- What did Paul boast about, and why (v. 14)?
- What counts in God's eyes (v. 15)?
- What "marks" (v. 17) was Paul talking about (see 2 Corinthians 11:23-25)? What did these marks say about Paul and his commitment to minister to others?

OBJECT LESSON

Items needed: Backpack, a couple of books, something too heavy for one person to carry alone (such as a table, a couple of concrete blocks, or a long ladder)

Illustrate the meanings of the two words translated as "burden" in Galatians 6. First, place the books in the backpack and have a student wear it. **This symbolizes carrying one's own burden (v. 5)—the Christian duties we must perform ourselves. Jesus called this burden "light" (Matthew 11:30).**

Now refer to the heavy item. **This represents the concept in verse 2— "Carry each other's burdens" (NIV). There are trials and needs we experience which we must not try to carry alone. Instead, we should reach out to a fellow believer for help.**

Have two volunteers lift the heavy item together.

Our Responsibility to the World

Study Text: Mark 16:15-20; Romans 13:1-14

Objective: To recognize that we represent Christ to the world and dedicate ourselves to reflect His values.

Golden Text: "[Jesus] said unto them, Go ye into all the world, and preach the gospel to every creature" (Mark 16:15).

Central Truth: Christians are responsible to represent Christ to the world.

PRINTED TEXT

Mark 16:15. And he said unto them, Go ye into all the world, and preach the gospel to every creature.

16. He that believeth and is baptized shall be saved; but he that believeth not shall be damned.

17. And these signs shall follow them that believe; In my name shall they cast out devils; they shall speak with new tongues;

18. They shall take up serpents; and if they drink any deadly thing, it shall not hurt them; they shall lay hands on the sick, and they shall recover.

Romans 13:1. Let every soul be subject unto the higher powers. For there is no power but of God: the powers that be are ordained of God.

2. Whosoever therefore resisteth the power, resisteth the ordinance of God: and they that resist shall receive to themselves damnation.

3. For rulers are not a terror to good works, but to the evil. Wilt thou then not be afraid of the power? do that which is good, and thou shalt have praise of the same:

4. For he is the minister of God to thee for good. But if thou do **that which is evil, be afraid; for he beareth not the sword in vain: for he is the minister of God, a revenger to execute wrath upon him that doeth evil.**

5. Wherefore ye must needs be subject, not only for wrath, but also for conscience sake.

6. For for this cause pay ye tribute also: for they are God's ministers, attending continually upon this very thing.

7. Render therefore to all their dues: tribute to whom tribute is due; custom to whom custom; fear to whom fear; honour to whom honour.

8. Owe no man any thing, but to love one another: for he that loveth another hath fulfilled the law.

9. For this, Thou shalt not commit adultery, Thou shalt not kill, Thou shalt not steal, Thou shalt not bear false witness, Thou shalt not covet; and if there be any other commandment, it is briefly comprehended in this saying, namely, Thou shalt love thy neighbour as thyself.

10. Love worketh no ill to his neighbour: therefore love is the fulfilling of the law.

DICTIONARY

rioting . . . chambering and wantonness—Romans 13:13—orgies, sexual promiscuity and sensuality

LESSON OUTLINE

I. EVANGELIZE THE WORLD
   A. The Great Commission
   B. Signs Following Believers
   C. The Ascension

II. SUBMIT TO AUTHORITY
   A. For Wrath's Sake
   B. For Conscience' Sake

III. WALK IN LOVE
   A. For Love's Sake
   B. For Christ's Sake

LESSON EXPOSITION

INTRODUCTION

The greatest event in human history had just taken place—the death, burial and resurrection of Jesus Christ. Mark records two sightings of the resurrected Christ before the events of our text; but the disciples remain skeptical until Jesus appears to the Eleven personally, chastises them for their lack of faith, and then gives them their marching orders that comprise the first portion of our study text for today's lesson.

The second and third portions of today's lesson come from the Book of Romans. It has been said that if one could preserve only one book of the New Testament, it should be the Book of Romans because the apostle Paul, under the inspiration of the Holy Spirit, deals with all the basic tenets of the Christian faith.

In chapter 13, Paul gives the Christians of Rome a lesson in their civic duties and responsibilities. In short, he tells them how to be politically correct in a pagan-dominated society and maintain their Christian testimony at the same time. If we substitute the word *secular* for *pagan* in the previous statement, we see that Paul's words have meaning for us today. How can we be good citizens and good Christians at the same time? Paul gives the simple answer in the latter verses of chapter 13—walk in love.

I. EVANGELIZE THE WORLD
   (Mark 16:15-20)

Modern scholars have debated whether the last 12 verses of Mark 16 were included in the original text. These verses are either missing altogether in the oldest known transcripts or have alternative endings. However, we accept verses 9-20 to be authentic based on long-standing Christian tradition and the fact that if the narrative were to end with verse 8, it would conclude on a negative note with frightened women unable to tell others about their encounter with the angel at the empty tomb. Also, there is nothing contradictory in these verses when compared to other New Testament accounts of these events.

A. The Great Commission (vv. 15, 16)

15. And he said unto them, Go ye into all the world, and preach the gospel to every creature.

16. He that believeth and is baptized shall be saved; but he that believeth not shall be damned.

The commissioning of the disciples recorded here contains most of the elements of Matthew's account except Mark uses the word *preach* instead of *teach.*

Creature is better understood as "all creation." Going "into all the world" means going everywhere people live.

Matthew used the phrase "all

nations" in his account of the Great Commission (28:18-20). *Nations* comes from the Greek word *ethnos*, meaning Gentile or pagan nations outside of Judea. It was always the Lord's plan that the gospel story be shared with the whole world. It took the disciples a little while to understand this broadened concept of salvation.

In verse 15 Mark gives us the method, scope and message of evangelism. The method is preaching, the scope is the world, and the message is the gospel. It is evident from Mark that the command of Christ obligates His church to preach to all nations. The world is the scope of our commission; the bounds of the earth are the church's only limitations. The gospel must be published among all nations, and every tribe and tongue must hear; such is the explicit will of the risen Lord.

Verse 16 ties together faith and water baptism. The person who has accepted Jesus as his or her Savior is to make an outward expression of this inward transformation by being baptized in water. Baptism is symbolic of the death, burial and resurrection of the Lord and is a public statement that the believer has embraced the Christian faith.

We tend to take baptism too lightly. It is not an option. Instead, it is a command of the Lord Jesus. In many countries today, water baptism represents a breaking away from the predominant religion and brings ostracism or even persecution to the baptized.

B. Signs Following Believers (vv. 17, 18)

17. And these signs shall follow them that believe; In my name shall they cast out devils; they shall speak with new tongues;

18. They shall take up serpents; and if they drink any deadly thing, **it shall not hurt them; they shall lay hands on the sick, and they shall recover.**

Verses 17 and 18 are some of the most controversial in New Testament Scripture, and this is one reason liberal scholars struggle with the authenticity of verses 9-20. Yet nothing is said here that is not later validated in New Testament history with the exception of drinking deadly poisons. The New Testament saints did speak with new tongues (Acts 2:4) and cast out demons (16:16-18). The apostle Paul accidentally picked up a poisonous viper with some firewood and though bitten, was not harmed (28:3-6).

Isaiah recorded God's promise, "When you pass through the waters, I will be with you; and when you pass through the rivers, they will not sweep over you. When you walk through the fire, you will not be burned; the flames will not set you ablaze" (43:2, *NIV*).

Modern missionaries to Muslim-dominated countries report that signs of healings and divine deliverance can help convince the Islamic populations of the superiority of Christianity over Islam. Jesus fortified His public ministry with signs and wonders (John 20:30) and so did Paul (Acts 14:3). Is it because the church today has grown so weak and cold that the signs intended to accompany the gospel message are lacking in our culture?

C. The Ascension (vv. 19, 20)

(Mark 16:19, 20 is not included in the printed text.)

Mark's account of the Ascension leaves out most of the 40-day period between the Resurrection and the Ascension. He comes right to the point and relates the disciples' reaction to their commission.

The witnesses saw Christ ascend bodily into the heavens and stood staring awestruck until the clouds received Him out of their sight (Acts 1:9-11). But the portion of Mark 16:19 that reads "and [He] sat on the right hand of God" had to come by divine revelation. The writer of Hebrews reported that Jesus, "when he had by himself purged our sins, sat down on the right hand of the Majesty on high" (1:3; see also 10:12).

The impact of the Ascension and the infilling of the Holy Spirit 10 days later transformed the body of believers into a mighty evangelistic force. "And they went forth, and preached every where, the Lord working with them, and confirming the word with signs following. Amen" (Mark 16:20).

By the time Paul penned 1 Corinthians, some of the 500 believers who witnessed the Ascension had died, but most were still alive (1 Corinthians 15:6). While people die, the Holy Spirit lives forever and inspires each new generation to tell the story of Jesus. The same Holy Spirit who inspired David to play his harp and sing the songs of Zion is alive and well today in the hearts of the saints.

II. SUBMIT TO AUTHORITY
   (Romans 13:1-7)

In Romans 13, Paul gives the body of believers four reasons why they should obey civic or secular government: (1) for wrath's sake, (2) for conscience' sake, (3) for love's sake, and (4) for the Savior's sake (Wiersbe). In this chapter, Paul discusses "the role of the state [secular government] as seen from a Christian perspective which honors and values good government" (James Dunn, *Word Biblical Commentary*).

A. For Wrath's Sake (vv. 1-4)

1. Let every soul be subject unto the higher powers. For there is no power but of God: the powers that be are ordained of God.

2. Whosoever therefore resisteth the power, resisteth the ordinance of God: and they that resist shall receive to themselves damnation.

3. For rulers are not a terror to good works, but to the evil. Wilt thou then not be afraid of the power? do that which is good, and thou shalt have praise of the same:

4. For he is the minister of God to thee for good. But if thou do that which is evil, be afraid; for he beareth not the sword in vain: for he is the minister of God, a revenger to execute wrath upon him that doeth evil.

The Christians in and around Rome were especially sensitive to civil authority, which could be unpredictable and repressive—especially toward believers. Paul advised believers to be good citizens, leading quiet lives and obeying secular law to avoid the wrath of civil authority. His approach to this subject must have surprised some of the saints. Paul told the Christians in Rome that even secular governmental officials are appointed by God (v. 1) and, therefore, those who resist or rebel against these constituted powers would really be rebelling against God himself and risk His judgment (v. 2).

"Be good, law-abiding citizens," Paul says, "and you will have nothing to fear from civil authorities. They have been placed in their positions to help maintain an orderly society by punishing evildoers and praising or rewarding good citizens" (v. 3, paraphrased). It is the old "carrot-and-stick" approach. Law-abiding citizens get the carrot and transgressors get the stick.

Paul was not advising the Christians to obey laws that might be in direct conflict with divine laws. In that case, Acts 5:29 is the principle to follow. This is where Peter and John informed their captors, "We ought to obey God rather than men."

The apostle went even further in verse 4 by equating civil authorities with ministers of God called to carry out His will. Paul may have been calling on his knowledge of Old Testament history, remembering how God had used foreign kings such as Nebuchadnezzar to punish Israel and Cyrus the Persian to restore Israel.

Paul's reference to the "sword" (v. 4) may have been a reference to capital punishment. The apostle himself would fall victim to Rome's capital punishment at the end of his earthly ministry. Christian tradition says he was beheaded for teaching sedition during the reign of Nero.

B. For Conscience' Sake (vv. 5-7)

5. Wherefore ye must needs be subject, not only for wrath, but also for conscience sake.

6. For for this cause pay ye tribute also: for they are God's ministers, attending continually upon this very thing.

7. Render therefore to all their dues: tribute to whom tribute is due; custom to whom custom; fear to whom fear; honour to whom honour.

Not just out of fear but out of a good conscience, Christians should submit themselves to civil authority. The obedient Christian has a good conscience (1 Timothy 1:5). To disobey leads to a defiled conscience (Titus 1:15), a seared or calloused conscience (1 Timothy 4:2), and finally, a rejected conscience (Romans 1:28) (Wiersbe).

Then as now, some Christians were reluctant to pay tribute or taxes to support a corrupt government. Paul advised the believers in Rome to pay their fair share of taxes (v. 6), thereby not drawing hostile attention to themselves but keeping a good conscience before God and people. This is in keeping with Jesus' teaching. The Lord once called for a coin and advised His audience, "Render therefore unto Caesar the things which are

Caesar's" (Matthew 22:21). In another occasion, Jesus also sent Peter fishing to pay their Temple tax (17:27).

In verse 7 of the text, the apostle named some of the dues we are to pay. *Tribute* is land tax; *custom* is mercantile tax; *fear*, or respect, is reverence for superiors; and *honor* is the respect due to persons of distinction.

Peter wrote, "Honour all men. Love the brotherhood. Fear God. Honour the king" (1 Peter 2:17).

III. WALK IN LOVE (Romans 13:8-14)

A. For Love's Sake (vv. 8-10)

8. Owe no man any thing, but to love one another: for he that loveth another hath fulfilled the law.

9. For this, Thou shalt not commit adultery, Thou shalt not kill, Thou shalt not steal, Thou shalt not bear false witness, Thou shalt not covet; and if there be any other commandment, it is briefly comprehended in this saying, namely, Thou shalt love thy neighbour as thyself.

10. Love worketh no ill to his neighbour: therefore love is the fulfilling of the law.

In verses 8-10, Paul extended the boundary lines from government officials to include all our neighbors. In the New Testament, the concept of "neighbor" had nothing to do with race, creed, color or geography, as seen in the story of the Good Samaritan (Luke 10:30-36).

Anybody could have written "Owe no man anything," but only a Christian would have included "but to love one another." Love is a continuing debt. It is a debt you can never discharge. When you have paid it you have only acknowledged it. When you love another person, you begin to realize the meaning of the Divine. John wrote: "Beloved, let us love one another: for love is of God; and every one that loveth is born of God, and knoweth God. He that loveth not knoweth not God; for God is love" (1 John 4:7, 8).

It is Paul's claim that if a person honestly seeks to discharge this debt of love, he will automatically keep all the commandments. If he discharges the debt of love, he will not commit adultery. In real love there is at once respect and restraint which saves a person from sin. If he pays the debt of love, he will not kill; for love never seeks to destroy but always to build up. If he discharges the debt of love, he will never steal; for love is always more concerned with giving than with getting. If he pays the debt of love, he will not covet; love cleanses the heart until the desire for the forbidden thing is gone.

Jesus said, "Thou shalt love the Lord thy God with all thy heart, and with all thy soul, and with all thy mind. This is the first and great commandment. And the second is like unto it, Thou shalt love thy neighbour as thyself. On these two commandments hang all the law and the prophets" (Matthew 22:37-40). Paul comes to this same conclusion in verse 10 of our text.

B. For Christ's Sake (vv. 11-14)

(Romans 13:11-14 is not included in the printed text.)

Obeying civil law for Christ's sake is Paul's strongest argument. Obedience out of fear is a weak motivator. Conscience is a good motivator, but can be dulled and diluted by repeated disobedience. Love is a superior motivator, working hand in glove with being motivated for Christ's sake. The love a believer has for the Lord and his or her neighbors is the primary motivating factor.

In verse 11, Paul reminded the Christians in Rome that the coming of the Lord is nearer than when they first believed. They were to be alert and vigilant.

It has been said that a great person passes through the dream of life as one awake. Genius is life at a higher power, at a greater intensity. The great person sees more clearly, feels more deeply, and wills more strenuously than ordinary people do. He is more thoroughly awake, more alive, than other people. The apostle calls upon all believers to become alert, alive and awake. We must deepen our love to God. We must open our eyes to see God and to do His will.

In verse 12, the believer is called upon to put aside the deeds of darkness. There is no place for sins and follies when we put on the garments of light. Christ has not come to save us *in* our sins but *from* our sins. The rags of sin must come off if we will put on the robe of Christ. There must be a taking away of the love of sin, there must be a renouncing of the practices and habits of sin, or else we cannot be Christians. We must be cleansed in the blood of Jesus before we can be clothed in the white linen which is the righteousness of the saints.

We are also called upon to "put on the armour of light." We are in an enemy's country, and we must dress appropriately. Conflicts are surely coming, so we must prepare by selecting the proper attire. Seek God that He will clothe us in such style that we may be ready for whatever comes.

In verse 13, Paul urged the believers to "walk their talk"—they were to be Christlike. They were not to get caught up in the immorality of Rome: "not in orgies and drunkenness, not in sexual immorality and debauchery, not in dissension and jealousy" (*NIV*).

Holiness is the highest decency, the most becoming apparel. We must walk as those who have the eye of God upon them. He will not walk with us unless we keep our garments unspotted from the world. Our raiment must be in keeping with our rank.

"But put ye on the Lord Jesus Christ, and make not provision for the flesh, to fulfil the lusts thereof" (v. 14).

Jesus must be in us before He can be on us. Grace puts Him within and enables us to put on Christ without. Christ must be in the heart by faith before He can be in the life by holiness. As we have Christ within as our Savior, the secret of our inner life, so we must put on Christ to be the beauty of our daily life.

Faith finds our manhood naked to its shame; faith sees that Christ Jesus is the robe of righteousness provided for our need. By faith the soul covers her weakness with His strength, her sin with His atonement, her folly with His wisdom, her failure with His triumphs, her death with His life, her wanderings with His constancy. By faith the soul hides itself in Jesus.

Jesus Christ is the answer to all things in our life. We go to Him for everything. To us, "Christ is all." According to Paul, God has made Jesus Christ "unto us wisdom, and righteousness, and sanctification, and redemption: that, according as it is written, He that glorieth, let him glory in the Lord" (1 Corinthians 1:30, 31).

Where do you look for garments that will be suitable for the courts of the Lord? Where should you look for armor that will protect you from the assaults of the foe? Where will you find a robe that will enable you to act as a priest and king unto God? The answer to each of these questions is, "Clothe yourselves with the Lord Jesus Christ" (Romans 13:14, *NIV*).

GOLDEN TEXT HOMILY

"[JESUS] SAID UNTO THEM, GO YE INTO ALL THE WORLD, AND PREACH THE GOSPEL TO EVERY CREATURE" (Mark 16:15).

The words of a recent international missions motto calls for "the *whole church* to take the *whole gospel* to the *whole world*." In that theme, and in the all-inclusive command of Jesus, there is a completeness and totality to our commission.

• *The whole church.* Jesus said to "them," the entire group of disciples—representing *all* the church. The command was not for just one special person or selected few but for everyone who follows Jesus. Acts 8:1, 4 says *all* the church was scattered and they "preached the word wherever they went" (*NIV*).

• *The whole gospel.* The whole (or "full") gospel is the good news that God's kingdom reign has come for everyone. Within itself the gospel has all the power for personal and social transformation, for "it is the power of God for the salvation of everyone who believes" (Romans 1:16, *NIV*).

• *The whole world.* Where are we to go with the message? Where is the gospel to penetrate? The *whole* world. It is for the whole world *geographically*—to the ends of the earth; every country, every city, every village, every neighborhood, and every family. The "world Christian," or "global believer," is also called to the whole world *sociologically*—every non-Christian religion, every unreached language and culture group, every segment of society (youth, children, professionals, immigrants, etc.), and every individual.

More insight on this and other "Great Commission" passages from Genesis to Revelation is available from the book *Globalbeliever.com: Connecting to God's Work in Your World* (Pathway Press, 2000).—**Grant McClung**

SENTENCE SERMONS

CHRISTIANS ARE RESPONSIBLE to represent Christ to the world.
—**Selected**

WHATEVER MAKES men good Christians makes them good citizens.
—**Daniel Webster**

WE ARE BORN SUBJECTS, and to obey God is perfect liberty.
—**Seneca**

EXAMPLE IS NOT the main thing in influencing others. It is the only thing.
—**Albert Schweitzer**

EVANGELISM APPLICATION

CHRISTIANS ARE RESPONSIBLE TO REPRESENT CHRIST TO THE WORLD.

Jesus knew when He issued the Great Commission and prayed for future generations in John 17 that Christians would be scattered throughout the world living under many different sets of civil laws. Yet Christ expects His followers to witness to the world through good citizenship, obeying the laws of the land unless they are in direct conflict with divine law.

We are Christ's ambassadors to the world.

ILLUMINATING THE LESSON

A missionary gave this account of an incident that happened to him which supports the portion of Mark 16:18 that says, "And if they drink any deadly thing, it shall not hurt them." The missionary had gone into a village to preach and was warned to expect opposition from the local witch doctor. However, when he arrived, the witch doctor invited him to his hut for a meal. The meal went well and the conversation was amiable. But after about an hour, the witch doctor became wide-eyed with excitement and fell at the missionary's feet begging forgiveness.

The missionary tried to comfort the witch doctor and asked what was troubling him. It was then that this village chairman confessed he had laced the missionary's food with enough poison to kill 20 men. When the missionary did not fall dead, the witch doctor knew the missionary must be the servant of the Most High God.

DAILY BIBLE READINGS

M. Humble Yourselves and Pray.
2 Chronicles 7:12-16
T. Warn of God's Judgment.
Jonah 3:1-10
W. God's Concern for the Lost.
Jonah 4:1-11
T. Integrity in the Workplace.
Ephesians 6:5-9
F. Pray for Those in Authority.
1 Timothy 2:1-4
S. Live With Integrity.
1 Peter 2:13-20

TRUTH SEARCH
Creatively Teaching the Word

DISCUSSION QUESTIONS

Mark 16:15-20
- What is the "good news"?
- Why should verse 16 motivate us to reach the unsaved?
- What "signs will accompany those who believe" (v. 17, *NIV*) as they spread the gospel? Why?
- How did the disciples respond to the commission?
- How is it that "the Lord [was] working with" the disciples in their ministry (v. 20) since He had already returned to heaven?

Romans 13:1-7
- Why should believers submit to government authorities (vv. 1, 5)?
- How does God view rebellion against government (v. 2)?
- How can one live without fear of authorities (v. 3)?
- How does God view those who hold public office (vv. 4, 6)?
- What specific obligations are outlined in verse 7?

Romans 13:8-14
- What "debt" should we never finish paying in this life (v. 8)?
- Explain the statement "love is the fulfilling of the law" (v. 10).
- According to verse 12, what are we to "cast off" and what are we to "put on"? Why?
- What do all the sins in verse 13 have in common?
- Why is it important to "not think about how to gratify the desires of the sinful nature" (v. 14, *NIV*)?

PRAYER FOCUS

During the introduction of today's lesson, point out that the Scripture texts concern the Christian's duty to various groups of people—the unsaved, people in authority, and fellow believers. One critical obligation believers have is to pray for people in each of these groups.

As you complete each section of today's lesson, pray for the group of people discussed in that portion. Make the prayers specific as suggested below:

1. Pray for unsaved friends and relatives.

2. Pray for local government officials by name.

3. Pray for fellow class members.

Invest in Eternal Treasure

Study Text: Matthew 6:19-34
Objective: To understand that lasting treasure is in heaven and seek first the kingdom of God.
Time: A.D. 28
Place: On a high hill near Capernaum in Galilee
Golden Text: "But seek ye first the kingdom of God, and his righteousness; and all these things shall be added unto you" (Matthew 6:33).
Central Truth: Christians invest in eternal treasure by seeking God and His kingdom.
Evangelism Emphasis: Seeking the kingdom of God motivates Christians to lead others to Christ.

PRINTED TEXT

Matthew 6:19. Lay not up for yourselves treasures upon earth, where moth and rust doth corrupt, and where thieves break through and steal:

20. But lay up for yourselves treasures in heaven, where neither moth nor rust doth corrupt, and where thieves do not break through nor steal:

21. For where your treasure is, there will your heart be also.

22. The light of the body is the eye: if therefore thine eye be single, thy whole body shall be full of light.

23. But if thine eye be evil, thy whole body shall be full of darkness. If therefore the light that is in thee be darkness, how great is that darkness!

24. No man can serve two masters: for either he will hate the one, and love the other; or else he will hold to the one, and despise the other. Ye cannot serve God and mammon.

25. Therefore I say unto you, Take no thought for your life, what ye shall eat, or what ye shall drink; nor yet for your body, what ye shall put on. Is not the life more than meat, and the body than raiment?

26. Behold the fowls of the air: for they sow not, neither do they reap, nor gather into barns; yet your heavenly Father feedeth them. Are ye not much better than they?

27. Which of you by taking thought can add one cubit unto his stature?

28. And why take ye thought for raiment? Consider the lilies of the field, how they grow; they toil not, neither do they spin:

29. And yet I say unto you, That even Solomon in all his glory was not arrayed like one of these.

30. Wherefore, if God so clothe the grass of the field, which to day is, and to morrow is cast into the oven, shall he not much more clothe you, O ye of little faith?

31. Therefore take no thought, saying, What shall we eat? or, What shall we drink? or, Wherewithal shall we be clothed?

32. (For after all these things do the Gentiles seek:) for your heavenly Father knoweth that ye have need of all these things.

33. But seek ye first the kingdom of God, and his righteousness; and all these things shall be added unto you.

34. Take therefore no thought

for the morrow: for the morrow shall take thought for the things of itself. **Sufficient unto the day is the evil thereof.**

LESSON OUTLINE
I. MAKE RIGHT CHOICES
   A. Two Types of Treasure
   B. Light and Darkness
II. TRUST IN GOD
   A. Do Not Worry
   B. Have Faith
III. PUT GOD FIRST
   A. The Father Knows
   B. The Father Provides

LESSON EXPOSITION
INTRODUCTION

The Scripture text comes from the middle portion of Jesus' Sermon on the Mount. Early in the sermon, Jesus gave His audience the Beatitudes (Matthew 5:1-12). In 6:1-18, Jesus preaches about the believer's worship. In verses 19-34, He preaches about the believer's wealth. In 7:1-12, Jesus teaches about the believer's walk.

Matthew was not commissioned as one of the Twelve until chapter 10; but since the Gospel of Matthew was not written in chronological order, he may have been an eyewitness to the Sermon on the Mount. He was a converted tax collector, so he viewed things through the eyes of an accountant. That is especially significant for today's lesson, which focuses on the believer and his or her wealth or material possessions.

I. MAKE RIGHT CHOICES
   (Matthew 6:19-24)

As Matthew was recording this portion of Jesus' sermon, he might have been thinking of his own life in the not-too-distant past when he was a willing pawn of imperial Rome collecting taxes from his own people. He had a quota to meet, and he could keep what he collected above his quota. Many tax collectors in Matthew's day became wealthy from skimming off the top of the tax base. So when he heard Jesus talking about laying up treasure in heaven rather than on earth (v. 19), he must have breathed a sigh of relief that he was a changed man who no longer hoarded excess taxes for personal gain.

In fact, to be one of the inner circle who traveled about with Jesus required the surrendering of one's personal wealth and depending on the generosity of their audiences for support. This was an act of faith on the disciples' part.

The disciples from time to time wrestled with the question of finances. Some had left prosperous businesses to follow Jesus. At least on one occasion, they asked Jesus what they would get out of it. His answer is the best financial deal ever offered—a hundredfold return in this life and eternal life in the future (19:27-30).

A. Two Types of Treasure (vv. 19-21)

19. Lay not up for yourselves treasures upon earth, where moth and rust doth corrupt, and where thieves break through and steal:

20. But lay up for yourselves treasures in heaven, where neither moth nor rust doth corrupt, and where thieves do not break through nor steal:

21. For where your treasure is, there will your heart be also.

Cloth or fabrics of various sorts have historically been important to the Jewish people, from the simple hand-woven tunic that Jesus wore to the fine linen imported from Egypt that the wealthy wore. Jesus cautioned His audience not to put their trust in expensive clothes that moths could eat, nor in hard currency that thieves could steal by digging through the houses made of mud or sun-baked brick. Rather, God's children are to store up wealth where moths and thieves have no entry.

Treasures that are laid up in heaven are unassailable and imperishable. What are these treasures? Luke quotes Jesus as saying: "Sell that ye have, and give alms; provide yourselves bags which wax not old, a treasure in the heavens that faileth not, where no thief approacheth, neither moth corrupteth" (Luke 12:33). Paul commented: "Set your affection on things above, not on things on the earth" (Colossians 3:2). The treasures we lay up in heaven are not fine garments or abundant food or earthly valuables, but deeds we do for others and for the Lord.

It has been said that if you were to examine a person's canceled checks, you could tell what was important to him. This seems to be Jesus' message in Matthew 6:21. Where a person places his material wealth is always very near where he stores his heart.

It is really about making right choices. A woman who chooses to spend all her wealth on herself may enjoy temporary success in this life but is bankrupt in eternity. A righteous person, on the other hand, may accumulate little material wealth here but be rich in the life to come. In addition, the selfish person is morally bankrupt here while the righteous one is rich in friends and human relations. The apostle Paul said he became poor (materially) while making others rich (spiritually) (2 Corinthians 6:10).

B. Light and Darkness (vv. 22-24)

22. The light of the body is the eye: if therefore thine eye be single, thy whole body shall be full of light.
23. But if thine eye be evil, thy whole body shall be full of darkness. If therefore the light that is in thee be darkness, how great is that darkness!

24. No man can serve two masters: for either he will hate the one, and love the other; or else he will hold to the one, and despise the other. Ye cannot serve God and mammon.

Jesus told His mountainside audience that in order to have true wealth, they must have their eye focused on the long-term goal and be single-minded in their resolve. Otherwise, it would be like the "blind leading the blind" (see 15:14). Furthermore, as James would write later, "A double minded man is unstable in all his ways" (1:8).

The eye is the one member of the body which acts as a lamp by which we see. Our perspective, then, depends on the spiritual quality of the eye. If the eye gazes constantly upon the things of the world, the soul will tend to respond to those things. If, on the other hand, the eye is fixed upon heavenly things, the soul will move toward those things.

If the eye is bad, that is, wicked and godless, the entire body will be full of darkness. When that is the case, the individual puts everything ahead of God and His kingdom. In such darkness, the soul perceives nothing as it is but is deceived into thinking that earthly treasures are more important than heavenly treasures.

Our inward purpose determines our character. If that light within us has become darkness, distorting our perspective, what kind of direction will our life take? What kind of character will we develop? How terrible is the nature and effects of that darkness? The total absence of light leaves room only for sin and evil.

In Matthew 6:24 Jesus said, "Ye cannot serve God and mammon [material wealth]." *Mammon* is defined as "wealth personified, avarice deified" (Strong).

Job said, "Naked came I out of my mother's womb and naked I shall return" (1:21). Centuries later, the apostle Paul would paraphrase this scripture to his young protégé, Timothy, warning him against the deceitfulness of riches and advising him to be content with food and clothing (1 Timothy 6:7-11).

It should be noted here that material wealth is not evil. It is "the love of money" that is the root of all evil (v. 10). When the seeking of wealth becomes one's all-consuming passion, wealth is deified.

II. TRUST IN GOD (Matthew 6:25-30)

A. Do Not Worry (vv. 25-27)

25. Therefore I say unto you, Take no thought for your life, what ye shall eat, or what ye shall drink; nor yet for your body, what ye shall put on. Is not the life more than meat, and the body than raiment?

26. Behold the fowls of the air: for they sow not, neither do they reap, nor gather into barns; yet your heavenly Father feedeth them. Are ye not much better than they?

27. Which of you by taking thought can add one cubit unto his stature?

The word *therefore* indicates that what follows is a spinoff from the principles taught in the previous verses. These principles include: Earthly wealth is temporal while heavenly wealth is eternal; a person's heart is located near his treasure; one must have his eye on the long-term goal and have singleness of purpose; one cannot serve God and materialism at the same time.

Now, "therefore," Jesus was saying, "If you understood what I just said to you, what follows will have more meaning." What follows is astounding: believers are not to worry or fret about going hungry, thirsty, or having clothes to wear.

That sounds good. But if we set our mind on spiritual things and become occupied with them, how will we care for the ordinary needs in life, such as food, clothing and shelter? It seems that Jesus' disciples were worrying about these things. The concern about drink alludes to the hot climate of Palestine and to the lack of water in that region. Food and drink represent daily needs. Clothes last longer and are mentioned last. Will He who gave us our life and the body fail to give us the little food we need and the few garments we require? Where is our faith?

"Take no thought" means not to be anxiously concerned about them. He did not mean that we were to give no forethought or consideration to temporal things. What we are to avoid is anxiety and doubtful misgivings. Paul summed it up beautifully, "Be anxious for nothing, but in everything by prayer and supplication with thanksgiving let your requests be made known to God" (Philippians 4:6, *NASB*).

In verse 26 of the text, Jesus illustrated His point with an example from nature. If God provides food for the wild animals, will He not provide food for His people? While God provides food for birds, He doesn't throw it into their nests. It is necessary for the mature adult birds to leave the nests daily and search out God's bounty. Baby birds, on the other hand, just sit in the nests with their mouths open waiting for food to be placed in their mouths. As Christians, we are not to be like the baby birds sitting around and chirping "Feed me!" Instead, we are to do all we can to provide for our needs and trust God to supply our lack.

People tend to worry or fret about those things they cannot change. Jesus makes this point in verse 27. Most translators see this verse as referring to one's life span rather than to

one's height. That interpretation is will of His Father His "food" (John
consistent with the context. The pro- 4:32). Jesus told the woman at the
longing of life by the supply of its well that if she drank of the water He
necessities of food and clothing is the would give her, she would never thirst
subject being discussed. Unless one is again (vv. 13, 14).
a midget, the thought of adding a foot   In Matthew 6:30, Jesus called the
and a half to one's height is not very attention of His disciples back to God.
appealing. But adding days to one's If God so beautifully dresses the grass
life is. However, Jesus cautions, all the which is green today but dry tomorrow,
worry in the world cannot add so how much more likely is He to clothe
much as a step to the length of your His followers. They are of much greater
life's journey. Worry does not lengthen worth to Him. His disciples should
life, it usually shortens life. trust in His faithfulness. The writer of
Hebrews admonished: "Let your con-
B. Have Faith (vv. 28-30) versation be without covetousness;
and be content with such things as ye
28. And why take ye thought for have: for he hath said, I will never leave
raiment? Consider the lilies of the thee, nor forsake thee" (13:5).
field, how they grow; they toil not,   On four different occasions in
neither do they spin: Matthew's Gospel, Jesus referred to
29. And yet I say unto you, That His disciples as men of little faith.
even Solomon in all his glory was The first reference was the occasion
not arrayed like one of these. of the text we are studying. The sec-
30. Wherefore, if God so clothe ond time was when He and His dis-
the grass of the field, which to day is, ciples were caught in a great tempest
and to morrow is cast into the oven, on the Sea of Galilee (8:26). Next, He
shall he not much more clothe you, used this term when Peter attempted
O ye of little faith? to walk on the water and failed
   Jesus returned to nature for His (14:31). Then, He used this expres-
next illustration. He told His audi- sion when His disciples did not
ence they should not worry about understand His warning to beware of
clothing because just as God clothes the leaven of the Pharisees (16:8). In
the wild flowers, even so He will each instance, their lack of faith came
clothe the faithful. under the pressure of earthly trials. It
   Solomon was the best-dressed man was His way of gently chiding them to
of his day. When the Queen of Sheba shake off the spirit of unbelief and
saw him, his wealth, his wisdom and trust in Him.
even the way his attendants were   In this middle portion of the
dressed, she was overwhelmed in her Sermon on the Mount, Jesus first told
spirit (2 Chronicles 9:3, 4). Yet the lilies the people how important it is to make
of the field were better dressed than right choices; then He taught them
Solomon. Of the lily someone has writ- not to fret about material needs; and
ten that it is "the most gorgeously then He came to His main point—
painted, the most conspicuous in putting God first.
spring, and the most universally
spread of all the floral treasures of the ## III. PUT GOD FIRST (Matthew 6:31-34)
Holy Land."
   Faith in God brings contentment. ## A. The Father Knows (vv. 31, 32)
The apostle Paul said he learned to be
content with little or much (Philippians **31. Therefore take no thought,**
4:11, 12). Jesus considered doing the **saying, What shall we eat? or, What**

shall we drink? or, Wherewithal shall we be clothed?

32. (For after all these things do the Gentiles seek:) for your heavenly Father knoweth that ye have need of all these things.

The admonition of not fretting over food and clothing is reiterated in verse 31 with two additional reasons given in verse 32. First, the Gentiles, or those outside the covenant blessing, fret about these things; second, our heavenly Father already knows we need food, water, and clothing and will provide them without our having to ask. Just as our own children do not have to beg us as parents for food, clothing and shelter because we are loving parents, so we do not have to beg God to meet our every need.

Worry is irreverent, wrote Myron S. Ausburger, for it fails to recognize the God who gave us life and is sustaining it. Worry is irrelevant; it does not change things, nor does it help us in coping with problems. And worry is irresponsible; it burns up energy without using it to apply constructive action to the problem.

B. The Father Provides (vv. 33, 34)

33. But seek ye first the kingdom of God, and his righteousness; and all these things shall be added unto you.

34. Take therefore no thought for the morrow: for the morrow shall take thought for the things of itself. Sufficient unto the day is the evil thereof.

The stage is now set for one of the most powerful statements in all of Scripture: "Seek first his kingdom and his righteousness, and all these things will be given to you as well" (v. 33, *NIV*).

God has never been willing to play second fiddle to anything or anybody. This was the first commandment:

"Thou shalt have no other gods before me" (Exodus 20:3). The Jews were taught from childhood that their first obligation was to "love the Lord thy God with all thine heart, . . . soul, and . . . might" (Deuteronomy 6:5).

In His Sermon on the Mount, Jesus coupled this commandment and obligation with a promise. If believers will seek after God and righteousness first, they will never have to worry about the necessities of life.

How can we put God first in all things? Wiersbe said that God should have the first of our time daily in devotional prayer and Bible reading. He should have the first of our week in regular attendance to the house of worship. He should have the first of our material means in tithing and giving. But most of all, He should have the first of our love and devotion as demonstrated by our daily walk with Him. If we do these things, Jesus said, material blessings will be added as well (v. 33).

While the Gentiles are seeking things that pertain to this life, believers are to be seeking the kingdom of God. This quest for the Kingdom, described earlier as hunger and thirst, is the mark of all true disciples. It consists of a longing to enter ever more fully into union with God. It recognizes God's royal rule which is a rule of grace leading to a rule of glory. This seeking acknowledges Him "who is the blessed and only Potentate, the King of kings, and Lord of lords; who only hath immortality, dwelling in the light which no man can approach unto; whom no man hath seen, nor can see: to whom be honour and power everlasting. Amen" (1 Timothy 6:15, 16).

In Matthew 6:34, Jesus teaches us how to live life one day at a time. We should not fret about tomorrow but just deal with the problems of each day as they arise. Jesus was not suggesting here that believers should not plan ahead. Planning and fretting are not the same things. Someone said, "He who fails to plan, plans to fail."

Each day will have cares and anxieties of its own, but it will also bring the proper provisions for those cares. Though you have needs, God will provide for them as they occur. Do not, therefore, increase the cares of this day by borrowing trouble from the future. Do your duty faithfully now, and depend on the mercy of God and His divine help for the troubles which are yet to come. As you care each day for the things God has trusted to you, your heavenly Father cares for your daily needs. God is faithful and will not fail to meet your needs.

GOLDEN TEXT HOMILY

"BUT SEEK YE FIRST THE KINGDOM OF GOD, AND HIS RIGHTEOUSNESS; AND ALL THESE THINGS SHALL BE ADDED UNTO YOU" (Matthew 6:33).

It is natural to have concern about food, drink, raiment (v. 25). And for the poverty-stricken people to whom Jesus spoke, concern often turned into worry.

In all matters relative to God's blessings and benevolence, it takes faith; first, to avoid worry, and second, to believe God will supply all our needs. Only through faith can we conceive of God even caring about our temporal needs. And the only way this faith can develop is to "seek first the kingdom of God."

As we turn our attention to the things of God, faith soars and therefore we will not worry.

The conjunction *but* at the beginning of verse 33 supplies a contrast between the unbeliever, whose only thinking can be of the needs of this life, and those who are sustained by the knowledge that when one's priorities are spiritual

there is absolutely no need to worry. The passage is in no way meant to encourage irresponsibility, but rather to build the believer's faith in God, who "shall supply all your need according to his riches in glory" (Philippians 4:19). When we understand this, our energies are free from worry of the cares of life and we can set our "affection on things above, not on things on the earth" (Colossians 3:2).—**Selected**

SENTENCE SERMONS

CHRISTIANS INVEST in eternal treasure by seeking God and His kingdom.

—Selected

WORRY DOES NOT empty tomorrow of its sorrow; it empties today of its strength.

—Corrie ten Boom

WORRY IS A THIN stream of fear trickling through the mind. If encouraged, it cuts a channel into which all other thoughts are drained.

—A.S. Roche

EVANGELISM APPLICATION

SEEKING THE KINGDOM OF GOD MOTIVATES CHRISTIANS TO LEAD OTHERS TO CHRIST.

As nonbelievers observe us as Christians making right choices, trusting God for material needs, and putting God first in all things, they will be attracted to the Christian way of life.

Also, when we put God first, we are reminded of our great commission (obligation) to win the lost and will look for opportunities to witness. Opportunities will come.

ILLUMINATING THE LESSON

A Bible College student had reached the end of his financial rope. His visit to the business office had not gone well. He was told he must pay at least $500 on his account or withdraw from school. The discouraged student informed the registrar of the situation. The registrar went to see the president of the Bible College to intercede for the student.

Hardly had the registrar finished telling the president of the student's plight when there was a knock at the door. The assistant business director entered with an envelope in his hand. "This check for $500 just came in," he said, "and the donor said to apply it to a student's account with an urgent need." The registrar returned to his office with a smile on his face and a check in his hand. God had supplied the student's need because he had "sought first the kingdom of God."

DAILY BIBLE READINGS

M. Courageous Decision.
   Joshua 2:1-14
T. Delight in God's Word.
   Psalm 1:1-6
W. Choosing God's Way.
   Daniel 1:8-21
T. Heirs With Christ.
   Romans 8:14-18
F. Faith's Choice.
   Hebrews 11:24-28
S. Eternal Dividends.
   Revelation 22:1-5

TRUTH SEARCH
Creatively Teaching the Word

DISCUSSION QUESTIONS

Matthew 6:19-24
• Name earthly treasures people store up.
• According to verse 21, where will our treasure be? Why?
• How does the discussion of the eye (vv. 22, 23) relate to our spiritual lives?
• Why can't a person serve two masters?
• Why is money pictured as a god?

Matthew 6:25-34
• Why do people tend to worry about the necessities of life? Why should we not worry?
• If the Father already knows our needs, why pray about them?
• What does it mean to seek God's kingdom?
• What does it mean to seek His righteousness?
• Does not worrying about tomorrow mean not preparing for tomorrow?

CHALLENGE

Have students name all types of things people seek after—whether positive or negative. List their responses on a marker board or poster board.

Here are some possible responses; career, fame, finances, God, education, families, sports, food, clothing, shelter, purpose in life, sexual pleasures, fun, knowledge, friendships, health, conveniences, hobbies and happiness. If students don't name some of the ones listed here, add them.

Have students decide which of these items are necessary. Mark out those deemed unnecessary.

God is not the only necessity in life. However, if we seek Him and His kingdom first, He promises that all the other things that really are necessary will be given to us as well!

Lead students in a renewed pledge to seek God first.

INTRODUCTION TO WINTER QUARTER

In his letters to the Corinthian church, Paul dealt with critical issues that are still facing the church today. Lessons 1, 2, 4-7 cover some of these vital topics.

Expositions for these lessons were written by the Reverend Dr. Jerald Daffe (B.A., M.A., D.Min.), who is professor of pastoral ministries at Lee University, Cleveland, Tennessee.

Dr. Daffe earned his bachelor of arts degree at Northwest Bible College, a master of arts degree at Wheaton College Graduate School, and his doctorate of ministry degree at Western Conservative Baptist Seminary. An ordained minister in the Church of God, Dr. Daffe has served in the pastoral ministry for 10 years and has been a faculty member at Northwest Bible College and Lee University for over 28 years.

Lesson 3 is the Christmas lesson, written by the Reverend Dr. R.B. Thomas (see page 16 for biographical information).

The second unit of lessons (8-13), "Lesser-Known People of the Bible," were written by Reverend Dr. Richard Keith Whitt (B.A., M.Div., Ph.D. cand.). Reverend Whitt earned his bachelor of arts degree at Lee University, a master of divinity at the Church of God Theological Seminary, and is completing the doctor of philosophy at the University of Nottingham (England). An ordained bishop in the Church of God, Keith has served his denomination as a pastor for 23 years, district overseer for 12 years, and as a member of various boards and committees. He has taught courses for the Church of God Theological Seminary and Lee University External Studies.

Promote Unity in the Church

Study Text: 1 Corinthians 1:10-13; 3:1-17
Objective: To understand that division is destructive and determine to maintain unity in the church.
Time: Written in A.D. 57
Place: Paul wrote this letter from Ephesus.
Golden Text: "I beseech you, brethren, by the name of our Lord Jesus Christ, that ye all speak the same thing, and that there be no divisions among you" (1 Corinthians 1:10).
Central Truth: Christians are called to live and work together in unity.
Evangelism Emphasis: Unity in the church helps to verify the gospel to the unsaved.

PRINTED TEXT

1 Corinthians 1:10. Now I beseech you, brethren, by the name of our Lord Jesus Christ, that ye all speak the same thing, and that there be no divisions among you; but that ye be perfectly joined together in the same mind and in the same judgment.

11. For it hath been declared unto me of you, my brethren, by them which are of the house of Chloe, that there are contentions among you.

12. Now this I say, that every one of you saith, I am of Paul; and I of Apollos; and I of Cephas; and I of Christ.

13. Is Christ divided? was Paul crucified for you? or were ye baptized in the name of Paul?

3:1. And I, brethren, could not speak unto you as unto spiritual, but as unto carnal, even as unto babes in Christ.

2. I have fed you with milk, and not with meat: for hitherto ye were not able to bear it, neither yet now are ye able.

3. For ye are yet carnal: for whereas there is among you envying, and strife, and divisions, are ye not carnal, and walk as men?

4. For while one saith, I am of Paul; and another, I am of Apollos; are ye not carnal?

5. Who then is Paul, and who is Apollos, but ministers by whom ye believed, even as the Lord gave to every man?

6. I have planted, Apollos watered; but God gave the increase.

7. So then neither is he that planteth any thing, neither he that watereth; but God that giveth the increase.

8. Now he that planteth and he that watereth are one: and every man shall receive his own reward according to his own labour.

9. For we are labourers together with God: ye are God's husbandry, ye are God's building.

10. According to the grace of God which is given unto me, as a wise masterbuilder, I have laid the foundation, and another buildeth thereon. But let every man take heed how he buildeth thereupon.

11. For other foundation can no man lay than that is laid, which is Jesus Christ.

12. Now if any man build upon this foundation gold, silver, precious stones, wood, hay, stubble;

13. Every man's work shall be made manifest: it shall be revealed by fire; and the fire shall try every man's work of what sort it is.

DICTIONARY

Chloe (KLO-eh)—1 Corinthians 1:11—A member of the Corinthian church whose servants informed Paul of the divisions there.

Apollos (uh-POL-lus)—1 Corinthians 1:12—A Jew from Alexandria, educated in Greek eloquence and the Scriptures. He was discipled by Aquila and Priscilla.

Cephas (SEE-fus)—1 Corinthians 1:12—The name Jesus gave Simon. It is a Syriac word answering to the Greek *petros* and signifying "a stone or rock."

LESSON OUTLINE

I. PURSUE UNITY

  A. Need for Agreement

  B. Needless Divisions

II. PURSUE SPIRITUAL MATURITY

  A. Immature Believers

  B. Signs of Immaturity

  C. Diverse Ministries

III. BUILD ON CHRIST

  A. The Only Foundation

  B. Building Materials

  C. God's Temple

LESSON EXPOSITION

INTRODUCTION

Our first lesson for this quarter encounters the divisions that were evident in the church at Corinth. Paul's letter appears to have been written about two years after his having started this congregation during a stay of some 18 months (Acts 18:1-18). This was a young congregation struggling with a variety of issues. This is normal when a church is planted with new Christians. Spiritual immaturity can reflect itself in negative actions and unbiblical beliefs.

Even though we refer to this letter as 1 Corinthians, it is in reality the second correspondence Paul sent to them (see 1 Corinthians 5:9). He wrote now in an attempt to correct some misunderstandings that had developed, to answer some of their questions and to encourage a change in

their lifestyles. Though he could have followed his introductory comments with addressing a variety of subjects, he chose the problem of their divisions within the church.

Paul wanted the Corinthians to understand how destructive disunity can be for the local body of believers as well as the extended corporate body of Christ. He also instructed them that unity is a choice; otherwise dispersions would continue to reign.

I. PURSUE UNITY
(1 Corinthians 1:10-13)

A. Need for Agreement (vv. 10, 11)

10. Now I beseech you, brethren, by the name of our Lord Jesus Christ, that ye all speak the same thing, and that there be no divisions among you; but that ye be perfectly joined together in the same mind and in the same judgment.

11. For it hath been declared unto me of you, my brethren, by them which are of the house of Chloe, that there are contentions among you.

The urgency of the apostle Paul's dealing with divisions can be seen in the way he addressed the subject. He issued a warning appeal. Danger and possible destruction stood in the future, if something wasn't done about the situation.

Notice also the authority by whom he asked the Corinthians to respond. Paul asked the Corinthian believers to place themselves before the Lord.

As they considered Christ's suffering for their salvation and His glorious resurrection, it became the basis for evaluating the divisive conditions in their church and making a change.

The goal which the apostle Paul projected for them is one of unity in mind and expression: "that all of you agree with one another so that there may be no divisions among you and that you may be perfectly united in mind and thought" (v. 10, *NIV*).

How can there be perfect unity with the variety of personalities, abilities and ideas within a congregation? Does this require believers to avoid diversity? Besides being "the spice of life," variety can provide strength if we see our differences as positive means to accomplish our common goal. Wouldn't it be chaotic if we attempted to build a church building and we had only plumbers and electricians but no carpenters and masons? That is why we need diversity. It enables us to accomplish far beyond than when limited in either perspective or abilities.

The Greek word for *divisions* refers to a "fissure." This implies a far greater problem than just a difference of opinion. Yet, we cannot forget that major divisions frequently have small beginnings in the form of opinion variances.

The agreement Paul desired for this church would come only when all subjected their individualism for the common good of the body. This meant seeking the mind of Christ and His revealed will for the church. While doing this, two extremes were to be avoided. First, no one was to simply give up his/her uniqueness without reason. On the other extreme, no one was to harbor or exhibit an unbrotherly attitude of dominance or superiority.

In verse 11 Paul addressed the Corinthians as his brothers in Christ. His concern stemmed from more than a supervisor's standpoint; it flowed from his spiritual relationship with them. Paul indicated how he knew of the church's current situation. Slaves from the household of Chloe apparently were in Ephesus and told Paul about the current difficulties. So Paul was speaking with accurate information.

B. Needless Divisions (vv. 12, 13)

12. Now this I say, that every one of you saith, I am of Paul; and I of Apollos; and I of Cephas; and I of Christ.

13. Is Christ divided? was Paul crucified for you? or were ye baptized in the name of Paul?

Paul specifically stated the four positions in the congregation. It appears that all of the people had picked a side. These divisions were not the result of the leaders seeking recruits. The believers chose sides because of their preferences.

Though the Scriptures do not state the reasons each of the individuals were preferred, we can make some educated assumptions. Very likely Paul and Apollos stood out for their preaching ability and wisdom. Some would prefer one above the other. The close ties of Peter (here called Cephas) to the Jewish religion would likely make him a favorite of the Judaistic teachers. Those who claimed to follow Christ received no commendation. Instead, they were grouped with the others as being divisive. All were reprimanded equally for their quarrelsome attitudes.

Verse 13 stands as the rebuke. Using three distinct questions, Paul pointed to the absurdity of their quarreling divisions. First, he asked, "Is Christ divided"? Surely no one would assume that Christ was the head over only part of His own body! And how could anyone suggest that Christ's mission here on earth was for only a select few?

Paul's second question further pursued the foolishness of their divisions: "Was Paul crucified for you?" Regardless of the role Paul played in beginning this church, it was nothing compared to Christ's sacrificial death. The ministry of Peter and Apollos also cannot compare to Christ's bearing the sins of all in His body.

Paul's final question pointed to water baptism, whereby the Corinthians had publicly declared their faith in Christ. Because of Christ's salvatory work, they had followed His example of being baptized in water. In verses 14-16, Paul pointed out his thankfulness in having administered the rite to only a few of them. Otherwise it might have caused more of the Corinthians to overemphasize their relationship with Paul, identifying him as the one they were following.

Verses 10-13 emphasize both the need for unity and the needless divisions that can occur. One can only wonder what the apostle Paul might write today. Very likely he would criticize some for being blind followers of human leaders rather than emphasizing the leadership of Christ. He might rebuke others for causing divisions by emphasizing particular styles of worship. Such preferences can become serious rifts which hinder the progress of the church. That definitely isn't the will of God for any congregation at any time or location!

II. PURSUE SPIRITUAL MATURITY (1 Corinthians 3:1-8)

A. Immature Believers (vv. 1, 2)

1. And I, brethren, could not speak unto you as unto spiritual, but as unto carnal, even as unto babes in Christ.

2. I have fed you with milk, and not with meat: for hitherto ye were not able to bear it, neither yet now are ye able.

In chapter 3 Paul returns to the previously mentioned problem of factions in the local church. Now he moves beyond the issue to the root cause, namely spiritual immaturity. This in turn raises questions for the contemporary church: (1) How is it possible for Spirit-filled individuals to be immature in their Christian walk? (2) What can be done to enable believers to grow out of their spiritual immaturity?

In chapter 2 Paul discussed the wisdom that comes from the ministry of the Holy Spirit in believers, stating in verse 12, "Now we have received, not the spirit of the world, but the spirit which is of God." However, in the Corinthian congregation, instead of spirituality, which should be evident, he spoke of their carnality (worldliness). True, it hadn't been too many years since they were unbelievers immersed in a heathen world. The problem was their failure to grow and move beyond the initial stage of spiritual infancy.

Paul addressed them as brethren, reflecting his seeing them as brothers and sisters in Christ. Yet, he also called them babes or mere infants. That probably didn't set too well with them.

The Corinthians' spiritual level was the same as when Paul previously had been with them. It's so easy to regard these believers with pity and possibly a sense of disdain. However, we should first evaluate our own spiritual growth. How much progress have we made in the past two or three years? All of us must remember that salvation is to be a process in which we advance to higher levels and deeper depths. Having simply accepted Christ as Savior is not sufficient for spiritual growth. It is to be followed with a deepening commitment to His lordship.

How do we perceive Paul's reference to these believers being fed milk rather than meat? Does this refer to preaching that is more worldly in content than Christ-centered? Absolutely not.

Paul constantly projected Christ as the central focus of his preaching. Does milk refer to a particular style of preaching? Once again, the answer is no.

The problem here was their not being ready to receive the richness and fullness of God's Word. The Corinthians were still within the clutches of a worldly, natural mindset. Even though having accepted Christ and experiencing the workings of the Holy Spirit, they were still having to be called to a place of surrender. Even though they had been served by some excellent ministers, they appeared to be one of holding on to aspects of their culture instead of fully yielding to the claims of Christ.

In the natural we grieve when a child is unable or hindered in the pursuit of physical or emotional growth. How much more should we be alarmed when believers never advance to spiritual maturity in the kingdom of God!

B. Signs of Immaturity (vv. 3, 4)

3. For ye are yet carnal: for whereas there is among you envying, and strife, and divisions, are ye not carnal, and walk as men?

4. For while one saith, I am of Paul; and another, I am of Apollos; are ye not carnal?

In verse 3 Paul pointedly stated their problem—worldliness. Otherwise, continual quarreling would not be present. He called them mere humans—people holding to earthly standards instead of Christ's. By their being so quick to align themselves with particular men, they had forgotten who was the source of their salvation and the head of the church. Even those who said they followed Christ apparently had digressed due to their being in competition with the other three factions of the congregation.

Notice the question at the end of verse 4. He forced them to think about the situation—"are ye not carnal?"

Spiritual maturity enables men and women to rise above such divisiveness.

C. Diverse Ministries (vv. 5-8)

5. Who then is Paul, and who is Apollos, but ministers by whom ye believed, even as the Lord gave to every man?

6. I have planted, Apollos watered; but God gave the increase.

7. So then neither is he that planteth any thing, neither he that watereth; but God that giveth the increase.

8. Now he that planteth and he that watereth are one: and every man shall receive his own reward according to his own labour.

These four verses are easy to understand but much harder to live by. It becomes so easy for individual believers and corporate bodies to place certain ministries on a pedestal of accomplishment while disregarding others whose work is equally important but not as public or seemingly not as fruitful.

Paul wanted the Corinthians to understand that a person's work is not the issue. The fact of their being the means by which God accomplishes His necessary work should be the emphasis. Each person's obedience and willingness to use their giftedness for Christ's service enables God to receive glory. Yes, Paul planted (founded) the congregation. Yes, Apollos offered care which enabled spiritual growth. But without God's direct involvement there could be no life and growth.

Paul and Apollos needed to be seen as being equal members of God's team fulfilling His will in their individual lives and in the lives of the church. God would reward each of these men for their labors. The obligation of the Corinthian church was to see each of them as God's worker sent for their benefit.

This passage reminds us not to expect every person to have the same ministry. Our obligation is to recognize each ministry as being just as vital as another. That definitely becomes a challenge for all of us due to our being swayed by numbers, buildings and completed projects.

III. BUILD ON CHRIST
(1 Corinthians 3:9-17)

A. The Only Foundation (vv. 9-11)

9. For we are labourers together with God: ye are God's husbandry, ye are God's building.
10. According to the grace of God which is given unto me, as a wise masterbuilder, I have laid the foundation, and another buildeth thereon. But let every man take heed how he buildeth thereupon.
11. For other foundation can no man lay than that is laid, which is Jesus Christ.

"We are God's fellow workers" (v. 9, NIV) could possibly be a reflection of Paul's relationship to the believers of the Corinthian church; however, that doesn't seem to fit the context. The most logical interpretation is his referring to Apollos and himself as being coworkers in the Kingdom. This continues the thought of there being no reason for division in the church.

Paul's description of the Corinthians being God's field reflected His ownership and continuing working among them. However, the apostle did not expand this description. Instead, he moved on to the second description of their being God's building. This life in Christ isn't a simple, instantaneous act. Rather, there is a block building process that enables the structure to take shape upon the foundation.

In verse 10 Paul refers to himself as a master builder in the spiritual realm. He realized this ability was not the result of his own righteousness.

Instead, this blessing proceeded due to God's grace having been made evident in his life. Though Paul was a willing vessel often experiencing suffering, he credited the grace of God for being the enabling power.

As the founder of the church, Paul laid the foundation. His bringing the message of Jesus Christ was not only the foundation for the church but also for the individual lives of believers. This foundation—Jesus Christ—was without defect and could not be replaced by anyone. The issue was how the building would be built upon this solid, true foundation, which was the responsibility of the Corinthian church and their teachers.

B. Building Materials (vv. 12-15)

(1 Corinthians 3:14, 15 is not included in the printed text.)

12. Now if any man build upon this foundation gold, silver, precious stones, wood, hay, stubble;
13. Every man's work shall be made manifest: it shall be revealed by fire; and the fire shall try every man's work of what sort it is.

These next verses are not a true reflection of the building process in the natural due to the materials mentioned. Gold, silver and precious stones are far beyond the scope of the average person's financial capabilities. And they are not basic building materials, but rather are used for expensive decoration. On the opposite side, neither are hay and straw normal building materials. For these reasons, it must be assumed that verses 12-15 are intended to emphasize a purity and character that will sustain the test.

Verse 13 points out the fact of a day of reckoning. At the final judgment each believer's work will be brought to light. This will test how appropriately each one has built on the foundation of Jesus Christ. Were our actions and attitudes in accord with the teachings and example of Jesus Christ himself? Were they consistent with the whole of Biblical teachings? Did they follow the guidance and empowerment of the Holy Spirit? Answering yes to these questions would indicate a building that will result in eternal rewards. In contrast, those with a negative response will find their buildings/works being destroyed. Those believers will be saved, but not experience the joy of other eternal rewards.

Paul confronted the Corinthians with the reality of their personal situation. By their having accepted Jesus Christ, each possessed the true foundation. Their challenge was how they would live their lives. Would their lifestyle be the words and activities reflective of precious metals which survive the refining fire? Or would theirs be the wood, straw and hay which fire destroys, leaving only a scattering of ashes?

One other dimension deserves consideration here. Those who teach are also a part of the building process. When errant teachers mislead the body with false doctrine or mix the secular with the spiritual, they become builders using wood, hay and straw. In contrast are godly teachers who enrich the believers by feeding them a balanced diet of God's Word. They are building with precious metals and stones. We need to carefully evaluate those whom we allow to be our spiritual mentors.

C. God's Temple (vv. 16, 17)

(1 Corinthians 3:16, 17 is not included in the printed text.)

"Know ye not," or "don't you know," was Paul's way of asking the Corinthians something they surely knew but had forgotten. He wanted to awaken them to their identity. As a church, they were God's temple, and His Holy Spirit dwelt among them. This is similar to the Tabernacle in the Old Testament as the cloud covered it and the glory of the Lord filled it. Just as the Tabernacle was built according to God's specifications for His glory, in the same way the church was to be built according to His divine guidelines.

With the status of the church established, Paul came back to the issue of those who would defile it. This speaks of individuals who damage the body of Christ through the preaching and teaching of false doctrine. Unless they repented and changed their ways, God would bring judgment on them. Since Paul uses the word *if*, there doesn't seem to be a particular person or issue being directly approached here. However, since immaturity with its worldly attitude was evident, the stage could be set for false teaching.

This verse reminds us that Satan's greatest weapon never has been persecution. Yes, millions of believers have physically died for their faith. But of greater impact has been the false doctrines that attacked the church from within, causing believers to lose their fervor and even their faith.

The last line of verse 17 reminded this church of their identity as God's temple. Since God's temple is to be holy, the believers had the obligation to strive for a life of holiness. This could be accomplished by walking and living in the Spirit (Galatians 5). In turn, this would produce unity in the church.

GOLDEN TEXT HOMILY

"I BESEECH YOU, BRETHREN, BY THE NAME OF OUR LORD JESUS CHRIST, THAT YE ALL SPEAK THE SAME THING, AND THAT THERE BE NO DIVISIONS AMONG YOU" (1 Corinthians 1:10).

Using the name of the Lord Jesus is a call to accept His lordship and authority. It is in His name that unity prevails in the church. He is the giver of gifts; He is the One who saves from sin; He is the One who will return in glory. To "speak the same thing" means to be in agreement with one another.

The word *divisions* does not mean the existence of different doctrines. The community was still a whole, although the apostle recognized the seeds of serious dissension that could split the church. Paul calls for a healing that would "perfectly" join together all the members of the church.

In the Greek text of the latter portion of this verse, being "perfectly joined together" means putting something in its proper condition, restoring and completing. Thus Paul calls for the church to be complete "in the same mind [observation, understanding] and in the same judgment [opinion, conviction]." Paul is calling for their unity to be based on a common understanding of the gospel that brings forth similar convictions of the nature of God's kingdom and how people should live. This can only come about when God's people are "complete" in terms of His Holy Spirit and power.—**Selected**

SENTENCE SERMONS

CHRISTIANS ARE CALLED to live and work together in unity.
—**Selected**

THE FELLOW who is pulling the oars usually doesn't have time to rock the boat.
—*Speaker's Sourcebook*

THE GREATEST HINDRANCES to the evangelization of the world are those within the church.
—**John Mott**

EVANGELISM APPLICATION

UNITY IN THE CHURCH HELPS TO VERIFY THE GOSPEL TO THE UNSAVED.

Division, schism, opposition—these are common happenings in business, politics and education. If these are regular happenings within the church as well, why should anyone want to accept Christ and become part of the church? If one exchanges six for a half a dozen, there's no difference, right? Exactly!

However, when Christians live in harmony and unity even with difference of opinion, it speaks of the difference Christ makes in believers' lives. Love for Christ and one another enables unity to reign rather than personal preference. That's a testimony.

ILLUMINATING THE LESSON

Have you ever had an invasion of ants and found spraying didn't work? Next resort is to get some ant bait. Worker ants take the poison back to the nest and there the entire colony becomes contaminated and dies.

In the same way, Satan desires to destroy the church from the inside by way of false doctrines and unbiblical divisions.

DAILY BIBLE READINGS

M. Unity Shattered by Sin.
     Genesis 11:1-9
T. Unity of Israel.
     2 Samuel 5:1-5
W. Pleasantness of Unity.
     Psalm 133:1-3
T. Jesus' Prayer for Unity.
     John 17:20-23
F. Unity of Believers.
     Acts 2:42-47
S. Endeavor to Keep Unity.
     Ephesians 4:1-6

TRUTH SEARCH
Creatively Teaching the Word

DISCUSSION QUESTIONS

Pursue Unity
(1 Corinthians 1:10-13)

1. What does it mean to be in "the same mind" and "the same judgment" (v. 10)?

2. How can a church become "perfectly joined together" (v. 10)?

3. What was dividing the Corinthian church (v. 12)?

4. How did Paul address this division?

5. What can divide a church today, and what can hold a church together?

Pursue Spiritual Maturity
(1 Corinthians 3:1-8)

1. What is the mark of a carnal church (vv. 1-4)?

2. What does it mean to be fed with spiritual milk instead of solid food (v. 2)?

3. How could the Corinthians move beyond carnality (vv. 5-7)?

4. What is the sign of a healthy ministry (v. 8)?

Build on Christ
(1 Corinthians 3:9-17)

1. How can Christians "take heed" of their "building" in doing God's work (vv. 9, 10)?

2. What are "other foundations" that Christians might build upon (v. 11)?

3. What types of believers' works will be burned up before Christ?

4. What types of believers' works will bring a reward?

5. What is the Holy Spirit's role in helping believers do good works in Christ (v. 16)?

6. How can a person "defile the temple of God," and what are the consequences (v. 17)?

WORD PLAY

Write the word *community* on the marker board in the following fashion:

        M
CO   UNITY
        M

Ask the students to think about why the word is written like this. Next, discuss the following questions:

• What message do you find in the way *community* is written here?

• What other words beginning with CO indicate that people are together?

• What traits might outsiders use to describe the community called the church?

• In our church, what do we do that reflects our unity of purpose?

Dealing With Moral Problems

Study Text: 1 Corinthians 5:1-13; 2 Corinthians 2:1-11; 6:14 through 7:1
Objective: To recognize that immorality must not be allowed in the church and encourage holy living.
Time: A.D. 57
Place: Paul's first Corinthian letter was written from Ephesus; the second, from Macedonia.
Golden Text: "Let us cleanse ourselves from all filthiness of the flesh and spirit, perfecting holiness in the fear of God" (2 Corinthians 7:1).
Central Truth: God commands His people to exemplify moral purity.
Evangelism Emphasis: A life of moral purity makes the Christian's witness more effective.

PRINTED TEXT

1 Corinthians 5:1. It is reported commonly that there is fornication among you, and such fornication as is not so much as named among the Gentiles, that one should have his father's wife.

2. And ye are puffed up, and have not rather mourned, that he that hath done this deed might be taken away from among you.

3. For I verily, as absent in body, but present in spirit, have judged already, as though I were present, concerning him that hath so done this deed,

4. In the name of our Lord Jesus Christ, when ye are gathered together, and my spirit, with the power of our Lord Jesus Christ,

5. To deliver such an one unto Satan for the destruction of the flesh, that the spirit may be saved in the day of the Lord Jesus.

2 Corinthians 2:4. For out of much affliction and anguish of heart I wrote unto you with many tears; not that ye should be grieved, but that ye might know the love which I have more abundantly unto you.

5. But if any have caused grief, he hath not grieved me, but in part: that I may not overcharge you all.

6. Sufficient to such a man is this punishment, which was inflicted of many.

7. So that contrariwise ye ought rather to forgive him, and comfort him, lest perhaps such a one should be swallowed up with overmuch sorrow.

8. Wherefore I beseech you that ye would confirm your love toward him.

6:14. Be ye not unequally yoked together with unbelievers: for what fellowship hath righteousness with unrighteousness? and what communion hath light with darkness?

15. And what concord hath Christ with Belial? or what part hath he that believeth with an infidel?

16. And what agreement hath the temple of God with idols? for ye are the temple of the living God; as God hath said, I will dwell in them, and walk in them; and I will be their God, and they shall be my people.

17. Wherefore come out from among them, and be ye separate, saith the Lord, and touch not the unclean thing; and I will receive you,

18. And will be a Father unto you, and ye shall be my sons and daughters, saith the Lord Almighty.

7:1. Having therefore these **promises, dearly beloved, let us cleanse ourselves from all filthiness of the flesh and spirit, perfecting holiness in the fear of God.**

DICTIONARY

Belial (be-LIE-ul)—2 Corinthians 6:15—an epithet of scorn or disdain which Paul used to describe someone opposed to Christ.

LESSON OUTLINE

I. JUDGE IMMORALITY

  A. Confronting the Sin
  B. Recognizing Sin's Influence
  C. Separating From Sinners

II. FORGIVE AND COMFORT

  A. The Pain
  B. The Sufficiency
  C. The Forgiveness

III. ENCOURAGE HOLY LIVING

  A. The Need for Separation
  B. The Desire for Purification

LESSON EXPOSITION

INTRODUCTION

Return to the basics! How often have we heard these words? It is a constant theme in education when students' test scores fall below the norm. Immediately there's a call to emphasize the basic courses needed for any successful curricular program. All the creative and specialty courses are given secondary emphasis to the core classes of reading, writing and math.

The same thing happens in sports. When a team fails to play up to its expectations or begins to make crucial errors, the coaches usually realize the need to return to the elementary principles of that sport. Several years ago the University of Tennessee's football team was floundering. Their offensive running game couldn't get off the ground. To solve the problem, the head coach announced that he personally was going to take over the coaching of the offensive line. He immediately drilled the linemen on the basic patterns of blocking. Those were patterns they surely learned in high school. But these men had either forgotten or become careless in performing them.

Today's lesson takes us back to the basics of moral living and disciplining those who either falter or flagrantly choose to live in opposition. The study text comes from both 1 and 2 Corinthians. There was a major problem of immorality evident within the Corinthian congregation. And of equal importance was their failure to deal with it.

Many individuals bemoan a believer's sin when it becomes known. But will they do anything to help the person? Will they rebuke in love and then offer their assistance to overcome this sin? Let's make it more personal: Are we confronting brothers and sisters who have fallen into some act of immorality? If the answer is "No," then we fall into the same category as the Corinthian believers.

Before proceeding, consideration needs to be given to what constitutes morality. Usually sexuality tends to be highlighted. Actions such as premarital sex, extramarital sex or homosexuality are discussed. However, morality incorporates a much broader dimension of action and attitude. To be *moral* means to be honest and refrain from lying or offering false insinuations. It includes respecting others' property, which means not stealing as well as doing an amount of work that equals or even supersedes the fair rate of pay. And that's only the beginning of morality.

The goal for individual believers and the corporate church should be to lead lives of morality. When there are immoral actions, we should hold individuals accountable before God. This action is for the purpose of restoration rather than punishment or public embarrassment. That doesn't mean there will be no occasions when a person is brought before the body or even disfellowshipped. Some actions of sin demand a more public action. But if the true spirit of discipleship prevails, it will always be done with love and kindness.

I. JUDGE IMMORALITY
    (1 Corinthians 5:1-11)

A. Confronting the Sin (vv. 1-5)

1. It is reported commonly that there is fornication among you, and such fornication as is not so much as named among the Gentiles, that one should have his father's wife.

2. And ye are puffed up, and have not rather mourned, that he that hath done this deed might be taken away from among you.

3. For I verily, as absent in body, but present in spirit, have judged already, as though I were present, concerning him that hath so done this deed,

4. In the name of our Lord Jesus Christ, when ye are gathered together, and my spirit, with the power of our Lord Jesus Christ,

5. To deliver such an one unto Satan for the destruction of the flesh, that the spirit may be saved in the day of the Lord Jesus.

The Corinthian believers had written Paul for answers on certain areas of concern; however, the issue discussed in chapter 5 was not one of them. The unusual incident of sexual immorality dealt with here had been spread by word of mouth. A general report spread throughout the churches until it reached Paul in Ephesus.

The cities of Corinth and Ephesus not only were different provinces but also separated by the sea.

The issue: A man had married his stepmother yet continued to be a member in good standing within the church. This relationship defied what even secular Gentile society would approve. This emphasizes the seriousness of the sin, since even a lewd society wouldn't approve of such a union. Within the heathen society, premarital sex, extramarital sex and even homosexuality were accepted. Sins of fornication were not considered taboo; but a man being united with his stepmother was too much.

The Old Testament records several cases in which a man had a sexual relationship with his father's wife. The first is when Reuben slept with Bilhah (Genesis 35:22). Reuben's father, Jacob, condemned this act when Jacob was on his deathbed (49:4). A second incident is when Absalom, David's son, publicly took his father's concubines as his own (2 Samuel 16:22). The defilement of this relationship can be seen by David's caring for the women but never again having a sexual relationship with them (20:3).

Paul chided the Corinthian church for being so puffed up with pride in themselves that they failed to mourn over the sin among them. They should have taken action prior to this point, removing the man from their fellowship. Instead, Paul now called for them to take proper disciplinary action.

Verses 3 and 4 indicate what Paul had done "in spirit" even though he was many miles from Corinth. His physical absence did not minimize his authority. Acting as though he were present, Paul passed judgment on the individual and then stated his decision. He directed the believers to gather as a congregation in the name of the Lord Jesus Christ and enact discipline. They were to take action just as if Paul were present with them.

Verse 5 creates some difficulty. What is meant by delivering a person to Satan? Second, how can the spirit be saved by destroying the flesh? To begin with, delivering this person to Satan would not destroy or change the man's sinful condition. Satan will never be a party to destroying that which separates a person from God. When the church banishes a sinner such as this from the church, they are putting him on notice of a physical separation which speaks of a spiritual separation from God. He or she is not allowed the luxury of assuming spiritual membership in the Kingdom while living in physical sin.

The second question isn't hinting that if the physical life is destroyed, it will produce an eternal spiritual future. Instead, Paul hoped this fornication would be brought to an end and spiritual restoration occur as a result of the church's discipline.

Genuine discipleship demands discipline. In the American church scene we frequently worry so much about the shame and guilt aspect, the possibility of losing a member and, in some circles, the possibility of a lawsuit, that the spiritual benefit of discipline is overlooked.

B. Recognizing Sin's Influence (vv. 6-8)

(1 Corinthians 5:6-8 is not included in the printed text.)

The Corinthian church's boasting and pride in who they were was "not good" (v. 6). While it is always good to boast in the Lord and what He has done, it is wrong to pridefully overlook gross sin and fail to recognize its destructiveness.

Paul used an analogy of yeast in dough. When yeast is used in making bread, it is impossible for the yeast to stay in just a small part of the dough. No way. It causes the entire batch to become leavened. In the same way,

the sinful fornication of one member will impact an entire congregation.

Paul said, "Get rid of the old yeast that you may be a new batch without yeast—as you really are" (v. 7, *NIV*). Leaven (yeast) symbolically represents sin. For that reason the Israelites always ate unleavened bread for seven days before celebrating the Passover. They also removed all yeast from their homes on the first day of preparation. This signified their separation from sin and historically their being liberated from the bondage of Egypt with all of its resident sinfulness. In the same way, the Corinthians were to separate themselves from the sinner who was defiling their entire congregation by his unrepentant lifestyle. They were to celebrate Jesus as their Passover, for it is by His shed blood they were liberated from sin.

In verse 8, Paul declares that celebrating and commemorating Christ's work at Calvary demands getting rid of all attitudes and actions that are sinful. He specifically mentions the sins of malice and wickedness. Divisions, quarrelings and sexual immorality have no place in the celebration of Christ and Christian living.

True believers will evidence sincerity. This begins in one's mind and then can be seen in one's outward lifestyle. Simply becoming a believer isn't sufficient. Belief needs to be followed with a dedicated effort to stay close to the Lord and grow spiritually stronger. Bible study, prayer, fasting, worship and fellowship with other believers are all part of the process.

Could it be that many congregations are lifeless due to the presence of sin? All the emotion of worship is useless form and ritual without inner holiness.

C. Separating From Sinners (vv. 9-11)

(1 Corinthians 5:9-11 is not included in the printed text.)

Verse 9 indicates Paul had previously written a letter that covered the same issues. Since nothing of the letter remains other than Paul's reference to it here, this has come to be known as the "lost letter."

In these three verses Paul specifically directed the church to be separated from those who were known to be sexually immoral. This was not a new directive, since it had been stated previously in the earlier letter. No believer's regular association should include people who are participating in sexual immorality. Paul added, "Not at all meaning the people of this world who are immoral, or the greedy and swindlers, or idolaters. In that case you would have to leave this world" (v. 10, *NIV*). In the day-to-day operation of business as well as general living, believers will mix with sinners. To avoid this type of contact would necessitate withdrawing and living in an isolated community. Christ never taught that form of separation. He prayed that we were to be in the world but not of the world (John 17:15-18).

In verse 11, Paul said the Christians "must not associate with anyone who calls himself a brother" (*NIV*) but is practicing a sinful lifestyle. In addition to fornicators, Paul named "the covetous" (individuals who want far more than a reasonable profit from their efforts), "extortioners" (swindlers looking for ways to take what isn't rightfully theirs), and "idolaters" (who place their faith in images of wood, stone or metal) as "Christians" whom believers should avoid.

Paul's interpretation of his directive for separation implies to the close fellowship which should exist among brothers and sisters in Christ. It is inconceivable for Christians to be in fellowship with believers who persist in their sinfulness. Holiness cannot be accomplished when individuals are allowed to remain in fellowship regardless of their constant indulgence in

sin. Not to be overlooked is the salvation of the one sinning. Concern for that person's spiritual condition will not allow "business as usual."

The situation described here does not apply to settings where a person mentors another who struggles with a particular sin but is seeking victory. Discipleship of this nature needs to be seen more often within the church. It builds spiritual character while deepening the bonds of brothers and sisters in Christ.

Verse 11 ends with the statement "With such a man do not even eat" (*NIV*). To better understand this statement, one must remember the cultural setting. Public places for eating were not available. So to eat would normally necessitate private hospitality in a home. This speaks of close fellowship, which Paul knew should not exist between immoral believers and fruitful believers.

II. FORGIVE AND COMFORT
(2 Corinthians 2:1-11)

A. The Pain (vv. 1-4)

(2 Corinthians 2:1-3 is not included in the printed text.)

4. For out of much affliction and anguish of heart I wrote unto you with many tears; not that ye should be grieved, but that ye might know the love which I have more abundantly unto you.

In these verses Paul reflects on the pain which he and the Corinthians had experienced. Apparently Paul had made a second visit to Corinth and dealt with problems (v. 1). However, he recognizes in verse 2 that the sorrow on both sides is what makes it possible for joy to occur. Without his writing a severe letter and without the painful encounter of his second visit, there would have been no change!

In verse 3 Paul pointed out the necessity of his previous letter. Without such a pointed approach there would have been a continued state of sorrow. Joy could not arise without there being a definite change.

It's important to notice the attitude with which the apostle Paul approached his discipline of the Corinthians. His genuine love for them caused grief over their sins of error and disloyalty. Even while having confidence there would be change, it didn't erase the anguish and distress due to the situation. Tears flowed as he sought their spiritual improvement.

These four verses provide an excellent example of the attitude that needs to be evident in those who discipline their brethren. It may require straight words motivated by love. The purpose never should be condemnation for the sake of injury. Instead, restoration should be in the forefront. This is possible when genuine love motivates words and actions.

B. The Sufficiency (vv. 5-9)

(2 Corinthians 2:9 is not included in the printed text.)

5. But if any have caused grief, he hath not grieved me, but in part: that I may not overcharge you all.

6. Sufficient to such a man is this punishment, which was inflicted of many.

7. So that contrariwise ye ought rather to forgive him, and comfort him, lest perhaps such a one should be swallowed up with overmuch sorrow.

8. Wherefore I beseech you that ye would confirm your love toward him.

There are two opinions as to the general identity of the offender in these verses. Modern commentators tend to believe this was the leader of a group who questioned Paul's integrity and apostleship. The traditional view sees the offender as the incestuous individual discussed in 1 Corinthians. It is this latter view that will be followed in this lesson. However, Paul's words seem to fit either application.

The problem that occurred did touch Paul; however, he pointed out that the believers also had experienced sorrow. Whenever someone chooses to be out of harmony in the Body, all of its members will be affected. Some may feel it more acutely than others. Yet all are hurt.

Without going into the specific details, Paul indicated that the church's discipline of the offender had been sufficient. He pointed out that this was the action of the majority. This reveals the presence of some church members who either chose a neutral position or were dissenters to the discipline. All that was in the past. The offender accepted their discipline and now they must open the door for repentance and reconciliation. In *The New International Commentary*, Philip E. Hughes stated, "Discipline which is so inflexible as to leave no place for repentance and reconciliation has ceased to be truly Christian, for it is no less a scandal to cut off the penitent sinner from all hope of re-entry into the comfort and security of the fellowship of the redeemed community than it is to permit flagrant wickedness to continue unpunished in the Body of Christ" (*The Second Epistle to the Corinthians*).

In verses 7 and 8 the Corinthians were instructed to open their arms and comfort the repentant sinner. He was to be affirmed by their love. To continue discipline once the problem had been corrected could lead to the individual being so overwhelmed that he could simply return to his old life. For this reason no specific time limit had been imposed. Instead, when genuine spiritual life evidenced itself, then that person should be restored to the membership and fellowship of the Body.

C. The Forgiveness (vv. 10, 11)

(2 Corinthians 2:10, 11 is not included in the printed text.)

These two verses can be called the bottom line of this whole matter. Yes, an offense had been committed. Yes, there had been appropriate discipline. Yes, the offender had been repentant. But, would the church forgive? There could be no restoration without forgiveness.

What does it mean to forgive? First, we no longer hold a person's sin against him or her. Second, we do not continue to discuss the sin. Third, when we think of it and feelings arise, we forgive again. Fourth, we remember it is only by God's forgiveness that we are in a harmonious relationship with Him.

Though Paul would not be there to experience the believers' acts of restoration, he wanted them to know of his forgiveness. He chose to follow their lead by forgiving. He trusted their discernment and observation of the situation. Also, any action other than forgiving would be inconsistent with Paul's desire to live in the presence of Christ.

In verse 11, Paul pointed out that failing to forgive a repentant sinner would be to fall into the scheme of Satan. A spirit of unforgiveness would not only harm the offender but create a spiritual problem in the lives of the Corinthian believers. The words of Jesus apply here: "But if ye do not forgive, neither will your Father which is in heaven forgive your trespasses" (Mark 11:26).

Our need to forgive has personal consequences. Failure to forgive others places a barrier in our relationship with God.

III. ENCOURAGE HOLY LIVING
(2 Corinthians 6:14-18; 7:1)

A. The Need for Separation (6:14-17)

14. Be ye not unequally yoked together with unbelievers: for what fellowship hath righteousness with unrighteousness? and what communion hath light with darkness?

15. And what concord hath Christ with Belial? or what part hath he that believeth with an infidel?

16. And what agreement hath the temple of God with idols? for ye are the temple of the living God; as God hath said, I will dwell in them, and walk in them; and I will be their God, and they shall be my people.

17. Wherefore come out from among them, and be ye separate, saith the Lord, and touch not the unclean thing; and I will receive you.

In a time period where it has become difficult to separate believers and unbelievers in terms of lifestyle, this part of our lesson demands special attention. Pentecostalism springs from the roots of holiness and emphasis on the sanctified life. And for many decades we emphasized the need to be separated from the world. Immediately there are those who would remind us of some of the unnecessary prohibitions which become a form of legalism. That is true. However, the fact of some extremism must not become the rationale to reject the entire concept. For example, we haven't stopped driving our cars simply because some putter down the freeway while others race at extreme speeds.

A brief historical review of other groups prior to Pentecostalism reflect similar separation decisions. Whether it is Pietism of the 17th century, the revival known as the Second Awakening in the 18th century, or the Holiness Movement of the 19th century, all taught that separation to God requires separation from certain activities of the world.

In the first century Paul pressed the believers to avoid close associations with their sinful, heathen culture. He used the analogy of a yoke which has two animals working side by side. Just as the Law forbade yoking an ox and a donkey together for plowing (Deuteronomy 22:10), so the apostle applied the same principle of believers and unbelievers being closely united. What do they have in common? The answer is nothing. Paul pointed this out by a series of opposites.

If we expect God to live and walk among us, we must place ourselves in such a position that He will delight in us. We need to reflect the characteristics of our heavenly Father, which requires our being found separate from the world even while living in it. Does this mean we cannot work in a company surrounded by unbelievers? Does it mean no believer should run for public office? No, of course not. Yet, at the same time there may be occasions when a job change, for example, may be necessary for our spiritual welfare.

There are areas where we can make some definite separations. For example, no believer should marry an unbeliever no matter how good a person he or she may be. Becoming a business partner with an unbeliever also fits this category. Consider some broader applications. It seems only logical for believers to be separated from language, entertainment, clothing styles and other practices that identify us with the world rather than with Jesus. (See Isaiah 52:11; Jeremiah 51:45; Ezekiel 20:34.)

B. The Desire for Purification
   (6:18; 7:1)

6:18. And will be a Father unto you, and ye shall be my sons and daughters, saith the Lord Almighty.

7:1. Having therefore these promises, dearly beloved, let us cleanse ourselves from all filthiness of the flesh and spirit, perfecting holiness in the fear of God.

Whenever God delivers a directive, He also follows with a promise. God's dealing with Abraham provides a classic example (Genesis 12:1-3). After instructing him to leave his homeland and family and go to an unnamed country, God said Abraham would have a great nation of descendants, and his name would become great. Many would be blessed through him.

Paul says when we choose to make a definite separation from the world, then the true Father/child relationship will be evident. He will be able to fulfill His will through us. In turn we will receive the benefits of being the spiritual children of God. What a fabulous promise! God wants to share with us all the blessings of His fatherhood!

Knowing God's desires and promises, Paul encouraged the Corinthians to cleanse themselves from everything that would separate them from God. His true affection for this congregation is seen by his addressing them as "beloved," or "dear friends."

Paul's asking them and himself to take on the actions of cleansing does not imply a salvation by works. But it does emphasize that each of us has the power of choice. We can choose to pursue righteous actions and attitudes which will impact us both physically and spiritually. This places each of us in the process of holiness. Though God through the Holy Spirit sanctifies, we decide to position ourselves for Him to work in and through us. So the question facing the Corinthians then, and us today, is, "Do we desire to experience the cleansing of holiness?"

GOLDEN TEXT HOMILY

"LET US CLEANSE OURSELVES FROM ALL FILTHINESS OF THE FLESH AND SPIRIT, PERFECTING HOLINESS IN THE FEAR OF GOD" (2 Corinthians 7:1).

Paul makes a call for "perfecting holiness out of reverence for God" (*NIV*). This holiness is based on the promises of God, yet many Christians attempt to live a holy life on the basis of their own strength and wisdom. Such an existence only becomes legalistic and sectarian.

True holiness does not consist in our pride. In fact, it may be argued that we are most holy (in God's sight) when we are most aware of our sinfulness. We then become dependent upon His mercy and holiness to cover us.

However, this verse makes it clear that we have a role to play in sanctification. We are exhorted to "cleanse ourselves" from the sin of this world in both flesh and spirit. Thus, by committing of our will to the will of the Spirit, we are able to reflect His holiness and love in our life.—**Selected**

SENTENCE SERMONS

GOD COMMANDS His people to exemplify moral purity.

—Selected

GOD IS MORE INTERESTED in making us what He wants us to be than giving us what we ought to have.
—Walter L. Wilson

THE SAINTS OF HISTORY have been people of discipline.

—Selected

SUBDUE YOUR PASSION or it will subdue you.
—Speaker's Sourcebook

EVANGELISM APPLICATION

A LIFE OF MORAL PURITY MAKES THE CHRISTIAN'S WITNESS MORE EFFECTIVE.

Greek mythology is filled with the various gods and goddesses who, though having a divine status, still experienced all the problems of humans. So the question that eventually surfaces is, What good did their status as gods really serve?

The same question needs to be directed toward believers: What do we have to offer in Christ if as believers we cannot demonstrate a morality that offers purity and honesty? Through the empowerment of the Holy Spirit, we can demonstrate the reality of the gospel we share.

ILLUMINATING THE LESSON

A college freshman went into the dorm laundry room with his clothes bundled into an old sweatshirt. Embarrassed by how dirty his clothes were, he never opened the bundle and pushed it into the washer. When the machine stopped, he put the bundle into the dryer. Later he took the dry bundle back to his room, still unopened. His discovery—the clothes had been wet and then dry, but never clean.

God says, "Don't keep your sins in a safe little bundle. I want to do a thorough cleaning in your life—all the dirty laundry of your life" (Michael P. Green and Haddon W. Robinson, *Illustrations for Biblical Preaching*).

DAILY BIBLE READINGS

M. God Commands Morality.
     Exodus 20:12-17
T. God Rewards Morality.
     Leviticus 26:3-12
W. God Punishes Immorality.
     2 Chronicles 36:14-20
T. Root of Immorality.
     Romans 1:24-32
F. Source of Christian Morality.
     Galatians 5:16-25
S. Moral Purity Commanded.
     Colossians 3:5-11

TRUTH SEARCH
Creatively Teaching the Word

REALITY TALK

Items needed: Marker board, marker

Have students name various moral problems that they have seen in others—problems of which at least one more person is aware (such as infidelity, addiction(s), cheating, abusive behavior, filthy tongue, lying, and so on). List the moral problems on the left side of the marker board.

We can recognize sin, and we can identify other people who are committing sins. But is that all we should do?

Have students think of ways Christians should and should not respond when they see a fellow believer get trapped in sinful living. Write their responses on the right side of the board. (Pray, speak the truth in love, forgive the repentant, follow the Biblical pattern. Do not attack the person, gossip, condone the sin nor ignore it.)

DISCUSSION QUESTIONS

Judge Immorality
(1 Corinthians 5:1-11)

1. What sin was present in the Corinthian church (v. 1)?
2. What had the church failed to do (v. 2)?
3. What was Paul's instruction regarding the matter (vv. 3-5)? Why?
4. What is the danger of "a little leaven," and what is the remedy (vv. 6, 7)?

5. Why were "sincerity and truth" needed in this case (v. 8)?
6. Practically speaking, how can we separate ourselves from church members who are living in sin (vv. 9-11)?

Forgive and Comfort
(2 Corinthians 2:6-11)

1. How had the church responded to Paul's instruction to discipline the immoral believer (v. 6)?
2. In what sense had the Corinthians passed a test (v. 9)?
3. What was the next step Paul said they must take, and why (v. 7)?
4. How could they confirm their love toward the man who had repented (v. 8)?
5. How could the Corinthians prevent Satan from gaining "an advantage" (v. 11)?

Encourage Holy Living
(2 Corinthians 6:14—7:1)

1. In what ways can Christians become "unequally yoked together with unbelievers" (v. 14)?
2. What are the dangers in such a partnership (vv. 14-16)?
3. What is God's promise to His people in verse 16?
4. What is God's command to His people in verse 17?
5. According to verse 18, why does God want us to be separate from immorality?

God With Us (Christmas)

Study Text: Matthew 1:1-25
Objective: To review Christ's lineage and events surrounding His birth and commit to love Him.
Time: 5 B.C.
Place: Nazareth and Bethlehem
Golden Text: "Behold, a virgin shall be with child, and shall bring forth a son, and they shall call his name Emmanuel" (Matthew 1:23).
Central Truth: Jesus Christ is the divinely conceived, virgin-born, Son of God.
Evangelism Emphasis: Jesus came to be the Savior of the world.

PRINTED TEXT

Matthew 1:1. The book of the generation of Jesus Christ, the son of David, the son of Abraham.

16. And Jacob begat Joseph the husband of Mary, of whom was born Jesus, who is called Christ.

17. So all the generations from Abraham to David are fourteen generations; and from David until the carrying away into Babylon are fourteen generations; and from the carrying away into Babylon unto Christ are fourteen generations.

18. Now the birth of Jesus Christ was on this wise: When as his mother Mary was espoused to Joseph, before they came together, she was found with child of the Holy Ghost.

19. Then Joseph her husband, being a just man, and not willing to make her a publick example, was minded to put her away privily.

20. But while he thought on these things, behold, the angel of the Lord appeared unto him in a dream, saying, Joseph, thou son of David, fear not to take unto thee Mary thy wife: for that which is conceived in her is of the Holy Ghost.

21. And she shall bring forth a son, and thou shalt call his name Jesus: for he shall save his people from their sins.

22. Now all this was done, that it might be fulfilled which was spoken of the Lord by the prophet, saying,

23. Behold, a virgin shall be with child, and shall bring forth a son, and they shall call his name Emmanuel, which being interpreted is, God with us.

24. Then Joseph being raised from sleep did as the angel of the Lord had bidden him, and took unto him his wife:

25. And knew her not till she had brought forth her firstborn son: and he called his name Jesus.

LESSON OUTLINE

I. FAMILY ROOTS
   A. God's Faithfulness
   B. God's Timing
   C. God's Strategy

II. DIVINE MESSAGE
   A. Divine Conception
   B. The Savior's Birth
   C. Prophetic Fulfillment
   D. God With Us

III. COURAGEOUS OBEDIENCE
   A. Divine Commission
   B. Courageous Action

LESSON EXPOSITION

INTRODUCTION

Matthew's account of the birth of Jesus is apologetic in nature. It was written to a Jewish audience and sought to counteract some of the views being circulated regarding the identity of Jesus.

The claim of a virgin birth drew criticism for Mary and Joseph even though Isaiah prophesied of a virgin birth. It is not difficult to see why people not versed in Scripture would find this story so hard to believe. Yet many people who knew the Scriptures were not prepared to accept Jesus' birth as the fulfillment of Isaiah's prophecy.

This is a most critical issue. If Mary had not conceived of the Holy Spirit, then Jesus was an illegitimate child. Matthew makes the case that Jesus' birth was the fulfillment of the prophecy of Isaiah and that Jesus is indeed the Messiah.

I. FAMILY ROOTS
   (Matthew 1:1-17)

A. God's Faithfulness (vv. 1-17)

(Matthew 1:2-15 is not included in the printed text.)

1. The book of the generation of Jesus Christ, the son of David, the son of Abraham.

16. And Jacob begat Joseph the husband of Mary, of whom was born Jesus, who is called Christ.

17. So all the generations from Abraham to David are fourteen generations; and from David until the carrying away into Babylon are fourteen generations; and from the carrying away into Babylon unto Christ are fourteen generations.

God promised Abraham that He would make of him a great nation, and that in him all the nations of the earth would be blessed (Genesis 12:1-3). Matthew begins his genealogy of Jesus with Abraham. Forty-two generations are represented from Abraham to the birth of Jesus. For all of these long years the descendants of Abraham looked for and longed for the Messiah.

Of course, the promise of a Redeemer preceded Abraham. Adam and Eve were the first two human beings to hear God say that a Deliverer would be raised up to crush the head and heel of Satan (Genesis 3:15). Matthew leaps over several generations and begins with Abraham because this is consistent with the purpose of his apology.

It is significant too that Matthew did not begin with Adam because Jesus did not come from Adam; He was conceived of the Holy Spirit, not of natural man. His birth was divine in nature, not human. Jesus, the Savior of the world, was not born of Adam's race. Joseph was the legal father of Jesus, but nowhere do we find that Joseph ever claimed to be Jesus' natural father.

Forty-two generations waited for the fulfillment of the promise of a Savior. Each person named by Matthew lived and died without seeing the Promised One. The fact that these people lived and died teaches us that God's plan does not depend on one or two people. It also teaches us to trust in God because in His own time God will keep His promise. Each one of us is a part of God's plan, and His plan does not die when we die. God made a promise to Abraham, Isaac, Jacob, David and to the world. He kept His promise.

Matthew included the good and the bad in his genealogy of Jesus. Even though ungodly people as well as godly people appear in the lineage of Jesus, God's plan was fulfilled. The evil deeds of unfaithful people will never defeat God's plan and purpose.

Matthew had no secrets, held nothing back, and protected no one. This brutal honesty demonstrates that, in spite of human frailty, God always keeps His promises.

B. God's Timing

God is not restricted by time. This is not to say that time and timing are not important to God. Scripture teaches that God is a God of order and structure. God has a plan and He always works consistently within that plan. In Scripture we find phrases such as "when the fulness of the time was come" (Galatians 4:4), "when the day of Pentecost was fully come" (Acts 2:1), and other passages that clearly show God follows a timetable.

However, God does not calculate time as we do. God does not follow the Roman or the Jewish calendar. Peter wrote, "With the Lord a day is like a thousand years, and a thousand years are like a day" (2 Peter 3:8, NIV). Following this observation about the Lord's timing, Peter commented about the Lord's promises. It may seem that the Lord has forgotten or reneged on His promise. But God never fails nor forgets. He will keep His promise no matter how long it takes.

We may suppose that from Adam to the Flood was 2,000 years, from the Flood to the birth of Jesus was 2,000 years, and it has been over 2,000 years since Jesus was born. This adds up to more than 6,000 years, which to us is a long time. To God 6,000 years is but a stroke of the clock.

Jesus was born when a course of preparation, unfolded through previous generations, was complete. Volumes could be written about the many aspects of readiness for the coming of Christ into the world. The political climate was right. Economic conditions were conducive to His arrival time. Spiritual conditions were in a state of readiness for His birth. What would take pages for us to express is put into a small package by the Holy Spirit. His Word says, "But when the fullness of the time had come, God sent forth His Son, born of a woman, born under the law, to redeem those who were under the law, that we might receive the adoption of sons" (Galatians 4:4, 5, NKJV).

All we need to understand about God's timing relative to the birth of Jesus is that it was not a day too soon nor a day too late. This is as it has always been and as it will always be. God's timing is perfect.

C. God's Strategy

God has a strategy, or plan, as well as a timetable. The strategy is classified in theological terms as soteriology, or the doctrine of salvation.

Looking at the genealogy of Jesus given by Matthew, we see the unfolding of God's strategy. Following the transgression by Adam and Eve, God set in motion a strategy that would restore humanity to fellowship with the Creator. This strategy was deliberate and methodical. It involved many different people over many generations of time. Peaks and valleys were experienced by those who had high hopes that the Messiah would come in their day. The writer of the Book of

Hebrews says that many of them lived by faith and died without seeing the promise (11:39).

Some of the major players in God's strategy were the Patriarchs, the Law, and the Prophets. Throughout the ages God used different phases of His plan to point and pave the way for the ultimate fulfillment of the promise (Hebrews 1:1). The birth, life, death, resurrection and eventual return of Jesus constitute the fulfillment of God's master plan. This plan was in the heart of God from the foundation of the world (Ephesians 1:4; Revelation 13:8).

II. DIVINE MESSAGE
(Matthew 1:18-23)

A. Divine Conception (vv. 18-20)

18. Now the birth of Jesus Christ was on this wise: When as his mother Mary was espoused to Joseph, before they came together, she was found with child of the Holy Ghost.

19. Then Joseph her husband, being a just man, and not willing to make her a publick example, was minded to put her away privily.

20. But while he thought on these things, behold, the angel of the Lord appeared unto him in a dream, saying, Joseph, thou son of David, fear not to take unto thee Mary thy wife: for that which is conceived in her is of the Holy Ghost.

Through the inspiration of the Holy Spirit, Matthew comes directly to the point. After Mary was betrothed to Joseph, before they came together, "she was found with child of the Holy Ghost." This fact cannot be ignored. This truth gives license to the term *virgin birth*.

Matthew introduced his account of the Gospel as "the genealogy of Jesus Christ, the son of David, the son of Abraham" (see v. 1). The word *begat* is used 39 times in the first 16 verses. In verse 16, in reference to the birth of Jesus, this changes. Here the reference moves from the male gender to Mary, and from the term *begat* to "Mary, of whom was born Jesus, who is called Christ."

Matthew makes no attempt to explain the divine mystery of the Virgin Birth. He simply states the facts and rests his case. Some critics say the story of the Virgin Birth is mythical. There are numerous accounts of virgin births in mythology, they point out. But these stories are pagan in origin and have absolutely nothing to do with the virgin birth of Christ. There is no evidence that Jesus was conceived through normal physical relations between a man and a woman. The virgin birth of Jesus is factual, not fictional nor mythical.

To understand these verses, we need to understand the three steps of a Jewish marriage. The first step was the engagement. Usually this was made between the parents while the couple were still children.

In the second step, the engaged couple was betrothed. Barclay observes that "once the betrothal was entered into it was absolutely binding." The betrothal lasted for one year; then the couple was considered legally married. This one-year period was so crucial that it took a bill of divorce to end the marriage contract.

Joseph and Mary were in the second phase of the marriage relationship when the Lord appeared to her.

The third step was the actual marriage. Then the sexual relationship could be consummated.

B. The Savior's Birth (v. 21)

21. And she shall bring forth a son, and thou shalt call his name Jesus: for he shall save his people from their sins.

The name *Jesus* addresses the

need for forgiveness and salvation. Since the transgression by Adam and Eve, God has progressively unfolded His plan of salvation whereby people can be forgiven and reinstated to fellowship and communion with God. A basis upon which God could be consistent with His divine attributes of mercy and justice had to be found. The answer to this need is Jesus, who took upon Himself the human condition and ultimately gave His life as the perfect, acceptable sacrifice for sin.

It is no wonder that we sing, "Joy to the world, the Lord is come!" Joy has come because God, through Jesus Christ, has brought the gift of salvation. The basis of a renewed fellowship with God has now been provided through the gift of His Son.

C. Prophetic Fulfillment (v. 22)

22. Now all this was done, that it might be fulfilled which was spoken of the Lord by the prophet, saying.

Isaiah 7:14 reads, "Therefore the Lord himself shall give you a sign: Behold, a virgin shall conceive, and bear a son, and shall call his name Immanuel." Matthew 1:23 connects this prophecy with Jesus' birth by quoting the Isaiah passage. It is important to connect not just the record of Jesus' birth with prophecy but the manner of His birth as well. The identity of Jesus as the Promised One hinges on the veracity of the Virgin Birth. If the birth of Jesus was an ordinary physical birth, then He is a sinner and not the Son of God. If Christ is a sinner, He cannot be a sacrifice for sin, neither can He forgive sin.

Other prophecies regarding the birth of Messiah authenticate Jesus as the Promised One. Baalam the prophet saw the coming Messiah. His vision is recorded in Numbers 24:17. He knew the time was not immediate but it was certain. He referred to Jesus as the "Star of Jacob" and the "Scepter of Israel." We see a New Testament connection in Luke 1:78, where Zacharias the priest referred to Jesus as the "dayspring," or the "daystar," from on high.

One of the better-known prophecies in the Old Testament is Isaiah 9:6, 7. Here Jesus is called "Wonderful, Counsellor, The mighty God, The everlasting Father, The Prince of Peace." Isaiah makes it clear that this person would sit on the throne of David to establish it. In fact, Jesus would establish a kingdom of justice and judgment forevermore.

D. God With Us (v. 23)

23. Behold, a virgin shall be with child, and shall bring forth a son, and they shall call his name Emmanuel, which being interpreted is, God with us.

The matter of fellowship and personal relationship with God is a benefit of the gift of Jesus to the world. His people are not only joyously saved from their sins, they now have an avenue of communion with their Creator. People are no longer alienated from God. The title, Emmanuel, conveys this restoration to fellowship in a powerful way. Nothing can be more important than the reality that God is with us. This is an overwhelming, incomprehensible reality. You can say, I can say, and all the redeemed of the earth can say, "God is with us."

Realizing that God is with us, we should strive to be *holy*. God is a holy God, and walking with Him mandates that we be holy.

Knowing God is with us should also make us *humble*. We certainly are not worthy that He should be with us. Each time I think of who I am and where I came from, I am amazed that God would be with me—but He is.

Because God is with us, we should also be *happy.* The Christian life is not drab, gloomy and depressing. Yet some representatives of Christ do not look or act like delivered people. Peace, tranquillity and contentment should be seen on the faces of those whom God is with.

Eight of the blessings Jesus pronounced in the Sermon on the Mount begin with the word *blessed,* or "happy." This is not a shallow, surface, giggly happiness the world knows; instead, it is a joy that surpasses all human understanding.

Because God is with us, we should be *helpful.* Serving others is the center of our response to God's presence with us. Christianity is not a passive way of life. Reaching out to serve others is the heart and soul of what Jesus did and what He wants His followers to do. He was about His Father's business and He expects the same of us.

That God is with us also makes us *hopeful.* Hope is one of the three great virtues espoused by the apostle Paul in his letter to the 1 Corinthians (13:13). Much has been written about love and faith, but not so much about hope. Hope is one of the major outcomes of the coming of Jesus into the world. He broke the back of sin, death and hell, and opened the way to eternal life, giving us a hope that is an anchor of the soul (Hebrews 6:19).

III. COURAGEOUS OBEDIENCE
   (Matthew 1:24, 25)

A. Divine Commission (v. 24)

24. Then Joseph being raised from sleep did as the angel of the Lord had bidden him, and took unto him his wife.

The birth of Jesus was the most significant event in history. God took on Himself the likeness of man to begin an earthly pilgrimage. The Incarnation was a cooperative effort

between Divinity and humanity. The Creator and the created joined together in an event of universal, eternal consequence.

Matthew's account of this drama begins with the genealogy of Jesus and then turns the focus on Joseph. Luke, on the other hand, begins with the focus on Mary and the great Annunciation. Both writers, under the guidance of the Holy Spirit, gravitated in the direction of a special emphasis for special reasons. Both Joseph and Mary were humble servants of the Lord and gladly responded to the call of God.

The depth of the piety and devotion of this young couple nearly defies human comprehension. Each of them was ready to do whatever God would dictate. God spoke to both of them through angelic messengers. The message of the angels was, in human terms, unbelievable. To Mary the angel said, "You are with child, and the child was conceived of the Holy Ghost" (see Luke 1:28-35). As shocking as this message was, Mary had no option but to believe. She knew this was not Joseph's child. She knew she had not had physical relations with any other man. The message of the angel must be correct. Mary was commissioned by God to give birth to the Son who would be the Savior of the world. What an incomparable honor! One can only begin to imagine the emotional roller-coaster Mary must have experienced.

What would Joseph say and do? How could she explain this pregnancy to her family and friends?

Joseph loved Mary. They were engaged to be married. Joseph, like any normal young man, looked forward to marriage and having a family with the woman of his dreams. He knew nothing of the special plan God had for his life. No one before or since was ever called upon for such a role. He would become the earthly parent of a child that was not his nor from the seed of any mortal man. He would provide a family atmosphere for the development of a divine child who would give His life to save the world. This was His destiny.

When Joseph learned from Mary that she was with child, he must have been stunned. He loved Mary, but how could he believe such a story? He had the option of having Mary stoned to death or putting her away in everlasting disgrace. But Matthew tells us that Joseph instead pondered how he could put her away privately and spare her any disgrace (v. 19). While in the throes of this dilemma, the angel of the Lord spoke to him.

Joseph walked close enough to the Lord to know that the angel's voice was real and that he was not hallucinating. In this, Joseph serves as a model for all of us. Many times God speaks to us, but we are not sensitive to His voice. Joseph knew in his heart that Mary had told him the truth, that he had heard God's voice and he must obey.

Jesus spoke to the issue of sensitivity to the voice of God in John 10:27: "My sheep hear my voice, and I know them, and they follow me." The safety of the sheep depended on their sensitivity to the shepherd's voice. They would not respond to the voice of a stranger. In the case of Joseph and Mary, one can only guess how history would have played out had they not been tuned in to the voice of God.

B. Courageous Action (v. 25)

25. And knew her not till she had brought forth her firstborn son: and he called his name Jesus.

When Joseph got the story correct and knew what the situation was, he arose and did exactly as the Lord had said. Months later, just as the angel had promised, Jesus the Savior was born.

It is one thing to hear God's voice and quite another to obey it. Often we know exactly what God would have us do but lack the courage to obey. Once it has been settled what God would have us do, we should proceed immediately with no hesitation whatsoever. It matters not how irrational the assignment may be.

It takes great courage to walk in a path never before traveled. We, like Joseph, can be sure that if we have the courage to act, the God who has commissioned us will go with us all the way. In time, God will give birth to whatever He had promised.

GOLDEN TEXT HOMILY

"BEHOLD, A VIRGIN SHALL BE WITH CHILD, AND SHALL BRING FORTH A SON, AND THEY SHALL CALL HIS NAME EMMANUEL" (Matthew 1:23).

From the miraculous union of the divine and human natures, Jesus, the Son of God, was born. Mary is the only virgin that ever became, or ever shall become, a mother in this fashion.

Secularists and even some so-called Christians try desperately to refute this miracle birth; but the Scriptures leave no room for doubt in the Christian believer as to the authenticity of the virgin birth of Jesus—Emmanuel.

Emmanuel—"God with us"—God with us then, God with us now! In the Old Testament ages God manifested Himself as Jehovah; in the Gospels, God manifested Himself in the person of Jesus Christ the Son; and after the Ascension, He manifests Himself in the indwelling, empowering Holy Spirit.

God is *with* us and *in* us through the gift of faith. God is with us to save, comfort, defend, enlighten, protect from Satan's darts, guide, sanctify, heal, and empower for service.

Jesus was born of God's nature and human nature; He is very God and perfect man. Because of His humanity He relates with humankind. He experienced all the temptations that we do. He felt pain, loneliness, hunger, thirst, weariness; He was poor; He shed tears (Hebrews 4:15).

We live in a sinful, sick, strife-ridden, suffering, cruel, revengeful world. So did Jesus! He understands our every need. He is all-knowing, ever-present, all-powerful to meet our every need.—**Selected**

SENTENCE SERMONS

JESUS CHRIST is the divinely conceived, virgin-born, Son of God.
—Selected

THE HINGE OF HISTORY is on the door of a Bethlehem stable.
—Ralph Sockman

THE MESSAGE OF CHRISTMAS is that the visible material world is bound to the invisible spiritual world.
—Anonymous

THE PURPOSE AND CAUSE of the Incarnation was that He might illuminate the world by His wisdom and excite it to the love of Himself.
—Peter Abelard

EVANGELISM APPLICATION

JESUS CAME TO BE THE SAVIOR OF THE WORLD.

Here we are in 2003, observing the birth of the Christ and even proclaiming that He is coming again. Yet many in the world do not know Jesus was ever here, not to mention He is coming again. To millions there is no babe of Bethlehem, no child wrapped in swaddling clothes, no shepherds and no wise men from the East. There is no guiding star, no angels singing, and no joy to the world.

The point is that while Christians celebrate the birth of Christ (and we should), we must be aware that multitudes have not heard His name. They do not know the Christ of Christmas. Christmas is such incredible news, and we must not rest until the whole world can celebrate.

ILLUMINATING THE LESSON

Two missionaries, captured by bandits and shut up in a filthy hole without fire, were miserably cold. To make things worse, the guard ordered them not to talk nor to even make signs to each other.

Christmas came. One of the missionaries, shivering and shaking, sat silently on the floor. His face suddenly lit up, for he thought of a way to communicate with his comrade. Idly toying with bits of hay around him, he spelled out a word on the hard-packed mud. With a glance he drew his friend's attention to it. Immediately his friend's face brightened with triumphant joy. The straws in the floor spelled out the word *Emmanuel*.

What if they were captives? What if they were in peril of death? What if their prison was dirty and cold? Inwardly they rejoiced because God was with them. This is the meaning of Christmas. God is with us everywhere, all the time!

DAILY BIBLE READINGS

M. Foretold by Prophets.
   Isaiah 7:10-14
T. Sent by God.
   Galatians 4:1-6
W. Born of the Virgin.
   Luke 1:26-31
T. Sought by Shepherds.
   Luke 2:8-18
F. Worshiped by Kings.
   Matthew 2:1-12
S. Protected by Angels.
   Matthew 2:13-21

TRUTH SEARCH
Creatively Teaching the Word

DISCUSSION QUESTIONS

1. Why is Jesus called "the son of David" (Matthew 1:1; see also Jeremiah 23:5)?

2. Why is Jesus called "the son of Abraham" (Matthew 1:1; see also Genesis 12:1-3)?

3. As you read through the earthly genealogy of Jesus (on Joseph's side), which names do you recognize (Matthew 1:2-16)? Were all men of God? What does this say about God's sovereignty and grace?

4. How did Mary become pregnant (v. 18)?

5. Why is the Virgin Birth of critical importance?

6. What is learned about Joseph's faith and character in verses 19, 20, 24, 25? Why do you suppose God chose him to be Jesus' earthly father?

7. What is the significance of the name *Jesus*?

8. In Isaiah 7:14, what did the prophet predict about Messiah's birth?

9. What is the significance of the name *Emmanuel* (Matthew 1:23)?

10. In 12 words or less, compose a sentence explaining the significance of Christ's birth.

ART BOX

Items needed: Gift-wrapped box, black permanent marker

Pass the box and the marker around the room. Students should take turns writing one adjective on the box describing the birth of Christ.

Once the box has made its way around the room, have someone read all the words.

Option: If you teach a large class, you might use two gift boxes and markers.

Living Right in a Wrong World

Study Text: 1 Corinthians 8:1-13; 9:24-27; 10:1-13, 23-33; 11:1
Objective: To know that Christian behavior must be in harmony with Scripture and determine to live by God's Word.
Time: A.D. 57
Place: Paul wrote 1 Corinthians from Ephesus.
Golden Text: "Whether therefore ye eat, or drink, or whatsoever ye do, do all to the glory of God" (1 Corinthians 10:31).
Central Truth: Christ calls us to live righteously in this sinful world.
Evangelism Emphasis: Christlike living is an essential part of a Christian's witness.

PRINTED TEXT

1 Corinthians 8:4. As concerning therefore the eating of those things that are offered in sacrifice unto idols, we know that an idol is nothing in the world, and that there is none other God but one.

7. Howbeit there is not in every man that knowledge: for some with conscience of the idol unto this hour eat it as a thing offered unto an idol; and their conscience being weak is defiled.

8. But meat commendeth us not to God: for neither, if we eat, are we the better; neither, if we eat not, are we the worse.

9. But take heed lest by any means this liberty of your's become a stumblingblock to them that are weak.

10. For if any man see thee which hast knowledge sit at meat in the idol's temple, shall not the conscience of him which is weak be emboldened to eat those things which are offered to idols;

11. And through thy knowledge shall the weak brother perish, for whom Christ died?

9:24. Know ye not that they which run in a race run all, but one receiveth the prize? So run, that ye may obtain.

25. And every man that striveth for the mastery is temperate in all things. Now they do it to obtain a corruptible crown; but we an incorruptible.

26. I therefore so run, not as uncertainly; so fight I, not as one that beateth the air:

27. But I keep under my body, and bring it into subjection: lest that by any means, when I have preached to others, I myself should be a castaway.

10:13. There hath no temptation taken you but such as is common to man: but God is faithful, who will not suffer you to be tempted above that ye are able; but will with the temptation also make a way to escape, that ye may be able to bear it.

27. If any of them that believe not bid you to a feast, and ye be disposed to go; whatsoever is set before you, eat, asking no question for conscience sake.

28. But if any man say unto you, This is offered in sacrifice unto idols, eat not for his sake that shewed it, and for conscience sake: for the earth is the Lord's, and the fulness thereof:

31. Whether therefore ye eat, or drink, or whatsoever ye do, do all to the glory of God.

32. Give none offence, neither to the Jews, nor to the Gentiles, nor to the church of God:

33. Even as I please all men in all things, not seeking mine own profit, but the profit of many, that they may be saved.

LESSON OUTLINE

I. CHRISTIAN LIBERTY
   A. Pitfall of Knowledge
   B. Sacrificed Food
   C. Exercise of Freedom

II. CHRISTIAN DISCIPLINE
   A. Qualifying for the Prize
   B. Battling Entanglements
   C. Overcoming Temptation

III. CONSIDERATION FOR OTHERS
   A. Seeking Their Good
 , B. Complying With Their
       Conscience
   C. Glorifying God

LESSON EXPOSITION

INTRODUCTION

The Corinthian believers of the first century never knew of the sinful opportunities offered through modern technology. Yet, they knew as well as us the powerful temptations which appeal to the sinful human nature. Their struggle definitely was not any less than our own.

The objective of this lesson is knowing that Christian behavior must be in harmony with Scripture and determining to live by God's Word. No one of us has the right to determine our own rules for living in a sinful world. To do so assumes that we are omnipotent and can take the place of God. This self-sufficient attitude guarantees spiritual decline at best and more than likely will produce spiritual shipwreck.

Equally devastating is to attempt, like the Pharisees did, to build protective walls of rules around Biblical principles so as not to break them. This results in a legalism that not only separates from the world but also from God.

Living right in a wrong world requires walking in the Spirit so the extremes of both sides are avoided. We have the wonderful opportunity to live in the world but not be of it. It demands our submission to the principles of the Word and the guidance of the Holy Spirit. At the same time, these actions involve thought and choice. None of us are robots who simply serve God without any personal input.

Right living involves more than just the big issues that occasionally come our way. We face choices on a daily basis even in more mundane areas such as what we eat or drink. It includes our speech or choice of vocabulary, our styles of dress and our forms of entertainment.

Today's lesson considers Christian living in three areas: Christian liberty, Christian discipline, and consideration for others. All of these are a vital component of living righteously in a sinful world.

I. CHRISTIAN LIBERTY
   (1 Corinthians 8:1-13)

A. Pitfall of Knowledge (vv. 1-3)

(1 Corinthians 8:1-3 is not included in the printed text.)

In chapter 8 Paul addresses the question of food sacrificed to idols. The Corinthians were concerned about this issue since there appears to have been an abundance of such food available in the markets of the city. He leads into this issue by addressing what he perceived to be an even more important item—the believer's pride in opinionated knowledge.

It is thought that the phrase "we know that we all have knowledge" came directly from the Corinthian believers' letter to Paul. Apparently they felt they possessed all the knowledge necessary to produce right religious actions. So why would they write to Paul about some of these areas? Probably there were a few practical details which they thought needed his input. Paul did not commend them for their knowledge. Instead, his words reproved them. Their knowledge was producing pride, which is sin.

Their lack of love contributed to the sinfulness of their emphasis on knowledge. Genuine love always edifies—it builds up. True knowledge in itself is not negative. However, emphasizing its value above love for others is wrong.

Verse 2 points out that those who rely on their own knowledge tend to believe that others should hold the same opinion. Self-generated knowledge tends to be faulty due to its source. Humans are not all-knowing, especially in spiritual matters. Cain demonstrated this when he chose a different manner of worship than what God required (Genesis 4:3-7). His sacrifice was not acceptable in God's sight and eventually led to more sin (v. 8).

A caution arises here for each of us. Knowledge gained through formal and informal means can be of value in the broad spectrum of life. Yet, it becomes a pitfall when facts and derived opinion supersede the principles of Scripture and the direction of the Holy Spirit.

B. Sacrificed Food (vv. 4-8)

(1 Corinthians 8:5, 6 is not included in the printed text.)

4. As concerning therefore the eating of those things that are offered in sacrifice unto idols, we know that an idol is nothing in the world, and that there is none other God but one.

7. Howbeit there is not in every man that knowledge: for some with conscience of the idol unto this hour eat it as a thing offered unto an idol; and their conscience being weak is defiled.

8. But meat commendeth us not to God: for neither, if we eat, are we the better; neither, if we eat not, are we the worse.

Part of the pagan worship of idols included burning the fat of meat due to their believing that the gods enjoyed the smell of vapors. At times the pagan worship would include banquets held at the temple of the god. Meat sacrificed to the idols frequently came to the markets when the priests sold their shares of the sacrificed food.

In verse 4 the "we know" once again refers to the Corinthians' letter. It indicates they knew the truth of there being one God and that idols were nothing more than fashioned images. This led them to the opinion that there was no problem in eating food sacrificed to these meaningless images.

Verses 5 and 6 state that even if there were other gods in the heavens and on earth, they would be limited to ruling over only a portion assigned. What a contrast to the Lord God who created all and has the final control! This could be referring to gods and goddesses of ancient mythology. Or possibly it could refer to the forces of evil. However, for the Corinthian Christians there was only one God—the One who brought all things into existence. He alone is worthy of praise.

Notice how correct the Corinthians were in the statements concerning Jesus Christ. They recognized His position in the Trinity and active participation in Creation. Verse 6 is similar to Paul's words to the Colossians regarding Christ's position and activities: "For by him all things were created: things in heaven and on earth, visible and invisible, whether thrones or powers or rulers or authorities; all things were created by him for him" (1:16, *NIV*).

The Corinthians also recognized that life comes from Christ. All human life stems from His creating man and woman on the sixth day of Creation.

All spiritual life comes through Christ as a result of His redemptive work on the cross of Calvary.

Even though the Corinthians as a whole recognized the neutral position of meat sacrificed to idols, not all of them were able to maintain this consistency of thought. The ideas of the past still lingered in the minds of some, focusing on the sacrificed meat as being part of their previous worship. This issue could be so significant as to destroy their weak spiritual life and return them to paganism.

Verse 8 notes that the food in itself was not a factor in the Corinthians' spirituality. The food would not make a difference in the believers' spiritual standing. However, individual conscience regarding the food was an issue.

A believer can be strong in overcoming temptations of one nature, yet susceptible to temptations of another type. Some believers have complete deliverance from past habits while others struggle and need the support of fellow believers.

C. Exercise of Freedom (vv. 9-13)

(1 Corinthians 8:12, 13 is not included in the printed text.)

9. But take heed lest by any means this liberty of your's become a stumblingblock to them that are weak.

10. For if any man see thee which hast knowledge sit at meat in the idol's temple, shall not the conscience of him which is weak be emboldened to eat those things which are offered to idols;

11. And through thy knowledge shall the weak brother perish, for whom Christ died?

To what extent will I go to help a weaker brother or sister in Christ? Will I abstain from attitudes and specific actions for their benefit even though I could in true Biblical conscience participate? Will I put my brother's or sister's spiritual growth ahead of my personal desire?

We are surrounded by the concepts of "having it our way" and exercising personal freedom. As a result, we can be pulled away from the Biblical obligation we have to those weaker members of the body who need us to help them by restricting our participation in certain activities. No, it may not be easy, but that's what God requires.

In verse 9 Paul recognizes Christian freedom. He agrees that eating food sacrificed to idols has no negative spiritual impact. His concern centers on those who are spiritually weak. How consistent is it to emphasize one's spiritual strength and knowledge at the expense of those who are not as advanced in their life in Christ? Brotherly love lifts the weak rather than causing them to stumble spiritually.

Verse 10 offers a situation without any expansion of how it could occur. Why would a believer eat a meal in a pagan temple? One suggestion is that if an official ceremony of city government were held in one of the halls of a temple, a believer might be part of that event. A strong, knowledgeable believer would not hesitate to eat the meal. He would know it was just regular food. However, a weaker believer seeing this might be induced to engage in idol worship.

How sad to even imagine that the strength and knowledge of one believer could lead to the spiritual destruction of another! Paul emphasized the consequences of such an action, seeing it as a double sin—sin against a brother and sin against Christ himself.

In conclusion, Paul provides a personal principle which Christians should follow. We must restrain from an action that could contribute to a fellow Christian's falling into sin. This philosophy flies in the face of the idea of satisfying self first. It offers personal sacrifice as a priority for the spiritual well-being of another—definitely not popular in the here and now but of eternal consequence.

Do we value our liberty above the spiritual development of a fellow believer? Do we want to satisfy self at the risk of sinning against Christ? Christlike living includes restraining our actions for the good of another believer.

II. CHRISTIAN DISCIPLINE
(1 Corinthians 9:24-27; 10:1-13)

A. Qualifying for the Prize (9:24-27)

24. Know ye not that they which run in a race run all, but one receiveth the prize? So run, that ye may obtain.

25. And every man that striveth for the mastery is temperate in all things. Now they do it to obtain a corruptible crown; but we an incorruptible.

26. I therefore so run, not as uncertainly; so fight I, not as one that beateth the air:

27. But I keep under my body, and bring it into subjection: lest that by any means, when I have preached to others, I myself should be a castaway.

In the previous verses of chapter 9 the apostle Paul explained what his rights as an apostle were. But as an example of refraining to use the extent of one's liberty or freedom, he chose to restrict himself so as to not cause a weaker brother or sister to sin. Their continuance in Christ and the furtherance of the gospel was what really mattered. Then, beginning in verse 24, he utilized the example of a runner in a race.

The Corinthians understood this analogy well since the Isthmian games were held close to their city. Paul used a favorite sport to emphasize the discipline required to qualify for the prize. His audience knew that all who entered the race had one goal in mind—winning to receive the prize. Though many would run, only the first one across the finish line would receive the winner's wreath. Winning demanded the discipline of preparation prior to the race and then an all-out effort during the race.

In the same way believers are to run the Christian race with the intention of winning. Winning needs to be defined as maintaining the Christian lifestyle, following God's will and then hearing the Lord say, "Well done, good and faithful servant." What a contrast to the prize that a runner in the games received! Though the wreath looked good for the moment, it did not last.

Paul used himself as an example of how the Christian race should be run. First, he indicated it cannot be accomplished by living without a goal. Switching to boxing as an example, Paul noted that fighters aren't content to fill the air with their fists. Their aim is to hit the opponent. That is the only way to win.

In verse 27 Paul continued his personal example by emphasizing the need for self-control. "I keep under my body," or "I beat my body" (*NIV*), does not mean physically punishing oneself. Rather, this speaks of placing oneself under subjection so actions and attitudes conform with the teachings and example of Christ. This mastery includes both body and spirit. Through this commitment Paul knew he would qualify for the prize at the end of the race.

One of the most encouraging concepts to remember is we do not run alone or only in our strength. The Holy Spirit is there to strengthen, comfort and encourage. He wants to work in and through us so we will be spiritually successful. Paul's words to the Philippians apply here: "Being confident of this very thing, that he which hath begun a good work in you will perform it until the day of Jesus Christ" (1:6).

B. Battling Entanglements (10:1-11)

(1 Corinthians 10:1-11 is not included in the printed text.)

Barbed wire, rose bushes, berry vines and cactus can snag your clothes and scratch your skin. Three of the four have left their mark on the skin and clothes of this writer. However, all of the physical thorns and barbs in the world are mild in comparison to how various sins can entrap and scar a person.

Chapter 10 begins another topic of concern as evidenced by Paul's opening words: "Moreover, brethren, I would not that ye should be ignorant." Where previously he spoke to the strong Christians, now the weak received special attention. He starts by turning their attention to some of Israel's history. Though these Gentile believers were not blood offspring, they were part of the extended spiritual family of God. For that reason Paul referred to the individuals of the past as "our fathers."

The historical perspective begins with the Israelites' leaving Egypt at the conclusion of the last plague. They "were under the cloud" (v. 1), referring to the pillar of cloud by day and the pillar of fire by night which led the Israelites (see Exodus 13:21). Passing "through the sea" (1 Corinthians 10:1) meant the miraculous opening of the Red Sea so God's people could cross on dry ground and escape the pursuing Egyptians.

Being "baptized unto Moses" (v. 2) refers to their being immersed in the leadership of this divinely ordained deliverer. They received spiritual food and drink (vv. 3, 4) beyond the mirac-

ulous provision of water, manna and quail. The expressions of God's grace in the wilderness foreshadowed His miraculous provision of salvation through Jesus Christ, which the first-century Corinthian church had received.

In verses 5-10 Paul moves to the problems of the Israelites. First, they repeatedly fell into idolatry even after seeing the judgment God brought upon the idol-worshiping Egyptians. Second, they engaged in sexual immorality even after having been given the Ten Commandments. Third, they repeatedly murmured and grumbled. Within three days of having walked through the Red Sea on dry ground, they were grumbling because of the undrinkable water at Marah.

Because of sin, only a very small percentage of those who left Egypt ever made it into the land of Canaan. It was not because of God's inability to take them through the desert with safety and sufficient provision. Rather, their sins forced God to bring judgment on them. Only those under the age of 20 (when leaving Egypt), except for Caleb and Joshua, ever entered the Promised Land.

Paul wanted the Corinthians to see these past examples as patterns for them to avoid some 15 centuries later. Though we live 34 centuries later, they still speak to us. Sin entangles regardless of the century or culture. Knowing this, it becomes our obligation through the empowerment of the Holy Spirit to strive to avoid sin's grasp.

C. Overcoming Temptation (vv. 12, 13)

(1 Corinthians 10:12 is not included in the printed text.)

13. There hath no temptation taken you but such as is common to man: but God is faithful, who will not suffer you to be tempted above that ye are able; but will with the temptation also make a way to

escape, that ye may be able to bear it.

In verse 12 Paul warned of the problem of deception which may undercut a believer: "If you think you are standing firm, be careful that you don't fall!" (*NIV*). Confidence in one's knowledge may lead to a boldness in liberty that may, in itself, not be a sin unless it causes a weaker brother or sister to sin. Also, we know that confidence in past experiences may lead to failure in not maintaining a fresh relationship with God. Confidence in our relationship and position with God is not the issue. The problem comes when we lose sensitivity to God's Word and His personal voice speaking to our heart.

Temptations come to all of us—they are "common to man" (v. 13). Satan strives to destroy us by drawing us into sin, but God faithfully watches over His children. He doesn't call us to Himself for the purpose of later neglecting us to situations that will cripple or destroy. In His love and care, He provides a way for each of us to withstand every tempting setting and come out stronger than before.

God never tempts us in the sense that Satan does. But our God does test us. Probably the greatest example of this is seen in the account of Abraham when God directed him to sacrifice Isaac (Genesis 22). In this request God tested and furthered the growth and quality of Abraham's faith.

III. CONSIDERATION FOR OTHERS (1 Corinthians 10:23-33; 11:1)

A. Seeking Their Good (10:23, 24)

(1 Corinthians 10:23, 24 is not included in the printed text.)

In the introduction to this lesson, four questions were asked which apply to the lifestyle of the believer. To those we add one more: How far should a believer go in seeking good for others?

It is much easier to talk about wanting the best for someone else than to bring it into reality. Words are cheap, but actions are costly when attempting to accomplish good for others at our own expense. That's what Paul had in mind when he stated, "Nobody should seek his own good, but the good of others" (v. 24, *NIV*).

Seeking the good of another means much more than hoping things will work out for them. It goes beyond helping a little for a short while. Here we must see *seeking* as an intensive effort on our part even though it may inconvenience or not be of any benefit for self. It implies restricting our personal liberty for the purpose of helping a weaker brother or sister. This consideration stems from not only a love for God but also from a love for the members of the family of God. Love develops selfless living.

B. Complying With Their Conscience (vv. 25-30)

(1 Corinthians 10:25, 26, 29, 30 is not included in the printed text.)

27. If any of them that believe not bid you to a feast, and ye be disposed to go; whatsoever is set before you, eat, asking no question for conscience sake.

28. But if any man say unto you, This is offered in sacrifice unto idols, eat not for his sake that shewed it, and for conscience sake: for the earth is the Lord's, and the fulness thereof.

In these six verses Paul becomes very specific in the actions which the Corinthians were to demonstrate. He begins with meat sold in the public markets. Even though the priests and butchers at the places of idol worship regularly sold meat at the market, it was not to hinder the believers' buying or eating meat purchased there. Paul did not expect them to abstain from meat or to seek some alternate source. Quoting from Psalm 24:1, he pointed out that the Lord's earth produces these foods. So there was no spiritual or physical reason why they should not eat such meat.

Paul then moved to the scenario of a believer's possibly being invited for a meal at the home of an unbeliever. He advised that the person accept the invitation. There shouldn't be a refusal due to fearing the meat may have been sacrificed to idols. However, if someone (more than likely a weaker believer) informed the believer of the meat's source, then not eating became a necessity! Refraining for the sake of a brother's or sister's conscience takes precedence over one's personal freedom and spiritual maturity.

C. Glorifying God (vv. 31-33; 11:1)

(1 Corinthians 11:1 is not included in the printed text.)

31. Whether therefore ye eat, or drink, or whatsoever ye do, do all to the glory of God.

32. Give none offence, neither to the Jews, nor to the Gentiles, nor to the church of God:

33. Even as I please all men in all things, not seeking mine own profit, but the profit of many, that they may be saved.

These verses provide a conclusion to the whole issue. Every aspect of life, from the most ordinary to the very extraordinary, needs to be seen within the total framework of serving God. Actions designed for personal satisfaction rather than seeking the good of the whole body of Christ must be avoided.

How do we put this principle into action?

Initially there is the temptation to simply say "I will do what Jesus would." That's good, provided you know the Gospel accounts of Jesus' example and teachings and interpret them accu-

rately. It demands a sensitivity to the Holy Spirit's leading. It also means glorifying God in all we do through personal commitment. Only when we put His kingdom above our wishes will everything fall in line.

In conclusion, we must all agree that it definitely is possible to live right in a wrong world. We can rise above the entanglements of sin and glorify God. Paul declared, "Follow my example, as I follow the example of Christ" (11:1, *NIV*). If Paul served Christ, so could the Corinthians . . . and so can we.

GOLDEN TEXT HOMILY

"WHETHER THEREFORE YE EAT, OR DRINK, OR WHATSOEVER YE DO, DO ALL TO THE GLORY OF GOD" (1 Corinthians 10:31).

The Living Bible expresses in modern language Paul's summation of the lesson he was trying to get across to his brothers in Christ:

"Why, you may ask, must I be guided and limited by what someone else thinks? If I can thank God for the food and enjoy it, why let someone spoil everything just because he thinks I am wrong? Well, I'll tell you why. It is because *you must do everything for the glory of God*, even your eating and drinking. So don't be a stumbling block to anyone. . . . I try to please everyone in everything I do, not doing what I like or what is best for me, but what is best for them, *so that they may be saved*" (1 Corinthians 10:29-33).

When we were sinners, we walked in the flesh, fulfilling our natural desires. But when we accepted Christ as Lord of our lives, instead of fulfilling the desires of the flesh—glorifying ourselves—our minds became attuned to bringing glory to God.

Christ, we understand, paid the price—a great price—for our liberty. We have been set free—free from the law, free from sin. And yet, freedom itself carries with it some responsibility. We *were* bound and led about by our carnal nature's desires. Those desires were alien to God's desires. They were self-serving ways, patterns of unproductive behavior, man-made ideas: "What's in it for me?"; "Look out for number one"; "What about my rights?" These were heard long enough until they became a normal attitude to assume. Now we have a new mind, a new mind-set. We are free—free to choose—to serve our Creator.

As believers, we are free to eat or drink; either is OK. So what is my basis for right choice here?

To win as many as possible is the issue. Self does not need this meat. Self does not have to have this thing I desire, not if it jeopardizes the salvation of another. NO. I choose my brother. I will no longer eat meat if it offends my brother or my sister.

"Though I am free and belong to no man, I make myself a slave to everyone, to win as many as possible" (1 Corinthians 9:19, *NIV*).

The glory of God comes through when we diminish and God increases.—**Ann Steely**

SENTENCE SERMONS

CHRIST CALLS US to live righteously in this sinful world.

—Selected

A STREAM is purest near its source. That is why we should live near Christ.

—*Notes and Quotes*

THE CHRISTIAN is not saved because he works, but he works because he is saved.

—Elmer Case

EVANGELISM APPLICATION

CHRISTLIKE LIVING IS AN ESSENTIAL PART OF A CHRISTIAN'S WITNESS.

It's one thing to tell a person about Christ and how he or she should live. But it is more effective when we are living daily the lifestyle being talked about.

Most children enjoy a show-and-tell session in their school. Every day should be "show and tell" in our Christian witness.

ILLUMINATING THE LESSON

It takes obedience in order to have true freedom. I can sit at a piano and be at liberty to play any keys that I want, but I don't have freedom, because I can't play anything but noise. I have no freedom to play Bach or even "Chopsticks." Why? Because it takes years of practice and obedience to lesson plans to be truly free at the piano. Then, and only then, does one have the freedom to play any piece of music.

The same is true of freedom of living. To be truly free, we must have the power and ability to be obedient (Green & Robinson, *Illustrations for Biblical Preaching*).

DAILY BIBLE READINGS

M. Right Living Though Tempted.
   Genesis 39:7-12
T. Right Living in Trouble.
   Job 2:1-10
W. Right Living Though Threatened.
   Daniel 3:13-18
T. Right Living Though Persecuted.
   Acts 16:19-26
F. Right Living by Faith.
   Hebrews 11:24-29
S. Right Living Commended.
   3 John 1-8

TRUTH SEARCH
Creatively Teaching the Word

DISCUSSION QUESTIONS

Liberty
(1 Corinthians 8:1-13)
1. How does Paul contrast love and knowledge in verse 1?

2. What knowledge is Paul discussing (v. 4)?

3. Is it wrong to eat food sacrificed to idols (vv. 4-8)? Why or why not?

4. Which is more important—a Christian's freedom or the conscience of others (v. 9)? In our freedom, how should we respond?

5. What damage can a Christian with a strong conscience do to a Christian with a weak conscience (vv. 10, 11)?

6. What damage can a Christian do to himself by violating another believer's conscience (v. 12)?

7. What personal commitment did Paul make, and why (v. 13)?

Discipline
(1 Corinthians 9:24-27)
1. How must we live to successfully run the Christian race (vv. 24, 25)?

2. How did Paul run the Christian race (vv. 26, 27)? How did he *not* run the race?

3. What could cause someone to be disqualified from the race?

Example
(1 Corinthians 10:1-13)
1. How did God minister to the Israelites through the Exodus (vv. 1-4)?

2. Why did judgment fall on the Israelites (vv. 5, 7-10)?

3. What does God want us to learn from Israel's example (vv. 6, 11)?

4. Explain the warning in verse 12.

5. What should we do when temptation comes (v. 13)? Name some escape routes God might provide.

6. Can the devil make a believer sin?

Purpose
(1 Corinthians 10:23—11:1)
1. How could a Christian's freedom become an idol?

2. Are there areas in life not declared off limits by Scripture that could lead to problems in one's walk with God (v. 23)? Can you name any such areas?

3. What principle does Paul give in verses 24 and 29?

4. How can a person "do all to the glory of God" (v. 31)?

5. What was Paul's ultimate purpose in ministering to others (10:32—11:1)?

DEMONSTRATION

Items needed: Blindfold, chair

Blindfold a volunteer who will walk across the front of the room. Have another person sit in a chair obstructing the blindfolded person's path. When the blindfolded one bumps into the person sitting in the chair, remove the blindfold and discuss these questions:

• Did the person in the chair cause the other person to stumble?

• Is it wrong to sit in a chair?

• What could the seated person have done to express love to the other one?

• How important is it for Christians to do all they can to help fellow Christians not to stumble?

Spiritual Gifts, Unity and Love

Study Text: 1 Corinthians 12:1 through 13:13
Objective: To review the work of the Holy Spirit among believers and minister in unity and love.
Time: A.D. 57
Place: Paul wrote this letter from Ephesus.
Golden Text: "Let all things be done unto edifying" (1 Corinthians 14:26).
Central Truth: When Christ's love rules our lives, we minister in unity.
Evangelism Emphasis: Gifts of the Spirit exercised in Christian love and unity make the church attractive to people desiring spiritual help.

PRINTED TEXT

1 Corinthians 12:4. Now there are diversities of gifts, but the same Spirit.

5. And there are differences of administrations, but the same Lord.

6. And there are diversities of operations, but it is the same God which worketh all in all.

7. But the manifestation of the Spirit is given to every man to profit withal.

8. For to one is given by the Spirit the word of wisdom; to another the word of knowledge by the same Spirit;

9. To another faith by the same Spirit; to another the gifts of healing by the same Spirit;

10. To another the working of miracles; to another prophecy; to another discerning of spirits; to another divers kinds of tongues; to another the interpretation of tongues:

11. But all these worketh that one and the selfsame Spirit, dividing to every man severally as he will.

12. For as the body is one, and hath many members, and all the members of that one body, being many, are one body: so also is Christ.

18. But now hath God set the members every one of them in the body, as it hath pleased him.

19. And if they were all one member, where were the body?

20. But now are they many members, yet but one body.

27. Now ye are the body of Christ, and members in particular.

28. And God hath set some in the church, first apostles, secondarily prophets, thirdly teachers, after that miracles, then gifts of healings, helps, governments, diversities of tongues.

13:4. Charity suffereth long, and is kind; charity envieth not; charity vaunteth not itself, is not puffed up,

5. Doth not behave itself unseemly, seeketh not her own, is not easily provoked, thinketh no evil;

6. Rejoiceth not in iniquity, but rejoiceth in the truth;

7. Beareth all things, believeth all things, hopeth all things, endureth all things.

8. Charity never faileth: but whether there be prophecies, they shall fail; whether there be tongues, they shall cease; whether there be knowledge, it shall vanish away.

13. And now abideth faith, hope, charity, these three; but the greatest of these is charity.

DICTIONARY
administrations—1 Corinthians 12:5—ways to serve

LESSON OUTLINE

I. GIFTS OF THE HOLY SPIRIT

  A. Knowledge of Spiritual Gifts

  B. Individual Spiritual Gifts

  C. Source of Spiritual Gifts

II. UNITED IN MINISTRY

  A. Unity in Diversity

  B. Value in Diversity

  C. Ministry With Diversity

III. PREEMINENCE OF LOVE

  A. Requirement of Love

  B. Definition of Love

  C. Continuation of Love

LESSON EXPOSITION

INTRODUCTION

Which chapters of the Bible are most significant to the operation of the local church?

John 3 speaks of the means of our salvation. Acts 2 describes the dramatic coming of the Holy Spirit to the believers in Jerusalem, just like Jesus promised. Not to be forgotten are chapters like Romans 12 and 1 Thessalonians 5 with their listings of the believers' duties. However, no two chapters have greater importance than 1 Corinthians 12 and 13. These chapters explore the attitudes, actions and abilities that are necessary for a church to truly function as Christ's church.

Our initial consideration is spiritual gifts, which are different than natural gifts. Many individuals perceive all their abilities to be spiritual gifts due to God's being the Creator of everyone. While we must recognize God's role in our total being, it is equally important to see the distinct means of His involvement.

Natural gifts are those we inherit from our gene pool. Because of our family genes, there are some abilities which come naturally or which we have the ability to develop. For example, some individuals can play instruments "by ear" without ever having any musical training. Others take lessons, and they too become skilled musicians. In contrast are those who will never make a musician or artist regardless of how many lessons they take.

Some individuals are natural athletes or have the ability to be trained in a certain sport. Their hand and eye coordination suits them for the task. In marked contrast are those who have difficulty "chewing gum and walking at the same time."

Spiritual gifts are endowments God gives us through the Holy Spirit. Supernaturally we are given an ability to do something that was not possible previously. It's not just an improvement in a skill already possessed. It is a new ability by which an individual can serve within the body of Christ. The empowerment never comes for the sake of personal glory but always for the glorification of Christ and His kingdom.

Yet an abundance of spiritual gifts in a congregation is not sufficient for its successful operation. Paul follows his teaching on spiritual gifts by speaking of the need for unity. Though members of the body have varied positions and abilities, no one should be considered of little or more importance. Everyone fulfills a vital function. No one is expendable.

Paul then moves to the topic of love. Love provides the atmosphere and stimulus for spiritual gifts and the unity of the body. Without love our words and actions are nothing more than meaningless activities.

In this study, focus on the relationship between spiritual gifts, unity and love. It is so easy to see them independently rather than as a total package required for the efficient ministry of the church.

I. GIFTS OF THE HOLY SPIRIT
(1 Corinthians 12:1-11)

A. Knowledge of Spiritual Gifts (vv. 1-6)

(1 Corinthians 12:1-3 is not included in the printed text.)

4. Now there are diversities of gifts, but the same Spirit.

5. And there are differences of administrations, but the same Lord.

6. And there are diversities of operations, but it is the same God which worketh all in all.

In verse 1 Paul addressed the Corinthians personally as his brothers and said he desired for them to be knowledgeable rather than ignorant. This reminds us how important it is to know the truth about how the Trinity in the various Persons—Father, Son and Holy Spirit—shape and influence our lives.

It can be easy to incorporate false concepts into one's spiritual life. This may result from attempting to base ideas on one's own imagination or faulty reasoning, shaped by secular influences such as non-Christian media or education. In verse 2 Paul reminded the Corinthians of their past steeped in paganism. Then they were led astray by images which could not even speak. Such ignorance never should be evident among the followers of Christ.

Paul's statement that no one speaking by the Holy Spirit says "Jesus be cursed" (v. 3, *NIV*) offers some interpretation difficulty. There are various views. It could refer to Christians who had been brought to trial for their faith and under persecution had renounced their faith. However, this doesn't seem too likely since persecution is not the topic of this passage.

More likely is that someone, in an ecstatic experience of unbridled emotionalism, had uttered a curse on Christ. If so, then the question arises whether or not everything spoken in the Spirit is good. Paul strongly declares that when the Holy Spirit speaks, He presents "Jesus as Lord" (see v. 3). What a contrast to pagan society in which emperor worship caused people to proclaim, "Caesar is Lord"! Also, what a contrast to the Jews who failed to see Jesus as the promised Messiah.

Here we need to be reminded of the need to test the spirits. If anyone speaks through the Holy Spirit, then Christ will be glorified. In John 16:14, Jesus said the Holy Spirit "will bring glory to me by taking from what is mine and making it known to you" (*NIV*). Any words or actions that do not bring honor to God are not of the Holy Spirit and need to be recognized as in error.

Having covered a negative situation, Paul moved to a positive presentation on spiritual gifts. He said there are a variety of spiritual gifts, but all of them operate through the empowerment of the Holy Spirit. The spiritual gifts are diverse from each other both in operation and impact, but their common source is God alone.

These verses present a clear challenge to each of us—especially if we claim to be baptized in the Holy Spirit. Are we as knowledgeable about the Spirit's working as we should be? Are we knowledgeable about the individual gifts of the Spirit and what each one accomplishes? Finally, are spiritual gifts evident in our lives?

B. Individual Spiritual Gifts (vv. 7-10)

7. But the manifestation of the Spirit is given to every man to profit withal.

8. For to one is given by the Spirit the word of wisdom; to another the word of knowledge by the same Spirit;

9. To another faith by the same Spirit; to another the gifts of healing by the same Spirit;

10. To another the working of miracles; to another prophecy; to another discerning of spirits; to another divers kinds of tongues; to another the interpretation of tongues.

Spiritual gifts are not limited to a select few. Through the indwelling of the Holy Spirit each believer receives a manifestation or gift. This quickly destroys the misconception that gifts of the Spirit are signs of superspirituality or special spiritual attainment. They are neither status symbols nor rewards! Gifts are the means by which believers can edify each other and further the kingdom of God. For that reason care needs to be taken that we do not become sidetracked by envying the gifts others receive.

Beginning with verse 8, Paul lists nine spiritual gifts. But there are many more than nine, as seen in a study of Romans 12:6-8; 1 Corinthians 12:28-30; Ephesians 4:11. However, even more important than the number is understanding the distinctiveness of each of the gifts.

The nine gifts listed here can be divided into three groups of three. *Wisdom, knowledge* and *discernment* are gifts of revelation. *Faith, miracles* and *healing* may be seen as gifts of power. Finally, *prophecy, tongues* and *interpretation* are gifts of inspiration.

Word of wisdom. This wisdom is not that which we acquire over the years through a variety of experiences. The word of wisdom operates by God

imparting divine intelligence which enables a person to have insight to a situation. This allows the gifted individual the ability to provide practical advice to another believer. Or, in some cases it could be the means by which an opponent is silenced.

Word of knowledge. Unlike the gift of wisdom, the word of knowledge has to do with specific facts or information. This gift enables a person to know something he or she could not know by normal means. An example of this is when Peter knew of the deception being attempted by Ananias and Sapphira (Acts 5).

Gift of faith. There is a difference between faith that brings salvation and the gift of faith. The gift can best be described as a mountain-moving faith. In his book *The Holy Spirit in Today's World,* W.A. Criswell described it as the power "to lay hold on God's promise for results beyond our own ability to achieve." This gift arises when an individual or even a church needs a supernatural intervention of God's power.

Gifts of healing. Due to its spectacular nature, many individuals desire this gift. It is listed in the plural because many forms of healing are required to minister to the whole person. Through this gift, divine healing of injuries, ills and diseases occurs apart from human skills or natural means. However, the presence of this gift never guarantees an automatic healing for every person.

Gift of miracles. Healing can be miraculous, but this gift includes miracles of all types. None of the actions produced through this gift could be produced by natural means. Examples include casting out evil spirits (Acts 8:7) and raising the dead (9:40).

Gift of prophecy. One of the great misconceptions concerning this gift is seeing it only as speaking of the future. The gift of prophecy is the means by which the whole counsel of God can be proclaimed. It can be predictive by the foretelling of the future. Or it can be proclamative by the forthtelling of God's Word (that which has already been stated in the Scriptures but needs emphasizing). Prophecy does not replace preaching or teaching. Its purpose consists of supplementing or reinforcing, and it always edifies.

Gift of discernment. This gift must not be confused with acquired skills that enable a person to understand or even predict human behavior. Through this gift, individual believers and the church as a whole can discern the source of an utterance or action. It unmasks the Enemy who would come to deceive through false prophets and false teachers. This gift does not allow us the luxury of not thinking, studying or applying the Word of God ourselves. The gift of discernment serves as a protection in situations that could cause considerable harm.

Gift of tongues. Through this gift, God speaks through an individual in a language or languages not known to the speaker. It necessitates interpretation into the vernacular for the people to hear the message of the Lord. The gift of tongues is not the same as the initial evidence of the Baptism or speaking in a prayer language. This gift serves to edify the entire body rather than one individual.

Gift of interpretation. This gift can be seen as a sister gift to the gift of tongues, for it has no function without the presence of tongues. It is the ability to interpret the meaning of a message given in an unknown tongue. It does not operate as a commentary on the message or as a word-for-word translation. The latter would not allow for a flowing language pattern in the vernacular of the congregation. Instead it states the content in an accurate translation.

C. Source of Spiritual Gifts (v. 11)

11. But all these worketh that one and the selfsame Spirit, dividing to every man severally as he will.

Verse 11 stands as a bottom-line statement. All of the gifts flow outward from a single source, the Holy Spirit. He distributes them according to His will. No one should be dissatisfied with his or her giftedness, since each gift is sovereignly provided. God knows what is best for us as individuals and for the edification of the church. Charles Conn wrote, "There is never any justification for an individual to claim that he possesses any particular gift, meaning, 'This belongs to me. God gave it to me and it is mine.' No, God retains the power of the gifts and manifests them through individuals as He will" (*A Balanced Church*).

II. UNITED IN MINISTRY
   (1 Corinthians 12:12-28)

A. Unity in Diversity (vv. 12-20)

   (1 Corinthians 12:13-17 is not included in the printed text.)

12. For as the body is one, and hath many members, and all the members of that one body, being many, are one body: so also is Christ.

18. But now hath God set the members every one of them in the body, as it hath pleased him.

19. And if they were all one member, where were the body?

20. But now are they many members, yet but one body.

In logical progression Paul moves to the topic of unity within the context of diversity. The need for various spiritual gifts and ministries in the body of Christ is just as necessary as the many parts of the human body. Only with the presence of all the functioning parts can the body truly be whole and operate appropriately. The church consists of many different people whose common denominator is their salvation and baptism in Christ. Even though they represent different nationalities and social status, in Christ all have a common unity and position of equality.

To demonstrate the need for unity in diversity while emphasizing the value of each member, Paul offers some absurd possibilities. What if the foot or ear would become dissatisfied by not being a seemingly more important member and declare itself separate from the body? Could it secede? Absolutely not! Regardless of its declaration, the physical unity would continue. Without such unity, the body would cease to function.

Next Paul asks what would happen if the whole body were an eye or ear. All of the other necessary aspects of the body would be absent. In the same way if all believers had the same spiritual gift, the church would lack all of the other necessary elements. The one strength would quickly be seen as a weakness, for the body would cease to exist.

With these absurdities as a framework, Paul reminded the Corinthians that just as God has designed the various parts of the human body, so has He designed the church. The diversity within the body enables it to be and to accomplish what God intends. Through the Holy Spirit, all of the different parts work in harmony as one body.

Diversity offers strength and possibilities of accomplishment that otherwise would be impossible. The beauty of sound an orchestra produces comes from the variety of instruments with their particular ranges of pitch and tone. As a group of musicians follows the musical score and the direction of the conductor, a harmonious blend fills the air.

B. Value in Diversity (vv. 21-27)

(1 Corinthians 12:21-26 is not included in the printed text.)

27. Now ye are the body of Christ, and members in particular.
Just as the eye cannot do without the hand and the head cannot operate without the feet, so should the church not devalue or reject any of its members and gifts. The body of Christ needs every individual and every gift.

Paul notes how certain parts of the body are necessary but out of modesty are covered when in public. Other parts are of equal value but due to their specific use and nature are not covered. And some parts of the body that appear weaker actually have tremendous value. For example, most of us take our thumbs and big toes for granted. However, sprain them or have one operated on and their role quickly comes to the forefront. This can be seen by the practices of ancient Oriental kings. Wanting to have human trophies of their conquests, victorious kings would cut off the big toes and thumbs of defeated kings. Unable to grip a sword or spear, they were of no danger. Unable to run, they could not escape.

The nature of the human body causes the whole body to feel the pain or discomfort of one member. Harm to even a smaller, weaker member can incapacitate the entire body. Just stub your toe and that reality quickly comes to mind. In the same way, when one member of the body of Christ suffers, then all should share in the pain. Likewise, when one member is exalted, all are to share in that joy. Within the body, diversity should result in equal value for all members. Regardless of strength, public presentation, or specific operation, each member serves a vital role.

C. Ministry With Diversity (v. 28)

28. And God hath set some in the church, first apostles, secondarily

prophets, thirdly teachers, after that miracles, then gifts of healings, helps, governments, diversities of tongues.

Continuing the thought of verse 27, Paul lists some examples of positions and giftedness which demonstrate the diversity of ministry within the body. He numbers the first three positions—apostles, prophets and teachers. In Ephesians 4:11, he also includes evangelists and pastors. Following the first three positions of 1 Corinthians 12:28 is a listing of five spiritual gifts.

An important principle is that ministry can be accomplished when holding a distinct office such as apostle or prophet or without holding a particular office. All gifted believers operate through the empowering of the Holy Spirit. This demonstrates the value of each person as they minister within the scope of their God-ordained setting. No believer should emphasize "me" or "I." Instead, everyone should speak in terms of "us" and "we." No one possesses greater value by virtue of their position or gift. All are needed for the church to operate in the manner Christ intended.

III. PREEMINENCE OF LOVE
    (1 Corinthians 13:1-13)

A. Requirement of Love (vv. 1-3)

(1 Corinthians 13:1-3 is not included in the printed text.)

Knowing the value that the Corinthians placed on spiritual gifts, Paul brought them face-to-face with a spiritual virtue that transcends all positions and gifts. It's the virtue of love. When writing to the Galatians concerning walking in the Spirit, Paul listed love as the first of the virtues of the Holy Spirit's fruit (5:22).

In verse 1 of the text, Paul used an example involving tongues. To exercise this gift without possessing a love that reaches out to others demotes the action to little more than an empty

pagan rite. The gong or cymbal seems to be a reference to pagan temples. Kenneth Chafin wrote, "In many of the temples there was hanging at the entrance a large cymbal. Often, as the would-be worshipers entered the temple, they struck it causing a loud noise. Some said the noise was for the purpose of rousing the gods. By the time Paul wrote this letter, the loud 'gong' which was made from striking the cymbal had become the symbol for superficial oratory" (*The Communicators' Commentary*).

Going further, Paul referred to the operation of four other gifts—*prophecy, wisdom, knowledge* and *faith* (v. 2). These can be seen as even more important spiritual gifts than tongues; yet, the operation of any one of these without love robs them of any importance. They might as well not exist.

In verse 3, the apostle moves to commendable actions of feeding the poor and suffering for the gospel. Charitable care for the poor at the cost of selling all of one's possessions definitely would be a great act. Sacrificing one's life in fire rather than recanting life in Christ would seem to be the ultimate act of commitment. Yet, neither sacrificial action would bring the Lord's reward unless accompanied with love.

Paul's inclusion of the personal pronoun "I" adds further emphasis to verse 3. Paul suffered much for the cause of Christ, eventually giving up his life. However, such sacrifices even by a man of his position would bring no benefit without the presence of love. That's powerful! There can be no heavenly reward for our religious and generous actions unless they are done with love.

B. Definition of Love (vv. 4-7)

4. Charity suffereth long, and is kind; charity envieth not; charity vaunteth not itself, is not puffed up,

5. Doth not behave itself unseemly, seeketh not her own, is not easily provoked, thinketh no evil;
6. Rejoiceth not in iniquity, but rejoiceth in the truth;
7. Beareth all things, believeth all things, hopeth all things, endureth all things.

Have a varied group of individuals give a definition of *love*. More than likely you will hear words of emotion and feeling. Though we know that love entails so much more, there is a tendency to project feelings and emotions over attitudes and actions. Human nature has not changed, as can be seen by Paul's careful, detailed approach in defining love. He wanted the Corinthians to have a complete view of what it means to love. To accomplish this goal, he used a string of short statements to explain love.

Love is patient even in the face of improper treatment.

Love is kind, causing a person to actively seek the good of others.

Love envies not—doesn't begrudge or become jealous of others' possessions or blessings.

Love does not boast, refusing to parade oneself or demand the attention of others.

Love is not puffed up, disallowing pride in self, possessions or accomplishments to create an inflated view of self.

Love doesn't behave itself unseemly, keeping us from rude, unpolite behavior regardless of how others may be attempting to provoke us.

Love is not self-seeking; instead, it looks to be of service to others.

Love is not easily provoked—doesn't become easily angered.

Love never keeps a record of wrongs no matter the number or the wrongdoer.

Love doesn't delight in evil—in contrast, it rejoices in those items of truth.

Verse 7 lists four aspects which are absolutes of love: Love *protects*, *trusts*, *hopes* and *perseveres* (*NIV*).

Such love is not of human origin. Only the Holy Spirit can impart divine love into our lives.

C. Continuation of Love (vv. 8-13)

(1 Corinthians 13:9-12 is not included in the printed text.)

8. Charity never faileth: but whether there be prophecies, they shall fail; whether there be tongues, they shall cease; whether there be knowledge, it shall vanish away.
13. And now abideth faith, hope, charity, these three; but the greatest of these is charity.

Love never disappears, love is always present, love works. Though some of the charismatic gifts may be silenced or become inoperative, love will continue. Even in situations of the imperfect and immature, love continues. How is this possible? The answer is simple: God *is* love.

As we grow and mature as God's children, godly love develops and flows outward. But love doesn't just happen. It becomes our obligation to cultivate each of the attitudes in partnership with the Holy Spirit.

GOLDEN TEXT HOMILY

"LET ALL THINGS BE DONE UNTO EDIFYING" (1 Corinthians 14:26).

Individual trees in a forest compete for sunlight, water and nutrients. They seek to outgrow each other to reach the sunlight necessary for their development.

People are similar. We selfishly focus on our own needs and wants often to the hurt of others. Lying, cheating, deception, stealing and fighting are just a few of the actions of the self-serving person.

The Old Testament compares the human heart to a stone. It is cold, hard and lacks compassion. Tears will not soften a stony heart, neither does pleading nor reasoning. There are many who feel nothing for the plight of others.

Now think again about trees. Researchers have discovered a unique fungus, when found growing among the roots in some forests, that will completely transform the natural order. Trees linked together by this fungus no longer compete but become a community. Nutrients needed are passed from tree to tree.

Similarly, something radical occurs when a person meets God. God's Holy Spirit transforms the selfish heart into one with warmth and consideration for others. Instead of viewing others as obstacles or competition, the born-again man or woman is filled with love and concern for them.

Building up each other is one of the foremost characteristics of the Christian. It is the sign that God is in our heart.—**Bill Helmstetter**

SENTENCE SERMONS

WHEN CHRIST'S LOVE rules our lives, we minister in unity.

—Selected

THE LOVE THAT UNITES Christians is stronger than the differences that divide them.

—Speaker's Sourcebook

THE MECHANICS OF MAN plus the dynamics of the Holy Spirit make a good combination.

—Milburn Miller

LOVE NEVER ASKS how much must I do, but how much can I do.

—Frederick Agar

EVANGELISM APPLICATION

GIFTS OF THE SPIRIT EXERCISED IN CHRISTIAN LOVE AND UNITY MAKE THE CHURCH ATTRACTIVE TO PEOPLE DESIRING SPIRITUAL HELP.

When speaking of spiritual gifts we usually associate them with edification of the believers. Rarely do we think of them as means of drawing unbelievers into the fellowship of Christ and the church. Why is that? Have we forgotten or overlooked the desire that many have to encounter the supernatural?

Spiritual gifts are evidence of the supernatural working through us by means of the Holy Spirit. When we exhibit the love of Christ and demonstrate the gifts of the Spirit, unbelievers searching for inner fulfillment will look to our churches.

ILLUMINATING THE LESSON

The diversity and abilities of the parts of the human body should continually remind us that we are fearfully and wonderfully made. Look at your hand. Of the 600 muscles in your body, 70 of them are in the hand. Working together, they enable a dexterity that is phenomenal. As they cooperate, you are able to pick up a button from the floor, type on a keyboard, turn a nut on a bolt, or handle your eating utensils.

DAILY BIBLE READINGS

M. Gifted Artisans.
   Exodus 31:1-11
T. Gifted Counselors.
   Numbers 11:16, 17, 24, 25
W. Gifted King.
   2 Samuel 23:1-5
T. Gifted Deacons.
   Acts 6:1-7
F. Gifted Ministries.
   Romans 12:4-8
S. Gifted Servants.
   1 Peter 4:7-11

TRUTH SEARCH
Creatively Teaching the Word

DISCUSSION QUESTIONS

1 Corinthians 12:1-11

1. Regarding spiritual gifts, what are we not to be (v. 1)? Why?

2. What was the spiritual background of the Corinthian Christians (v. 2)? How had they been enabled to confess Jesus as Lord (v. 3)?

3. Why does Paul sound so redundant in verses 3-6? What is his point?

4. What is the purpose of spiritual gifts (v. 7)?

5. List the gifts recorded in verses 8-10. Who decides who gets what gift (v. 11)?

1 Corinthians 12:12-28

1. How do people become part of the body of Christ (vv. 12-14)?

2. Why is the word *body* an accurate description of the church?

3. What is the danger if some members of the body feel less important than others, or if some feel more important than others (vv. 15-21)?

4. How does God view the various gifts He has placed in the church, and why (vv. 24, 25)?

5. How should the people of God minister to each other (vv. 26, 27)?

6. Why did God place so many different gifts in the church (vv. 28-30)?

7. What are the "best gifts," and what is the "more excellent way" (v. 31)?

1 Corinthians 13:1-13

1. What good is it to be gifted but fail to minister in love (vv. 1-3)?

2. What are the actions of love (vv. 4-7)?

3. Why is love more important than spiritual gifts and greater than hope and faith (vv. 8, 9, 13)?

4. What awaits the body of Christ (vv. 10-12)?

OBJECT LESSON

Items needed: Computer mouse, keyboard, cable or a notebook computer

Do we have any computer nerds here today? Are there any people here who do not like computers?

Display the computer parts or the notebook computer.

A computer has many parts. Besides the obvious ones—such as the keyboard, the mouse, the monitor and the cable—there are microchips and processors we usually do not see. There are many kinds of parts with all kinds of functions. This computer could not function with just one part, nor could it function properly if a single piece were missing.

This computer is like the body of Christ. There are different gifts in the church, and each one is necessary for the functioning of the whole.

Also, just as the computer has an operating system to make it function properly, so is there an operating system that enables the church to work in unity and power.

Ministry Principles

Study Text: 2 Corinthians 3:1 through 5:21
Objective: To learn and apply Biblical principles for Christian ministry.
Time: A.D. 57
Place: Written from Macedonia
Golden Text: "Not that we are sufficient of ourselves to think any thing as of ourselves; but our sufficiency is of God" (2 Corinthians 3:5).
Central Truth: For effective Christian ministry, we must depend on the power of God's Spirit.
Evangelism Emphasis: Successful evangelism is the result of God working through us.

PRINTED TEXT

2 Corinthians 3:5. Not that we are sufficient of ourselves to think any thing as of ourselves; but our sufficiency is of God;

6. Who also hath made us able ministers of the new testament; not of the letter, but of the spirit: for the letter killeth, but the spirit giveth life.

7. But if the ministration of death, written and engraven in stones, was glorious, so that the children of Israel could not stedfastly behold the face of Moses for the glory of his countenance; which glory was to be done away:

8. How shall not the ministration of the spirit be rather glorious?

17. Now the Lord is that Spirit: and where the Spirit of the Lord is, there is liberty.

18. But we all, with open face beholding as in a glass the glory of the Lord, are changed into the same image from glory to glory, even as by the Spirit of the Lord.

4:1. Therefore seeing we have this ministry, as we have received mercy, we faint not;

2. But have renounced the hidden things of dishonesty, not walking in craftiness, nor handling the word of God deceitfully; but by manifestation of the truth commending ourselves to every man's conscience in the sight of God.

5. For we preach not ourselves, but Christ Jesus the Lord; and ourselves your servants for Jesus' sake.

7. But we have this treasure in earthen vessels, that the excellency of the power may be of God, and not of us.

15. For all things are for your sakes, that the abundant grace might through the thanksgiving of many redound to the glory of God.

16. For which cause we faint not; but though our outward man perish, yet the inward man is renewed day by day.

5:14. For the love of Christ constraineth us; because we thus judge, that if one died for all, then were all dead:

15. And that he died for all, that they which live should not henceforth live unto themselves, but unto him which died for them, and rose again.

18. And all things are of God, who hath reconciled us to himself by Jesus Christ, and hath given to us the ministry of reconciliation;

19. To wit, that God was in Christ, reconciling the world unto himself, not imputing their trespasses unto them; and hath committed unto us the word of reconciliation.

DICTIONARY

ministration—2 Corinthians 3:7, 8—ministry

constraineth—2 Corinthians 5:14—Holds or confines to one object. Christ's love was the constraining force that compelled Paul to preach the gospel.

LESSON OUTLINE

I. SUFFICIENCY

  A. Competence From God

  B. Ministry in the Spirit

II. PERSEVERANCE

  A. Courage in Ministry

  B. Strength in Weakness

  C. Renewal in Dying

III. RECONCILIATION

  A. Source of Reconciliation

  B. Ministry of Reconciliation

LESSON EXPOSITION

INTRODUCTION

What comes to mind when you hear someone speak of "being in the ministry"? Or, if you have ever heard it said, "we're all ministers," what does that mean?

In more traditional churches, "being in the ministry" usually speaks of the role for clergy. It paints the picture of an ordained minister holding a church position. Associated with it is the spouse of this person. This phrase, in the near historical past, never included anyone categorized as laity.

In stark contrast, the common phrase "we're all ministers" seems to disregard any sense of qualification or activity. By virtue of being a member of the body of Christ, each person can be called a minister. Initially this should be seen in the positive, since no one is overlooked or exempted from ministering. However, it can be negative when people assume that their relationship as a believer automatically provides this action title.

Here is a good place to consider three terms commonly used in the church—*laity, clergy* and *minister*. In the Greek language, *laity* means "people." It carries no sense of being secondary or of lesser value and ability within the kingdom of God. No one should ever say, "I'm *just* a layperson," for within the church, *laity* means "the people of God."

Clergy comes from a Greek word meaning "lot" or "inheritance." It does not imply an upper level of importance or higher distinction. By definition *clergy* indicates being given a certain task or position to fill. Knowing the specific meanings of *laity* and *clergy* should enable us to see there is no gulf from dividing these groups of believers.

Minister can be translated as "servant" or "deacon." *Ministry* means "service" or "mission." This contains some important implications. A minister is someone who is actively serving and helping others. Remember, in the New Testament church the deacons helped the widows and served others in need.

As you study the lesson, remember that Paul wrote under the inspiration of the Holy Spirit, and not about unproven theories. Paul lived the ministry principles he wrote about.

I. SUFFICIENCY

    (2 Corinthians 3:5-8, 17, 18)

A. Competence From God (vv. 5, 6)

5. Not that we are sufficient of ourselves to think any thing as of ourselves; but our sufficiency is of God;

6. Who also hath made us able ministers of the new testament;

not of the letter, but of the spirit: for the letter killeth, but the spirit giveth life.

Apparently some individuals had come to Corinth and seriously questioned and criticized Paul's ministry. Carrying impressive letters of recommendation from someone in Jerusalem, these critics had quickly integrated themselves into the church. They even asked the Corinthians if Paul had brought letters of introduction when coming to their city, the implication being that a person without credentials could not be trusted or was a fake. How ridiculous! When Paul arrived in Corinth there was no Christian church. Through his ministry, individuals came to Christ and a church arose within a pagan city. What greater recommendation than that could possibly be needed!

With this as the context, Paul chose to maintain a humble posture rather than boast in personal abilities. He knew his inability to change the heart of any person. For that reason he knew better than to claim competence in himself. Does that mean he lacked confidence in his own skills? No! But he recognized that only through the sufficiency of God's grace could his efforts produce spiritual fruit.

In verse 6 Paul referred to the day when God miraculously stopped him on the road to Damascus and changed him spiritually (Acts 9). Where once he lived dominated by the law of the Old Testament (previous covenant), now he lived and ministered the new covenant of Christ. This change came not from his own merit but through God's grace. The sufficiency of genuine, fruitful ministry stems from the Holy Spirit's renewal and continued work in one's life.

When Paul says "the letter killeth," it is not a condemnation of the Old Testament law. The Law served God's purpose for a certain time. Paul is speaking of how a self-righteous, slavish adherence to every detail of the Law becomes a cloak of hypocrisy. In marked contrast is life in the Spirit. The Holy Spirit lives and works within. His grace works from the inside out, providing a freshness of life instead of dead conformity. In Romans 7:6, Paul writes, "But now, by dying to what once bound us, we have been released from the law so that we serve in the new way of the Spirit, and not in the old way of the written code" (*NIV*).

B. Ministry in the Spirit
   (vv. 7, 8, 17, 18)

7. But if the ministration of death, written and engraven in stones, was glorious, so that the children of Israel could not stedfastly behold the face of Moses for the glory of his countenance; which glory was to be done away:

8. How shall not the ministration of the spirit be rather glorious?

17. Now the Lord is that Spirit: and where the Spirit of the Lord is, there is liberty.

18. But we all, with open face beholding as in a glass the glory of the Lord, are changed into the same image from glory to glory, even as by the Spirit of the Lord.

In verses 7 and 8 Paul continues the comparison between the previous covenant and the new covenant. Moses stands as the representative of that first covenant. His reception of the tablets of stone from God was a glorious moment in Israel's history. Moses' encounter with God produced a physical radiance resulting from the brightness of God's glory.

"When Moses came down from Mount Sinai with the two tablets of the Testimony in his hands, he was not aware that his face was radiant because he had spoken with the Lord.

When Aaron and all the Israelites saw Moses, his face was radiant, and they were afraid to come near him" (Exodus 34:29, 30, *NIV*). As a result, "When Moses finished speaking to them, he put a veil over his face" (v. 33, *NIV*).

In 2 Corinthians 3:13-15, Paul equated the veil Moses wore to the veil of dullness that remained on those who clung to the old covenant. Thus they continued to be shielded from an even greater glory of God. What a sad spiritual state when they could have been experiencing the glory of God to a greater extent than that which Moses saw. Through Jesus Christ and the Holy Spirit's imputing of righteousness which replaces sin, all believers are partakers of God's glorious revelation of the new covenant.

Verse 17 stands as a point of contrast. Through the Spirit of the Lord in our hearts there is freedom rather than the darkness of bondage. But it doesn't stop there. The Spirit continues to work in us. Through His empowerment we are able to grow into the image of Christ (v. 18). This is the process of sanctification—a striving for holiness. And as this occurs in each of our lives, a greater dimension of God's glory is revealed. Salvation and the process of Christian maturity take away the veil of darkness and releases the rays of God's glory.

II. PERSEVERANCE
(2 Corinthians 4:1-9, 15, 16)

A. Courage in Ministry (vv. 1-6)

(2 Corinthians 4:3, 4, 6 is not included in the printed text.)

1. Therefore seeing we have this ministry, as we have received mercy, we faint not;
2. But have renounced the hidden things of dishonesty, not walking in craftiness, nor handling the word of God deceitfully; but by manifestation of the truth commending ourselves to every man's conscience in the sight of God.

5. For we preach not ourselves, but Christ Jesus the Lord; and ourselves your servants for Jesus' sake.

Ministering the gospel of the Lord Jesus Christ through words and actions during good times is enjoyable. But then there are those difficult times. The gospel continues to be glorious, but human limitations and discouragement can take its toll. So how can believers continue in the face of varied forms of opposition? Paul addressed this matter in verse 1, saying we can persevere since it is God who has called us and through His mercy given us the gospel. As partakers of this glorious truth, we can continue without succumbing to weaknesses or discouragement.

Beginning in verse 2, Paul wrote about his own ministerial conduct. As a result of conversion and a continued commitment to Christ, he had *renounced*, or "disowned," evil actions others were following. Neither was he using trickery nor distortion to convince people to accept his message. In marked contrast to impostors claiming to be apostles, Paul spoke the truth of Christ plainly. There were no hidden agendas or ideas that would surface later. With boldness he openly proclaimed the truth. No one could ever accuse him of emptying the gospel so that it was nothing more than another vain religion.

In verses 3 and 4 Paul dealt with the reason for people's not accepting the gospel even when given an authentic presentation. The prince of this world, Satan, does his best to keep a veil of blindness over people's spiritual eyes even when the gospel comes in clarity and power. This veil evidences itself in various forms, such as human reason, which suggests the gospel account could not be true. For others the veil is an attitude of self-sufficiency, while selfish pleasure blinds others.

No matter the response, the true apostle never preaches his own devised gospel. Paul declared, "We do not preach ourselves, but Jesus Christ as Lord" (v. 5, *NIV*). Even though Paul was the messenger, there would not be any exaltation of self. He was a servant to those receiving the ministry of the gospel.

Verse 6 further demonstrates why there can be no room for projection of self in ministry. We are nothing but for the message. The message of light comes from God. In Creation He called light into existence in the presence of darkness. Through Jesus Christ the light of salvation pierces the darkness of sin. No wonder we should be courageous in ministry. Our life-changing message comes from God himself.

B. Strength in Weakness (vv. 7-9)

(2 Corinthians 4:8, 9 is not included in the printed text.)

7. But we have this treasure in earthen vessels, that the excellency of the power may be of God, and not of us.

Along with Romans 8:31-39, these verses show the strength and perseverance which the believer can experience in the face of adversity.

The frailty of the human body and the pressures of the surrounding world would seem to guarantee destruction. However, Paul described a different result. He compared the human body with common, inexpensive pottery lamps. Though weak, the body holds a treasure—salvation through the empowering of the Holy Spirit, and the good news of this salvation.

Placing valued treasures in nearly valueless containers apparently was a common practice. Plutarch, the Greek biographer who lived in the second century A.D., records how the Romans transported a huge shipment of silver coins in 750 earthen vessels after their Macedonian victory in 167 B.C. What a tremendous difference between the value of the container and its content! The same continues to be true of each of us as believers.

In spite of our weakness, through the power of God residing within we can withstand. Verses 8 and 9 describe difficulties through which we can survive victoriously. Hostile forces or situations may press hard upon us without our being crushed. Though perplexed and without understanding the "why" or "how" of our problems, we do not fall into despair. Even when the forces of evil unleash painful persecution, we can know God is still there. When we are thrown to the ground in seeming defeat, destruction does not have its way.

Paul could speak with so much assurance because of his personal experience. In chapter 11 we read of the sufferings he incurred for the sake of Christ, yet he came through boasting in the power of God (vv. 21-33). Paul's example reminds us that in ourselves we are weak. But when we are filled with the treasure of salvation and the empowering of the Holy Spirit, we stand victorious even in death!

C. Renewal in Dying (vv. 15, 16)

15. For all things are for your sakes, that the abundant grace might through the thanksgiving of many redound to the glory of God.

16. For which cause we faint not; but though our outward man perish, yet the inward man is renewed day by day.

No matter how much we may want to avoid the subject, death is a constant reality. From the day we were born, each of us has been on a path toward death. That is the reality for each of our human bodies.

The truth we must never forget is the provision for our bodily resurrection. "The one who raised the Lord

Jesus from the dead will also raise us with Jesus" (v. 14, *NIV*). What a hope! God's grace provides this benefit for all. It needs to be a truth for which we continually give thanks. Our lives will span far beyond the shortness of human life. We will live forever in our resurrected bodies.

This promise enables us to be strong rather than fainthearted in the middle of overwhelming struggles. Even when disease strikes or aging takes its toll and our body appears to be shrinking, our inner being remains strong. In fact, we can be growing spiritually while the physical process of dying continues until all life is gone. That is a marvelous paradox—increasing spiritually while decreasing physically.

Paul suffered for the gospel's sake, bringing glory to God and drawing people to Christ. He did not *faint* ("lose heart"); instead, God's grace enabled him to endure and accomplish far more than he could have possibly imagined. He ran the race triumphantly even though tragedy, illness and death attempted to stop him.

III. RECONCILIATION
(2 Corinthians 5:14, 15, 18, 19)

A. Source of Reconciliation
(vv. 14, 15)

14. For the love of Christ constraineth us; because we thus judge, that if one died for all, then were all dead:

15. And that he died for all, that they which live should not henceforth live unto themselves, but unto him which died for them, and rose again.

What drives men and women to sacrificially spread the gospel of Christ? What causes them to leave their comfort zones and enter unknown areas of ridicule, separation and hardship? There can be no other motive than their personal relation-

ship with Jesus. Paul spoke of the love of Christ constraining him—"For Christ's love compels us" (v. 14, *NIV*).

In verse 11, Paul initiated the subject of reconciliation in terms of persuading people to come to Christ. Coming to Christ includes much more than accepting Him as a good teacher whose message has some value for personal living. Paul preached so people would accept Jesus as Savior and Lord and experience the restoration of spiritual fellowship.

Paul's passion for Christ may have caused some to think he was not in his right mind (v. 13). They might have even suggested his Damascus-road experience was nothing more than a hallucination. Such detractors failed to understand what it is to grasp the love of Christ.

Paul recognized the tremendous love of God for all humankind. Because of love, God sent His Son, Jesus, to become the sacrifice for the sins of all humans. Love kept Jesus on the cross through the gruesome act of crucifixion.

Paul's writing that "all died" (v. 14, *NIV*) refers to Adam's sin and the resulting spiritual death of the human race. "Just as sin entered the world through one man, and death through sin, and in this way death came to all men, because all sinned" (Romans 5:12, *NIV*). It's a hopeless situation but for Christ. Where Adam's action brought death, Christ's death brings life.

There is a new motivation and life direction for those who experience the love of God through salvation. Instead of yielding to the old selfish nature which urges living for personal choice, the emphasis now becomes living for Jesus Christ. Christ's resurrection guarantees spiritual life now and eternal life with God in the future. Not only do we believers have this wonderful truth, but we can offer it to others!

B. Ministry of Reconciliation
(vv. 18, 19)

18. And all things are of God, who hath reconciled us to himself by Jesus Christ, and hath given to us the ministry of reconciliation;

19. To wit, that God was in Christ, reconciling the world unto himself, not imputing their trespasses unto them; and hath committed unto us the word of reconciliation.

These two verses put the entire lesson into perspective. If we are going to minister to others, we must depend on a competency that comes through God's empowerment. We also must recognize the need for perseverance in the task.

Because of salvation, each one of us stands as a newborn creation. No longer does a gulf of guilt and sin separate us from God. It is just as though we had never sinned and been alienated from our Creator. As a result of this marvelous transformation, we have new positions as ministers of reconciliation. In other words, we are to be witnesses to the world.

To fulfill a ministry of reconciliation we must have something concrete to offer. And we do! It's the Biblical account of Jesus. Here's the basic outline:

* Jesus Christ is the divine Son of God.
* Jesus Christ came to earth in human flesh.
* Jesus Christ died on the cross of Calvary.
* Jesus Christ was buried in a tomb.
* Jesus Christ was miraculously raised from the dead.
* Jesus Christ ascended into heaven.
* Jesus Christ will come again to take His children to heaven.

That's the formal outline. But the personal message looks like this:

* Jesus loves you so much that He died for you.
* His blood can cover your sins and remove all guilt.
* He offers life everlasting.
* He brings peace and comfort.
* Will you accept Him as your Savior and Lord?

GOLDEN TEXT HOMILY

"NOT THAT WE ARE SUFFICIENT OF OURSELVES TO THINK ANY THING AS OF OURSELVES; BUT OUR SUFFICIENCY IS OF GOD" (2 Corinthians 3:5).

Many times we question if we are fit for ministry. Sometimes others question if we are qualified for ministry. Paul faced this question from the Corinthians. There was a faction in the church who was questioning his authority, his qualifications and even his apostleship. They were asking, "Why should we listen to you?"

Who and *what* qualify us to do ministry? From *where* do we get our credentials? Our qualifications come from God. It is El Shaddai, "the all-sufficient One," who makes us adequate for ministry purposes.

Many Christians try to rely on their own talents and abilities. Paul states that we are not to think so highly of ourselves. We, in ourselves, cannot change a soul—only God can. Peter also warned against relying on our own abilities: "If any man minister, let him do it as of the ability which God giveth" (1 Peter 4:11).

We become personally qualified and competent for ministry when God calls us. He will enable and equip us, by His Holy Spirit, to become effective Christian ministers.

All qualifications come from God. He gives us the ability; we do not have it on our own, nor would we want to do it on our own.—**Greg Baird**

SENTENCE SERMONS

FOR EFFECTIVE CHRISTIAN MINISTRY, we must depend on the power of God's Spirit.

—Selected

GOD LOVES TO SEE in me not His servant, but Himself, who serves all.

—Rabindranath Tagore

A REAL CHRISTIAN never boasts of his service and sacrifice. He enjoys their fruits in silence.

—*Notes and Quotes*

EVEN JESUS CHRIST relied on the enablement of the Holy Spirit.

—Selected

EVANGELISM APPLICATION

SUCCESSFUL EVANGELISM IS THE RESULT OF GOD WORKING THROUGH US.

Methods, patterns and approaches are all important aspects of any evangelism program. But the bottom line remains the same. We are only the instruments presenting the gospel message. However, that doesn't remove responsibility from us. As messengers we must let God work through us.

Just as God's Spirit opens the heart and mind of the hearer to the gospel, so He should be operating through us. Through Him we can have boldness to speak, wisdom as to how to speak, and knowledge when we have said enough. The Holy Spirit enables us to be a means of evangelism rather than a hindrance.

ILLUMINATING THE LESSON

For 18½ years Pastor M.Y. Chan was in prison and assigned to a soil pit (human excrement), filling buckets with waste to be spread as fertilizer. Without protection of any type, he often stood in this filth up to his waist, but never was sick for one day. During this time his parishioners prayed for him and witnessed. His church grew from 300 to 5,000 during his imprisonment.

DAILY BIBLE READINGS

M. Chosen for Ministry.
    Numbers 3:5-9
T. Devoted to Ministry.
    1 Samuel 12:18-25
W. Authority for Ministry.
    Jeremiah 1:4-10
T. Addicted to Ministry.
    1 Corinthians 16:13-18
F. Placed Into Ministry.
    1 Timothy 1:12-17
S. More Excellent Ministry.
    Hebrews 8:1-6

TRUTH SEARCH
Creatively Teaching the Word

BUZZ GROUPS

Items needed: Index cards, pencils

Divide the class into groups of three or four students each. Give each group an index card and pencil, and have them write down their answers to this question: **List five reasons why Christians become discouraged and sometimes give up in ministering to others.**

Next, ask them to turn their cards over and write their answer to this question: **What is the key to persevering in ministry?**

Have the groups report their findings.

DISCUSSION QUESTIONS

Sufficiency
(2 Corinthians 3:1-9, 17, 18)

1. According to verses 1-3, what was the evidence of Paul's success in ministry?

2. What was the secret of Paul's ministry (v. 5)?

3. What made the ministry of Paul different from the religion of the Pharisees (v. 6)?

4. What makes the Holy Spirit's work "more glorious" (vv. 7-9)?

5. Describe the liberty of life and ministry in the Spirit (v. 17).

6. According to verse 18, what is the work of the Spirit in the believer's heart?

Perseverance
(2 Corinthians 4:1-10, 15-17)

1. From verses 1 and 2, list the things Paul did to help him not lose heart.

2. How do verses 3 and 4 describe people who are without Christ? How should believers pray for them?

3. What is the "treasure" in believers' "earthen vessels" (vv. 5-7)?

4. What battles do ministers of the gospel face (vv. 8, 9)?

5. What does God want to manifest in believers' lives (v. 10)?

6. How does the treasure within help believers not to "lose heart" (v. 16, *NIV*)?

7. How could Paul call the persecutions and sufferings he endured "light affliction" (v. 17)?

Reconciliation
(2 Corinthians 5:14-20)

1. What is the proper motive for ministry to others (vv. 14, 15)?

2. What does *reconciliation* mean (vv. 17, 18)?

3. Who has been given the ministry of reconciliation (vv. 18, 19)?

4. In light of what Christ has done for us, why do so many Christians not reach out to unsaved people?

5. What is the message God wants believers to spread (v. 20)?

Christian Authority

Study Text: 2 Corinthians 10:1 through 13:10
Objective: To comprehend the nature and purpose of Christian authority and exercise it accordingly.
Time: A.D. 57
Place: Written from Macedonia
Golden Text: "For the weapons of our warfare are not carnal, but mighty through God to the pulling down of strong holds" (2 Corinthians 10:4).
Central Truth: Christians have God-given authority to minister for Christ.
Evangelism Emphasis: Christ has authorized the church to make the gospel known to all people.

PRINTED TEXT

2 Corinthians 10:3. For though we walk in the flesh, we do not war after the flesh:

4. (For the weapons of our warfare are not carnal, but mighty through God to the pulling down of strong holds;)

5. Casting down imaginations, and every high thing that exalteth itself against the knowledge of God, and bringing into captivity every thought to the obedience of Christ.

17. But he that glorieth, let him glory in the Lord.

18. For not he that commendeth himself is approved, but whom the Lord commendeth.

11:2. For I am jealous over you with godly jealousy: for I have espoused you to one husband, that I may present you as a chaste virgin to Christ.

3. But I fear, lest by any means, as the serpent beguiled Eve through his subtlety, so your minds should be corrupted from the simplicity that is in Christ.

12:14. Behold, the third time I am ready to come to you; and I will not be burdensome to you: for I seek not your's, but you: for the children ought not to lay up for the parents, but the parents for the children.

15. And I will very gladly spend and be spent for you; though the more abundantly I love you, the less I be loved.

16. But be it so, I did not burden you: nevertheless, being crafty, I caught you with guile.

17. Did I make a gain of you by any of them whom I sent unto you?

18. I desired Titus, and with him I sent a brother. Did Titus make a gain of you? walked we not in the same spirit? walked we not in the same steps?

19. Again, think ye that we excuse ourselves unto you? we speak before God in Christ: but we do all things, dearly beloved, for your edifying.

13:2. I told you before, and foretell you, as if I were present, the second time; and being absent now I write to them which heretofore have sinned, and to all other, that, if I come again, I will not spare:

8. For we can do nothing against the truth, but for the truth.

9. For we are glad, when we are weak, and ye are strong: and this also we wish, even your perfection.

10. Therefore I write these things being absent, lest being present I should use sharpness, according to the power which the Lord hath given me to edification, and not to destruction.

DICTIONARY
imaginations—2 Corinthians 10:5—reasonings
simplicity—2 Corinthians 11:3—sincerity
perfection—2 Corinthians 13:9—"a making fit"; a process leading to completion

LESSON OUTLINE

I. NATURE OF AUTHORITY

   A. Belongs to the Lord

   B. Boasts in the Lord

II. PURPOSE OF AUTHORITY

   A. Preserve Truth

   B. Strengthen Believers

III. EXERCISING AUTHORITY

   A. Spirit of Humility

   B. The Goal of Edification

LESSON EXPOSITION

INTRODUCTION

Which is worse—little authority accompanied by disorder or unbridled authority that dominates people?

Both extremes are equally unacceptable and create problems within any institution. Denominations, local churches and parachurch groups, regretfully, are not exempt from these opposites. When one occurs, the purpose of the believers' mission cannot be accomplished.

Why do such unacceptable exercises of authority occur? Consider these possibilities: (1) Individuals are elevated to positions beyond their abilities or experience. (2) Egotism in leaders dominates the opportunity to serve. (3) Leaders fail to understand either the nature or purpose of authority.

In order to be effective, leaders need vision and communication skills, but authority must also be part of the leadership package. Otherwise, decisions of importance will never take place. Without authority a vacuum exists.

At the same time, authority that seeks to serve self will lead a group on a tangent far from the path of truth and brotherly love. It will inflict pain and suffering instead of edifying those under its rule. Just as there are dictators who use an iron hand in governing a country, so there are dictatorial leaders in too many Christian churches.

When Christ instituted the church as an organization here on earth, He did not provide a flowchart or chain of command. As He ascended to heaven, the initial disciples were left to provide an informal system of leadership. Not one of them could produce a written job description designed by Christ. Yet, as Christ's called and trained disciples, they possessed an authority to lead. Furthermore, the infilling of the Holy Spirit enabled them to minister and lead with wisdom and authority.

In our lesson today we will study authority in light of the apostle Paul's supervision of the Corinthians. Though he likely had been hurt by some of their rebellious actions and attitudes, he strove to demonstrate an authority that would change the situation rather than simply satisfying the right to yield power.

Look around you for examples of Christian leaders who demonstrate the Biblical authority Paul practiced. Then do some introspection. Ask yourself, "When I'm in a position of leadership, what is the pattern of authority I project?"

I. NATURE OF AUTHORITY
(2 Corinthians 10:3-5, 8, 12, 13, 17, 18)

A. Belongs to the Lord (vv. 3-5, 8)

(2 Corinthians 10:8 is not included in the printed text.)

3. For though we walk in the flesh, we do not war after the flesh:

4. (For the weapons of our warfare are not carnal, but mighty through God to the pulling down of strong holds;)

5. Casting down imaginations, and every high thing that exalteth itself against the knowledge of God, and bringing into captivity every thought to the obedience of Christ.

Chapter 10 begins the last section of Paul's letter we call Second Corinthians. This entire letter stands as an example of the restraint he continually exhibited while attempting to defend himself and correct problems. Even while being firm he expressed love and affection. Especially noticeable is the presence of humility instead of a domineering boasting of his authority as an apostle. Paul demonstrated boldness and confidence instead of an authoritarian spirit.

Paul understood his humanity with all its weaknesses and limitations. However, he knew that as a believer engaged against the forces of evil, he could not depend on the frailty of human ability. Instead, he fought in the authority and ability of God. Only by this means could the power of Satan and his forces be overcome.

Human wisdom, philosophical ideas and a secular religion not only are ineffective but in reality are methods of the Enemy. They tend to offer arguments that are in opposition to God's nature and His Word.

The authority in our warfare comes from God through the Holy Spirit. He enables us to demolish the arguments of mere mortals and take them captive. Their capture enables true liberation to occur. Rather than living in fear of defeat, we can stand triumphantly.

In verses 7 and 8 Paul says it is right to boast in the Lord. Anyone who can claim God as Father through the saving grace of Jesus Christ can rightfully delight in authority over evil. No believer can personally generate or claim this authority based on his or her years in the church. All authority over sin and evil resides in God himself. Even civil authority here on earth derives its power from God (Romans 13:1).

Paul's authority as a spiritual overseer came from God enabling him to govern the church. Yes, there are occasions when forceful words may need to be verbalized or written in an attempt to right a situation. They aren't just scare tactics. They are words of truth intended to bring individual believers and the church closer to God.

B. Boasts in the Lord
(vv. 12, 13, 17, 18)

(2 Corinthians 10:12, 13 is not included in the printed text.)

17. But he that glorieth, let him glory in the Lord.

18. For not he that commendeth himself is approved, but whom the Lord commendeth.

In verse 12 the apostle pens one of the most descriptive verses of how we humans often justify our actions. Instead of using a standard of excellence determined by God, we tend to choose a human standard. When we measure ourselves against mediocre standards, our mediocrity appears to be meeting the standard. It is like a teacher grading on the curve, giving some students an excellent grade despite their mediocre performance. Paul said, "When they measure themselves by themselves and compare themselves with themselves, they are not wise" (*NIV*).

Verse 13 contrasts Paul's approach against the intruders who were attempting to turn the Corinthians against him. Apparently they made claims of position and ministry that were not from God. How different from Paul's pattern! He knew the calling and pattern God had laid out for him and continued in it. His claims and activities of ministry were confined to what God had done through Paul and his coworkers.

Paul's desire was for the Corinthian believers to spiritually mature to the point that they could partner with him in taking the gospel to outer regions still needing to hear the gospel (vv. 15, 16). He had no desire to move into another person's area of ministry and attempt to claim the results of their efforts and God's glory.

The last two verses of chapter 10 are a strong statement against self-commendation. Anyone who constantly boasts of the results of their labors needs to be viewed with suspicion. Since we know that spiritual growth comes directly through the ministry of the Holy Spirit, anyone who commends himself for such growth needs to be seen as one who has strayed from the truth. Instead of seeing themselves as instruments for the glory of God, they are reveling in self-glory.

These verses have practical application to us. When individuals come to Christ, we may be the vessels or instruments of the message; but without the work of the Holy Spirit, all efforts are meaningless. For that reason we should boast in God's work.

II. PURPOSE OF AUTHORITY
(2 Corinthians 11:1-8; 12:14-19)

A. Preserve Truth (11:1-8)

(2 Corinthians 11:1, 4-8 is not included in the printed text.)

2. For I am jealous over you with godly jealousy: for I have espoused you to one husband, that I may present you as a chaste virgin to Christ.

3. But I fear, lest by any means, as the serpent beguiled Eve through his subtlety, so your minds should be corrupted from the simplicity that is in Christ.

Authority in the church goes beyond the need for organization and leadership. In these eight verses the apostle Paul continued to defend himself against the false apostles, and in doing so he emphasized the role of authority in preserving truth among the believers.

In verse 1 Paul requested their indulgence while he continued to speak of himself. His purpose was not self-commendation but to further reveal the falseness of the intruders who claimed to be apostles. He then proceeded to describe his tremendous possessiveness for the Corinthians. This was not on the level of human jealousy—he wasn't possessive of them for his own glory or reputation. This possessiveness was directed toward and for God. The apostle desired to present this church to God untouched by the sins of heresy and deception.

The example of Eve in verse 3 provides an excellent review of how "good people" can be led astray. Using the body of the snake, Satan cunningly corrupted her thinking. Satan began with a statement intended to produce doubt and then followed with a counterstatement to what God had said. Having heard Satan's words, Eve looked at the fruit. Seeing its pleasing appearance, she desired it and finally ate of it. How quickly it all took place! That scenario is exactly what Paul wanted to prevent.

In verse 4 Paul was concerned about the relative ease with which false apostles and their less-than-edifying concepts had been accepted. He warned the believers against accepting a Jesus different than the One through whom they had experienced salvation. Also, it was vital that they not accept a spirit that returned them to bondage instead of remaining in a spirit of liberty that brought peace, joy and comfort. The apostle's concern continued to be for the preservation of truth that the believers had already received.

According to verses 5-8, apparently it had been suggested that Paul was lesser in position and ability than the intruders who were causing the difficulties. While Paul recognized that he might not have the same rhetorical skills as others, he possessed all the necessary knowledge for a man of his authority.

To further defend the genuineness of his concern and actions, Paul pointed out that believers from other regions had supported him financially. For instance, the Philippians generously supplied his needs. This eliminated any possible accusation from the Corinthians of his being a financial burden or taking advantage of them.

B. Strengthen Believers (12:14-19)

14. Behold, the third time I am ready to come to you; and I will not be burdensome to you: for I seek not your's, but you: for the children ought not to lay up for the parents, but the parents for the children.

15. And I will very gladly spend and be spent for you; though the more abundantly I love you, the less I be loved.

16. But be it so, I did not burden you: nevertheless, being crafty, I caught you with guile.

17. Did I make a gain of you by any of them whom I sent unto you?

18. I desired Titus, and with him I sent a brother. Did Titus make a gain of you? walked we not in the same spirit? walked we not in the same steps?

19. Again, think ye that we excuse ourselves unto you? we speak before God in Christ: but we do all things, dearly beloved, for your edifying.

Paul indicates preparations to visit Corinth for a third time. We read of his first visit in Acts 18. The second visit is apparently referred to in 2 Corinthians 2:1, where he spoke of "a painful visit"

(*NIV*). The time and details of this sorrowful visit are unknown.

Right up front, in 12:14, the financial conditions for his coming visit are explained. He was not coming for personal gain at their expense. Unlike unscrupulous individuals who used the gospel to fleece the believers and accumulate possessions, Paul would gladly use all of his own funds for their benefit. Willingly he would expend his physical strength to minister for their common good. Here is the image of a father willingly giving of his possessions and self for the love of his children.

At the end of verse 15 Paul pointed to the problem. Even while he attempted to extend more of his love to them, they offered less in return than before. The reason is seen in verse 16—a lie or deceptive insinuation apparently had been circulated about him. While he did not depend on the Corinthians' support while ministering there, what about the collection that had been received from Corinth for the needy saints in Jerusalem? Had some of that money found its way into Paul's pocket?

To counter this accusation, he asked a very pointed question in verse 17: "Did I exploit you through any of the men I sent you?" (*NIV*). Paul had sent Titus and another brother to the Corinthians, and Titus did not take advantage of them. Paul then asked, "Did we not act in the same spirit and follow the same course?" (v. 18, *NIV*).

In verse 19 Paul turned the Corinthians' attention back to his true purpose. He was not interested in gaining popularity or personal possessions. Any use of authority he exercised continued to be for the sole purpose of strengthening their faith as believers. He wanted them to be grounded in Christ.

Anyone who is in a leadership position possesses a certain level of authority. Every person in leadership needs to seriously consider his or her motives while fulfilling the various responsibilities. Am I doing this so others will grow spiritually? Are my decisions made with the intention of furthering the Kingdom or benefiting my image and position? Have I begun to believe others owe me because of the amount of service rendered?

Everyone in Christian leadership should use their authority for the specific purpose of preserving truth and strengthening believers.

III. EXERCISING AUTHORITY
(2 Corinthians 12:20, 21; 13:1-10)

A. A Spirit of Humility (12:20, 21)

(2 Corinthians 12:20, 21 is not included in the printed text.)

Knowing their history and the ease with which many had adopted a negative attitude toward him, Paul was concerned about the problems and weaknesses he might find on his arrival.

Look at the listing: "quarreling, jealousy, outbursts of anger, factions, slander, gossip, arrogance and disorder" (v. 20, *NIV*). These were the very issues which helped prompt the writing of 1 Corinthians (see 3:3; 4:6, 18, 19; 6:1). If there were a few unspiritual, rebellious individuals not walking in the Spirit but in the flesh, it could be understood earlier. However, if these problems were widespread, this church needed a major revival.

Paul also indicated that some in the church might not be satisfied with him. Barnes observed, "That is, 'that I shall be compelled to administer discipline, and that my visit may not be as pleasant to you as you would desire.' For this reason he wished all disorder corrected, and all offences removed; that everything might be pleasant when he should come."

In verse 21 Paul repeated the concern over what he might find. Here he mentioned three other areas: "impurity, sexual sin and debauchery" (*NIV*). This too brings to remembrance issues covered in the first epistle (5:1, 10, 11; 6:9, 13, 18). He feared that some members were continuing a pattern of sin instead of repenting after having been confronted. If he found this to be true, it would be a humbling experience for Paul.

In speaking of God's humbling him, it doesn't mean that Paul lacked humility. However, whenever a leader faces the spiritual defeat of those whom he helped bring to Christ, it is humbling. No, we cannot force people to live right. We cannot keep them from abandoning their faith to pursue the desires of the flesh. But when it becomes known, it delivers a devastating blow.

If the worst scenario were true, Paul would sorrow over those believers' spiritual deaths in the same way family and close friends mourn a loved one's physical death. In light of the eternal consequences, the apostle would grieve over them as a father would grieve for his children.

These verses remind us not to become prideful in spiritual accomplishments. It is humbling when converts choose to return to their old life. We may put forth extraordinary effort to win them back, but without God's grace and the moving of the Holy Spirit, it is all in vain. So even when surrounded with the most amazing spiritual success stories, we as leaders must maintain a spirit of humility.

B. The Goal of Edification (13:1-10)

(2 Corinthians 13:1, 3-7 is not included in the printed text.)

2. I told you before, and foretell you, as if I were present, the second time; and being absent now I write to them which heretofore have sinned, and to all other, that, if I come again, I will not spare:

8. For we can do nothing against the truth, but for the truth.

9. For we are glad, when we are weak, and ye are strong: and this

also we wish, even your perfection.
10. Therefore I write these things being absent, lest being present I should use sharpness, according to the power which the Lord hath given me to edification, and not to destruction.

As the apostle Paul ends this letter, he offers some final warnings. Authority never is to be used for tearing down people. Such abusive use of authority never should be found within the body of Christ. Instead, when the authority of leadership enables others to mature in their knowledge and experience of Christ, its goal has been accomplished.

After repeating the fact of his upcoming third visit, Paul gave warning to those who had been warned previously but were continuing in sin. They were now put on notice. If their pattern of sinfulness was still in evidence upon his arrival, there would be strong discipline.

Their rebellion needed to be put in proper perspective. Instead of challenging Paul, they were in reality rebelling against God. The apostle continued as the humble messenger who would confront them through the power of God so righteousness would prevail.

In verse 5, the tables are turned. Stirred up by the false apostles, the Corinthians had been challenging Paul to show proof of his apostleship. Now he asked them to examine themselves and show proof of their being in Christ. If they had truly experienced the grace of God in their lives, there should be no problem in recognizing that Paul had proclaimed Christ to them. Only because of his passion for the gospel and willingness to serve were they able to hear the good news of Jesus Christ as Savior and Lord.

In verses 8 and 9 Paul pointed out that if truth were predominant upon his arrival in Corinth, there would be

no need to take stern measures which demonstrated his authority. He would much rather come to minister with a weak projection of authority due to their having already repented of their sins. A genuine leader with a heart for ministry wants to be involved in encouragement and teaching of the Word rather than being forced to administer the heavy hand of discipline.

Verse 10 reminds us of the heart of a true apostle. Paul knew that certain situations may demand the use of strong measures to correct and to restore, yet his goal was to build up people in the faith of the Lord Jesus Christ!

GOLDEN TEXT HOMILY

"FOR THE WEAPONS OF OUR WARFARE ARE NOT CARNAL, BUT MIGHTY THROUGH GOD TO THE PULLING DOWN OF STRONG HOLDS" (2 Corinthians 10:4).

Every generation since Adam and Eve has experienced some kind of military warfare, whether it was local, regional or national. Since the birth of America, we have encountered some terrible wars. We experienced the Civil War, World War I, World War II, Vietnam, the Persian Gulf War, and the war against terrorism.

Currently there is a war going on between Israel and the Palestinians with many innocent people being killed on both sides. It is a tragedy when anyone dies because of war.

There has been, however, another kind of war going on in the world that began when Adam and Eve were in the tranquil Garden of Eden. Doesn't this sound strange? Only two people who had everything so lovely, yet a war broke out between Adam and Eve and the devil. We call it spiritual warfare.

The children of God have an enemy, Satan. His cause is to separate

God's children from their Father, the Lord God Most High. Since the devil cannot come against God directly, he constantly comes against the apple of God's eye, humanity in general, and Christians in particular. His strategies and weapons to defeat Christians in their faith walk with God are more than the mind can imagine. The truth is people are no match for the devil. Believers must lean on God to be victorious.

The text says God's weapons are mighty ones that can pull down any stronghold that Satan establishes against us. The battlefield for our souls is the mind; Satan seeks to establish strongholds in the mind through deception, fear and worry.

However, weapons of faith, fortitude and fire that God gives us are not of man's doings. Anyone who has faith, fortitude and fire in their soul through Christ will overcome Satan. We are more than conquerors through Jesus Christ.—**Ted Gray**

SENTENCE SERMONS

CHRISTIANS HAVE God-given authority to minister for Christ.
—Selected

A GREAT LEADER never sets himself above his followers except in carrying out responsibilities.
—Jules Ormont

YOU PLAN A TOWER that will pierce the clouds? Lay first the foundation of humility.
—Augustine

EVANGELISM APPLICATION

CHRIST HAS AUTHORIZED THE CHURCH TO MAKE THE GOSPEL KNOWN TO ALL PEOPLE.

Authorization basically means to be given the power. It includes both the aspects of right and abilities.

The church, namely we believers, have been given the power to spread the gospel. Through walking in the Spirit we can daily exhibit a lifestyle that witnesses to the grace of God. What we do frequently speaks much louder than what we say. However, that's no excuse for failing to verbalize our faith in a way that creates interest in the minds and hearts of unbelievers.

Our authorization is not limited to a few select people groups. It applies to all people regardless of geographic location, ethnic background or skin color. That's because God loves people of the world equally.

ILLUMINATING THE LESSON

On July 22, 1980, Mount St. Helens exploded ash 100,000 feet into the air. The plume looked like an atomic blast. It was a fascinating sight. Though powerful, it wasn't like the preceding blast on May 18, which ripped 1,300 feet off the mountain with a force of 10 million tons of TNT. That is equal to about 500 times the explosive force when Hiroshima was bombed at the end of World War II.

Power can be positive or destructive, depending on how it is harnessed and under whose authority it operates.

DAILY BIBLE READINGS

M. Authority of Humans.
   Genesis 1:26-31
T. Authority of Prophets.
   Deuteronomy 18:15-22
W. Authority of a King.
   Nehemiah 2:1-11
T. Authority of Jesus.
   Matthew 7:24-29
F. Authority of Rulers.
   Romans 13:1-7
S. Authority of Ministers.
   1 Peter 5:1-4

TRUTH SEARCH
Creatively Teaching the Word

DISCUSSION QUESTIONS

**Nature of Authority
(2 Corinthians 10:3-5, 8, 12, 13, 17, 18)**

1. What can be accomplished through spiritual power (vv. 3-5)?

2. Why does God appoint spiritual authorities in the church (v. 8)?

3. What mistake do some church leaders make (v. 12)? Why is this unwise?

4. What was the sphere of Paul's God-given authority (v. 13)?

**Purpose of Authority
(2 Corinthians 11:1-8; 12:14-19)**

1. What was Paul's attitude toward the Corinthians, and why (v. 2)?

2. What was Paul's great concern regarding the Corinthian Christians (vv. 3, 4)?

3. What kind of authority figure was Paul—dictatorial, weak, servant-leader, or nonchalant (vv. 5-8)? How did he prove himself?

4. Explain Paul's statement about parents and children (12:14).

5. How did Paul spend himself for the Corinthians (v. 15)?

6. What was Paul's motivation in everything he did for the Corinthians (v. 19)?

**Exercising Authority
(2 Corinthians 12:20, 21; 13:1-10)**

1. How did Paul express his pastoral heart in 12:20, 21?

2. Was Paul being cruel to hold people accountable for their actions (13:1-3)?

3. What is the connection between authority and weakness (v. 4)?

4. What did Paul tell the Corinthians to do (v. 5)?

5. Was pride part of Paul's motive in seeing the Corinthians serve Christ (vv. 7, 8)?

6. For what purpose does God grant spiritual authority to leaders (vv. 9, 10)?

OBJECT LESSON

Item needed: Whistle

Blow the whistle.

How is it that a 175-pound policeman can blow a whistle and hold out his hand and stop an 18-wheeler carrying tons of cargo? Is that police officer using his own power to stop the big truck? Of course not! It is the authority of the Police Department, represented by the officer's badge and uniform, that causes the trucker to stop.

Blow the whistle again. Then say that Paul exercised authority even though he did not wear a uniform or a badge. **Paul walked not in his own authority but in God's power. Some Corinthians had a wrong perception of him. But Paul used his God-given authority to help them grow up into perfection.**

What is your perception of the spiritual authorities in your life? Our spiritual authorities need our prayers and understanding as they fulfill their calling.

Lead the students in praying for your church's spiritual authorities.

A-Good-King Gone-Bad

Nathan, Reprover and Counselor

Study Text: 2 Samuel 12:1-18; 1 Chronicles 17:1-15
Objective: To acknowledge that a true friend may give either reproof or counsel and be willing to accept both.
Time: Around 1035 B.C.
Place: Jerusalem
Golden Text: "He that refuseth instruction despiseth his own soul: but he that heareth reproof getteth understanding" (Proverbs 15:32).
Central Truth: Sometimes, wise reproof and counsel are needed.
Evangelism Emphasis: The unsaved need to hear the reproof and counsel of the gospel.

a good King gone bad

PRINTED TEXT

2 Samuel 12:7. And Nathan said to David, Thou art the man. Thus saith the Lord God of Israel, I anointed thee king over Israel, and I delivered thee out of the hand of Saul;

9. Wherefore hast thou despised the commandment of the Lord, to do evil in his sight? thou hast killed Uriah the Hittite with the sword, and hast taken his wife to be thy wife, and hast slain him with the sword of the children of Ammon.

10. Now therefore the sword shall never depart from thine house; because thou hast despised me, and hast taken the wife of Uriah the Hittite to be thy wife.

11. Thus saith the Lord, Behold, I will raise up evil against thee out of thine own house, and I will take thy wives before thine eyes, and give them unto thy neighbour, and he shall lie with thy wives in the sight of this sun.

12. For thou didst it secretly: but I will do this thing before all Israel, and before the sun.

13. And David said unto Nathan, I have sinned against the Lord. And Nathan said unto David, The Lord also hath put away thy sin; thou shalt not die.

14. Howbeit, because by this deed thou hast given great occasion to the enemies of the Lord to blaspheme, the child also that is born unto thee shall surely die.

15. And Nathan departed unto his house. And the Lord struck the child that Uriah's wife bare unto David, and it was very sick.

1 Chronicles 17:2. Then Nathan said unto David, Do all that is in thine heart; for God is with thee.

3. And it came to pass the same night, that the word of God came to Nathan, saying,

4. Go and tell David my servant, Thus saith the Lord, Thou shalt not build me an house to dwell in:

11. And it shall come to pass, when thy days be expired that thou must go to be with thy fathers, that I will raise up thy seed after thee, which shall be of thy sons; and I will establish his kingdom.

12. He shall build me an house, and I will establish his throne for ever.

14. But I will settle him in mine house and in my kingdom for ever: and his throne shall be established for evermore.

15. According to all these words, and according to all this vision, so did Nathan speak unto David.

DICTIONARY

Uriah (you-RYE-uh)—2 Samuel 12:9—the husband of Bathsheba and a loyal soldier of David who, although not born an Israelite, apparently was a worshiper of Jehovah

LESSON OUTLINE

I. A FRIEND GIVES REPROOF

    A. The Parable of Contrasts

    B. The Outrage of the Hypocritical King

    C. The Rebuke of God's Prophet

II. JUDGMENT AND FORGIVE-NESS DECLARED

    A. The Sentence

    B. Repentance, Forgiveness and Consequences

    C. Judgment Effected

III. PROPHETIC COUNSEL GIVEN

    A. David's Desire

    B. God's Interruption

    C. Nathan's Prophecy

LESSON EXPOSITION

INTRODUCTION

Second Samuel 11, the passage that sets the background for this lesson, records one of the most tragic accounts of a fallen human leader—David's sin with the wife of Uriah. At a time when he should have been with his troops fighting against the Ammonites, David was lounging on his bed and observing his kingdom. He was at the height of his political power and influence, but his relationship with God was not where it needed to be. David became aware that he was the king and he began taking that position—a position bestowed upon him by God—for granted.

David saw. He looked. He lusted. He took. He manipulated. He murdered. He sighed relief. His transgressions were hidden . . . so he thought. However, God saw what had happened *in* David with its consequential behavior and it was evil in His eyes (v. 27).

God had the right man for the job of bringing David's focus back to God and spiritual health, for He knew that what happened in David would also affect the rest of the kingdom.

Nathan appears in chapter 12 much like Elijah does in 1 Kings 17—without fanfare or introduction. He arrives on the scene with the prophetic anointing, representing God to the people and delivering the word of the Lord. What he delivers in the first portion of this lesson is the tragic judgment upon a good king gone bad.

Nathan means "the given one," and he lived up to his name and destiny in life. He was given to David to assist him faithfully, counsel him wisely, pray for him continually and confront him when necessary. These are the marks of a true friend (Proverbs 17:17; 18:24; 22:11; 27:6, 9). This lesson will examine two times Nathan gives counsel to David—reproving him of his sin with Bathsheba, and giving instruction concerning the building of the Temple.

Elsewhere in Scripture, we find Nathan helped David choose his kingly successor (1 Kings 1:5-39), and served as the historian of David and Solomon's reign (1 Chronicles 29:29; 2 Chronicles 9:29). When he received news of Solomon's birth, he gave him the name *Jedidiah*, meaning "friend of God" (2 Samuel 12:25). The prophet had two sons: Azariah, who was over the officers in Solomon's administration, and Zabud, a priest, who is described quite aptly as "the king's friend" (1 Kings 4:5), no doubt following in his father's footsteps.

I. A FRIEND GIVES REPROOF
(2 Samuel 12:1-9)

A. The Parable of Contrasts (vv. 1-4)

(2 Samuel 12:1-4 is not included in the printed text.)

On 10 occasions in 2 Samuel 11, someone or something is sent *to* or *from* David and always because of him. Now, Nathan is "sent" to him by God himself in this passage (v. 1). The term *send* in the Bible often means "to send with a purpose or commission." Nathan had a commission to confront the king of his evil heart and wicked deeds with the purpose of bringing him to repentance. ⨍ 4 - 23 - 07

God's acts in the life of His people are redemptive rather than retributive in nature. He does expose unrepentant sin. His purpose, however, is to gain our attention, convict us of our sin, and restore our fellowship with Him (see Psalm 85; Jeremiah 30; Titus 2:14). He confronts us—whether through His Word, the Holy Spirit, or His servants—to correct us, not to condemn us. Those whom He sends understand the gravity of their responsibility and approach the task with prayer, humility and wisdom.

Nathan entered the king's presence and began his parable in a way that would gain David's attention. Some see this as a common story utilized by Nathan. However, the parallels to David's situation are too striking to have been part of folklore. He carefully used a very specific word for *poor*. It is the same word David used to describe himself in 1 Samuel 18:23. David understood that those who are rich (blessed) and powerful (in authority), whether in material goods or spiritual blessings, have a responsibility to those who are less fortunate (Proverbs 14:21, 31; 19:17; 21:13). David probably thought Nathan was asking for his advice in judging this matter, for such was the king's duty (1 Samuel 8:5, 6; 2 Samuel 15:2-4).

In verse 2, little description is given of the rich man. He had everything he needed and more. Yet in verse 3, Nathan provides great detail of the poor man's poverty and his relationship with his ewe lamb, a relationship with which David, the poor shepherd who became king, could identify. The little lamb was not something the poor man was given or inherited, but something he purchased from his own meager funds. He "nourished" it (literally, "kept it alive or revived it") and fed it from "his own cup." It grew up as a member of the family, just "like a daughter to him" (*NKJV*). He let it lie "in his bosom," or sleep on his lap.

This is a story of contrasts: the rich (David) robbing from the poor (Uriah); many sheep and cattle (a harem) compared to one cherished lamb (Bathsheba); a man who took what he wanted (the king) against a man who gave of himself (a soldier); one who cared for nothing except himself (lust and adultery) versus one who cared deeply for others (transparent integrity); a man with everything (God's anointed one) against a man with just one thing (hope).

The rich man *took* the poor man's lamb (v. 4). It is the same word used in 2 Samuel 11:4 to describe David's messengers who "took" Bathsheba from her home with Uriah, and in 1 Samuel 8:11-19 to anticipate self-absorbed kings—of which David was now one—who only "take" from the people they govern. This vivid description would come back to haunt the unsuspecting David later in the narrative. 4 - 07

B. The Outrage of the Hypocritical King (vv. 5, 6)

(2 Samuel 12:5, 6 is not included in the printed text.)

The language of verse 5 reveals that David's emotion was intense and quick. He exploded with rage, something perhaps he was prone to do (see

Psalm 39:3), at such shameful behavior. A person who would do what Nathan described was callous, self-centered, concerned with appearances, and a transgressor of God's law and justice. He deserved "to die" (literally, was a son of death) and that was David's judgment, even though it was the appropriate penalty for adultery and murder (Exodus 21:12; Deuteronomy 22:22), not stealing sheep (Exodus 22:1). It was to be swift and certain—"as surely as the Lord lives" (2 Samuel 12:5, NIV). However, before the sentence of the indignant king would be carried out, the sentence of the Torah would be fulfilled and the man would restore four times over what he had stolen from the poor man (v. 6).

The rich man showed "no pity" or compassion on the poor man; therefore, no compassion would be shown to him. The king would see to it that this offense against God's law and His people was adequately punished! David unknowingly condemned and passed judgment on himself. Transgressors tend to do that.

It is easy to observe and condemn the "sins" of others and overlook our own "weaknesses." Jesus said we must examine ourselves first before going to others (Matthew 7:1-5). We must examine our own lives under the scrutiny of the Spirit's light, not on the basis of what we see in others (see Acts 4:34—5:11). We must examine our actions, our attitudes and our motives before we minister to others. We find here and elsewhere (see Galatians 2:11) that God does use people to reprove others. Certainly, there is a need for wise counsel in every person's life, but before we offer such without invitation, we must determine our motives for doing so.

C. The Rebuke of God's Prophet
   (vv. 7-9)

(2 Samuel 12:8 is not included in the printed text.)

7. And Nathan said to David, Thou art the man. Thus saith the Lord God of Israel, I anointed thee king over Israel, and I delivered thee out of the hand of Saul;
9. Wherefore hast thou despised the commandment of the Lord, to do evil in his sight? thou hast killed Uriah the Hittite with the sword, and hast taken his wife to be thy wife, and hast slain him with the sword of the children of Ammon.

The language changes. It is no longer the language of a parable or a matter to be discussed. It is the bold and direct pronouncement of God through His servant. Think of Nathan's courage! In verse 7, he stands in the face of the man who has the power to banish or even execute him and declares, "You are the man!"

Here we do not see a court prophet like those of Ahab, there for the whim of the king (1 Kings 18:19). Instead we see a man who has been in the presence of God, rather than the king, and fears the Lord more than the king.

Verses 7-12 give a long speech from God that begins by reviewing His gracious action on David's behalf (vv. 7, 8). In contrast to David's *taking*, God graciously *gave* him everything he needed and more. In Nathan's parable, the rich man had taken the lamb from "the bosom" of the poor man (see v. 3). Verse 8 says literally that God had given into David's *bosom* ("into his keeping") the house and wives of his predecessor. This was a euphemistic way of saying God had given him the kingdom and most likely the wealth of Saul. It was also a reminder to David that he was not king because of his ability or lineage. Instead, he was king because God chose and anointed him king over Israel (v. 7; see also 1 Samuel 16:12).

Saul could have easily killed David, but God protected him. As such, he was responsible to God first and foremost. Positions and ministries are not to be taken for granted. When one ceases to serve God, one can expect a visitation from Him, along with its consequences (see Luke 12:48).

In verse 9 of the text, God asked David why he despised the word of the Lord and did "evil in his sight." David's actions revealed that he placed himself above and had contempt for the word of the Lord, so the word of the Lord came to him. David violated at least three of the Ten Commandments—adultery, murder, covetousness—and probably the first one also; his position, power and desire usurped the place of God in his life (see Exodus 20:1-17). He not only violated the Torah, he violated the covenant relationship he had with God and the gifts and claims God had on his life (see 2 Samuel 7).

The one whom God raised up "struck down" Uriah (NIV); the one to whom God gave everything his heart desired "took" Uriah's wife; the one whom God protected from Saul "killed" through his enemy to protect his honor. David got what he wanted, but not what he expected.

We too must be careful in the things we desire. There always seems to be something else that we *think* we need. Second Peter 1:3, 4 says, "His divine power has given to us all things that pertain to life and godliness, through the knowledge of Him who called us by glory and virtue, by which have been given to us exceedingly great and precious promises, that through these you may be partakers of the divine nature, having escaped the corruption that is in the world through lust" (NKJV). We need to stop and see what we really have before we lust for what we do not have.

II. JUDGMENT AND FORGIVENESS DECLARED (2 Samuel 12:10-18)

A. The Sentence (vv. 10-12)

10. Now therefore the sword shall never depart from thine house; because thou hast despised me, and hast taken the wife of Uriah the Hittite to be thy wife.

11. Thus saith the Lord, Behold, I will raise up evil against thee out of thine own house, and I will take thy wives before thine eyes, and give them unto thy neighbour, and he shall lie with thy wives in the sight of this sun.

12. For thou didst it secretly: but I will do this thing before all Israel, and before the sun.

"Therefore" (v. 10) indicates that what follows is the result of David's sin recorded in the previous verses. All actions have reactions and consequences (see Genesis 4:7). David's sin was against God, Uriah and Bathsheba. Walter Brueggemann notes that the language of 2 Samuel 11:4 and 12:4 may indicate she was not a completely willing participant in David's sin (*First and Second Samuel,* Interpretation). Certainly, God and Uriah were not willing participants.

The effect of David's sin was immense and extensive, and ironically, fitting. It was by the sword in the hand of the Ammonites (2 Samuel 11:1, 17) that David passed judgment upon Uriah (see James 4:11, 12 for a modern-day application), justified himself and comforted Joab (2 Samuel 11:25). And now that same judgment, a sword in the hands of others, would come upon him and his descendants (see 2 Kings 24; 25). Jesus reminds us that those who live by "the sword will perish by the sword" (Matthew 26:52, NKJV). Three of David's sons died violent deaths (see 2 Samuel 13:28, 29; 18:14; 1 Kings 2:24, 25). Sin never affects just the sinner. It is far-reaching in its scope and destructive in its power.

In 2 Samuel 12:11, God declared that adversity from within David's own family would afflict him. This was fulfilled through his son Absalom, who later attempted to claim the throne and defiled David's concubines in a public display to establish his claim on the throne and embarrass his father (2 Samuel 16:20-22). What David did in private would be done publicly ("in the sight of this sun"), as 12:12 reemphasizes. Favor and anointing do not condone evil attitudes or actions (see Amos 3:1, 2).

B. Repentance, Forgiveness and Consequences (vv. 13, 14)

13. And David said unto Nathan, I have sinned against the Lord. And Nathan said unto David, The Lord also hath put away thy sin; thou shalt not die.

14. Howbeit, because by this deed thou hast given great occasion to the enemies of the Lord to blaspheme, the child also that is born unto thee shall surely die.

One of David's strengths, both as a person and a leader, was his ability to be honest before God and accept responsibility for his actions (see Psalms 32; 38; 51). For at least the better part of a year, he had lived with the guilt and secret. Every time he looked at Bathsheba and the newborn child, he was reminded of his sin. Now he came clean.

There are times when the weight of the sin is worse than the judgment for that sin (Proverbs 13:15). That is, once a person's sin is exposed, it gives him or her an opportunity to repent and find restoration and peace (Romans 5:1).

David proclaimed death upon the rich man before he knew he was "the man" (2 Samuel 12:5), yet Nathan revealed to him God's mercy. David was outraged because the rich man did not show compassion or mercy. Now, in contrast to David's lust, covetousness, murderous actions, and contempt for God and His Word—all lacking in mercy—God would allow him to live (v. 13).

David not only sinned against God, his family, Bathsheba and Uriah, he gave "great occasion to the enemies of the Lord to blaspheme," or treat with contempt the name of the Lord (v. 14). He brought a reproach upon the Divine Name, the very Name by which David declared judgment upon the rich man of Nathan's parable (v. 5). David lost sight of the awe and holiness of God and caused others to do the same. He violated the Hittites through his actions against Uriah, and the Ammonites by using them without their knowledge to accomplish his plan.

We must act honorably even in dealing with our enemies so that a reproach is not brought against God or His church. People are not objects to be used to accomplish our personal goals. Our treatment of others affects our relationship with God, both now and in the future (Matthew 5:21-24; 22:37-39; 25:31-46; 1 John 4:20).

C. Judgment Effected (vv. 15-18)

(2 Samuel 12:16-18 is not included in the printed text.)

15. And Nathan departed unto his house. And the Lord struck the child that Uriah's wife bare unto David, and it was very sick.

Nathan departed, and the child born as the result of David's sin with the wife of Uriah immediately became ill. God's judgment had begun. Forgiveness sought and received did not absolve David of sin's consequences (see Psalm 99:8). Notice Bathsheba's name is never mentioned in this account. The emphasis is upon her position as Uriah's wife (also see Matthew 1:6).

David "pleaded with God for the child, and . . . fasted and went in and lay all night on the ground" (2 Samuel 12:16, *NKJV*). These actions are associated with humility and mourning, especially mourning for sin, both personal and corporate. It is not the only time we should fast, but it is certainly a time for fasting (see Isaiah 58:1-9). The elders saw David's sorrow and tried to intervene, but he would not listen (v. 17). He knew what he must do. These actions of repentance were as much for David's well-being as the child's. When tragedy strikes, our priorities become very clear.

After a week of illness, the child died (v. 18). The servants were afraid to approach the king with the news. Note the contrast with Nathan, who heard from God and did what needed to be done (v. 7). The servants also needed to convey a message to the king, but fear prevented them from doing so. His remorse was so genuine and heartfelt that they were afraid of what David would do to himself.

Second Samuel 8:15, apparently a commentary over David's entire reign, says, "David reigned over all Israel; and David executed judgment and justice unto all his people." Nathan's very difficult message of reproof was not in vain.

III. PROPHETIC COUNSEL GIVEN (1 Chronicles 17:1-15)

A. David's Desire (vv. 1, 2)

(1 Chronicles 17:1 is not included in the printed text.)

2. Then Nathan said unto David, Do all that is in thine heart; for God is with thee.

Chronologically, this event precedes the above (see 2 Samuel 7 for the parallel account); however, 1 Chronicles was written after 2 Samuel. This account enables the positive side of Nathan's ministry to David to be seen, revealing that reproof and wise counsel go together.

David was dissatisfied and shared his feelings with Nathan (v. 1). He was living in "a house of cedar," or an elegant house paneled with cedar. The ark of the covenant, the symbol of God's presence and power, was in a tent made of goats' hair (see Exodus 26:7). The contrast bothered the king. The narrative of 1 Chronicles 17 reveals that David had not heard from the Lord concerning building the Temple (see v. 6). This is something *he* wanted to do. Two other times in 1 Chronicles, David jumped ahead of God (chs. 13, 21). However, here David is not rebuked for such. His intentions were honorable.

Nathan simply told David to do what God had put in his heart, for God was with him (v. 2). The supposition was God had put it there. No prophetic formula introduces Nathan's words in this verse. This was counsel from Nathan, not the prophetic word from God.

B. God's Interruption (v. 3)

3. And it came to pass the same night, that the word of God came to Nathan, saying.

Even the best of counselors can get it wrong. We must not mistake our words for God's. What we say is always subject to the confirmation of God. The manifestation of the gifts of the Spirit, including personal and corporate prophecy, is to be confirmed by others (1 Corinthians 14:29). God has a way of letting His will be known to those who seek Him (Psalm 16:11; Jeremiah 33:3).

That night God's word came to Nathan (1 Chronicles 17:3). This must have been in response to prayer or may have been a divine revelation. The result was the same. David's desire and Nathan's counsel were both overturned.

In Scripture there is not much distinction made between the appearance of God and the declaration of His word. If God speaks, it is an event that will come to pass. It will be an occasion for the appearance of God's power. God could have easily spoken to David. The Davidic Psalms are proof of that. But here He chose to speak through a messenger or counselor.

The role of the prophetic voice has diminished in the church today. A few abuses have caused many to neglect a gift that God has given to the church (see 1 Corinthians 12:10; 14:1). We must hear from God, and having heard, we must speak what "thus saith the Lord!" This is one of the ways God reproves and directs His people.

C. Nathan's Prophecy (vv. 4-15)

(1 Chronicles 17:5-10, 13 is not included in the printed text.)

4. Go and tell David my servant, Thus saith the Lord, Thou shalt not build me an house to dwell in:

11. And it shall come to pass, when thy days be expired that thou must go to be with thy fathers, that I will raise up thy seed after thee, which shall be of thy sons; and I will establish his kingdom.

12. He shall build me an house, and I will establish his throne for ever.

14. But I will settle him in mine house and in my kingdom for ever: and his throne shall be established for evermore.

15. According to all these words, and according to all this vision, so did Nathan speak unto David.

The prophecy, with its classical formulary, is divided into two parts, each with the instruction to relay the information to "my servant David" (vv. 4, 7). These words softened what God had to say. It also reminded David that he belonged to God.

In the first section (vv. 4-6), God, through the prophet, told David that he would "not build me an house to dwell in" (v. 4). Notice the number of times *house* is used in this passage (see vv. 1, 4-6, 10, 12, 14). The term starts out as a reference to the Temple and takes on an eschatological meaning. Israel had been a nomadic people until the call for a king. God's presence had been on the move "from tent to tent, and from one tabernacle to another" (v. 5). For approximately 500 years, the ark had dwelt in movable tents. He had not directed any of the judges to build a house for the ark (v. 6), a reminder that God is not confined to time or space, even church buildings.

The second section of the prophecy (vv. 7-15) reminded David that "the Lord of hosts"—the source of power and position who has an undefeatable entire army at His disposal—had taken him from following sheep to leading God's people, Israel (v. 7). David was king because of God. Divine presence, provision and protection had been with him wherever he went to give him victory over his enemies and to make him a person of renown and respect (v. 8).

Verses 9 and 10 mark a change in Israel's situation. In contrast to His wandering (vv. 5, 6), God would designate a place for them to develop roots and stability, a fulfillment of Deuteronomy 12:10, 11. He also promised to bring rest from the oppression of their enemies.

The man who wanted to build a house for the Lord could not, because the Lord was building David's house (1 Chronicles 17:10)—He was establishing His covenant with David. When David's reign ended, God promised to establish his kingdom through his sons (v. 11). Although this is a reference to his progeny who would sit upon the throne, Christ's lineage is traced through two of David's sons—Solomon (Matthew 1:6) and Nathan (Luke 3:31). Charles Stanley reminds us that our children are a message we send to a time we shall not see. God will build His own house—through people. David could not build what God was already building.

David's son, his successor, would build the Temple (1 Chronicles 17:12). This verse does not indicate it would be Solomon, but 23:1 does. Here, the focus is not on the building of the Temple, but the building of David's heritage in the divine plan. In verse 13 of the text, God further promised He would not remove His mercy or favor as He did with Saul (see 1 Samuel 16:14; 18:12; 28:15, 16). The permanence of the Davidic line is emphasized no less than five times (1 Chronicles 17:11-14). This promise was accomplished through the messianic fulfillment (Isaiah 11:1-5) in Jesus Christ, the Son of David (Matthew 1:1, 6, 17), who was born in Bethlehem, the ancestral home of David (1 Samuel 17:12).

Verse 13 of the text also emphasizes the father-son language of adoption and intimacy ("I will be his father, and he shall be my son"). There is a shift from "your house" to "My house" and "My kingdom" (v. 14, NKJV). God was still the real King of Israel, and He would raise up One who was righteous and legitimate to sit on the throne (Jeremiah 23:5). The King still sits upon that throne.

Nathan only spoke what God gave him, but he spoke all that God gave him (v. 15). He gave full and faithful counsel to David. Nathan's friendship apparently had a great influence on David, who named one of his sons (also born of Bathsheba) after the prophet (2 Samuel 5:14). It was through this Nathan that Luke recorded the biological genealogy of Jesus, while Matthew recorded His royal genealogy through Solomon.

The prophet Nathan was instrumental in establishing the course of events that would correct a king's heart and lead to the entrance of the King of all kings. Many times what we do (or don't do) has an effect that lasts far beyond our life span.

GOLDEN TEXT HOMILY

"HE THAT REFUSETH INSTRUCTION DESPISETH HIS OWN SOUL: BUT HE THAT HEARETH REPROOF GETTETH UNDERSTANDING" (Proverbs 15:32).

This proverb categorizes people into two groups: those who are willing to accept instruction and those who are not.

The word *instruction* means "discipline." There are many people who *refuse*—"despise" and "reject"—discipline. They want to do their own thing without being held accountable to anyone.

The writer says those who despise instruction actually are living as if they hate themselves. They are on a suicidal path.

Then there are those who *hear*—"give heed to" and "obey"—godly correction. They respond positively to discipline and thereby gain the understanding they need to progress in life.

We must not "despise the Lord's discipline [nor] resent his rebuke, because the Lord disciplines those he loves" (Proverbs 3:11, 12, NIV).—**Lance Colkmire**

SENTENCE SERMONS

SOMETIMES, wise reproof and counsel are needed.

—Selected

IT TAKES A GREAT MAN to give sound advice tactfully, but a greater to accept it graciously.

—J.C. Macaulay

ADVICE IS SELDOM WELCOME. Those who need it most like it least.
—Quotable Quotations

EVANGELISM APPLICATION

THE UNSAVED NEED TO HEAR THE REPROOF AND COUNSEL OF THE GOSPEL.

Visitors can be seen walking around Oxford, England, observing the university architecture. At times they get so caught up in the inspiring buildings that they lose track of where they are. Tourists can be seen asking directions from those who look like they know where they are going.

In this world with all its distractions, it is easy to lose track of where a person is on the road to eternity. Christians have the ability to reveal in love the error of those who have lost their way and point them to the road that will lead them to eternal life.

ILLUMINATING THE LESSON

A minister was on a plane from Chicago to New York when the Lord revealed to him that the businessman across the aisle was ensnared in adultery. As he was looking at the man, trying to figure out how to approach him, the man snapped at him, "What do you want?"

The pastor asked the gentleman if a certain lady's first name meant anything to him. The man turned pale and said, "We've got to talk." He wanted to know how the minister knew about the adultery, to which the minister replied, "God told me."

The minister further told the man that unless he repented, God was going to take his life. The man asked what he should do, and the minister led him in a prayer of confession of his sin and repentance in the sky far above the earth (*Power Evangelism: Signs and Wonders Today*, by John Wimber with Kevin Springer).

DAILY BIBLE READINGS

M. Reproving a Neighbor.
    Genesis 21:22-26
T. Wisdom's Counsel and Reproof.
    Proverbs 1:20-33
W. An Ominous Reproof.
    Daniel 4:24-28
T. Wise Counsel Given.
    Acts 5:34-39
F. An Apostle Reproved.
    Galatians 2:11-16
S. Counsel to a Colleague.
    1 Timothy 4:7-16

TRUTH SEARCH
Creatively Teaching the Word

DISCUSSION QUESTIONS

**Nathan's Rebuke
(2 Samuel 12:1-19)**

1. Summarize Nathan's story (vv. 1-4).

2. What was David's response to the story (vv. 5, 6)?

3. Why did Nathan tell David, "You are the man!" (v. 7, NKJV)?

4. What sins was David guilty of committing (vv. 8, 9)?

5. List the ways David would suffer because of his sins (vv. 10-12, 14).

6. How did David respond to Nathan's rebuke (v. 13)?

7. What did the Lord do for David because of his repentance (v. 13)?

8. What did the Lord not do for David despite his prayers (vv. 15-19)? Why?

**Nathan's Prophecy
(1 Chronicles 17:1-16)**

1. What was David's concern (v. 1)?

2. What was Nathan's initial response to David (v. 2)?

3. Why did Nathan's response change (vv. 3, 4)?

4. What had God never asked for (vv. 5, 6)?

5. What had God done for David (vv. 7, 8)?

6. What did the Lord mean by telling David, "I will build you a house" (see vv. 10, 11)?

7. Who would finally build a permanent house for the Lord, and what would God do for him (vv. 12, 13)?

8. How could the throne of David's son be established "forever" (v. 14)?

9. Describe David's response to Nathan's prophecy (v. 16). What does this say about David?

OBJECT LESSON

Items needed: Rubber ball and glue

Hold the items in your hands as you talk.

There's an old saying that goes, "I'm rubber and you're glue; whatever you say bounces off of me and sticks on to you."

When Nathan approached King David to rebuke him, the prophet did not know if David would respond like rubber—letting the rebuke bounce off—or like glue, letting the rebuke stick.

If we are to grow as believers, we must not let God-sent words of rebuke simply bounce off us; instead, we should let them stick to our heart, bringing us to repentance.

Micaiah, Devoted to Truthfulness

Study Text: 1 Kings 22:1-38
Objective: To understand the importance of truthfulness and be a truthful person.
Time: Around 865 B.C.
Place: Samaria and Ramoth Gilead
Golden Text: "As the Lord liveth, what the Lord saith unto me, that will I speak" (1 Kings 22:14).
Central Truth: Christians are called to speak the truth in love.
Evangelism Emphasis: Christians must proclaim the truth of the gospel to all people.

PRINTED TEXT

1 Kings 22:7. And Jehoshaphat said, Is there not here a prophet of the Lord besides, that we might enquire of him?

8. And the king of Israel said unto Jehoshaphat, There is yet one man, Micaiah the son of Imlah, by whom we may enquire of the Lord: but I hate him; for he doth not prophesy good concerning me, but evil. And Jehoshaphat said, Let not the king say so.

9. Then the king of Israel called an officer, and said, Hasten hither Micaiah the son of Imlah.

14. And Micaiah said, As the Lord liveth, what the Lord saith unto me, that will I speak.

19. And he said, Hear thou therefore the word of the Lord: I saw the Lord sitting on his throne, and all the host of heaven standing by him on his right hand and on his left.

20. And the Lord said, Who shall persuade Ahab, that he may go up and fall at Ramoth-gilead? And one said on this manner, and another said on that manner.

21. And there came forth a spirit, and stood before the Lord, and said, I will persuade him.

22. And the Lord said unto him, Wherewith? And he said, I will go forth, and I will be a lying spirit in the mouth of all his prophets. And he said, Thou shalt persuade him, and prevail also: go forth, and do so.

23. Now therefore, behold, the Lord hath put a lying spirit in the mouth of all these thy prophets, and the Lord hath spoken evil concerning thee.

26. And the king of Israel said, Take Micaiah, and carry him back unto Amon the governor of the city, and to Joash the king's son;

27. And say, Thus saith the king, Put this fellow in the prison, and feed him with bread of affliction and with water of affliction, until I come in peace.

28. And Micaiah said, If thou return at all in peace, the Lord hath not spoken by me. And he said, Hearken, O people, every one of you.

29. So the king of Israel and Jehoshaphat the king of Judah went up to Ramoth-gilead.

34. And a certain man drew a bow at a venture, and smote the king of Israel between the joints of the harness: wherefore he said unto the driver of his chariot, Turn thine hand, and carry me out of the host; for I am wounded.

37. So the king died, and was brought to Samaria; and they buried the king in Samaria.

DICTIONARY

Jehoshaphat (jeh-HOSH-uh-fat)—1 Kings 22:7—king of Judah who reigned from about 873 to 849 B.C.

Micaiah (mi-KAY-uh)—1 Kings 22:9—a bold and righteous prophet of Jehovah

Ramoth-gilead (RAY-moth-GIL-ee-ad)—1 Kings 22:20—one of Israel's cities of refuge in the tribe of Gad, captured by Syria

---

LESSON OUTLINE

I. TRUTH SOUGHT

  A. An Alliance of Convenience

  B. The Need to Hear From God

  C. Confirmation or Truth?

II. TRUTH SPOKEN

  A. A Whimsical Prophecy

  B. A Tale of Two Visions

  C. Abuse, Affliction and Affirmation

III. TRUTH CONFIRMED

  A. Disregard and Deception

  B. Prophecy Fulfilled

  C. Death and Dogs

LESSON EXPOSITION

INTRODUCTION

First Kings 22 brings to an end the 22-year saga of Ahab, king of Israel (northern kingdom), begun in 1 Kings 16:28. It is a fascinating narrative with twists and turns that keep the reader on the edge of his or her seat. It is the chronicle of a young man living in the shadow of his ambitious, successful and corrupt father, Omri. Unfortunately, he excelled above his father in that he "did more to provoke the Lord God of Israel to anger than all the kings of Israel who were before him" (v. 33). His marriage to Jezebel only compounded his spiritual and moral corruption (21:25).

God sent prophet after prophet into his life in an effort to bring him to spiritual wholeness. These included Elijah (chs. 17-19, 21), an anonymous prophet (20:35-43), and Micaiah throughout Ahab's reign; but each time Ahab rejected the truth in favor of his own ambitions and the false prophecies of his court prophets. God also sent prophets to give Ahab successful directions in warfare (20:13, 22, 28), but political victories did not change his spiritual outlook. He is the consummate example of what not to do, both as a leader and a person.

Chapter 22 records the third in a series of three battles Ahab led against Syria (see 2 Chronicles 18 for a parallel account). The two previous campaigns ended in victory (1 Kings 20:20, 21, 28-30). For three years Israel and Syria lived in peace, following Ahab's second victory and the promise of Ben-Hadad, king of Syria, to return Ramoth Gilead and other cities that his father took from Israel (v. 34).

Ramoth Gilead was a city that carried historical and political significance for Israel. Solomon made it one of his administrative centers east of the Jordan (4:13) because of its proximity with Syria. Ahab was in the right to want the city. However, he was under God's judgment (20:42; 21:17-26) in spite of a temporary reprieve (21:28, 29). God did His part to bring Ahab to a right relationship and righteous reign (see 2 Kings 17:13), but Ahab kept rejecting the truth.

I. TRUTH SOUGHT
  (1 Kings 22:1-14)

A. An Alliance of Convenience
  (vv. 1-4)

(1 Kings 22:1-4 is not included in the printed text.)

Jehoshaphat, king of Judah, came down to visit the king of Israel. Curiously, Ahab is not named throughout this passage, except in verse 20. He is referred to simply as "the king of Israel" or "the king." A council was called and Ahab set forth his plan to recapture the city of Ramoth Gilead, reminding his audience that it is "ours" (v. 3). No doubt his speech was designed to stir national emotion.

Ahab sought and received the support of Jehoshaphat in this campaign (v. 4). Syria was a common enemy, and it served both of the kings to defeat this continued threat to their well-being. But Jehoshaphat was unwise to place himself and his army under Ahab's corrupt leadership.

B. The Need to Hear From God (vv. 5-12)

(1 Kings 22:5, 6, 10-12 is not included in the printed text.)

7. And Jehoshaphat said, Is there not here a prophet of the Lord besides, that we might enquire of him?

8. And the king of Israel said unto Jehoshaphat, There is yet one man, Micaiah the son of Imlah, by whom we may enquire of the Lord: but I hate him; for he doth not prophesy good concerning me, but evil. And Jehoshaphat said, Let not the king say so.

9. Then the king of Israel called an officer, and said, Hasten hither Micaiah the son of Imlah.

Jehoshaphat is generally depicted in a positive light in Scripture and here reveals his spiritual sensitivity by asking Ahab to "please inquire for the word of the Lord today" (v. 5, *NKJV*), even after agreeing to go to battle. Jehoshaphat was looking for a special word of confirmation or direction from *Yahweh*, the special and intimate name of God, usually designated in the English translations by capital letters (LORD). It was common for a leader to seek guidance prior to engaging in battle, usually from a prophet or prophetess (Judges 4:12-16); priest (1 Samuel 14:36, 37); or the Lord himself, as David often did (1 Samuel 23:1-5; 30:7, 8). This was a practice that even Ahab had engaged in previously (1 Kings 20:13, 14).

There are two categories of prophets in this passage: (1) the 400 court prophets of Ahab (22:6), who were prophets for hire (see Micah 3:5, 11), and (2) the prophet of God, Micaiah (1 Kings 22:8). During this period, there were several other true prophets, including Elijah (ch. 17 ff.) and an anonymous prophet seen in 20:13. Presumably, the 400 hired prophets were the ones of Asherah who ate "at Jezebel's table" (18:19), and escaped judgment during Elijah's encounter with the prophets of Baal.

When Ahab asked the prophets, "Shall I go against Ramoth Gilead to fight?" (22:6, *NKJV*), he did not include Jehoshaphat or the combined armies in his statement. This could be a depiction of his arrogance or a subtle hint to the prophets to return a favorable verdict. That is exactly what he received. They encouraged him to take the city, assuring him that God was in the plan. Their livelihood depended on pleasing the king, not seeking and proclaiming the truth.

There is a contrast between Ahab's view of the prophetic gift and Jehoshaphat's view. Ahab seemed to consider prophets as agents of magic to accomplish his purpose. Jehoshaphat regarded prophets as God's instrument to bring to His people the revelation of Himself and His plan.

Jehoshaphat was dissatisfied with what he heard from the court prophets. He discerned that something was not right and asked for "a prophet of the Lord" (v. 7) because he wanted to hear from the Lord, not those who had a vested interest in pleasing the king. His life was on the line and he wanted a sure answer.

Ahab told him of Micaiah but added, "I hate him, because he does not prophesy good concerning me, but evil" (v. 8, *NKJV*). *Evil* can mean "disaster" and is reminiscent of Elijah's language in 21:20, 21, where the prophet predicted that Ahab and his progeny would be cut off. Ahab's strong statement shows contempt for those who would disagree with him. It also shows contempt for God and His messenger.

Perhaps Micaiah's name ("Who is like Yahweh?") was an unpleasant reminder that Ahab was engaged in relationships with inferior gods, such as Baal. The name certainly provides a striking parallel between the messenger of God and the request of Jehoshaphat for a word from Yahweh.

There is no record of any previous encounters between Ahab and Micaiah, but apparently this was not their first meeting. Ahab did not want to seek him out, but did so because of Jehoshaphat's swift rebuke (22:8, 9). Micaiah was not with the 400 prophets, nor in the court of the king. He maintained his distance and independence, as all true prophets must. The Old Testament reveals that prophetic correction of a corrupt system or reign requires maintaining a particular detachment from the influence of that system. Ahab's encounters with God's prophets often ended with the prophet receiving the blame for the problems Ahab created (see 18:17). It was a telling flaw in his character to blame others, rather than examining the truth for relevance to his life. Intriguingly, Elijah, who had been Ahab's "nemesis," is not a direct part of this event, though what he prophesied (21:19) does come to pass.

The kings prepared for battle on the "threshing floor" (22:10, *NKJV*), a large open space used to separate grain from chaff and convenient for a large gathering. The false prophets continued to prophesy good things in their presence.

Zedekiah, a leader or spokesman for the court prophets, used "horns of iron," symbols of power and victory (v. 11; see Deuteronomy 33:17), to illustrate what he thought would be a victory for Ahab and his soldiers. Zedekiah's behavior in this whole episode, especially toward Micaiah (see v. 24), contradicts his name, which means "Yahweh is righteousness." His enactment was confirmed by his colleagues, who prophesied a third time the assurance of victory (v. 12).

C. Confirmation or Truth? (vv. 13, 14)

(1 Kings 22:13 is not included in the printed text.)

14. And Micaiah said, As the Lord liveth, what the Lord saith unto me, that will I speak.

The messenger sent to retrieve Micaiah informed him of the declarations of the prophets, and pleaded with him to confirm their forecast and speak words of "encouragement" (v 13, *NKJV*). The messenger had the same view of prophecy as Ahab. It was a tool utilized to obtain blessings upon what he wanted to do, not an opportunity to hear the truth. It was a method utilized to fortify the official position. This verse also reveals how pervasive the influence of a leader can be, even to a messenger.

Micaiah declared, "As the Lord lives, whatever the Lord says to me, that I will speak" (v. 14, *NKJV*). He made it clear that he would only speak when the Lord spoke and that the content will be what the Lord spoke to him. He would not be one of Ahab's "yes" men.

II. TRUTH SPOKEN
   (1 Kings 22:15-28)

A. A Whimsical Prophecy
   (vv. 15, 16)

(1 Kings 22:15, 16 is not included in the printed text.)

Micaiah told the king exactly what he wanted to hear, but there was something about Micaiah's words, perhaps his tone or behavior, that communicated to the king this was not God's genuine message that he needed to hear. Ahab had heard Micaiah prophesy before and knew the difference between the true prophetic utterance and a message of comfort. In light of verse 14, apparently Micaiah had been instructed by the Lord to take the king by surprise and gain his full attention, much like Nathan did with David (2 Samuel 12:1-4).

Verse 16 is one of the few shining moments of Ahab's reign, as he insisted on hearing "the truth in the name of the Lord" (*NIV*). Somewhere deep inside of him there was a desire for truth. It may have been due to the influence of Jehoshaphat or the presence of God with the prophet or his awareness of previous prophecies; but something gripped his heart and he needed the facts. Sometimes, however, the truth can be difficult to receive even when we think we are prepared for it. Difficult truth should not only be shared in love, but received with a heart bathed in prayer.

B. A Tale of Two Visions (vv. 17-23)

(1 Kings 22:17, 18 is not included in the printed text.)

19. And he said, Hear thou therefore the word of the Lord: I saw the Lord sitting on his throne, and all the host of heaven standing by him on his right hand and on his left.

20. And the Lord said, Who shall persuade Ahab, that he may go up and fall at Ramoth-gilead? And one said on this manner, and another said on that manner.

21. And there came forth a spirit, and stood before the Lord, and said, I will persuade him.

22. And the Lord said unto him, Wherewith? And he said, I will go forth, and I will be a lying spirit in the mouth of all his prophets. And he said, Thou shalt persuade him, and prevail also: go forth, and do so.

23. Now therefore, behold, the Lord hath put a lying spirit in the mouth of all these thy prophets, and the Lord hath spoken evil concerning thee.

The prophet Micaiah had an authoritative message for the king, received through two visions. His first vision depicted Israel as scattered sheep without a shepherd. It is a clear allusion to the death of the king.

The image of a shepherd communicated that kings were to feed and protect the flock under their care (2 Samuel 5:2; also see Zechariah 13:7). It was an image of self-sacrifice and concern for others above concern for self. The king would soon die, leaving Israel with no leader ("master"), and yet his death would result in peace for the nation. It was a separation of the well-being of the nation from that of the king. God was beginning to communicate to His people a need for a personal relationship with Him apart from their identity as the nation of Israel. Just being with the right crowd is insufficient.

Verse 18 relays one of the humorous aspects of this story. Ahab turned to Jehoshaphat and effectively said, "I told you so!" It indicates Ahab understood exactly what Micaiah was saying. Unfortunately, he did not act upon it. Receiving the truth and applying it are two different issues.

Micaiah then gave "the word of the Lord" he received through a second vision (vv. 19-23). Visions convey truth without assuming literal interpretation of all the details. For example, Peter's vision of Acts 10:9-16 reveals that everyone redeemed by God is to be accepted into the church, not that there are sheets and unclean animals in heaven.

In the first segment of the vision, Micaiah says, "I saw the Lord sitting on his throne," surrounded by a heavenly host (v. 19). It was a clear message that God was still reigning over all the kingdoms of the earth, including Israel, and that He was in control of the events that would transpire.

In verse 20, the vision depicts a meeting of the heavenly host, or council, to discuss Ahab's situation. This too is consistent with other visions of the throne room of God (see Job 1:6-12; 2:1-6; Psalm 82:1; cf. Genesis 1:26; 3:22; 11:7; Psalm 89:5-7; Isaiah 6:8).

The heavenly host is viewed in Scripture as God's army under His control utilized to accomplish His will (see Psalm 103:21), but still with free will like humanity (see v. 20). This is a method of communicating to finite human beings the interaction of the Godhead with His created order.

In the midst of this scene, the Lord asks, "Who will persuade Ahab to go up?" (1 Kings 22:20, *NKJV*). The imagery behind this verse is that of convincing Ahab to do what is already in his heart to do. Ahab is now named (the only time in this encounter) and it is made clear that God's judgment is upon him. After a discussion ensued, "a spirit [came forward] and stood before the Lord" (v. 21) and volunteered to use Ahab's own prophets to bring about his judgment.

The Hebrew term has an article, so the translation would normally be "the spirit." Some have suggested this is a reference to the Holy Spirit. This explanation is inconsistent with His nature as the Spirit of truth (John 16:13). It is also inconsistent with this verse. The spirit "stood before the Lord," which is an indication of subordination (cf. Genesis 19:27). The Spirit as the third person of the Trinity is fully God.

Others have suggested that this spirit was one of the angels who volunteered to become an agent of deception to bring about Ahab's demise. While there is no mention of Satan here, it is not difficult to see a correlation with Job 1:6 and 2:1, where Satan appeared with the heavenly host and desired to afflict Job. It would be consistent with his destructive nature to bring about the judgment of Ahab through deceit and lies (see John 8:44), making him the unnamed "spirit." The New Testament concept of Satan as ruler over the realm of evil is not fully developed in the Old Testament, where all events are attributed to God, who is ultimately in control of this world (2 Samuel 24:1; Isaiah 45:7).

When God asked how this would be accomplished, the spirit replied, "I will go [out] and . . . be a lying spirit in the mouth of all his prophets" (1 Kings 22:22). The word *lying* can also mean "empty promises." In a sense, the spirit would inspire the false prophets to bring forth empty promises, which by its nature is the characteristic of false prophecy. God gave His permission for the spirit to accomplish the task (see Job 1:12; 2:6).

This vision teaches several truths.

1. *God utilizes what is already in the hearts of humanity to accomplish His purposes.* The spirit inspired the false prophets to prophesy the things they were inclined to speak anyway. As with Pharaoh, God used what was in their hearts to accomplish His will. However, God does not violate humanity's free will. Ahab had a choice. He knew the declaration of his prophets was an illusion, not truth. Yet he chose to listen to them rather than Micaiah's true prophecy (v. 18).

2. *Mercy always precedes judgment.* Jehoshaphat's desire for a "word from the Lord" and Micaiah's presence were both instruments of God's mercy to Ahab. He could have repented and acknowledged God, which would have averted his judgment again (see 1 Kings 21:29). Instead, he chose to press on with his plans.

3. *Wise counsel must be listened to and heeded.* God, who knows all things, is still willing to listen to others; but Ahab, who did not know all things, rejected that with which he disagreed.

4. *Judgment is redemptive in nature.* God brought the opportunity of

salvation to Israel through the death of Ahab and the end of his evil presence.

5. *Our faith and trust must be in God even when we do not understand His will or His ways.*

C. Abuse, Affliction and Affirmation (vv. 24-28)

(1 Kings 22:24, 25 is not included in the printed text.)

26. And the king of Israel said, Take Micaiah, and carry him back unto Amon the governor of the city, and to Joash the king's son;

27. And say, Thus saith the king, Put this fellow in the prison, and feed him with bread of affliction and with water of affliction, until I come in peace.

28. And Micaiah said, If thou return at all in peace, the Lord hath not spoken by me. And he said, Hearken, O people, every one of you.

Zedekiah, who had previously enacted a scene of victory, slapped the man of God and made it clear that he believed his own prophecy to be of God. Zedekiah asked Micaiah, "When did the Spirit of the Lord leave me to speak to you?" (v. 24, *NLT*). His act of violence may have been a second symbolic action to express his "prophetic" superiority over Micaiah. Micaiah responded wisely by not returning evil with further evil, in contrast to Zedekiah and Ahab. Not unlike today, this passage reveals a continuing conflict between those who always prophesy prosperity, peace and success, and those who deliver the true message of God, which at this time happened to be impending judgment.

Prophets were often imprisoned when their oracles did not suit those in charge. They were removed from the sphere of influence in an effort to keep them from unsettling the people (see Jeremiah 37; 38). Ahab's punishment of Micaiah may have been designed to threaten the prophet. He was entrusted to the "governor of the city" and placed in confinement and

fed prison food—the "bread of affliction and . . . water of affliction" (1 Kings 22:26, 27). This was probably designed to weaken Micaiah and the power of his prophetic utterance.

Before being removed from Ahab's presence, Micaiah communicated three things to his hearers. First, he informed Zedekiah that he would hear from God. The truth would be confirmed to Zedekiah in secret, his inner chamber as a place of hiding (v. 25). This appears to be a prophetic word of impending judgment for Zedekiah. The fulfillment of this is not reported, since it is not crucial to the story.

Second, Micaiah lay his calling and reputation as a prophet on the line before all those gathered, but especially with Ahab: "If you ever return in peace, the Lord has not spoken by me" (v. 28, *NKJV*). Deuteronomy 18:21, 22 and Jeremiah 28:8, 9 (in a strikingly similar situation) both reveal the classic test of a true prophet: whatever a prophet speaks must come to pass or the prophet is not to be feared or regarded. In a play on words, Micaiah noted there would be peace, but it would be for Israel and not Ahab (1 Kings 22:28; cf. v. 17).

Third, he warned those listening to "hearken"—take heed. The events were not just a message to Ahab, but to all Israel (and us) to learn from the tragic circumstances of a person who rejects truth.

III. TRUTH CONFIRMED
(1 Kings 22:29-38)

A. Disregard and Deception (vv. 29-33)

(1 Kings 22:30-33 is not included in the printed text.)

29. So the king of Israel and Jehoshaphat the king of Judah went up to Ramoth-gilead.

Ahab and Jehoshaphat disregarded the message of Micaiah and went to reclaim Ramoth Gilead. However, Ahab was disconcerted by the prophecy enough to disguise himself as a soldier, rather than appear as a king. In a picture of his true character, he wanted Jehoshaphat, however, to remain in his royal robes (v. 30). Perhaps he thought he could outwit the prophetic declaration and deceive his way through the battle. He is the image of a person devoid of truth.

Thirty-two of the Syrian captains received orders from the king of Syria to find Ahab (v. 31). They found Jehoshaphat in his royal robes and believed him to be Ahab, but when he "cried out" (v. 32), apparently informing them of his identity and uttering a prayer, they left him alone (v. 33; see also 2 Chronicles 18:31).

B. Prophecy Fulfilled (vv. 34-36)

(1 Kings 22:35, 36 is not included in the printed text.)

34. And a certain man drew a bow at a venture, and smote the king of Israel between the joints of the harness: wherefore he said unto the driver of his chariot, Turn thine hand, and carry me out of the host; for I am wounded.

"A certain man" at *random* ("with integrity" or "in innocence") drew his bow and let an arrow fly. Of course, God is in control of even coincidental circumstances (see Ruth 2:3). In a compelling confirmation of several prophecies given to him (1 Kings 20:42; 21:20-24), Ahab was struck "between the joints of [his armor]," where the solid armor covering his chest and the flexible mesh armor covering his abdomen, which allowed him to move about, came together.

Seriously wounded, Ahab asked to be removed from the battle, but because of the intensity of the fight, that proved to be impossible (v. 35). He was propped up in his chariot to rally his troops and deceive the Syrians. The wound resulted in a substantial loss of blood and in death later that evening. Reminiscent of Micaiah's words (v. 17), the cry came for the troops to return home because their leader was dead (v. 36).

C. Death and Dogs (vv. 37, 38)

(1 Kings 22:38 is not included in the printed text.)

37. So the king died, and was brought to Samaria; and they buried the king in Samaria.

The king and his chariot were returned to Samaria, where he was buried. As the blood was being washed from his chariot by a cistern, the dogs licked his blood in fulfillment of Elijah's prophecy and his treatment of Naboth (21:19; also see 2 Kings 9:25, 26, 30-36).

According to verse 38 of the text (*NKJV*), in a disgraceful act, the harlots bathed in the pool with the king's blood. Some suggest that the prostitutes did this in superstitious hope of enhancing their beauty, vitality, or even receiving magical power, through contact with royal blood. However, this is probably best seen as commentary on Ahab's own spiritual and physical infidelity (see 1 Kings 16:31).

The word of the Lord sought earlier in this text (v. 5) was fulfilled. Micaiah was vindicated. Truth prevailed once again.

GOLDEN TEXT HOMILY

"AS THE LORD LIVETH, WHAT THE LORD SAITH UNTO ME, THAT WILL I SPEAK" (1 Kings 22:14).

As a child I often heard my father say during a business transaction, "A man is as good as his word." There were no contracts or legal documents to sign, just a smile and a handshake. The phrase meant "Whatever this man says, one can believe it is true."

Today, in a world driven by social acceptance, power, position, greed and conformity, a man of his word is a rare commodity.

Paul warned Timothy that the last days would be characterized by hypocrisy; that dishonesty would flourish and people would be inclined to say one thing when they really mean something different (1 Timothy 4:1, 2).

Yet, Paul states in Ephesians 6:14 we are to have our "loins girt about with truth." Truth is the Christian soldier's belt, and all truth and honesty originates in Christ.

Therefore, when we take on the likeness of Christ either by action or by mouth, we speak the word of the Lord. The Bible says that Jesus was "full of grace and truth" (John 1:14). As Christians, we must also be "grace-full" and "truth-full." We must be full of truth under all circumstances.

Throughout history, stories have been recorded of men and women who, for the smallest moment of gratification, have compromised the absolutes of Scripture just to gain acceptance and praise only to have their "word" tarnished for life.

As a child of God, our most treasured and guarded possession should be "our word."—**Kathy Sanders**

SENTENCE SERMONS

CHRISTIANS are called to speak the truth in love.

—Selected

APART FROM BLUNT TRUTH, our lives sink decadently amid the perfume of hints and suggestions.

—Alfred Whitehead

SOME PEOPLE live their whole lives just around the corner from the world of truth.

—Carl F.H. Henry

ILLUMINATING THE LESSON

A Mercedes Benz TV commercial featured one of their cars crashing into a cement wall to show the energy-absorbing design, which keeps passengers safer in the event of a crash. Because of its success, the design was subsequently copied by other car manufacturers. Someone then asked the company spokesman why Mercedes does not keep others from copying the patented design. He replied, "Because some things in life are too important not to share."

Jesus said, "And ye shall know the truth, and the truth shall make you free" (John 8:32). People need to know the truth before that truth can set them free. Christians have and know the truth, and the truth is too important not to share. Lives are depending on it.—**Adapted from Jim Beranek, "To Illustrate," Leadership, Summer 1991**

DAILY BIBLE READINGS

M. Truthful Judges.
   Exodus 18:15-26
T. God's Law Is Truth.
   Psalm 119:137-144
W. Speak the Truth.
   Zechariah 8:13-17
T. Truth Makes Free.
   John 8:28-32
F. Christ Is Truth.
   John 14:1-7
S. God's Word Is Truth.
   John 17:14-19

TRUTH SEARCH
Creatively Teaching the Word

DISCUSSION QUESTIONS

1 Kings 22:1-14

1. What request did Ahab, the king of Israel, make of Jehoshaphat, king of Judah (vv. 1-4)?

2. What did Jehoshaphat request (v. 5)? Why?

3. What did Jehoshaphat think about the 400 prophets who spoke with one voice (vv. 6, 7)?

4. What was the reputation of the prophet Micaiah (v. 8)?

5. How did King Ahab feel about Micaiah, and why (v. 8)?

6. What was the message of Zedekiah and his fellow prophets (vv. 11, 12)?

7. What did Micaiah promise to do (vv. 13, 14)?

1 Kings 22:15-28

1. What was Micaiah's first message to the king of Israel (vv. 15, 16), and why?

2. Explain the prophecy the Lord had actually given him (v. 17).

3. According to Micaiah, what was the source of the other prophets' advice (vv. 19-23)?

4. What prophecy did Micaiah make concerning the prophet Zedekiah (v. 25)?

5. How did Micaiah suffer because of his brave stand for truth (vv. 24, 26, 27)?

6. How certain was Micaiah that he had heard from the Lord (v. 28)?

1 Kings 22:29-37

1. What was the two kings' decision about fighting Syria (v. 29)?

2. What was Ahab's scheme to protect himself (v. 30)?

3. How did Jehoshaphat save his own life (vv. 31-33)?

4. In what sense was a soldier's arrow shot at random (v. 34)? In what sense was it not a random shot?

5. Describe the accuracy of Micaiah's prophecy (vv. 36, 37).

DRAMA SKETCH

Write each of the following statements on a different slip of paper:

• Truth is relevant—what is wrong for you might be right for me.

• Homosexuality is a positive alternative lifestyle.

• All religions lead to the same God.

• Tolerance is the most important value.

• Lying is acceptable in certain situations.

• Abortion is a woman's right.

Have a person come forward. Introduce him or her as a Christian who wants to take a strong stand for truth. Tell this volunteer to be ready to respond to worldly ideas.

Before class, give the papers to six people and explain their roles. First, each will stand and make the statement on the paper as if it is a personal belief. As the person standing for truth begins to respond, the second person should stand and make his or her statement. This pattern continues until all six statements are made.

Next, the six people should take turns coming forward, repeating their statements as they come. They will finally surround the Christian and repeatedly shout their statements at the same time.

After the sketch, talk about how difficult it can be to stand up for truth in today's world. Then move into the Bible study.

Jehoiada, Righteous Statesman

Study Text: 2 Kings 11:1-21; 2 Chronicles 24:1-16
Objective: To recognize that righteousness is beneficial to society and live righteously in Christ.
Time: Between 890 and 850 B.C.
Place: Jerusalem
Golden Text: "When the righteous are in authority, the people rejoice" (Proverbs 29:2).
Central Truth: Righteous people are needed throughout society.
Evangelism Emphasis: The church's appeal to sinners to repent and believe the gospel is a call to righteous living.

PRINTED TEXT

2 Kings 11:4. And the seventh year Jehoiada sent and fetched the rulers over hundreds, with the captains and the guard, and brought them to him into the house of the Lord, and made a covenant with them, and took an oath of them in the house of the Lord, and shewed them the king's son.

11. And the guard stood, every man with his weapons in his hand, round about the king, from the right corner of the temple to the left corner of the temple, along by the altar and the temple.

12. And he brought forth the king's son, and put the crown upon him, and gave him the testimony; and they made him king, and anointed him; and they clapped their hands, and said, God save the king.

17. And Jehoiada made a covenant between the Lord and the king and the people, that they should be the Lord's people; between the king also and the people.

18. And all the people of the land went into the house of Baal, and brake it down; his altars and his images brake they in pieces thoroughly, and slew Mattan the priest of Baal before the altars. And the priest appointed officers over the house of the Lord.

19. And he took the rulers over hundreds, and the captains, and the guard, and all the people of the land; and they brought down the king from the house of the Lord, and came by the way of the gate of the guard to the king's house. And he sat on the throne of the kings.

20. And all the people of the land rejoiced, and the city was in quiet: and they slew Athaliah with the sword beside the king's house.

21. Seven years old was Jehoash when he began to reign.

2 Chronicles 24:1. Joash was seven years old when he began to reign, and he reigned forty years in Jerusalem. His mother's name also was Zibiah of Beer-sheba.

2. And Joash did that which was right in the sight of the Lord all the days of Jehoiada the priest.

15. But Jehoiada waxed old, and was full of days when he died; an hundred and thirty years old was he when he died.

16. And they buried him in the city of David among the kings, because he had done good in Israel, both toward God, and toward his house.

DICTIONARY

Jehoiada (jeh-HOY-uh-duh)—2 Kings 11:4—a godly high priest whom God used to preserve the Messianic line
Mattan (MAT-un)—2 Kings 11:18—a priest of the idol **Baal (BAY-ul)**
Athaliah (ath-uh-LIE-uh)—2 Kings 11:20—the only woman to ever reign over Judah, whose evil reign lasted six years
Jehoash (jeh-HO-ash)—2 Kings 11:21—or **Joash (JO-ash)—**
(2 Chronicles 24:1)—ruler of Judah who became king at age 7

LESSON OUTLINE

I. COMMITTED TO RIGHTEOUS GOVERNMENT

  A. The Concern of the Righteous

  B. The Commission of the Soldiers

  C. The Crowning of the King

  D. The Cure for Evil

II. COMMITTED TO RIGHTEOUS LIVING

  A. The Covenants

  B. The Cleansing of the Land

  C. The Celebration of the People

III. LIFELONG RIGHTEOUS INFLUENCE

  A. The Reign of the King

  B. The Restoration of the Temple

  C. The Reputation of Jehoiada

LESSON EXPOSITION

INTRODUCTION

The narrative of 2 Kings can be challenging to follow because there are so many people with the same names ruling the two Jewish kingdoms, and the action moves along at a rapid pace.

King Jehoram of Judah (southern kingdom) married Athaliah, the daughter of Ahab and Jezebel (8:18), and had a son named Ahaziah. This Ahaziah was the grandson of Ahab and not to be confused with Ahaziah, the son of Ahab, whose reign over Israel (northern kingdom) was very brief (1 Kings 22:40—2 Kings 1:18). At the death of Jehoram of Judah, Ahaziah became king of that nation (2 Kings 8:24-27). Following the example set by her mother, Jezebel, Athaliah taught Ahaziah to rebel against the Lord (2 Chronicles 22:3). The influence of the northern kingdom had now infiltrated the southern kingdom.

God commissioned Jehu, king of Israel, through Elisha to rid the land of the evil influence from the house of Ahab (2 Kings 9:7; 2 Chronicles 22:7). Jehu is an interesting character. He was zealous *for* the Lord but not zealous *in* the Lord, especially at the end of his life (2 Kings 10:31). He is an example of one who does righteous deeds but is not righteous. He fulfilled his commission, killing Ahab's son, King Joram of Israel (9:24), and Ahab's grandson, King Ahaziah of Judah (v. 27), at the plot of Naboth's garden (see 1 Kings 21). This brings us to the passage at hand.

Second Kings 11 is a story of how one righteous man inspired a nation to do what was right. God, who is not mentioned directly, was at work through the lives of those who were righteous. Even in times of seeming inactivity and detachment, God is an agent of action and presence. He is working behind the scene to bring about His plan to deliver His people from evil. God's promise to David came down to the fate of one baby boy (Joash) and the people placed in his life. Even in the midst of a perverse and wicked land, God had a righteous remnant. He knew who they were and where they were.

Absent from this passage are the prophets who had been so active in the lives of the kings and the people (Samuel, Nathan, Elijah, Micaiah, Elisha, and others). The primary person in this narrative is a priest, Jehoiada. It indicates that the church needs both the prophet, who represents God to the people, and the priest, who represents the people to God. Proclamation and intercession are both part of the church's mission. Jehoiada was a true priest who offered himself as an agent of God, ministering to the people in tangible ways to bring about God's righteousness and justice in the land.

Righteousness is a rich and complex term whose many facets of meaning must be determined based on the context in which it is found. It can mean *legitimacy* in reference to a relationship or reign. In order to be a legitimate king, one had to have a connection or right to the throne, and was therefore a righteous king who was expected to do righteousness (see Jeremiah 23:5).

Righteousness is closely related to several other concepts in Scripture, including justice (Psalm 72:2, *NKJV*). Without justice, there is no righteousness. It is aligned with the covenantal faithfulness of God's love (Psalm 36:10) and associated with His peace (Isaiah 32:17). In its essence, righteousness is *living in a covenant relationship with God.* Today's study reveals Jehoiada as a truly righteous person.

I. COMMITTED TO RIGHTEOUS GOVERNMENT
   (2 Kings 11:1-16)

A. The Concern of the Righteous (vv. 1-3)

(2 Kings 11:1-3 is not included in the printed text.)

Athaliah, the mother of Ahaziah, seized the throne of Judah and killed all the heirs to that throne she could locate, which included her own grandchildren (v. 1). She is not introduced as the queen because she was not the legitimate queen. She was from the house of Omri and Ahab, not the Davidic line. Scripture does not provide her with the usual introduction

and summary for that reason. She is treated as an interregnum—a temporary suspension of government between successive reigns. Her story serves to emphasize God's promise to David (8:19; 2 Samuel 7:16).

Joash ("God is strong") was rescued ("stolen"), which carries the idea of being kidnapped, or snatched away (see 2 Kings 11:2). Joash, also called Jehoash, is to be distinguished from the king of the northern kingdom by the same name(s) (13:9-13). It was Ahaziah's own sister, Jehosheba, who secured the child from certain death at the hands of Athaliah. The parallel account in 2 Chronicles 22 reveals that Jehosheba was the wife of the high priest Jehoiada (v. 11). She does not appear to have been the daughter of Athaliah.

Jehosheba's actions not only secured the child's life but certified his identity and legitimized his Davidic lineage. He and his nurse were hidden in the priest's quarters of the Temple for six years (2 Kings 11:2, 3). His identity could have been easily concealed. He would pass as one of the children of the priests or as a protégé, much like Samuel (1 Samuel 1—3).

Two significant images are raised by 2 Kings 11:3. On one level, the true king hid (albeit temporarily) while the false queen reigned openly, a classic picture of this world. Evil is not ashamed, while the righteous must often ensure their safety from those who would extinguish the flame of God in this world.

On another level, the legitimate king was in the Temple being prepared for service, while the queen, a usurper, operated through the wisdom and values of the world in the pursuit of power. She worshiped at the altars of Baal; he received and fulfilled the instruction of God. Joash is associated with the presence of God throughout the narrative.

Notice the contrast that develops throughout the story between the Temple ("house of the Lord") and the palace ("the king's house"). It must have been a difficult six years of waiting for Jehoiada, Jehosheba and Joash. In the end, righteousness would prevail in the Temple and the palace.

B. The Commission of the Soldiers (vv. 4-8)

(2 Kings 11:5-8 is not included in the printed text.)

4. And the seventh year Jehoiada sent and fetched the rulers over hundreds, with the captains and the guard, and brought them to him into the house of the Lord, and made a covenant with them, and took an oath of them in the house of the Lord, and shewed them the king's son.

In the seventh year, the year of restoration in Scripture (Exodus 23:11; Deuteronomy 15:12), the time came for the restoration of the Davidic king to the throne. Jehoiada appears in the narrative without explanation or background, much like the prophets of 1 and 2 Kings. It is not until verse 9 that he is described as a priest. He was the high priest (see 12:10; 2 Chronicles 24:6), which enabled him to secure the confidence of and give commands to the Temple and palace guard.

Jehoiada approached the captains commanding troops of a hundred, both of "the bodyguards," an elite group trained to protect royalty, and "the escorts," those who ran before the monarch as he or she was moving from one place to another (v. 4, NKJV). He "brought them into the house of the Lord." This is more than a statement to reveal the location of Joash, though it serves that purpose also. In the presence of God, they entered into a covenant (sacred agreement) to be the servants of God in placing Joash on the throne of promise. Next, "the king's son" was revealed to the captains.

Jehoiada devised a complex plan to protect the king during his coronation (vv. 5-8). Normally during the week, two-thirds of the troops were assigned to protect the queen and one-third to protect the Temple. However on the Sabbath, the order was reversed. Jehoiada's plan was designed to take full advantage of the changing of the guard. No one would notice the confluence of the troops at the Temple on a Sabbath, which would provide for the little king to be protected on all sides and deprive Athaliah of any troops to foil the plan or protect her from judgment.

C. The Crowning of the King (vv. 9-12)

(2 Kings 11:9, 10 is not included in the printed text.)

11. And the guard stood, every man with his weapons in his hand, round about the king, from the right corner of the temple to the left corner of the temple, along by the altar and the temple.

12. And he brought forth the king's son, and put the crown upon him, and gave him the testimony; and they made him king, and anointed him; and they clapped their hands, and said, God save the king.

On the day of the coronation, when all of the troops would have been in movement, the plan was executed and all the captains and troops reported to Jehoiada (v. 9). Some suggest that this particular Sabbath may have been the start of the New Year, a time when kings were normally crowned. David's ceremonial shields and spears added authenticity and authority to the event (v. 10). These were normally carried by the Temple guard during the visits of royalty. Now they would not only be used to recognize the new king, but his connection to David as well. The escorts formed a semicircle around the entrance to the Temple and the altar in front of it, awaiting the presence of the well-guarded king, who would be surrounded as he emerged, presumably by the bodyguards (v. 11).

In verse 12, Joash was brought out of the Temple into the Temple courtyard between the porch and the altar (see 2 Chronicles 8:12; Joel 2:17) and crowned with the diadem, signifying his royalty and his consecration. It symbolized (1) his authority under God as His representative to bring righteousness and justice to the people on a national level and (2) his separation unto the office in which God was placing him. He would be confirmed by the people, but the crown was a reminder that he answered ultimately to God. Jehoiada also gave Joash "the testimony." There are different opinions concerning the contents of this scroll. However, the evidence suggests it was the king's personal copy of the Torah, to guide him and remind him of his awesome responsibilities as a political and spiritual leader (see Deuteronomy 17:18-20; 1 Kings 2:3; Psalm 132:12). That he offers the written Torah to the new king, rather than a prophetic proclamation, is significant. God's people need both the written word and the prophetic voice to effectively fulfill His will.

Joash was proclaimed king and anointed. Those inducted into the offices of the priest (Exodus 30:30), prophet (1 Kings 19:16) and king (2 Samuel 12:7) were anointed upon the head, usually with designated oil (see Exodus 30:22-25) poured from a horn to symbolize the following:
• Separation from the masses unto consecrated service for God (Numbers 8:14; Leviticus 8:12)
• Recognition of a special calling by God upon the life of the person (1 Samuel 16:12)
• Increased accountability (15:17, 19)
• The manifestation of God's presence and divine enablement through the Holy Spirit (10:6; 16:13)
• In anticipation and as a type of the Messiah, "the Anointed One" (Psalm 2:2; Isaiah 9:1-7; 11:1-5; 61:1-3)

When the anointing was accomplished, the people clapped and proclaimed, "Long live the king," like Solomon received at the Gihon spring (1 Kings 1:38-40).

D. The Cure for Evil (vv. 13-16)

(2 Kings 11:13-16 is not included in the printed text.)

Athaliah heard the commotion of the "guard and of the people" and made her way to the source of the noise, "the temple of the Lord," where she found "the king" (vv. 13, 14). In addition to the facts mentioned above, there are two truths in verse 14 that indicate Joash's legitimacy and God's sanction. First, he was "standing by a pillar according to custom" (NKJV). This was one of the two bronze pillars that marked the entrance to the Temple. The pillars were named Jachin, "He shall establish," and Boaz, "in its strength" (1 Kings 7:15-22). These signified the abiding presence of Yahweh. Joash was most likely standing by Jachin to confirm that it is God who was establishing the king. The word translated as "custom" can also mean "justice." The usurper was about to get her due, the heir of David was being placed on the throne, and God's promise was being fulfilled in His presence.

Second, "all the people of the land were rejoicing and blowing trumpets" (v. 14, NKJV). Though God selected, He made provision for the people to confirm the king, as with Saul (1 Samuel 10:24), David (2 Samuel 5:1-3), and Solomon (1 Kings 1:38, 39).

The exact meaning of the phrase "the people of the land" is difficult to determine. It could refer to landowners, or patriots who heard about the king (or were worshiping in the Temple) and were there to celebrate. In addition, the phrase often signifies those who are disenfranchised by those in authority. Those who have no voice in the political structures of this world, however, are given a voice through righteousness (Proverbs 29:2). When the structures of this world fail, God still hears the cries of the people. It serves as a reminder that kings (leaders) exist for the benefit of the people and not vice versa.

In a humorous display of irony, the one who had blasphemed God tore her clothes in an act designed to show her deep spiritual sorrow. The one who seized the throne illegally yelled, "Treason! Treason!" (2 Kings 11:14).

Athaliah was seized and removed from the Temple area by the soldiers under Jehoiada's directive (v. 15). Anyone who followed her out of the Temple was to be killed as well. "Those who follow her" is not a metaphorical reference to her loyal servants and subjects, but limited to those who actually left with her. None are recorded doing so. There is no wholesale slaughter here, in contrast to Jehu's zealous actions in the northern kingdom. Jehoiada was careful to maintain the sanctity of the Temple, ordering that she not be killed in the court or Temple area. Jehoiada used wisdom, rather than force, to purge the wickedness from Judah. Athaliah was removed "by way of the horses' entrance into the king's house" and slain there (v. 16, NKJV).

While the true king was crowned in the front of the Temple, the false queen was slain in the back of the palace.

Righteousness has positive and negative implications. It is not just the receiving of God's provision (life and relationship) and our response to His provision (communion and obedience); it includes the removal of those things that are unrighteous or cause unrighteousness (see Matthew 5:29, 30).

II. COMMITTED TO RIGHTEOUS LIVING (2 Kings 11:17-21)

A. The Covenants (v. 17)

17. And Jehoiada made a covenant between the Lord and the king and the people, that they should be the Lord's people; between the king also and the people.

Three covenants are made here. The first was a covenant between the Lord and the king. It was most likely a renewal of the covenant God made

with David (2 Samuel 7:8-16). Athaliah's seizure of the throne made the renewal advisable for the sake of the people, as well as Joash, who needed to know why he was receiving the throne and what the promises were in connection to his coronation (see 2 Kings 8:19).

The second covenant was between the Lord and the people, that they should be wholly dedicated to God (Deuteronomy 4:20; 26:18; 27:9). He was their God; they were His people (Exodus 6:7; 19:5; Deuteronomy 5:2; Joshua 24:25).

The third covenant was between the king and the people (see 2 Kings 23:3). This covenant links back to "the testimony" (11:12). It was a reminder that the kingship was based on covenant relationship with God that was also expressed to the people. The king was the guardian of the covenant law, the Torah. It was his responsibility to see that justice and righteousness prevail in the land (1 Kings 10:9).

D. The Cleansing of the Land (v. 18)

18. And all the people of the land went into the house of Baal, and brake it down; his altars and his images brake they in pieces thoroughly, and slew Mattan the priest of Baal before the altars. And the priest appointed officers over the house of the Lord.

Purification was the result of covenant renewal. Again, "all the people of the land" descended upon the temple of Baal to destroy it and remove its presence and influence from the land. Athaliah had apparently built and furnished the temple, following the example set by her parents, Ahab and Jezebel (1 Kings 16:30, 31). The images of foreign idols were smashed, along with the altars. Mattan, the priest of Baal, was killed before the altar of Baal.

In a sense, this was a desecration of that which had been wrongly considered "holy." The exact location of Baal's temple is difficult to ascertain, but is believed to have been in the court of the Temple or palace, revealing just how perverse Athaliah was. Jehoiada appointed guards for the Temple to prevent any uprising or retaliation from the worshipers of Baal.

C. The Celebration of the People (vv. 19-21)

19. And he took the rulers over hundreds, and the captains, and the guard, and all the people of the land; and they brought down the king from the house of the Lord, and came by the way of the gate of the guard to the king's house. And he sat on the throne of the kings.
20. And all the people of the land rejoiced, and the city was in quiet: and they slew Athaliah with the sword beside the king's house.
21. Seven years old was Jehoash when he began to reign.

The entourage of troops, people of the land, and probably the priests carried the king from the Temple court to the king's palace, through a different gate than the area in which Athaliah was killed. Joash entered through the gate normally used by royalty. To this point, Joash had been passive. He went where he was led or carried. For the first time in the narrative, he did something proactively. He sat upon the throne and lay claim to his right to rule Judah (v. 19). The people rejoiced and "the city was in quiet" (calm) because evil had been removed from the land (v. 20).

Jehoash (a variation of Joash) was only 7 as he began his reign (v. 21). This story is a reminder of what his aunt and uncle did to bring the legitimate ruler to the throne, help reestablish the Davidic line, remove the presence of evil, and motivate the people to a commitment to righteous living.

III. LIFELONG RIGHTEOUS INFLUENCE (2 Chronicles 24:1-16)

A. The Reign of the King (vv. 1-3)

(2 Chronicles 24:3 is not included in the printed text.)

1. Joash was seven years old when he began to reign, and he reigned forty years in Jerusalem. His mother's name also was Zibiah of Beer-sheba.
2. And Joash did that which was right in the sight of the Lord all the days of Jehoiada the priest.

In 2 Chronicles 24, the reign of Joash is divided into two distinct segments: (1) the period of blessings and obedience, during which he was influenced by Jehoiada (vv. 1-16), and (2) the period of disobedience and judgment, following Jehoiada's death (vv. 17-27). The passage under study concentrates on the positive influence Jehoiada had on Joash.

Through Jehoiada's (and his wife's) efforts, the king came to the throne at 7 years of age and reigned for 40 years in Jerusalem, the capital of Judah (v. 1). The inclusion of his mother's name may indicate she was somehow spared in Athaliah's revenge and had a part in shaping his character and administration, but certainly highlights the fact that Joash was of pure Jewish lineage, as Beersheba was at the southern edge of Judah.

The chronicler leaves no doubt as to the powerful effect one person can have on others. He notes that Joash "did that which was right in the sight of the Lord" under Jehoiada's guidance (v. 2). This speaks of his vision and focus, which was *to look straight ahead and follow that course*. It highlights his ethical and moral conduct with God and humanity, in that he was upright and blameless in all his dealings. It reveals that his spiritual relationship was one of obedience and submission to God, all of which received God's approval.

Verse 3 is a commentary on the effectiveness of Athaliah's efforts to rid the land of successors to the throne. Jehoiada chose two wives for Joash, enabling him to rebuild and broaden the lineage of David. Children were a sign of God's blessings, especially in the life of a king (1 Chronicles 14:2-7; 25:4, 5; Psalm 127:4, 5). This points to the proactive role that Jehoiada had in the king's life. He serves not only as priest to the king, but in a sense as a substitute father also.

B. The Restoration of the Temple (vv. 4-14)

(2 Chronicles 24:4-14 is not included in the printed text.)

"And it came to pass after this" (v. 4) is a phrase that means "some time after this." The time is difficult to determine, but probably somewhere toward the middle of his reign, Joash "set his heart on repairing [the Temple]" (*NKJV*). It was an act of restoration required by a particular situation, rather than daily neglect (see v. 7).

Joash attempted to motivate the priests and Levites to gather money for the restoration of the Temple (v. 5). Joash told them to go to "all Israel" to gather money, emphasizing the continuity of the present people with that of previous generations of Israelites and Moses (see v. 9). However, his instruction was received with less than an enthusiastic response.

Joash summoned Jehoiada to inquire about the delayed response in producing the "collection" (contribution or gift) for the "tabernacle of witness" (v. 6). This reference connected Moses' collection of funds to construct the Tabernacle with Joash's desire to restore the Temple built by Solomon. It was not an arbitrary decree, but an obligation based on the half-shekel tax (approximately a day's wage) used to construct the Tabernacle (Exodus 30:11-16).

In verses 6 and 7 of the text, Joash explained fully the basis for his appeal and why he wanted the funds. Athaliah most likely financed the temple of Baal by robbing the Temple of the valuable vessels and instruments.

The Temple needed to be restored to its holy state.

The king ordered the method (v. 8). A chest was to be placed outside the Temple gate, which would be in the vicinity of the altar and accessible to the people. The shift was to a more voluntary appeal to the people and removed the obligation of fund-raising from the Levites. It is not solely a decree of the king, but a plan forged in relationship with Jehoiada and possibly the priests ("they," v. 9). It was to be a wide appeal throughout Judah and Jerusalem.

The response of the people in verse 10 is the proper response for an offering made unto God—they "rejoiced" and participated "until all had given" (*NKJV*). Everyone gave and everyone gave with enthusiasm (every pastor's dream!). The response of the people on a continual basis was such that the chest had to be emptied on a daily basis, and more was gathered than needed (cf. Exodus 36:4-7).

The workers were secured and the Temple was restored to its original condition, strengthened and refurbished (2 Chronicles 24:12-14) to the design and specifications given by God himself (1 Chronicles 28:11-19), as was the Tabernacle. The Hebrew behind the phrase "was perfected" ("completed," v. 13, *NKJV*) is also used in the poetry sections of the Old Testament to signify *healing*. The work not only affected the facade and structure of the Temple, it also erased the memories of the Temple's desecration for the worship of Baal and healing resulted. The verse speaks as much to the spiritual element of the Temple as the physical. The condition of the building does affect the human spirit and, therefore, the Holy Spirit.

C. The Reputation of Jehoiada (vv. 15, 16)

15. But Jehoiada waxed old, and was full of days when he died; an hundred and thirty years old was he when he died.

16. And they buried him in the city of David among the kings, because he had done good in Israel, both toward God, and toward his house.

The phrases used of Jehoiada in this passage are generally reserved for kings. He "grew old and was full of days" (*NKJV*), a designation of honor (see 1 Chronicles 23:1). He died at the age of 130, older than Sarah (127, Genesis 23:1); Joseph (110, Genesis 50:26); Aaron (123, Numbers 33:39); Moses (120, Deuteronomy 34:7; and Joshua (110, Joshua 24:29). His long life signifies God's blessing upon him. He was buried "in the city of David among the kings." This expression depicts the character and service of the person given such an honor (see 21:20; 24:25). It is one of the highest honors that a person, whether priest or king, could receive.

Jehoiada was honored for the exceptional contribution he made to the nation through his assistance rendered to the king, God, and the Temple. His relationship with God positively affected the spiritual and political climate of a king, a Temple and a nation. His righteousness was not something distinctly inward. He lived out his righteousness—the life and power of his relationship with God—in a way that blessed all those in his life.

SENTENCE SERMONS

RIGHTEOUS PEOPLE are needed throughout society.
—Selected

A CHRISTIAN is a blot or a blessing; a blank he cannot be.
—*This Day*

A HOLY LIFE has a voice. It speaks when the tongue is silent, and is either a constant attraction or a perpetual reproof.
—Hinton

EVANGELISM APPLICATION

THE CHURCH'S APPEAL TO SINNERS TO REPENT AND BELIEVE THE GOSPEL IS A CALL TO RIGHTEOUS LIVING.

It is the church's task to help unbelievers see that the power to do right comes from God, not ourselves. As we live in relationship with Him, He gives us the power to live the life consistent with His desire for us. It is not by our ability or our strength, but through the Holy Spirit that we prevail over sin and live righteously.

ILLUMINATING THE LESSON

A student in Charissa Cole's kindergarten class in Kannapolis, North Carolina, grew frustrated and declared, "Oh my God!"—no doubt imitating what he learned at home. At his declaration of frustration, another little boy stood up and swiftly rebuked him, stating, "You're not supposed to take the Lord's name in Spain!"

This young man understood there are times when we need to be the voice crying out against things that are unrighteous. It is easy to ignore those things that bother us, but this allows the problem to continue and it also desensitizes us. We become accustomed to the evil around us. Before long, it is too easy for the evil around us to become evil within us.

DAILY BIBLE READINGS

M. Righteous Leader's Influence.
Joshua 24:22-31
T. Righteous King's Good Works.
2 Kings 23:21-25
W. Motivated by Righteous Prophets.
Ezra 4:23 through 5:2
T. Encouraged by a Righteous Man.
Acts 11:19-24
F. Helped by a Righteous Woman.
Acts 16:11-15
S. Live Righteously.
Titus 2:11-14

TRUTH SEARCH
Creatively Teaching the Word

DISCUSSION QUESTIONS

2 Kings 11

1. How was the life of young Joash spared from wicked Queen Athaliah (vv. 1-3)?

2. What was the covenant and oath Jehoiada made with the leaders of Judah (v. 4)?

3. What was Jehoiada's plan for protecting the 7-year-old boy (vv. 5-8)?

4. How well did the plan develop (vv. 9-12)?

5. What was the response of Queen Athaliah (vv. 13, 14), and what was her fate (vv. 15, 16)?

6. With the evil queen deposed, what did the priest challenge the people to do (v. 17)?

7. How did the people show the seriousness of their commitment (v. 18)?

8. Why did the people of Judah rejoice (vv. 19-21)?

2 Chronicles 24:1, 2, 15-18

1. Describe the nature of Joash's reign (vv. 1, 2).

2. How did Jehoiada influence Joash (v. 2)?

3. What happened to Joash and the people of Judah after the faithful priest's death (vv. 17, 18)? Why?

BUZZ GROUPS

Break the class into pairs or trios. Ask each group to come up with the name of a layperson in your church who is making a significant influence for righteousness, and why that person is having such an influence. After a few minutes, bring everyone back together and talk about the people they named and why.

Next, ask the students to think about whether or not they would make it on anyone's "Righteous Influencers" list. Why would they make (or not make) such a list?

Huldah, Prophetess of Encouragement

Study Text: 2 Chronicles 34:1-33
Objective: To appreciate the value of encouraging others and be an encourager.
Time: Around 630 B.C.
Place: Jerusalem
Golden Text: "Let us consider one another to provoke unto love and to good works" (Hebrews 10:24).
Central Truth: Everyone needs to be encouraged to do good.
Evangelism Emphasis: Christians should encourage the unsaved to accept Christ.

PRINTED TEXT

2 Chronicles 34:1. Josiah was eight years old when he began to reign, and he reigned in Jerusalem one and thirty years.

2. And he did that which was right in the sight of the Lord, and walked in the ways of David his father, and declined neither to the right hand, nor to the left.

14. And when they brought out the money that was brought into the house of the Lord, Hilkiah the priest found a book of the law of the Lord given by Moses.

15. And Hilkiah answered and said to Shaphan the scribe, I have found the book of the law in the house of the Lord. And Hilkiah delivered the book to Shaphan.

19. And it came to pass, when the king had heard the words of the law, that he rent his clothes.

20. And the king commanded Hilkiah, and Ahikam the son of Shaphan, and Abdon the son of Micah, and Shaphan the scribe, and Asaiah a servant of the king's, saying,

21. Go, enquire of the Lord for me, and for them that are left in Israel and in Judah, concerning the words of the book that is found: for great is the wrath of the Lord that is poured out upon us, because our fathers have not kept the word of the Lord, to do after all that is written in this book.

22. And Hilkiah, and they that the king had appointed, went to Huldah the prophetess, the wife of Shallum the son of Tikvath, the son of Hasrah, keeper of the wardrobe; (now she dwelt in Jerusalem in the college:) and they spake to her to that effect.

23. And she answered them, Thus saith the Lord God of Israel, Tell ye the man that sent you to me.

27. Because thine heart was tender, and thou didst humble thyself before God, when thou heardest his words against this place, and against the inhabitants thereof, and humbledst thyself before me, and didst rend thy clothes, and weep before me; I have even heard thee also, saith the Lord.

28. Behold, I will gather thee to thy fathers, and thou shalt be gathered to thy grave in peace, neither shall thine eyes see all the evil that I will bring upon this place, and upon the inhabitants of the same. So they brought the king word again.

DICTIONARY

Josiah (jo-SIGH-ah)—2 Chronicles 34:1—righteous king of Judah who reigned 31 years

Hilkiah (hill-KIGH-uh)—2 Chronicles 34:14—high priest during Josiah's reign, and probably Ezra's great-grandfather

Shaphan (SHAY-fan)—2 Chronicles 34:15—the secretary-financial officer of Josiah

Ahikam (uh-HIGH-cam)—2 Chronicles 34:20—a minister of Josiah, and the sole protector of Jeremiah from death under Jehoiakim (Jeremiah 26:24).

Abdon (AB-don) . . . and Asaiah (uh-ZAY-yuh)—2 Chronicles 34:20— two more of Josiah's officials

Huldah (HULL-dah)—2 Chronicles 34:22—one of the few women who filled the office of prophetess in the Bible.

LESSON OUTLINE

I. GOD'S WORD FOUND
   A. Purification of the Land
   B. Repairing of the Temple
   C. The Grand Discovery

II. UNCERTAINTY EXPRESSED
   A. An Awareness of Sin
   B. An Action of Sincerity
   C. An Official of God

III. ENCOURAGEMENT GIVEN
   A. The Introductory Prophecy
   B. The Prophecy for the People
   C. The Prophecy for Josiah
   D. The Covenant to Keep the Covenant

LESSON EXPOSITION

INTRODUCTION

Josiah was one of the greatest kings that ever reigned in Judah. His continued dedication and sensitivity to the Lord guided his personal life and made him a great leader. He is known as the great reformer of the Old Testament who sought the Lord early in life, listened to the direction God gave him, and acted upon the Word of God. His efforts resulted in a renewal in the land that came as close to bringing Israel, both the northern and southern kingdoms, back to the glory days of David and Solomon as any other king in Israel's history. His dedication to God resulted in the impending exile being delayed until the end of his life. As with all great leaders, he did not accomplish his task alone.

There were persons whom God placed in Josiah's life that assisted and encouraged him along the pathway of righteousness, including Huldah the prophetess. All that we know of her is contained in the seven verses that 2 Chronicles 34 and 2 Kings 22 record of her and her message to the nation and the king. She was a faithful wife, dedicated prophetess of God, and an encourager to King Josiah. Her encouragement gave him the strength to do what was right even though it would not change the appointed outcome.

Her ministry in the life of Josiah is an excellent example of what encouragement is—enabling a person to grow stronger. At times that may include encouraging those who are weak to keep the faith. Other times it may require that we are a sure and steadfast presence in others' lives, helping them to prevail in difficult circumstances. It may even include helping people see things from a proper perspective— God's perspective. Encouragement can be something as simple as cheering a person up and speaking words of comfort. Every believer is called and equipped to be an encourager in the kingdom of God (1 Thessalonians 5:11; Hebrews 3:13).

I. GOD'S WORD FOUND
(2 Chronicles 34:1-17)

A. Purification of the Land (vv. 1-7)

(2 Chronicles 34:3-7 is not included in the printed text.)

1. Josiah was eight years old when he began to reign, and he reigned in Jerusalem one and thirty years.

2. And he did that which was right in the sight of the Lord, and walked in the ways of David his father, and declined neither to the right hand, nor to the left.

Josiah ("supported by Jehovah") was 8 years old when he came to the throne. His reign lasted 31 years and was pleasing "in the sight of the Lord" (v. 2). That he "walked in the ways of David his father" indicates he was of the lineage of David, but also that he served God faithfully with an upright heart and did not participate or condone idolatry as many before him (see also 2 Chronicles 6:16). Throughout his lifetime, he followed God wholeheartedly, unlike Joash (24:17-25), who became king at age 7.

When Josiah reached age 16 during his eighth year on the throne, he "began to seek" God (34:3), the first step of his journey. This certainly contrasts with Saul, who does not seek ("inquire of") the Lord, but rather the medium at Endor (1 Samuel 28:7). At this age, Josiah's desire was due to his own spiritual stirring, rather than the influence of a regent or counselor, such as Jehoiada with Joash (2 Chronicles 24:2). Young kings were provided with individuals who guided them until they reached the age of majority, which was age 20 (his 12th year as king). This was the age of eligibility for military service (Numbers 1:3) and contributions to the sanctuary fund (Exodus 30:14).

Upon reaching the age of majority, when he could act without the inter-ference of a regent who could be an adherent of idolatry, Josiah took the next step and began to purge the land (Judah and Jerusalem) of everything associated with idolatry. The Temple of God is not mentioned specifically here as in 2 Kings 23:4, but it is safe to assume this was one of the first things purged of the presence of idols (see 1 Chronicles 23:28, where the Levites were to cleanse all things holy). The temples of Baal and foreign gods often had pillars with the images of these deities carved or molded into them. The things re-erected by Amon were now destroyed (2 Chronicles 33:22). Though not stated explicitly, it can be assumed that the priests of these temples were killed, following the precedent of Jehu (2 Kings 10:25) and Jehoiada (11:18).

Verse 4 of the text reveals something of Josiah's leadership. The altars were destroyed by his army "in his presence." His zeal and conviction required that he personally supervise and participate in this cleansing, rather than delegate it. Some things should not be delegated. *They* tore down the altar, but *he* destroyed the other items of worship. The incense altars which were above the altars is a play on Hebrew words depicting those things which are placed in a position of prominence, a place reserved for God, and thus are treacherous to one's spiritual well-being.

Everything was ground to dust and scattered on the graves of "them that had sacrificed" to Baal (v. 4). This includes those who worshiped Baal, not just the priests. This act both contained the pollution of idolatry and further defiled the already polluted.

Josiah burned the bones of the priests (v. 5) who were killed and even those who were removed from the graves (2 Kings 23:16). Again, it was the ultimate act of defiling (pollution of the dead) the already defiled. The punishment was consistent with their crime. The priests had burned sacrifices on the altars, now they burned upon them. In Scripture, to crush the bones of the enemy was to cut off their hope and destroy them forever (Numbers 24:8).

Josiah's campaign of reform extended to the deep south and far north (2 Chronicles 34:3-5, Jerusalem and Judah; vv. 6, 7, the north). It included the highlands of Manasseh and Ephraim, Simeon in the farthest south, and Naphtali in northernmost Galilee. It was a north-to-south-to-north movement, denoting comprehensive purification of the land. This does not seem to have been a political endeavor on the part of Josiah. However, the dating of his cleansing the land and bringing reform does correlate with the diminishing influence of the Assyrian Empire; therefore, he did not encounter the resistance that Hezekiah did (ch. 32). As he was faithful to God, God was faithful to deal with his enemy. The northern kingdom, Israel, which had been taken captive approximately a century earlier, was now a land without leadership. Josiah extended the boundaries of his reform into that region.

B. Repairing of the Temple (vv. 8-13)

(2 Chronicles 34:8-13 is not included in the printed text.)

In his 18th year (approximately age 26), after Josiah had purified the land, he turned his attention to repairing the Temple (v. 8). The focus here is on the repair of the "house of the Lord his God." This was not just the God of his father David (see v. 3), but the God he worshiped also. The writer emphasized Josiah's personal relationship with God. The funds for the repairs were provided through the methods initiated by Joash (see previous lesson). In verse 9 and the following verses, the chronicler is careful to describe how carefully the funds were handled. The money was first brought to the high priest, Hilkiah ("The Lord is my portion"). There is a chain of responsibility, as this money was to be used only for its intended purpose. The

emphasis was on the total participation of all Israel.

Construction and repair of the Temple occurred during the reigns of David, who was active in the planning and fund-raising stage; Solomon, who constructed the Temple; Joash and Hezekiah, both of whom repaired it. Verse 11 is most likely a reference to the sections of the Temple complex which had been destroyed by previous kings. Josiah was repairing the physical and spiritual damage that Manasseh, Amon and Ahaz had done (2 Kings 23:12). It was a sacred task which the workers took seriously and performed "faithfully"—with honesty (2 Chronicles 34:12). Musicians were often used on construction projects in the Middle East of that period, much like the radios found now on sites. However, here the emphasis seems to be on a supervisory role for the musicians.

In light of verse 13, it can be surmised that the writer was emphasizing three facts in this passage: (1) Everyone worked according to his or her ability, (2) worshipers were intricately involved in the repair of the Temple, and (3) it was a spiritual and physical endeavor. In view of 1 Chronicles 16 and 25, Temple renovation was more than a task of repairing the physical structure. It was a reaffirmation of God's existence, supremacy, and redemptive actions in the life of those who worshiped Him.

C. The Grand Discovery (vv. 14-17)

(2 Chronicles 34:16, 17 is not included in the printed text.)

14. And when they brought out the money that was brought into the house of the Lord, Hilkiah the priest found a book of the law of the Lord given by Moses.

15. And Hilkiah answered and said to Shaphan the scribe, I have found the book of the law in the house of the Lord. And Hilkiah delivered the book to Shaphan.

Opinions are divided as to whether the Book of the Law that Hilkiah found was the entire Pentateuch or the Book of Deuteronomy. Because of the many parallels with the Josiah reform, it was most likely the Book of Deuteronomy. This book admonishes Israel to destroy anything that rivals the worship of God (Deuteronomy 12), contains large sections of blessings and curses (chs. 27-29), and its structure fits that of a covenant. Either way, God's Word was found in the house of God and its presence had an effect upon the rest of the community.

The question arises as to how such an important book could be lost. The threat of invasion during Hezekiah's reign or the apostasy of Amon and Manasseh could have motivated a conscientious priest to hide the scroll for protection, and subsequently it was forgotten.

The message is clear. As all of Israel fulfilled their responsibilities to the Lord, the heritage and life of the nation were rediscovered. It was passed from person to person and affected the highest rank of leadership in the land. The heritage was not just a collection of past histories, but a living entity that transformed both king and community. To give unto God that which He so richly deserves is to receive the best God has to give to His people (see 2 Chronicles 15:2).

Shaphan is the picture of a servant who wanted to keep the king happy. First he told the king his orders had been followed, then he told him of the find (34:16-18).

Verse 17 could be viewed in two different ways. The money could have been melted down and used as the precious metals for the Temple repairs. Or, the emphasis could be on taking care of those who did the work of God. It is difficult to determine which the writer had in mind.

II. UNCERTAINTY EXPRESSED
(2 Chronicles 34:18-22)

A. An Awareness of Sin (vv. 18, 19)

(2 Chronicles 34:18 is not included in the printed text.)

19. And it came to pass, when the king had heard the words of the law, that he rent his clothes.

Shaphan read the book to the king, who ripped his clothes in an act of humility and mourning (rending of the heart). His actions revealed he was aware of the difference between the nation's current actions and God's requirements. His purging may have removed the evil items from the landscape, but had not addressed the issues of the people's hearts.

B. An Action of Sincerity (vv. 20, 21)

20. And the king commanded Hilkiah, and Ahikam the son of Shaphan, and Abdon the son of Micah, and Shaphan the scribe, and Asaiah a servant of the king's, saying,

21. Go, enquire of the Lord for me, and for them that are left in Israel and in Judah, concerning the words of the book that is found: for great is the wrath of the Lord that is poured out upon us, because our fathers have not kept the word of the Lord, to do after all that is written in this book.

Five high officials were dispatched "to enquire of the Lord" (seek, cf. v. 3) on his behalf, as well as the nations ("them that are left"—the faithful of the land or the remnant of true believers). His actions show the intensity of his concern. He had already acknowledged the presence of sin through the tearing of his garments. Now he was looking for intercessors, as "seeking" carries the idea of diligent prayer. The group was to pray that the imminent wrath of God be stayed (see Jeremiah 21:2).

Josiah acknowledged the authority of the book and the presence of sin in the land. He recognized the imminent wrath because of earlier generations in the lineage of David who did not keep God's Word. The Holy Spirit was at work confirming the Word and acting as an agent of conviction (John 16:8). God is not looking for mere obedience, but a covenant relationship that results in harmony.

C. An Official of God (v. 22)

22. And Hilkiah, and they that the king had appointed, went to Huldah the prophetess, the wife of Shallum the son of Tikvath, the son of Hasrah, keeper of the wardrobe; (now she dwelt in Jerusalem in the college:) and they spake to her to that effect.

Josiah did not give the group specific directions to seek out a prophet or prophetess. However, Hilkiah and the group approached Huldah. Her husband was the "keeper of the wardrobe," which refers to the production and care of the necessary garments for the Levites, priests and the high priest. These garments were quite elaborate (see Exodus 28; Leviticus 8:7-9) and were changed within the ceremonies (Leviticus 6:10, 11; 16:4-32), requiring the aid of the keeper. Shallum, her husband, was probably of Levitical status in light of the genealogy given to show proper status and claim.

Huldah and her husband dwelt in "the college," or "the Second Quarter" (NKJV) of Jerusalem. It is probably a reference to the work of Hezekiah, who expanded the walls of the city to include the hill to the west of Jerusalem (32:5) for military purposes and perhaps to accommodate the increase in population or the refugees from the north. Care for the less fortunate appears to have been taken more seriously in Judah than the northern kingdom.

III. ENCOURAGEMENT GIVEN
(2 Chronicles 34:23-33)

A. The Introductory Prophecy (v. 23)

23. And she answered them, Thus saith the Lord God of Israel, Tell ye the man that sent you to me.

Huldah's response to their infor-

mation is the classic prophetic formula ("Thus saith the Lord") to which is added here "God of Israel." It accentuates the authority and gravity of what follows for all of Israel. It also serves as a reminder of relationship. God had not forsaken them, even though the judgment for disobedience was about to fall.

Huldah was not speaking on her own authority, wisdom or knowledge, but as an instrument of God. The Lord's words, "Tell . . . the man that sent you to me," are a reminder that status with God is not a matter of position, but of relationship; not of birth, but of obedience.

B. The Prophecy for the People
(vv. 24, 25)

(2 Chronicles 34:24, 25 is not included in the printed text.)

Again there is the prophetic formula (v. 24). The normal order of judgment is reversed here. Usually, the reason for the judgment is given first (for past transgressions), then the verdict (cf. 12:5). Here the verdict is given first, then the reason. If "the book" is indeed Deuteronomy, chapter 28 spells out the blessings that Israel could expect to participate in if she was obedient to God (vv. 1-14), but also spells out the curses for disobedience and idolatry (vv. 15 68). If it is the entire Torah, then this could be a reference to Leviticus 26:3-39, as well as the Deuteronomy passages.

The people not only were disobedient but they had "forsaken" or rejected God. They had denied Him His divine rights. He called them to be a people wholly devoted to Him (Exodus 19:5, 6), but they had taken "other gods" and provoked Him by "the works of their hands" (see 2 Chronicles 28:25).

God had warned His people of the futility and absurdity of worshiping that which they created (Isaiah 44:9-20). Thus, God's wrath would be "poured out" and "not be quenched"

(2 Chronicles 34:25; see also v. 21). It is the imagery of a fire that refuses to be extinguished. It is a reference to the Babylonian exile that would befall in less than 25 years. Judah would be taken captive because she did not heed the voices of the prophets nor the example of the northern kingdom, which had also been warned, given opportunities to repent, but ignored the warnings and was taken captive.

The passage serves to remind us there are sins of commission and omission. It is not just what we do that matters to God. It is also the things we don't do that count (James 4:17). The people had seen the idolatry taking over their land, but did nothing to stop it. There is a price to be paid for ignoring sin. Believers must also be aware of the sins of the heart, the attitude and mind, especially those directed toward God and His requirements. Our image of God and attitude toward Him will shape our attitude toward the rest of His creation.

C. The Prophecy for Josiah (vv. 26-28)

(2 Chronicles 34:26 is not included in the printed text.)

27. Because thine heart was tender, and thou didst humble thyself before God, when thou heardest his words against this place, and against the inhabitants thereof, and humbledst thyself before me, and didst rend thy clothes, and weep before me; I have even heard thee also, saith the Lord.

28. Behold, I will gather thee to thy fathers, and thou shalt be gathered to thy grave in peace, neither shall thine eyes see all the evil that I will bring upon this place, and upon the inhabitants of the same. So they brought the king word again.

The formulary is again used to emphasize this was not Huldah's message for the king, but God's (v. 26). In verses 27 and 28, there is a two-part message of promised blessing, con-

sisting of the reason and the blessing itself. Josiah's "heart was tender" (susceptible or soft) and he had "humbled himself" upon hearing the words of the Law. He proved himself to be open to the will and correction of God (see 2 Chronicles 7:14). Thus the judgment would be delayed until after his reign was over. He would die "in peace," meaning he would not see Jerusalem taken captive. The delegation reported Huldah's encouraging word to him.

God's promise concerned the impending exile. The remainder of Josiah's life, however, was conditional; when Josiah failed to trust God fully in the face of Necho's Egyptian aggression, it cost him his life (35:20-24).

Most of the promises of God are conditional. We must do our part to trust God fully with our minds, hearts and bodies, then He will do His part.

D. The Covenant to Keep the Covenant (vv. 29-33)

(2 Chronicles 34:29-33 is not included in the printed text.)

Josiah called "all the elders" of the southern kingdom to Jerusalem, as representatives of the whole community of Israel (v. 29). Everyone gathered at the Temple ("the house of the Lord"), including the priests, Levites and everyone "great and small" (v. 30). There is no class or cultural status with God. All must come before Him.

The great multitude of people listened as Josiah himself read "the book of the covenant." The designation of the book has changed. It is not called "the book of the law" as in verse 15. Josiah understood the book to be one of grace, promise and relationship. The Law was not given to be oppressive, but to engender relationship with God. *Torah* (law) has as its basic meaning "instruction" or "direction."

Verse 31 reveals that the king made a covenant with the people to keep the words of the covenant, to do what was right before the Lord, follow Him, give Him the position and prominence He deserved. David (1 Chronicles 11:1-3), Jehoiada and Joash (2 Kings 11:17), Asa (2 Chronicles 15:10-15) and Hezekiah (29:10) had made similar covenants. The use of "to keep" and "to perform" place an emphasis on actions that correspond to the commitment one makes (see Deuteronomy 29:9). Josiah dedicated the entirety of his being to fulfill the expectations of God.

The king made *all* the people present take a stand, which they gladly did (2 Chronicles 34:32). This is reminiscent of Joshua standing before the children of Israel asking them to choose whose side they were on (Joshua 24:15). This is interesting in light of the prophecy received from Huldah, which said the outcome had been determined and was unchangeable (2 Chronicles 34:25). Yet Josiah sensed the need to do what was right even if it would not change the impending judgment. It was an admirable trait of the king, witnessing to the fact that living in right relationship with God is sufficient reward within itself, apart from what happens in the future.

The remainder of the abominable things were removed from the people's possessions (v. 33), as opposed to "the land" which had previously been purged. Josiah zealously enforced their decision to serve God, holding them accountable, apparently without the drastic measures taken during Asa's covenant renewal ceremony (15:12-15). The verse also serves as a summary. All the country united in worship and, during the reign of Josiah, "did not depart from following the Lord God" (*NKJV*). Josiah's seeking the Lord (see v. 3) had come full circle.

The word of encouragement from Huldah to Josiah had a positive effect on the people. Judgment averted for him was judgment averted for them. His faithfulness in heeding the encouraging word of Huldah and the Book of the Covenant allowed his reign to go down in history as one in which he never looked to the right or the left, but worshiped God alone. The Exile did not occur on his watch.

GOLDEN TEXT HOMILY

"LET US CONSIDER ONE ANOTHER TO PROVOKE UNTO LOVE AND TO GOOD WORKS" (Hebrews 10:24).

The exercise of love is the outward attitude of the Christian. We are to consider one another with the special object of stirring our fellow Christians to love and "good works."

Through the use of the word *provoke*, the author gives us a beautiful paradox. It expresses the Greek word, which is transliterated in English as *paroxysm*. This is the only "exasperation" that is permissible, and it is impossible to have too much of it. We are to "exasperate" our fellow Christians in the sense of "provoking," or motivating, them to love and good works.

F.B. Meyer made a beautiful statement on this concept of love: "Love is the passion of self-giving. It never stays to ask what it can afford or what it may expect in return, but it is ever shedding forth its perfume, breaking its alabaster boxes, and shedding its heart's blood. It will pine to death if it cannot give. It must share its possessions. It is prodigal of costliest service. Such love is in the heart of God and should also be in us, and we may increase it materially by considering one another and associating with our fellow believers."—**Selected**

SENTENCE SERMONS

EVERYONE needs to be encouraged to do good.

—Selected

THE DEEPEST PRINCIPLE in human nature is the craving to be appreciated.

—William James

HE WHO LIVES only to benefit himself confers on the world a benefit when he dies.

—Tertullian

CORRECTION DOES MUCH, but encouragement does more.

—Goethe

EVANGELISM APPLICATION

CHRISTIANS SHOULD ENCOURAGE THE UNSAVED TO ACCEPT CHRIST.

Many Christians are afraid of offending the unsaved through witnessing. We don't want to be pushy. However, the world is not concerned with offending Christians through the language, stories and actions that are displayed in front of us every day. Some take great delight in attempting to shock Christians with their actions. Christians are regularly depicted in the media as second-class citizens.

While the message of the Cross is offensive (1 Corinthians 1:18), it is the message of salvation God has entrusted to us. We cannot afford to bury it in the ground like the servant who was afraid (Matthew 25:14-30). A little offense is worth the salvation of a soul.

ILLUMINATING THE LESSON

Joseph Burgess, a young preacher, had been dispatched to Ireland to minister the gospel. He found the territory difficult, the work tiring, and grew discouraged. It was not long before he received a letter from an aged minister, who wrote, "My dear brother, you are called to do all the good you can for the present in Ireland; by your staying there a little longer may be a blessing to many souls . . . a little difficulty on setting out is a good omen! Wishing all happiness to you and yours. I am, dear Joseph, your affectionate brother."

The letter served its purpose. John Wesley, the great preacher, who experienced difficulty and discouragement in his own early ministry, took the time to encourage a young colleague. Wesley knew the value of encouraging those around us, for we never know whom God is raising up through our efforts (taken from *The Letters of John Wesley*).

DAILY BIBLE READINGS

M. Encouraged in the Lord.
    1 Samuel 30:1-8
T. God's Ministers Encouraged.
    2 Chronicles 31:2-6
W. Captives Encouraged.
    Jeremiah 29:1-14
T. Jesus Encouraged Faith.
    Mark 11:20-24
F. Encouraged to Do Good.
    Galatians 6:1-10
S. Encouraged to Persevere.
    Hebrews 12:1-11

TRUTH SEARCH
Creatively Teaching the Word

DISCUSSION QUESTIONS

2 Chronicles 34

1. Describe the reign of Josiah, as seen in verses 1-3.

2. Describe Josiah's restoration project and its success (vv. 8-13).

3. The item found by Hilkiah the priest had gone forgotten and unused for many years (vv. 14, 15). What does this say about Judah's spiritual condition?

4. When Hilkiah read God's Word to the king, how did he respond (vv. 18, 19)?

5. Why did Josiah send messengers to Huldah the prophetess (vv. 20-22)?

6. What calamities did Huldah predict, and why (vv. 23-25)?

7. What was the prophecy regarding Josiah, and why (vv. 26-28)?

8. How did Josiah respond to Huldah's prophecies (vv. 29-33)?

OBJECT LESSON

Item needed: Newspaper

Read the headlines and summarize a couple of bad-news stories. Next, read the headlines and summarize a couple of good-news stories.

All of these stories were obviously written after the events described had already taken place. The reporters simply described what happened, according to the information they gathered.

It's incredible to think that God could have penned these stories in perfect detail days, weeks or even years before they happened.

In the Bible we read about the eternal future God has in store for His children, knowing that every wonderful detail will come to pass. We must encourage ourselves and others with this incredible news.

Three Notable Disciples

Study Text: John 1:35-51; 12:20-22

Objective: To examine and emulate the practical virtues revealed in the examples of three disciples.

Golden Text: "Jesus saw Nathanael coming to him, and saith of him, Behold an Israelite indeed, in whom is no guile!" (John 1:47).

Central Truth: Faithful disciples of Jesus set good examples for others to follow.

Evangelism Emphasis: Jesus calls all who will to become His disciples.

PRINTED TEXT

John 1:35. Again the next day after John stood, and two of his disciples;

36. And looking upon Jesus as he walked, he saith, Behold the Lamb of God!

37. And the two disciples heard him speak, and they followed Jesus.

38. Then Jesus turned, and saw them following, and saith unto them, What seek ye? They said unto him, Rabbi, (which is to say, being interpreted, Master,) where dwellest thou?

39. He saith unto them, Come and see. They came and saw where he dwelt, and abode with him that day: for it was about the tenth hour.

40. One of the two which heard John speak, and followed him, was Andrew, Simon Peter's brother.

41. He first findeth his own brother Simon, and saith unto him, We have found the Messias, which is, being interpreted, the Christ.

42. And he brought him to Jesus. And when Jesus beheld him, he said, Thou art Simon the son of Jona: thou shalt be called Cephas, which is by interpretation, A stone.

43. The day following Jesus would go forth into Galilee, and findeth Philip, and saith unto him, Follow me.

44. Now Philip was of Bethsaida, the city of Andrew and Peter.

45. Philip findeth Nathanael, and saith unto him, We have found him, of whom Moses in the law, and the prophets, did write, Jesus of Nazareth, the son of Joseph.

46. And Nathanael said unto him, Can there any good thing come out of Nazareth? Philip saith unto him, Come and see.

47. Jesus saw Nathanael coming to him, and saith of him, Behold an Israelite indeed, in whom is no guile!

48. Nathanael saith unto him, Whence knowest thou me? Jesus answered and said unto him, Before that Philip called thee, when thou wast under the fig tree, I saw thee.

49. Nathanael answered and saith unto him, Rabbi, thou art the Son of God; thou art the King of Israel.

12:20. And there were certain Greeks among them that came up to worship at the feast:

21. The same came therefore to Philip, which was of Bethsaida of Galilee, and desired him, saying, Sir, we would see Jesus.

22. Philip cometh and telleth Andrew: and again Andrew and Philip tell Jesus.

DICTIONARY

Cephas (SEE-fuss)—John 1:42—the Aramaic word for the name *Peter*, meaning "a rock" or "a stone"

Bethsaida (beth-SAY-ih-dah)—John 1:44—a city in Galilee on the west coast of the Sea of Galilee, the native place of Peter, Andrew and Philip, located near Capernaum

Nathanael (na-THAN-yell)—John 1:45—from the Hebrew meaning "God has given"; a disciple of Jesus commonly identified as Bartholomew

Greeks—John 12:20—from the Greek word which means "persons born Greek or Gentile," as distinguished from Jews who spoke Greek

---

LESSON OUTLINE

I. ANDREW: NO HESITATION
   A. John the Baptist
   B. Jesus' Call
   C. Andrew and Peter
   D. Jesus and Peter
II. PHILIP: EAGER WITNESS
   A. The Finding of Philip
   B. Leading Others to Jesus
III. NATHANAEL: AN HONEST MAN
   A. Skepticism Displayed
   B. Skepticism Convinced
   C. The Promise of Things Greater

LESSON EXPOSITION

INTRODUCTION

John 1:35-51 contains a multitude of themes. Just prior to these verses, John the Baptist identifies Jesus as "the Lamb of God who takes away the sin of the world" (v. 29, *NKJV*). The next day, two of his disciples leave him to follow Jesus. His role in the Kingdom diminishes so that the ministry of Jesus can be established (3:30).

God uses many people to accomplish His will. It requires cooperation with others to fulfill our ministries effectively. The focus, as always, must be on Jesus.

Methods of evangelism are revealed in the passage, such as the power of personal experience in witnessing. The most effective program of evangelism is telling others what God has done for you.

The promise of greater things—including revelation of the knowledge of God, the majesty of Jesus Christ, and the manifestation of the power of God—is made in verses 50 and 51.

The Gospels provide examples that teach us what God expects from us. The supreme example for all believers is Jesus Christ, who operated in the Spirit, had compassion on those whom He met, did the will of the Father, and glorified God in all He did. Andrew, Philip and Nathanael are examples of what a disciple should know, be and do.

I. ANDREW: NO HESITATION
   (John 1:35-42)

A. John the Baptist (vv. 35-37)

35. Again the next day after John stood, and two of his disciples;

36. And looking upon Jesus as he walked, he saith, Behold the Lamb of God!

37. And the two disciples heard him speak, and they followed Jesus.

The second day, John the Baptist preached to a crowd and bore witness of Jesus Christ, the Son of God (vv. 29-34). On the third day of the narrative, he stood with "two of his disciples" (v. 35). The Baptist knew how to minister to the multitudes, but also was available to provide personal attention to those who needed it.

Later on in the narrative, we find that one of these two was Andrew (v. 40). The other is never named, yet even this might be a clue. The writer of the Gospel, the apostle John according to tradition, only referred to himself as "the disciple whom Jesus loved" (19:26; 21:20). Like John the Baptist, he wanted to step out of the spotlight so the ministry of Jesus could be the focus. Therefore, it seems logical that the apostle John is the unnamed disciple. In the lists of the 12 disciples, his name occurs as one of the first four, and the order is consistent with the order of calling by Jesus (Matthew 10:2-4; Luke 6:14-16).

As they stood there, the Baptist was "looking upon Jesus" (John 1:36). This was not just a glancing awareness, but an intentional observation that saw with insight and perception, even recognition. It was a poignant moment for John. The previous day Jesus was walking toward him. John's ministry was at its peak. This day, Jesus was walking away from him (see v. 38), not in abandonment but as a shift in the strategy of God. John had accomplished his role (v. 23) and fulfilled it well (v. 34). People now knew who Jesus was.

At that moment, for the sake of the two disciples, John proclaimed, "Behold the Lamb of God!" It was the same testimony as the day before (v. 29), but for a different audience and purpose. He was preparing the hearts of his disciples.

The "Lamb" reference could be understood as the Paschal Lamb (Exodus 12; 13; see John 19:36; 1 Corinthians 5:7) since the Passover was approaching (John 2:13). It could be viewed as the lamb for the daily offering in the Temple (Numbers 28:4) or the lamb of Isaiah 53 (vv. 6, 7). Jesus is the fulfillment of each and all of these (see 1 Peter 1:19, 22).

It was the declaration of John that convinced these two disciples to follow Jesus. Because of his unselfish actions, several people "found" Jesus on this day. Notice the number of times that "found" is used: Andrew and the unnamed disciple found Jesus (v. 41); Andrew found Simon (v. 41); Jesus found Philip (v. 43) and Philip found Jesus (v. 45); and Philip found Nathanael (v. 45).

"Followed" (v. 37) is often used in the Gospels to signify acceptance of discipleship and commitment of faith (see Matthew 9:9; Mark 8:34), as it is here and elsewhere in John (8:12; 10:4, 27).

B. Jesus' Call (vv. 38, 39)

38. Then Jesus turned, and saw them following, and saith unto them, What seek ye? They said unto him, Rabbi, (which is to say, being interpreted, Master,) where dwellest thou?

39. He saith unto them, Come and see. They came and saw where he dwelt, and abode with him that day: for it was about the tenth hour.

Jesus turned around and "saw" Andrew and John following Him. Given what is revealed about Jesus in this passage, it is evident He knew they were behind Him (see v. 48). The two were "following" Jesus, choosing to become disciples.

In the first century, a disciple entered into a relationship with a teacher. The disciple became identified with the teacher and was considered to be a reliable source of the teacher's wisdom and doctrine. The disciple's destiny was also tied to that of the teacher.

The first words spoken by Jesus in the Gospel of John are directed to these two disciples. He asked them, "What do you seek?" (*What are you searching for?*). He did not ask, "Whom do you seek," but "what." It has been said that this is the first question to be answered by everyone coming to Jesus.

The two followers addressed Him as "Rabbi," which John interpreted for his readers. It is an Aramaic term of polite address, meaning "teacher" or "master," or literally, "my great one." The Gospel of John can be divided easily into two sections: the Book of Signs (chs. 1-12) and the Book of Glory (chs. 13-21). "Rabbi" is used predominantly in the Book of Signs, while "Lord" is used in the Book of Glory, as Jesus is heading to the cross and the disciples are learning more about Him.

The two disciples responded to Jesus with a puzzling, "Where are You staying?" (*NKJV*). Perhaps they were unsure how to respond, or were asking if He had a school with which they could become associated, as teachers often did.

Jesus' response was not one of rebuke or annoyance. He simply replied, "Come and see" (v. 39). It was an invitation to those who wanted uninterrupted time with Jesus. The invitation still stands. They saw where He was staying and their following led to "abiding" ("remaining," *NKJV*) with Jesus. There is probably a play on words here, implying that the remaining went beyond the day. It was a permanent relationship.

The reference to the "tenth hour" is probably 4 o'clock in the afternoon. The Jewish method of tracking time consisted of counting the hours from sunrise to sunset (6 a.m. to 6 p.m.). The conversation made such an impact on John's life that he remembered the exact hour.

C. Andrew and Peter (vv. 40, 41)

40. One of the two which heard John speak, and followed him, was Andrew, Simon Peter's brother.

41. He first findeth his own brother Simon, and saith unto him, We have found the Messias, which is, being interpreted, the Christ.

In verse 40 John identifies one of the two as Andrew, a Greek name meaning "manly." He is further identified as "Simon Peter's brother." At this point, Simon Peter has not been introduced in the narrative, but by the time the Gospel was written, he was well known to those who read it.

Andrew "first" found Simon (v. 41). Before doing anything else, he wanted his brother to share in the discovery he made. Some see the meaning of this verse to imply that he found *his* brother first, before the other disciple found his brother, James.

Andrew informed Simon that he and John had found "the Messias," a Hebrew word meaning "Anointed One." In the Old Testament, several offices were set apart through anointing. The king of Israel was known as "the Lord's anointed" (1 Samuel 16:6; 2 Samuel 1:14). The high priest (Exodus 29:7; Leviticus 4:3) and prophets (1 Kings 19:16) were anointed. Jesus, as the Messiah, the Anointed One, fulfilled the offices of prophet, priest and king. The anticipation and searching for the Messiah, the declaration of John the Baptist, and the daylong visit convinced them beyond any shadow of doubt that Jesus was "the Christ" (Greek equivalent of *Messiah*).

D. Jesus and Peter (v. 42)

42. And he brought him to Jesus. And when Jesus beheld him, he said, Thou art Simon the son of Jona: thou shalt be called Cephas, which is by interpretation, A stone.

Andrew "brought" Simon Peter "to Jesus." This is evangelism. It is also the natural order of evangelism: we lead people to the same place we received help. The place to start is with our family and friends.

From this point on, wherever Andrew is highlighted, he is bringing someone to Jesus. He brings Simon Peter here. When the multitude has remained with Jesus and is in need of food, it is Andrew who brings the lad with the loaves and fish (6:8, 9). It is also Andrew, along with Philip, who brings the Greeks to Jesus, discussed later in the lesson (12:22).

"Jesus beheld" Simon. The phrase denotes intentionality—Jesus looked him over. He looked deep within. Jesus knew who he was and knew his name, even though the narrative gives no indication of a previous meeting. The work of the Holy Spirit can and does reveal what is in the hearts of humanity (Matthew 9:4; 1 Corinthians 14:25). Jesus' statement is a prophecy of what Simon would become, not a declaration of what he then was. Before Simon ever spoke a word, Jesus accepted him as a disciple and gave him a new name, a new character, and a new work to fulfill in the unfolding of God's redemptive plan. He would be a "stone." The Greek term John used to translate the Aramaic "Cephas" is *Petros*, "a large rock or boulder." It was the type of stone used to mark the boundaries of property. (Also see Matthew 16:18.)

There are those who see a needless contradiction between the call of Andrew and Peter here and their call in the synoptic Gospels (Matthew, Mark and Luke; the term *synoptic* means "to see together," or "parallel accounts"). The calling of the first disciples in the Synoptics is by the sea (Matthew 4:18-22; Luke 5:1-11), yet John locates them in Bethabara, where John the Baptist is (John 1:28). The Synoptics have them engaged in fishing, whereas John has them coming to Jesus, some as disciples of John the Baptist.

Two solutions have been offered. It is believed that Jesus did encounter them first as John reveals, then they returned to their homes to set things in order. Next, Jesus called them to active discipleship, which is recorded in the Synoptics. Philip is the only one to whom Jesus issues a call in the Gospel of John account. The others in this event come to Him in Bethabara, but are actually called by the sea.

The second proposal is that Jesus called them to be disciples (believers) as recorded by John, and apostles (messengers of the Kingdom) in the other Gospels. Both are possible, but the first seems most logical.

II. PHILIP: EAGER WITNESS
   (John 1:43-46; 12:20-22)

A. The Finding of Philip (1:43-46)

43. The day following Jesus would go forth into Galilee, and findeth Philip, and saith unto him, Follow me.

44. Now Philip was of Bethsaida, the city of Andrew and Peter.

45. Philip findeth Nathanael, and saith unto him, We have found him, of whom Moses in the law, and the prophets, did write, Jesus of Nazareth, the son of Joseph.

46. And Nathanael said unto him, Can there any good thing come out of Nazareth? Philip saith unto him, Come and see.

Verse 43 begins the last of the four consecutive days in the first chapter. Jesus is still at Bethabara beyond the Jordan, also known as Bethany beyond the Jordan, but distinct from the village of Bethany outside of Jerusalem. He desires to go to Galilee, which would require crossing over the Jordan and traveling west. Perhaps while making preparations, He finds or *seeks out* Philip (whose Greek name means "lover of horses") and issues him the call to discipleship—"Follow Me." This is a different person than Philip the deacon and evangelist of Acts 6 and 8.

John also tells the readers that Philip, like Andrew and Simon Peter, was originally from Bethsaida ("house of fishing"), a fishing village in a predominantly Greek area (v. 44; also see 12:21). In the account of the feeding of the 5,000, Jesus asked him about feeding the multitude. Philip focused on the cost, while Andrew found the lad (John 6:5-9). On another occasion Philip was slow to understand that one purpose of Jesus' mission was to reveal the Father (14:8, 9). He did tend to examine things from a natural perspective.

Part of the process of discipleship is to move the eyes of the disciple from the human perspective to God's perspective. This is an ongoing process. If the disciple is confident he or she has reached that goal, the change in perspective is not complete.

Philip immediately found Nathanael (1:45), who was from Cana in Galilee (21:2). Philip's declaration displayed great enthusiasm. The reference to the Law and the Prophets usually means the entire Old Testament. Moses did speak of a "Prophet" like him who would bring forth the Word of God (Deuteronomy 18:15-19). The Prophets also contain numerous references to a coming Deliverer (e.g., Isaiah 42:1-4).

That Philip referred to Jesus as the "son of Joseph" was not a denial of the Virgin Birth. Philip, according to the custom of his day, identified Jesus by His native home and His legal father, which was Joseph (see Matthew 1:16). John wrote after Matthew and Luke and, therefore, did not need to defend the accepted belief of the Virgin Birth.

The point of the verse is just as Jesus found Philip, Philip found Nathanael. Philip's enthusiasm, however, was met with skepticism: "Can there any good thing come out of Nazareth?" (v. 46). Philip's reply, "Come and see," imitated Jesus (see v. 39). Some things a person just has to experience to be convinced of (see Psalm 34:8).

B. Leading Others to Jesus
   (12:20-22)

20. And there were certain Greeks among them that came up to worship at the feast:

21. The same came therefore to Philip, which was of Bethsaida of Galilee, and desired him, saying, Sir, we would see Jesus.

22. Philip cometh and telleth Andrew: and again Andrew and Philip tell Jesus.

Nathanael was not the only one that Philip brought to Jesus. In verse 20 "certain Greeks" came to Jerusalem for the Passover (see v. 1). These were not Greek-speaking Jews, but Gentiles who came from the Greek-speaking world. They probably were God-fearers (see Acts 10:2; 13:42, 43; 17:4), uncircumcised Greeks who had given up worshiping other gods to worship the one true God of Israel, but had not become official converts or proselytes. They were allowed as far as the Court of the Gentiles in the Temple complex.

They approached Philip perhaps because he was from their area, was known to them, or just looked approachable. John made a distinct point to give the reader Philip's geographical information again. Their request was simple enough, "Sir, we wish to see Jesus" (v. 21, NKJV). The verb to see indicated they wanted a personal interview with Jesus to learn more about Him. No doubt their interest was stimulated by the raising of Lazarus and the Triumphal Entry into Jerusalem (see vv. 1, 9-18). Desiring time with Jesus, they enlisted the help of an intermediary, since they did not know if Jesus would see them or not.

The request of the Greeks presented a twofold question: (1) In light of what Jesus said elsewhere, would He accept an audience with the Greeks (see Matthew 10:5; 15:24)? (2) What would be the response of the Jews, especially if this interview was held in the Temple area (see Acts 21:28)? The first problem is easily dismissed. Jesus' attitude was one of acceptance. He stated that He had "other sheep"

(John 10:16). His focus was on the person, not the national heritage or racial identification. He ministered to (or for) and commended the faith of the Roman centurion (Matthew 8:5-10) and the Canaanite woman (15:21-28). The second part is more troublesome in light of John 12:19. The Jews were looking for anything that would give them cause to confront Jesus.

After Philip's consulting Andrew, the two of them approached Jesus with the request—an excellent approach in any situation. It also reveals that cooperation is needed to accomplish the difficult tasks of evangelism and discipleship.

III. NATHANAEL: AN HONEST MAN (John 1:46-51)

A. Skepticism Displayed (v. 46)

46. And Nathanael said unto him, Can there any good thing come out of Nazareth? Philip saith unto him, Come and see.

Nathanael ("God has given") was found by Philip and received the news that the Messiah had been found (v. 45). His name does not appear in the lists given in the Synoptics, but a close examination of the lists reveals that *Bartholomew* ("son of Tolmai") comes immediately after Philip (Matthew 10:3; Mark 3:18; Luke 6:14). Thus, Nathanael would be his proper Hebrew name, but he is identified in the Synoptics by his ancestral name, Bartholomew.

Nathanael was skeptical about Philip's assertion that the Messiah was from Nazareth (John 1:46). Perhaps he objected to the Messiah having such a lowly origin, as did the Jews (6:42; 7:52). The idea that the Messiah could come from Nazareth was as offensive as His being born in a stable, or dying for people's sins, and taking on the flesh of humanity to suffer what we suffer and feel what we feel. Or perhaps Nathanael's objection was based on the understanding that neither the anticipated Prophet nor

the Messiah would come out of Galilee (7:40-42). This then would depict Nathanael as a student of the Scriptures, though he misunderstood them.

B. Skepticism Convinced (vv. 47-49)

47. Jesus saw Nathanael coming to him, and saith of him, Behold an Israelite indeed, in whom is no guile!

48. Nathanael saith unto him, Whence knowest thou me? Jesus answered and said unto him, Before that Philip called thee, when thou wast under the fig tree, I saw thee.

49. Nathanael answered and saith unto him, Rabbi, thou art the Son of God; thou art the King of Israel.

Nathanael agreed to go with Philip to see Jesus, who saw him approaching and declared that he was a true "Israelite" (v. 47), a member of God's chosen community. Jesus further declared that Nathanael had "no deceit" (*NKJV*)—visible integrity! Such a person is blessed (Psalm 32:2) and an example for all to emulate.

The original meaning of *deceit*, or *guile*, is "bait for fishing." It carries the idea of "that which is not as it seems" and, therefore, is a "snare." The reference later by Jesus to Jacob's vision (John 1:51) may be a contrast between Nathanael and Jacob the deceiver (see Genesis 27:19-27; 28:12). Previously, Jesus knew Simon's name (John 1:42). Now He knows the very character of Nathanael. Even people of integrity and high morals still need a Savior (Romans 3:23).

Jesus' description hit its mark and surprised Nathanael, who responded, "How do you know me?" (John 1:48, *NKJV*), or it can also mean, "From where do You know me?" He may have thought Philip told Jesus more about him than he desired. Jesus quickly cleared up that misconception, telling him that "before Philip" ever approached him, He saw him "under the fig tree."

In rabbinical tradition, fig trees were the places that master teachers often discussed the Scriptures with their students, or studied in the excellent shade they provided. For this reason some believe Nathanael was a scribe or rabbi. The Old Testament identifies fig trees as a place of peace and security through the provision of God (Micah 4:4; Zechariah 3:10). Therefore, some believe Jesus was not speaking of Nathanael's physical location but rather his spiritual condition. In essence, Jesus was saying, "Before you saw Me, I saw you sheltered, blessed, secure, saved in the midst of the messianic kingdom." While that may be part of the message, Jesus was communicating to Nathanael that He actually "saw" him before Philip called him.

Jesus' power is associated with a relationship of intimacy and union with the Father (John 11:42; 13:3). The implication is that those who follow His example can have the same. Jesus knows those who believe and those who refuse to believe (10:26-29). He also knows the past of those who follow Him, but calls them anyway. If Jesus saw Nathanael under the fig tree, He could have heard him disparage His hometown, yet He still accepted him.

Nathanael was convinced of Jesus' ability and status. With deep emotion he cried, "Rabbi, You are the Son of God! You are the King of Israel!" (1:49, *NKJV*). It is a confession of faith and a statement of revelation (see Matthew 16:16, 17). While he may not have understood the full implication of his statement, he did see Jesus as the restorer of the kingship of God to Israel (see Psalm 2).

In the Gospel of John, those who *come* to Jesus, *look* on Him, and *believe* on Him are promised eternal life (5:40; 6:40, 47). All three actions are considered the same, for those who come to Him are making a commitment of faith to follow Him; those who

see Him see who He really is and share in His provision; and those who believe on Him accept Him for who He is and what He offers.

C. The Promise of Things Greater
   (vv. 50, 51)

(John 1:50, 51 is not included in the printed text.)

Jesus responded with a rhetorical question to Nathanael's declaration (v. 50). There was no hint of rebuke or disparagement for either Nathanael or his utterance. Instead, there was a personal promise to Nathanael of greater things to come. However, while it was directed toward Nathanael, others would share in this promise also.

Greater can be taken in a qualitative or quantitative sense. Jesus could be saying to Nathanael, "You will see things of a greater nature than My ability to see you under a fig tree." Or He could be saying, "You will see a greater number of works like this in the future." It seems to be inclusive of both. There would be works that revealed a greater power than the ability to see beyond His physical location, and they would be numerous. Three years later, Nathanael was one of seven disciples who saw the risen Lord by the Sea of Tiberias (21:2).

The reward for faithful discipleship is participation in the splendor of God's presence, promise, power and provision (14:12). Faith must be based on more than what we see in terms of miracles. It must be based on the person of Jesus Christ, not just His performance (4:48; 14:11) or even our own performance (Matthew 7:21-23).

In verse 51 of the text, Jesus used the Aramaic *amen, amen* ("verily, verily"), which often introduced a statement that summed up the preceding discussion. It was designed to call attention to the statement that followed. Jesus shifts His words from a promise to Nathanael to a promise for many that began at that point in time ("hereafter"). "Ye [plural] shall see heaven open."

Whenever the heavens are opened in Scripture, a revelation of great magnitude follows. When the heavens were opened, Ezekiel saw the presence of God (Ezekiel 1:1); John the Baptist and the crowd saw the Spirit descend upon Jesus and heard the Father speak (Matthew 3:16, 17); Peter understood that the church was for all those cleansed by the blood of Christ (Acts 10:11); Stephen saw Jesus standing at the Father's right hand waiting to usher him into heaven (7:56); John saw the splendor of the throne room of God (Revelation 4:1) and the victorious white horse Rider (19:11). When the heavens open, there is mediation between God and humanity and a special union is established. Through Jesus the gateway to heaven is now open.

The next element of the promise speaks of the angels "ascending and descending." This recalls Jacob's covenant dream in Genesis 28:11-15. As he lay down with a stone for a pillow and fell asleep, he saw a ladder upon which the angels were moving between heaven and earth. God spoke to him to renew and personalize the covenant of his fathers (see Genesis 15; 26). Jacob arose and called the place Bethel—"the house of God," or "the place to meet God."

In John 1:51, Jesus declared Himself to be the Messiah, our Bethel, the house of God, the holy place where the presence of God is manifest. His presence makes His disciples the temple of God, the place where the presence of God abides (1 Corinthians 3:16; see also Matthew 1:23; 18:20; 28:20).

The angels descend upon the "Son of Man," a reference to Daniel 7 (see Matthew 26:64). This title establishes a connection with humanity. It reveals the full spectrum of who Jesus is and what He accomplishes, which His disciples would see. He is the Son of Man who suffers humiliation and pain that He might reconcile people to God. He is also the Son of Man who receives dominion and glory, whose kingdom is eternal (Daniel 7:13, 14). In John 1 we see the two natures, divine and human, of Jesus Christ— the Son of God (v. 49) and Son of Man (v. 51).

The disciples could not grasp all that at this point, but they would before their journey on earth with Jesus was complete (see 6:66-71; 13:7). It was after the Resurrection that they began to understand the full significance of their time with Jesus (2:22; 12:16). It is an example that reveals to us that our "theology," or organized thinking and understanding of God, need not be complete to accept who He is and what He has to offer to us. He is just looking for disciples who will answer His call to know, be, and do greater things.

GOLDEN TEXT HOMILY

"JESUS SAW NATHANAEL COMING TO HIM, AND SAITH OF HIM, BEHOLD AN ISRAELITE INDEED, IN WHOM IS NO GUILE!" (John 1:47).

Jesus, seeing deep into Nathanael's heart, said of him as he approached, "Here is a genuine Israelite with no deceit in him!" It took quite a bit of doing on the part of Nathanael even to come near Jesus; the fact that he did come proved to the Master that he indeed was without "guile."

The word translated "guile" here is the Greek word signifying "bait" used to catch fish. Even though Nathanael had been dead wrong concerning Jesus, he was sincere in what he did say; and he came to Jesus with an open mind and a hungry heart. He was indeed a blessed man, for the Lord found no guile in his spirit (see Psalm 32:2).

Anyone coming to Jesus as did Nathanael will truly find favor with the Lord.—**Selected**

SENTENCE SERMONS

FAITHFUL DISCIPLES OF JESUS set good examples for others to follow.
—**Selected**

THE HEART OF RELIGION lies in its personal pronouns.
—**Martin Luther**

WHAT I GAVE, I have; what I spent, I had; what I kept, I lost.
—**Selected**

I'D RATHER SEE a sermon than hear one any day.
—**Edgar Guest**

EVANGELISM APPLICATION

JESUS CALLS ALL WHO WILL TO BECOME HIS DISCIPLES.

God is not looking for perfect people to become His disciples. He is looking for people willing to be made perfect (*whole* or *complete*). We do not need to have everything in our lives lined up with God's expectations to answer the call to discipleship. Discipleship is a process. While our destination is heaven, the journey, a lifetime of discipleship, is just as important as the destination. The journey prepares us for the destination.

ILLUMINATING THE LESSON

Dissatisfied with his success as an author and theology professor, a young man sat down at his desk and noticed a magazine. It was not his magazine, but had been left there for him by his housekeeper. He pushed it aside, but that evening he picked it up to move it again and the magazine fell open to an article titled "The Needs of the Congo Mission." It caught his attention, so he picked it up and read that the mission in the Congo did not have enough workers to minister to the people.

The author, Alfred Boegner, wrote that he hoped someone reading the article would be touched by "the Master's eyes" and respond to the "Master's call" and reply, "Lord, I am coming." At that moment, Albert Schweitzer knew his search for God's call to service was over. He resolved to become a medical doctor and use his skills to minister to the people in Africa.

Discipleship is being willing to do and go where God directs (from Albert Schweitzer, *My Life and Thought: An Autobiography*).

DAILY BIBLE READINGS

M. Following the Lord Completely.
Joshua 14:6-14
T. Following the Man of God.
2 Kings 2:1-10
W. Twelve Disciples.
Matthew 10:1-8
T. Seventy Disciples.
Luke 10:1-9
F. One-Hundred-Twenty Disciples.
Acts 1:9-15
S. Disciples Multiplied.
Acts 6:1-7

TRUTH SEARCH
Creatively Teaching the Word

DISCUSSION QUESTIONS
Andrew
(John 1:35-42)

1. What title did John the Baptist use in reference to Jesus, and why?

2. What was Andrew's relationship with John the Baptist?

3. What did Andrew call Jesus in verse 38? Why?

4. What did Jesus invite Andrew to do, and how did Andrew respond (v. 39)?

5. After hearing Jesus teach, what did Andrew call Jesus (v. 41)? What is the significance of this title?

6. Once Andrew realized Jesus was the Messiah, what did he do first? What does this say about Andrew?

Philip
(John 1:43-46; 12:20-22)

1. What did Jesus mean by saying, "Follow me" (1:43)?

2. What did Philip believe about Jesus (v. 45)?

3. Why did Philip say, "We have found him," since Jesus actually came to Philip?

4. Why did Philip tell Nathanael, "Come and see" (v. 46)?

5. In John 12:20-22, how did Philip respond to some Greeks who came to see Jesus?

Nathanael
(John 1:46-51)

1. Why did Nathanael initially doubt that Jesus could be the Messiah?

2. What insightful knowledge did Jesus have about Nathanael (v. 47)? Explain Jesus' statement.

3. Explain Jesus' response to Nathanael's question, "How do You know me?" (v. 48, *NKJV*).

4. Why did Nathanael now begin to believe Jesus was God's Son?

5. What promises did Jesus make to Nathanael (vv. 50, 51)?

TESTIMONIES

Have students divide into trios to briefly give their salvation testimonies to one another. Each person should answer the following questions:

1. What was your earliest belief about Jesus?

2. When did you first realize Jesus was calling you to follow Him?

3. How and where did you begin following Jesus?

Ministry Colleagues of Paul

Study Text: Acts 18:1-3, 18, 19, 24-26; Romans 16:1-16; Philippians 2:25-30; 2 Timothy 1:15-18

Objective: To acknowledge that every Christian needs helpers and work with other believers in Christ.

Golden Text: "I thank my God upon every remembrance of you, . . . for your fellowship in the gospel from the first day until now" (Philippians 1:3, 5).

Central Truth: Believers in Christ are colleagues in faith and ministry.

Evangelism Emphasis: Christians must work together to make the gospel known to all the world.

PRINTED TEXT

Romans 16:1. I commend unto you Phebe our sister, which is a servant of the church which is at Cenchrea:

2. That ye receive her in the Lord, as becometh saints, and that ye assist her in whatsoever business she hath need of you: for she hath been a succourer of many, and of myself also.

6. Greet Mary, who bestowed much labour on us.

12. Salute Tryphena and Tryphosa, who labour in the Lord. Salute the beloved Persis, which laboured much in the Lord.

Acts 18:1. After these things Paul departed from Athens, and came to Corinth;

2. And found a certain Jew named Aquila, born in Pontus, lately come from Italy, with his wife Priscilla; (because that Claudius had commanded all Jews to depart from Rome:) and came unto them.

3. And because he was of the same craft, he abode with them, and wrought: for by their occupation they were tentmakers.

Romans 16:3. Greet Priscilla and Aquila my helpers in Christ Jesus:

4. Who have for my life laid down their own necks: unto whom not only

I give thanks, but also all the churches of the Gentiles.

5. Likewise greet the church that is in their house. Salute my well-beloved Epaenetus, who is the firstfruits of Achaia unto Christ.

Philippians 2:25. Yet I supposed it necessary to send to you Epaphroditus, my brother, and companion in labour, and fellowsoldier, but your messenger, and he that ministered to my wants.

29. Receive him therefore in the Lord with all gladness; and hold such in reputation:

30. Because for the work of Christ he was nigh unto death, not regarding his life, to supply your lack of service toward me.

2 Timothy 1:16. The Lord give mercy unto the house of Onesiphorus; for he oft refreshed me, and was not ashamed of my chain:

17. But, when he was in Rome, he sought me out very diligently, and found me.

18. The Lord grant unto him that he may find mercy of the Lord in that day: and in how many things he ministered unto me at Ephesus, thou knowest very well.

DICTIONARY

Phebe (FEE-bee)—Romans 16:1—a woman who ministered as a deacon

Cenchrea (SIN-kree-uh)—Romans 16:1—a little town on the eastern harbor of Corinth

Tryphena (tri-FE-na) and Tryphosa (tri-PHOS-ah) . . . Persis (PUR-sis)—Romans 16:12—friends of Paul

Aquila (ACK-wi-lah) and Priscilla (prih-SIL-ah)—Acts 18:2—Jewish tentmakers, this married couple converted to Christianity.

Epaenetus (eep-EE-nee-tus)—Romans 16:5—a Christian from the Roman province of Achaia (uh-KAY-yuh)

Epaphroditus (ee-paf-row-DIE-tus)—Philippians 2:25—a messenger delegated by the church at Philippi

Onesiphorus (ON-eh-SIF-oh-rus)—2 Timothy 1:16—an Ephesian who ministered to Paul in prison

---

LESSON OUTLINE

I. WOMEN IN MINISTRY

   A. Phoebe

   B. Mary

   C. Junia

   D. Tryphena, Tryphosa, Persis

   E. And Others

II. HUSBAND-WIFE COWORKERS

   A. A Forged Relationship

   B. A Fruitful Relationship

III. TWO LOYAL FRIENDS

   A. Epaphroditus

   B. Onesiphorus

LESSON EXPOSITION

INTRODUCTION

We are living in a post-Christian era according to sociologists. It is a day when the gospel needs to be spread and ministry extended, as happened in the early church. God has called every Christian to ministry (1 Peter 2:5-10) and each has different gifts (Romans 12:6). Some are called to the front line. Others are support personnel, enabling those in more public ministry to continue their work. It is when we all utilize our gifts for the Lord that we will see the Kingdom expanded.

In Romans 16, Paul sends greetings to a church he had never visited, but hoped to minister to in the near future (see 15:22-24). This last chapter has often been overlooked as a salutation of Paul that has little theological merit. However, an examination of the people he greets gives us insight into the character of the early church and reminds us that even great apostles do not work alone and were not the only ones ministering the gospel in the first century. In addition, it gives us a picture of what the church should look like today. It reveals that there were people rich and poor, slave and free, male and female who pressed forward the cause of Christ (see Galatians 3:28). The focus of much of this lesson will be on the women Paul mentions in Romans 16, as well as Priscilla and Aquila.

John Goldengay says, "Arguably the greatest of the judges in the Book of Judges, after all, is a woman. But as Israel grew up (!?), it became more patriarchal, as happened to the church" (*Men Behaving Badly*). The early church accepted women as ministers in their own right during the first two centuries, recognizing that God called women to preach, teach, baptize, utilize the gifts of the Spirit, and hold positions of authority. It was not until the third and fourth centuries that women were relegated to limited ministry. It was also about this time that the charismatic gifts began to disappear from the church.

On the basis of 1 Corinthians 14:34, 35 and 1 Timothy 2:9-15, some have taught that women are not to exercise public ministry. However, Romans 16 and other passages in Scripture where women (such as Deborah and Huldah) exercised public ministries should cause us to examine that position carefully to see if Paul was giving a directive to local situations or a declaration for all time. Scripture cannot violate itself, and the overwhelming evidence points to women as active and effective participants in the plan of God.

The picture of the church at Rome is one that not only included women and men, but couples who exercised ministry in the home, the church, and the workplace. Priscilla and Aquila not only put into service their own ministry, they enabled Paul to carry out his own work in the Lord. They were mobile, moving as God directed. This reveals an attitude of self-sacrifice that is worthy of emulation today.

Later in Paul's ministry and life, he was imprisoned in Rome for at least two years. This was a difficult time for him and hindered (but did not stop) his preaching and public ministry. It was during this time that he needed workers to come alongside of him, not only to assist him in public ministry but also to provide financial and moral support.

I. WOMEN IN MINISTRY
(Romans 16:1, 2, 6, 7, 12)

A. Phoebe (vv. 1, 2)

1. I commend unto you Phebe our sister, which is a servant of the church which is at Cenchrea:

2. That ye receive her in the Lord, as becometh saints, and that ye assist her in whatsoever business she hath need of you: for she hath been a succourer of many, and of myself also.

Paul begins the chapter by introducing the Roman church to a person of importance to him and them, "I commend to you Phoebe our sister" (*NKJV*). Her name indicates that she was most likely a Gentile. The word *commend* literally means "to stand with or alongside of." Paul was giving her a high recommendation to the church at Rome, recognizing her contribution to the ministry. He then used three terms to describe Phoebe and why he was commending her.

First, he noted she was a Christian by calling her "our sister." As such, she was a member of the spiritual family that transcends genealogies, cultures, languages, and other earthly boundaries.

Second, he qualified her as a servant of the church in Cenchrea, a seaport just east of Corinth. Here he uses a term that has been much debated. In referring to her as "a servant," he used the term *deacon* (*diakonos*). This is the same word Paul used to describe an element of Christ's ministry in Romans 15:8. It is also used by Paul of himself, where it is rendered *minister* (1 Corinthians 3:5; 2 Corinthians 3:6; 6:4; Colossians 1:25). It was used also of Apollos (1 Corinthians 3:5), Timothy (1 Thessalonians 3:2), and the office of deacons in the church (1 Timothy 3:8-13). While the term is used elsewhere in the New Testament to refer to servants (e.g., Matthew 22:13; John 2:5), Paul's use of the term consistently carried the connotation of *minister*.

Paul did not differentiate between Phoebe's ministry and that of men by using other terms at his disposal which would indicate a subordinate ministry, or by calling her a *deaconess* (*diakonissa*), a term not found in the Bible. The office of deaconess was developed by the church later on, when the ministry of women was being curtailed. Phoebe appears to have been responsible for the local congregation and ministry reaching beyond that congregation.

Third, Phoebe was introduced as "a helper" (Romans 16:2, *NKJV*). This is the only place in the New Testament where this Greek word (*prostatis*) is found. It is used in secular literature to indicate a woman who uses her resources to help others, or a *patroness*. Paul said she had been a helper of many, including him. This would seem to indicate she supported Paul and others financially. She probably was a woman of means, with a house large enough in which the Cenchrean church could meet.

He instructed the congregation to receive and *assist* (literal meaning, "to stand with") her. Four things stand out here: (1) Phoebe was to be received as a representative of Paul, most probably with the epistle they were receiving. (2) She was to be received "in the Lord," a phrase Paul used seven times in Romans 16. (3) She was to be received "in a manner worthy of the saints" (*NKJV*), the *holy* or *called-out ones*. (4) She was to be given whatever assistance she needed during her stay in Rome.

B. Mary (v. 6)

6. Greet Mary, who bestowed much labour on us.

Mary stands in contrast to Phoebe. Whereas Phoebe was noted to have an official leadership position in the early church, Mary apparently did not have a formal office (see discussion of v. 12 below). Paul described her as one who "labored much" (*NKJV*). The verb used here means "working to the point of weariness" (see Matthew 11:28). She was sensitive to the needs of the church, as well as Paul's, and acted voluntarily out of love and labored beyond what was normal or expected. She found a way to minister to those in need. Her name indicates she was probably Jewish, given there are at least five women named Mary in the New Testament.

C. Junia (v. 7)

(Romans 16:7 is not included in the printed text.)

Because Junia and Andronicus (probably her husband, cf. v. 3) are mentioned as being "of note among the apostles," some commentators assume that Junia is a shortened version of a man's name. There are several problems with that view.

First, the supposed masculine name is not found elsewhere in surviving literature, whereas *Junia* is found throughout secular writings of that time. Second, the best manuscripts do not support that view. Third, the early-church fathers accepted this as a reference to a woman. Chrysostom said, "How great the dedication of this woman Junia must have been, that she should be worthy to be called an apostle [and] . . . be considered outstanding among the apostles" (*Homilies on Romans*).

She and Andronicus are distinguished in four ways in this verse. (1) They were Paul's "kinsmen," which probably indicates they were Jewish (cf. Romans 9:3). (2) Both were his "fellowprisoners," signifying they had been imprisoned for their faith and apparently with Paul at some point, though the location is difficult to determine. (3) Together they were "of note among the apostles." (4) They had distinguished themselves as *outstanding* or *prominent* among the apostles through their labor for the Lord.

Apostles is used in Scripture to indicate the Twelve (the 11 faithful and Matthias, see Acts 1:26); those who had seen and were commissioned by the risen Lord (1 Corinthians 15:7); and a group of *messengers* who served as emissaries of the gospel and were recognized as a distinct group by the church (see 2 Corinthians 8:23; 1 Corinthians 12:28). Apparently, Junia and Andronicus were members of the second group. Paul notes they "were in Christ before me," revealing that they were among the earliest leaders of the church. The apostle leaves no doubt that Junia was valuable to him and the ministry of the church.

D. Tryphena, Tryphosa, Persis (v. 12)

12. Salute Tryphena and Tryphosa, who labour in the Lord. Salute the beloved Persis, which laboured much in the Lord.

Tryphena and Tryphosa, probably sisters, labored in the Lord. In contrast to their names ("dainty" and "delicate"), their exhausting work for the Kingdom is highlighted. Paul's use of *labored* in his writings is used either of missionaries (see 1 Corinthians 15:10; Galatians 4:11) or those active in the local church, and he consistently admonished his readers to be subject to them (see 1 Corinthians 16:16; 1 Thessalonians 5:12; 1 Timothy 5:17). The ability of these two women to conduct the work of the church means they were probably freed slaves. Their ministry merited Paul's recognition and approval.

Persis also was praised for her labor in the Kingdom, but Paul added *much* to point to the abundance of her ministry. Her name means "Persian" and, as a Gentile Christian, she may have felt the need to overcome others' perception of her, or perhaps she wanted to utilize to the fullest the opportunity she had to work "in the Lord." She certainly distinguished herself, as Paul called her "the beloved," a term of endearment (see Matthew 12:18). It is of interest that in Romans 16, Paul reserves the phrase "labored much" for women (see v. 6). The early-church fathers took note of this and challenged men to follow the example of these women.

E. And Others (vv. 13, 15)

(Romans 16:13, 15 is not included in the printed text.)

Little is known concerning the remaining women of this chapter. Paul greets "Rufus, chosen in the Lord, and his mother and mine" (v. 13). Rufus' mother had apparently extended the gift of hospitality to Paul at some point in his ministry and became a "mother in Israel" to him (see Judges 5:7).

The other two women to whom Paul sends greetings are Julia and the sister of Nereus (v. 15). These women, and the men mentioned in this verse, appear to be Gentile Christians who had some leadership responsibility or influence in the church, though the capacity is unknown.

Romans 16 reveals that Paul took the ministry and leadership of women seriously. He was neither patriarchal nor feminist, but recognized that both women and men are called by God to meaningful work in the kingdom of God.

II. HUSBAND-WIFE, COWORKERS (Acts 18:1-3; Romans 16:3-5)

A. A Forged Relationship (Acts 18:1-3)

1. After these things Paul departed from Athens, and came to Corinth;

2. And found a certain Jew named Aquila, born in Pontus, lately come from Italy, with his wife Priscilla; (because that Claudius had commanded all Jews to depart from Rome:) and came unto them.

3. And because he was of the same craft, he abode with them, and wrought: for by their occupation they were tentmakers.

In this passage, Luke, the author of Acts, describes Paul's encounter with Aquila and Priscilla during his second missionary journey (also see vv. 18, 19, 24-26; 2 Timothy 4:19). Paul had departed Athens, where his message of the resurrected Lord was met with cynicism; however, even in the midst of what might have appeared to be defeat, there were those who believed (see Acts 17:16-34). He traveled to Corinth (18:1), a city that was on two major trade routes. The large numbers of travelers and sailors passing through, along with the temple to Aphrodite, contributed to its reputation for immorality. As such, Corinth was ripe for the preaching of the gospel, and the apostle Paul stayed there for 18 months (v. 11).

Once in Corinth, Paul "found a certain Jew named Aquila" (v. 2). Aquila ("eagle") is described as "born in Pontus," a Roman province. He and his wife, Priscilla (also known as Prisca in 2 Timothy 4:19), were both probably freeborn, but not Roman citizens or they would not have been ejected from Rome. At some point Aquila moved from Pontus to Rome before arriving in Corinth. The fact that Paul "found" them can mean either that he looked for fellow Jews when he entered the city, or he sought them out because they were known to him. The former was probably the case, as this was his usual method when entering a new area (see Acts 13:5, 6; 14:1; 19:8).

Aquila and Priscilla were in Corinth because Claudius had expelled all the Jews from Rome (A.D. 49 or 50). Paul "came to them" or lived with them after arriving in Corinth before being joined by Silas and Timothy (v. 5) and moving to the house of Justus (v. 7). Apparently, Aquila and Priscilla were Christians prior to leaving Rome, since there is no mention of their conversion. And Luke describes their teaching Apollos in verses 24-26.

Paul not only stayed in their home, but worked with them, probably in Aquila's shop, since they were tentmakers also (v. 3). Tentmakers of that period worked either in leather or in woven goat's hair cloth. It was an acceptable profession, but not considered worthy of Paul's social status. It does reveal his dedication to the cause of Christ. He was willing to work in a menial occupation in order to provide for himself an opportunity to share Christ.

Not only was Priscilla a coworker in the gospel, she worked with her husband in tentmaking. She appears to have been an industrious woman.

Today the bi-vocational minister is often viewed as less than a "full" minister. Those who are willing to dedicate themselves to the gospel and provide their own support are to be commended and honored.

B. A Fruitful Relationship (Romans 16:3-5)

3. Greet Priscilla and Aquila my helpers in Christ Jesus:
4. Who have for my life laid down their own necks: unto whom not only I give thanks, but also all the churches of the Gentiles.
5. Likewise greet the church that is in their house. Salute my well-beloved Epaenetus, who is the first-fruits of Achaia unto Christ.

Paul called the ministerial couple his "fellow workers" (v. 3, *NKJV*), a title used of Apollos (1 Corinthians 3:9); Titus (2 Corinthians 8:23); Timothy (Romans 16:21; 1 Thessalonians 3:2); Urbanus (Romans 16:9); and Euodia and Syntyche, two women in the Philippian church (Philippians 4:2, 3). His use of this term seemed to refer primarily to those who were establishing new churches and preaching the gospel. Some worked alongside of Paul for a while, then returned to their home churches (as did Phoebe), or were dispatched by him to other areas (as Timothy, Acts 19:22). In Romans 16 we find that Priscilla and Aquila had returned to Rome sometime after moving with Paul from Corinth to Ephesus (Acts 18:18).

Paul expressed a debt to the couple, saying they "risked their own necks for my life" (Romans 16:4, NKJV). The occasion is difficult to determine. It could be a reference to the riot in Ephesus, where Paul's life was in danger (Acts 19:23-40; 1 Corinthians 15:32; 2 Corinthians 1:8, 9). Wherever it was, Paul informed the Roman church that Priscilla and Aquila placed their own lives in jeopardy to assist him.

Further, this couple was owed a debt of gratitude from "all the churches of the Gentiles." This is a sweeping statement. It could be viewed as a reference to the saving of Paul's life, the apostle to the Gentiles (see Romans 11:13). That is, since Priscilla and Aquila rescued him from the danger in mind, those churches he established owed them a debt of thanks. Given the apostle's tone of gratitude for the ministry of others in the midst of this chapter, as well as the tone of humility in all of his writings, it is difficult to understand this as a reference to himself, the self-proclaimed "least of the apostles" (1 Corinthians 15:9; 2 Corinthians 11:5).

Aquila and Priscilla's influence is better explained as an acknowledgment and endorsement of the couple's work in the Gentile churches. It reveals this couple had a significant ministry that influenced more than the three known cities associated with their ministry in Acts and Paul's writings (Rome and Corinth, Acts 18:2; Ephesus, Acts 18:18, 19; Rome again, here; Ephesus a second time, 2 Timothy 4:19).

Paul also sent greetings to the church worshiping in their house (Romans 16:5). From this it can be ascertained that the church in Rome consisted of more than one congregation, most meeting in the homes of individuals. In all probability, a house church would meet at least weekly (see Acts 20:6, 7; 1 Corinthians 16:2), then the congregations ("whole church") would meet together on a regular basis (Romans 16:23; 1 Corinthians 14:23). This couple started or pastored a congregation in their house at Rome, as well as Corinth and Ephesus.

In three of the six references to the couple, Priscilla's name precedes Aquila's (Romans 16:3; Acts 18:18; 2 Timothy 4:19). Some believe this indicates Priscilla had a higher social standing than Aquila. However, Paul was not one to allow social standing to influence his writings. In fact, he usually listed the prominent people last. It probably indicates Priscilla was more active in missionary work, as well as the church that met in their house, than Aquila. Support for this may be found in Acts 18, where Luke listed Aquila first in verse 2, then Priscilla first in verse 18, where they were traveling with Paul.

Paul sent greetings to his "wellbeloved Epaenetus, who is the firstfruits of Achaia [Asia] unto Christ" (Romans 16:5). The inclusion of Epaenetus here could indicate he was converted under Priscilla and Aquila in Ephesus (capital of Achaia) and moved with them to Rome. Since he is mentioned with them, it is probable he was a part of their congregation. Priscilla and Aquila's ministry reveals they cared for both Jewish and Gentile Christians. Their emphasis was on revealing Christ to those in need. The apostle showed no indication of exerting authority over them in any of the places they are mentioned. He considered them to be true coworkers with him in God's field (see 1 Corinthians 3:9).

III. TWO LOYAL FRIENDS
(Philippians 2:25-30; 2 Timothy 1:16-18)

A. Epaphroditus (Philippians 2:25-30)

(Philippians 2:26-28 is not included in the printed text.)

25. Yet I supposed it necessary

to send to you Epaphroditus, my brother, and companion in labour, and fellowsoldier, but your messenger, and he that ministered to my wants.

29. Receive him therefore in the Lord with all gladness; and hold such in reputation:

30. Because for the work of Christ he was nigh unto death, not regarding his life, to supply your lack of service toward me.

The Philippian church had sent Epaphroditus ("charming") to be a help to Paul during one of his imprisonments, probably at Rome around A.D. 61-63 (see 1:13). He carried the offering the church raised for Paul's needs (4:18), and apparently had been commissioned by the congregation to be with Paul in his time of need.

Paul's words for Epaphroditus are reminiscent of Romans 16. He expressed genuine feelings of appreciation in explaining that he considered it necessary to send Epaphroditus to Philippi from Rome. The apostle's tone was almost apologetic. Paul made it clear that Epaphroditus had done all Paul could ask. He was not being dismissed nor deserting. He had loyally completed his service to the apostle (see Philippians 2:30).

In verse 25, Paul described the character and conduct of Epaphroditus in five different ways:

1. *My brother.* Certainly this refers to Epaphroditus' Christian experience, but probably was also a reference to the personal relationship he and Paul developed during their time together.

2. *Fellow worker.* He was a colleague in spreading the gospel.

3. *Fellow soldier.* This military imagery suggests determination in the midst of suffering and opposition. Paul used words of confrontation in Philippians 1:27, 30 and military terms to describe difficult conditions (see 1 Corinthians 9:7; 2 Corinthians 10:3).

4. *Your messenger (apostle).* Epaphroditus was in the third category of apostles mentioned above in the discussion of Junia.

5. *The one who ministered to me in my need.* No doubt this was a reference in part to Philippians 4:18 and his delivering the congregation's offering, but *ministered* also refers to one who exercises public ministry.

In Philippians 2:21, Paul notes his lack of true friends in Rome. Epaphroditus was there to deliver the congregation's offering, assist the apostle in ministry, and be a friend to one imprisoned. He apparently had gone through a very difficult time and spiritual struggle along with Paul, perhaps the reason he almost died (v. 26). His resolve during this struggle had not gone unnoticed by Paul, who held him in high regard.

Epaphroditus' concern for the Philippian church is described in verses 26-28. He was "full of heaviness" ("distressed," *NKJV*), indicating a mental and spiritual anguish (see Mark 14:33), because of their concern for him during his deathly illness. Therefore, Paul decided to send him back to Philippi to ease their minds and his sorrow (v. 28), for Paul too was concerned about the church and knew Epaphroditus could minister to them in his absence.

Paul instructed the church to "receive him . . . in the Lord with all gladness" (v. 29).

They were to honor him, as the apostle did, for his diligence in accomplishing their commission, ministering to Paul's needs, and being faithful in ministry while in Rome. He was so diligent in "the work of Christ" (v. 30) that he came close to death. This does not seem to be a reference to the illness described in verse 26. Paul used a strong term to describe Epaphroditus' disregard for his life. The imagery is that of risking his life for the cause of Christ, just as Priscilla and Aquila had risked their own necks for Paul.

What the Philippians could not do, Epaphroditus did in their place. In Philippians 2, Paul never commented on Epaphroditus' concern for himself but only his concern for others. He embodied what Paul instructed the Philippian church to do and be in the epistle he carried.

B. Onesiphorus (2 Timothy 1:16-18)

16. The Lord give mercy unto the house of Onesiphorus; for he oft refreshed me, and was not ashamed of my chain:

17. But, when he was in Rome, he sought me out very diligently, and found me.

18. The Lord grant unto him that he may find mercy of the Lord in that day: and in how many things he ministered unto me at Ephesus, thou knowest very well.

In contrast to those who left him, Paul lifted up Onesiphorus in this letter as an example for Timothy of one who is faithful and loyal. Paul was abandoned by Phygellus and Hermogenes (v. 15). Demas deserted him for the world, and Titus left on a mission (4:10). But Onesiphorus was there for him in his time of need.

Verse 16 of the text begins with an expression of desire for mercy to be extended to the household of Onesiphorus (also see 4:19). *Mercy* is an "emotion, attitude and demonstration of compassion extended to one in need." Mercy must result in definite ministry to be true mercy. Paul desired this for Onesiphorus, because Onesiphorus often "refreshed" him. He supplied the necessities of life, fellowship, encouragement, hospitality, and ministry to Paul, which enabled Paul to promote the gospel.

Further, he was not ashamed of Paul's "chain," or imprisonment. He did not allow Paul's situation or circumstance to be a hindrance to him or his desire to bring to the apostle those things necessary (see Matthew 25:31-46). In fact, he eagerly sought out Paul when he arrived in Rome (2 Timothy 1:17). The language of this verse reveals that he sought him zealously, looking diligently until he found him. He was determined to get to a brother in need.

The passage ends as it began, with an expression of desire for mercy—that Onesiphorus "may find mercy of the Lord" (v. 18). It is a play on words: just as Onesiphorus found Paul, Paul desired that Onesiphorus find mercy (see Galatians 6:8). "In that day" is a reference to 1:12 of this letter and the appearing of the Lord.

Paul further pointed out to Timothy how Onesiphorus had been faithful in ministering to him at Ephesus. He did not extend ministry to Paul just once, but on at least two occasions.

GOLDEN TEXT HOMILY

"I THANK MY GOD UPON EVERY REMEMBRANCE OF YOU, . . . FOR YOUR FELLOWSHIP IN THE GOSPEL FROM THE FIRST DAY UNTIL NOW" (Philippians 1:3, 5).

Philippians is perhaps the most personal of all the apostle Paul's letters. It was written to the saints in Christ Jesus who were at Philippi, where the first European church was founded by Paul, representing the first major penetration of the gospel into Gentile territory.

Paul expressed thanksgiving for the saints "upon every remembrance of you," or "my whole memory of you." The Philippians had actively supported Paul's ministry even though they were poor. The fruit of their faith was abundant.

Paul acknowledged their "partnership in the gospel from the first day" (v. 5, *NIV*)—that is, from the first coming of the gospel among them. On several occasions they collected funds for Paul and also aided him while in prison. He recognized their generous devotedness to the service of Christ as

God's work in them, and therefore as a pledge of their perseverance in their Christian calling until their salvation should be "completed" at the time of Christ's return (see v. 6).

Paul teaches us that *ministry* describes action, not a person. Ministry represents function, not a station. Every believer is an agent of ministry, as well as an object of ministry.—**Gerald Johnson**

SENTENCE SERMONS

BELIEVERS IN CHRIST are colleagues in faith and ministry.
—Selected

WHEN LOVE AND SKILL work together, expect a masterpiece.
—John Ruskin

WHEN BROTHER STANDS with brother, a war is already half won.
—Selected

EVANGELISM APPLICATION

CHRISTIANS MUST WORK TOGETHER TO MAKE THE GOSPEL KNOWN TO ALL THE WORLD.

In this lesson we have a mix of women, men, couples and family members active in ministry. These Christians put aside their own concerns and focused on the goal of sharing the gospel and ministering to a dying world, while being attentive to the needs of those in the church. Some individuals left their physical families and homes to share the good news. Others came alongside the full-time workers to be a help during difficult periods of ministry. Some provided the funding to promote the

message of salvation. Churches were started in homes and the unsaved were led to Jesus Christ.

The work of many resulted in the spread of the gospel and the growth of the church in the first century. It is an excellent example for the church in the 21st century.

ILLUMINATING THE LESSON

Several years ago a popular TV evangelist made the statement that God had called him to reach the world with the gospel. The emphasis of his statement was not one of teamwork, but implied that he alone was capable of such a task. Sadly, he was wrong. God does not lay the work of the ministry upon one or two highly gifted individuals, whether it is ministry around the world or in the local church. He uses all kinds of people.

In Deuteronomy 32:30 we are told that one can chase 1,000 and two can put 10,000 to flight. This verse reveals the power of cooperation. When we partner with others, share our resources and pool our efforts, we are more productive and effective in the kingdom of God.

DAILY BIBLE READINGS

M. Supportive Assistants.
Exodus 17:8-13
T. Best of Friends.
1 Samuel 20:11-17
W. Loyal Proxy.
Jeremiah 36:4-8
T. Fellow Ministers.
Acts 12:24 through 13:4
F. Trustworthy Associate.
Philippians 2:19-23
S. Companion and Fellow Soldier.
Philippians 2:25-30

TRUTH SEARCH
Creatively Teaching the Word

DISCUSSION QUESTIONS

Women in Ministry
(Romans 16:1, 2, 6, 12)

1. How did Paul describe Phoebe's ministry (vv. 1, 2)?

2. What requests did Paul make of the Roman Christians regarding Phoebe?

3. How did Paul describe the women named in verses 6 and 12? What was the reputation of Persis?

Husband-Wife Coworkers
(Acts 18:1-3, 24-26; Romans 16:3-5)

1. Why had Aquila and Priscilla moved from Rome to Corinth (Acts 18:2)?

2. How did this couple team up with Paul (v. 3)?

3. How did this couple minister to Apollos (vv. 24-26)?

4. How did Paul feel about Aquila and Priscilla (Romans 16:3, 4)?

5. What ministry did this couple establish in Rome (v. 5)?

Two Loyal Friends
(Philippians 2:25-30; 2 Timothy 1:16-18)

1. What five phrases did Paul use to describe Epaphroditus (Philippians 2:25)?

2. Describe the bond between Paul and Epaphroditus (vv. 27, 28).

3. How had Epaphroditus proven His love for Christ and for Paul (v. 30)?

4. How did Paul say the church should treat such faithful servants of God (v. 29)?

5. Under what circumstances did Onesiphorus minister to Paul, and how did he serve Paul (2 Timothy 1:16, 17)?

6. What was Paul's prayer for Onesiphorus?

OBJECT LESSON

Items needed: Hearts made from construction paper, pencils and a stapler

Give a heart to each student. **If each of us were to write on our heart things that are dear to us, we would have some similar responses and some differing responses.**

Ask everyone to write the word *Christ* on their heart. **As believers, Christ should be most precious to us. He unites us as one family.**

Sadly, a person who loves Christ can come to a church with other Christians yet fail to feel he or she belongs; after a while, that person will probably leave.

Ask everyone to add the word *Ministry* to their heart.

When we as Christians take the step of not merely loving Christ in a passive way but actively getting involved in ministry with each other, we are brought together in a strong Christian bond.

As students pass the hearts forward, have them name ministry opportunities in your church. Once you have received the hearts, staple them together.

Doing ministry together will bind our hearts together in love for Christ, the people we serve, and one another.

INTRODUCTION TO SPRING QUARTER

Lessons 1-5 are studies from Jeremiah and Lamentations. The expositions were written by the Reverend Dr. Homer G. Rhea, who is an ordained minister in the Church of God and has held positions as district overseer and member of the Mississippi State Council and the State Youth and Christian Education Board. (See page 16 for more biographical information).

The Easter lesson was written by the Reverend Dr. R.B. Thomas. An ordained minister, Dr. Thomas is a recipient of the Distinguished Educator Award in the Church of God and is listed as an Outstanding Educator of America. (See page 16 for more biographical information).

The second unit, "Out of Exile (Ezra and Nehemiah)," includes lessons 7-13, and was written by the Reverend Dr. Jerald Daffe (B.A., M.A., D.Min.). Dr. Daffe received the Excellence in Advising award (1999) at Lee University. His two latest books are *Life Challenges for Men* and *Revival: God's Plan for His People*. (See page 136 for more biographical information).

Called to Serve

Study Text: Jeremiah 1:1-19
Objective: To review Jeremiah's call to serve God and offer ourselves in service to God.
Time: Jeremiah was called by God in 626 B.C.
Place: Anathoth in Judah
Golden Text: "I beseech you therefore, brethren, by the mercies of God, that ye present your bodies a living sacrifice, holy, acceptable unto God, which is your reasonable service" (Romans 12:1).
Central Truth: God calls and equips every Christian to serve.
Evangelism Emphasis: God calls every Christian to witness to the lost.

PRINTED TEXT

Jeremiah 1:4. Then the word of the Lord came unto me, saying,

5. Before I formed thee in the belly I knew thee; and before thou camest forth out of the womb I sanctified thee, and I ordained thee a prophet unto the nations.

6. Then said I, Ah, Lord God! behold, I cannot speak: for I am a child.

7. But the Lord said unto me, Say not, I am a child: for thou shalt go to all that I shall send thee, and whatsoever I command thee thou shalt speak.

8. Be not afraid of their faces: for I am with thee to deliver thee, saith the Lord.

9. Then the Lord put forth his hand, and touched my mouth. And the Lord said unto me, Behold, I have put my words in thy mouth.

10. See, I have this day set thee over the nations and over the kingdoms, to root out, and to pull down, and to destroy, and to throw down, to build, and to plant.

11. Moreover the word of the Lord came unto me, saying, Jeremiah, what seest thou? And I said, I see a rod of an almond tree.

12. Then said the Lord unto me, Thou hast well seen: for I will hasten my word to perform it.

13. And the word of the Lord came unto me the second time, saying, What seest thou? And I said, I see a seething pot; and the face thereof is toward the north.

14. Then the Lord said unto me, Out of the north an evil shall break forth upon all the inhabitants of the land.

16. And I will utter my judgments against them touching all their wickedness, who have forsaken me, and have burned incense unto other gods, and worshipped the works of their own hands.

17. Thou therefore gird up thy loins, and arise, and speak unto them all that I command thee: be not dismayed at their faces, lest I confound thee before them.

18. For, behold, I have made thee this day a defenced city, and an iron pillar, and brasen walls against the whole land, against the kings of Judah, against the princes thereof, against the priests thereof, and against the people of the land.

19. And they shall fight against thee; but they shall not prevail against thee; for I am with thee, saith the Lord, to deliver thee.

LESSON OUTLINE

I. CALL OF JEREMIAH

   A. The Time and Place of Jeremiah's Ministry

   B. The Word of the Lord

   C. The Authority of the Prophet

II. VISIONS OF JEREMIAH

   A. The Vision of the Almond Branch

   B. The Vision of the Boiling Pot

III. PROMISES TO JEREMIAH

   A. A Command to Proclaim

   B. A Promise of Strength

   C. A Promise of Deliverance

LESSON EXPOSITION

INTRODUCTION

Jeremiah is unique among the prophets in that he reveals more of his own personal life, concerns and frustrations than any other prophet. It may be this personal approach that led Jeremiah to open the book with the statement "The words of Jeremiah." All other prophetic books except for Amos open with a statement similar to "The word of the Lord that came to. . . ."

The ministry of Jeremiah was aimed at the southern kingdom of Judah. To illustrate the severity of Jeremiah's prophecies of judgment, he was commanded not to marry or have children (16:2). His prophecy for Judah was that judgment was pending and the next generation would bear the brunt of God's wrath. It was this pending judgment and angry outpouring that God intended to amplify by commanding Jeremiah not to wed or have children.

I. CALL OF JEREMIAH
(Jeremiah 1:1-10)

Nothing is more personal and life-altering than God calling someone to preach the gospel. Though many contrasts may be drawn from God's calling of preachers today and His calling of prophets in Jeremiah's day, many similarities may be seen as well. Preachers are called to declare God's Word to all who will hear. Prophets were called to fulfill the same calling. Preachers are called to be God's representative to the world. Prophets too were God's ambassadors who spoke in behalf of and with the authority of God.

Those who receive a calling from God today can reflect upon the calling of Jeremiah and envision their calling as being fundamentally the same as his. Jeremiah's calling was intensely personal, as are the ministry callings God gives to His children today.

A. The Time and Place of Jeremiah's Ministry (vv. 1-3)

(Jeremiah 1:1-3 is not included in the printed text.)

Anathoth was a town in the territory of Benjamin, set aside for residence of the priests and Levites (see Joshua 21:18). It is located two and one-half miles northeast of Jerusalem and is called Anata today. It was at Anathoth that God came to Jeremiah and called him to prophesy. One might be a priest in Judah by birth, but to become a prophet required a special calling from God. This was the case for Jeremiah. As he served Judah as a member of the priestly society, God called him to an even greater ministry as a prophet.

God's call came to Jeremiah in the 13th year of the reign of Josiah, king of Judah. Josiah was the last of the good kings in Judah and instituted reforms in the religious practices of God's people. Although he was a good king who pleased the Lord, God had already determined the fate of Judah. Josiah would not be able to turn away God's wrath.

The 13th year of Josiah's reign was actually 626 B.C., and he would remain on the throne of Judah for the next 18 years. Jeremiah's ministry lasted throughout the life of Josiah, through the brief reign of Jehoahaz, who was taken to Egypt, through 11 years of the reign of Jehoiakim, and finally through the reign of Zedekiah, who was Judah's final king.

After the fall of Jerusalem in 586 B.C., Nebuchadnezzar gave Jeremiah the option of either staying in Jerusalem with the poor remnant or going to Babylon. Jeremiah chose to stay in Jerusalem, but was later forced to go to Egypt with many of the remnant, where he probably died.

B. The Word of the Lord (vv. 4-9)

4. Then the word of the Lord came unto me, saying,

5. Before I formed thee in the belly I knew thee; and before thou camest forth out of the womb I sanctified thee, and I ordained thee a prophet unto the nations.

6. Then said I, Ah, Lord God! behold, I cannot speak: for I am a child.

7. But the Lord said unto me, Say not, I am a child: for thou shalt go to all that I shall send thee, and whatsoever I command thee thou shalt speak.

8. Be not afraid of their faces: for I am with thee to deliver thee, saith the Lord.

9. Then the Lord put forth his hand, and touched my mouth. And the Lord said unto me, Behold, I have put my words in thy mouth.

It is interesting to compare the ways Isaiah and Jeremiah received their call to be prophets of God. Both callings came unexpectedly. Isaiah and Jeremiah received their calls through a vision and an audible command. Both men then attempted to evade the call by playing upon their weaknesses. Isaiah proclaimed himself unworthy because he was a man of "unclean lips" dwelling in the midst of a people of unclean lips (see Isaiah 6:1-8). Jeremiah's reply was, "Behold, I cannot speak: for I am a child" (1:6). God duly noted their objections and took certain measures in both cases to remove any doubt or reluctance either prophet might have had.

The symbolism of God's enablement for both Isaiah and Jeremiah was a tactile experience in which their mouths were touched and the authority to proclaim God's word was given. For Isaiah, one of the seraphim touched his mouth with a coal from the altar of God in the Temple. For Jeremiah, it was the hand of God that touched his lips. In both instances, the touch of God was sufficient to set aside all doubt and feelings of inadequacy for the prophets.

In the call of Jeremiah, God reveled His preparation of Jeremiah—preparations that predated the prophet's birth. Before Jeremiah was formed in the womb, he was known of God. Prior to his birth, he was sanctified and ordained a prophet. However, Jeremiah did not begin to fulfill the role of a prophet until the fullness of time came for God to give him prophetic utterances. The earlier years of Jeremiah passed without any recognition or suspicion of such a call.

God always works according to His time schedule. Who is to say whether someone in your classroom is about to be awakened to a dramatic call from God? Who is to say whether that rowdy child at church has been ordained of God to perform a tremendous ministry in adulthood? God knows all individuals intimately even prior to their conception in the womb. His plans for each life are to be honored and obeyed.

C. The Authority of the Prophet (v. 10)

10. See, I have this day set thee over the nations and over the kingdoms, to root out, and to pull down, and to destroy, and to throw down, to build, and to plant.

The statement that God made to Jeremiah regarding the authority and force of his calling reveals to us the power God instilled in Jeremiah and his words. He was *set over*, or "given authority over," nations and kingdoms to either pull down or to build up. Of course, this authority was not Jeremiah's, but God's; and the decisions to either build up or pull down would not be made by Jeremiah. God would decide and send the verdict through the mouth of Jeremiah.

As in the ministry of prophesying, the preaching of the Word of God is serious business. God calls ministers to proclaim the Word of Life to all who will hear. It is God's delight to save individuals through the ministry of preaching. It is also His judgment to hold accountable those who do not receive the preached Word and refuse to repent. In this sense, modern preaching and the modern preacher hold the same authority as the prophets of old.

II. VISIONS OF JEREMIAH
(Jeremiah 1:11-16)

Once Jeremiah was called into ministry, God began to give him messages of prophetic importance. God never calls individuals to a ministry and then leaves them idle. His callings are punctual in that the fullness of time has arrived for the ministry to be performed. When God calls, it is time to work. For Jeremiah there was no time for him to adjust to the calling God had just given him; it was time to speak.

A. The Vision of the Almond Branch
(vv. 11, 12)

11. Moreover the word of the Lord came unto me, saying, Jeremiah, what seest thou? And I said, I see a rod of an almond tree.

12. Then said the Lord unto me, Thou hast well seen: for I will hasten my word to perform it.

The first vision Jeremiah received was filled with symbolism. It was a simple vision of an almond branch. The Hebrew word for *almond tree* is *shaqed*, derived from the word *shaqad*, which means "to be ready, to hasten, to watch for an opportunity to do a thing." Because the almond tree was the first to bloom each year, and the root word meant "to hasten," the vision meant that God was hastening to bring about judgment upon Judah. The prophesies of Jeremiah were going to be timely and fulfilled presently.

Such a simple message was intended to spark the ministry of Jeremiah and provide him with the self-confidence he would need to boldly speak the messages God would give him. God was not only telling Jeremiah that He was ready to begin His judgment of Judah; He was also telling Jeremiah that it was time for him to take his place among the prophets.

B. The Vision of the Boiling Pot
(vv. 13-16)

(Jeremiah 1:15 is not included in the printed text.)

13. And the word of the Lord came unto me the second time, saying, What seest thou? And I said, I see a seething pot; and the face thereof is toward the north.

14. Then the Lord said unto me, Out of the north an evil shall break forth upon all the inhabitants of the land.

16. And I will utter my judgments against them touching all

their wickedness, who have forsaken me, and have burned incense unto other gods, and worshipped the works of their own hands.

While the first vision dealt with God's intent to quickly bring about His judgment, the second vision got right to the point of God's intentions. Jeremiah saw a boiling pot that faced the north. The message of this vision would not be pleasing to those in Judah to whom it was sent. From the north "an evil" was coming whose "families" would set up their thrones at the entrance gates of Jerusalem (vv. 14, 15). Specifically, the various races and peoples who made up the Babylonian empire were coming to bring judgment upon an idolatrous Jerusalem and Judah.

It was not unusual for God to use idolatrous nations to bring His judgments upon Israel and Judah, even though this seems to be contrary to what we might think of as appropriate action on God's part. Therein was the source of the anger and animosity directed toward Jeremiah. It was unthinkable to the inhabitants of Jerusalem and Judah that God would allow a heathen nation to rule over them. For this priest turned prophet to herald such a prediction was to invite the disdain and anger of the masses.

Judah had become idolatrous—the people "burned incense unto other gods, and worshipped the works of their own hands" (v. 16). God, therefore, had begun to display His judgment through the prophecies of Jeremiah and the vehicle of an idolatrous nation. The anger of the people of Judah would find its focus on the messenger.

III. PROMISES TO JEREMIAH
(Jeremiah 1:17-19)

God's call to Jeremiah was not one that he would be able to refuse. There can be no rejection, denial, or divorcing of oneself from God's call. For Jeremiah to attempt to avoid the call in some way would have resulted in something similar to what happened to Jonah.

To proclaim the message God had ordained, Jeremiah would place himself in harm's way. He was to become a very unpopular individual in the coming months and years. Therefore, immediately after giving Jeremiah his first prophetic revelations, the Lord gave Jeremiah several promises of divine protection and comfort.

A. A Command to Proclaim (v. 17)

17. Thou therefore gird up thy loins, and arise, and speak unto them all that I command thee: be not dismayed at their faces, lest I confound thee before them.

Jeremiah's calling came with a stern warning concerning the demeanor he should have as he delivered the words of God. God told Jeremiah, "Get yourself ready! Stand up and say to them whatever I command you. Do not be terrified by them, or I will terrify you before them" (NIV). It is not surprising that God expected Jeremiah to speak with authority and readiness. The phrase "gird up thy loins" meant to make oneself ready for action or, in this case, to show oneself to be a person in readiness to speak God's word with authority.

Should Jeremiah become afraid or ashamed to speak as God directed when he came face-to-face with those to whom God would send His word, God would then confound or confuse Jeremiah before them and increase his embarrassment many times over. Jeremiah had no alternative but to speak boldly and forcefully as God gave him the message. This should be the way all individuals who speak in behalf of God should conduct themselves.

God's messengers should never be timid when speaking to this world in His behalf. Whether we are preaching a sermon, teaching a lesson or witnessing to the lost, we should be bold and vigorous for His glory.

B. A Promise of Strength (v. 18)

18. For, behold, I have made thee this day a defenced city, and an iron pillar, and brasen walls against the whole land, against the kings of Judah, against the princes thereof, against the priests thereof, and against the people of the land.

God is always faithful to provide His servants with the strength to fulfill the tasks He is sending them to perform. In Jeremiah's case, God's assurance was phenomenal. God's instruction to "prepare yourself and arise" (v. 17, *NKJV*) was bolstered by the statement "Behold, I have made you this day a fortified city and an iron pillar, and bronze walls against the whole land" (v. 18, *NKJV*).

God was assuring Jeremiah he could deliver the prophecies without fear of being harmed by those angered by the prophecies. Jeremiah would have spiritual defense walls around him—strong walls, like walls of bronze. In addition, Jeremiah also would be like an "iron pillar."

The need for this great defense is quickly on the heels of God's promise. Jeremiah was going to become an enemy of almost everyone in the land of Judah. His bronze defense and iron demeanor would set him against the kings of Judah, the leaders or princes of Judah, the priests of the Temple, and the very people themselves. God's call to Jeremiah was a life sentence of hatred. With so many people angry and vengeful toward him, it was indeed the best for Jeremiah that he live without a wife or children lest they too be objects of Judah's hatred.

C. A Promise of Deliverance (v. 19)

19. And they shall fight against thee; but they shall not prevail against thee; for I am with thee, saith the Lord, to deliver thee.

Few people enjoy always being in some type of battle with another individual, group or organization. To be constantly at odds with a single person is difficult enough—much less being at odds with the entire world. But that was God's word to Jeremiah—his life would be a constant routine of battles, revolts and anger.

The entire company listed in verse 18 would be at war with this prophet. This war was likely to be more than a battle of words. Though Jeremiah would only have words at his disposal, they would be words given him directly from the throne of God. People would not be able to avoid the impact those words would bring upon Judah, so their anger would smolder toward the messenger Jeremiah.

God's promise to Jeremiah was that even though the entire nation of Judah would rise up against him, God would deliver him from whatever traps or assaults the people brought against him.

It should always be on the mind and heart of the believer that if we are bold in pressing forward with our witness of Jesus Christ, God will be standing at our side able to deliver us at the slightest threat of the world. His promise to us is, "I will never leave thee, nor forsake thee" (Hebrews 13:5).

GOLDEN TEXT HOMILY

"I BESEECH YOU THEREFORE, BRETHREN, BY THE MERCIES OF GOD, THAT YE PRESENT YOUR BODIES A LIVING SACRIFICE, HOLY, ACCEPTABLE UNTO GOD,

WHICH IS YOUR REASONABLE SERVICE" (Romans 12:1).

The apostle alludes to the sacrifices that were offered under the Law. The victims were brought to the door of the Tabernacle and were there slain. The bodies were then disposed of according to the particular directions given in the Law.

In reference to these Old Testament sacrifices, we are to present our bodies as a living sacrifice unto the Lord. The term *body* is used here to represent our total personality or self. No part of us should be under the dominion of any other lord. As we have in the past yielded ourselves instruments of sin, we must now yield ourselves completely to God. Every sin, of whatever kind, must be mortified; and every grace, however difficult and self-denying, must be put into the service of God.

God calls us to holiness. He says, "Be ye holy; for I am holy" (1 Peter 1:16). The sacrifices in the Old Testament were to be without spot or blemish; and so must we. We are to present ourselves a living sacrifice, holy. It is true that we cannot be holy until we are renewed by the Holy Spirit; but it is equally true that when we come to Christ in faith, He will give us that which we need to be clean and holy.

A holy sacrifice will be acceptable to God. Absolutely nothing so pleases God as a broken and contrite heart (Psalm 51:17). As for all the legal sacrifices, He had no delight in them except as they pointed to the Lord Jesus Christ, and were offered with reference to Him. A heart filled with gratitude to Him, devoted to His service, is worth more than all the Old Testament sacrifices. Every act of obedience proceeding from faith and love is, in God's sight, the most acceptable tribute that anyone can possibly offer to Him.—**Selected**

SENTENCE SERMONS

GOD CALLS AND EQUIPS every Christian to serve.

—Selected

MOST PEOPLE want to serve God—but in an advisory capacity only.

—Sunday Express

SERVICE CAN NEVER become slavery to those who love.

—J.L. Masse

ILLUMINATING THE LESSON

Jeremiah was called to live a lonely existence as the bearer of bad tidings to the nation of Judah. In our earthly way of viewing things, we might think it was cruel of God to ask Jeremiah to be a prophet rejected and hated by those whom he served. He was not allowed to take a wife who might have been a source of companionship for him during those hard times of solitude. He was never allowed to father children who could have brought him moments of joy and happiness. God sentenced him to a life of solitude.

But Jeremiah's solitude was only in the earthly realm. We do not see the companionship and fellowship Jeremiah enjoyed with God. God may have placed him in a life of solitude in the flesh, but Jeremiah lived an exciting and fulfilling life in the spirit with the constant companionship of God.

DAILY BIBLE READINGS

M. God Calls the Insignificant.
    Judges 6:11-16
T. Sound the Warning.
    Ezekiel 33:7-11
W. All Ages Can Serve.
    Joel 2:28-32
T. Bravely Face Opposition.
    Philippians 1:14-29
F. God's Judgment Is Right.
    2 Thessalonians 1:3-12
S. Use Your Gift in Service.
    2 Timothy 1:6-9

TRUTH SEARCH
Creatively Teaching the Word

DISCUSSION QUESTIONS

Call of Jeremiah
(Jeremiah 1:1-10)

1. What was difficult about the time period when Jeremiah lived (v. 3)?

2. What did the Lord determine about Jeremiah before his birth (vv. 4, 5)?

3. Describe and explain Jeremiah's initial response to God's call (v. 6).

4. What did the Lord tell Jeremiah to do (v. 7)?

5. What did the Lord promise him (v. 8)?

6. Describe the authority God gave to Jeremiah (vv. 9, 10).

Visions of Jeremiah
(Jeremiah 1:11-16)

1. Understanding that the almond tree blossoms very early, what might be the significance of this first vision (vv. 11, 12)?

2. What did the vision of the boiling pot symbolize (vv. 13, 14)?

3. What would Jerusalem soon face (v. 15)?

4. Why was God sending judgment (v. 16)?

Promises to Jeremiah
(Jeremiah 1:17-19)

1. What did the Lord command Jeremiah to do (v. 17)?

2. What personal warning did the Lord give to Jeremiah in verse 17?

3. Who would oppose Jeremiah, and what would the Lord do for him (v. 18)?

4. What guarantee did the Lord make in verse 19?

OBJECT LESSON

Items needed: Marker board and marker

Make two columns on the board. Title one "Commanded"; name the other one "Called."

Ask students to name a variety of things the Bible commands all Christians to do, and write responses on the board. (Love God, love other people, pray, read the Word, obey God's commands, reach out to the needy, witness for Christ, worship God, attend church, give offerings, etc.)

All these commands and many more are to be followed by all believers. They demonstrate our relationship with Christ and bring Him praise.

Next, have students name specific callings God places on some believers but not on others. (Preaching, directing worship, teaching, prophecy, leadership, missions, etc.)

Whatever specific ministries God has called us to perform, and even if we're not yet certain of His calling, He has ordained each of us to serve Him by fulfilling the commands in His Word. Every believer is a minister with a ministry.

The One True God

Study Text: Jeremiah 10:1-16
Objective: To contrast the nature of the one true God with idols and praise God for who He is.
Time: 607 B.C.
Place: The Temple in Jerusalem
Golden Text: "Forasmuch as there is none like unto thee, O Lord; thou art great, and thy name is great in might" (Jeremiah 10:6).
Central Truth: God is the only true and living God.
Evangelism Emphasis: By proclaiming Jesus Christ, Christians lead sinners to know the one true God.

PRINTED TEXT

Jeremiah 10:1. Hear ye the word which the Lord speaketh unto you, O house of Israel:

2. Thus saith the Lord, Learn not the way of the heathen, and be not dismayed at the signs of heaven; for the heathen are dismayed at them.

3. For the customs of the people are vain: for one cutteth a tree out of the forest, the work of the hands of the workman, with the axe.

4. They deck it with silver and with gold; they fasten it with nails and with hammers, that it move not.

5. They are upright as the palm tree, but speak not: they must needs be borne, because they cannot go. Be not afraid of them; for they cannot do evil, neither also is it in them to do good.

6. Forasmuch as there is none like unto thee, O Lord; thou art great, and thy name is great in might.

7. Who would not fear thee, O King of nations? for to thee doth it appertain: forasmuch as among all the wise men of the nations, and in all their kingdoms, there is none like unto thee.

10. But the Lord is the true God, he is the living God, and an ever-lasting king: at his wrath the earth shall tremble, and the nations shall not be able to abide his indignation.

11. Thus shall ye say unto them, The gods that have not made the heavens and the earth, even they shall perish from the earth, and from under these heavens.

12. He hath made the earth by his power, he hath established the world by his wisdom, and hath stretched out the heavens by his discretion.

13. When he uttereth his voice, there is a multitude of waters in the heavens, and he causeth the vapours to ascend from the ends of the earth; he maketh lightnings with rain, and bringeth forth the wind out of his treasures.

14. Every man is brutish in his knowledge: every founder is confounded by the graven image: for his molten image is falsehood, and there is no breath in them.

15. They are vanity, and the work of errors: in the time of their visitation they shall perish.

16. The portion of Jacob is not like them: for he is the former of all things; and Israel is the rod of his inheritance: The Lord of hosts is his name.

LESSON OUTLINE

I. IDOLATROUS RELIGIONS
   A. Created Gods
   B. Mute Gods
   C. Immobile Gods
   D. Impotent Gods
II. THE MAJESTY OF GOD
   A. God Is Great
   B. Idols Are Man-Made
   C. The Lord Is the True God
III. CREATOR OF ALL THINGS
   A. The Destruction of Idols
   B. The Creator God
   C. The End of Idol-Makers
   D. The Fate of God's People

LESSON EXPOSITION

INTRODUCTION

When God called Jeremiah to pronounce His judgments against Judah, the idolatry of the people of Judah was one of the primary catalysts. God told Jeremiah that He would utter His judgments against those "who have forsaken me, and have burned incense unto other gods, and worshipped the works of their own hands" (Jeremiah 1:16). Though the classic concept of idolatry is uncommon today in contemporary societies, it is very much a part of native religious activities in many developing countries.

Another version of idolatry, however, is a common practice in every society. The idols are as many and as varied as the individual interests and habits of the masses. In fact, anything can become an idol to the person who becomes devoted to it. Consider the fascination and devotion that some people have with sports such as football or baseball. Consider also how many people are so attracted to specific types of music and particular entertainers. Money and the pursuit of money is a common form of idolatry throughout the world. Anything that holds the devoted person's affection and prompts a worship-like action has become his or her idol.

Idolatry is a sin no matter what form it takes. Whether it is materialism, fanaticism or greed, anything a person places more affection on than God becomes god to them and they become idolaters. *yes Lord*

I. IDOLATROUS RELIGIONS
   (Jeremiah 10:1-5)

The future of Israel and especially that of Judah was going to be one of intermingling with foreign nations. Through the conquering by Babylon many would be taken away into captivity and exposed to the idolatrous practices of their conquerors. Those left behind would be exposed to the idolatry of the peoples that would be transplanted in Judah from foreign lands. Eventually, the remnant of Judah would travel to Egypt, taking Jeremiah against his will. There they would be exposed to the idolatry of Egypt.

With such exposure to various forms of idolatry, along with the idolatry that had already crept into Judah's population, God's warning was adamant. The people must not only remain free of idols ("Learn not the way of the heathen"), they must also keep themselves aloof from their superstitions—"and be not dismayed at the signs of heaven; for the heathen are dismayed at them" (v. 2).

It was God's intention that even in captivity or under foreign rule, the people who had been chosen by the living God not demean themselves by worshiping idols or observing vain superstitions. God's people, even in the harshest of situations, were still His chosen nation and should conduct themselves as such.

A. Created Gods (vv. 1-4)

   1. Hear ye the word which the

Lord speaketh unto you, O house of Israel:

2. Thus saith the Lord, Learn not the way of the heathen, and be not dismayed at the signs of heaven; for the heathen are dismayed at them.

3. For the customs of the people are vain: for one cutteth a tree out of the forest, the work of the hands of the workman, with the axe.

4. They deck it with silver and with gold; they fasten it with nails and with hammers, that it move not.

To emphasize the foolishness of idol worship, Jeremiah describes the common and quite ordinary process of creating an idol. There are no magical spells, no miraculous events, not even a bolt of lightning or clap of thunder. It is a simple task of putting an ax to a tree, and then hewing some type of image out of the tree trunk.

Next, the most absurd part of idol building takes place. This chunk of glorified kindling is bedecked with gold and silver. A common log cut by a woodman in the forest is dragged out of the woods, carved into an image, and then, in the height of foolishness, is made a thing of value by adorning it with gold and silver. Since the Hebrew society was strictly forbidden to create sculpted images, there was no artistic value to be applied to the image itself. The only value it would have was the gold and silver that adorned it.

When the idol was adequately decorated, it was taken to the place where it would stand before its worshipers and fastened to its foundation by hammer and nails. This action was necessary lest the idol should fall on its face or rock with the gusting of the wind.

This brief but clear explanation of the fashioning and erecting of an idol illustrated for the people of Judah the utter foolishness of idolatry. The very idea that a chunk of wood could become a god to be feared and worshiped was ridiculous. Yet this form of religion was not only common in the day of Jeremiah, it was prominent. Many in Judah had already succumbed to the enticements of idolatry despite its foolishness.

in to day TO,

B. Mute Gods (v. 5a)

5a. They are upright as the palm tree, but speak not.

When all of the carving, decorating and erecting were completed, the finished product—the god of fools—stood erect "as the palm tree," but as silent as any other block of wood. It would seem reasonable to assume that a god—any god—would possess the ability to communicate.

Even the birds of the air, the animals of the field, and the most primitive people are able to communicate at a basic level. The birds and animals communicate territorial boundaries, sound alarms, and demonstrate various sentiments with simple sounds understood by creatures of their own kind. The most isolated and undeveloped tribes of the world have ample communication skills. The ability to verbally communicate to others is routinely developed in early childhood so that small children are capable of understanding and being understood.

The idol, however, stands like a cigar-store statue with neither the ability to understand nor respond to any type of communication. Speech is the simplest and most basic facet of civilization, yet those civilizations exalted and deified things that were unable to utter the first syllable.

C. Immobile Gods (v. 5b)

5b. They must needs be borne, because they cannot go.

The ark of the covenant was for Israel the closest thing they had to an idol. The similarities between the ark and idols were that both sat in sacred places and both relied upon people for transportation. The differences between them, however, were profound.

The ark was merely a symbol of God's presence and mercy to Israel. Its contents—the tablets of stone, the rod of Aaron and the bowl of manna—were not items to be worshiped but reminders of the great miracles God had performed in redeeming Israel from captivity in Egypt. The cover for the ark was the mercy seat, which represented God's ever-present grace and mercy available to the children of Israel.

When being transported from one location to another, it was required by God that the ark be carried upon the shoulders of the descendants of the Kohathites from the tribe of Levi (see Numbers 3:30, 31). This too was bathed in symbolism, indicating that wherever the presence of the true and living God journeyed, it would do so on the shoulders of sanctified children of God.   hol Y

Idols, however, were not symbols of the presence of a deity; they *were* the deity. Whereas the presence of Jehovah filled the universe, idols filled only the space where they stood. Whereas the symbolism of the ark and its contents brought to mind for Israel the great works of God on their behalf, the idols held no symbolism. The power of Jehovah could be traced back to Creation. The idol could be traced back to a stump in the forest from whence it was carried by men. Just as Jeremiah said, "They must be carried because they cannot walk" (10:5b, *NIV*).

D. Impotent Gods (v. 5c)

5c. Be not afraid of them; for they cannot do evil, neither also is it in them to do good.

To Judah, God said, "Do not fear them; they can do no harm," and to the idolaters He would say, "nor can they do any good" (*NIV*).

For a god to be feared by its enemies, it must be able to inflict harm upon them. For a god to be worthy of worship, it must be able to provide some need. One wonders how the idolatrous nations maintained any kind of faith in their gods simply because of their impotence against enemies and toward worshipers. How futile it must have been to pray day after day before an idol for a specific need, only to see the idol—immobile and mute—stare into space without regard for one's prayers. It must have been this futility that eventually led to human sacrifice, trying to get the attention of a lifeless god. hE1p

From God's vantage point, it must have stirred His anger greatly when He observed His creation carving, adorning and kneeling before lifeless gods. Even His chosen people had given themselves to such vanity. But as always, God would have the last word: "I am the Lord: that is my name: and my glory will I not give to another, neither my praise to graven images" (Isaiah 42:8).

II. THE MAJESTY OF GOD
(Jeremiah 10:6-10)

Having exposed the foolishness of idolatry, Jeremiah focuses his attention on the greatness and glory of God. There are some comparisons that simply cannot be made. Simple things such as apples and oranges are easily set in juxtaposition to each other and comparisons to size, shape, color and aroma can be observed. However, attempt a comparison of an apple and the planet Earth. While one may be easily observed, the other is of such a vast size that we can hardly observe even a small community.

This is a fraction of the juxtaposition Jeremiah faced when he set out to compare idols with the one true God, Jehovah.

A. God Is Great (vv. 6, 7)

6. Forasmuch as there is none like unto thee, O Lord; thou art great, and thy name is great in might.

7. Who would not fear thee, O King of nations? for to thee doth it

appertain: forasmuch as among all the wise men of the nations, and in all their kingdoms, there is none like unto thee.

Having eloquently defined the origins and weaknesses of idolatry, Jeremiah turns to the topic of Jehovah, the true and living God. However, he is without words to express the greatness of Jehovah. He is at a loss to speak of His origins. He can find no words powerful enough to explain God's authority and might. To describe God's appearance exceeds his imagination. So, Jeremiah is left with a simple statement uttered in complete awe of God: "No one is like you, O Lord; you are great, and your name is mighty in power" (v. 6, *NIV*). Idols are easily explained and described, but Jehovah is beyond description and defies explanation.

"Who would not fear thee?" asks Jeremiah. Then he proclaims Jehovah as the "King of nations," indicating that even though a nation might worship an idol, it is still the property of and answerable to Jehovah. All nations should fear God because among all of the wise people of the earth and all of the great people of the nations, there is no one who begins to compare with the living God. All comparisons fail and all attempts at explanation are met with exasperation. All that can be uttered in the presence of Jehovah is, "God is great."

B. Idols Are Man-Made (vv. 8, 9)

(Jeremiah 10:8, 9 is not included in the printed text.)

Again, in comparison to the awesomeness of God, Jeremiah defames the foolishness of idolatry. The word translated "stock" in the King James Version refers to the wooden trunk of the tree carved into the form of a creature. The *New King James Version* says, "But they are altogether dull-hearted and foolish; a wooden idol is a worthless doctrine" (v. 8). The "dull-hearted and foolish" are those who make and serve the idol as though it

were a living and powerful deity. Further, the whole idea of idol worship is a "doctrine of vanities," or a "worthless doctrine."

The worthless pieces of wood that became idols were by no means unattractive or haphazardly built icons; they were crafted carefully and adorned with the finest of materials. Jeremiah describes the typical idol as being coated with "hammered silver . . . brought from Tarshish and gold from Uphaz" (v. 9, *NIV*). After the work of the goldsmith was done, tailors crafted garments of blue and purple to further adorn the image.

Jeremiah's point is that the idols of heathen nations are examples of the best work of their most skilled craftsmen. Crafted to perfection in the smallest detail, adorned with the most precious and expertly created appointments, these idols were nonetheless vain and worthless when contrasted to Jehovah.

C. The Lord Is the True God (v. 10)

10. But the Lord is the true God, he is the living God, and an everlasting king: at his wrath the earth shall tremble, and the nations shall not be able to abide his indignation.

The clear distinction between idols and Jehovah is that Jehovah is first of all true. To be truly God, you must owe no one any credit for your existence. Idols are derived from natural elements fashioned by human hands. In this regard, humanity becomes creator of god. But Jehovah is totally underived. He is from everlasting to everlasting, without beginning and without end.

Further, Jehovah—as opposed to idols—is alive. In the creation of an idol, the wooden image moves from life to death. The tree was probably alive at the beginning of the process, but after being felled and hewn into an image, life left the wood. Idolatry is always a moving from life to death while serving God is always moving from death to life.

III. CREATOR OF ALL THINGS
  (Jeremiah 10:11-16)

In the Day of Judgment, all idolaters will meet their fate with as useless a defense as their god was. In complete subjugation and honor, the various elements and trees used to form images for worship will themselves be given in worship of Jehovah. Just as Dagon, the god of the Philistines, fell on its face before the ark of God (1 Samuel 5:1-4), so shall every idol and idolater bow before Jehovah one day.

A. The Destruction of Idols (v. 11)

11. Thus shall ye say unto them, The gods that have not made the heavens and the earth, even they shall perish from the earth, and from under these heavens.

The Lord God brings into one classification all of the false gods and idols of the earth. Opposite them is the only Creator God—the true and living God. The detailed account of Creation in the Book of Genesis leaves no room for argument or debate—"In the beginning God created the heaven and the earth" (1:1). Jeremiah's message to the idolaters was simple: Any god that did not create the heavens and the earth will perish.

As an eraser can wipe a marker board clean, idols (and, by implication, idolaters) will "perish from the earth, and from under these heavens" (Jeremiah 10:11). The intent of God in calling attention to His judgment based on the creation of heaven and earth was to prepare the way so He might again declare His mighty creative work.

B. The Creator God (vv. 12, 13)

12. He hath made the earth by his power, he hath established the world by his wisdom, and hath stretched out the heavens by his discretion.
13. When he uttereth his voice, there is a multitude of waters in the heavens, and he causeth the vapours to ascend from the ends of the earth; he maketh lightnings with rain, and bringeth forth the wind out of his treasures.

Creation is the foundation of the mighty works of God. God lays claim to the role of Creator and consistently reaffirms that role throughout the Bible. It is the single most powerful demonstration of His glory and might seen both through nature and through the Bible. Only Jehovah is powerful enough to have set the stars in the heavens and hung the sun in its place.

God's work in nature was not completed at Creation, however. It is His continual activity and care for the universe that keeps all things functioning properly. God's constant attention holds His creation in perfect symmetry. Paul spoke of this in Colossians 1:17: "And he is before all things, and by him all things consist." Paul also stated, "For of him, and through him, and to him, are all things: to whom be glory for ever. Amen" (Romans 11:36).

Jeremiah saw God in the thunder, lightning and rains as they fell upon the earth. What idol could possibly bring such powerful demonstrations to pass? The Lord God is beyond comparison.

C. The End of Idol-Makers (vv. 14, 15)

14. Every man is brutish in his knowledge: every founder is confounded by the graven image: for his molten image is falsehood, and there is no breath in them.
15. They are vanity, and the work of errors: in the time of their visitation they shall perish.

The making of idols is a senseless and futile activity. It is particularly a folly to the craftsman who creates the idol. "Every goldsmith is shamed by his idols. His images are a fraud; they have no breath in them" (v. 14, NIV).

At the end of all the carving of the woodsman, at the end of the work of the silversmith and goldsmith, at the end of the work of the tailor and other skillful craftsmen, there emerges a worthless and vain icon that is an embarrassment to all who took part in its construction. It does not matter how beautiful it is to the eye, nor how valuable the materials were that went into its making; when the image is given a place of worship and is saluted as god, it becomes the most useless creation in all of the earth. The workmen have labored in vain and the skills of the craftsmen have been wasted.

When the time of judgment comes, the craftsmen will not be judged on the artistry and skill of their work; they will be judged as idolaters who have betrayed the one true God to serve the works of their own hands.

D. The Fate of God's People (v. 16)

16. The portion of Jacob is not like them: for he is the former of all things; and Israel is the rod of his inheritance: The Lord of hosts is his name.

Those who follow the true and living God will never be ashamed. This is not the case of the worshiper creating his god, but of the God creating His worshiper. God is the "Maker of all things" and Israel is "the tribe of his inheritance" (NIV). Just as God chose to create all things, He also chose to make Israel His people and the church His people through Christ.

Idols are still very much a part of our world. When people value the work of their own hands more than they value their relationship with God, they have developed a form of idolatry. When people value a particular activity or pastime enough to focus their life's affection, attention and energies upon it, they have developed a form of idolatry.

We should always remind ourselves that all forms of idolatry will be condemned and every idolater will be judged. The Bible says, "Set your affection on things above, not on things on the earth. For ye are dead,

and your life is hid with Christ in God" (Colossians 3:2, 3).

GOLDEN TEXT HOMILY

"FORASMUCH AS THERE IS NONE LIKE UNTO THEE, O LORD; THOU ART GREAT, AND THY NAME IS GREAT IN MIGHT" (Jeremiah 10:6).

A buffet lunch or dinner is a marvelous example of freedom in contemporary dining pleasure. In most of the world, variety or choices regarding the items of culinary delight simply do not exist. Many people can remember the time when they simply ate what was put before them. This is not a picture of what God revealed through His prophet. God is not saying, "Take Me because I am all you have to choose." God is saying, "I reveal Myself to be the best." In a world that offers buffets of religious idols, God calls for true relationship with His people of faith.

Idolatry is misunderstood when it is limited to figures of stone, wood, gold or silver. An idol can be anything of reverence where God is defined as second best. Idolatry can involve ego, relationships, children, money, position, or anything of value. The greatest form of idolatry is to attempt to define God. Even the Bible does not define God but reveals Him to be who He is! God has chosen to reveal Himself as the great "I AM." Whatever you have need of in life, God will meet you at that point of need and provide for your needs by faith!

As the prophet of truth, Jeremiah could only proclaim the revelation given by God to meet the needs of His people: There is none to compare with the true God. Majestic and mighty, God is revealed to be the answer to their backsliding, to their unfaithfulness, and to their helplessness in the face of their adversaries! That is not a buffet; that is God providing for His true remnant! Doubt and unbelief press in on the unbelieving heart to say, "No one can help me in my time of despair." But God is there for the believer!

In the name of Christ Jesus, God has promised to respond. He is not a religious buffet, nor is He the only choice, but He is the best choice you will ever make! Trust Him.—**Eugene Wigelsworth**

SENTENCE SERMONS

GOD IS the only true and living God.
—Selected

MAN IS CERTAINLY STARK MAD; he cannot make a worm, yet he will be making gods by dozens.
—Michel de Montaigne

WHATEVER YOU LOVE more than God is your idol.
—D.L. Moody

EVANGELISM APPLICATION

BY PROCLAIMING JESUS CHRIST, CHRISTIANS LEAD SINNERS TO KNOW THE ONE TRUE GOD.

Our modern world is a mixture of various cultures and religions brought into direct contact with each other on a daily basis. The immigration policies of the United States and the poverty and oppression that people face in other countries have made America even more of a melting pot than it has been throughout history. This presents America with a grand and urgent challenge. How do we bring the knowledge of the one true and living God into the lives of those so different from ourselves?

The means may be different for each of us, but the answer will be the same for all. If you are devoted to Jesus Christ and serve Him with all your heart, your witness of Him will inevitably come through. Your words will praise Him and your actions will show the love and kindness that exemplifies His followers. Just live your life as a Christian and love will find a way to witness.

ILLUMINATING THE LESSON

What is the most lifelike portrait you have ever seen? What is the most lifelike still-life painting, sculpture, or other work of art you have ever seen? Skillful artists can make their works of art seem so real that you almost expect them to move or speak. Other artists however, never set out to create something realistic-looking; they want to create something abstract and unusual.

However, the truth is that the most abstract painting you have ever seen is as close to real life as the most realistic painting you have ever seen. Neither one can lay claim to life at all.

Lifelike does not mean alive. God is alive and wants His church to be alive as well. Idolaters settle for being lifelike, but Christians settle for nothing less than abundant life.

DAILY BIBLE READINGS

M. Dagon Bows Before God.
1 Samuel 5:1-12
T. Greatness of God.
Psalm 95:1-7
W. Worthless Idols.
Habakkuk 2:18-20
T. Wisdom of God.
Romans 11:33-36
F. God of Grace.
Ephesians 3:1-9
S. God the Judge.
Revelation 20:11 through 21:4

TRUTH SEARCH
Creatively Teaching the Word

DISCUSSION QUESTIONS

Idolatrous Religions
(Jeremiah 10:1-5)

1. Why are some people "terrified by signs in the sky" (v. 2, *NIV*)? What do they believe?

2. What "customs" are referred to in verse 3?

3. What powers do idols have, and what powers do they not have?

4. Knowing the origin of idols, why would people still fear them?

The Majesty of God
(Jeremiah 10:6-11)

1. What is "great" about the name of the Lord (v. 6)?

2. Answer the question in verse 7: "Who would not fear thee, O King of nations?"

3. How do many "wise" people prove themselves to be "dull-hearted and foolish" (vv. 7, 8, *NKJV*)?

4. Describe the contrasts made between idols and the living God (vv. 9-11).

Creator of All Things
(Jeremiah 10:12-16)

1. What resources did God use to make the world (v. 12)?

2. How does God control nature (v. 13)?

3. What idols of "falsehood" and "no breath" (v. 14) do people worship today? Why?

4. Do most people believe their idols will one day "perish" in "punishment" (v. 15, *NKJV*)?

5. List and explain the names of God given in verse 16.

DRAWING ACTIVITY

Items needed: Paper, pens or pencils, trash can

Pass out a piece of paper to each student. Ask all to draw a picture of something people put first in place of the living God. When they are finished drawing, have them show their pictures to one another.

Just as with handmade statues that are worshiped in some cultures, the life in these modern idols comes from the allegiance people give to them. The more people bow to them, the more power these things exert.

To illustrate the fact that all false gods will eventually perish under God's judgment, have students wad up their drawings and throw them away.

God Bless Joe

Messages From the Potter's House

Study Text: Jeremiah 18:1 through 19:15; 30:1-24
Objective: To acknowledge God's sovereignty and live in obedience to His Word.
Time: 607—590 B.C.
Place: Jerusalem
Golden Text: "O house of Israel, cannot I do with you as this potter? saith the Lord. Behold, as the clay is in the potter's hand, so are ye in mine hand, O house of Israel" (Jeremiah 18:6).
Central Truth: God shapes the lives of those who yield to Him.
Evangelism Emphasis: God shapes the lives of those who yield to Him.

PRINTED TEXT

Jeremiah 18:3. Then I went down to the potter's house, and, behold, he wrought a work on the wheels.

4. And the vessel that he made of clay was marred in the hand of the potter: so he made it again another vessel, as seemed good to the potter to make it.

5. Then the word of the Lord came to me, saying,

6. O house of Israel, cannot I do with you as this potter? saith the Lord. Behold, as the clay is in the potter's hand, so are ye in mine hand, O house of Israel.

15. Because my people have forgotten me, they have burned incense to vanity, and they have caused them to stumble in their ways from the ancient paths, to walk in paths, in a way not cast up;

16. To make their land desolate, and a perpetual hissing; every one that passeth thereby shall be astonished, and wag his head.

17. I will scatter them as with an east wind before the enemy; I will shew them the back, and not the face, in the day of their calamity.

19:1. Thus saith the Lord, Go and get a potter's earthen bottle, and take of the ancients of the people, and of the ancients of the priests;

10. Then shalt thou break the bottle in the sight of the men that go with thee,

11. And shalt say unto them, Thus saith the Lord of hosts; Even so will I break this people and this city, as one breaketh a potter's vessel, that cannot be made whole again: and they shall bury them in Tophet, till there be no place to bury.

30:18. Thus saith the Lord; Behold, I will bring again the captivity of Jacob's tents, and have mercy on his dwellingplaces; and the city shall be builded upon her own heap, and the palace shall remain after the manner thereof.

19. And out of them shall proceed thanksgiving and the voice of them that make merry: and I will multiply them, and they shall not be few; I will also glorify them, and they shall not be small.

21. And their nobles shall be of themselves, and their governor shall proceed from the midst of them; and I will cause him to draw near, and he shall approach unto me: for who is this that engaged his heart to approach unto me? saith the Lord.

22. And ye shall be my people, and I will be your God.

LESSON OUTLINE

I. GOD IS SOVEREIGN

  A. The Potter's Wheel

  B. God's Sovereignty

  C. God's Plea

II. GOD WILL JUDGE

  A. Judah's Folly

  B. Judah's Hardness

  C. God's Judgment

III. GOD WILL RESTORE

  A. The Land Restored

  B. Joy and Thanksgiving Restored

  C. The People Restored

LESSON EXPOSITION

INTRODUCTION

The story of Jeremiah's visit to the potter's house is an example of the vivid and poetic interaction between the prophets and God as He brought about His revelations. Often the interaction and revelation was aimed at bringing about repentance—even on the heels of the sternest of judgments. In the Book of Jonah, for instance, Jonah pronounced God's judgment against Nineveh without any indication that God would allow an opportunity for them to repent. Yet, when Nineveh did repent, God withdrew His judgment and showed them His mercy. *Love Them*

In our text, however, God first offers mercy to Judah in lieu of judgment. His desire was for Judah to repent rather than suffer His wrath. But in their hardness of heart, Judah declined God's offer of mercy and settled in to await His judgment. How foolish can any group of people be to hear a kind and compassionate offer of mercy and choose rather to suffer punishment!

This same attitude seems to be prevalent in our world today. Facing the unavoidable judgment of God, society continues to drift deeper and deeper into the morass of sinfulness and immorality that makes our day akin to the days of Sodom and Gomorrah. So intent on propagating immorality and sinfulness is our world that it rarely pauses to acknowledge God's offer of salvation. When such an acknowledgment takes place, it is mocked as the ravings of religious zealots who are stuck in the past.

God's mercy, however, continues to be compassionately proclaimed through the preached Word and the printed page. As the day of God's wrath draws nearer each day, His offer of mercy becomes more and more urgent. *mocked God*

I. GOD IS SOVEREIGN *word*
(Jeremiah 18:1-12)

The sovereignty of God, clearly stated, is His power and authority over all of creation to do as He pleases. The Lord God is *omnipotent* (all-powerful), *omniscient* (all-knowing), and *omnipresent* (everywhere present). To be sovereign over all creation requires God to be all of these things and more. The highest and most important facet of God's sovereignty is His holy love. It is this innate quality of total goodness that causes God to perform His acts of sovereignty based on mercy and grace rather than might.

As Jeremiah experienced at the potter's house, God's mercy takes precedent over judgment. He desires to re-create rather than destroy.

A. The Potter's Wheel (vv. 1-4)

(Jeremiah 18:1, 2 is not included in the printed text.)

3. Then I went down to the potter's house, and, behold, he wrought a work on the wheels.

4. And the vessel that he made of clay was marred in the hand of the potter: so he made it again another vessel, as seemed good to the potter to make it.

God had a message that He wanted to give to Jeremiah, but this particular message required a specific atmosphere for it to have the desired impact. He told Jeremiah to go to the potter's house and await the message He had for him. As Jeremiah awaited the word of the Lord, he watched the potter at work making a vessel on the wheel.

The process of working with clay, whether on a wheel or molding an image by hand, requires that the clay be put through a somewhat lengthy and aggressive process to rid it of any air bubbles that might cause it to break in the heat of the kiln. A kneading trough is made by stretching a strong string between two sides of a wooden box, which forms a work space for the kneading of the clay. Repeatedly, the clay is cut into two halves on the stretched string and is slammed together on the bottom of the wooden box and kneaded with the occasional addition of a little water. This process continues until the clay reaches the desired consistency and the potter is sure that the clay is free of any air bubbles. The clay is then taken from the kneading trough and placed in the center of the wheel where the skillful hands of the potter continually fashions the clay into the desired shape.   *Here we see*

Should the potter's vessel somehow become broken—the clay possibly folding in upon itself—the potter will return the clay to the kneading trough and perform the purging process over again before he returns the clay to the wheel.

This was the event Jeremiah witnessed at the potter's house while he waited for the word of the Lord. While the potter worked with a lump of clay on the wheel, it somehow became broken and unfit to be fashioned into the vessel the potter had intended to make. Without comment and without any sign of disappointment, the potter once again prepared the lump of clay

and returned it to the wheel where he again fashioned a vessel to his liking.

Watching a potter work with the potter's wheel is a fascinating experience. It is impressive when out of a lump of clay there emerges a beautiful piece of pottery through the touch of the potter's hands. It must have been this type of impression that Jeremiah experienced as he watched the potter refuse to give up on that single lump of clay and instead create from it a useful and whole work of art.

B. God's Sovereignty (vv. 5-10)

(Jeremiah 18:7-10 is not included in the printed text.)

5. Then the word of the Lord came to me, saying,

6. O house of Israel, cannot I do with you as this potter? saith the Lord. Behold, as the clay is in the potter's hand, so are ye in mine hand, O house of Israel.

The message God had for Jeremiah was as dramatic as the image of the potter at the wheel. There are two important statements made in verse 6—one plainly spoken and the second implied. First, there is the powerful description of Judah being in the hands of God as a lump of clay in the hands of a potter. God was emphatically saying that He could reform and rebuild Judah as a nation pleasing unto Him and return them to days of glory. Second, however, the statement implied that Judah had the ability to reject God's mercy and continue on the road to judgment. Unlike the clay, Judah could refuse the touch of the Potter's hands and remain a broken work. Strangely enough, this was the choice they made.   *fool choosing*

Choosing not to accept God's mercy, however, did not free Judah from the Potter's hands. Simply because a person refuses to accept the idea that God has sovereign authority over him does not in any way free him from answering to God on the Day of

Judgment. Indeed, millions of people who think they have become too wise to believe in God or too sophisticated to believe the Bible will one day face the reality of God's sovereignty as He sits in judgment over them.

God's message through Jeremiah was that the status quo did not have to be—that the wicked nation did not have to remain wicked and the righteous nation should not take God's blessings for granted. A nation that repents under the judgment of God will of God receive mercy. A nation that sins after receiving God's blessing "to build and to plant it" (v. 9) will prompt the retraction of God's blessing and invite God's judgment.

C. God's Plea (vv. 11, 12)

(Jeremiah 18:11, 12 is not included in the printed text.)

God's warning to Judah and Jerusalem was by no means softened or broken to them gently. He told Jeremiah to boldly tell them, "I am preparing a disaster for you and devising a plan against you." As is so often the case with God's warnings to His people, this warning was immediately followed with an invitation to repent: "Turn from your evil ways, each one of you, and reform your ways and your actions" (v. 11, *NIV*).

The reply Judah gave to God was almost unbelievable. It did not indicate that Judah doubted God's judgment, nor was there a sense of apathy toward their situation. If anything, there was a sense of acceptance of any punishment God intended to pronounce upon them. "And they said, There is no hope: but we will walk after our own devices, and we will every one do the imagination of his evil heart" (v. 12).

Judah's response started with an admission that their way of life—their typical routine from day to day—offered no hope of stirring God's compassion and mercy. Yet, repentance

and a change of lifestyle were out of the question. While admitting that their plans and imaginations were evil, Judah resolved to await God's wrath while living in sinfulness. There was no railing against God in anger, no evidence of fear or dread, not even a denial of sinful acts warranting such judgment. They simply decided to enjoy their sinful lives as long as they could and accept God's judgment when it arrived.

They Choice To wait

II. GOD WILL JUDGE
    (Jeremiah 18:13-17; 19:1-11)

As surely as the sun will come up in the morning and as surely as the rain will eventually fall from heaven, a day is coming in which God will judge all things. The psalmist said, "For he cometh to judge the earth: he shall judge the world with righteousness, and the people with his truth" (96:13). In addition to this ultimate judgment of God, the Bible clearly states that He sits in constant judgment on the nations of the earth (see Jeremiah 18:7-10).

We have little difficulty believing the judgments of God that took place in the Old Testament because history verifies how God punished the nations that withstood Him. Even Israel and Judah—the chosen people of God—suffered His wrath because of their disobedience and idolatry. Why then do we have difficulty believing God still sits in judgment on nations today? More exactly, why do we have difficulty believing God will withdraw His blessings on our country if it persists in waywardness and wickedness? *NOT ME Lord?*

A. Judah's Folly (18:13-17)

(Jeremiah 18:13, 14 is not included in the printed text.)

15. Because my people have forgotten me, they have burned incense to vanity, and they have caused them to stumble in their

ways from the ancient paths, to walk in paths, in a way not cast up;

16. To make their land desolate, and a perpetual hissing; every one that passeth thereby shall be astonished, and wag his head.

17. I will scatter them as with an east wind before the enemy; I will shew them the back, and not the face, in the day of their calamity.

The northern kingdom of Israel had already fallen to its enemies, and now the southern kingdom of Judah was following the same path. Idolatry had caused them to forsake God, burning incense to idols as any other heathen nation. Jeremiah likened it to a pure virgin who becomes defiled with sinfulness. The purity or virginity of Israel and Judah had become whoredom—an astonishing impurity replacing the holy worship of Jehovah.

Their idolatry is likened to someone who leaves the pure waters resulting from the snows of Lebanon, which was the highest mountain in Judea. The melting snow continually watered the land below. In essence, Judah had abandoned a pure, fertile land watered by the purest of streams to dwell in a desert place—a foolish action that even the heathen would mock. Judah would become "an object of lasting scorn; all who pass by will be appalled and shake their heads" (v. 16, *NIV*).

In reward of such stupidity and arrogance, God determined to allow the enemies of Judah to scatter them abroad. In their day of calamity they would seek after the face of God, only to find He had turned His back on them and that they were at the mercy of their enemy.

Mercy was Not found

B. Judah's Hardness (19:1-6)

(Jeremiah 19:2-6 is not included in the printed text.)

1. Thus saith the Lord, Go and get a potter's earthen bottle, and take of the ancients of the people, and of the ancients of the priests.

Jeremiah's first encounter with the potter was marked by God's willingness to show mercy to Judah and allow them to be remolded into a nation once again pleasing unto God. That opportunity, however, was met by Judah's rejection and apathy.

On this occasion, God told Jeremiah to take a piece of pottery that had already passed through the kiln and gather the elders of the people and the elders of the priests of Jerusalem to the east gate (Potsherd Gate) for a message from God. The vessel Jeremiah used had been baked into the hardened shape that it would forever have. This time, the clay could not be refashioned nor watered so that it might become pliable once again. Having passed through the kiln, this piece of clay was unchangeable even by the hands of the most skillful potter. Any attempt to change its form would result in the destruction of the vessel.

This was the case with Judah's heart. The people had become so entrenched in their idolatry that they could not be separated from it. They had become bloodthirsty in offering human sacrifices to Baal. They had even burned their sons as offerings. They had filled Judah with high places and sites for idol worship. They were so corrupt that they could not be changed nor reasoned with. In every sense, they were as they had said in Jeremiah 18:12—hopeless.

C. God's Judgment (vv. 7-11)

(Jeremiah 19:7-9 is not included in the printed text.)

10. Then shalt thou break the bottle in the sight of the men that go with thee,

11. And shalt say unto them, Thus saith the Lord of hosts; Even so will I break this people and this city, as one breaketh a potter's vessel, that cannot be made whole again: and they shall bury them in Tophet, till there be no place to bury.

God's sentence upon them was that they would be conquered and slaughtered with the sword, and their flesh would become meat for the buzzards. In the process of their destruction they would be forced into cannibalism, eating the very flesh of their children. God's judgment against Jerusalem would be so astounding and complete that everyone who passed that way would "hiss" at the savagery and ruin (see vv. 7-9).

After delivering his message to the people at the eastern gate to Jerusalem, Jeremiah—as instructed by God—was to break the piece of pottery that he had taken from the potter's house. The shattering of the earthen vessel clearly illustrated the intent of God for Judah and Jerusalem. He would break them so thoroughly that they could not be "made whole again" (v. 11).

The people of Judah would be buried in the valley of Tophet until there would be no more room to bury them. Tophet was the place where Judah had willingly sacrificed innocent children to idol gods, but it would become the valley of slaughter where guilty people would be condemned by the living God.

God's judgment is certain. Though many may think He will not judge today as He did then, the Bible assures us that He will. "Be not deceived; God is not mocked: for whatsoever a man soweth, that shall he also reap" (Galatians 6:7).

III. GOD WILL RESTORE
(Jeremiah 30:18-22)

Though God's anger is intense and fearsome, His mercy is plenteous and enduring. As the psalmist has said, "The Lord is merciful and gracious, slow to anger, and plenteous in mercy. He will not always chide: neither will he keep his anger for ever" (103:8, 9).

Jeremiah was given a promise to pass on to those who would go into captivity from Jerusalem—a promise that God's anger would eventually abate and that they would be able to return home.

The various pronouncements of God's judgment against His people in Scripture (excluding the final judgments revealed in the Book of Revelation) are tempered with a promise of mercy when His people return to Him and repent. God's justice is repeatedly overshadowed by His mercy.

A. The Land Restored (v. 18)

18. Thus saith the Lord; Behold, I will bring again the captivity of Jacob's tents, and have mercy on his dwellingplaces; and the city shall be builded upon her own heap, and the palace shall remain after the manner thereof.

Even though the city of Jerusalem was in ruins, it would be rebuilt. The city where Solomon's temple once stood would be restored. How fitting that the capital city would be the first tract of land returned to the Israelites.

God would not only have mercy on the people but on the land that had been cursed for the people's sake. God would "restore the fortunes of Jacob's tents and have compassion on his dwellings" (NIV). Homes would be rebuilt upon the "heap" formed by her rubble.

The palace to be rebuilt was God's palace—the Temple. It would stand upon its rightful site.

B. Joy and Thanksgiving Restored (19a)

19a. And out of them shall proceed thanksgiving and the voice of them that make merry.

In the face of judgment that would bring much sorrow, God promised His people that He would eventually restore their joy and give them ample reason to practice thanksgiving. Out of the remnant that would return to Jerusalem, there would proceed the sound of rejoicing in gratitude for what God had done for them.

This stands in stark contrast to the

previous predictions of Jeremiah. The same city that would be forced to devour the flesh of its own children, and would see its eastern gate visited with such a slaughter that the valley before it would be filled to overflowing with graves, would in time see rejoicing and praising of God for His deliverance. "Then shall the virgin rejoice in the dance, both young men and old together: for I will turn their mourning into joy, and will comfort them, and make them rejoice from their sorrow" (31:13). *Thanks God for mercy*

C. The People Restored (19b-22)

(Jeremiah 30:20 is not included in the printed text.)

19b. And I will multiply them, and they shall not be few; I will also glorify them, and they shall not be small.

21. And their nobles shall be of themselves, and their governor shall proceed from the midst of them; and I will cause him to draw near, and he shall approach unto me: for who is this that engaged his heart to approach unto me? saith the Lord.

22. And ye shall be my people, and I will be your God.

The people of Israel, having been decimated by war and captivity, would again be blessed of God and multiply in number. The promise of God was that their number "shall not be few" and their glory "shall not be small" (v. 19). When God's blessing is upon a people, their numbers grow as well as their reputation. God grants strength to those that are His and He covers them with His glory that others will respect them. This was to be the case for the remnant that would return to Jerusalem. Anyone that might attempt to oppress this restored people of God would face divine punishment.

God further promised that He would raise up leaders from within the ranks of those He restored to Jerusalem. In essence, He was stating

that He would once again make a nation out of His people and would restore self-determination to them as a sovereign state.

The ultimate promise He made to those who would be restored to Jerusalem was a return to the promise He made to Israel upon delivering them from Egypt: "And I will walk among you, and will be your God, and ye shall be my people" (Leviticus 26:12). God assured them that not only would the returning remnant be *a* nation but that they would be *His* nation—"And ye shall be my people, and I will be your God" (Jeremiah 30:22).

Two messages were given to Jeremiah from the potter's house. One was a message of mercy and the other a message of judgment. Each message emanated from the same location, yet each message had a drastically different tone and intent. The first—if heeded—would produce harmony, purity and peace. The second—resulting from the neglect of the first—would produce an unalterable doom.

God's messages are still the same today. He stands ready to forgive and renew anyone who would come unto Him in repentance. Jesus said, "Him that cometh to me I will in no wise cast out" (John 6:37). But those who refuse this invitation will unavoidably face God's judgment.

GOLDEN TEXT HOMILY

"O HOUSE OF ISRAEL, CANNOT I DO WITH YOU AS THIS POTTER? SAITH THE LORD. BEHOLD, AS THE CLAY IS IN THE POTTER'S HAND, SO ARE YE IN MINE HAND, O HOUSE OF ISRAEL" (Jeremiah 18:6).

In the face of the marred pottery and the skill of the potter in making something else, Jeremiah heard from the Lord the meaning of this "show-and-tell" event.

There were two lessons to be

learned. The first came as a form of judgment, "Cannot I do with you as this potter?" It was the Lord's way of saying He had the power to reshape the life of His people.

It was obvious that Israel was not the quality He desired. But this lack of quality was not due to the Lord; rather it was due to Israel's refusal to obey and her willingness to be controlled by sin. Thus, the Lord spoke this word of judgment upon His people.

The second lesson was the message of grace—"So are ye in mine hand." While it is a fearful thing to fall into the hands of an angry God, it is more fearful to fall out of God's hands.

Behind the message of judgment stands the message of grace. God disciplines because He loves. He loves because He has created us and desires to be loved in return. His discipline is not intended to destroy, but to lead to repentance and life. His will is for us to enjoy this life in His will, thus He shapes and reshapes us to make such a life possible.—**Selected**

SENTENCE SERMONS

GOD SHAPES THE LIVES of those who yield to Him.

Choosing Him.—**Selected**

BLESSED IS THE MAN who finds out which way God is moving and then gets going in the same direction.
—**Anonymous**

WE SHOULD GIVE GOD the same place in our heart that He holds in the universe.
—**Selected**

EVANGELISM APPLICATION

GOD SHAPES THE LIVES OF THOSE WHO YIELD TO HIM.

There is a children's song titled "He's Still Working on Me," and its message is that God constantly molds and fashions our lives from day to day. God's hands have never left the clay.

Every day God is working with us, tenderly remolding us closer to the vessel He would have us become. Sometimes He even breaks us so we will lose our resemblance to the world and be renewed in the image He has in mind for us.

Will He ever be through with His work of molding our lives? Not until we come "unto the measure of the stature of the fulness of Christ" (Ephesians 4:13).

ILLUMINATING THE LESSON

After Richard Nixon resigned from the presidency of the United States in 1974, President Gerald Ford offered him a presidential pardon. Nixon accepted the pardon and was freed from any impending legal action. To some Americans, Nixon's acceptance of the pardon was tantamount to an admission of guilt.

The offer of forgiveness is always tentative. It must be accepted if it is to be valid. As long as the person to whom the offer is made refuses to admit to culpability or simply refuses to accept the offer, forgiveness has not been completed. Guilt must be confessed to and the offer of forgiveness must be accepted before forgiveness passes from God to people.

DAILY BIBLE READINGS

M. Chosen by God.
   Deuteronomy 4:32-40
T. Loyal Hearts.
   1 Chronicles 29:10-18
W. Things God Hates.
   Proverbs 6:16-19
T. Foolish Choice.
   Luke 12:13-23
F. Believing Removes Condemnation.
   John 3:16-21
S. God's Sovereign Choice.
   Romans 9:18-26

God You Bless me

TRUTH SEARCH
Creatively Teaching the Word

DISCUSSION QUESTIONS
God Is Sovereign
(Jeremiah 18:1-10)

1. Why didn't the Lord speak His message to Jeremiah on the spot? Why did God send him elsewhere first (vv. 1-3)?

2. In verses 4-6, what did God communicate through the illustration of the potter?

3. What power does God have over nations?

4. What promise does God make to sinful nations who repent (vv. 7, 8)?

5. What warning does God give to nations who turn away from Him (vv. 9, 10)?

God Will Judge
(Jeremiah 18:11-18; 19:7-11)

1. What message did God send through Jeremiah to Jerusalem (v. 11)?

2. How did the people respond (v. 12)?

3. What image did God use to illustrate the people's rebellion (vv. 13, 14)?

4. Why was God going to punish Jerusalem (vv. 15, 16)?

5. What would the punishment be (v. 17)?

6. How did the people respond to this message (v. 18)?

7. In 19:7-11, what judgments did Jeremiah prophesy?

God Will Restore
(Jeremiah 30:18-22)

1. Even though the Jews faced impending captivity, what long-term promise did God make regarding Jerusalem (v. 18)?

2. What sounds would be heard in the restored city (v. 19)?

3. What did God say about Jerusalem's future government (vv. 20, 21)?

4. What was the ultimate purpose of God's restoration plan (v. 22)?

BUZZ GROUPS

Divide your class into groups of three or four students each. Within the groups, have students discuss punishments they received when they were growing up, answering these questions:

• Why were you disciplined?

• How were you disciplined?

• Did the punishment accomplish its purpose?

Let the students summarize their discussions for the entire class, then compare God's acts of discipline.

When God disciplines us, His purpose is always redemptive—to bring us back into close fellowship with Him. However, people who resist God's discipline and continue headlong into rebellion are headed for divine judgment.

The New Covenant

Study Text: Jeremiah 31:31-34; Matthew 26:27, 28; 2 Corinthians 3:7-18; Hebrews 10:1-18

Objective: To examine God's establishment of the new covenant and receive its benefits.

Golden Text: "This is my blood of the new testament [covenant], which is shed for many for the remission of sins" (Matthew 26:28).

Central Truth: Christ established a new covenant that brings life, freedom, and forgiveness to those who receive Him.

Evangelism Emphasis: Christ established a new covenant that brings salvation to those who receive Him.

PRINTED TEXT

Jeremiah 31:31. Behold, the days come, saith the Lord, that I will make a new covenant with the house of Israel, and with the house of Judah:

32. Not according to the covenant that I made with their fathers in the day that I took them by the hand to bring them out of the land of Egypt; which my covenant they brake, although I was an husband unto them, saith the Lord.

Hebrews 10:1. For the law having a shadow of good things to come, and not the very image of the things, can never with those sacrifices which they offered year by year continually make the comers thereunto perfect.

2. For then would they not have ceased to be offered? because that the worshippers once purged should have had no more conscience of sins.

3. But in those sacrifices there is a remembrance again made of sins every year.

4. For it is not possible that the blood of bulls and of goats should take away sins.

Jeremiah 31:33. But this shall be the covenant that I will make with the house of Israel; After those days, saith the Lord, I will put my law in their inward parts, and write it in their hearts; and will be their God, and they shall be my people.

34. And they shall teach no more every man his neighbour, and every man his brother, saying, Know the Lord: for they shall all know me, from the least of them unto the greatest of them, saith the Lord: for I will forgive their iniquity, and I will remember their sin no more.

Hebrews 10:12. But this man, after he had offered one sacrifice for sins for ever, sat down on the right hand of God;

13. From henceforth expecting till his enemies be made his footstool.

14. For by one offering he hath perfected for ever them that are sanctified.

Matthew 26:28. For this is my blood of the new testament, which is shed for many for the remission of sins.

2 Corinthians 3:7. But if the ministration of death, written and engraven in stones, was glorious, so that the children of Israel could not stedfastly behold the face of Moses for the glory of his countenance; which glory was to be done away:

8. How shall not the ministration of the spirit be rather glorious?

9. For if the ministration of condemnation be glory, much more doth the ministration of righteousness exceed in glory.

LESSON OUTLINE

I. NEED FOR A NEW COVENANT
   A. Broken Covenant
   B. Only a Shadow
   C. Inadequate Covenant
II. PROMISE OF THE NEW COVENANT
   A. An Intimate Covenant
   B. A Perfect Sacrifice
   C. A Complete Sacrifice
III. FULFILLMENT OF THE NEW COVENANT
   A. Blood of the New Covenant
   B. Veil of the Old Covenant
   C. Veil Lifted in Christ

LESSON EXPOSITION

INTRODUCTION

Throughout history God has dealt with humanity through covenants. A covenant relationship is a logical and functional way for God to develop and maintain His interaction with people. A covenant requires something specific from people and a reciprocal commitment from God.

In Eden, the covenant was as simple as two people observing a single rule in return for which God provided the blessings and benefit of the rest of the garden. In the Abrahamic covenant, God promised Abraham that he would be the father of nations; in return, Abraham devoted himself to worshiping Jehovah, the true and living God. The Mosaic covenant was an expansion of the Abrahamic covenant in that God renewed His promise to the descendants of Abraham and gave them a clear set of laws to guide them into fulfilling their end of the covenant.

In each of these covenants the sanctions and promises were material even though spiritual issues were involved. Therefore, each of these covenants was by its nature temporary. The new covenant Jeremiah foresaw was a spiritual covenant—written upon the hearts of the covenanted people. This new covenant then would be drastically different from any previous covenant God had made with humanity.

I. NEED FOR A NEW COVENANT
   (Jeremiah 31:31, 32; Hebrews 10:1-4)

If the previous covenants dealt with people on a material and physical level, the resulting relationships with God were inadequate at best. The Bible tells us, "God is a Spirit: and they that worship him must worship him in spirit and in truth" (John 4:24).

The blood of bulls and goats, the burning of incense, and all other material forms of worship were for people's benefit, illustrating humanity's fallen condition and the righteous requirements of God's justice. For God to lift people to the next level of relationship with Himself and prepare them for the indwelling of the Holy Spirit, a new covenant based on personal relationships and a spiritual new birth had to be established.

A. Broken Covenant
   (Jeremiah 31:31, 32)

31. Behold, the days come, saith the Lord, that I will make a new covenant with the house of Israel, and with the house of Judah:

32. Not according to the covenant that I made with their fathers in the day that I took them by the hand to bring them out of the land of Egypt; which my covenant they brake, although I was an husband unto them, saith the Lord.

God's covenant with Israel had its origins in the covenant He made with Abram in Genesis 15. That covenant was renewed in Isaac and Jacob with the same promises and the same symbol—circumcision.

The covenant between God and Israel was established when God gave Moses the tenets of the covenant on Mount Sinai (Exodus 20:1—31:18). Israel, and ultimately Judah, often violated that covenant and repeatedly faced God's wrath. The repetitive breaking of the covenant by Israel frustrated God because He had been faithful—"a husband"—to them.

The violations of the covenant actually began before Israel left the wilderness and began to inhabit the Promised Land. In fact, the first rebellion took place before God had completed the work of giving the Law to Moses. From the golden calf that Aaron made (Exodus 32:1-35), to the rebellions of Miriam and Aaron (Numbers 12) and Korah, Dathan and Abiram (16:1-35), to Balak's success in turning Israel from the Lord (25:1-18), the road from Sinai to the Promised Land was fraught with covenant rebellions. Obviously, the laws written in stone on Sinai had not reached the hearts of the general population of Israel. Therein lay the first inadequacy of the old covenant.

B. Only a Shadow (Hebrews 10:1, 2)

1. For the law having a shadow of good things to come, and not the very image of the things, can never with those sacrifices which they offered year by year continually make the comers thereunto perfect.

2. For then would they not have ceased to be offered? because that the worshippers once purged should have had no more conscience of sins.

A second inadequacy of the old covenant was in its authority to pardon sin. The writer describes the old covenant as a "shadow" and "not the very image" of the sacrifice for sin. This language focuses on the difference between the animal sacrifices of the old covenant and the sacrifice of Jesus in the new covenant.

The sin offering of the old covenant revealed the severity of God's anger against sin by demanding the brutal death of a spotless and choice animal from the flock. The greatest inadequacy of this offering was in its limited effectiveness and scope. The sacrifice of a single animal might pardon the sins of a man's household for a season, but the offering would have to be repeated on a regular basis to assure God's mercy. Because of this limited effectiveness, the consciousness of sin and subsequent judgment would return, requiring further sacrifice.

The consistent repetition of such sacrifices served to act as a shadow of the perfect sacrifice that would come in the person of Jesus. In the regular shedding of blood and in the specific requirements that constituted an acceptable sacrifice, a pattern was set that would find fulfillment only in Christ.

C. Inadequate Covenant (vv. 3, 4)

3. But in those sacrifices there is a remembrance again made of sins every year.

4. For it is not possible that the blood of bulls and of goats should take away sins.

With the sacrificial sin offering each year, a constant reminder was given to each individual that he or she was still captive to sin and that regular and repetitive measures had to be taken to assure forgiveness. Thus, the old covenant provided for temporary atonement through animal sacrifice while reminding the worshiper of the consequences of sin. In obedience of the law of Moses, the blood of an animal was shed and God accepted that sacrifice in atonement for the household for which it was offered. God accepted the sacrifice in lieu of the perfect sacrifice that would be offered in Jesus.

The blood of animals was offered only as a testament of that covenant to come in Jesus Christ. There was absolutely nothing of intrinsic value in the blood of animals other than the fact that the Mosaic covenant provided for such sacrifices for sin. God honored His commitment to Israel by pardoning the sins of those who brought their sin offering in sincerity to take part in the covenant God had made with them.

There came a time, however, when such sacrifices were taken for granted and were seen as a license to commit evil. In His anger, God said, "To what purpose is the multitude of your sacrifices unto me? saith the Lord: I am full of the burnt-offerings of rams, and the fat of fed beasts; and I delight not in the blood of bullocks, or of lambs, or of he goats" (Isaiah 1:11). The obvious reason for this rejection of animal sacrifice was that God intended such sacrifices to be performed in a heartfelt remorse for sin. Those who casually or flippantly made animal sacrifice as a matter of routine had angered God. Here was His counsel to His people:

"Wash yourselves, make yourselves clean; put away the evil of your doings from before My eyes. Cease to do evil, learn to do good; seek justice, rebuke the oppressor; defend the fatherless, plead for the widow. Come now, and let us reason together," says the Lord, "Though your sins are like scarlet, they shall be as white as snow; though they are red like crimson, they shall be as wool" (vv. 16-18, NKJV).

The provisions of animal sacrifice in the old covenant, then, could be nullified by insincerity and false worship. Though the offerings foretold of a more perfect sacrifice that was to come and were accepted by God when offered in submission, their only true value lay in the surrendered heart(s) of the person(s) making the sacrifice. The blood of animals could not atone for people's sins. Such sacrifices served only to prove the hearts of the worshipers and point ahead to a more perfect sacrifice.

II. PROMISE OF THE NEW COVENANT (Jeremiah 31:33, 34; Hebrews 10:11-18)

The old covenant promised certain advantages that were to be fulfilled in the new covenant. Though the old covenant was far superior to the idolatrous religions of surrounding nations, it was still only an incomplete shadow of the true faith God intended to bring into the world.

A. An Intimate Covenant (Jeremiah 31:33, 34)

33. But this shall be the covenant that I will make with the house of Israel; After those days, saith the Lord, I will put my law in their inward parts, and write it in their hearts; and will be their God, and they shall be my people.

34. And they shall teach no more every man his neighbour, and every man his brother, saying, Know the Lord: for they shall all know me, from the least of them unto the greatest of them, saith the Lord: for I will forgive their iniquity, and I will remember their sin no more.

As indicated earlier, the sin offerings of the old covenant could be nullified if the heart of the worshiper was not deeply involved in the blood sacrifice as it was offered. The weakest point of the old covenant's sin offering was that it was performed in the physical realm and subject to all the distractions of the flesh. The text defining the sacrifice was written on scrolls of animal skin or papyrus, the actions of the priest were performed in a perfunctory manner, and the offering could be completed without ever truly acknowledging the righteousness or demands of the God to whom the sacrifice was made.

By design, the new covenant would not be fraught with all of the encumbrances of the flesh. The law would be written upon the heart, the means of observing the demands of the law would be conscripted through the soul, and the sacrifice that enabled the covenant would be offered once for all through the Son of God.

When the new covenant arrived, the intervention of both priest and prophet would not be necessary, for "they shall all know me, from the least of them unto the greatest" (v. 34).

B. A Perfect Sacrifice
(Hebrews 10:11-14)

(Hebrews 10:11 is not included in the printed text.)

12. But this man, after he had offered one sacrifice for sins for ever, sat down on the right hand of God;

13. From henceforth expecting till his enemies be made his footstool.

14. For by one offering he hath perfected for ever them that are sanctified.

The priest of the old covenant served as an intermediary between people and God in the offering up of the sacrifice for sin. Filling such an important role, the priest could exercise authority over the person(s) offering up the sin offering.

He could decide if the sin offering was an acceptable animal or refuse to deem it appropriate. He could perform the rite of sacrificing the sin offering or he could refuse. There was always a man standing between an Israelite and his God.

A similar scenario existed in the Middle Ages. The priests gained dominant authority over all of their constituents by mandating that salvation was obtained only through the sacraments and that only the priests could administer the sacraments. Thus, the local priest could supposedly determine who was saved and who was not by either administering or refusing to administer the sacraments.

In Christ, however, we not only have the perfect sacrifice, we also have the perfect priest. Jesus offered Himself up as the perfect sin offering,

then ascended into heaven to sit at the right hand of the Father to intercede for us as the perfect High Priest. Sitting at the right hand of the Father is the Lamb who was offered in atonement for the sins of all people. That Lamb, who is also the only High Priest, now grants salvation to anyone who will accept His atoning sacrifice as having been offered in his or her stead.

Verse 14 can be translated, "By one sacrifice he has made perfect forever those who are being made holy" (*NIV*). The blood of Christ has made believers holy, is making them holy, and will keep them holy.

C. A Complete Sacrifice (vv. 15-18)

(Hebrews 10:15-18 is not included in the printed text.)

The function of the Holy Spirit in administering the new covenant is one of internal and eternal instruction. He has put the laws of the new covenant into our hearts and upon our minds (v. 16). The gift of the Holy Spirit is not only an empowerment for service to the kingdom of God; it is an empowerment to be. By the presence of the Holy Spirit within us, Spirit-filled believers are walking repositories of the laws of God written upon our hearts and minds. We walk not after the letter of the law but in the Spirit of the law, giving praise to Jesus our Lord.

As recipients of the grace of God through Jesus, our sins are atoned for once and for all through His blood. Never again will a sacrifice have to be made—human or animal—for the blood of Jesus made it possible for God to permanently forget our sins. "And their sins and iniquities will I remember no more" (v. 17).

With such a complete atonement and such a perfect sacrifice, there can be nothing left to be atoned for and no further sacrifice necessary. "Now where remission of these is, there is no more offering for sin" (v. 18). The "remission" that the writer of Hebrews mentions here is the sin that has been surrendered to Christ in repentance. Jesus forgives such sin perfectly. A perfect atonement forgives sin perfectly, rendering the repentant soul as spotless and pure as though he or she had never sinned. What more could be desired from such a wonderful covenant?

III. FULFILLMENT OF THE NEW COVENANT (Matthew 26:27, 28; 2 Corinthians 3:7-18)

The narratives of the New Testament provide us with the story of how the new covenant came into being through the fulfillment of the prophecies in and shadows of the old covenant. We can follow the story of Jesus' suffering and sacrifice in each of the Gospels and observe how He guaranteed all of the promises of the new covenant through the shedding of His own blood.

A. Blood of the New Covenant (Matthew 26:27, 28)

(Matthew 26:27 is not included in the printed text.)

28. For this is my blood of the new testament, which is shed for many for the remission of sins.

Jesus intended for the final Passover He spent with His disciples to be a watershed event for them and for the church that would spring from their leadership. Jesus even gave special meaning to the task of selecting a place to celebrate the Passover by foretelling the means His disciples would find the room:

And he said unto them, Behold, when ye are entered into the city, there shall a man meet you, bearing a pitcher of water; follow him into the house where he entereth in. And ye shall say unto the goodman of the house, The Master saith unto thee, Where is the guestchamber, where I shall eat the passover with

my disciples? And he shall shew you a large upper room furnished: there make ready. And they went, and found as he had said unto them: and they made ready the passover (Luke 22:10-13).

As the Lord and His disciples gathered in the room that had been prepared for them, the air must have been filled with expectancy because of the recent revelations Jesus had made concerning His arrest and death. Matthew 16:21 says, "From that time forth began Jesus to shew unto his disciples, how that he must go unto Jerusalem, and suffer many things of the elders and chief priests and scribes, and be killed, and be raised again the third day." Jesus had tried to prepare them for the hour that was soon to come, and they possibly wondered if the fulfillment of His words was at hand. His actions during the feast would prove to confirm their fears.

Jesus took bread, blessed it and gave it to His disciples with the instructions, "Take, eat; this is my body" (26:26). Then He took a cup and gave it to them, saying, "Drink ye all of it; for this is my blood of the new testament [covenant], which is shed for many for the remission of sins" (vv. 27, 28). As the blood of lambs and bulls had been the blood of the old covenant, His blood would now become the blood of the new covenant. There would be no more animal sacrifices, for their blood was never sufficient to remove sins. The blood of God's Son would now once and for all eradicate the sins of those who would believe on Him.

B. Veil of the Old Covenant (2 Corinthians 3:7-16)

(2 Corinthians 3:10-16 is not included in the printed text.)

7. But if the ministration of death, written and engraven in stones, was glorious, so that the

**children of Israel could not sted-
fastly behold the face of Moses for
the glory of his countenance; which
glory was to be done away:**

**8. How shall not the ministration
of the spirit be rather glorious?**

**9. For if the ministration of con-
demnation be glory, much more
doth the ministration of righteousness exceed in glory.**

After receiving the laws of the old
covenant that required the death of
animal sacrifices, Moses came down
from Sinai with a glorious shining
countenance. The glory upon his face,
having been in the presence of God,
was a source of fear for the children of
Israel. To alleviate their fears, a veil
was placed over Moses' face to conceal
the glory of God that was upon him
(see Exodus 34:29-35).

Paul said the glory that shown on
Moses' face was the product of a
covenant based upon death (2
Corinthians 3:7-16). He posed the
question that if a covenant based
upon death brought glory, "how will
the ministry of the Spirit not be more
glorious? For . . . the ministry of righteousness exceeds much more in
glory" (vv. 7-9, *NKJV*).

The veil placed on Moses' face is
symbolic of the veil that still conceals
the glory of God from those who refuse to accept Christ. Paul said when
the Law given through Moses was
read in the hearing of the Israelites, a
spiritual veil rested upon them, so
they could not see that it foretold of a
new covenant sealed by the blood of
Jesus. Only in accepting the blood of
Jesus as atonement for sins could
they have the veil removed and see
clearly the new covenant.

C. Veil Lifted in Christ (vv. 17, 18)

(2 Corinthians 3:17, 18 is not included in the printed text.)

The grand finale of Paul's description of the new covenant focuses on
three specific glories received by every
believer in Christ.

The first glory is *liberty*. The veil has
been removed and the believer has
been set free. We can see not only the
shadows and intents of the old
covenant, but we can also see the
advantages and the glories of the new.
The blood of Jesus Christ has set us
free, and "if the Son therefore shall
make you free, ye shall be free indeed"
(John 8:36).

The second glory is *intimacy*—
"beholding . . . the glory of the Lord" (2
Corinthians 3:18). Whereas in the old
covenant there was a man—the
priest—who stood between God and
the worshiper, the new covenant
made provisions for every believer to
"come boldly unto the throne of grace"
(Hebrews 4:16).

The third glory is *transformation*—
we "are changed into the same image
from glory to glory, even as by the
Spirit of the Lord" (2 Corinthians
3:18). Through the new covenant God
not only forgives our sins, but He
transforms us into His image through
sanctification and the indwelling and
infilling of the Holy Spirit.

The new covenant has overshadowed the old, not to the point of dis-
solving the old, for the old covenant
prepared the way for the new. The
overshadowing of the old was simply
a work of completion, as in adding the
final stanza to a wonderful hymn that
was beautiful but incomplete. What
was seen in shadows in the old covenant can now be seen in the light of
Jesus Christ, and the believer is by far
the better for it.

GOLDEN TEXT HOMILY

"THIS IS MY BLOOD OF THE
NEW TESTAMENT [COVENANT],
WHICH IS SHED FOR MANY FOR
THE REMISSION OF SINS" (Matthew
26:28).

The "new testament" does not refer
to our book by that name, but rather
means the new covenant. The death
of Christ, represented by the blood,
is God's seal of the new covenant

whereby He agrees to save all who accept Jesus Christ and believe the gospel.

The first covenant with Israel was ratified with the blood of animals; but the new covenant with the whole world was ratified with the blood of Jesus Christ. This blood was shed "for many." Christ's body was broken and His blood poured out to save people from their sins.

Through observing Communion we testify that through Christ alone comes the remission of sins.— **Selected**

SENTENCE SERMONS

CHRIST ESTABLISHED A NEW COVENANT that brings life, freedom, and forgiveness to those who receive Him.

—Selected

WHEN JESUS COMES, the shadows depart.

—Inscription

THE CROSS is the sign of addition.
—George Sweeting

EVANGELISM APPLICATION

CHRIST ESTABLISHED A NEW COVENANT THAT BRINGS SALVATION TO THOSE WHO RECEIVE HIM.

The new covenant established in Jesus' blood is complete in its plan of salvation. The blood of Jesus was sufficient to cover the sins of every man, woman and child who has ever lived upon this earth. Every detail of God's pardon and atonement has been assured—every detail but one, that is.

As complete and final as the new covenant in Jesus' blood is, it is of no effect until the repentant sinner accepts it. The sinner must accept God's atoning work in Jesus or its saving power is void. Jesus said, "He that believeth and is baptized shall be saved; but he that believeth not shall be damned" (Mark 16:16).

ILLUMINATING THE LESSON

Have you ever watched a rose grow into its glory? It begins as a small green bulb on the rose bush. The gardener nurtures the plant and waters it from the roots up. He uses the best nutrients and fertilizers in hope of one day glimpsing a long-stem American beauty.

Finally the small green bulb parts and the rosebud appears. The bud itself is a thing of beauty, but it is not the most glorious stage of the flower. Patiently the gardener waits, and when the time is right he watches the bud open fully to the grand and glorious, perfectly developed rose.

Such was the case with God's development of His plan of salvation. The green bulb sprang up in Abraham, the rosebud appeared in the Mosaic covenant, but the rose did not reach fulfillment until Jesus came and shed His crimson blood on Calvary.

DAILY BIBLE READINGS

M. Judah Breaks the Covenant.
   Jeremiah 11:1-13
T. A New Heart.
   Ezekiel 36:24-28
W. A Covenant People.
   Hosea 2:14-23
T. Set Free From Sin.
   Romans 8:1-4
F. Promise of the Spirit.
   Galatians 3:1-14
S. Jesus the Mediator.
   Hebrews 12:22-29

TRUTH SEARCH
Creatively Teaching the Word

OBJECT LESSON

Items needed: Two or three products labeled "New and Improved" or "More Than Before" or something similar

Display the objects. Talk about the ways these items are supposed to be better than their former versions.

Many times an item labeled "New and Improved" isn't all that different from the original product. However, in today's lesson we will see how God took what was good—the old covenant He made with humanity—and made it into something perfect.

DISCUSSION QUESTIONS

Need for a New Covenant (Jeremiah 31:31, 32; Hebrews 10:1-4)

1. How had God carried out His part in the old covenant (Jeremiah 31:31, 32)?

2. How had the people carried out their part?

3. What had to be continually repeated under the old covenant (Hebrews 10:1)?

4. Why did sacrifices have to be offered again and again (vv. 1, 2)?

5. What could not be accomplished under the old covenant (vv. 3, 4)?

Promise of the New Covenant (Jeremiah 31:33, 34; Hebrews 10:11-18)

1. According to Jeremiah 31:33,

why did God want to make a new covenant?

2. How would the writing of this covenant be different than the old one?

3. What would the new covenant do that the old one could not (v. 34)?

4. Contrast the sacrifices made by the Old Testament priests with the sacrifice of Jesus (Hebrews 10:11, 12).

5. What did Christ's "one offering" accomplish (v. 14)?

6. Who writes God's laws in His children's hearts (vv. 15-17)?

Fulfillment of the New Covenant (Matthew 26:27, 28; 2 Corinthians 3:7-18)

1. How was the new covenant established, and what is its purpose (Matthew 26:27, 28)?

2. What makes the new covenant more glorious than the old one (2 Corinthians 3:7, 8, 10, 11)?

3. Why is the old covenant called the "ministry of death" (v. 7, *NKJV*) but the new one the "ministry of righteousness" (v. 9, *NKJV*)?

4. What "veil" has been removed through Christ's sacrifice (vv. 13-16)?

5. In what ways does the indwelling Holy Spirit bring liberty (v. 17)?

6. What transformation is God's Spirit working in believers' lives (v. 18)?

Hope in God

Study Text: Lamentations 1:1 through 5:22

Objective: To highlight the message of Lamentations and place our hope in God.

Time: Written by Jeremiah after Jerusalem's destruction in 586 B.C.

Golden Text: "This I recall to my mind, therefore have I hope. It is of the Lord's mercies that we are not consumed, because his compassions fail not" (Lamentations 3:21, 22).

Central Truth: God judges sin, but He is also compassionate and forgiving.

Evangelism Emphasis: God is faithful to save sinners who call on Him for salvation.

PRINTED TEXT

Lamentations 1:3. Judah is gone into captivity because of affliction, and because of great servitude: she dwelleth among the heathen, she findeth no rest: all her persecutors overtook her between the straits.

4. The ways of Zion do mourn, because none come to the solemn feasts: all her gates are desolate: her priests sigh, her virgins are afflicted, and she is in bitterness.

8. Jerusalem hath grievously sinned; therefore she is removed: all that honoured her despise her, because they have seen her nakedness: yea, she sigheth, and turneth backward.

9. Her filthiness is in her skirts; she remembereth not her last end; therefore she came down wonderfully: she had no comforter. O Lord, behold my affliction: for the enemy hath magnified himself.

2:11. Mine eyes do fail with tears, my bowels are troubled, my liver is poured upon the earth, for the destruction of the daughter of my people; because the children and the sucklings swoon in the streets of the city.

15. All that pass by clap their hands at thee; they hiss and wag their head at the daughter of Jerusalem, saying, Is this the city that men call The perfection of beauty, The joy of the whole earth?

16. All thine enemies have opened their mouth against thee: they hiss and gnash the teeth: they say, We have swallowed her up: certainly this is the day that we looked for; we have found, we have seen it.

17. The Lord hath done that which he had devised; he hath fulfilled his word that he had commanded in the days of old: he hath thrown down, and hath not pitied: and he hath caused thine enemy to rejoice over thee, he hath set up the horn of thine adversaries.

3:18. And I said, My strength and my hope is perished from the Lord:

19. Remembering mine affliction and my misery, the wormwood and the gall.

20. My soul hath them still in remembrance, and is humbled in me.

21. This I recall to my mind, therefore have I hope.

22. It is of the Lord's mercies that we are not consumed, because his compassions fail not.

23. They are new every morning: great is thy faithfulness.

24. The Lord is my portion, saith my soul; therefore will I hope in him.

25. The Lord is good unto them that wait for him, to the soul that seeketh him.

DICTIONARY

between the straits—Lamentations 1:3—in dire straits, trapped by one's pursuers with no chance of escape

wormwood—Lamentations 3:19—an aromatic plant which yielded a bitter, dark green oil; represents bitter sorrow

---

LESSON OUTLINE

I. JERUSALEM'S DOWNFALL

  A. The Captivity of Jerusalem

  B. The Result of Jerusalem's Sin

  C. The Sorrow of Jerusalem

II. LAMENTING JERUSALEM'S DESTRUCTION

  A. Jerusalem in Mourning

  B. Jerusalem's Shame

  C. Jerusalem's Enemies Rejoice

III. GOD'S MERCY BRINGS HOPE

  A. Hope Amid Distress

  B. The Virtues of Patience

  C. Mercy on the Repentant

LESSON EXPOSITION

INTRODUCTION

The five chapters of Lamentations form a literary mountain. The first two chapters ascend to the peak of chapter 3 and the last two chapters descend to the mountain base. Lamentations 3:23 forms the apex of the mountain with the powerful and emotional expression, "Great is thy faithfulness."

This book's focus is on the suffering of the people of Judah. Chapters 1 and 5 tell us of the siege and fall of Jerusalem, while chapters 2 and 4 reveal more explicitly the horrors of the city's destruction. In the center of these four poems concerning the suffering of Judah lies chapter 3 and its revelation of God's ever-present compassions. The overall purpose of the book's structure seems to be the revelation that even in the most grievous of times the compassions and faithfulness of God will lift the faithful above the distress and anguish of the day.

I. JERUSALEM'S DOWNFALL
(Lamentations 1:3-12)

With the fall of the northern kingdom (Israel) and the backsliding of the southern kingdom (Judah), it was only a matter of time until the same fate suffered in the north would be faced in the south. Judah's sins against God forced Him into the position of having to bring judgment upon Judah for His righteousness' sake.

As the center of the kingdom of Judah and the heart of all Israel, Jerusalem became the last bastion of the Hebrew faith and way of life. Within her walls the Temple stood, the king held court, and the prophet Jeremiah prophesied and lamented her eventual destruction while the Babylonians surrounded and laid siege to her. Following the fall of Jerusalem and the destruction of the city and the Temple of God in 586 B.C., Jeremiah penned the Book of Lamentations.

A. The Captivity of Jerusalem (vv. 3, 4)

3. Judah is gone into captivity because of affliction, and because of great servitude: she dwelleth among the heathen, she findeth no rest: all her persecutors overtook her between the straits.

4. The ways of Zion do mourn, because none come to the solemn feasts: all her gates are desolate: her priests sigh, her virgins are afflicted, and she is in bitterness.

Jeremiah launched his lament with a vivid description of Jerusalem's fallen condition. As someone who loved the Holy City greatly, his words seem to be bathed in tears: "How lonely sits the city that was full of people! How like a widow is she, who was great among the nations! The princess among the provinces has become a slave!" (Lamentations 1:1, *NKJV*).

No longer the capital of a sovereign nation, Jerusalem is now a "widow" (without a king). The remaining inhabitants had to pay tribute to a foreign and pagan conqueror.

Jerusalem was once the focal point of a tremendous kingdom whose fame had spread throughout the world. Solomon had brought wealth and fame to the nation of Israel in general and to Jerusalem in particular. Though the kingdom of Israel was split through the foolishness of Solomon's son Rehoboam, the glory and esteem of the city of Jerusalem lasted for generation after generation. The Jewish people were proud and their city was in no small way a source of their pride.

Now, however, "she weepeth sore in the night . . . she hath none to comfort her" (v. 2). Those who were once her friends had become her enemies. In affliction and under hard labor in captivity, Jerusalem's inhabitants became lost "among the nations" (v. 3, *NKJV*) and no longer had a place to call their own. What a severe blow that must have been for such a proud people from such a grand city!

No longer did the throngs travel the roads to Jerusalem, for her great feasts no longer took place and all of her holidays were now just as every other day—of no consequence. Lost in captivity, Jerusalem lived "in bitterness" (v. 4).

B. The Result of Jerusalem's Sin
  (vv. 5-9)

(Lamentations 1:5-7 is not included in the printed text.)

8. Jerusalem hath grievously sinned; therefore she is removed: all that honoured her despise her, because they have seen her nakedness: yea, she sigheth, and turneth backward.

9. Her filthiness is in her skirts; she remembereth not her last end; therefore she came down wonderfully: she had no comforter. O Lord,

behold my affliction: for the enemy hath magnified himself.

The harsh circumstances that had overtaken Jerusalem should not have come as a surprise. Jeremiah and Isaiah had both foretold of these consequences awaiting Jerusalem because of the sins of her people. It might even be said that God had shown Jerusalem more patience and mercy than she actually deserved. But as is always the way with God, their sins found them out: "The Lord hath afflicted her for the multitude of her transgressions" (v. 5).

The results of sin are always the same whether we are considering the fall of Jerusalem or the sinful condition of people today. Whatever might have been considered beautiful becomes ugly, and those things that may have been considered regal become feral. Jeremiah said that the beauty of the daughters of Zion had departed and the "princes" had become as a wild deer pursued by hunters (v. 6). The sins of Jerusalem had turned her beauty to ugliness. Where an extravagant and beautiful Temple sat, there stood a heap of unsightly rubble. Where once a palace and regal throne had been, there was ashes and dust.

Under the chastening of God the memories of the good things of old were magnified. Jerusalem remembered those better days, making their sufferings more grievous. The memories of the days of blessings keenly reminded them of the sins that had brought about the destruction of their beloved city.

C. The Sorrow of Jerusalem
  (vv. 10-12)

(Lamentations 1:10-12 is not included in the printed text.)

The sense of violation expressed by Jeremiah for Jerusalem is profound. Like the groping hands of a rapist, the hands of Jerusalem's enemy had reached out and fondled "all her pleasant things" (v. 10). The heathen that was never to enter the Temple of God had not only entered the sanctuary but had ravaged and plundered it. The precious instruments, utensils and objects within the Temple had been taken away to be held in the coffers of an idol god. Even the precious things of the people of Jerusalem had been lost—given in exchange for a morsel of food. What good is gold if you are starving? The people had become so degraded that they were self-abhorrent and "vile" in their own eyes (v. 11).

In astonishment Jerusalem wondered at the lack of sympathy in those who witnessed her shame. "Is it nothing to you, all ye that pass by?" (v. 12). Jerusalem's sorrow was devastating and profound, yet no one seemed to care—her grief was hers alone.

II. LAMENTING JERUSALEM'S DESTRUCTION
(Lamentations 2:10-17)

Jeremiah was not a spectator at the sufferings of Jerusalem; he was a participant. He endured the time of the siege and overthrow of the city; he suffered along with the remnant left in the city after the Babylonians' victory; his eyes beheld every level of suffering that the people of Jerusalem endured and his body endured them as well.

It is significant, however, that Jeremiah never lamented his own sufferings but only the sufferings of those around him. His grief for the pain of his neighbors seems to have been more agonizing than the hunger that gripped his own body. His sensitivity and caring distinguish Jeremiah as a true servant of God.

A. Jerusalem in Mourning (vv. 10-12)

(Lamentations 2:10, 12 is not included in the printed text.)

11. Mine eyes do fail with tears, my bowels are troubled, my liver is poured upon the earth, for the destruction of the daughter of my people; because the children and the sucklings swoon in the streets of the city.

A heavy pall hung over the city of Jerusalem as they endured the anger of God. Jeremiah saw Jerusalem as though she had been engulfed in a "cloud" and her beauty "cast down" to the earth (v. 1). God "hath swallowed up" the people of the city and "hath not pitied" (v. 2).

Verse 10 says the elders of the city had put on sackcloth and covered their heads with dust. The virgins of the city hung their heads "to the ground" because with the ruin of Jerusalem came also the ruin of their hopes for husbands and families.

Jeremiah seems to have taken Jerusalem's devastation with more grief than even the elders and virgins displayed. We can assume this to be true not only because of our text but because he knew these terrible things need not have happened. His prophesying to the inhabitants of Jerusalem had fallen on deaf ears. His warnings were never heeded. If indeed these elders who now sat in sackcloth and dust had taken heed to his warnings, they could have still been dressed in rich apparel and the virgins would be filled with joy at the prospects of finding husbands and building families.

As Jeremiah watched the needless suffering of his people, he grieved so deeply that his body began to show the intense pains of sorrow. His eyes had shed so many tears that they had run dry. Though the pain was still severe, his eyes could no longer dampen his cheeks with their salty drops.

Jeremiah described his pain by saying, "My bowels are troubled, my liver is poured upon the earth" (v. 11). The phrase "my liver is poured upon the earth" is found nowhere else in Scripture and is difficult to interpret. The *New King James Version* translates the word *liver* as "bile," while the *New International Version* translates it as "heart." Either way, we know Jeremiah wept so severely and grieved so deeply that he became physically ill, possibly even regurgitating wretched-tasting bile upon the ground.

The horror of Jerusalem's suffering is vividly expressed when Jeremiah speaks of the starvation of the children and infants. This catastrophe seemed to stir Jeremiah's emotions the most. He saw children "swoon [faint] in the streets of the city" (v. 11) because of hunger. He witnessed infants' lives ebbing away in their mothers' bosom (v. 12). It is no wonder that Jeremiah grieved until his body was tormented with illness.

B. Jerusalem's Shame (vv. 13-15)

(Lamentations 2:13, 14 is not included in the printed text.)

15. All that pass by clap their hands at thee; they hiss and wag their head at the daughter of Jerusalem, saying, Is this the city that men call The perfection of beauty, The joy of the whole earth?

Jeremiah not only was ill because of the heavy grief that he experienced, he was also perplexed at how to compare Jerusalem's suffering to any other event in history that he might draw forth some comfort for himself and his people. "How shall I console you?" (v. 13, *NKJV*), Jeremiah asked.

To Jeremiah, Jerusalem's destruction and ensuing famine were incomparable. This, of course, was not true, for many other cities had experienced war and besiegement at the hands of the Babylonians as well as other aggressive nations. Jerusalem was not the first to suffer such torment, nor would she be the last.

Jerusalem, however, had been a blessed city. Though difficult times had visited her, she had always endured and regained her place as a city blessed by God. The city that Jeremiah now saw held no rescm blance to the blessed city he had previously known. "Your ruin is spread wide as the sea," Jeremiah lamented. "Who can heal you?" (v. 13, *NKJV*).

Jerusalem's prophets had failed her. Not Jeremiah, for he had warned Jerusalem in faithfulness and integrity—and had suffered for his efforts. Numerous prophets, however, had filled the city with rosy predictions of continued blessings. Eager to please their listeners, false prophets are always willing to paint a picture that excuses the sins of the people without calling them to repentance. "They have not uncovered your iniquity," Jeremiah said of the false prophets (v. 14, *NKJV*). Instead, they had filled Jerusalem with "delusions," which made the city's downfall even more painful.

Those who viewed Jerusalem's downfall were now astonished at her grave condition, and they mocked her. "[They] clap their hands at thee; they hiss and wag their head" (v. 15).

Psalmists had called Jerusalem "beautiful for situation, the joy of the whole earth" (Psalm 48:2) and "the perfection of beauty" (50:2). But now Jerusalem's enemies used those same words to taunt her, saying, "Is this the city that is called 'The perfection of beauty, the joy of the whole earth'?" (v. 15, *NKJV*).

C. Jerusalem's Enemies Rejoice (vv. 16, 17)

16. All thine enemies have opened their mouth against thee: they hiss and gnash the teeth: they say, We have swallowed her up: certainly this is the day that we looked for; we have found, we have seen it.

17. The Lord hath done that which he had devised; he hath fulfilled his word that he had commanded in the days of old: he hath thrown down, and hath not pitied: and he hath caused thine enemy to rejoice over thee, he hath set up the horn of thine adversaries.

Just as her prophets had deceived Jerusalem, her enemies were deceived by their victory. They had never been able to defeat Jerusalem before because of God's divine protection. Every attempt had met with a sound defeat either by God's empowerment of her army or by miraculous intervention. The only difference in those defeats and the current victory was the change in God's attitude toward Jerusalem.

Foolishly, Jerusalem's enemies rejoiced, saying, "We have swallowed her up" (v. 16). A victory long desired and anticipated had come for them, yet they did not know or did not recognize its source. To them, their strength and military might had won the victory.

The truth was that God had brought them this victory just as He had brought them down to defeat at other times. How agonizing it must have been for the people of Jerusalem to realize God had delivered them into the hands of their enemies. How painful it must have been when they realized that their own sins had evoked such an act of God.

III. GOD'S MERCY BRINGS HOPE
(Lamentations 3:18-32)

As Jeremiah began his third poem (ch. 3), he lamented all of the suffering and distress he had experienced personally throughout the ministry and life God assigned to him. All of the sufferings of Jerusalem he suffered as well. All of the pain and anguish of the people of the city became his pain and anguish. Finding himself deep in a state of remorse and grief, Jeremiah reflected upon past experiences and came to an astounding conclusion: Even in great distress, God is faithful.

A. Hope Amid Distress (vv. 18-23)

18. And I said, My strength and my hope is perished from the Lord:

19. Remembering mine affliction and my misery, the wormwood and the gall.

20. My soul hath them still in remembrance, and is humbled in me.

21. This I recall to my mind, therefore have I hope.

22. It is of the Lord's mercies that we are not consumed, because

his compassions fail not.

23. They are new every morning: great is thy faithfulness.

Jeremiah came to the point where he cried out that all he hoped for had perished. As he focused on his past afflictions and wanderings, "the wormwood [bitterness] and the gall" (v. 19), he was filled with despair.

However, in verse 20 "we find a different feeling," says Adam Clarke. There Jeremiah "humbles himself under the mighty hand of God, and then his hope revives." It is a broken and humbled heart that always attracts the attention of God. The psalmist said, "The Lord is nigh unto them that are of a broken heart; and saveth such as be of a contrite spirit" (Psalm 34:18).

Jeremiah was reminded that through all of the situations he had faced, throughout all of his sufferings and trials, God had been gracious to him and had sustained him. His spirits lifted, the prophet said, "This I recall to my mind, therefore have I hope" (v. 21).

Knowing that sin had brought the judgment of God upon Jerusalem and that God was just in all He had done, Jeremiah realized that God's judgment could have been much worse. He realized God had been merciful even in His wrath. "Through the Lord's mercies we are not consumed" (v. 22, NKJV). God could have annihilated the inhabitants of Jerusalem from the face of the earth, but He didn't. They had not been "consumed," so there was hope for the future.

Jeremiah realized the compassions of the Lord had been with him even during the fall of Jerusalem. God's compassion never ceased but was as fresh each morning as the day before. His love would not fail to cover the faithful. With such a realization fresh in his mind, Jeremiah penned one of the most inspiring and renowned statements of the Bible: "Great is thy faithfulness" (v. 23).

B. The Virtues of Patience (vv. 24-26)

(Lamentations 3:26 is not included in the printed text.)

24. The Lord is my portion, saith my soul; therefore will I hope in him.

25. The Lord is good unto them that wait for him, to the soul that seeketh him.

A common refrain throughout the Psalms is the statement "The Lord is my portion." This statement bears the connotation of inheritance or a choice made between material things or spiritual things. To claim the Lord as one's "portion" means to choose Him over and above all things of this world.

Jeremiah used this refrain as a foundation for his expression of hope. The sentiment expressed in verse 24 is one of faith and common sense: If I choose God to be my "portion" over all that is in the world, then it stands to reason that God will honor my commitment to Him by caring for me not only in my time of need, but in all circumstances. Paul said, "And we know that all things work together for good to them that love God, to them who are the called according to his purpose" (Romans 8:28).

This does not mean all things that take place in a believer's life will be good, but that in time God will make even the painful things—the agonies and sorrows—work for the believer's benefit. This fact brings us to a point of personal participation in the plan of God. Often all that God's plan requires is patience. We are to wait until God's perfect time arrives for the benefit to be realized.

Jeremiah stressed two important activities for the believer in verse 25—waiting and seeking: "The Lord is good to those who wait for Him, to the soul who seeks Him" (*NKJV*). To *wait* on God really means to *hope* in Him. Waiting is hoping.

Jeremiah expressed the surety of God's eventual salvation in verse 23 with the statement "Great is thy faithfulness." The actualization of God's faithfulness, however, may be a while in coming. Jeremiah reminds us, however, of the importance of patience in hopefulness: "It is good that [one] should both hope and quietly wait for the salvation of the Lord" (v. 26).

C. Mercy on the Repentant (vv. 27-32)

(Lamentations 3:27-32 is not included in the printed text.)

When a time of trial and suffering comes our way, our typical response is to immediately begin to seek the Lord for an end to our pain and sorrow. Christians today seldom see suffering as God's will; it is viewed rather as an intrusion of Satan into an otherwise blessed existence. Jeremiah stands out as an example to the contrary. Often it is the case that the righteous suffer along with the wicked. Such sufferings are to be endured in patient hope of God's restoration.

Jeremiah's advice to the righteous sufferer is, "Let him sit alone and keep silent, because God has laid it on him" (v. 28, *NKJV*). He also advises the sufferer to repent, to "put his mouth in the dust" in humble submission because "there may yet be hope" (see v. 29). If the repentant person "gives his cheek to the one who strikes him" and humbles himself, being "full of reproach," God's compassions will be stirred and He will come to his aid (see v. 30).

In the midst of destruction and sorrow, Jeremiah came to remember the grace of God. He remembered that even God's anger has a limit and "the Lord will not cast off for ever" (v. 31). He recognized that the God who allowed this tragedy to befall Jerusalem was the same God who had shown Israel His great mercy in times past. The truth and resolution of the whole matter was, "Though he cause grief, yet will he have compassion according to the multitude of his mercies" (v. 32).

GOLDEN TEXT HOMILY

"THIS I RECALL TO MY MIND, THEREFORE HAVE I HOPE. IT IS OF THE LORD'S MERCIES THAT WE ARE NOT CONSUMED, BECAUSE HIS COMPASSIONS FAIL NOT" (Lamentations 3:21, 22).

Jeremiah gives us a model for dealing with disappointment and distress. In essence, he shows us how to reach the place Paul talks about in 2 Corinthians 4:16, "But though our outward man perish, yet the inward man is renewed day by day." God's goodness and provision is greater than our struggle. "Where sin abounds, grace abounds much more" (see Romans 5:20).

His faithfulness to us goes beyond the obvious and into areas we fail to recognize or seldom consider. For example, Romans 5:3 tells us that even when we face tribulations we are able to "glory" because they work for our good, building perseverance and character in us. He purposefully conditions us with these qualities that become strengths to carry us through tough times. He never allows anything to come upon us that is more than we can bear. Paul declares in 1 Corinthians 10:13, "There hath no temptation taken you but such as is common to man: but God is faithful, who will not suffer you to be tempted above that ye are able; but will with the temptation also make a way to escape, that ye may be able to bear it." Yes, God is faithful!

God is also merciful. Someone said that grace is God giving you what you do not deserve, and mercy is evidenced when God does not give you what you really do deserve. Each of us are recipients of His mercy and compassion. If He gave us what we deserved, all of us would be in serious trouble. Therefore, when life hits us hard, and we feel like giving up, let's remember the goodness of God! As Paul reminds us in Romans 2:4, "The goodness of God leadeth thee to repentance."—**J. David Stephens**

SENTENCE SERMONS

GOD JUDGES SIN, but He is also compassionate and forgiving.
                                        —Selected

OTHER MEN SEE ONLY A HOPELESS END, but the Christian rejoices in an endless hope.
                              —Gilbert Beenken

THERE ARE NO HOPELESS SITUATIONS; there are only people who have grown hopeless about them.
                            —Clare Boothe Luce

ILLUMINATING THE LESSON

One of the most inspiring statements of the Bible occurs in one of the most unlikely places. Lamentations is a book of weeping and lamenting because of the destruction of Jerusalem. Of all the books of the Bible, only Job might be considered more sorrowful.

The deep emotional pain of the writer of Lamentations constantly strikes the reader. Yet, there in the middle of all that pain and sorrow is this powerful statement of praise:

Through the Lord's mercies we are
  not consumed,
Because His compassions fail not.
They are new every morning;
Great is Your faithfulness
(3:22, 23, NKJV).

DAILY BIBLE READINGS

M. The Fall of Jerusalem.
    Jeremiah 52:4-16
T. Remembering Zion.
    Psalm 137:1-6
W. End of the Exile.
    Daniel 9:1-6, 17-19
T. God's Great Love.
    Ephesians 2:1-10
F. God Remains Faithful.
    2 Timothy 2:8-13
S. Hope of Eternal Life.
    Titus 3:3-8

TRUTH SEARCH
Creatively Teaching the Word

DISCUSSION QUESTIONS

Seeing Jerusalem's Downfall
(Lamentations 1:3-12)

1. What happened to Judah and its capital, Jerusalem (v. 3)?

2. Why did this happen (vv. 5, 8)?

3. What was the impact on Judah's priests (v. 4) and leaders (v. 6)?

4. What help was available to Jerusalem (vv. 7, 9)?

5. What happened to the Temple (v. 10)?

6. What did the people do to survive (v. 11)?

Lamenting Jerusalem's Destruction
(Lamentations 2:10-17)

1. How did the elders and virgins display their grief (v. 10)?

2. What was the fate of Jerusalem's children, and how did it affect the writer (vv. 11, 12)?

3. What questions did the writer raise (v. 13)?

4. Despite Jerusalem's fall, what did the false prophets say, and what did they not say (v. 14)?

5. How did the enemies of Jerusalem react to her fall (v. 15, 16)?

6. Was the writer surprised by Jerusalem's destruction? Why or why not (v. 17)?

Hoping in God's Mercy
(Lamentations 3:19-33)

1. What enabled the writer not to lose all hope?

2. How could the writer declare the Lord's mercies despite the destruction he saw (vv. 22-24)?

3. What is the connection between waiting on and hoping in the Lord (vv. 25-27)?

4. What should one's response be when experiencing judgment for sins (vv. 28-30)?

5. What does the Lord not do "forever" (v. 31) and what does He not do "willingly" (v. 33)?

6. When the Lord does "cause grief," what is His purpose (v. 32)?

OBJECT LESSON

Items needed: Coin

Hold a coin in your hand and ask a student to guess "heads or tails," then flip the coin and see if their guess was correct.

Some people think God's actions are like a coin toss—He might be merciful or He might be harsh and judgmental. You just never know.

However, the truth is that God is always the same. All of His actions toward us flow out of His compassion and mercy. Even when He punishes us, His purpose is redemptive—to bring us close to Himself.

Resurrection Hope (Easter)

Study Text: 1 Corinthians 15:1-58
Objective: To investigate the effects of Christ's death and resurrection and rejoice in the hope this brings.
Time: Around A.D. 56
Place: Written at Ephesus
Golden Text: "As in Adam all die, even so in Christ shall all be made alive" (1 Corinthians 15:22).
Central Truth: Christ's resurrection confirms the promise of eternal life to believers.
Evangelism Emphasis: The only hope of obtaining eternal life is by accepting Christ as Savior.

PRINTED TEXT

1 Corinthians 15:3. For I delivered unto you first of all that which I also received, how that Christ died for our sins according to the scriptures;

4. And that he was buried, and that he rose again the third day according to the scriptures:

5. And that he was seen of Cephas, then of the twelve:

6. After that, he was seen of above five hundred brethren at once; of whom the greater part remain unto this present, but some are fallen asleep.

7 After that, he was seen of James; then of all the apostles.

8. And last of all he was seen of me also, as of one born out of due time.

12. Now if Christ be preached that he rose from the dead, how say some among you that there is no resurrection of the dead?

13. But if there be no resurrection of the dead, then is Christ not risen:

14. And if Christ be not risen, then is our preaching vain, and your faith is also vain.

15. Yea, and we are found false witnesses of God; because we have testified of God that he raised up Christ: whom he raised not up, if so be that the dead rise not.

16. For if the dead rise not, then is not Christ raised:

17. And if Christ be not raised, your faith is vain; ye are yet in your sins.

18. Then they also which are fallen asleep in Christ are perished.

19. If in this life only we have hope in Christ, we are of all men most miserable.

20. But now is Christ risen from the dead, and become the firstfruits of them that slept.

24. Then cometh the end, when he shall have delivered up the kingdom to God, even the Father; when he shall have put down all rule and all authority and power.

25. For he must reign, till he hath put all enemies under his feet.

26. The last enemy that shall be destroyed is death.

52. In a moment, in the twinkling of an eye, at the last trump: for the trumpet shall sound, and the dead shall be raised incorruptible, and we shall be changed.

53. For this corruptible must put on incorruption, and this mortal must put on immortality.

LESSON OUTLINE

I. CHRIST'S DEATH AND RESUR-
   RECTION
   A. The Purpose of His Death
   B. The Meaning of His Burial
   C. The Reality of His Resurrection

II. RESURRECTION ASSURED
   A. The Necessity of the
      Resurrection
   B. The Scope of the Resurrection

III. ALL ENEMIES DESTROYED
   A. Evildoers and Satan
   B. Death

IV. THE BELIEVER'S HOPE
   A. A New Body
   B. A New Life
   C. A Steadfast Life

LESSON EXPOSITION

INTRODUCTION

The credibility of Christianity rests on the reality of the resurrection of Jesus Christ. If He did not rise from the dead, it does not matter that He was crucified. The meaning of resurrection in a sense is the reversal of death. This is exactly what Jesus did. He conquered death. The grave could not hold Him. Of course, He died as a sacrifice for the sin of the world. This was necessary, and must not be downplayed. Yet it was the Resurrection that provided the evidence needed to confirm His mission and ministry.

In this lesson we see the bold argument of the apostle Paul for the significance of the veracity of the resurrection of Jesus. Everything we preach or claim is empty if Jesus is not risen. Connected to the resurrection of Jesus is the resurrection of believers. The doctrine of immortality, an afterlife, or more accurately the extension of life for believers is connected to the

resurrection of Jesus. We will examine both His resurrection and the resurrection of believers in the unfolding of the 15th chapter of 1 Corinthians.

I. CHRIST'S DEATH AND RESUR-
   RECTION (1 Corinthians 15:1-11)

A. The Purpose of His Death (vv. 1-3)

(1 Corinthians 15:1, 2 is not included in the printed text.)

3. For I delivered unto you first of all that which I also received, how that Christ died for our sins according to the scriptures.

In verses 1 and 2 Paul is referring to the personal salvation experience of the Corinthians. They were saved through the gospel Paul had preached to them. However, questions seemed to be creeping in about the resurrection of Jesus. The way Paul dealt with this was to go directly to their faith. The relationship they now had with God was due to the death and the resurrection of Jesus.

In verse 3 the apostle declared, "Christ died for our sins according to the scriptures." The purpose of the death of Jesus could not be in doubt. Long before Jesus came to earth the prophet identified the purpose of His coming and of His death. He came to die as the supreme, perfect sacrifice for sin. John the Baptist, upon seeing Jesus, proclaimed, "Behold! The Lamb of God who takes away the sin of the world!" (John 1:29, *NKJV*).

B. The Meaning of His Burial (v. 4)

4. And that he was buried, and that he rose again the third day according to the scriptures.

Jesus was placed in a grave. One of His followers made arrangements for Jesus to occupy his own personal tomb. No previous arrangement had been made for the burial of Jesus. It was significant that Jesus be buried and that His followers would know the place. Some critics of the Resurrection said that the disciples stole the body of Jesus, hid it, and produced a substitute to try to prove the Resurrection.

The burial of Jesus was important because during the time He was in the heart of the earth, He carried out a most important mission. In 1 Peter 3:19, 20 we are told that Jesus went and preached to the spirits in prison. These were individuals who, waiting for the Messiah, went as far in their faith as they could go. On this mission Jesus included them in the plan of redemption. *in prison*

The burial of Jesus is important because it symbolizes an important aspect of the salvation experience— the dying that must take place before a spiritual resurrection can occur. We are buried with Christ in baptism. "Therefore we were buried with Him through baptism into death, that just as Christ was raised from the dead by the glory of the Father, even so we also should walk in newness of life" (Romans 6:4, *NKJV*). When new believers are baptized in water, they give testimony to the death, burial and resurrection of Jesus. They rise out of the water to walk in newness of life.

The burial of Jesus is referred to in each of the four accounts of the Gospels. It is a vital part of Christian evidences. Also, the phrase "according to the scriptures" signals the value and important significance of His burial.

C. The Reality of His Resurrection (vv. 5-11)

(1 Corinthians 15:9-11 is not included in the printed text.)

5. And that he was seen of Cephas, then of the twelve:

6. After that, he was seen of above five hundred brethren at once; of whom the greater part remain unto this present, but some are fallen asleep.

7. After that, he was seen of James; then of all the apostles.

8. And last of all he was seen of me also, as of one born out of due time.

Christ appeared to Peter (Cephas) and then to the other apostles. He was seen by more than 500 followers all at once, most of whom were still alive when Paul wrote this letter. This particular appearance is not recorded elsewhere in the Scriptures. This is also the only record that the resurrected Christ appeared to James, but there are other records of His appearance to the apostles and the later appearance to Paul himself.

The resurrection of Jesus really did take place. Paul carefully identifies the persons who were eyewitnesses. To have seen Christ, the risen Lord, was one of the requirements for apostleship. This gives credibility not only to the reality of the Resurrection, but to the apostleship of Paul.

A view known as the "swoon theory" holds that Jesus did not actually die, He only fainted. There is no credible evidence for this. The death of Jesus was a true death; thus His resurrection was a true resurrection. The people who crucified Him, the ones who prepared His body for burial, and those who went to the tomb and found it empty were convinced beyond doubt that Jesus died. An easy way to deny the Resurrection would be to deny His death. Neither of these will suffice.

II. RESURRECTION ASSURED (1 Corinthians 15:12-23)

A. The Necessity of the Resurrection (vv. 12-19)

12. Now if Christ be preached that he rose from the dead, how say some among you that there is no resurrection of the dead?

13. But if there be no resurrection of the dead, then is Christ not risen:

14. And if Christ be not risen, then is our preaching vain, and your faith is also vain.

15. Yea, and we are found false witnesses of God; because we have testified of God that he raised up Christ: whom he raised not up, if so be that the dead rise not.

16. For if the dead rise not, then is not Christ raised:

17. And if Christ be not raised, your faith is vain; ye are yet in your sins.

18. Then they also which are fallen asleep in Christ are perished.

19. If in this life only we have hope in Christ, we are of all men most miserable.

The Resurrection is the most fundamental doctrine of Christianity. According to Paul, everything stands or falls on the truth of the Resurrection. If Jesus was not raised, all of our preaching is vain, our faith is vain, and we are still in our sins. If Jesus did not rise, the dead perish with no hope, and living Christians are miserable, for they live without hope. The resurrection of Jesus is mentioned over 100 times in the New Testament and was a major theme in apostolic preaching.

It was important that the resurrected Christ show Himself alive after He was raised from the dead. It must be established beyond doubt that this was the same Jesus who was crucified, buried, and came out of the tomb victorious. The Book of Acts addresses this issue in the opening statements, "To whom He also presented Himself alive after His suffering by many infallible proofs, being seen by them during forty days and speaking of the things pertaining to the kingdom of God" (1:3, *NKJV*). In so doing Jesus established His deity, emphasized the purpose of His coming into the world, provided assurance and hope to His followers, and provided motivation and inspiration for launching the church into its mission.

The resurrection of Jesus is important for the message and provisions it brings to His followers for all generations. It assures the resurrection of all who are in Christ Jesus. Paul argues that the resurrection of the saints could not take place if Christ is not risen from the dead. The point made in 1 Corinthians 15:13-17 is that the resurrection of Christ and the resurrection of the saints are dependent one upon the other. If one is not a fact, neither can the other be a fact. He further states that if Christ is significant only as it pertains to this life, we all are left in misery (vv. 18, 19).

Jesus was raised from the dead by His own power, though we know He was acting in harmony with the two other persons of the Trinity. The entire Godhead acted as the source of His bodily resurrection. The resurrected body of Jesus was a real body. The women who came to the grave site on the morning of the Resurrection saw Him, recognized Him, and worshiped at His feet (Matthew 28:9).

In the evening of the Resurrection, Christ appeared to the Eleven and invited them to view the nail prints in His hands and feet. He asked them to "handle His hands and feet" that they may know this was the same Jesus they knew before the Crucifixion and Resurrection (see Luke 24:39). These scars of Jesus were very special scars. They were a necessary part of the evidence that was so essential in establishing the reality of the Resurrection. In no way does this suggest that risen saints will have scars, missing limbs, flaws and blemishes. In truth we will have new bodies, fully restored, for they have been redeemed by the blood of the Lamb that was slain!

B. The Scope of the Resurrection (vv. 20-23)

(1 Corinthians 15:21-23 is not included in the printed text.)

20. But now is Christ risen from the dead, and become the firstfruits of them that slept.

Christ has risen from the dead, and as such He became the "firstfruits" of those who die. The analogy of fruit that springs forth from the earth is suggested by this terminology. Through the long ages, in all places in the earth thousands of souls were in a sense sleeping. Just as literal fields wait for spring to awaken them, these sleeping souls were waiting for the touch of life to awaken them. Here the apostle is saying that the resurrection of Jesus makes it possible that all who died in the faith will rise again.

The resurrection of Jesus signals that springtime has come. Those who sleep in the earth will be quickened by the power of the Resurrection and will see life once again.

From the concept of the firstfruits the writer turns to the contrast of what he calls the first Adam and the last Adam (vv. 21, 22). In the first Adam all of humanity dies. In the last Adam (Jesus) all will be brought back to life. The actions of the first Adam brought death to the human race. The action of the last Adam means everyone will have an eternal existence. All members of the human race were affected by the first Adam, and all members of the human race were affected by the last Adam.

There is an order to the resurrections. This is alluded to in verse 23: "But each one in his own order: Christ the firstfruits, afterward those who are Christ's at His coming" (NKJV). The word translated as "order" is a military term speaking of rank. Christ, the commander over life and death, rose from the dead first. His children will follow Him in resurrection to eternal life. In Revelation 20:13-15 we read that the wicked dead will not be raised up until the final resurrection.

III. ALL ENEMIES DESTROYED
(1 Corinthians 15:24-28)

A. Evildoers and Satan (vv. 24, 25)

24. Then cometh the end, when he shall have delivered up the kingdom to God, even the Father; when he shall have put down all rule and all authority and power.
25. For he must reign, till he hath put all enemies under his feet.

The authority and power inherent in Jesus, confirmed by His resurrection, will result in a radical change in the status quo of humanity. After the resurrections (of both good and evil people), Christ will establish a new kingdom. He will put an end to all other rule, authority and powers. He will put everything under His feet. At last the hope of Israel, the promise to Abraham, and the covenant with David will be fulfilled. The kingdom of God will be established forever.

The saints of the past were unable to imagine that to establish the Kingdom, Christ must die, be buried and resurrected. To them, establishing the Kingdom was a military issue. Of course, we know that earthly wars and fighting did not and could not bring in the Kingdom. Christ became the Victor through His ministry as the suffering Servant, but He will one day reign as the all-powerful King of kings and Lord of lords.

Meanwhile, we know that the ultimate evil behind the acts and deeds of evil people is the devil himself. Numbers of so-called enlightened scholars deny the existence of a personal devil. But how could anyone believe the Bible is the Word of God and not believe in a personal devil? Satan is the original and ultimate enemy of God. He sought to displace God and cause the world to worship him. He was responsible for the temptation of Adam and Eve that resulted in their sin. He was the force behind the murderers who killed the sinless Son of God. He is behind all evil in the world past and present.

Because of the resurrection of Jesus from the dead, Satan's days are numbered. It is only a matter of time. Soon Satan will be conquered and confined forever. Sin and all of its heartaches will have vanished, and paradise that was lost will be restored. Of course, we know that a final fight will occur. But we also know what the outcome of that fight will be. The reality is that the devil is a defeated foe. He was defeated when Jesus conquered the grave!

B. Death (vv. 26-28)

(1 Corinthians 15:27, 28 is not included in the printed text.)

26. The last enemy that shall be destroyed is death.

Death is the constant reminder of Adam's sin. It was the sentence promised and given for violating the law of God. This is why Paul says that in the first Adam all die. Those of us who live do so knowing that we will die. We look at our loved ones and friends and know that they will die. We experience the pain of leaving the earthly remains of our families in the cemetery. This hurts even though we know we shall see them again if they were in Christ and we remain in Him.

The vision of the Kingdom as revealed to John includes a straightforward statement regarding this last enemy. "There shall be no more death" is as matter of fact as it could be (Revelation 21:4). Death is considered a vicious enemy because it is associated with sin and is the cause of separation from God.

With all of God's enemies defeated, "then the Son himself will be made subject to him who put everything under him, so that God may be all in all" (1 Corinthians 15:28, *NIV*).

IV. THE BELIEVER'S HOPE
(1 Corinthians 15:50-58)

A. A New Body (vv. 50-53)

(1 Corinthians 15:50, 51 is not included in the printed text.)

52. In a moment, in the twinkling of an eye, at the last trump: for the trumpet shall sound, and the dead shall be raised incorruptible, and we shall be changed.

53. For this corruptible must put on incorruption, and this mortal must put on immortality.

"Flesh and blood cannot inherit the kingdom of God; neither doth corruption inherit incorruption" (v. 50). For men and women to inherit the Kingdom, a mysterious change must take place. We cannot get there from here in our present form. In verses 52 and 53, Paul reveals an instant change that will take place with those who are asleep, as well as those who are alive at the return of Christ. This change is an absolute necessity.

When this change takes place, all aspects of contamination, weakness, infirmity and blemishes associated with sin will no longer exist. Damaged hearts, cancerous livers, missing limbs, ruptured blood vessels will not be a part of the new body. The new body will not be a return of the sin-cursed form that we possess due to Adam's transgression. We are not talking about a reconditioned body— we are talking about a new one.

Questions are raised as to the identity of the new bodies. Will we recognize loved ones? Will I recognize my mother as my mother? There are elements of the mystery we will never understand in this life. We should rejoice in what we do know rather than being disturbed by what we do not understand. Jesus taught that our way of relating to others in the new heaven and the new earth will be different than the way we relate in this life. However, we know all will be wonderful and joyous.

B. A New Life (vv. 54-57)

(1 Corinthians 15:54-57 is not included in the printed text.)

A new body that does not relate to the old necessitates a new life. An incorruptible body cannot function in a corruptible environment. Heaven has been referred to as "a prepared place for a prepared people." Although this is not a Scriptural quotation, it is consistent with Scripture.

In verses 54 and 55, Paul is so caught up in the glory of what he is writing that his heart sings out quotations from the prophets: "He will swallow up death in victory; and the Lord God will wipe away tears from off all faces; and the rebuke of his people shall he take away from off all the earth: for the Lord hath spoken it" (Isaiah 25:8). "I will ransom them from the power of the grave; I will redeem them from death: O death, I will be thy plagues; O grave, I will be thy destruction" (Hosea 13:14).

Just as believers have questions about the nature of the new body, we also wonder about the nature of the new environment. Probably the Book of Revelation is the best source for discovering truths about our new home and new life. There are details that arouse our curiosity, but we must not be unduly concerned about them. What we do know about the new life is sufficient to make the desire worthwhile.

We know that there will be no more sin, tears, sorrow nor death in our new life (Revelation 21:4). We know that we will never again contend with the devil in our new life (20:10). We will be free from all of the restrictions of the earthly life. We know that in our new life we will rejoice and sing praises to God (19:1-7). Our fellowship will be pure and genuine—no more rivalry with others. The lion and the lamb shall lie together without hostility (Isaiah 11:6). Everything we ever wanted in terms of wholesome living will be incorporated into this new life.

There will be no night, for the Lamb is the light (Revelation 21:23). The river of life will be there (22:1). The great and wonderful fruit tree with 12 different kinds of fruit will be there (v. 2). Questions are often raised as to how much of what we know is symbolic and how much of it is to be taken literally. God has revealed everything of an essential nature to us. Paul makes the resurrection of Christ and the resurrection of the saints the necessary transitional experience for getting from here to there.

C. A Steadfast Life (v. 58)

One of the active consequences of faith in the resurrection is a steadfast life. No man can be slack in his living who truly believes that the Lord is coming and that the dead will rise in resurrection.

GOLDEN TEXT HOMILY

"AS IN ADAM ALL DIE, EVEN SO IN CHRIST SHALL ALL BE MADE ALIVE" (1 Corinthians 15:22).

To think that a dead body could resume life again—eat, walk and talk with its friends for 40 days—causes pseudo-Christians to spiritualize Christ's resurrection, and enemies to doubt it. But Christ experienced a bodily resurrection. And the "all" of verse 22 means that the bodies of the saved and the unsaved will one day be resurrected.

Verse 23 uses a military word, *order*, meaning "rank" or "company." The first rank is "Christ the firstfruits." Christ rose 2,000 years ago, and a great number of Old Testament saints rose bodily and ascended with Christ. This second rank to experience the resurrection of the body will be all who have received Jesus Christ. The third rank is the *telos* ("end," v. 24), or "last ones," to be raised after the Millennium to stand in judgment at the Great White Throne.—**Selected**

SENTENCE SERMONS

CHRIST'S RESURRECTION confirms the promise of eternal life to believers.

—Selected

BELIEF IN THE RESURRECTION is not an appendage to the Christian faith; it is the Christian faith.

—John S. Whale

THE GOSPELS DO NOT EXPLAIN the Resurrection. The Resurrection explains the Gospels.

—John S. Whale

EVANGELISM APPLICATION

THE ONLY HOPE OF OBTAINING ETERNAL LIFE IS BY ACCEPTING CHRIST AS SAVIOR.

All we want and need has been provided. The new body, the new life, the new world (without all that we do not need, yet with everything we do need) is wonderful. God has planned it, prepared it, and made it available to us by faith in the Son of God.

The tragedy is that all the wonderful works of God on our behalf will not profit us unless we make a commitment to Him. The glorious world God has prepared for us is free, but we must claim it through the confession of our sins. No one understood this better than the apostle Paul, who wrote, "That I may know Him and the power of His resurrection, and the fellowship of His sufferings, being conformed to His death, if, by any means, I may attain to the resurrection from the dead" (Philippians 3:10, 11, *NKJV*).

ILLUMINATING THE LESSON

In the Tate Gallery, London, there is a beautiful picture illustrating the Christian hope of immortality. In the center of the painting there is a marble tomb from which flowers are springing up, among them beautiful white lilies, which in art represent immortality. Standing in the midst is an entreating figure of a young woman clad in green drapery, who holds her hands upward in prayer and longing.

The stars are shining in the sky, but they are paling because it is at the hour of dawn. The thought of the artist is revealed in the words engraved beneath: "If hope were not, life would break."

Hope is the anchor of the soul. It is the one virtue that keeps us moving toward the goal. It has been said that three things are needed in life: (1) someone to love, (2) something to do, and (3) something to hope for. Imagine attending a funeral and knowing or believing nothing about the Resurrection!

DAILY BIBLE READINGS

M. Origin of Death.
    Genesis 3:17-19
T. Death Is Certain.
    Job 14:1-14
W. Triumph of Faith.
    Job 19-23-27
T. Promise of Resurrection.
    John 11:21-25
F. Order of Resurrection.
    1 Thessalonians 4:13-18
S. Future of the Saints.
    Revelation 20:4-6

TRUTH SEARCH
Creatively Teaching the Word

DISCUSSION QUESTIONS

Christ's Death and Resurrection
(1 Corinthians 15:1-11)

1. How important is the gospel of Christ's death and resurrection (vv. 1, 2)?

2. Why does Paul use the phrase "according to the Scriptures" in verses 3 and 4?

3. Who saw the resurrected Christ, and why is this important (vv. 5-8)?

4. How had the Corinthians responded to Paul's preaching about Christ (v. 11)?

Resurrection Assured
(1 Corinthians 15:12-23)

1. How important is the doctrine of Christ's resurrection (vv. 12-16)?

2. If Christ was not raised from the dead, what would be our condition and the condition of believers who have died (vv. 17-19)?

3. What did Paul mean by calling Christ's resurrection the "firstfruits" (vv. 20, 23)?

4. Contrast Adam's influence on humanity with Christ's influence (vv. 21, 22).

All Enemies Destroyed
(1 Corinthians 15:24-28)

1. Name some of the authorities and powers Christ will completely defeat (vv. 24, 25).

2. Why is death called the "last enemy" (v. 26)?

3. After the Son of God conquers every enemy, to whom will He subject Himself, and why (vv. 27, 28)?

The Believer's Hope
(1 Corinthians 15:50-58)

1. What cannot enter heaven, and why (v. 50)?

2. What "mystery" does Paul reveal (v. 51)?

3. Describe the process of events and the time involved in our coming change (v. 52).

4. How will we be changed (vv. 53, 54)?

5. What will Christ give us victory over (vv. 55-57)?

6. Understanding the truths about death and resurrection, how should we live (v. 58)?

NEWS REPORT

Item needed: Obituaries from recent newspaper

Read aloud the names and ages of people in the obituary section of your local newspaper.

At their moment of death, there is only one issue that mattered to these people: Had they trusted in the resurrected Christ for salvation? Each of those individuals has stepped into an eternity of joy with Christ or into unending torment without Him.

Where will we spend our eternal future?

Return From Exile

Study Text: 2 Chronicles 36:15-21; Ezra 1:1 through 3:13; Jeremiah 29:10-14
Objective: To survey the events of Israel's exile and restoration, and trust in God's promises.
Time: Around 600 B.C. until 535 B.C.
Place: Jerusalem
Golden Text: "Ye shall seek me, and find me, when ye shall search for me with all your heart" (Jeremiah 29:13).
Central Truth: God will forgive and restore those who return to Him.
Evangelism Emphasis: God will forgive and save those who turn to Him repenting.

PRINTED TEXT

2 Chronicles 36:19. And they burnt the house of God, and brake down the wall of Jerusalem, and burnt all the palaces thereof with fire, and destroyed all the goodly vessels thereof.

20. And them that had escaped from the sword carried he away to Babylon; where they were servants to him and his sons until the reign of the kingdom of Persia:

21. To fulfil the word of the Lord by the mouth of Jeremiah, until the land had enjoyed her sabbaths: for as long as she lay desolate she kept sabbath, to fulfil threescore and ten years.

Ezra 1:1. Now in the first year of Cyrus king of Persia, that the word of the Lord by the mouth of Jeremiah might be fulfilled, the Lord stirred up the spirit of Cyrus king of Persia, that he made a proclamation throughout all his kingdom, and put it also in writing, saying,

2. Thus saith Cyrus king of Persia, The Lord God of heaven hath given me all the kingdoms of the earth; and he hath charged me to build him an house at Jerusalem, which is in Judah.

3. Who is there among you of all his people? his God be with him, **and let him go up to Jerusalem, which is in Judah, and build the house of the Lord God of Israel, (he is the God,) which is in Jerusalem.**

5. Then rose up the chief of the fathers of Judah and Benjamin, and the priests, and the Levites, with all them whose spirit God had raised, to go up to build the house of the Lord which is in Jerusalem.

3:1. And when the seventh month was come, and the children of Israel were in the cities, the people gathered themselves together as one man to Jerusalem.

2. Then stood up Jeshua the son of Jozadak, and his brethren the priests, and Zerubbabel the son of Shealtiel, and his brethren, and builded the altar of the God of Israel, to offer burnt-offerings thereon, as it is written in the law of Moses the man of God.

3. And they set the altar upon his bases; for fear was upon them because of the people of those countries: and they offered burnt-offerings thereon unto the Lord, even burnt-offerings morning and evening.

DICTIONARY

Jeshua (JESH-you-ah) . . . Jozadak (JOZ-ah-dak)—Ezra 3:2—the priest who returned to Jerusalem with Zerubbabel; Jozadak was his father.

Zerubbabel (zeh-RUB-uh-bell) . . . Shealtiel (she-ALL-ti-el)—Ezra 3:2—grandson and son of King Jehoiachin

---

LESSON OUTLINE

I. DESOLATION AND BONDAGE

  A. The Rebellion

  B. The Invasion

  C. The Exile

II. PROMISE OF RESTORATION

  A. The Promise

  B. The Fulfillment

III. RESTORATION BRING CHANGE

  A. The Preparation

  B. The Rebuilding

LESSON EXPOSITION

INTRODUCTION

How is it possible for a nation with so much promise to find itself enslaved in a distant land? Why would they give up the blessings of God for the disastrous pursuit of self-determination?

Today's lesson provides an opportunity for an overview of an extended period of Israel's history. Though most of the lesson focuses on the sixth century B.C., it reaches back into previous centuries. There the seeds for destruction were not only planted but repeatedly watered until Judah reaped the harvest of God's judgment.

After the death of King Solomon, 10 tribes refused to remain loyal to Rehoboam, who ascended to the throne. This stemmed from his refusal to lighten the tax load imposed by the previous king (see 1 Kings 12). This resulted in the people of Israel being divided into two separate nations. The 10 tribes are referred to as Israel, or the northern kingdom. At times they are also called Ephraim, the name of the largest tribe in the coalition. The two remaining tribes use the name Judah, or the southern kingdom.

God's judgment came upon the northern tribes through the invasion of the Assyrians in 722 B.C. Many of the people were transferred to other lands. Those who remained intermarried with other people groups whom the Assyrians relocated in their land. This resulted in the people known as the Samaritans. Second Kings 17 records these events.

Judah continued as an independent nation for over 100 years beyond the dismantling of Israel. Eventually their sins became so great that God had no other choice than to bring justice upon them. Repeatedly, as we will see in this lesson, God warned them, but they disregarded His warnings. A study of the Book of Habakkuk reveals how specifically God spoke of their future. He revealed to the prophet how the Babylonians would be the means of His judgment.

Today's lesson is the first of six which deal with the return from exile in Babylon. Except for two sections of Scripture from 2 Chronicles and Jeremiah, the lesson texts come from the Books of Ezra and Nehemiah.

We will experience the joys and struggles that accompanied the resettlement and reconstruction. Repeatedly the frailties of human weakness will appear; however, there will be the examples of faith and repentance that brought joy and a restoration of relationship with God. We will be reminded of the influence that one person who follows righteousness can make on a group of people.

I. DESOLATION AND BONDAGE
(2 Chronicles 36:15-21)

A. The Rebellion (vv. 15, 16)

(2 Chronicles 36:15, 16 is not included in the printed text.)

The last chapter of 2 Chronicles summarizes the final years of Judah as a nation steadily falling under the political influence of other nations. Initially it was Egypt flexing its military muscle and political influence. However, Judah's final three kings came under the domination of King Nebuchadnezzar of Babylon. On three separate occasions, beginning about 605 B.C., his armies entered the land and took captives into exile. Daniel and the three Hebrew children were taken in the first group. The prophet Ezekiel was taken in the second group in 597 B.C. When Zedekiah rebelled a decade later, Nebuchadnezzar's forces marched against Jerusalem and lay siege.

After months of siege they broke through the walls. All the important buildings of the city were burned, including Solomon's temple (after plundering its contents). Only some of the poorest of the people were left behind. The rest were relocated as exiles in the land of the Babylonians. (Read 2 Kings 25.)

Unless the rest of the story is seen, it could simply be perceived as the misfortunes of a weaker nation in the face of an expanding empire. Verses 15 and 16 of the text summarize the divine influence on these events. They were the direct result of God's punishing His people for their disobedience and total disregard of previous warnings. This demonstrates God's mercy. He did not thunder judgment in haste due to sins creeping into Israelites' lives. It is their continued pattern of straying and staying away from Him that brought such severe repercussions.

Consider the ministry of Isaiah.

Beginning around 740 B.C. and continuing for nearly 50 years, he spoke the words of the Lord. Isaiah 1 reflects the conditions more than 100 years before the Exile. In verse 4, Isaiah describes God's children as a sinful nation who had forsaken and provoked Him. In verses 9 and 10 he compares them to Sodom and Gomorrah. They continued to worship as though they were in a right relationship with God (vv. 11-15). God's response was to ask them to put away the evil and experience spiritual cleansings; otherwise, they would suffer judgment.

Jeremiah began his ministry over 100 years later than Isaiah; however, he too suffered due to the people's spiritual rebellion. Two verses state the condition: "They have forsaken me, the spring of living water. . . . Long ago you broke off your yoke and tore off your bonds; you said, 'I will not serve you!'" (Jeremiah 2:13, 20, *NIV*). And as a result they would experience the judgment of an invading nation: "Your towns will lie in ruins without inhabitant. So put on sackcloth, lament and wail, for the fierce anger of the Lord has not turned away from us" (4:7, 8, *NIV*).

B. The Invasion (vv. 17-19)

(2 Chronicles 36:17, 18 is not included in the printed text.)

19. And they burnt the house of God, and brake down the wall of Jerusalem, and burnt all the palaces thereof with fire, and destroyed all the goodly vessels thereof.

God raised up a short-lived empire, the Babylonians, for the purpose of bringing judgment through an invasion and deportation of His people along with great destruction and desolation. This is clearly in God's answer to Habakkuk's complaint: "I am raising up the Babylonians, that ruthless and impetuous people, who sweep across the whole earth to seize dwelling places not their own" (Habakkuk 1:6, *NIV*).

The Babylonians launched three major invasions over an 18-year period. When Judah's King Zedekiah rebelled against Babylon, Nebuchadnezzar lay siege to Jerusalem in January 587 B.C. until July 586 B.C. Famine finally caused the city to break as the army attempted to flee. Zedekiah's rebellion resulted in extremely cruel personal punishment. His sons were killed before him. Then his eyes were poked out and in chains he was taken prisoner to Babylon (2 Kings 25:7). Many people of all ages in the city were killed. Then the city itself was ruthlessly destroyed as the invaders dismantled Solomon's temple block-by-block for the precious metals. The walls of the city were dismantled, private homes as well as public buildings were razed to the ground, and 60 officers of the city and Temple were executed.

This final picture of devastation graphically reminds us that God fulfills His word. His mercy and love extend far beyond the boundaries of what could be expected. But there comes a point where His justice and judgment become a reality. One can only wonder what the people who survived were thinking as the events unfolded.

C. The Exile (vv. 20, 21)

20. And them that had escaped from the sword carried he away to Babylon; where they were servants to him and his sons until the reign of the kingdom of Persia:

21. To fulfil the word of the Lord by the mouth of Jeremiah, until the land had enjoyed her sabbaths: for as long as she lay desolate she kept sabbath, to fulfil threescore and ten years.

A small group from Jerusalem were taken into exile to serve the royal family. Jeremiah records the number of the captives to be 832 (52:29). For the next 50 years these individuals and their descendants became the servants of Nebuchadnezzar and his sons.

Second Chronicles 36:21 speaks of two separate issues. First is the length of the Captivity. It continued for 70 years (606-536 B.C.), exactly as prophesied by Jeremiah (25:12). "For thus saith the Lord, That after seventy years be accomplished at Babylon I will visit you, and perform my good word toward you, in causing you to return to this place" (29:10). The 70 years date from Nebuchadnezzar's first invasion of Judah to the first return of captives from Babylon under the leadership of Zerubbabel.

The second issue included here is the apparent failure to observe the sabbatical year during the latter years of Judah's independence. During the seventh year the land was not to be seeded or cultivated, and the people would live on the abundance of the sixth year's harvest. This demonstrated their dependence and faith in God's provision. However, due to their failure, God would allow the land to rest for a period of 70 sabbatical years—the time of captivity.

II. PROMISE OF RESTORATION
(Jeremiah 29:10-14; Ezra 1:1-4)

A. The Promise (Jeremiah 29:10-14)

(Jeremiah 29:10-14 is not included in the printed text.)

These verses are an excerpt from a letter Jeremiah sent to the people who were in Babylonian exile (see v. 1). False prophets with false information were circulating among the people stating that the Exile would be short-lived. In view of that, nothing permanent should be attempted in their current location.

Attempting to correct this error, Jeremiah encouraged the people to live normally—settle down with homes and gardens, marry and have children, work for the peace and prosperity of their towns (vv. 4-9).

Then, beginning with verse 10, the prophet indicated the exact length of the Captivity. No one would be going home until 70 years had passed.

In verse 11 the word of the Lord declared His planning for the future. Just as He desired peace and prosperity for the Jews in the past, the same held true in the future. They were still His chosen people in spite of their sins. Blessings were part of the plan for them. However, this continued to be a two-way street. The promise depended on their sincere seeking of Him. Only when they avidly sought God with the fullness of their innermost being could they expect Him to restore them from captivity (vv. 13, 14).

The promise of restoration from captivity did not depend on political connections and bearing arms. God himself would accomplish it. All the people needed to do was be found in fellowship with Him. The physical location and national barriers would pose no problem in this restoration. Just as God allowed them to be exiled, so He would enable them to return.

In recent decades, some groups have taken verse 11 out of context and made it a promise for physical safety and material prosperity now. True, God still does bless His people. But just because we are spiritually in close fellowship with God and seeking to serve Him doesn't guarantee we will not suffer physical harm or live with less than an abundance of material goods. Besides, these verses were given to a select group of people at a precise location for a particular time.

B. The Fulfillment (Ezra 1:1-4)

(Ezra 1:4 is not included in the printed text.)

1. Now in the first year of Cyrus king of Persia, that the word of the Lord by the mouth of Jeremiah might be fulfilled, the Lord stirred up the spirit of Cyrus king of Persia, that he made a proclamation throughout all his kingdom, and put it also in writing, saying,

2. Thus saith Cyrus king of Persia, The Lord God of heaven hath given me all the kingdoms of the earth; and he hath charged me to build him an house at Jerusalem, which is in Judah.

3. Who is there among you of all his people? his God be with him, and let him go up to Jerusalem, which is in Judah, and build the house of the Lord God of Israel, (he is the God,) which is in Jerusalem.

Cyrus became the king of the Medes and Persians in 557 B.C. Ezra 1:1 refers to his first year of ruling in Babylon. This dates the decree in 538 or 537 B.C. Thus, the 70 years of predicted captivity were drawing to a close. The releasing of captives and providing them financial support was an unusual procedure for an Oriental ruler. Yet, here we are again reminded of God's sovereignty and His involvement in human history.

Exactly as prophesied by Isaiah nearly 200 years before these events, Cyrus made a formal proclamation which provided for captives to return to Jerusalem and for the rebuilding of the Temple. How did this come about? The Persians were mainly Zoroastrian, worshiping a god called Ormazd. Was Cyrus personally committed to a monotheistic religion? There's no way to know. How was he influenced? Josephus, the first-century Jewish historian, suggests some Jew showed Cyrus the passages in Isaiah (44:28; 45:1-3) and he then chose to fulfill the divine will.

It becomes easy to speculate on these possibilities and, in the process, overlook the specifics of Scripture. The key aspect we must focus on is God's taking the initiative to fulfill His will exactly as previously stated. He can and does work in the hearts of individuals who do not know Him in a personal relationship. The Lord's stirring up the spirit of Cyrus is the experience of the Holy Spirit constraining an individual toward a particular viewpoint and action.

Cyrus recognized that God Jehovah not only had given him this extensive kingdom but wanted His house to be built in Jerusalem (Ezra 1:2). The means of this knowledge remains unknown to us. And even if we had that information, it would not change the narrative.

The building of the Temple in Jerusalem demanded a call for volunteers to return to Palestine. No coercion or lottery was used to guarantee a suitable number of people were available; it was strictly voluntary. To support the rebuilding effort, Cyrus instituted a tax that the returning Jews did not have to pay. Some scholars believe no Jews had to pay this tax. Regardless, the king made financial provision. These funds, along with freewill offerings, were given to help the emigrants in their huge task (v. 4). And, as is noted in later verses, Cyrus gave all the vessels of Solomon's temple for furnishing the new structure.

III. RESTORATION BRINGS CHANGE (Ezra 1:5-11; 2:68—3:13)

A. The Preparation (1:5-11)

(Ezra 1:6-11 is not included in the printed text.)

5. Then rose up the chief of the fathers of Judah and Benjamin, and the priests, and the Levites, with all them whose spirit God had raised, to go up to build the house of the Lord which is in Jerusalem.

God's preparation for the restoration included dealing with the hearts of His people. Unless there were people willing to accept the opportunity being offered, nothing would be accomplished. In the natural sense, return to Jerusalem wasn't a wonderful change. They would be leaving a comfortable setting in a foreign land to travel to a city that was in a state of destruction. However, God's Spirit inspired the leadership to desire to fulfill this chance to rebuild their Temple. And in doing so, they would return to their homeland.

Those individuals not making the trip generously provided the necessary items (v. 6). Willingly they gave of precious metals, goods and animals. The group leaving for Jerusalem would have everything needed for the task at hand.

Cyrus' policy after conquering Babylon was to restore all of the images/gods to their original shrines. Belshazzar, the previous co-regent of Babylon, had taken the gods from other cities and relocated them in the capital city of Babylon hoping they would overcome the power of the advancing armies of Cyrus. This return policy endeared Cyrus to the cities and people receiving their idols.

In the case of the Israelites, there were no images for return. Instead, Cyrus made a gift to the Jews of all the sacred vessels which had been taken decades earlier from Solomon's temple. Verse 11 records the total number of all the various types to be 5,400. Just imagine the weight and space needed for transportation!

Through the moving of the Spirit in their hearts, nearly 50,000 Jews chose to return to Palestine for the purpose of rebuilding the Temple. (The exact total is 49,697—see 2:64, 65). Since no census of Jews in Babylon at that point in time was available, one can only speculate at the percentage of Jews returning to the homeland. Most scholars assume it was a relatively small group in comparison to the total Jewish population.

B. The Rebuilding (2:68—3:13)

(Ezra 2:68-70; 3:4-13 is not included in the printed text.)

3:1. And when the seventh month was come, and the children of Israel were in the cities, the people gathered themselves together as one man to Jerusalem.

2. Then stood up Jeshua the son of Jozadak, and his brethren the priests, and Zerubbabel the son of Shealtiel, and his brethren, and builded the altar of the God of Israel, to offer burnt-offerings thereon, as it is written in the law of Moses the man of God.

3. And they set the altar upon his bases; for fear was upon them because of the people of those countries: and they offered burnt-offerings thereon unto the Lord, even burnt-offerings morning and evening.

Upon arriving in Jerusalem, the heads of the families immediately gave a generous freewill offering to the Temple treasury (2:68, 69). (It appears that some of the Jews had prospered financially while in captivity.) After that, they dispersed and settled in the various cities of the land. More than likely they returned to the home cities of their families.

Notice the priority that existed; they restored worship prior to building the house of God (3:1-6). Relationship definitely stood above a dwelling place. Besides, God alone could provide protection from neighboring peoples who did not want to see any restoration of Jerusalem. Though it occurred many decades later, the opposition given to Nehemiah's rebuilding of the walls spoke of the attitudes toward the Jews and their sacred city.

Note the leadership God provided (vv. 8, 9). Zerubbabel gave the civil leadership and Jeshua the spiritual leadership. Working together they led the people. About 18 months after leaving Babylon, the foundation of the Temple was laid. Verse 11 records how the people rejoiced and offered praise for the Lord's goodness. However, the next two verses indicate weeping by many of the older men, so that the sounds of joy and weeping were intermingled. Maybe they wept in a spirit of gladness for God's beginning to restore their heritage. Or, they could have wept in sorrow knowing it was sin that brought the captivity and destruction. The past can't always be completely forgotten in the joy of the present.

What a change occurred in a relatively short period of time! A king allowed captive people to return home and helped finance the trip. Nearly 50,000 people traveled 600 miles over a four-month period to return to their homeland. The foundation of a new Temple stood completed, ready for further construction.

GOLDEN TEXT HOMILY

"YE SHALL SEEK ME, AND FIND ME, WHEN YE SHALL SEARCH FOR ME WITH ALL YOUR HEART" (Jeremiah 29:13).

The Hebrews were in captivity in a foreign land, Babylon. Some among them had aroused false hopes of returning soon to Jerusalem. Jeremiah urged them to patience and to prayer. Through prayer God could be found "by the rivers of Babylon" (see Psalm 137). God said, "I will listen to you . . . when you seek me with all your heart" (Jeremiah 29:12, 13, NIV). Prayer here is more than words; it is the whole heart reaching out to God.

Prayer has been defined as talking to God. All petitions and supplications directed to heaven do not qualify as prayer. They may seem to be ardent enough and framed in the proper words, but rise no higher than the ceiling. Unless commitment is present, words addressed to God are not real prayer.

Real prayer assumes commitment to Christ and the gospel. When full commitment undergirds prayer, our hearts reach out to God and our souls are poured out to give clarity to the real desires of the heart. Should that be, the apostle Paul assures us that "the Spirit helps us in our weakness; for we do not know how to pray as we ought, but the Spirit himself intercedes for us with sighs too deep for words. And He who searches the hearts of men knows what is the mind of the Spirit, because the Spirit intercedes for the saints according to the will of God" (Romans 8:26, 27, free translation).—**French L. Arrington**

SENTENCE SERMONS

GOD WILL FORGIVE AND RESTORE those who return to Him.
—Selected

NO ONE IS HOPELESS whose hope is in God.
—Selected

REPENTANCE does not mean remorse. It means giving up sin.
—W.E. Biederwolf

BEFORE GOD can deliver us, we must undeceive ourselves.
—Augustine

EVANGELISM APPLICATION

GOD WILL FORGIVE AND SAVE THOSE WHO TURN TO HIM REPENTING.

"But my sins are so many and so awful! It has been my lifestyle for years. God couldn't love me after all I have done!"

Yes, He can and does.

Though God hates sin and punishes it, He loves sinners. He eagerly awaits their turning to Him so Christ's blood shed on the cross of Calvary can cover them. He sends the Holy Spirit to draw them to Himself. No one who repents of their sins, no matter how many or how awful, will be turned away from the heavenly Father.

ILLUMINATING THE LESSON

"When Crowfoot, the great chief of the Blackfoot confederacy in southern Alberta, gave the Canadian Pacific Railroad permission to cross the Blackfoot land from Medicine Hat to Calgary, he was given in return a lifetime railroad pass. Crowfoot put it in a leather case and carried it around his neck for the rest of his life. There is no record, however, that he ever availed himself of the right to travel anywhere on CPR trains.

"The promises of God are often treated in this way by Christians."—**Michael P. Green, *Illustrations for Biblical Preaching***

DAILY BIBLE READINGS

M.	God Restores Joy.
	Psalm 30:1-12
T.	A Rebellious Nation.
	Isaiah 1:2-9
W.	Restoration Promised.
	Isaiah 43:1-7
T.	Sins Forgiven.
	Acts 3:19-26
F.	A New Creature.
	2 Corinthians 5:17-21
S.	Great and Precious Promises.
	2 Peter 1:2-11

TRUTH SEARCH
Creatively Teaching the Word

DISCUSSION QUESTIONS
Desolation and Bondage
(2 Chronicles 36:15-21)

1. How had God tried to convince His people to return to Him, and why (v. 15)?

2. In what ways had the people responded (v. 16)?

3. How did the people finally pay for their rebellion (vv. 17, 20, 21)?

4. What happened to the Temple, and why was this significant (vv. 18, 19)?

Promise of Restoration
(Ezra 1:1-4; Jeremiah 29:10-14)

1. Seven decades after the Jews were taken into captivity, how did God's Spirit move in the heart of Persia's king (Ezra 1:1, 2)?

2. What decrees did Cyrus make regarding Jerusalem (vv. 3, 4)?

3. Before the Captivity, what had Jeremiah prophesied (Jeremiah 29:10, 14)?

4. What plans did the Lord have for His people (v. 11)?

5. How would the people find God (vv. 12, 13)?

Restoration Brings Change
(Ezra 1:5-11; 2:68—3:13)

1. What motivated people to return to Jerusalem and rebuild, and in what ways did others help them (Ezra 1:5, 6)?

2. How did the Lord again work through the king of Persia to accomplish His purposes (vv. 7-11)?

3. What significant events took place in 2:68-70?

4. What did the returning exiles do despite their fears (3:1-3)?

5. What had not yet happened, and how did this affect the people's worship (vv. 4-6)?

6. What was the cause of great celebration (vv. 7-13)?

7. Why did some of the older Jews weep?

OBJECT LESSON

Items needed: Inexpensive ceramic figurine and a hammer

Display the figurine.

Let this nice, complete figurine remind us of the people of Israel. They had it all! They were living in the wonderful land God had promised them, and He had driven out their enemies so they could live in peace. He gave them His laws and a magnificent place of worship so they could serve Him.

However, the people slowly began moving away from God, drawn by materialism and false religions. Pick up the hammer. **Year after year, God sent prophet after prophet to warn His people that they would be judged and punished if they continued rebelling. But they would not listen. So the Lord had to act.**

Bust the ceramic with the hammer. **The people and their land were so devastated that only God would be able to restore them. He finally did, but it was a long, hard process.**

The Lord still brings judgment on His people today in an effort to turn their hearts toward Him. Let's act wisely, letting Him make and remake us without fighting against His plan.

Overcoming Opposition

Study Text: Ezra 4:1 through 6:22
Objective: To realize we may face opposition in doing good and believe God for success.
Time: 535-516 B.C.
Place: Judah
Golden Text: "Deliver me from mine enemies, O my God: defend me from them that rise up against me" (Psalm 59:1).
Central Truth: God empowers His servants to overcome opposition.
Evangelism Emphasis: God empowers His servants to witness to the lost.

PRINTED TEXT

Ezra 4:1. Now when the adversaries of Judah and Benjamin heard that the children of the captivity builded the temple unto the Lord God of Israel;

2. Then they came to Zerubbabel, and to the chief of the fathers, and said unto them, Let us build with you: for we seek your God, as ye do; and we do sacrifice unto him since the days of Esarhaddon king of Assur, which brought us up hither.

3. But Zerubbabel, and Jeshua, and the rest of the chief of the fathers of Israel, said unto them, Ye have nothing to do with us to build an house unto our God; but we ourselves together will build unto the Lord God of Israel, as king Cyrus the king of Persia hath commanded us.

4. Then the people of the land weakened the hands of the people of Judah, and troubled them in building.

5:1. Then the prophets, Haggai the prophet, and Zechariah the son of Iddo, prophesied unto the Jews that were in Judah and Jerusalem in the name of the God of Israel, even unto them.

5. But the eye of their God was upon the elders of the Jews, that they could not cause them to cease, till the matter came to Darius: and then they returned answer by letter concerning this matter.

6:3. In the first year of Cyrus the king the same Cyrus the king made a decree concerning the house of God at Jerusalem, Let the house be builded, the place where they offered sacrifices, and let the foundations thereof be strongly laid; the height thereof threescore cubits, and the breadth thereof threescore cubits;

7. Let the work of this house of God alone; let the governor of the Jews and the elders of the Jews build this house of God in his place.

14. And the elders of the Jews builded, and they prospered through the prophesying of Haggai the prophet and Zechariah the son of Iddo. And they builded, and finished it, according to the commandment of the God of Israel, and according to the commandment of Cyrus, and Darius, and Artaxerxes king of Persia.

15. And this house was finished on the third day of the month Adar, which was in the sixth year of the reign of Darius the king.

16. And the children of Israel, the priests, and the Levites, and the rest of the children of the captivity, kept the dedication of this house of God with joy.

DICTIONARY

Zerubbabel (zeh-RUB-uh-bel)—Ezra 4:2—When the Jews were allowed to return home from exile, Zerubbabel was appointed governor by King Cyrus of Persia.

Esar-haddon (EE-sar-HAD-uhn)—Ezra 4:2—king of Assyria (Assur) from 681 to 669 B.C.

Jeshua (JESH-you-uh)—Ezra 4:3—high priest who helped to rebuild the altar and the house of God

Artaxerxes (ar-tuh-ZERK-seez)—Ezra 6:14—Persian king who opposed the liberal policies of Cyrus and thus prohibited the Jews from building the Temple; his reign lasted only seven months.

Darius (duh-RYE-us)—Ezra 5:5—the Persian king who allowed the restoration of Jerusalem's walls and its Temple to be completed

---

LESSON OUTLINE

I. FACING OPPOSITION

    A. Necessary Separation

    B. False Charges

    C. Work Stoppage

II. GOD'S INTERVENTION

    A. Prophetic Direction

    B. Opposition's Inquiry

    C. Official Sanction

III. VICTORIOUS CELEBRATION

    A. Temple Completed

    B. Temple Dedicated

LESSON EXPOSITION

INTRODUCTION

How quickly victory can turn into defeat! How quickly the sounds of progress can be replaced with the silence of inactivity! How quickly following God's will can be redefined into doing for self!

All of this will be seen in today's lesson. Opposition was allowed to sidetrack the Jews from rebuilding the Temple. The length of this delay wasn't a few weeks or months. Rather, for 15 years the people who through divine provision were returned to their homeland for the express purpose of building God's house chose to allow their enemies to hinder the purpose of God.

This lesson should be a strong reminder that whenever we attempt to do great things for God, there will be both detractors and bitter opponents. Detractors will mock our efforts and possibly make progress more difficult. They are like irritating mosquitoes who inflict no harm greater than discomfort and minor frustrations.

Opponents are a different story. They work to create roadblocks that hinder progress or totally stop it. The opponents of the Jews returning from exile were ready to do whatever was necessary to stop this building project.

Know that opposition to God's will on earth will always arise from the forces of Satan. The challenge facing believers continues to be one of choice. Will we back off from the forces that try to stop us? Will we edge slowly in the direction we are being pushed? Or will we stand firm, waiting for God's intervention so we can faithfully move forward?

When Moses and the Hebrews fled from Egypt after the last plague, they suddenly found themselves trapped—Red Sea in front, mountain ranges on either side, and Pharaoh's army behind them. Then came Moses' directions of faith: "Fear ye not, stand still, and see the salvation of the Lord, which he will shew to you to day: for the Egyptians whom ye have seen to day, ye shall see them again no more for ever. The Lord shall fight for you, and ye shall hold your peace" (Exodus 14:13, 14).

I. FACING OPPOSITION
(Ezra 4:1-24)

A. Necessary Separation (vv. 1-3)

1. Now when the adversaries of Judah and Benjamin heard that the children of the captivity builded the temple unto the Lord God of Israel;

2. Then they came to Zerubbabel, and to the chief of the fathers, and said unto them, Let us build with you: for we seek your God, as ye do; and we do sacrifice unto him since the days of Esarhaddon king of Assur, which brought us up hither.

3. But Zerubbabel, and Jeshua, and the rest of the chief of the fathers of Israel, said unto them, Ye have nothing to do with us to build an house unto our God; but we ourselves together will build unto the Lord God of Israel, as king Cyrus the king of Persia hath commanded us.

When success becomes evident, it is amazing who may want to join us. This happens in religious circles as well as business. When people flock to a religious phenomenon, discernment needs to be evident. Otherwise, we can open the door to Satan himself.

When Zerubbabel and the returning Jews began rebuilding the Temple, their adversaries came under the guise of seeking the same God and asked to help with the building project. Their reference to Esarhaddon indicates them to be Samaritans— people who followed a mixture of religious practices, combining elements of Judaism and idolatry.

At this point Zerubbabel and Jeshua, the civil and spiritual leaders, made a crucial decision. They chose to

unmask these apparent brothers for who they really were. Yes, there were some similarities in their form of worship. They used some of the same words and concepts. But they were not true worshipers of the Lord God of Israel. For that reason these wise leaders of the Jews rejected their help. Instead, the Jews alone would build the house of God as directed by King Cyrus.

Does God ever lead unbelievers to give assistance to believers and their projects? Yes, He does. Cyrus stands as an excellent example. Also, many contemporary stories can be found of unbelievers donating labor, land, buildings and money to help churches and Christian organizations fulfill their mission. However, the desire to help, coupled with charitable deeds, doesn't make unbelievers brothers and sisters in Christ! Nor does it qualify them for responsibilities and positions in the body of Christ.

The current rise of pluralism with its push for accepting everyone's beliefs and actions as being equally true must not be allowed within the church. There is only one Savior, one way and one truth—Jesus Christ as revealed through the Bible. This distinction must not be blurred. Doctrinal truth and relationship with God are priorities.

B. False Charges (vv. 4-22)

(Ezra 4:5-22 is not included in the printed text)

4. Then the people of the land weakened the hands of the people of Judah, and troubled them in building.

In just a few words verse 4 sums up the events which follow. The true colors of those previously offering help and identifying themselves as one in faith quickly came to light. After being rejected, their efforts turned toward stopping the project. Their serious intent can be seen by the willingness to hire professionals who could influence the royal court in their favor. Verse 5 indicates their efforts continued over a period of time—"all the days of Cyrus . . . even until the reign of Darius." The Samaritans were serious in attempting to keep Jerusalem and its inhabitants oppressed.

When unbelievers seek their own will, truth quickly gets put to the side. Babylon was 600 miles from Jerusalem. It's doubtful that a royal representative would be sent to check on the truth of the situation. Without hesitation, their enemies stated that the Jews were rebuilding the walls of the city (vv. 12, 13). Then, to color this lie with the possibility of rebellion, they referred to Jerusalem's history (v. 15). Had this city not possessed a history of rebellion against its ruling king which in turn necessitated its previous destruction? This was true. Jerusalem had rebelled against King Nebuchadnezzar, but that happened more than half a century before.

Without checking all the facts, the letter from the Samaritans was accepted at face value. The king ordered that all work on the city cease and that the Samaritans look out after their interests by causing their will to be accomplished (vv. 21, 22).

C. Work Stoppage (vv. 23, 24)

(Ezra 4:23, 24 is not included in the printed text.)

With the king's letter in hand and what appears to have been an armed force, the Samaritans went to Jerusalem and forced the Jews to stop building on the Temple. Apparently without protest the people stopped their labors. How could that be? After such unbelievable events brought them back to Jerusalem, it is hard to understand their willingness to quit so easily. They had the irrevocable decree of Cyrus on their side. Why didn't they invoke it and continue their right to build?

We can only suggest some possibilities. First, it appears their initial enthusiasm had worn off. Once the foundation of the Temple was laid and the celebration ended, the hard aspects of day-to-day living took over. More than likely, the people were "camping out" due to the lack of permanent homes.

Second, once they were confronted with this opposition, they seemed to make assumptions that favored their interests rather than God's will. We see this in Haggai's message written some 15 years after the building stopped: "This people say, The time is not come, the time that the Lord's house should be built" (1:2). So the people then turned their efforts to building personal residences. Hear God's rebuke: "Is it time for you, O ye, to dwell in your cieled [paneled] houses, and this house lie waste?" (v. 4).

II. GOD'S INTERVENTION
(Ezra 5:1-17; 6:1-12)

A. Prophetic Direction (5:1-5)

(Ezra 5:2-4 is not included in the printed text.)

1. Then the prophets, Haggai the prophet, and Zechariah the son of Iddo, prophesied unto the Jews that were in Judah and Jerusalem in the name of the God of Israel, even unto them.

5. But the eye of their God was upon the elders of the Jews, that they could not cause them to cease, till the matter came to Darius: and then they returned answer by letter concerning this matter.

In his own time frame God chose to send two prophets, Haggai and Zechariah, to stimulate the Jews back to their original project. For 15 years the building of the Temple remained idle. Then these two fiery prophets of the Lord burst on the scene. Their accusations against the people and their leaders focused on their faithlessness. Haggai specifically called them to consider the recent events: "Ye have sown much, and bring in little; ye eat, but ye have not enough; ye drink, but ye are not filled with drink; ye clothe you, but there is none warm; and he that earneth wages earneth wages to put it into a bag with holes" (Haggai 1:6). Spiritual blindness kept them from recognizing the drought and crop failures as God's calling them back to the building of His house (vv. 9-11).

To the credit of the leaders and the people was their response to the prophetic messages. Stirred by their words, the project commenced again in 520 B.C. Even when opposition arose to question their authority to build, the work continued. Tatnai (TAT-nigh), governor of the province which included Palestine, came to Jerusalem and asked for the names of the key people in the project. More than likely he intended to incriminate in his correspondence. Undaunted, the Jews maintained their construction activities.

Verse 5 of the text speaks of a special care God gave to His now obedient servants. Where in the past they were persuaded to stop, now they kept on working during the exchange of correspondence. It's amazing what obstacles and hindrances can be overcome when choosing to follow God's will in a particular situation. When there are failures it is not due to God's inability to protect and deliver. It always comes down to our commitment to be people of faith in the face of difficulty!

B. Opposition's Inquiry (vv. 6-17)

(Ezra 5:6-17 is not included in the printed text.)

It is easy to bypass these verses of chapter 5 in our haste to follow the major parts of the story; however, in doing so, one misses how God can use an opposer for the good of His people. Here a copy of the governor's letter to King Darius is included. Notice how

Tatnai carefully included all the details pertinent to the circumstances.

The governor began with noting he had personally visited Jerusalem and was an eyewitness to the events taking place. He referred to the Temple as "the house of the great God" (v. 8). Maybe he knew of some of the exploits of Jehovah in the past. Next he gave a brief description of the progress. Giant stones and wooden timbers were being erected at a fast pace. Through their diligent efforts the construction was progressing rapidly.

In verses 9 and 10 he described their interrogation to secure the needed information. The key question was, "Who authorized you to rebuild this temple?" (NIV). They then asked for the Jewish leaders' names.

The majority of the letter contains the Jews' response. It didn't become necessary for them to send a separate letter. Their account went to King Darius via the governor's letter. Notice how they identified themselves in verse 11, "the servants of the God of heaven and earth." They mentioned their ties to the "great king," Solomon, who first built the house of God. However, due to their disobedience of God, He allowed King Nebuchadnezzar and the Babylonians to not only destroy the Temple but also take many into exile.

Then in great detail, yet with brevity, they listed the events that led to their construction work. King Cyrus in his first year in Babylon made the official decree to build God's house. They pointed out how the original vessels from the first Temple had been returned to the Jews (by Cyrus' order) for the purpose of taking them to Jerusalem. Once the Temple was rebuilt, they were to be placed therein. It was also by Cyrus' order that Sheshbazzar (also known as Zerubbabel) received the title of governor. And under his leadership the initial foundations were laid.

Tatnai then requested King Darius to search the official records to determine whether or not a decree to rebuild the Temple existed. The "treasure house" (v. 17) served as an official depository of royal decrees as well as royal monies. Many years had passed. Would a true search be made? Or would the request be seen as inconsequential to the overall operation of the empire?

C. Official Sanction (6:1-12)

(Ezra 6:1, 2, 4-6, 8-12 is not included in the printed text.)

3. In the first year of Cyrus the king the same Cyrus the king made a decree concerning the house of God at Jerusalem, Let the house be builded, the place where they offered sacrifices, and let the foundations thereof be strongly laid; the height thereof threescore cubits, and the breadth thereof threescore cubits;
7. Let the work of this house of God alone; let the governor of the Jews and the elders of the Jews build this house of God in his place.

God never fails in His promises. His word is fulfilled as long as His people are faithful and complete their responsibilities. So it is no surprise that a search of the treasury documents was made.

It is doubtful that Tatnai expected such a document to be found. There were four separate cities used as the capital by the Median-Persian kings. Each depository might need to be searched. Would sufficient effort be exerted, if the decree were not found initially? But that's what took place. Eventually the officials at Achmetha, the usual summer residence, found the decree of Cyrus just as claimed by the Jews (v. 2). More than likely this would not have been the first location searched. But once again God's providence stands forth.

The official decree is slightly different from that recorded in chapter 1. That one seems to be the popular or common version delivered to the people. This one would be the official version and contained precise language even to the inclusion of dimensions and some of the design. It also identified the vessels of the Temple as being those taken by Nebuchadnezzar and brought to Babylon (vv. 3-5).

Upon seeing the decree, King Darius replied to his governor's inquiry. It began with a warning to Tatnai and other rulers in neighboring provinces. They were to keep their distance from the building project and not interfere in any way (vv. 6, 7). The Jews were to be left alone to continue the building. However, Darius did not stop with the prohibitions. He followed with some positive directions. These civil leaders were to help the Jews in whatever way needed. If money for construction was needed, tax monies normally sent to the emperor should be directed to them. They were to be given any animals and other supplies needed for sacrifices to God (vv. 8-10).

Darius concluded his decree with a somber warning. Anyone who stood in the way of any of these directives should be hanged using timbers from his own home as the hanging platform. Also, his home should become a pile of rubble (v. 11). The king concluded, "Let it be carried out with diligence" (v. 12, NIV).

III. VICTORIOUS CELEBRATION (Ezra 6:13-22)

A. Temple Completed (vv. 13-15)

(Ezra 6:13 is not included in the printed text.)

14. And the elders of the Jews builded, and they prospered through the prophesying of Haggai the prophet and Zechariah the son of Iddo. And they builded, and finished it, according to the commandment of

the God of Israel, and according to the commandment of Cyrus, and Darius, and Artaxerxes king of Persia.

15. And this house was finished on the third day of the month Adar, which was in the sixth year of the reign of Darius the king.

Once the construction project resumed, they completed it within four years (520-516 B.C.). This may seem rather lengthy; however, the original construction (Solomon's temple) took more than seven years (1 Kings 6:38). No doubt the cooperation of Tatnai and other area governors greatly assisted. They followed Darius' directive of speedily making all the necessary provisions available (Ezra 6:13).

Verse 14 provides a summary of events. With the elders of the Jews taking the lead, they continued the building project until its completion. This time there were no stoppages. Once they obediently did the work of God, He removed the hindrances of drought and crop failure. They experienced a material prosperity as they heard and followed the prophetic messages of Haggai and Zechariah. Today we still need prophets who boldly declare the word of God regardless of how people respond. We need prophets who speak what God wants the people to hear. And God doesn't limit Himself to truth being spoken by males. He uses women in spiritual gifts without consideration of gender.

Notice how the people fulfilled the directions of both God and the human ruler. True, Cyrus was the instrument of God, but he held the earthly position of authority. As individuals under his sovereign rule and benefactors of his kindness, the Jews had an obligation to complete the work as directed by him. Much more important was the responsibility of fulfilling the commands of their sovereign God!

Verse 15 provides a chronological time marker. This reminds us that Biblical history correlates with secular history, reinforcing the correctness of the Scriptures. We do not read and abide by a sacred book that covers only the spiritual dimension of life.

B. Temple Dedicated (vv. 16-22)

(Ezra 6:17-22 is not included in the printed text.)

16. And the children of Israel, the priests, and the Levites, and the rest of the children of the captivity, kept the dedication of this house of God with joy.

Once again, there was a house of God for the Jews to offer their worship through sacrifice. Seventy years had passed since the forces of Nebuchadnezzar had razed the Temple. Generations had been born without the privilege of going to the house of God. Even though the sins of rebellion and God's judgment were history, they were to be remembered. God's chastisement was not intended just for the immediate but hopefully would serve as a deterrent in the future.

This short description of the second Temple definitely speaks of a much smaller celebration than that of the first Temple constructed by Solomon. Then Israel stood as a powerful nation basking in the glory of Solomon's splendid rule. The coffers of Israel's treasury continually received the tribute of subdued neighboring nations and the profits of many trade agreements. Thousands of animals were sacrificed and offered to the Lord (1 Kings 8:5, 62-64). This time the scenario differed greatly. There was no longer a free Israel. Palestine was under the power of the Medo-Persian Empire. It did not even qualify as an individual province. The capital city of Jerusalem no longer stood with beauty but now showed the scars of destruction and the feeble attempts at reconstruction. No city wall existed for protection.

In spite of the previous description, this dedication still was a day for rejoicing. God's word of restoration of His people could be seen. Miraculously God had moved civil leaders to do the unusual so the house of God could be built. Another Temple stood on the original site. Rejoicing needed to be the order of the day.

Carefully the celebration followed the order which provided for a spiritual relationship with God and the continuing pattern of worship. Notice how these Jews still perceived themselves as 12 tribes. They did not speak of the 10 lost tribes as a result of the Assyrian conquest which destroyed the northern kingdom in 722 B.C. Israel as a complete nation stood in their perception.

Four distinctive worship elements were enacted: (1) The priests offered a sin offering for all Israel (v. 17). (2) They reestablished the rotation structure so all priests would serve a turn ministering in the Temple (v. 18). (3) They celebrated the Passover, which once again reminded them of God's deliverance of their forefathers from Egyptian bondage (v. 19). (4) As a people they dedicated themselves to the purity of holiness of seeking their Lord God (vv. 20-22).

All the splendor of the first dedication was not there. However, notice what did shine through. Here was a people now committed to holy living and obediently following God's law. Could there be any greater occasion?

True, descendants of these people would fail miserably in the future. They would experience the pain and desolation of God's judgment. But that would take place in the future and would not be the fault of these people! Now they could celebrate. God had done marvelous feats before their eyes. They were in harmony with the Lord their God!

GOLDEN TEXT HOMILY

"DELIVER ME FROM MINE ENEMIES, O MY GOD: DEFEND ME FROM THEM THAT RISE UP AGAINST ME" (Psalm 59:1).

The Psalms uniquely enrich our lives by the experience of relating to God as did David, Moses, Solomon, Asaph and other Psalm writers. We identify with their fears, joys and triumphs and find in them models for personal praise and prayer. Indeed, John Calvin called the Psalms "an anatomy of all parts of the soul; for no one will find in himself a single feeling of which the image is not reflected in this mirror."

Perhaps no single scripture in the Psalms is more descriptive of our claim to make an existing prayer our prayer than is Psalm 59:1. David cries out as one who is persecuted and innocent. His cry is with confidence, for his prayer is to "my God"—the One who is able to deliver him.

It is clear that God had come to the rescue of the psalmist before, so his confidence is high. In Psalm 18, David reflects on a time of God's deliverance. "He delivered me from my strong enemy, and from them which hated me; for they were too strong for me" (v. 17).

Sometimes our cry is for deliverance, but it might of necessity come through a defense. "Defend me from them that rise up against me." Ezra faced opposition in his effort to rebuild the Temple; but with God's intervention and a confirmation of the original decree to rebuild, a defense was honored and the work was completed and a dedication celebrated.

While King David faced bloodthirsty enemies determined to destroy him, we face spiritual opposition trying to hinder our efforts to do service for God or to draw near to Him in fellowship. The psalmist certainly expressed a deep need for the Lord's presence when he wrote, "As the hart panteth after the water brooks, so panteth my soul after thee, O God" (42:1).

While we are certain to be opposed by the enemies of our souls, we are assured of God's help to deliver and defend us against our enemies. "The [uncompromisingly] righteous shall flourish like the palm tree . . . they shall grow like a cedar in Lebanon. . . . They shall still bring forth fruit in old age; they shall be full of sap [of spiritual vitality] and [rich in the] verdure [of trust, love, and contentment]" (92:12, 14, *Amp.*).—**James E. Humbertson**

SENTENCE SERMONS

GOD EMPOWERS His servants to overcome opposition.

—Selected

WE LOOK UPON the enemy of our souls as a conquered foe, so he is, but only to God, not to us.

—Oswald Chambers

NEXT TO A HAPPY FAMILY and a few good friends, the best human gift that God can give to any man is a worthy adversary.

—*Quotable Quotations*

VICTORY IS GAINED only through conflict.

—Selected

EVANGELISM APPLICATION

GOD EMPOWERS HIS SERVANTS TO WITNESS TO THE LOST.

Usually, when speaking of God's empowering us for witnessing, the emphasis is on the ministry of the Holy Spirit through us. We think of Christ's final words promising power for witnessing once the Holy Spirit comes upon us (Acts 1:8). And our interpretation focuses on speaking the truths of God and giving our testimonies. All this definitely should be happening.

But what about witnessing through our lifestyle? God's Spirit empowers us to demonstrate peace in times of crisis and calmness in the face of the unknown. The fruit of the Spirit is a vital part of our witness to individuals who have never accepted Christ. Our lives should loudly proclaim the difference Christ's presence makes.

ILLUMINATING THE LESSON

In his book *Games Church Bosses Play*, Carl R. Hobbs includes a folklore story from the Vietnam War concerning a detachment of marines who were surrounded and cut off from reinforcements. "The battle was fierce and sometimes hand to hand. Wave after wave of the North Vietnamese forces were driven back only to charge again with renewed energy and determination.

"When the marines realized they might not survive the next attack, they decided to die laughing. When the next wave of Vietcong hit their line, they all broke into loud laughter. It so demoralized the enemy that they retreated in confusion and did not launch another attack!" (p. 105).

DAILY BIBLE READINGS

M. God Gives Victory.
   Joshua 21:43-45
T. God Is a Stronghold.
   Psalm 9:1-10
W. God Will Rescue.
   Psalm 55:16-23
T. Overcoming Through Love.
   Luke 6:27-36
F. Divine Authority.
   Luke 10:17-20
S. Miraculous Deliverance.
   Acts 12:5-11

TRUTH SEARCH
Creatively Teaching the Word

DISCUSSION QUESTIONS

Facing Opposition
(Ezra 4:1-6, 11-13, 23, 24)

1. Why did Zerubbabel decline the offer made by the adversaries of Judah (vv. 1-3)?

2. What efforts did the enemies make to try to stop the rebuilding of Jerusalem (vv. 4-6)?

3. Describe the contents of the letter written to King Artaxerxes (vv. 11-13).

4. What impact did the letter have (vv. 23, 24)?

God's Intervention
(Ezra 5:1-5; 6:1-3, 6-12)

1. How did God intervene through His prophets (5:1, 2)?

2. How was their work able to continue despite the complaints (5:3-5)?

3. What did King Darius discover in the archives (6:1-3)?

4. List all the orders Darius gave in verses 6-12.

Victorious Celebration
(Ezra 6:13-22)

1. How did the enemies of Jerusalem respond to King Darius' decree (v. 13)?

2. How long did it take to rebuild the Temple, and who were the key players (vv. 14, 15)?

3. Describe the dedication celebration (vv. 16, 17).

4. What Scriptural worship practices were restored (vv. 18-20)?

5. Who celebrated the feast together, and what preparation did they make (vv. 20, 21)?

6. According to verse 22, in what ways had the Lord worked to restore the Temple?

BRICK TALK

Items needed: Bricks, paper sacks and markers

Divide the class into small groups of three or four students each, and give each group a brick, a paper sack and a marker.

The bricks remind us that God wants to build us into faithful followers. But just as there were people who tried to stop the rebuilding of the Temple, so there are individuals who will try to hinder our Christian walk.

Have each group place its brick inside a sack. On the sack they should write ways people have come against them as Christians.

Next, group members can tell each other about any opposition they are currently facing. Then they should pray for one another.

Finally, have the students remove the bricks from the sacks and stack them together in front of the room as a reminder that God can complete His work in them.

Returning to God's Way

Study Text: Ezra 9:1 through 10:17
Objective: To acknowledge the results of our sins and turn to God in repentance.
Time: 457 B.C. and later
Place: Judah
Golden Text: "Repent ye therefore, and be converted, that your sins may be blotted out, when the times of refreshing shall come from the presence of the Lord" (Acts 3:19).
Central Truth: Believers must forsake sin to maintain a holy lifestyle.
Evangelism Emphasis: Unbelievers must repent of sin to be saved.

PRINTED TEXT

Ezra 9:1. Now when these things were done, the princes came to me, saying, The people of Israel, and the priests, and the Levites, have not separated themselves from the people of the lands, doing according to their abominations, even of the Canaanites, the Hittites, the Perizzites, the Jebusites, the Ammonites, the Moabites, the Egyptians, and the Amorites.

2. For they have taken of their daughters for themselves, and for their sons: so that the holy seed have mingled themselves with the people of those lands: yea, the hand of the princes and rulers hath been chief in this trespass.

3. And when I heard this thing, I rent my garment and my mantle, and plucked off the hair of my head and of my beard, and sat down astonied.

5. And at the evening sacrifice I arose up from my heaviness; and having rent my garment and my mantle, I fell upon my knees, and spread out my hands unto the Lord my God,

6. And said, O my God, I am ashamed and blush to lift up my face to thee, my God: for our iniquities are increased over our head, and our trespass is grown up unto the heavens.

14. Should we again break thy commandments, and join in affinity with the people of these abominations? wouldest not thou be angry with us till thou hadst consumed us, so that there should be no remnant nor escaping?

15. O Lord God of Israel, thou art righteous: for we remain yet escaped, as it is this day: behold, we are before thee in our trespasses: for we cannot stand before thee because of this.

10:1. Now when Ezra had prayed, and when he had confessed, weeping and casting himself down before the house of God, there assembled unto him out of Israel a very great congregation of men and women and children: for the people wept very sore.

2. And Shechaniah the son of Jehiel, one of the sons of Elam, answered and said unto Ezra, We have trespassed against our God, and have taken strange wives of the people of the land: yet now there is hope in Israel concerning this thing.

3. Now therefore let us make a covenant with our God to put away all the wives, and such as are born of them, according to the counsel of my lord, and of those that tremble at the commandment of our God; and let it be done according to the law.

DICTIONARY
Shechaniah (shek-uh-NIGH-uh)—Ezra 10:2—leading man in Ezra's time who proposed making a covenant with God to end all marriages to foreign women; he was the son of Jehiel (gee-HI-el)

LESSON OUTLINE

I. SORROW FOR SIN

   A. Sin of Intermarriage

   B. Anguish Over Sin

II. CONFESS SIN

   A. Past Reviewed

   B. Guilt Recognized

III. REPENT OF SIN

   A. Covenant of Change

   B. Covenant Proclaimed

   C. Covenant Accomplished

LESSON EXPOSITION

INTRODUCTION

The Book of Ezra records the account of two restorations of Jews to the land of Canaan. Zerubbabel led nearly 50,000 back in 536 B.C. Their return eventually resulted in the rebuilding of the Temple. A second restoration took place in 457 B.C. when Ezra brought another party of immigrants to Canaan. Once again we see divine intervention as King Artaxerxes generously contributed to the financial part of their trip as well as removing any legal barriers from anyone desiring to leave the empire. (See Artaxerxes' letter as recorded in Ezra 7:12-26). Nearly 6,000 Jews chose to make the move under Ezra, the newly appointed governor.

Chapter 8 details how Ezra and the people prepared spiritually to trust God for safe passage on the trip. Knowing that the tremendous amount of precious metals they were carrying made them a target for marauding bands of thieves, they fasted and prayed for God's protection. Ezra could have asked for a military escort, but he saw that as a smudge on the testimony which they had given of God's care and protection. With wisdom and trust in God they journeyed safely to their destination. However, upon arriving in Jerusalem, Ezra found a major sin problem among the people.

This leads us to consideration of an important question: Why do God's people sometimes fall into sinful practices which are denounced in His Word? How do believers slip into sins for which previous generations have been punished?

A quick review of the Book of Judges reveals the spiritual cycle of the Israelites. A period of spirituality would decline into a time of spiritual indifference which eventually led to outright spiritual rebellion. Only after God sent judgment on them would they cry out in repentance, and eventually He would send a deliverer.

This pattern of spiritual decline can also be seen in what is known as the third-generation problem. The first generation experiences the fullness of the Spirit and maintains a close relationship with God. The second generation sees the working of God but never owns it for themselves. Then the third generation arises. They haven't seen or personally experienced the work of God.

Martin Marty, a noted contemporary historian, describes these three stages as the tent, the temple and the tomb. It reflects a trend toward respectability within society with an eventually moving away from God. A group eventually has beautiful buildings but lacks the spirit of life within.

How can this sin trend be reversed? Well, it can't be legislated. Morality and spirituality aren't a matter of law. They come through choice and inner renewal. However, human facilitators are important. Someone needs to stand up with love and authority to declare truth and God's will.

I. SORROW FOR SIN (Ezra 9:1-4)

A. Sin of Intermarriage (vv. 1, 2)

1. Now when these things were done, the princes came to me, saying, The people of Israel, and the priests, and the Levites, have not separated themselves from the people of the lands, doing according to their abominations, even of the Canaanites, the Hittites, the Perizzites, the Jebusites, the Ammonites, the Moabites, the Egyptians, and the Amorites.
2. For they have taken of their daughters for themselves, and for their sons: so that the holy seed have mingled themselves with the people of those lands: yea, the hand of the princes and rulers hath been chief in this trespass.

Within days of arriving in Jerusalem, Ezra was confronted with a critical problem. Instead of maintaining a separate identity from their pagan neighbors in obedience to God's law, the Jews had been intermarrying with a host of other nationalities.

Verse 1 shares the breadth of this sin. There were not just a few incidents involving a small number of people. Rather, this intermarriage problem included a wide variety of people. It crossed the classes of the inhabitants from the common people all the way to the religious leaders. Another group is mentioned in verse 2. Even some of the princes of the people were involved. In fact, they were the ones who led the way into this sin.

Leaders set a standard which others follow. It is difficult to expect a group of people to adhere to a lifestyle that supersedes the one being demonstrated regularly before them by both civil and religious leaders. The Jews were no different than any other group. Many of them chose to follow the example of the wayward princes, Levites and priests.

Notice how verse 1 lists the specific people with whom there had been intermarriage. Not only does it point out the widespread association with pagan neighbors, but it also notes the various ones which God had specifically forbidden involvement with. What made these pagan neighbors so attractive? Were there no women to marry from among their own people? Of course there were.

We must assume that the choice to intermarry reflected the pitiful spiritual condition which dominated. Simply having a temple and offering sacrifices does not speak of a commitment to God's truth. Religious acts can be nothing more than a following of ritual, as is seen in many congregations of all denominations today. More than likely the law of God was unknown to the Jews. Note that some years later Ezra's public reading of God's Word became the stimulus for a major spiritual renewal (Nehemiah 8).

Before leaving these two verses, it is important to recognize that there still were some people who knew right from wrong. And they were willing to bring the problem to the forefront. Frequently we find people who know the truth of what is happening but are afraid to speak out. And it is understandable since in many cases they, instead of the wrongdoers, are the ones who receive the repercussions.

B. Anguish Over Sin (vv. 3, 4)

(Ezra 9:4 is not included in the printed text.)

3. And when I heard this thing, I rent my garment and my mantle, and plucked off the hair of my head and of my beard, and sat down astonied.

What a reaction to the news of sin's grip on the people! Ezra didn't weep or wail at the report; he followed a custom of expressing grief by tearing his clothes to demonstrate the anguish. But instead of shaving his facial hair or the hair of his head, he literally began to pull it out. How painful! Was this really necessary? For Ezra the answer stands as a definite "yes." As a scribe he knew the law of God very well and understood the consequences of the people's actions. Widespread intermarriage would lead to eventually losing their national identity as Jews, God's chosen people. Plus intermarriage would lead to their adopting manners, customs and religious practices that would separate them from God.

After having demonstrated his grief so visibly, Ezra sat in silence for some hours, completely aghast at how the exiles had given themselves into the hands of pagan women. It's comforting to know he didn't sit alone. Those individuals who were of like concern and respect for God's law gathered around him. They didn't need to say a word; just being there made a statement of their identity and support.

Let's reflect on the need to anguish over sin when it overtakes God's people. If we really believe that sin separates us from God, then when brothers or sisters in Christ become entrapped we should mourn this spiritual illness or even spiritual death. How can we claim love for the family of God and not grieve over sin's domination of their lives? We hurt with deep compassion for family members when they experience injury, loss or illness. Should we not do the same for the members of our spiritual family?

II. CONFESS SIN (Ezra 9:5-15)

A. Past Reviewed (vv. 5-12)

(Ezra 9:7-12 is not included in the printed text.)

5. And at the evening sacrifice I arose up from my heaviness; and having rent my garment and my mantle, I fell upon my knees, and spread out my hands unto the Lord my God,

6. And said, O my God, I am ashamed and blush to lift up my face to thee, my God: for our iniquities are increased over our head, and our trespass is grown up unto the heavens.

At the hour of the evening sacrifice, Ezra arose from sitting in silent anguish only to fall on his knees and begin verbally expressing the torment of his heart. Grasp the picture here. The newly arrived governor of the colony, with torn garments and outstretched hands, began to pray in repentance before the Lord. Immediately evident was his identification with the sinful element. He did not separate himself by stating he was praying on behalf of those who had left the law of God. Instead, he bowed in solidarity, understanding the corporate nature of the Jews as God's people.

Ezra knew that when sin pervades a nation, even the innocent will experience the judgment of God. For this reason he used the pronoun *our*. This inclusiveness identified him with the shame and sin of his brethren. He felt the burden to the point of not feeling worthy to lift his face in prayer to God. How unlike many believers who do not understand the bonds of the body of Christ. When one sins, all of us are affected.

After identifying with his brethren, Ezra prayed, "Because of our sins, we and our kings and our priests have been subjected to the sword and captivity, to pillage and humiliation at the hand of foreign kings, as it is today" (v. 7, *NIV*). Being under the domination of the Persian king was far from the glorious days of David and Solomon's reign over Israel!

In verses 8 and 9 Ezra recognized the grace of God which enabled a remnant of the captive people to return and build the Temple. Only through God's divine intervention were they able to find some security in returning to the Promised Land. His sovereign will provided the opportunity for them to worship as prescribed in the Law. And now, sin cast a dark shadow on their future. A sense of helplessness dominated. Nothing could be said. There was no excuse. They had disregarded God's commandments for them.

As he continued praying, Ezra recalled God's requirements for His people (vv. 11, 12). Because of the spiritual corruption practiced by the people of Canaan, the Jews were to abstain from any intermarriage with them. In fact, God's will was for Israel to destroy the inhabitants of the land. There were to be no peace treaties. By following these directions, Israel would prosper and the land would continue to be an inheritance for their children. However, Israel failed miserably in this calling. We first see it in the treaty with the deceiving Gibeonites (Joshua 9) and then later in their failure to drive out the idolatrous people, instead choosing to tax them (Judges 1:28).

B. Guilt Recognized (vv. 13-15)

(Ezra 9:13 is not included in the printed text.)

14. Should we again break thy commandments, and join in affinity with the people of these abominations? wouldest not thou be angry with us till thou hadst consumed us, so that there should be no remnant nor escaping?

15. O Lord God of Israel, thou art righteous: for we remain yet escaped, as it is this day: behold, we are before thee in our trespasses: for we cannot stand before thee because of this.

The last section of Ezra's prayer recognized the people's guilt and God's previous mercy even in His judgment. Referring back to verse 7, it is evident there had been an abundance of sin in the past. And God punished the Jews for it; however, their sins were so many and of such a nature to have deserved far greater retribution. God would have been justified in destroying them.

In view of this, it is almost inconceivable for the remnant to have so easily slipped back into the sins of their forefathers. God's destruction of both the northern and southern kingdoms of Israel should still be in their historical memories even though removed by several generations. Yet, this seems to be a constant problem with people. We sometimes forget the past, or we assume it doesn't apply to the present. Then there are always those who simply follow their passions regardless of the possible consequences.

Contrasting with their sinfulness is God's righteousness. It made them unworthy to stand before Him. They had no reason to continue to exist. Complete destruction for their sins would be justified. For that reason Ezra made no petition for mercy. He did not ask for God's forgiveness. Instead, in complete humility, he bowed before the Lord in acceptance of God's choice of action. How different from the prayers we might be tempted to pray!

III. REPENT OF SIN (Ezra 10:1-17)

A. Covenant of Change (vv. 1-6)

(Ezra 10:4-6 is not included in the printed text.)

1. Now when Ezra had prayed, and when he had confessed, weeping and casting himself down before the house of God, there assembled unto him out of Israel a very great congregation of men and women and children: for the people wept very sore.

2. And Shechaniah the son of Jehiel, one of the sons of Elam, answered and said unto Ezra, We have trespassed against our God, and have taken strange wives of the people of the land: yet now there is hope in Israel concerning this thing.

3. Now therefore let us make a covenant with our God to put away all the wives, and such as are born of them, according to the counsel of my lord, and of those that tremble at the commandment of our God; and let it be done according to the law.

The posture and passion of Ezra's prayer deeply touched those who witnessed it. With tears of contrition and prostrating himself on the ground, their governor displayed the anguish of his heart. Apparently word spread and a large assembly of people gathered around Ezra. This would seem to include more than those who initially were with him earlier in the day (9:4). Soon the people gathered to reflect the same spirit of confession as they too wept bitterly.

In that scenario one man led the way to change. It is not sufficient to just confess one's sins. True repentance includes a turnabout, a going in the opposite direction. Shechaniah chose to be the spokesman for those who had committed the sin of intermarriage. He began by publicly stating the nature of their sin against God. Then he offered hope for the situation by suggesting all the guilty men enter a covenant of separating from their foreign wives and the children born of such unions. Only through such drastic action would they be in accord with God's law.

Notice there was no sermon or religious exhortation given on that day. Absent were any declarations of damnation upon those who were guilty of this sin. Missing were the verbal barrages against leaders who should have known better. All of this change came because of Ezra's identifying this sin as a corporate problem and choosing to passionately feel the shame and separation as his own.

Shechaniah encouraged Ezra to rise from his sorrowing and put the plan into effect. The people pledged to support him in this difficult process. Having this type of support, Ezra immediately began by asking the men to enter into a covenant of separation. Upon completion of this first step, Ezra entered a room and for three days fasted from both food and water. He mourned over the serious sins of Israel. He possibly mourned the need for such dire consequences. Surely he was not without feelings and understanding of the trauma of these family breakups.

Our compassion surely causes us to ask, "Couldn't there have been another way?" The problem here is that our compassion might cause us to lose sight of the consequences of sin. True repentance never allows confession of sin without change! It's never enough to just say, "I have sinned." Those words must be followed with steps in the other direction. Sin, even when forgiven, leaves marks which do not fade away easily or quickly. For example, God forgives sexual immorality, but it doesn't necessarily keep a person from becoming HIV positive and later developing AIDS.

B. Covenant Proclaimed (vv. 7-15)

(Ezra 10:7-15 is not included in the printed text.)

Having reached a decision on the process to be followed, an order was sent throughout Judah for all Jews to assemble in Jerusalem within three days. The ruling princes and elders placed a stiff sentence on any who refused to cooperate and attend the meeting. Not only would such individuals forfeit all their property, but they would be expelled from the congregation. The leaders definitely meant business once having come to a true sense of their sins.

On the appointed day all the males of the region gathered in Jerusalem. There was no happiness here, only distress. They recognized their sins and separation from God. Physically they were uncomfortable due to the rain that fell. It was appropriate there were no rays of sunshine on such a solemn occasion. More than likely, word of Shechaniah's suggestion already had spread. Difficult times were ahead.

Ezra spoke to the crowd of men. He put it straight and to the point. Their unfaithfulness to God by marrying women from the neighboring pagan peoples added to the guilt of Israel as a nation. These actions added to the history of the Jews turning from the commands of God. Then, without an extended exhortation with all types of explanations, he gave them three steps to take: (1) Confess their sin of intermarriage, (2) obediently do God's will, and (3) separate themselves from the heathen peoples and their foreign wives. There would be no vote on the adoption of the plan. These men recognized the task demanded, and responded accordingly. With a loud voice the body responded to the correctness of the plan and their need to fulfill it.

The audience of men requested that a procedure be established which would allow the process to be completed in the days ahead. First, the inclement weather made it impossible to accomplish the separation outdoors at that time. Second, the process would take more than one day due to the large number of families involved. Third, a divorce court was established with the individuals coming to Jerusalem from their areas at set times. The elders and judges from the city would accompany those coming to Jerusalem. Using this process, the divorce court would be able to pass judgment on all cases within three months.

Verse 14 speaks of God's fierce anger. The reality of God's hatred of sin and bringing judgment stood as a stark reality to these people. Only when their confession and repentance was complete could they expect to be within God's covenant care again. However, verse 15 identifies four men who were not in agreement with the plan. This doesn't mean they did not attend the meeting in Jerusalem. But a review of the listing of men who divorced their wives (vv. 18-43) does not include their names. How pitiful for these men to assume knowledge greater than the body or to be so hardhearted not to feel the guilt of sin.

C. Covenant Accomplished
   (vv. 16, 17)

(Ezra 10:16, 17 is not included in the printed text.)

With a distinct system of organization, the plan of separation was implemented and completed. Using heads of the various families to serve in the investigation process, they were able to evaluate each case and bring it to a conclusion. Would this solve the problem forever? No! It would reappear again in a later time. The issue was not for the future but for their present. The sins were eradicated. A right relationship with God could now function in their hearts and lives.

GOLDEN TEXT HOMILY

"REPENT YE THEREFORE, AND BE CONVERTED, THAT YOUR SINS MAY BE BLOTTED OUT, WHEN THE TIMES OF REFRESHING SHALL COME FROM THE PRESENCE OF THE LORD" (Acts 3:19).

In the tension-packed society that we live in today, Peter gives us a remedy that will bring the refreshing breezes from the throne room of God. He declares to the crowd gathered that repentance and the blotting out of sins will bring a refreshing from the Lord. Unloading the guilt of sins committed will release a person from the weight of sin. Sin will stay the zephyrs of God from moving upon our lives. The Bible says that if we will confess our sins, He is faithful and just to forgive us of our sins (1 John 1:9).

Repentance calls for a turning from our sinful ways and to a commitment to Christ. The freedom from sin and blessed winds of God come as a result of complete repentance. God wants us to walk in freedom, joy and peace—the beginning that starts with repentance.

Search our hearts today, Lord, and know our thoughts. Forgive us of any hidden sins and restore us with Your refreshing today.—**Richard Fowler**

SENTENCE SERMONS

BELIEVERS MUST forsake sin to maintain a holy lifestyle.
—Selected

REPENTANCE is the spring beneath our virtues.
—Chinese proverb

REPENTANCE is the tear in the eye of faith.
—D.L. Moody

EVANGELISM APPLICATION

UNBELIEVERS MUST REPENT OF SIN TO BE SAVED.

All religions do not lead to the same future. There aren't a variety of ways to obtain salvation. The road to heaven and eternal life comes only by believing in Jesus Christ and repenting of one's sins.

Jesus said, "I tell you, Nay: but, except ye repent, ye shall all likewise perish" (Luke 13:3). And then, for emphasis, He repeated this statement in verse 5.

His message continues to be, "Repent of your sins and accept Me as Savior and Lord."

ILLUMINATING THE LESSON

The story of Bobby Leach demonstrates how what we consider minor issues can bring greater harm than some of the seemingly major ones. Leach went over Niagara Falls in a barrel and somehow emerged unscathed. However, sometime later he slipped on an orange peel while walking down the street. His injury? A badly fractured leg.

DAILY BIBLE READINGS

M. God Forgives the Repentant.
    1 Kings 8:46-52
T. God Offers Cleansing.
    Isaiah 1:18-20
W. God's Way Is Just.
    Ezekiel 18:21-32
T. Go and Sin No More.
    John 8:1-11
F. God's Acts Bring Conviction.
    Acts 19:11-20
S. God Is an Impartial Judge.
    Romans 2:1-11

TRUTH SEARCH
Creatively Teaching the Word

DISCUSSION QUESTIONS

Sorrow for Sin
(Ezra 9:1-4)

1. Who was guilty of sin, and what sins were they committing (vv. 1, 2)?

2. Who was primarily responsible for the sinful acts?

3. Describe and explain Ezra's response to the report about Israel's sins (vv. 3, 4).

4. Who joined together with Ezra in dismay (v. 4)?

Confess Sin
(Ezra 9:5-15)

1. How did Ezra express his sorrow for Israel's sin (v. 5)?

2. What did Ezra say about Israel's current sins (v. 6) and their past sins (v. 7)?

3. How had the Lord shown grace to Israel (vv. 8, 9)?

4. Which commandments had been broken by many of the returned exiles (vv. 10-14)?

5. Restate the conclusion to Ezra's confession in your own words (v. 15).

6. Since Ezra was not personally guilty of the sins committed, why was he confessing to the Lord?

Repent of Sin
(Ezra 10:1-10)

1. How did the people respond to Ezra's leadership (v. 1)?

2. What did Shechaniah say he and the other transgressors should do (vv. 2-4)?

3. What three steps did Ezra take?
- v. 5:
- v. 6:
- vv. 7, 8:

4. What did Ezra command the transgressors to do (vv. 9-11)?

5. What was the response of nearly all the people (vv. 12-15)?

6. What was done as an act of repentance (vv. 18, 19)?

TRENDS

According to a poll released by Barna Research Group, most Americans do not live by an absolute standard of right and wrong.

Only 22 percent of the adults questioned said moral truth is unchanging, 14 percent said they don't know if there is an unchanging standard, and 64 percent said moral truth depends on the situation.

When asked how they make a moral or ethical choice, only 13 percent said they follow Biblical principles, while 30 percent said they do whatever "feels right or comfortable in that situation" (2002, Barna).

Knowing and Doing God's Will

Study Text: Nehemiah 1:1 through 2:20
Objective: To become aware of needs around us and find our place in God's plan to meet them.
Time: 444 B.C.
Place: Events begin in the Persian capital of Shushan and in Jerusalem.
Golden Text: "Whoso hath this world's good, and seeth his brother have need, and shutteth up his bowels of compassion from him, how dwelleth the love of God in him?" (1 John 3:17).
Central Truth: God uses concern for others to motivate His people to action.
Evangelism Emphasis: God uses concern for the lost to motivate His people to witness.

PRINTED TEXT

Nehemiah 1:1. The words of Nehemiah the son of Hachaliah. And it came to pass in the month Chisleu, in the twentieth year, as I was in Shushan the palace,

2. That Hanani, one of my brethren, came, he and certain men of Judah; and I asked them concerning the Jews that had escaped, which were left of the captivity, and concerning Jerusalem.

3. And they said unto me, The remnant that are left of the captivity there in the province are in great affliction and reproach: the wall of Jerusalem also is broken down, and the gates thereof are burned with fire.

4. And it came to pass, when I heard these words, that I sat down and wept, and mourned certain days, and fasted, and prayed before the God of heaven,

11. O Lord, I beseech thee, let now thine ear be attentive to the prayer of thy servant, and to the prayer of thy servants, who desire to fear thy name: and prosper, I pray thee, thy servant this day, and grant him mercy in the sight of this man. For I was the king's cupbearer.

2:1. And it came to pass in the month Nisan, in the twentieth year of Artaxerxes the king, that wine was before him: and I took up the wine, and gave it unto the king. Now I had not been beforetime sad in his presence.

2. Wherefore the king said unto me, Why is thy countenance sad, seeing thou art not sick? this is nothing else but sorrow of heart. Then I was very sore afraid,

4. Then the king said unto me, For what dost thou make request? So I prayed to the God of heaven.

5. And I said unto the king, If it please the king, and if thy servant have found favour in thy sight, that thou wouldest send me unto Judah, unto the city of my fathers' sepulchres, that I may build it.

11. So I came to Jerusalem, and was there three days.

17. Then said I unto them, Ye see the distress that we are in, how Jerusalem lieth waste, and the gates thereof are burned with fire: come, and let us build up the wall of Jerusalem, that we be no more a reproach.

18. Then I told them of the hand of my God which was good upon me; as also the king's words that he had spoken unto me. And they said, Let us rise up and build. So they strengthened their hands for this good work.

DICTIONARY

Nehemiah (knee-ha-MY-ah)—Nehemiah 1:1—a cupbearer of the Persian king who made him governor of Judah so he could supervise rebuilding the walls

Hachaliah (HAK-ah-LIE-ah)—Nehemiah 1:1—Nehemiah's father

Chisleu (KIZ-lew)—Nehemiah 1:1—the ninth month of the Hebrew ritual year

Shushan (SHOO-shan)—Nehemiah 1:1—one of the capital cities of the Persian Empire

Hanani (ha-NAY-nigh)—Nehemiah 1:2—He reported the sad state of Jerusalem to his brother, Nehemiah.

Nisan (NI-san)—Nehemiah 2:1—first month of the Hebrew calendar (March-April)

Artaxerxes (AR-tah-ZERK-sees)—Nehemiah 2:1—a Persian king who gave permission to Ezra in 457 B.C. and Nehemiah in 444 B.C. to go to Jerusalem and gave them supplies and authority.

LESSON OUTLINE

I. PRAY FOR GOD'S HELP

   A. The Dilemma

   B. The Sorrow

   C. The Prayer

II. SEIZE OPPORTUNITIES

   A. The Opportunity

   B. The Request

III. TAKE ACTION

   A. The Survey

   B. The Presentation

LESSON EXPOSITION

INTRODUCTION

It is important that the decisions of our life be made within the context of God's will. This involves two separate dimensions. The first is following the principles and commandments of Scripture. This demands studying the Word and becoming knowledgeable of its content. The second dimension deals with decisions for which there are no specific written guidelines and the process of basic reasoning doesn't apply. Whom should I marry? Should I change jobs? Is this the right investment for our money? Should we adopt a child? Is this the right ministry involvement for me?

Whether or not these types of questions are brought to God depends on how involved an individual perceives God to be in their personal life. Some believers simply follow the broad principles offered within Scripture in making critical decisions. Others seek God's specific guidance through fervent prayer.

It is inconceivable to this writer that we, God's special creation, would not be given definite guidance in key areas of our lives. In today's lesson we can see the importance of knowing God's will and then taking the proper steps to fulfill it. Nehemiah was a leader who knew how to pray and yearned to fulfill God's will.

I. PRAY FOR GOD'S HELP
    Nehemiah 1:1-11)

A. The Dilemma (vv. 1-3)

1. The words of Nehemiah the son of Hachaliah. And it came to pass in the month Chisleu, in the twentieth year, as I was in Shushan the palace,

2. That Hanani, one of my brethren, came, he and certain men of Judah; and I asked them concerning the Jews that had escaped, which were left of the captivity, and concerning Jerusalem.

3. And they said unto me, The remnant that are left of the captivity there in the province are in great affliction and reproach: the wall of Jerusalem also is broken down, and the gates thereof are burned with fire.

Without personal introduction, other than naming his father, Nehemiah immediately sets the stage for the situation. He was in Shushan (Susa), one of the four capital cities of the Persian Empire. Located about 150 miles from the Persian Gulf in southwest Persia, it served as the winter palace.

The last verse of the chapter indicates Nehemiah's prestigious position of being the king's cupbearer. Traditionally the cupbearer stood as the doorkeeper to the royal living quarters. Not only would he be responsible for safeguarding the royal family, but he controlled who had the opportunity for an audience with the king. This shows Nehemiah not only was a trusted employee but held considerable influence with the ruler.

Nehemiah received a disturbing report concerning the conditions in Jerusalem. Hanani, Nehemiah's brother, along with several others returned from a personal survey of what was taking place. As Nehemiah questioned them concerning the people and the city, the sad state of affairs quickly became evident. Those living there were in an atmosphere of shame and disgrace. The city stood defenseless, since the walls were broken down and the gates had been burned. These conditions apparently came not just from the Babylonians' destruction of the city in 586 B.C. It appears there had been some recent attacks from the Samaritans.

The dilemma was evident. On two occasions, groups of Jewish exiles had returned to Jerusalem and Judah. Though still under the control of an outside nation, it would be thought that some progress had been made over the decades. Instead, those living in Jerusalem were at the mercy of those who would attack, pillage and destroy. Who would care enough to make a difference?

B. The Sorrow (v. 4)

4. And it came to pass, when I heard these words, that I sat down and wept, and mourned certain days, and fasted, and prayed before the God of heaven.

Hearing the disastrous situation in Jerusalem, Nehemiah was touched so deeply that he entered a period of mourning and spiritual entreaty. He wept. Instead of offering a few words of heartfelt sorrow and wishing for improvement, Nehemiah expressed an identification with the situation as though he were personally there.

What drove this employee of royalty to feel so intensely for his people? Having never visited Jerusalem, as far as can be determined, what caused such concern? To begin with, Nehemiah revealed the true brotherhood of God's people. The people in Jerusalem were his blood relatives. Also, as will be seen in his prayer, Nehemiah understood the covenant relationship between God and the Jews, and he knew the ramifications when those guidelines were neglected or rejected. So for him this was a physical, emotional and spiritual issue.

This one verse provides practical implications for believers. When the ministries of God's people or the conditions of their personal lives are in shambles, feelings of pity are insufficient. There needs to be personal identification accompanied with true sorrow, followed by spiritual actions. We too are a family who should care and intercede when our brothers and sisters in Christ are in dire circumstances.

C. The Prayer (vv. 5-11)

(Nehemiah 1:5-10 is not included in the printed text.)

11. O Lord, I beseech thee, let now thine ear be attentive to the prayer of thy servant, and to the prayer of thy servants, who desire to fear thy name: and prosper, I pray thee, thy servant this day, and grant him mercy in the sight of this man. For I was the king's cupbearer.

Nehemiah's prayer easily divides into four sections. In the first section (vv. 5, 6) Nehemiah recognizes the greatness of God. The word *terrible* in the King James Version is better translated "awesome." People must be reverent in approaching God. Nehemiah further describes God in terms of His love, referring to His covenant with His children. God offers protection and provision on the basis of people's obedience. In verse 6 Nehemiah appeals for God's attention. This does not mean Nehemiah was unaware that God knows everything. Instead, he was requesting God's attention to what he desired.

The second section of the prayer begins in the middle of verse 6 as Nehemiah confessed the previous sins of Israel. He personally identified with the wickedness of disobedience which occurred several centuries prior to his own lifetime and which forced judgment. Yes, several groups of Jews had returned from captivity. However, the marks of God's judgment continued to be seen. Thus, remembering the past sins was appropriate even this far from the initial destruction.

Section three of the prayer begins in verse 8 as Nehemiah again referred to God's covenant with Israel. Disobedience or transgression against God's law brings punishment. In contrast is obedience. When God's people began returning to His law, God miraculously began restoring them to their homeland as He had promised (v. 9).

In the final section of the prayer (vv. 10, 11), Nehemiah proceeded to his request, first honoring God for redeeming the Jews by His strength

and power. Humanly it would have been an impossibility to expect an Oriental ruler to allow captives to return home and finance the expeditions through various means, but God had accomplished it. Now Nehemiah asked for the same type of intervention in this situation. He desired God to be involved in the arrangements so the king would be favorable toward his requests.

In view of Nehemiah's prayer, it appears he had a plan in mind. He didn't know when or how it would work. But one thing stood out: The key person was his employer, King Artaxerxes. Only if God entered the setting and influenced this man could the task be accomplished.

II. SEIZE OPPORTUNITIES
(Nehemiah 2:1-10)

A. The Opportunity (vv. 1-3)

(Nehemiah 2:3 is not included in the printed text).

1. And it came to pass in the month Nisan, in the twentieth year of Artaxerxes the king, that wine was before him: and I took up the wine, and gave it unto the king. Now I had not been beforetime sad in his presence.

2. Wherefore the king said unto me, Why is thy countenance sad, seeing thou art not sick? this is nothing else but sorrow of heart. Then I was very sore afraid.

Nehemiah's private sorrow and prayerful preparation eventually were placed in the public arena of King Artaxerxes' presence. Three or four months had passed after Nehemiah's first hearing of the plight of the Jews in Jerusalem. Even after this period of time his grief continued to be so great that his physical appearance revealed it. Up to this point he had hidden his sorrow from the king. There were probably several cupbearers serving in rotation, so Nehemiah did not personally serve the king every day. Or it could have been that a cupbearer resided in each of the royal palaces rather than traveling from location to location with the royal party, so Nehemiah might not have been with the king for some time.

Verse 2 indicates the presence of fear when King Artaxerxes questioned Nehemiah concerning the apparent sadness. The king's servants were required to be joyful in his presence. Though knowing this, Nehemiah still could not hide his grief. This indicates how completely the situation dominated his inner being. Yet, this visible sign opened the door of opportunity. So here was the choice: either seize the moment or attempt some feeble excuse.

With the stage set, Nehemiah properly addressed his king and then stated the situation (v. 3). Why shouldn't he grieve over the desolation of his heritage capital? He described the widespread ruin of the city. The absence of city gates spoke loudly of its defenselessness without having to explain any further.

Nehemiah was naturally terrified because he stood in danger before the king. However, fear and faith in God can be present at the same time without hindering the progress God intends. The human side of us is prone to fear when it recognizes the difficulty of a situation. However, faith enables us to step beyond fear and continue in the direction God intends.

B. The Request (vv. 4-10)

(Nehemiah 2:6-10 is not included in the printed text.)

4. Then the king said unto me, For what dost thou make request? So I prayed to the God of heaven.

5. And I said unto the king, If it please the king, and if thy servant have found favour in thy sight, that thou wouldest send me unto Judah, unto the city of my fathers' sepulchres, that I may build it.

What a favorable response to Nehemiah's reply! It reminds us how God can prepare any heart regardless of the person's position. Without any further questioning concerning the situation, the king asked a simple question of Nehemiah. It can be paraphrased as, "What do you want?" He couldn't ask for anything more.

Rather than immediately forge ahead, Nehemiah quietly prayed. The words of that prayer aren't recorded. The important fact was his pausing for prayer prior to speaking.

Continuous prayer should be part of one's daily life. This goes beyond having a special time for devotions. Moments of prayer throughout the day should be normal.

Verse 5 shows Nehemiah's getting right to the heart of the situation. His request was to be allowed to go to Jerusalem and build the wall of the city of his fathers. This focus on one's heritage would seem normal to the king. The king's reply indicated his agreement with the request. However, he moved to some of the specifics of personal importance. How long would he be without the services of Nehemiah? He wanted to know the length of his journey and the total absence from the royal court.

The last line of verse 6 summarizes the overall atmosphere. With a willingness to allow Nehemiah's request, the king demonstrated his approval of both the person and the project. Looking further ahead to the last part of verse 8, we see God's hand in King Artaxerxes' graciousness in granting all that Nehemiah asked of him. Notice that the Scriptural narrative doesn't include the amount of time which Nehemiah allowed for the trip and the task. However, it met the king's approval.

Knowing there were other needs, Nehemiah continued his requests. To facilitate quick and safe travel, he asked for letters directing the provincial governors to provide military escorts. He also asked for a letter authorizing the head forester to provide the necessary wood for building city gates and a residence for Nehemiah.

Once again the king responded favorably. All Nehemiah desired was provided. Then, going a step further, King Artaxerxes provided a personal escort of military officers and mounted soldiers. This would be consistent with Nehemiah's new position as governor of Judah.

The last verse of this segment (v. 10) drastically changes the atmosphere. The ugly head of opposition arose in the persons of Sanballat and Tobiah, two influential men who did not want the Jewish people to reestablish a homeland. What was good for the inhabitants of Jerusalem was in direct opposition to this pair's desire of personal power and prosperity. Times haven't changed nor have unscrupulous leaders. Self-interest always comes in conflict with interest in others.

III. TAKE ACTION
(Nehemiah 2:11-20)

A. The Survey (vv. 11-16)

(Nehemiah 2:12-16 is not included in the printed text.)

11. So I came to Jerusalem, and was there three days.

After completing the journey to Jerusalem, Nehemiah took a few days to recuperate and to acquaint himself with the city. Using wisdom, the new governor did not immediately reveal the primary purpose for his arrival. Instead, he initiated his work with a secret nighttime survey.

Verses 12 through 15 provide a short yet detailed picture of what took place. A few men were selected to accompany him. No names are given, but no doubt they were individuals who were trustworthy and would be important to the project in the days

ahead. Only the governor was mounted. Verse 14 shows why the rest had to walk. The debris from the destruction of the wall made mounted travel impossible at places.

Nehemiah and his small group traveled around the perimeter of the city. Carefully they examined each of the gates of the city and the sections of the walls between each. Even then, in 444 B.C., the effectiveness of Nebuchadnezzar's troops in destroying the city walls in 586 B.C. was evident. Though the conditions were deplorable, the situation wasn't hopeless. Plenty of building materials from the previous wall remained ready to be reused. The main issue would be motivating the people to provide the necessary construction workers.

Verse 16 emphasizes the secrecy which Nehemiah maintained. No one, regardless of position, was given even the slightest hint of the project which burned in his heart and motivated him. This particular action is one of many leadership principles that the governor demonstrated as the building of the wall became a reality. Here we see the need for tactical timing when publicizing a plan of action. The leader must, of necessity, understand the totality of the task before opening the discussion. This enables one to speak of an attainable goal rather than some "pie in the sky" possibility. Knowledge enables a leader to speak with confidence which can be transmitted to the followers.

Another factor that entered the aspect of secrecy was not providing an opportunity for enemies and "wet blanket" thinkers to sabotage the effort before it even got off the ground. Sometimes just a very few can hinder the majority from accomplishing great tasks for the Kingdom.

B. The Presentation (vv. 17-20)

(Nehemiah 2:19, 20 is not included in the printed text.)

17. Then said I unto them, Ye see the distress that we are in, how Jerusalem lieth waste, and the gates thereof are burned with fire: come, and let us build up the wall of Jerusalem, that we be no more a reproach.

18. Then I told them of the hand of my God which was good upon me; as also the king's words that he had spoken unto me. And they said, Let us rise up and build. So they strengthened their hands for this good work.

At the right moment Nehemiah presented his plan to the populace of Jerusalem. First, he pointed to the problem by calling attention to their current setting. They were in trouble. All of the city's defenses lay in ruins. However, he did not dwell on the problem or rehash the historical circumstances which brought it about. Now was the time to move forward.

Second, Nehemiah offered them the opportunity to change this condition. He opened the door to action without demanding their involvement. He wanted them to volunteer rather than feel driven by their new governor. Instead of saying, "You build," he said, "Let us build." He desired side-by-side involvement with them. How could anyone resist the task and the spirit in which it was given? By rebuilding the wall, the people would "no longer be in disgrace" (v. 17, NIV).

Before asking for their response, Nehemiah included a third part to the presentation. He gave his personal testimony of the events that led to his coming to Jerusalem. His story included how King Artaxerxes responded to Nehemiah's sadness and his subsequent requests.

At this point the people responded affirmatively. They were ready to immediately initiate the project. They didn't just respond verbally and then stand around and wait.

Once again Sanballat and Tobiah promptly appeared along with a third detractor, Geshem the Arab. Sanballat was a leader among the Samaritans, while Tobiah was a leading Ammonite who had married into a Jewish family. Their initial response to the project was mocking and ridicule. They asked, "What is this you are doing? . . . Are you rebelling against the king?" (v. 19, NIV).

In verse 20 we see Nehemiah's response to this first attempt to hinder the building. He said God in heaven would prosper them. With His blessing they were going to start rebuilding the wall. The governor then pointed out Sanballat's, Tobiah's and Geshem's separation from these people and the project. They were not Jews by blood nor were they followers of the God of heaven. They had no rights, no ownership, and no future in Jerusalem.

What does Nehemiah's response teach us when individuals would hinder our work for the Lord? This question deserves consideration while studying the continuing encounters with Sanballat and Tobiah.

GOLDEN TEXT HOMILY

"WHOSO HATH THIS WORLD'S GOOD, AND SEETH HIS BROTHER HAVE NEED, AND SHUTTETH UP HIS BOWELS OF COMPASSION FROM HIM, HOW DWELLETH THE LOVE OF GOD IN HIM?" (1 John 3:17).

The writer knew the poor firsthand. He and Peter did not have money for the disadvantaged cripple at the gate to the Temple, but through Christ's power they could give healing. His question is as relevant today as when written—how can we possess God's love and ignore the poor? In his commentary R.R. Williams puts it this way: "If you have enough to live on, and can peacefully see your brother in need, the divine love cannot be in you. . . . A famine relief project is as much a Christian concern as a coin for a beggar at the door."

Practically every book of the Bible discusses the poor, usually admonishing the reader to help. For example, Psalm 41:1 says, "Blessed is he who considers the poor; the Lord will deliver him in time of trouble" (NKJV). Christ spoke often of the poor with compassion; in fact, He said He was sent to preach the gospel to the poor (Luke 4:18). The only time the Bible uses the term "pure religion" is when discussing our helping widows and orphans in need (James 1:27).

If your local church is not actually involved in caring for people in need, you should ask, "What can we do this week to start an outreach ministry?" Be certain to have a planned answer to the question.—**Clyne W. Buxton**

SENTENCE SERMONS

GOD USES concern for others to motivate His people to action.
—Selected

BECAUSE WE CANNOT SEE CHRIST we cannot express our love to Him; but our neighbors we can always see, and we can do to them what, if we saw Him, we would like to do for Christ.
—Mother Teresa

LOVE IS APPEALING, but its practice is appallingly difficult.
—Anonymous

EVANGELISM APPLICATION

GOD USES CONCERN FOR THE LOST TO MOTIVATE HIS PEOPLE TO WITNESS.

When we can see and feel someone's pain and suffering and hopelessness, it grips our heart and makes us want to get involved. This transcends distance, culture and language.

When God burdens us for individuals who do not know Jesus Christ and we reflect on their hopeless future, it drives us to witness about Jesus. This witness may be through spoken words, a well-placed tract or works of kindness.

ILLUMINATING THE LESSON

A story passed down through the decades tells of a football player who hired out to a farmer with the intent of doing heavy physical labor. Prior to the use of weight machines to develop muscle, this appeared to be a good way to build muscle and develop stamina.

The farmer obliged the young man by giving him long hours pitching hay and shoveling grain. One day, however, the farmer gave him a break. The day's assignment was to separate the newly dug potatoes according to predetermined size standards.

After several hours the farmer went to see how the work was progressing. Much to his amazement, little had been accomplished. In great frustration the young man explained, "This work isn't hard. But the decisions are killing me!"

Actually, nothing is more stressful than trying to make the right decision. As Christians, however, we can depend on godly wisdom in making decisions.

One clear direction God has already given us is to minister to others in need. The only question is how.

DAILY BIBLE READINGS

M. Obey God's Commands.
   Deuteronomy 8:1-10
T. Desire to Do God's Will.
   Psalm 40:4-8
W. Minister by the Spirit.
   Isaiah 61:1-8
T. Give in Secret.
   Matthew 6:1-4
F. Pray to Know God's Will.
   Colossians 1:9-14
S. Show Faith With Action.
   James 2:14-24

TRUTH SEARCH
Creatively Teaching the Word

DISCUSSION QUESTIONS

**Pray for God's Help
(Nehemiah 1:1-11)**

1. Where was Nehemiah living, and what did he ask about (vv. 1, 2)?

2. What report was Nehemiah given (v. 3)?

3. How did Nehemiah respond, and why (v. 4)?

4. Summarize the first part of Nehemiah's prayer (vv. 5-7) in one short sentence.

5. What did Nehemiah "remind" the Lord of in verses 8-10?

6. What request did he make in verse 11?

**Seize Opportunities
(Nehemiah 2:1-10)**

1. How did the news about Jerusalem's condition affect Nehemiah (vv. 1, 2)?

2. How did Nehemiah explain his sadness to the king (v. 3)?

3. What was Nehemiah's initial request, and how did the king reply (vv. 4-6)?

4. According to verse 8, why did King Artaxerxes respond so favorably to all of Nehemiah's requests?

5. Why were some people "grieved" (v. 10) to hear about Nehemiah's concern for Jerusalem?

**Take Action
(Nehemiah 2:11-20)**

1. Why do you suppose Nehemiah was secretive about his mission to Jerusalem (vv. 11, 12, 15, 16)?

2. What did he discover about Jerusalem's condition (vv. 13, 14)?

3. What did Nehemiah announce that must be done (v. 17)?

4. How did he encourage the people to work with him (v. 18)?

5. How did Nehemiah answer the enemies who scoffed at this plan (vv. 19, 20)?

PICTURE MESSAGE

Items needed: Marker board, marker

Have a volunteer draw a simple picture of a church building—representing your church—in the center of the board.

Next, have students name various spiritual, material and social needs that exist in your community. Write these on the board surrounding the church.

There are many needs in our community. As members of this church, how are we responding to our community's needs?

Just like Nehemiah could have kept his cupbearer's job in the palace of Persia's king, so we can choose to stay within the church's secure walls and ignore our community's needs. Or we can move out of the "palace"—the church—and serve others.

Leadership During Crises

Study Text: Nehemiah 4:1 through 7:3
Objective: To study Nehemiah's leadership skills and apply them during daily responsibilities.
Time: 444 B.C.
Place: Jerusalem
Golden Text: "I told them of the hand of my God which was good upon me. . . . And they said, Let us rise up and build. So they strengthened their hands for this good work" (Nehemiah 2:18).
Central Truth: God gives leaders wisdom for their tasks.
Evangelism Emphasis: God gives believers wisdom to witness.

PRINTED TEXT

Nehemiah 4:1. But it came to pass, that when Sanballat heard that we builded the wall, he was wroth, and took great indignation, and mocked the Jews.

14. And I looked, and rose up, and said unto the nobles, and to the rulers, and to the rest of the people, Be not ye afraid of them: remember the Lord, which is great and terrible, and fight for your brethren, your sons, and your daughters, your wives, and your houses.

15. And it came to pass, when our enemies heard that it was known unto us, and God had brought their counsel to nought, that we returned all of us to the wall, every one unto his work.

16. And it came to pass from that time forth, that the half of my servants wrought in the work, and the other half of them held both the spears, the shields, and the bows, and the habergeons; and the rulers were behind all the house of Judah.

5:1. And there was a great cry of the people and of their wives against their brethren the Jews.

6. And I was very angry when I heard their cry and these words.

7. Then I consulted with myself, and I rebuked the nobles, and the rulers, and said unto them, Ye exact usury, every one of his brother. And I set a great assembly against them.

9. Also I said, It is not good that ye do: ought ye not to walk in the fear of our God because of the reproach of the heathen our enemies?

11. Restore, I pray you, to them, even this day, their lands, their vineyards, their oliveyards, and their houses, also the hundredth part of the money, and of the corn, the wine, and the oil, that ye exact of them.

6:2. That Sanballat and Geshem sent unto me, saying, Come, let us meet together in some one of the villages in the plain of Ono. But they thought to do me mischief.

3. And I sent messengers unto them, saying, I am doing a great work, so that I cannot come down: why should the work cease, whilst I leave it, and come down to you?

15. So the wall was finished in the twenty and fifth day of the month Elul, in fifty and two days.

16. And it came to pass, that when all our enemies heard thereof, and all the heathen that were about us saw these things, they were much cast down in their own eyes: for they perceived that this work was wrought of our God.

DICTIONARY

Sanballat (san-BAL-lat)—Nehemiah 4:1—a Samaritan who apparently held some office in service of Persia's king

habergeons (HA-ber-jens)—Nehemiah 4:16—leather coats covered with thin plates of metal

Geshem (GEE-shem)—Nehemiah 6:2—evidently an inhabitant of the Arabian desert who was a tribal leader

Elul (eh-LOWL)—Nehemiah 6:15—the sixth month of the Hebrew calendar, approximately August-September

---

LESSON OUTLINE

I. DEVISE AN EFFECTIVE STRATEGY
   A. The Opposition
   B. The Challenge
   C. The Plan

II. SOLVE INTERNAL DISPUTES
   A. The Injustice
   B. The Confrontation

III. MAINTAIN FOCUS
   A. The Dialogue
   B. The Completion

LESSON EXPOSITION

INTRODUCTION

Have you ever asked the question "Do we really need leaders?" When a person in leadership flubs up, this question might arise. Forgetting the leader's humanity, it becomes easy to believe either we could do a better job or we could get along without him or her.

Any organization or group of people may continue for a period of time without a distinct leader in position. Some "muddle" along, frequently following a trial-and-error approach. Others are quite successful due to capable individuals fulfilling their job responsibilities. But, in spite of surviving or succeeding, leaders are needed. They generate vision and then bring others on board to help fulfill it. They provide encouragement to continue seeing the task in terms of the end result. And in crisis the leader becomes the point person responsible to seek solutions to the problems while keeping the project or group on course. A wise leader seeks counsel from others, but the bottom line is "The buck stops here."

We need leaders! Committees are great for planning and providing information, but they can't take the place of that one individual who must keep the proper perspectives. Perhaps you have heard the statement that "a camel is a horse designed by a committee." This saying emphasizes how no group of people can take the place of individual leadership. This is especially true in times of crises. The dogged leadership of Winston Churchill in the face of Nazi aggression stands out. Realistically at the onset he promised the British citizens nothing other than blood, sweat and tears in their conflict, yet they followed his leadership and eventually prevailed.

Anyone can sit in the position of leadership and hold a title. The test comes in the face of crisis which would destroy not only progress but the project itself. And it needs to be noted that passion to see something done isn't sufficient in itself. In the previous lesson, we saw Nehemiah's heart for the city of Jerusalem and his willingness to make a bold request of his employer, King Artaxerxes. His careful preparation prior to presenting the project to the inhabitants was laced with wisdom. He also passed the test when the first opposition became evident. However, the true character of his leadership would be seen only when intense, organized efforts were made to halt the process.

Today's lesson provides much more than a Biblical, historical review of Nehemiah. It teaches how we can overcome the hindrances of others through prayer, hard work and keeping our eyes focused on the task.

I. DEVISE AN EFFECTIVE STRATEGY
    (Nehemiah 4:1-23)

A. The Opposition (vv. 1-9)

(Nehemiah 4:2-9 is not included in the printed text.)

1. But it came to pass, that when Sanballat heard that we builded the wall, he was wroth, and took great indignation, and mocked the Jews.

In chapter 3 we see how the people of Jerusalem followed up their words with work. Even Eliashib the high priest and his fellow priests joined in the rebuilding of the wall (v. 1). Of course, there were a few who thought their noble birth placed them above manual labor (v. 5); however, the people as a whole put their backs into restoring the city wall. Imagine the shock Sanballat must have experienced upon hearing of the progress on the wall. It quickly turned into intense anger. He was incensed that this could actually be taking place.

To vent his anger and frustration, Sanballat launched into a tirade of ridicule. Notice the audience to whom this Samaritan spoke—associates and the army of Samaria (4:2). That should say something about his personality. The five questions he mockingly asked were intended to demean the Jews and their efforts in the eyes of those within his hearing. On the one hand, he seemed to be saying they would not be successful. On the other hand, maybe fear generated his response as he heard of their corporate effort.

Tobiah, Sanballat's Ammonite colleague, quickly joined in the ridicule. He suggested that even if a fox (despite its little weight) were to jump on the wall, it would break. When ridicule reaches such exaggeration, it appears to be rather desperate.

Verse 4 indicates the words of Sanballat and Tobiah were spread to the general populace or at least were directed in some manner so Nehemiah would hear them. In his usual pattern, Nehemiah's first response was prayer. First, he asked for the Lord to hear him. This should be understood in terms of desiring for God to answer the following petition. Second, he stated the lowliness with which he and the people were regarded by neighboring peoples and the local leadership. Third, he prayed for judgment to come upon the opposition. He saw these opponents in direct conflict with God himself and worthy only of His punishment. He said they were worthy of being plunder to an invading people. Those were strong words!

Even though the words of mockery and ridicule were flung at them, the people didn't hesitate or falter. They continued to work. Verse 6 says "the people had a mind to work." The *New International Version* states "the people worked with all their heart." Both means of description indicate their commitment to work regardless of the opinion of others. Their full effort of thought and physical action were focused on this project.

Having failed in their initial attempt to stop the building project and hearing of its continuance, Sanballat and Tobiah—along with the Arabs, the Ammonites and the Ashdodites—both responded in anger. Something had to be done! The breaches in the wall were being closed quickly. So the logical conclusion for their next attempt was armed force. "They all plotted together to come and fight against Jerusalem" (v. 8, *NIV*).

Nehemiah responded to the threat by first praying and placing the situation in God's hands. Second, he set watchmen in place to preclude a surprise attack. This provided balance. Trust in God does not mean neglecting what can be done by human hands.

B. The Challenge (vv. 10-12)

(Nehemiah 4:10-12 is not included in the printed text.)

Verse 10 indicates how the laborers had been pushing themselves and were experiencing fatigue. Complicating their efforts was the amount of rubbish they had to work around as well as sort through for building materials. A hint of frustration appeared.

The next two verses indicate how Sanballat's forces were planning to attack. They wanted to mount a sneak attack, killing the workers and thus stopping the project. They hoped one invasion would be sufficient. They planned to attack from all sides, so no one working on any part of the wall would escape the confrontation. This threat not only needed to be taken seriously, but demanded a team effort along with divine intervention.

C. The Plan (vv. 13-23)

(Nehemiah 4:13, 17-23 is not included in the printed text.)

14. And I looked, and rose up, and said unto the nobles, and to the rulers, and to the rest of the people, Be not ye afraid of them: remember the Lord, which is great and terrible, and fight for your brethren, your sons, and your daughters, your wives, and your houses.

15. And it came to pass, when our enemies heard that it was known unto us, and God had brought their counsel to nought, that we returned all of us to the wall, every one unto his work.

16. And it came to pass from that time forth, that the half of my servants wrought in the work, and

the other half of them held both the spears, the shields, and the bows, and the habergeons; and the rulers were behind all the house of Judah.

Without delay, Nehemiah responded to the threat by posting armed individuals at the most vulnerable points on the wall. Some portions of the wall were higher and thus of a stronger fortification; the lower portions needed protection.

After addressing the physical situation, Nehemiah turned his attention to the people who were gathered. All groups were represented. Nehemiah began with a statement of confidence and direction, saying there was no reason to be afraid. If they would remember their God, they could stand strong and fight.

Nehemiah's words remind us how we can be confident when God stands with us. He enables the weak to overcome the strong. Remember how Moses stood before the Hebrews and said, "Do not be afraid. Stand firm and you will see the deliverance the Lord will bring you today" (Exodus 14:13, NIV).

In urging people to stand firm and fight if necessary, Nehemiah began with the sense of community, saying to fight for one's fellow believers. Next, he moved to family and finally pointed to material possessions. Nehemiah was stating that the value of the whole continued to be more important than the small group. And people always take precedent over things.

Verse 15 indicates God's hand in frustrating Sanballat's efforts. The Lord enabled the Jews to know in advance and make the necessary preparations to stymie any attack. In response to Nehemiah's urging and God's involvement, the builders returned to the building project. However, they maintained a vigilance. Half of the men stood guard while the other half worked. The workers also carried a weapon even as they constructed the wall. If an attack were to happen, they could immediately spring to defend. Another precaution was an alarm system which would call additional help if an attack came to a more isolated, sparsely defended portion of the wall. A trumpeter stood by Nehemiah ready to sound the alarm.

One other safeguard was instituted. Nehemiah instructed all the workmen from outside of the city to remain within the walls during the night. This provided more men to share night guard duty as well as bolstered the number of men available to fight, if attacked. Also, they were to sleep fully dressed. What a sense of readiness! Yes, they depended on God, but at the same time they recognized the need to participate as God's instrument.

II. SOLVE INTERNAL DISPUTES
(Nehemiah 5:1-12)

A. The Injustice (vv. 1-6)

(Nehemiah 5:2-5 is not included in the printed text.)

1. And there was a great cry of the people and of their wives against their brethren the Jews.

6. And I was very angry when I heard their cry and these words.

Not only did Nehemiah have to deal with opposition from the enemies of the Jews, but now problems developed from within. While the governor worked to lead them in a successful construction project which would provide security, some people were seeking personal gain. Because of the current famine and the builders' dedication to working on the wall, the poorer Jews found themselves in financial crisis. In order to purchase food for their families and pay the heavy taxation required by the Persians, they turned to their wealthier brethren for assistance. Instead of responding with brotherly love and fulfilling the Law, the wealthier Jews treated them as though they were foreigners.

Needing to feed their families caused some to mortgage their land. Others, pushed to desperation, committed their children to slavery to obtain the necessary funds. This desperate move resulted from their land having been foreclosed because of previous indebtedness. Can you imagine the hurt and frustration they were feeling? No wonder they appealed to Nehemiah! They had no control over the circumstances which brought famine, and they were trying to fulfill both their civic and spiritual duties. Instead of their fellow Jews attempting to assist them, just the opposite occurred.

Nehemiah's initial response was one of anger. How could this unscrupulous behavior take place during a time of crisis? Now the challenge of leadership came from another direction. How would he handle it? Would his indignation be channeled through righteousness and wisdom? Or, would he allow the heat of the moment to cause a reflex action which might be regretted later?

B. The Confrontation (vv. 7-12)

(Nehemiah 5:8, 10, 12 is not included in the printed text.)

7. Then I consulted with myself, and I rebuked the nobles, and the rulers, and said unto them, Ye exact usury, every one of his brother. And I set a great assembly against them.

9. Also I said, It is not good that ye do: ought ye not to walk in the fear of our God because of the reproach of the heathen our enemies?

11. Restore, I pray you, to them, even this day, their lands, their vineyards, their oliveyards, and their houses, also the hundredth part of the money, and of the corn, the wine, and the oil, that ye exact of them.

Once again, Nehemiah demonstrated marvelous wisdom in his leadership. Before doing anything, he took time to think through the situation. In verse 7 he said, "Then I consulted with myself." A modern translation makes it clear by stating, "I pondered them in my mind" (*NIV*). Something had to be done, but in such a manner to bring change rather than further the problem.

After thinking about this oppression, Nehemiah called for a meeting of the people. He knew the nobility and ruling officials were in the wrong; however, there must be a public forum for the confrontation, enabling all to hear rather than keep it within the cloak of privacy.

Can you imagine the shame the rich felt as Nehemiah outlined the problem? Their loaning money with interest due was in direct violation to the Mosaic Law (see Exodus 22:25; Deuteronomy 23:19, 20). And the taking of their own into slavery defied logic. After God's punishment through captivity, efforts had been made to bring the people back home only now to see them being in captivity (slavery) in their own land! Then the governor pointed to his own example of providing food and loaning money at no interest.

Then Nehemiah directed the wealthy to stop lending money at interest. But he did not stop there. He ordered them to return all the property that had been foreclosed and all interest charged. The "hundredth part of the money" (v. 11) indicates a 12 percent interest rate. Without any attempt at rebuttal and apparently in complete agreement, the guilty individuals indicated their compliance to Nehemiah's demands. They went even further by binding themselves in an oath to fulfill their words.

Not every situation of division and profiteering ends with such a positive response. However, this account reminds us of the need for skillful leadership which evaluates and then takes appropriate action to bring a healing conclusion to the problem.

III. MAINTAIN FOCUS
(Nehemiah 6:1-4, 15, 16)

A. The Dialogue (vv. 1-4)

(Nehemiah 6:1, 4 is not included in the printed text.)

2. That Sanballat and Geshem sent unto me, saying, Come, let us meet together in some one of the villages in the plain of Ono. But they thought to do me mischief.

3. And I sent messengers unto them, saying, I am doing a great work, so that I cannot come down: why should the work cease, whilst I leave it, and come down to you?

There is a time to talk and a time to work. Failure to understand the need of the hour may lead to the destruction or, at best, the delay of a project. As will be seen in this section, Nehemiah understood the importance of remaining focused on the opportunity despite efforts to divert one's attention.

One has to admire the persistence of Sanballat in his attempts to stop the rebuilding of the wall. Though misdirected, he demonstrates a sense of focus. Having already used mockery and the threat of attack unsuccessfully, he chose a seemingly innocent third method. This time Sanballat sent a messenger inviting Nehemiah to a personal conference. The location, Ono, was some 20 miles north of Jerusalem. If Nehemiah chose to accept, it meant being absent from the work site for several days and being removed from the relative safety of the city. Any type of physical harm could come during such a trip.

Wisely Nehemiah refused to be led into this subtle trap. However, rather than blatantly charging Sanballat with trickery and an invitation under false pretenses, he responded with a positive message in declining this opportunity for dialogue. He pointed out the importance and magnitude of the building project and his unwillingness to leave it. Then he asked a straightforward question: "Why should the work cease, whilst I leave it, and come down to you?" (v. 3). He put the ball back into their court. It now became their responsibility to develop an argument which would merit such action on his part.

Undaunted by the refusal, Sanballat persisted. On four more occasions he sent the same request (v. 4). But he never provided an answer to Nehemiah's question. Rather than waste time and effort in producing further correspondence, Nehemiah simply responded with his first statement on each of the three successive occasions. However, with the fifth request, Sanballat also sent an unsealed letter which he intended to send to the king (v. 5). It spoke of a revolt in Judah and the people setting up an independent king (vv. 6, 7).

Instead of a long letter refuting these false charges, Nehemiah's response was nothing more than a brief denial. He recognized the enemies' attempt to frighten him. Also, he surely knew and relied on his personal relationship with the Persian king.

This segment of the lesson reminds us to be discerning as to whom we dialogue with while working for the Lord. We always should be open to hearts seeking the truth. Yet we need to carefully watch the amount of time given talking with those who intend to hinder our progress and inflict harm.

B. The Completion (vv. 15, 16)

15. So the wall was finished in the twenty and fifth day of the month Elul, in fifty and two days.

16. And it came to pass, that when all our enemies heard thereof, and all the heathen that were about us saw these things, they were much cast down in their own eyes: for they perceived that this work was wrought of our God.

There was one final attempt to stop Nehemiah and the building project. A man named Shemaiah tried to propagate fear in Nehemiah by telling of a plot to kill him at night. He encouraged Nehemiah to hide within the locked doors of the Temple (v. 10). His enemies were hopeful the seed of fear would take root and grow. However, Nehemiah's prayer in verse 9 was already in effect. He had prayed for his hands to be strengthened so fear could not hinder the work.

As a result of Nehemiah's skillful, spiritual leadership, coupled with the people's committed work, the wall was rebuilt in 52 days. This made a strong impact on the surrounding nations and Jerusalem's enemies. Realizing this work could have been accomplished only through the help of God, the self-confidence of the surrounding peoples evaporated and their fears mushroomed. Apparently they realized the inadequacy of their gods in comparison to God Jehovah. Here we see the double impact of Nehemiah's leadership—the wall was a reality and their enemies were demoralized.

GOLDEN TEXT HOMILY

"I TOLD THEM OF THE HAND OF MY GOD WHICH WAS GOOD UPON ME. . . . AND THEY SAID, LET US RISE UP AND BUILD. SO THEY STRENGTHENED THEIR HANDS FOR THIS GOOD WORK" (Nehemiah 2:18).

Nehemiah had to face many difficulties. His first task was by no means his easiest; namely, to win the confidence and stir the enthusiasm of the Jewish people. This, of course, is what leadership of any kind involves. And it is one thing to have a concern yourself, and to be capable of doing a job yourself; but it's quite another to rouse and stir others to work with you.

The Jews at Jerusalem were gazing constantly at their devastated walls, but there was no one with the conviction and confidence to deal with the situation. They needed a leader. Now they had one! And Nehemiah was ready to call for workers.

Mark the two features of his call: (1) "Take another look at our sad situation!" (see v. 17). (2) "See how God has already begun to work for us!" (see v. 18). In other words, he drew attention to the need, and fixed people's gaze upon the power of God. Nehemiah succeeded, like other great leaders, because he knew just what he wanted to do. Lack of this fundamental quality is a major weakness in the Christian ministry at any time.—**Selected**

SENTENCE SERMONS

GOD GIVES LEADERS wisdom for their tasks.

—Selected

A TRUE AND SAFE LEADER is likely to be one who has no desire to lead, but is forced into a position of leadership by the inward pressure of the Holy Spirit and the press of external situations.

—A.W. Tozer

PERHAPS THE MOST IMPORTANT ISSUE for leaders responsible for implementing dreams is . . . will they come through it with their vision intact, or will their vision die?

—Aubrey Malphurs

EVANGELISM APPLICATION

GOD GIVES BELIEVERS WISDOM TO WITNESS.

Even the most "people-skilled" person is in need of divine wisdom to lead during times of stress and crisis. God selects individuals for positions of leadership and then offers the necessary equipping. He wants them to be successful and overcome the pitfalls which Satan and evildoers place in their way.

We may never have the opportunity to request anything we want from God such as did King Solomon. We may never be considered the wisest person in our town or even in our church. But we do know God offers wisdom to anyone who asks, especially for witnessing.

ILLUMINATING THE LESSON

Churches generally overstate their ability to handle conflict. The real danger is their fear of conflict, as they blindly believe all conflict is wrong or unchristian. Dealing openly with conflict is an affirmation that the issues are worth fighting over and that we can resolve our differences without destroying one another.

Conflict makes all of us draw upon the resources of our faith to handle the matter at hand. . . . Even in a congregation's darkest hours, the Christian faith provides the resources necessary for making sense out of difficult situations and surviving them.—**James D. Berkley, Gen. Ed.,** *Leadership Handbook of Management and Administration*

DAILY BIBLE READINGS

M. Build According to God's Plan.
    Exodus 25:1-9
T. God's Plan of Hope.
    Jeremiah 29:10-14
W. What the Lord Requires.
    Micah 6:6-8
T. Do Right.
    Ephesians 4:25-32
F. Focus on Things Above.
    Colossians 3:1-10
S. Plan According to God's Will.
    James 4:13-17

TRUTH SEARCH
Creatively Teaching the Word

DISCUSSION QUESTIONS

**Devise an Effective Strategy
(Nehemiah 4:1-23)**

1. How did Sanballat and Tobiah try to discourage the Jews from rebuilding Jerusalem's walls (vv. 1-3)?

2. What was Nehemiah's prayer concerning Sanballat and Tobiah (vv. 4, 5)?

3. What further angered the enemies of Jerusalem and what did they do (vv. 6-8)?

4. What action did Nehemiah take (v. 9)?

5. How did the enemies continue their opposition (vv. 10-12)?

6. How did Nehemiah respond, and what was the result (vv. 13-15)?

7. Explain the various strategies Nehemiah used to continue the work:
   - vv. 15-18:
   - vv. 19, 20:
   - vv. 21-23:

**Solve Internal Disputes
(Nehemiah 5:1-13)**

1. What crisis did the common people of Jerusalem face (vv. 1-3)?

2. How were the richer people taking advantage of the poorer (vv. 4, 5)?

3. What charges did Nehemiah bring against the richer people (vv. 6-8)?

4. What did Nehemiah tell them to do, and how did they respond (vv. 9-12)?

5. Explain the object lesson Nehemiah used (v. 13).

**Maintain Focus
(Nehemiah 6:1-4, 9, 13, 15, 16)**

1. What did Nehemiah accomplish (v. 1)?

2. How do you suppose Nehemiah knew what Sanballat and Geshem's intentions were (vv. 2-4)?

3. What was the underlying element the enemies used to try to stop Nehemiah (vv. 9, 13)?

4. Explain the response of Jerusalem's enemies and the surrounding nations (vv. 15, 16).

SELF-EVALUATION

Items needed: Index cards and pencils

Hand out a card and a pencil to each student, and have them number the card from 1 to 3.

Next to number 1, each person should write something he or she knows God has called them to do.

Next to number 2, they should describe opposition they are facing regarding that calling.

Next to number 3, they should write a sentence prayer asking for God's help in following His plan.

Lead everyone in a time of prayer.

Repentance Brings Spiritual Renewal

Study Text: Nehemiah 7:73 through 10:39

Objective: To recognize our need for repentance and renew ourselves through God's Word, prayer, and dedication to God.

Time: About 445 B.C.

Place: Jerusalem

Golden Text: "If my people, which are called by my name, shall humble themselves, and pray, and seek my face, and turn from their wicked ways; then will I hear from heaven, and will forgive their sin, and will heal their land" (2 Chronicles 7:14).

Central Truth: Revival comes when God's people humble themselves and repent.

Evangelism Emphasis: God saves sinners when they humble themselves and repent.

PRINTED TEXT

Nehemiah 8:2. And Ezra the priest brought the law before the congregation both of men and women, and all that could hear with understanding, upon the first day of the seventh month.

3. And he read therein before the street that was before the water gate from the morning until midday, before the men and women, and those that could understand; and the ears of all the people were attentive unto the book of the law.

5. And Ezra opened the book in the sight of all the people; (for he was above all the people;) and when he opened it, all the people stood up:

6. And Ezra blessed the Lord, the great God. And all the people answered, Amen, Amen, with lifting up their hands: and they bowed their heads, and worshipped the Lord with their faces to the ground.

9:1. Now in the twenty and fourth day of this month the children of Israel were assembled with fasting, and with sackclothes, and earth upon them.

5. Then the Levites, Jeshua, and Kadmiel, Bani, Hashabniah, Sherebiah, Hodijah, Shebaniah, and Pethahiah, said, Stand up and bless the Lord your God for ever and ever: and blessed be thy glorious name, which is exalted above all blessing and praise.

6. Thou, even thou, art Lord alone; thou hast made heaven, the heaven of heavens, with all their host, the earth, and all things that are therein, the seas, and all that is therein, and thou preservest them all; and the host of heaven worshippeth thee.

19. Yet thou in thy manifold mercies forsookest them not in the wilderness: the pillar of the cloud departed not from them by day, to lead them in the way; neither the pillar of fire by night, to shew them light, and the way wherein they should go.

10:28. And the rest of the people, the priests, the Levites, the porters, the singers, the Nethinims, and all they that had separated themselves from the people of the lands unto the law of God, their wives, their sons, and their daughters, every one having knowledge, and having understanding;

29. They clave to their brethren, their nobles, and entered into a curse, and into an oath, to walk in God's law, which was given by

Moses the servant of God, and to observe and do all the command- **ments of the Lord our Lord, and his judgments and his statutes.**

DICTIONARY
the street that was before the water gate—Nehemiah 8:3—a broad place near the Temple's southeast corner
Nethinims (NETH-ih-nims)—Nehemiah 10:28—a large group of Temple servants

LESSON OUTLINE

I. TAKE GOD'S WORD TO HEART
  A. Hearing the Word
  B. Following the Word
II. RECOUNT GOD'S MERCIES
  A. A Gathering of Confession
  B. Establishment of Israel
  C. Rebellion Against God
III. ASSUME GODLY RESPONSIBILITIES
  A. Committing to a Covenant
  B. Bringing the Firstfruits

LESSON EXPOSITION

INTRODUCTION

Leonard Ravenhill said, "True revival is God's coming to the aid of His sick church." It is crucial for us to understand revival in terms of Christian renewal from a Scriptural as well as historical standpoint. This renewal is seen in three major areas.

1. *There is a change in people's perspectives and lifestyles.* A changed moral climate occurs as individuals return to the Biblical standards of personal integrity, modesty and moral purity. Alcohol and other drugs are put aside and recognized for their harmful effects. People not only leave the encounter differently—they live differently.

2. *Revival influences people in their commitment to the church.* This is seen in increased membership, service attendance and financial receipts. Of greater importance is renewed commitment to the Bible as the infallible

Word of God, to holiness as God's standard for His people, and to salvation by faith in Jesus Christ.

3. *Revival includes conversion.* Backsliders (former believers) reestablish their relationship with Christ, and sinners experience the redemptive work of Jesus Christ in their lives. Evangelism of the lost cannot help but be a part of revival.

Today's lesson covers one of the great Biblical revivals. It demonstrates foremost the power of the Scriptures to touch people's hearts so their lives will be changed.

I. TAKE GOD'S WORD TO HEART
  (Nehemiah 7:73—8:18)

A. Hearing the Word (7:73—8:12)

(Nehemiah 7:73; 8:1, 4, 7-12 is not included in the printed text.)

8:2. And Ezra the priest brought the law before the congregation both of men and women, and all that could hear with understanding, upon the first day of the seventh month.

3. And he read therein before the street that was before the water gate from the morning until midday, before the men and women, and those that could understand; and the ears of all the people were attentive unto the book of the law.

5. And Ezra opened the book in the sight of all the people; (for he was above all the people;) and when he opened it, all the people stood up:

6. And Ezra blessed the Lord, the great God. And all the people

answered, Amen, Amen, with lifting up their hands: and they bowed their heads, and worshipped the Lord with their faces to the ground.

We now enter a study of one of the most fascinating revivals recorded in the past 25 centuries. Ezra the scribe had been in Jerusalem for 13 years following the Exile. During these years he had likely been teaching the Law with the distinctive directives of the various festivals and appointed seasons which were to be celebrated. Otherwise, there would be no need to mention the month of Tishri and the people gathering in Jerusalem. This was the time for celebrating the Feast of Trumpets.

In the presence of this large assembly the leaders requested Ezra to read from the Law. Though not a normal part of the celebration, it appears his previous teaching must have influenced them to the point of desiring to hear the Word. In compliance with their request, Ezra brought the Law before them to publicly read it.

Nehemiah 8:2, 3 emphasizes the makeup of this congregation. Both men and women were in attendance, along with children. The phrases "all that could hear with understanding" (v. 2) and "those that could understand" (v. 3) refer to children who were old enough to comprehend the words of the Law and respond even though not old enough to be categorized as adults. This concept has application for churches today. It is possible to so segregate children from the adult congregation that it inhibits their spiritual development. Too many children of Pentecostal parents are growing up without regularly taking part in corporate worship. While specialized children's ministry is important, children need spiritual education and nurture that come from corporate worship.

Verse 4 says a wooden platform was constructed on which Ezra stood. This enabled the people to see him and aided in the projection of his

voice. The people came to listen attentively. They wanted to hear, and it was made possible.

As Ezra opened the scroll to read, all the people stood in reverence. Surrounding him on both sides was a group of men. Their exact function is not mentioned; however, it is believed they participated in the presentation. Possibly Ezra read in Hebrew and various of these may have translated it in Chaldaic or Aramaic, the language of the Exile. Or they may have helped further understanding by explaining what was being said, as did the men described in verses 7 and 8.

After hearing God's Word, the people bowed before the Lord in worship. They also sorrowed when their sins and God's requirements became evident. Reading the Scriptures brought conviction. Today we must grasp the importance of the public reading of Scripture in the presence of the congregation. In many churches the Word of God rarely is read even as a text for the sermon. How can we expect people to read the Word in private if it isn't read in the worship service? Another lesson comes from the people's posture—they bowed in humility. Surely we need to give more attention to kneeling as a posture of response and worship.

At a certain point Nehemiah, Ezra and the Levites calmed the people and asked them to stop mourning. Now they were to rejoice, for that day had been set aside for the Lord. They were encouraged to eat, drink, and allow the joy of the Lord to be their strength (v. 10). What a balance is projected here! Yes, we should mourn over our sins and disobedience. But once there has been repentance, our sorrow turns into joy.

B. Following the Word (vv. 13-18)

(Nehemiah 8:13-18 is not included in the printed text.)

There is no value in hearing the Word and then failing to follow it. In fact, it would seem better to be ignorant of the truth than to be guilty of not following it. Hearing and obeying brings great reward.

When the Israelites heard of the need to celebrate the Feast of Tabernacles, they immediately proceeded to make the necessary preparations. They spread the word throughout the towns outside of Jerusalem so all could obediently follow God's Law.

This feast began four days after the Day of Atonement and marked the end of the harvest. For seven days the people lived in makeshift booths made of tree boughs. The purpose was to remember the years of tent life in the wilderness. They would be reminded of the disobedience at Kadesh-barnea, which led to the 38 years of wilderness wandering (Numbers 14). During this seven-day commemoration, daily burnt and meal offerings were presented to the Lord. Then, on the eighth day, all of the people gathered for a joint assembly (Nehemiah 8:18).

This was the first time Israel celebrated the Feast of Tabernacles since the 70-year exile. And it was the most joyous observance since the time of Joshua some 900 years earlier. No wonder the people mourned and grieved upon hearing the Law read, realizing that the religious observances had been neglected. However, following the encouragement of Nehemiah, their obedience and fulfillment of the Law became a tremendous source of joy (v. 17).

II. RECOUNT GOD'S MERCIES
     (Nehemiah 9:1-25)

A. A Gathering of Confession (vv. 1-5)

(Nehemiah 9:2-4 is not included in the printed text.)

1. Now in the twenty and fourth day of this month the children of Israel were assembled with fasting, and with sackclothes, and earth upon them.

5. Then the Levites, Jeshua, and Kadmiel, Bani, Hashabniah, Sherebiah, Hodijah, Shebaniah, and Pethahiah, said, Stand up and bless the Lord your God for ever and ever: and blessed be thy glorious name, which is exalted above all blessing and praise.

Nehemiah 9 lifts up the power of Scripture when people listen to it and are taught its significance to their personal lives. A short time after celebrating the Feast of Tabernacles, the people returned to deal with the Scriptural admonitions which had been presented to them during Ezra's reading of God's Law. They understood their plight and chose to right it in the presence of God. Verse 1 graphically presents their state of mourning over sin. Not only did they fast and wear sackcloth, but they proceeded to throw dust on their heads. This added step further indicated the seriousness of their spiritual concern.

Many people weep over their wrong actions but fail to go any further. That wasn't the case of these people. They took a major step in changing their ways by separating themselves from all foreigners. This doesn't seem to be a separation from marriage with non-Jews such as recorded in Ezra 10. Instead, it appears to be a separation from non-Jewish customs and other negative foreign influences.

Their process of spiritual renewal covered a six-hour period. For three hours the group stood and listened to the reading of the Law. After hearing the Word, the next three hours were spent in confessing their sins in a worship setting which revealed their dedication to God. Standing on a platform were eight Levites who led the people in their praises. Notice their directive to stand up. Apparently there was a change of posture after hearing the Word read. Possibly they had prostrated themselves during the time of confession.

Their praise started with a declaration of God's eternal being—without beginning and without ending. In our own prayers we always should begin with a recognition of who God is in terms of His characteristics and attributes rather than simply asking for His intervention in our lives.

B. Establishment of Israel (vv. 6-15)

(Nehemiah 9:7-15 is not included in the printed text.)

6. Thou, even thou, art Lord alone; thou hast made heaven, the heaven of heavens, with all their host, the earth, and all things that are therein, the seas, and all that is therein, and thou preservest them all; and the host of heaven worshippeth thee.

Following the normal pattern of recounting the past, Ezra's prayer reviews some of the key events in God's establishing Israel as a nation. Setting the stage is his recognition of God as Creator. Having made the heavens and earth, this great God surely can determine events among the people to whom He has given life. And in turn the multitudes are to offer their worship.

Verses 7 and 8 describe God's selection of Abraham and the covenant promising future events beyond his lifetime. In two verses Ezra summarized the events described in Genesis 11, 12, 13, 15 and 17. He pointed out Abraham's ethnic and geographic heritage, and then emphasized the reason for Abraham's being God's man—God valued his faithful heart. Though Abraham was not perfect, he demonstrated tremendous commitment to God as seen by his leaving a cultured city environment for an unknown destiny.

God promised Abraham the land of Canaan, which was then occupied by many heathen peoples. When Abraham died, the only piece of land in his possession was the field purchased so he could bury Sarah

(Genesis 23). However, the covenant came to pass more than 400 years later when Joshua triumphantly led Israel into Canaan. So Ezra prayed, "You have kept your promise because you are righteous" (Nehemiah 9:8, NIV).

Verses 9-12 reveal God's rescue of the Hebrews from Egypt through the means of miraculous events. He saw their suffering under the yoke of Egyptian slavery, and at the right time He answered with plagues which devastated the nation. Egypt's polytheism, coupled with disregard for God and His people, brought them destruction beyond imagination. When Pharaoh made a last effort to keep the Israelites, God provided escape by opening the Red Sea. God's people passed safely through on dry ground, but when the Egyptian army attempted the same crossing, the waters closed on them and destroyed all (Exodus 14). "In the day" and "in the night" God led His people (Nehemiah 9:12). What security!

Upon arrival at Mount Sinai, God encamped His people for some 13 months. During this time they became an established nation with religious and social guidelines. In a most dramatic means God spoke audibly to His people the basic laws which were to govern their lives. The Ten Commandments were followed with expanded guidelines providing for their social and physical well-being as well as their spiritual relationship with God.

Before moving to the next major section of his prayer, Ezra expressed God's total care for His people. Miraculously He provided bread and water. Manna was found on the ground six out of every seven days. On two occasions God caused a river of water to flow from a rock to quench their thirst. Also, God directed them to take possession of the Promised Land. But it is at this point where rebellion occurred, so it became necessary for

Ezra's prayer to remind the people of their heritage of sin in the face of God's care and provision.

C. Rebellion Against God (vv. 16-25)

(Nehemiah 9:16-18, 20-25 is not included in the printed text.)

19. Yet thou in thy manifold mercies forsookest them not in the wilderness: the pillar of the cloud departed not from them by day, to lead them in the way; neither the pillar of fire by night, to shew them light, and the way wherein they should go.

These 10 verses provide an overview of the sinful pride that entered the Israelites' hearts. It caused them to believe their powers of reason superseded God's divine power to provide and guide. First was their desiring an idol at Mount Sinai to represent the god who brought them from Egypt. This took place only a few weeks after hearing God speak against idolatry.

The second rebellion was at Kadesh-barnea when they refused to enter Canaan. They even went as far as to elect a leader to return them to the slavery of Egypt. Notice the stupidity that evidences itself when sin dominates. There was nothing back in Egypt except death and destruction.

Ezra prayed, "Because of your great compassion you did not abandon them in the desert" (v. 19, NIV). God chose to fulfill His covenant with Abraham even though the descendants were uncooperative. God led them, fed them, and taught them day by day. Their clothes never wore out. And they suffered no sore, swollen feet, which would normally occur with so much walking. Then, true to His word, God brought Israel into Canaan.

Verse 25 summarizes the completeness of God's actions. The Israelites defeated heavily fortified cities and took possession of the fertile land. Now they moved from living in tents to residing in permanent houses. Instead of having to plant vineyards, olive groves and fruit trees, they simply took possession of those in the land—no hard labor of digging in the soil or years of waiting for the first crop. Immediately the people were able to enjoy a diet of fresh crops.

Even in the times of God's discipline He doesn't forget either His promises or our needs. The big issue is whether or not His discipline and provision will lead us to mend our ways for the future. The rest of Ezra's prayer indicates that Israel didn't set an example which future generations could benefit from and follow. Instead, their disobedience forced God to allow judgment to come on them just as experienced by their forefathers.

III. ASSUME GODLY RESPONSIBILITIES (Nehemiah 10:28-39)

A. Committing to a Covenant (vv. 28-34)

(Nehemiah 10:30-34 is not included in the printed text.)

28. And the rest of the people, the priests, the Levites, the porters, the singers, the Nethinims, and all they that had separated themselves from the people of the lands unto the law of God, their wives, their sons, and their daughters, every one having knowledge, and having understanding;

29. They clave to their brethren, their nobles, and entered into a curse, and into an oath, to walk in God's law, which was given by Moses the servant of God, and to observe and do all the commandments of the Lord our Lord, and his judgments and his statutes.

Chapter 10 records the people's committing to a covenant of future godly actions which would fulfill God's Law. The initial verses record those individual family heads who chose to lead in separating themselves unto God. Verse 28 indicates the inclusiveness of this action by the people. It went beyond the heads of family to include all those who had both the knowledge and understanding of their actions.

Though this covenant covers the broadest application of the entire Law, notice some of the distinct issues which are highlighted. Each of them had a special application to these people at this point in time.

First of the five is the commitment to not intermarry with heathen tribes (v. 30). Could they expect to serve God in His holiness if they broke the laws of intermarriage which always contributed to idolatry? Of course not, so it is only logical for this to be at the top of the list.

Second is the commitment to keep the Sabbath holy as required in the Ten Commandments (v. 31). Not only must they refrain from merchandising on this day, but they would go a step further. They were to keep the sabbatical year, which included allowing the land to rest every seventh year as explained in the Book of the Law (Exodus 23:10, 11). What a step of faith, since it meant believing that the harvest of the sixth year would be sufficient until the next harvest two years later! There also was the canceling of all debts.

The next three commitments are tied to the ministry of the Temple and the Levites. If they were going to serve God, then provision must be made for the continuance of public worship.

The third commitment was for every man to pay a yearly Temple tax which covered the expenses for such items as the shewbread and sacrificial animals (vv. 32, 33). The Temple tax initiated under Moses was a half shekel (Exodus 30:13). But due to the financial poverty of the people, it was lowered to a one-third shekel.

Their fourth commitment provided

firewood for the altar sacrifices (v. 34). The need for fuel can easily be overlooked in our study, but to the ministering priests it was an absolute necessity. Their chosen means of selection for providing the wood was a rotation system determined by casting lots. The Law required the constant use of wood for the daily altar fires, but did not include the means of procuring it. Nehemiah chose to make this the people's responsibility (see 13:31).

The final commitment provides for the support of those ministering in the Temple (10:35-39). This will be discussed below.

B. Bringing the Firstfruits (vv. 35-39)

(Nehemiah 10:35-39 is not included in the printed text.)

The completeness of their spiritual renewal continued to be evident by the people's commitment to return to the Law by bringing the firstfruits of their crops to the Temple. This pattern of recognition of God's provision and their need to support the ministering tribe is seen repeatedly in the Pentateuch (Exodus 23:19; 34:26; Numbers 18:13-16; Deuteronomy 26:2).

In today's church there always should be a balance between spiritual blessings and practical responsibilities. We are to enjoy the benefits of relationship with God and His material blessings. Yet, at the same time each one of us has an obligation to obediently use a portion of our blessings for the support of those who are given the responsibility for spiritual ministry. Anyone who purposefully withholds tithes and offerings becomes guilty of robbing God (see Malachi 3:8).

GOLDEN TEXT HOMILY

"IF MY PEOPLE, WHICH ARE CALLED BY MY NAME, SHALL HUMBLE THEMSELVES, AND PRAY,

AND SEEK MY FACE, AND TURN FROM THEIR WICKED WAYS; THEN WILL I HEAR FROM HEAVEN, AND WILL FORGIVE THEIR SIN, AND WILL HEAL THEIR LAND" (2 Chronicles 7:14).

After Solomon's prayer of dedication of the Temple and the offering of sacrifices, the Lord appeared to Solomon by night and said, "I have heard thy prayer" (v. 12). In His appearance, the Lord called for the repentance of His people, prayer and reformation. God expects His people to recognize His right to rule their lives and to obey Him.

The blessings of God are conditional to nations and people. God will not continue to overlook a nation or people who does not sincerely serve Him. The answer to Solomon's prayer was conditionally promised. If God's people dishonored His name by their iniquity, then they could only expect His judgment. His people were to humble themselves before God and pray for the removal of the judgment, and seek the face and favor of God. This is a test of faith, a motive of obedience, and a rule of discipline.

God has not changed His command of obedience to His people. Today He calls for our total surrender and dedication; then we can expect His blessings upon us.—**Selected**

SENTENCE SERMONS

REVIVAL COMES when God's people humble themselves and repent.

—Selected

REVIVAL IS ABSOLUTELY ESSENTIAL to restrain the righteous anger of God, to restore the conscious awareness of God, and to reveal the gracious activity of God.

—Stephen Olford

PEOPLE SAY they are going to hold a revival; it doesn't matter if revival happens or not, as long as they hold one.

—J. Edwin Orr

ILLUMINATING THE LESSON

In 1734 revival began at Jonathan Edward's Congregational Church in Northampton, Massachusetts, after his having preached a series of sermons on justification by faith. These truths, along with the fear of God's having withdrawn from the land, unsettled the people and opened the floodgates of spiritual renewal. Soon both the community and the church were experiencing misery over sin followed by the marvelous joy of forgiveness. Some 300 individuals wept their way to conversion. Changes took place in their society, with strife, gossiping and backbiting disappearing. This is the true test of revival!

DAILY BIBLE READINGS

M. Know God's Word.
   Joshua 1:6-9
T. A Fallen Hero Redeemed.
   Judges 16:26-30
W. God Is Compassionate.
   Psalm 103:2-12
T. Repent or Perish.
   Luke 13:1-5
F. Born Again by the Word.
   1 Peter 1:17-23
S. Return to Your First Love.
   Revelation 2:1-7

TRUTH SEARCH
Creatively Teaching the Word

INTRODUCTORY DRAMA

Start today's lesson by having everyone stand. Ask them to remain standing as you read the entire books of Genesis through Deuteronomy. After you read the first few verses of Genesis, one student (whom you talked with before class) should sit down and complain that he is not going to keep standing while you read all those books—that will take hours!

At first you should act surprised at the response, then say that it all was an act, and have everyone sit down.

Today we're going to explore a time when the people of Israel were so hungry for God's Word that they listened to the Scriptures being read for many hours.

DISCUSSION QUESTIONS

**Take God's Word to Heart
(Nehemiah 7:73—8:18)**

1. After many years in exile, how had life changed for the Israelites (7:73)?

2. What did the people of Israel want Ezra to do? Why was this significant (8:1)?

3. Describe the people's hunger for God and His Word (8:1-6).

4. Explain the process described in verses 7 and 8.

5. Explain the Israelites' initial response to the Scriptures (v. 9).

6. Why did the Levites urge the people to respond differently (vv. 10-12)?

7. Describe the events depicted in verses 13-18 and their significance.

**Recount God's Mercies
(Nehemiah 9:1-8, 19-25)**

1. Explain the actions of the people in 9:1, 2.

2. In what ways did the people respond to the reading of God's Word (vv. 3, 4)?

3. List the specific blessings for which the people worshiped God (vv. 5-8).

4. From verses 19-25, how did God express mercies to Israel in these areas?

- Guidance:
- Instruction:
- Sustenance:
- Deliverance:
- Family:
- Shelter:
- Security:

**Assume Godly Responsibilities
(Nehemiah 10:28-39)**

1. Who entered into the covenant (10:28)?

2. What did the Israelites promise to do (v. 29)?

3. What confession did they specifically promise not to do (vv. 30, 31)? Why?

4. How did the people pledge to serve the Lord through giving (vv. 32, 33)?

5. How did the people pledge to bless the Lord from their possessions (vv. 35-38)?

6. What did the people promise to no longer neglect (v. 39)?

Promise of the Holy Spirit (Pentecost)

Study Text: Joel 2:28-32; Acts 2:1-39

Objective: To know the baptism in the Holy Spirit is available to every believer and accept this blessing by faith.

Golden Text: "The promise is unto you, and to your children, and to all that are afar off, even as many as the Lord our God shall call" (Acts 2:39).

Central Truth: The baptism in the Holy Spirit is promised to every believer.

Evangelism Emphasis: The Holy Spirit empowers believers to win the lost to Christ.

PRINTED TEXT

Joel 2:28. And it shall come to pass afterward, that I will pour out my spirit upon all flesh; and your sons and your daughters shall prophesy, your old men shall dream dreams, your young men shall see visions:

29. And also upon the servants and upon the handmaids in those days will I pour out my spirit.

30. And I will shew wonders in the heavens and in the earth, blood, and fire, and pillars of smoke.

31. The sun shall be turned into darkness, and the moon into blood, before the great and the terrible day of the Lord come.

32. And it shall come to pass, that whosoever shall call on the name of the Lord shall be delivered: for in mount Zion and in Jerusalem shall be deliverance, as the Lord hath said, and in the remnant whom the Lord shall call.

Acts 2:14. But Peter, standing up with the eleven, lifted up his voice, and said unto them, Ye men of Judaea, and all ye that dwell at Jerusalem, be this known unto you, and hearken to my words:

15. For these are not drunken, as ye suppose, seeing it is but the third hour of the day.

16. But this is that which was spoken by the prophet Joel;

17. And it shall come to pass in the last days, saith God, I will pour out of my Spirit upon all flesh: and your sons and your daughters shall prophesy, and your young men shall see visions, and your old men shall dream dreams:

18. And on my servants and on my handmaidens I will pour out in those days of my Spirit; and they shall prophesy.

37. Now when they heard this, they were pricked in their heart, and said unto Peter and to the rest of the apostles, Men and brethren, what shall we do?

38. Then Peter said unto them, Repent, and be baptized every one of you in the name of Jesus Christ for the remission of sins, and ye shall receive the gift of the Holy Ghost.

39. For the promise is unto you, and to your children, and to all that are afar off, even as many as the Lord our God shall call.

LESSON OUTLINE

I. PROMISE GIVEN
  A. The Spirit's Work
  B. The Judgment to Come
II. PROMISE FULFILLED
  A. The Outpouring
  B. The People's Response
  C. The Disciples' Sermon
III. PROMISE TO ALL
  A. The Conviction
  B. The Promise

LESSON EXPOSITION

INTRODUCTION

Return to the basics. Repeatedly this four-word phrase or some variation appears. In education we think of emphasizing the basic subjects of reading, writing and mathematics. In sports it means returning to the fundamental skills of the game. In theology it speaks of emphasizing the major doctrines of the faith. And to Pentecostals and Charismatics it reminds us of the need to return to the major passages which provide the foundations for our distinctive experience and life in the Spirit.

Even if we've heard people teach or preach from Joel 2 or Acts 2 many times, if we listen carefully, the old story will flow with freshness as though hearing it for the first time. Such teaching can transport us back to our spiritual heritage as Pentecostals.

This really shouldn't be amazing. When we gather with friends and relive past times together, we tell the same old stories. Laughter and even tears may be present. What happens the next time we get together? Some of the same old but special conversations flow again. We don't tire of them.

Shouldn't the same be true of those passages of Scripture which are the foundation for belief and experience? The answer should be a resounding "yes." Now, having established this principle, let's explore these special passages in Joel and Acts.

I. PROMISE GIVEN (Joel 2:28-32)

A. The Spirit's Work (vv. 28, 29)

28. And it shall come to pass afterward, that I will pour out my spirit upon all flesh; and your sons and your daughters shall prophesy, your old men shall dream dreams, your young men shall see visions:

29. And also upon the servants and upon the handmaids in those days will I pour out my spirit.

The passage in Joel precedes the events of Acts 2 by as many as 850 years. Very little is known about this prophet except for his being "the son of Pethuel" (Joel 1:1). He could have been a citizen of Judah, perhaps even residing in Jerusalem, in light of his references to Zion, Judah and Jerusalem. An invasion of locusts provided the opportunity for Joel to speak of the judgment which would come on the enemies of God. He also spoke of the blessings which would come to those who repented.   *Yes*

To grasp the seriousness of the setting, it's important to understand the dread and terror that locust invasions could strike in people's hearts. In a relatively short period of time all the vegetation in an area could be stripped completely from every stalk and branch. The intensity of this particular invasion had not been seen for several generations (1:2). It set the stage for the terrible judgments of God described in chapters 1 and 2. However, if the people would repent, there would be a tremendous spiritual harvest. Not to be overlooked are the material blessings which would accompany their repentance (2:21-27).

In verses 28 and 29 the prophet foretells of a distinct outpouring of the Holy Spirit which would be comprehensive. In the Old Testament a limited number of individuals experienced an outpouring of the Holy Spirit. Examples include the Spirit's coming on the 70 elders of Israel and their prophesying (Numbers 11:24-30) as well as the distinct power which came to the judges, of whom Samson stands out (Judges 14:6, 19; 15:14). But in the future the Holy Spirit's filling and empowerment would cross many boundaries, Joel proclaimed.

This future spiritual outpouring would reach beyond the borders of God's chosen people, Israel. Regardless of race, ethnic distinction or language, countless people would be included in this marvelous experience. There will also be no gender barriers. Instead of being reserved only for men in these patriarchal societies, this spiritual blessing would be given equally to both men and women.

The prophet further pointed out that age would not be a boundary. Old and young would be blessed equally. Both young and old would be active participants and vessels through whom the Holy Spirit would move.

Verse 28 speaks specifically of three ways the Spirit would speak—prophecy, dreams and visions. All of these are evident in the Old Testament among individuals chosen for the selective work of the Spirit for that time period. In the future the Spirit's work would explode beyond the limited usage of the past.

The word *prophesy* in the Hebrew text came from *naba*, which meant "to speak as moved upon by another." The prophet does not speak something on his or her own but something which has been initiated by God. The outpouring of God's Spirit would cause people in great numbers to be used by Him to speak His words.

The other two terms that amplify the result of the outpouring of the Spirit are *dreams* and *visions*. In the context of the concept just mentioned, prophecy, dreams and visions are to be understood as part of the manner in which God will communicate by the power of the Spirit unto those who would be caused to speak His word—those who would prophesy.

This passage is not to be interpreted as an exclusive description of God's means. That is, God speaks through more than just dreams and visions. Further, visions are not restricted to young men, and dreams are not restricted to old men. Finally, *prophesying* is not the only term which can describe the communication of God's Word. There are other concepts such as "preaching" and "witnessing" that could be used.

Verse 29 indicates the final boundary which this outpouring of the Holy Spirit would cross—social position. What a contrast! Not just prophets and judges, but even male and female servants would experience the outpouring of the Holy Spirit.

This prophecy has special significance when considering the social groups of the Roman Empire at the time of its fulfillment. It is estimated that more than half of the empire's population were in some form of slavery—forced or voluntary. Now they could be participants in this blessing.

B. The Judgment to Come (vv. 30-32)

30. And I will shew wonders in the heavens and in the earth, blood, and fire, and pillars of smoke.

31. The sun shall be turned into darkness, and the moon into blood, before the great and the terrible day of the Lord come.

32. And it shall come to pass, that whosoever shall call on the name of the Lord shall be delivered: for in mount Zion and in Jerusalem shall be deliverance, as the Lord hath said, and in the remnant whom the Lord shall call.

Verses 30 and 31 provide a brief description of the judgment which will come on those who fail to repent and follow the Lord. The word *wonder* came from a Hebrew word meaning "extraordinary event which serves as a sign." Just as the Spirit is being poured out on all nations, so will divine judgment. Some of the forerunners to this great and terrible day will be earthshaking. Blood, fire and smoke not only speak of war but are reminders of the plagues which God sent on Egypt—water turning to blood and horrendous lightning accompanying the hail (Exodus 7:19-21; 9:22-24). Pillars or columns of smoke can result from cities being captured and burned.

The blotting out of the sun and the moon turning the color of blood probably refers to God's miraculously obscuring the light of the sun and changing the color of the moon. Solar and lunar eclipses do not seem to qualify as an explanation here due to their running in cycles and being able to be predicted. A precedent for this can be seen in the plague of darkness which God sent on Egypt as the ninth plague (Exodus 10:21-23).

All of these events are preparatory for the Judgment Day. They send fear. Yet, God doesn't allow for hopelessness. There is deliverance and salvation for those who repent.

Verse 32 isn't talking about a closet believer, but rather someone making a public confession. If the Lord is enthroned in one's heart spiritually in the same manner as Jerusalem had become the physical center for worship, that person will be saved in that day of the Great Judgment which will be poured out on all humankind.

The word *delivered* comes from a Hebrew root concept which meant "to be smooth" or "to slip through." Those who call upon the name of the Lord will be able to literally "slip out of" and avoid the final judgment of the Lord. They will be the remnant—"those who escape."

In our rush to study the marvelous spiritual renewal of the Holy Spirit, it's imperative that we not overlook the reality of God's judgment. Since the outpouring of the Holy Spirit took place on the Day of Pentecost nearly 2,000 years ago, it means we are that much closer to God's reckoning.

II. PROMISE FULFILLED
(Acts 2:1-36)

A. The Outpouring (vv. 1-4)

(Acts 2:1-4 is not included in the printed text.)

The events of Acts 2 mark the beginning of the fulfillment of the prophecy in Joel 2:28-32. The three elements found in these verses—the outpouring of the Spirit, the evidence of God's final judgment, and the deliverance of all who call upon the name of the Lord—are all found in Acts 2. As the believers were gathered in the Upper Room in unity and obedience, they experienced phenomena that touched their hearing, vision and speech. First, they heard the sound of a violent wind that filled the entire structure in which they were meeting. They did not feel the force—they just heard it. Second, "they saw what seemed to be tongues of fire that separated and came to rest on each of them" (v. 3, *NIV*). Yet, there was no smell of smoke, singeing of their clothing or sensation of heat. Third, everyone of them began to speak in a language they had not learned.

Wind and fire are symbols of the Holy Spirit. Speaking in a language previously unlearned indicates a distinct sign of having experienced the baptism of the Holy Spirit.

B. The People's Response (vv. 5-13)

(Acts 2:5-13 is not included in the printed text.)

Apparently the disciples moved from the Upper Room to an open place in the city, perhaps near the Temple. Jews from all parts of the Roman Empire were visiting for the celebration of the Feast of Pentecost. And much to their amazement they heard Galilean Jews speaking the languages of their adopted lands. Realizing the impossibility of these Galileans having traveled and/or been schooled to speak so many languages, they were utterly amazed.

The wonders of God were being dramatically spoken through these tongues (v. 11). What a witness! Empowered by the Holy Spirit, God used the disciples to reach out to unbelievers with a distinct message.

The question arose as to the meaning of such an event. But some in attendance weren't nearly as intrigued or inquisitive. They simply dismissed the disciples' actions as the result of drinking too much wine. You wonder how they could come to this conclusion. One of the results of drunkenness never is the ability to speak fluently in a language never learned!

C. The Disciples' Sermon (vv. 14-36)

(Acts 2:19-36 is not included in the printed text.)

14. But Peter, standing up with the eleven, lifted up his voice, and said unto them, Ye men of Judaea, and all ye that dwell at Jerusalem, be this known unto you, and hearken to my words:

15. For these are not drunken, as ye suppose, seeing it is but the third hour of the day.

16. But this is that which was spoken by the prophet Joel;

17. And it shall come to pass in the last days, saith God, I will pour out of my Spirit upon all flesh: and your sons and your daughters shall prophesy, and your young men shall see visions, and your old men shall dream dreams:

18. And on my servants and on my handmaidens I will pour out in those days of my Spirit; and they shall prophesy.

With Peter being the chief spokesperson, the 12 disciples took full advantage of this unique opportunity for witness. They intended to explain precisely what the crowd was witnessing and desired their close attention. However, first Peter addressed the accusation of drunkenness. It was only 9 o'clock in the morning, so a large group of people heavily indulging in wine wasn't even a reasonable possibility. Having laid that to rest, Peter turned to Joel's prophecy. Emphatically he stated they were witnessing the fulfillment of Joel's words. As promised, God was pouring out His Spirit.

Remember that the 12 disciples represented only 10 percent of the people who received the Spirit on Pentecost. There were 108 other believers—male and female, young and old—who received this baptism, just as Joel had prophesied. But this was just the beginning. Pentecost was only a few drops of the coming shower.

Notice verse 21. After highlighting Joel's prophecy, Peter turned the crowd's attention to Jesus Christ. To fully grasp the Spirit's coming, they must see it within the framework of Christ's life. He clearly pointed out that God's intention for Christ's earthly ministry included His suffering on the cross.

Moving beyond Christ's death and burial, Peter emphasized Christ's resurrection from the grave and current position at the right hand of the Father. He added that the current outpouring of the Holy Spirit fulfilled the divine plan and promise (v. 33).

Peter's sermon on the Day of Pentecost set the pattern of New Testament preaching in the early church. It all centered on Christ's death, burial, resurrection, ascension and return. This doesn't mean Christ's teachings and miracles were minimized, but rather they served as support to the reality of His being the God-man sent for a divine purpose.

Peter quoted David from the Book of Psalms (16:8-11; 110:1) as support for Christ's resurrection and glorification (see Acts 2:25-28, 34, 35). He declared that though King David occupied an important place in Israel's history, Jesus is far greater. They saw fit to crucify Him, but God exalted Him as "both Lord and Christ" (v. 36). Not only did His death and resurrection provide salvation, but He rules over all.

III. PROMISE TO ALL (Acts 2:37-39)

A. The Conviction (v. 37)

37. Now when they heard this, they were pricked in their heart, and said unto Peter and to the rest of the apostles, Men and brethren, what shall we do?

What began with a mass of people inquiring concerning some unusual sights and sounds led to a point of spiritual conviction. The truth of fulfilled prophecy and the true identity of Jesus forced them to a point of decision. Would they reject this marvelous opportunity, attempt to subdue the conviction and go away? Or would they take the next step by believing on Jesus Christ?

The crowd was feeling much more than a slight twinge of conscience or a passing sense of guilt. Conviction penetrated deeply. One modern translation states they were "cut to the heart" (NIV). It demanded their finding a solution to their inner agony.

Notice how they addressed the apostles as "brothers" (NIV). They were brothers in terms of their being Jewish. Now they would be given the opportunity to become brothers in Christ.

The question asked is very simple. They didn't spend time in idle discussion on insignificant questions. Only one thing mattered! They wanted to know, "What shall we do?"

Before moving to the next two verses, consideration needs to be given to the power of the spoken (preached) Word. Filled with the Holy Spirit the disciples had boldly witnessed to the gathered crowd as Jesus had said they would be empowered to do (Acts 1:8). This same powerful witnessing through the work of the Holy Spirit needs to be evident today in the pulpit and in personal witnessing. His power can and will be evident provided each of us walks daily in the Holy Spirit and seeks His ministry through us.

B. The Promise (vv. 38, 39)

38. Then Peter said unto them, Repent, and be baptized every one of you in the name of Jesus Christ for the remission of sins, and ye shall receive the gift of the Holy Ghost.

39. For the promise is unto you, and to your children, and to all that are afar off, even as many as the Lord our God shall call.

Peter's response provided several simple steps. Though salvation involves the complexity of Divinity interacting with humanity, becoming a believer continues to be a simple process. There are no complex rigors to be completed. The requirement is humility which allows one to repent. Repentance cannot occur unless an individual humbly looks to God and recognizes his or her condition as a sinner.

Self-righteousness separates us from God and keeps us from realizing the joy of salvation. But when we say, "I am a sinner needing Your forgiveness," it opens the door for cleansing and spiritual rebirth.

In ourselves repentance doesn't come easy because it requires confronting our sin and personal inability to develop an acceptable relationship with God. Yet as the Holy Spirit convicts and draws us to Christ, we recognize it as the only feasible action.

Repentance which brings salvation is more than being sorry for sins.

It means making a turnaround. Through the drawing of the Holy Spirit, a person determines to begin a new life direction in obedience to the directives and principles of Scripture. Without this Spirit-enabled about-face there is no salvation.

Next, Peter stated their need to be baptized. Water baptism by immersion was a practice known to Jews prior to the preaching and practice of John the Baptist. When non-Jews converted to Judaism, water baptism became the sign of this major religious transition. However, when John the Baptist's ministry began, the focus of his message was to *repent* and be baptized. After experiencing inner spiritual renewal, it was to be followed by an outward, public sign of one's commitment.

Obedience to these steps opens the door for Spirit baptism. Receiving "the gift of the Holy Spirit" (v. 38, *NIV*) isn't a referral to the initial work of the Spirit as He regenerates and begins the process of sanctification. Rather, this "promise" (v. 39) points to the baptism of the Holy Spirit as had just been experienced by those assembled in the Upper Room. It is a work of God's grace separate from salvation.

Peter was pointing them to the opportunity for Joel's prophecy to become a reality in their lives. They too could experience the empowerment and the initial evidence of speaking in tongues just as they had witnessed.

This marvelous truth continues nearly 20 centuries later. Joel's prophecy of the Spirit's outpouring continues. It is for us who are far removed in time from the Day of Pentecost.

GOLDEN TEXT HOMILY

"THE PROMISE IS UNTO YOU, AND TO YOUR CHILDREN, AND TO ALL THAT ARE AFAR OFF, EVEN AS MANY AS THE LORD OUR GOD SHALL CALL" (Acts 2:39).

It is unlikely that the writer of this scripture had a full conception of just how far the scope of his statements would extend. He may have visualized "to all that are afar off" in terms of the area of the Middle East or even of the then-known world. But there is no way he could have fully grasped the vast sweep of the promise of this scripture.

Many times we are too small in our thinking when it comes to the promises of God. Even while we are thinking of the infinite possibilities of what God can accomplish, we are probably underestimating Him.

There is an old saying, "What the human mind can conceive, it can achieve." But God can achieve those things that the human mind can never conceive or comprehend. It is impossible to cast the promises of God in such cosmic terms that they fully explore the range of His power.

See the promise of Acts 2 being lived out today. According to the *World Christian Encyclopedia*, there are now more than 500 million Pentecostals worldwide. They primarily live in Latin America, Asia and Africa.

If current growth rates continue, there will be 811 million Pentecostals by 2025.—**Selected**

SENTENCE SERMONS

THE BAPTISM in the Holy Spirit is promised to every believer.

—Selected

GOD COMMANDS US to be filled with the Spirit; and if we aren't filled, it's because we're living beneath our privileges.

—D.L. Moody

THERE MUST BE an emptying before there can be a filling.

—George Sweeting

EVANGELISM APPLICATION

THE HOLY SPIRIT EMPOWERS BELIEVERS TO WIN THE LOST TO CHRIST.

In ourselves we cannot bring an unbeliever to change his/her ways and enter a new relationship with Jesus Christ. And few of us would ever encourage people to consider the claims of Christ but for His giving us the desire and drive to do so.

The Holy Spirit empowers some Christians to win unbelievers through anointed preaching and persuasive logic based on the Word of God. Others are behind-the-scenes people who tell the good news of Jesus Christ in personal conversations. Each way demonstrates the ability to boldly speak of the Savior and the gift of eternal life.

ILLUMINATING THE LESSON

What changes a shy 14-year-old from an economically deprived home into an aggressive, confident young man who led his high school athletic teams to state recognition? How would this same young man excel in higher education until he earned a doctorate?

His pastor loved to tell the story of the boy who would hardly lift his eyes to shake hands, yet who dramatically changed after receiving the baptism of the Holy Spirit. Now that's empowerment!

DAILY BIBLE READINGS

M. Anointed by the Spirit.
   Numbers 11:25-29
T. Led by the Spirit.
   Ezekiel 3:10–14
W. Born of the Spirit.
   John 3:1-8
T. Ministry of the Spirit.
   John 16:5-15
F. Witness of the Spirit.
   Romans 8:12-17
S. Filled With the Spirit.
   Ephesians 5:15-21

TRUTH SEARCH
Creatively Teaching the Word

DISCUSSION QUESTIONS

Promise Given
(Joel 2:28-32)

1. Explain the meaning of God's promise, "I will pour out my Spirit" (v. 28).

2. What does "upon all flesh" mean (v. 28)?

3. When would the outpouring take place?

4. Through what three means did God promise to speak (v. 28)? What is different about these three, and what is the same?

5. What is the significance of the signs mentioned in verses 30 and 31?

6. To whom would salvation be available (v. 32)?

Promise Fulfilled
(Acts 2:14-18)

1. What did some onlookers say about those who had been filled with the Spirit (v. 15)? Why?

2. According to the apostle Peter, when did Joel's prophecy begin to be fulfilled (v. 16)?

3. If that Pentecost outpouring took place "in the last days" (v. 17), what days are we living in now? What does the term "last days" mean?

4. Is the outpouring of the Spirit limited by age or gender (vv. 17, 18)?

Promise to All
(Acts 2:37-39)

1. As Peter preached his Pentecost message, the people were "cut to the heart" (v. 37, *NIV*). What does this mean, and how did it happen?

2. What question did the people ask, and why (v. 37)?

3. What must a person do to be able to receive the gift of the Spirit (v. 38)?

4. What does the phrase "to all that are afar off" mean (v. 39)?

5. Who can receive the gift of the Spirit (v. 39)?

TESTIMONIES

Have adults from different age groups—senior adult, middle adult, and young adult—testify about being filled with the Spirit and the difference this gift has made in their lives.

INTRODUCTION TO SUMMER QUARTER

S ome of the most valuable Christian doctrine was penned by Paul while he was in prison. Lessons 1-8 focus on some of these principles as found in Ephesians, Philippians, Colossians and Philemon.

The second unit (lessons 9-13) address "Revival and Renewal," with lessons drawn from various books.

Lesson expositions for the summer quarter were written by the Reverend Rodney Hodge (A.B.), an ordained minister who has served as minister of music for 30 years at Northwood Temple Pentecostal Holiness Church in Fayetteville, North Carolina. He holds degrees from Emmanuel College and the University of Georgia and did graduate studies in history at the University of Georgia.

Reverend Hodge has written numerous Bible study programs, as well as dramas and music productions, and has produced an entire series of theater productions for church use. The Reverend Hodge presently writes adult Sunday school literature for the International Pentecostal Holiness Church.

Spiritual Blessings in Christ

Study Text: Ephesians 1:1-23
Objective: To acknowledge the many spiritual blessings we have in Christ and rejoice in the redemption He provided.
Time: Probably in A.D. 61
Place: Written from a Roman prison
Golden Text: "Blessed be the God and Father of our Lord Jesus Christ, who hath blessed us with all spiritual blessings in heavenly places in Christ" (Ephesians 1:3).
Central Truth: The blessings of redemption come through Christ.
Evangelism Emphasis: Christians should testify to the lost of the blessings of redemption.

PRINTED TEXT

Ephesians 1:3. Blessed be the God and Father of our Lord Jesus Christ, who hath blessed us with all spiritual blessings in heavenly places in Christ:

4. According as he hath chosen us in him before the foundation of the world, that we should be holy and without blame before him in love:

5 Having predestinated us unto the adoption of children by Jesus Christ to himself, according to the good pleasure of his will,

6. To the praise of the glory of his grace, wherein he hath made us accepted in the beloved.

7. In whom we have redemption through his blood, the forgiveness of sins, according to the riches of his grace;

13. In whom ye also trusted, after that ye heard the word of truth, the gospel of your salvation: in whom also after that ye believed, ye were sealed with that holy Spirit of promise,

14. Which is the earnest of our inheritance until the redemption of the purchased possession, unto the praise of his glory.

15. Wherefore I also, after I heard of your faith in the Lord Jesus, and love unto all the saints,

16. Cease not to give thanks for you, making mention of you in my prayers;

17. That the God of our Lord Jesus Christ, the Father of glory, may give unto you the spirit of wisdom and revelation in the knowledge of him:

18. The eyes of your understanding being enlightened; that ye may know what is the hope of his calling, and what the riches of the glory of his inheritance in the saints,

19. And what is the exceeding greatness of his power to us-ward who believe, according to the working of his mighty power,

20. Which he wrought in Christ, when he raised him from the dead, and set him at his own right hand in the heavenly places,

21. Far above all principality, and power, and might, and dominion, and every name that is named, not only in this world, but also in that which is to come:

22. And hath put all things under his feet, and gave him to be the head over all things to the church,

23. Which is his body, the fulness of him that filleth all in all.

LESSON OUTLINE

I. BLESSINGS OF REDEMPTION
   A. Blessings From the Father
   B. Chosen for Blessings
   C. Blessings From God's Son

II. GUARANTEE OF REDEMPTION
   A. For His Glory
   B. Blessings Through the Holy Spirit

III. GOD'S POWER TO REDEEM
   A. Paul's Prayers
   B. Inherited Riches
   C. Christ's Power in Us
   D. Christ's Church

LESSON EXPOSITION

INTRODUCTION

The first unit of this quarter consists of eight lessons on Paul's four *prison epistles* (Ephesians, Philippians, Colossians, Philemon). An epistle is simply a letter between two or more parties, although it generally carries the connotation of a more formal, extended correspondence. Bearing this in mind, Philemon might be considered less of an epistle and more of a personal letter. Still, all of Paul's four works written during his first imprisonment carry a personal, intimate quality to them.

During New Testament times there was no postal service under Roman rule except for official state documents. Private correspondence had to be sent by messengers, or by merchants and travelers who happened to be going in the right direction. All of Paul's letters (with the possible exception of Ephesians), were addressed to particular churches. The other epistles of the New Testament were general letters, intended to be doctrinal teachings that were circulated from congregation to congregation, city to city. Some say that Ephesians falls into this category.

Our first three lessons will be studies on this letter. In Ephesians, Paul has no bones to pick, no doctrinal controversies to correct, no false teachers to expose. Instead, he overflows with profound truths revealed to him in his life of faith. He wants every believer to grow in faith, love, wisdom, and understanding of the depths of God's love for humanity.

Paul was the missionary to the Gentile world. While winding his way back to Antioch during his second missionary journey (A.D. 53), he stopped at Ephesus briefly (Acts 18:19-21). He left his ministry friends, Aquila and Priscilla, there to pioneer a church. Two years later, while on his third journey, he stayed in Ephesus for two years and evangelized the entire area (Acts 19, 20). The letter to the Ephesians was written some 10 years later while in prison in Rome. Though he was waiting to go on trial for his own life, he was more concerned about the spiritual health of the churches he had founded. Paul felt a major obligation to teach the Word of God accurately and build up the saints in a true faith.

Paul addresses his letter to the *saints* at Ephesus. Were these people particularly holy that they should be given such a lofty title? No. The word has suffered from misuse. A saint is simply a person who has trusted Jesus Christ as Savior. He or she is alive both physically and spiritually, and has been called for the Lord's purposes.

Our lesson is centered on *riches in Christ*. In the Old Testament, God promised Israel material blessing as a reward for obedience (see Deuteronomy 28:1-13). The blessings for saints in Christ are primarily spiritual, though our physical and material needs while still on earth will be met. The Lord promises to supply *all* our needs "according to his riches in glory by Christ Jesus" (Philippians 4:19). How are these needs met? What is the conduit through which Christ's riches become ours? The Holy Spirit channels Christ's blessings to us.

Our spiritual blessings are obviously more important than our material ones. Paul had caught a glimpse of all that would belong to the saints in glory. The Christian has a dual citizenship—one on earth and one in heaven. Heaven is where Jesus is right now (Ephesians 1:20), and also where the believer is seated with Him (2:6). Physically, the saints are still in human bodies, but spiritually are in a higher place. That higher place provides the direction and motivation to deal with the present earthly place.

The fact that Paul writes about riches is significant because Ephesus was a wealthy city. The Temple of Diana, one of the seven wonders of the ancient world, was there, and was the depository for many of the great art works of the time. Paul compares the church of Jesus Christ to a temple and shows that the wealth Christ gives is far beyond anything that might be seen in a heathen temple.

I. BLESSINGS OF REDEMPTION (Ephesians 1:3-11)

A. Blessings From the Father (v. 3)

3 Blessed be the God and Father of our Lord Jesus Christ, who hath blessed us with all spiritual blessings in heavenly places in Christ.

God the Father has made us rich. Paul directs his praise to the Father for the wonderful grace He bestowed in sending Jesus to earth. Jesus became the visible representation of the Father to humanity. Until Jesus came, we could picture the Father only in ethereal terms. Jesus put flesh and blood to the eternal God.

God had begun to reveal Himself to humanity through the shadows and types of the Old Testament, but few

men and women actually understood and had any type of personal relationship with Him. Jesus makes this relationship possible, restoring what had been lost in the Garden of Eden. Through Christ, we share in the riches of God's wonderful grace.

There are many rich people on earth today, but none as rich as God the Father. Also, earthly riches will all be left behind as people die, but the spiritual riches we are granted will last for eternity.

B. Chosen for Blessings (vv. 4-6)

4. According as he hath chosen us in him before the foundation of the world, that we should be holy and without blame before him in love:

5. Having predestinated us unto the adoption of children by Jesus Christ to himself, according to the good pleasure of his will,

6. To the praise of the glory of his grace, wherein he hath made us accepted in the beloved.

Here Paul declares the doctrine of election. Before Adam was ever created, God knew he would fail. He knew the human heart, given the right of choice, would at some point fall prey to Satan's temptation. So the entire plan of salvation was foreordained before Adam was formed in the Garden. Thus, salvation begins with God.

It has been said that most world religions are people seeking God. However, Christianity is God seeking us. Jesus said, "Ye have not chosen me, but I have chosen you" (John 15:16). Paul said, "There is none that seeketh after God" (Romans 3:11). The plan of salvation is based entirely on God's grace, not on anything we can do of ourselves.

Why would God choose us? Paul is amazed at the grace bestowed on lowly humanity. We are totally undeserving. The plan for our salvation would not be possible without the work of Jesus. Because of Jesus, we are made holy and blameless in the Father's sight. There is nothing we could do to merit this, and neither can we take any credit. The plan was initiated by God and carried out by His Son. We are merely the heirs.

Are there any costs involved for us to pay? Certainly. Paul says, "Now if we are children, then we are heirs—heirs of God and co-heirs with Christ, if indeed we share in his sufferings in order that we may also share in his glory" (Romans 8:17, *NIV*). Along with the treasures, there are potential sufferings we must face. We say *potential,* because God's plan is different for every follower. However, all will face some type of suffering. Economic and social deprivation, as well as martyrdom, have been typical of the costs to many believers down through the centuries. Bearing the name of Jesus means giving up certain rights while on this earth. However, the ultimate glories are more than worth any costs incurred now.

A key word in this passage is *adoption.* Entrance into God's family is by the new birth. The new birth gives us the rights of adopted children—but with adult standing. God gives us the eternal privileges and responsibilities of His kingdom. Rather than being guaranteed by an earthly legal process, the adoption is secured by "the good pleasure of his [God's] will" (Ephesians 1:5).

God's marvelous grace is displayed by the act of adoption into God's family (v. 6). The believer is "accepted" (an act of unmerited favor) into "the beloved"—into Christ. Paul explains in Romans 8:23, 24 that we cannot fully see our adoption status while here on earth, but we wait for it patiently by hope when Jesus returns.

C. Blessings From God's Son
   (vv. 7-11)

(Ephesians 1:8-11 is not included in the printed text.)

7. In whom we have redemption through his blood, the forgiveness of sins, according to the riches of his grace.

All three persons of the Godhead are involved in our salvation. The Father chose us to be in Christ from eternity past. However, that alone will not save us, for He gives us free will. Jesus died on the cross as a ransom for our sins. The Holy Spirit convicts us and draws us to yield our hearts to Christ's wooing.

All three persons are involved, yet there are specific blessings Christ has brought us:

1. *He has redeemed us* (v. 7). To *redeem* means to purchase and then set free. A slave could be bought by a master and then given permanent freedom. The price Jesus paid for us was His own blood (1 Peter 1:18, 19). Our slave masters were sin, the law, Satan and the world. We are free from the bondage of each of these.

2. *He has forgiven us* (v. 7). Every year on the Day of Atonement, the sins of the people were ceremonially placed on a scapegoat, who was then carried away into the wilderness. Christ carried our sins away. Nothing can accuse us of the past. In God's sight we are free from the consequences of all the wrongs we committed before coming to Christ.

3. *He has revealed the mystery of God's will* (vv. 8-10). The Old Testament prophets caught glimpses of what God was planning. They saw things but had limited understanding of what they were seeing. The entire story, from Genesis to Malachi, is one ever-broadening revelation of how God was going to restore humanity.

Jesus' life, ministry, sacrifice and death ended the mystery. All things will finally reunite under the authority of Jesus. "Sin is tearing everything apart, but in Christ, God will gather everything together in the culmination of the ages. We are part of this great eternal program" (Wiersbe).

The prophets of old would have given everything to have the benefits we have. They only saw glimpses of God's plan, but we have seen the Son revealed.

One great benefit of redemption is that wisdom and spiritual discernment accompany it. Even the most uneducated believer can be wise because of God's provision. How many Christians over the ages who have had little education, or even limited ability to comprehend the Scriptures, still have been wise in the ways of God! God imparts wisdom and discernment. It is not humanly learned.

4. *We both have and are an inheritance* (v. 11). Paul says that in Christ "we have obtained an inheritance." However, it is also possible to translate this to say "we *were made* an inheritance." We are an inheritance for the Lord's enjoyment. The Westminster Confessional says the purpose of humanity "is to glorify God and enjoy Him forever." We were valuable enough to God that He paid the price of His own Son's life to purchase us.

Peter communicates a similar message in 1 Peter 1:1-4. Peter calls believers God's *elect* who have been chosen for "an inheritance incorruptible." God gave us His Son as a gift. At the same time, we are His gift to His Son.

II. GUARANTEE OF REDEMPTION (Ephesians 1:12-14)

A. For His Glory (v. 12)

(Ephesians 1:12 is not included in the printed text.)

The *we* Paul speaks of in this verse is believed by many to indicate the Jews who had longed for the coming of the Messiah over the centuries. Others believe he meant the Jews who accepted the gospel before it was widely preached to the Gentiles. However, he might simply have meant those who had first believed the

gospel and went on to preach it everywhere. Whatever the case, all became equal partakers of the same privileges in Christ. "Paul pointed out the timing of God's plan of bringing the gospel message through the Jews and then offering it to the Gentiles. Yet throughout this eulogy, Paul continued to focus on the unity in Christ of all believers, resulting in the praise of his glory" (*Life Application Commentary Series*).

B. Blessings Through the Holy Spirit (vv. 13, 14)

13. In whom ye also trusted, after that ye heard the word of truth, the gospel of your salvation: in whom also after that ye believed, ye were sealed with that holy Spirit of promise,

14. Which is the earnest of our inheritance until the redemption of the purchased possession, unto the praise of his glory.

The process of salvation is outlined here. First, we hear the gospel—that Christ died for our sins, was buried, and rose again. Although the message came first to the Jews (Romans 1:16), God sent Paul to bring the good news to the Gentile world. The Ephesians heard the message and realized it was for them. They believed, and their faith brought salvation. The Spirit sealed them immediately. The sealing was the evidence that salvation had occurred. Paul said to the Romans, "You, however, are controlled not by the sinful nature but by the Spirit, if the Spirit of God lives in you. And if anyone does not have the Spirit of Christ, he does not belong to Christ" (Romans 8:9, *NIV*).

Is this sealing the same as the baptism of the Holy Spirit as described in Acts 2? No. Look at what happened when Jesus appeared to the disciples after His resurrection: "He breathed on them and said, 'Receive the Holy Spirit'" (John 20:22, *NIV*). Here the disciples moved from an old covenant relationship to a new covenant one. They were sealed with the Spirit in that room, but it was not until some weeks later that the fullness of Pentecost arrived. They had been sealed earlier, but at Pentecost they were empowered (Acts 1:8).

What does it mean to be sealed? In the ancient world, ownership was indicated by attaching one's seal to his possessions. The Spirit is the One who tags us with His mark, sealing us for ownership by the Father. Paul said, "The Spirit himself testifies with our spirit that we are God's children. Now if we are children, then we are heirs—heirs of God and co-heirs with Christ, if indeed we share in his sufferings in order that we may also share in his glory" (Romans 8:16, 17, NIV). The seal of the Spirit indicates ownership, but also assures us of divine protection. "We are owned by our Lord and are under His protection until the great day of redemption" (R. Kent Hughes, *The Mystery of the Body of Christ*).

Paul says the Holy Spirit is the "earnest of our inheritance" (Ephesians 1:14). The Holy Spirit is our deposit, or down payment, that guarantees our inheritance. In ancient Greek and Roman cultures it was customary to make an *arrabon*, or deposit, for a major purchase. This was simply the first installment payment. In today's real estate market this is called *earnest money*. The Holy Spirit operating in our lives is a foretaste of what our glorified life in heaven will be like. Thus, we say the blessing of the Father has been lavished to us who are "in Christ," but the conduit for these blessings is the Holy Spirit. We need to be open, available, and hungry for the Spirit to move in us.

III. GOD'S POWER TO REDEEM
(Ephesians 1:15-23)

A. Paul's Prayers (vv. 15, 16)

15. Wherefore I also, after I heard of your faith in the Lord Jesus, and love unto all the saints,

16. Cease not to give thanks for you, making mention of you in my prayers.

Paul faithfully prayed for the Ephesian believers. His prayers included thanksgiving for these believers' faith and Christian love. His prayers were unceasing.

In the rest of this chapter we read the content of Paul's prayers for the Ephesians.

B. Inherited Riches (vv. 17, 18)

17. That the God of our Lord Jesus Christ, the Father of glory, may give unto you the spirit of wisdom and revelation in the knowledge of him:

18. The eyes of your understanding being enlightened; that ye may know what is the hope of his calling, and what the riches of the glory of his inheritance in the saints.

An old saying speaks of a baby born with a "silver spoon in his mouth." That's exactly what happens when a person comes to Christ. He or she is born again, and also born rich. However, a child rarely has an understanding of his or her inheritance. As believers, we have to be educated as to who we are, what our inheritance is, and how to wisely use it. Paul was anxious for the Ephesians to look beyond their physical circumstances to see just how wealthy they were. The real riches of God's grace were within their grasps—if they could only look with spiritual eyes to see them.

"The eyes of your understanding" is translated in other versions as "the eyes of your heart." From a Biblical perspective, the heart is the center of one's being. Proverbs 4:23 says, "Above all else, guard your heart, for it is the wellspring of life" (NIV).

My heart is the real me. It is everything about me that departs from this body when I die. The body is nothing but flesh and blood. When it dies, it decays and goes back to dust. However, the real me lives on. The spiritual self operates in a different set of dimensions from the physical man, so it has to have senses that fit that environment.

Back in Ephesians 1:3, Paul speaks of the *heavenly realms*. Look at the definition for this term: "the immaterial reign, the unseen universe, which lies beyond the world of sense" (J. Armitage Robinson, *The Epistle to the Ephesians*). The spiritual world is not just heaven; it is the unseen operation of God that is going on all around us right now. If we are in Christ, we were given spiritual senses when we were sealed by the Holy Spirit. The spiritual senses are the means by which we can feel, see, hear, smell, and taste the things of the spiritual realm—that is, the kingdom of God. With the natural senses, we can't discern what the Lord is saying. This can only be done with spiritual senses. From Scripture we can see that the Christian has spiritual senses that correspond to the physical senses:

1. *The inner person can see.* The psalmist said, "Open thou mine eyes, that I may behold wondrous things out of thy law" (119:18). Jesus said to Nicodemus, "No one can see the kingdom of God unless he is born again" (John 3:3, *NIV*).

2. *The inner person can hear.* Jesus said, "Who hath ears to hear, let him hear" (Matthew 13:9). The writer of Hebrews speaks of drifting saints as becoming "dull of hearing" (5:11).

3. *The inner person can taste.* David said, "Taste and see that the Lord is good: blessed is the man that trusteth in him" (Psalm 34:8).

4. *The inner person can smell.* Paul said, "I am amply supplied, now that I have received from Epaphroditus the gifts you sent. They are a fragrant offering, an acceptable sacrifice, pleasing to God" (Philippians 4:18, *NIV*). He also said, "But thanks be to God, who always leads us in triumphal procession in Christ and through us spreads everywhere the fragrance of the knowledge of him" (2 Corinthians 2:14, *NIV*).

5. *The inner person can touch.* Paul said in Athens, "[God did this] so that they should seek the Lord, in the hope that they might grope for Him and find Him, though He is not far from each one of us" (Acts 17:27, *NKJV*).

The ability to see, hear, smell, taste, and touch spiritual things doesn't come through the intellect (physical self), but through our heart (the spiritual self). Our spiritual senses must be opened by the Spirit of God. Paul prayed that the spiritual senses of the Ephesians be opened so that they might clearly know just what was theirs in the spiritual realm. The senses help us with daily life, but also give us the ability to look ahead to all the riches of the future.

Verse 18 speaks of the believer's *calling*. This is an important word in the Christian vocabulary. Peter speaks of us being called by God "out of darkness into his marvellous light" (1 Peter 2:9). We have been called by God's grace to a hope of a wonderful future. We have been called out of terrible darkness and given a tremendous life ahead. This prospect should be the dynamic force in our lives that encourages us to live worthy of the promises made to us.

We also see here that Christ has an inheritance—the saints. Not only do we have an inheritance in Christ, but He has one in us. He sees us as part of His wealth. He will not be fully satisfied until the church is in glory with Him. In His prayer at the close of the Last Supper, He said, "Father, I will that they also, whom thou hast given me, be with me where I am; that they may behold my glory, which thou hast given me: for thou lovedst me before the foundation of the world" (John 17:24).

C. Christ's Power in Us (vv. 19-21)

19. And what is the exceeding greatness of his power to us-ward who believe, according to the working of his mighty power,
20. Which he wrought in Christ, when he raised him from the dead, and set him at his own right hand in the heavenly places,
21. Far above all principality, and power, and might, and dominion, and every name that is named, not only in this world, but also in that which is to come.

By making us His inheritance, not only has God given us a great future, but we also have all the power of heaven available to us while still in this life. The "greatness of his power" is extended to us. The word *power* in Greek is *dunamis,* from which we get the English words *dynamite* and *dynamic.* Eternal energy becomes ours.

How many times have we heard stories of men and women who had great earthly wealth, but their personal health was so poor that they couldn't enjoy it! It is said that John D. Rockefeller lived for many years on simple crackers and milk because of stomach problems—when he could have afforded the most delicious food available to mankind. He was wealthy, but miserable at the same time. In the same sense, though we have great heavenly riches promised to us, we can still live pitiful earthly lives. Matthew 26:41 says, "The spirit indeed is willing, but the flesh is weak."

We live in fallen, corrupted fleshly bodies that are prone to succumb to temptations. We cannot defeat our spiritual enemies on our own. Also, there are times when we simply don't have the physical energy to do all that is required of us. That's why we need the power of heaven to energize us. "Paul wants us to know the greatness of God's power so that we will not fail to use our wealth, and so that the

enemy will not deprive us of our wealth" (Wiersbe).

The power that raised Christ from the dead (and by which He ascended back to heaven) is available to us through the Holy Spirit. We have to believe for that power, however. Grace supplies us the wealth, but our faith brings it to our disposal.

A perfect example of this is seen in the transition from the four Gospels to the Book of Acts. In the Gospels we see the power of God at work through the life of His Son. In Acts we see that same power, but now it is operating through simple men and women who lay hold of it by faith. Especially visible is the transition we see in Peter. The difference in this man was the resurrection power of Jesus.

D. Christ's Church (vv. 22, 23)

22. And hath put all things under his feet, and gave him to be the head over all things to the church,
23. Which is his body, the fulness of him that filleth all in all.

Paul ends the prayer by referring to the vital relationship between Christ and the church. Christ is the head of the church, and the church is to be the fullness of Christ. Filled with Christ, the church serves as an extension of Christ to the world.

GOLDEN TEXT HOMILY

"BLESSED BE THE GOD AND FATHER OF OUR LORD JESUS CHRIST, WHO HATH BLESSED US WITH ALL SPIRITUAL BLESSINGS IN HEAVENLY PLACES IN CHRIST" (Ephesians 1:3).

As God's children we are blessed when we receive His blessings, and God is blessed when we give Him praise for all that He freely bestows on us. We bless God because He blesses us. No wonder the psalmist cried, "Bless the Lord, O my soul, and forget not all his benefits" (Psalm 103:2).

"*Blessed be . . . God.*" How can we bless Him? We bless Him by esteeming Him above anything or anyone else and by desiring that others esteem Him as we do. In blessing God we desire to do good to Him as He has done to us. When we long for others to love and serve the Lord, we are blessing Him. When we have a burning desire to love Him more ourselves, we are blessing Him. When we tell others of the good news which glorifies God, we bless Him.

"*Blessed be the God and Father of our Lord Jesus Christ.*" When our heavenly Father is viewed aright, He becomes the object of our affection, not of our dread. We do not come trembling before Him as someone who is going to cut off our head, but we rejoice in Him as a tender, loving Father. To view the Father aright we must regard Him as the God of our Savior, Jesus Christ. After Jesus was resurrected, He called God "my Father, and your Father . . . my God, and your God" (John 20:17).

"*Who hath blessed us.*" There can be no blessing like that of God. Even here on earth, we enjoy and experience heavenly blessings. Our new nature is a heavenly one, and the love, joy, peace, safety and acceptance we receive as His children are all heavenly. Every day we should say, "The Lord has blessed me."

"*With all spiritual blessings.*" The word *spiritual* generally describes that which is produced by the Spirit. The blessings are spiritual because they come from, and are applied by, the warm and wonderful person of the Spirit.

"*In heavenly places in Christ.*" Christians are said to be raised up and made to "sit together in heavenly places in Christ Jesus" (Ephesians 2:6). This kind of life is lifted above the commonplace. We are in the world but not of the world . . . unlimited by the materialistic things that pass away. Life now, that is really and truly in Christ, is in the heavenly realm.— **Fred G. Swank**

SENTENCE SERMONS

THE BLESSINGS OF REDEMPTION come through Christ.
—Selected

LIFE WOULD BE MORE PLEASANT if we could forget our troubles as easily as we forget our blessings.
—Tom Haggai

TRY CLAIMING God's blessings instead of merely longing for them.
—Herry Jacobsen

EVANGELISM APPLICATION

CHRISTIANS SHOULD TESTIFY TO THE LOST OF THE BLESSINGS OF REDEMPTION.

Under the old covenant, the blessings of God were material and focused on this life. Deuteronomy 28:1-14 lists a bounty for those who obeyed the commandments: many children, flourishing crops, abundant flocks, plentiful bread, financial prosperity, and even world influence—everything the natural person desires today.

Under the new covenant, Jesus promises to take care of us materially . . . as long as we seek His kingdom first. Seeking His kingdom first brings greater blessings, which are mostly spiritual in nature. Jeremiah saw this coming and said, "'This is the covenant I will make with the house of Israel after that time,' declares the Lord. 'I will put my law in their minds and write it on their hearts. I will be their God, and they will be my people'" (31:33, *NIV*).

New covenant blessings are for the inner person, but the Lord doesn't forget our physical needs. Charles Spurgeon said, "We shall have enough spending money on the road to glory; for he who has guaranteed to bring us there will not starve us along the way."

What is it that draws people to Christ? Jesus said, "And I, if I be lifted up from the earth, will draw all men unto me" (John 12:32). Jesus was referring to His being lifted on a cross and crucified. Still, *we* can lift Him up as well. As the world sees serenity, peace and joy in us—as well as the fact that God supplies our physical needs—they will be attracted to Him. There is no greater witness than the person who trusts Christ for everything. There is no poorer witness than the person who claims Christ but cannot see the blessings that are already present.

ILLUMINATING THE LESSON

In Ephesians 1:14, Paul says that the Holy Spirit in our lives is the "earnest of our inheritance," or the "deposit guaranteeing our inheritance" (*NIV*). All believers have places along their journey where the Spirit has manifested Himself in a very real way. Try to imagine the most treasured experience you ever had with the Lord. Was it possibly the moment you fully recognized that you had been saved from your sins? Was it the first time you experienced a prayer language after receiving the Spirit baptism? Was it the time the Spirit moved on you and used you vitally in someone else's life? Perhaps it was the time He prompted you to some unusual decision or action—which you later found out was absolutely

providential, or which might have saved your life. Perhaps it was simply a time of praise and worship where the presence of the Spirit brought on rapturous joy.

Whatever that time was, realize that this is simply a foretaste of what heaven will be like. Multiply what you felt by millions to sense what one day you will have. "Here on earth we have experienced the first dollar of a million celestial dollars—the earnest. We have the dawning of knowledge, but then we will have the midday sun" (Hughes). Paul quoted to the Corinthians something Isaiah had already seen by faith: "'No eye has seen, no ear has heard, no mind has conceived what God has prepared for those who love him'—but God has revealed it to us by his Spirit" (1 Corinthians 2:9, 10, *NIV*).

DAILY BIBLE READINGS

M. A Covenant Established.
     Genesis 17:1-8
T. Benefits of Redemption.
     Psalm 107:1-9
W. The God of Blessing.
     Isaiah 44:1-8
T. Promise of Blessing.
     Matthew 5:1-12
F. Song of Redemption.
     Luke 1:46-55
S. Christ, the Mediator.
     Hebrews 9:11-15

TRUTH SEARCH
Creatively Teaching the Word

DISCUSSION QUESTIONS

Blessings of Redemption
(Ephesians 1:3-10)

1. The word *blessed* is used twice in verse 3. What does it mean?

2. When did God choose us to be His children (v. 4)?

3. How does God expect His children to live (v. 4)?

4. Describe God's ministry of adoption (vv. 5, 6).

5. What blessings did Christ provide for us through His sacrifice (v. 7)?

6. What *mystery* has been shown to God's children (vv. 9, 10)?

Guarantee of Redemption
(Ephesians 1:11-14)

1. What brings glory to Christ (vv. 11, 12)?

2. Describe the salvation process as depicted in verse 13:

    a. We _____ the word of _____.

    b. We t_____ and b_____ Christ for salvation.

    c. We are s_____ with the _____ _____.

3. What is the *earnest* ("guarantee") that we have been saved (v. 14)?

God's Power to Redeem
(Ephesians 1:15-23)

1. What positive report had Paul heard about the Ephesian church (v. 15)?

2. How and why did Paul minister to the Ephesians while he was away from them (v. 16)?

3. What did Paul ask God to give to the Ephesians (v. 17), and why (vv. 18, 19)?

4. Describe the extent of Christ's power and authority (vv. 20, 21).

5. Describe Christ's relationship with the church (vv. 22, 23).

ACROSTIC

Items needed: Marker board, marker

Write the word *GRACE* on the board vertically.

All of the spiritual blessings God offers us come from one source— His grace, manifested through the sacrifice of Jesus Christ. Let's use the word *grace* as an acrostic as we list divine blessings. Possible answers are given below.

    G: Goodness, Guidance
    R: Righteousness, Redemption
    A: Answered prayer, Assurance
    C: Compassion, Church
    E: Eternal life, Equality

Transforming Power of Grace

Study Text: Ephesians 2:1-22
Objective: To realize our need for saving grace and praise God for His transforming power.
Time: Around A.D. 61
Place: Written by Paul from a Roman prison
Golden Text: "For by grace are ye saved through faith; and that not of yourselves: it is the gift of God" (Ephesians 2:8).
Central Truth: Salvation is the gift of God through Jesus Christ.
Evangelism Emphasis: Christians are called to proclaim God's transforming grace to sinners.

PRINTED TEXT

Ephesians 2:1. And you hath he quickened, who were dead in trespasses and sins:

2. Wherein in time past ye walked according to the course of this world, according to the prince of the power of the air, the spirit that now worketh in the children of disobedience:

3. Among whom also we all had our conversation in times past in the lusts of our flesh, fulfilling the desires of the flesh and of the mind; and were by nature the children of wrath, even as others.

4. But God, who is rich in mercy, for his great love wherewith he loved us,

5. Even when we were dead in sins, hath quickened us together with Christ, (by grace ye are saved;)

6. And hath raised us up together, and made us sit together in heavenly places in Christ Jesus:

7. That in the ages to come he might shew the exceeding riches of his grace in his kindness toward us through Christ Jesus.

8. For by grace are ye saved through faith; and that not of yourselves: it is the gift of God:

9. Not of works, lest any man should boast.

10. For we are his workmanship, created in Christ Jesus unto good works, which God hath before ordained that we should walk in them.

11. Wherefore remember, that ye being in time past Gentiles in the flesh, who are called Uncircumcision by that which is called the Circumcision in the flesh made by hands;

12. That at that time ye were without Christ, being aliens from the commonwealth of Israel, and strangers from the covenants of promise, having no hope, and without God in the world:

13. But now in Christ Jesus ye who sometimes were far off are made nigh by the blood of Christ.

14. For he is our peace, who hath made both one, and hath broken down the middle wall of partition between us;

15. Having abolished in his flesh the enmity, even the law of commandments contained in ordinances; for to make in himself of twain one new man, so making peace;

16. And that he might reconcile both unto God in one body by the cross, having slain the enmity thereby.

LESSON OUTLINE

I. DEAD IN SIN
  A. Trespasses and Sins
  B. Children of Disobedience
  C. Children of Wrath
II. MADE ALIVE IN CHRIST
  A. Quickened With Christ
  B. The Believer Exalted
  C. Saved by Grace
  D. Created in Christ
III. MADE ONE IN CHRIST
  A. The Greatest Peace Mission
  B. No Longer Aliens

LESSON EXPOSITION

INTRODUCTION

In last week's lesson, Paul gave the Ephesian believers a grand picture of their spiritual riches (ch. 1). These include not only the wonderful things they would see in heaven, but the wealth that was available to them for this life. This wealth had to be perceived and received—and it could only be done so by faith, and with spiritual senses.

In Ephesians 2, Paul turns to a complimentary truth: our spiritual *position* in Christ. He begins by saying that the Ephesians (like all of us) were spiritually *dead*. Just as someone physically dead cannot respond to stimuli, neither can a person spiritually dead respond. A corpse cannot hear or see or feel. Neither can an unsaved person respond to spiritual things. The unbeliever is not just sick—he or she is dead and needs resurrection.

This lesson deals with the power of Christ to transform us from dead people to new creatures fully alive in Him. It is only His grace, however, that causes Him to look down on the undeserving creatures we are and give us abundant life.

I. DEAD IN SIN (Ephesians 2:1-3)

A. Trespasses and Sins (v. 1)

1. And you hath he quickened, who were dead in trespasses and sins.

Anyone without Christ is dead. There are no exceptions, either Jew or Gentile. The dead person doesn't need to be resuscitated; he or she needs resurrection. "All lost sinners are dead, and the only difference between one sinner and another is the state of decay. The lost derelict on skid row may be more decayed outwardly than the unsaved society leader, but both are dead in sin—and one corpse cannot be more dead than another!" (Wiersbe, *Be Rich*).

Paul wrote to Timothy, "But the widow who lives for pleasure is dead even while she lives" (1 Timothy 5:6, *NIV*). A spiritually dead person has no spiritual faculties. He or she may be alive physically, but is dead to the things that matter most—the matters of the soul. The unbeliever cannot see or hear, nor otherwise sense spiritual things. What brought about this terrible state? Trespasses and sin, going all the way back to the Garden of Eden.

"We should not hesitate to reaffirm that a life without God (however physically fit and mentally alert that person may be) is a living death, and that those who live it are dead even while they are living" (John R.W. Stott, *God's New Society*).

B. Children of Disobedience (v. 2)

2. Wherein in time past ye walked according to the course of this world, according to the prince of the power of the air, the spirit that now worketh in the children of disobedience.

Walking is a Biblical term that usually denotes the believer's progress in the faith. Here, however, Paul looks to a believer's old walk—the way of death. There are three enemies of the soul that brought about this state of death—the world, the devil and the flesh:

1. *The world*—The Greek word for "world" is *kosmos*, and is frequently used with an evil connotation. Anyone without Christ is a prisoner of the social and value systems of the present evil age, which is radically opposed to Christ.

2. *The devil*—The kingdom of God is outside the grasp of humanity's physical senses. And there is another kingdom operating in this realm, one ruled by Satan, whom Jesus called "the prince of this world" (John 12:31). Paul called Satan "the god of this world" (2 Corinthians 4:4). Unlike God, however, Satan cannot be everywhere at one time, and neither can he know everything. He is still a created being, and he must use evil tricks to influence people. He holds sway over unsaved humanity, and also seeks to sway believers. He longs for all people to live as "children of disobedience."

3. *The flesh*—All of us were born with a sinful nature because of what happened in the Garden of Eden. Someone may say, "The devil made me do it," but usually the idea originated right in one's own wicked heart.

C. Children of Wrath (v. 3)

3. Among whom also we all had our conversation in times past in the lusts of our flesh, fulfilling the desires of the flesh and of the mind; and were by nature the children of wrath, even as others.

Before Christ came into their lives, the Ephesians (like all believers) had been children of wrath, just as the rest of the world still is. All are children of Adam, and thus are all guilty and tainted by sin. John the Baptist said, "He that believeth on the Son hath everlasting life: and he that believeth not the Son shall not see life; but the wrath of God abideth on him" (John 3:36).

It is as natural for the unsaved person to live in disobedience to God as it is for a dog to act like a dog. A dog has a dog's nature, and a sinner has a sinner's nature. The sinner cannot overcome the three forces controlling him or her. The sinner must have outside help, and that can only come from God.

In Luke 6:33, Jesus spoke of sinners doing good for each other. We know that even pagans generally love and do their best for their own children. However, no one apart from Christ can do anything to please God.

II. MADE ALIVE IN CHRIST
(Ephesians 2:4-10)

A. Quickened With Christ (vv. 4, 5)

4. But God, who is rich in mercy, for his great love wherewith he loved us,

5. Even when we were dead in sins, hath quickened us together with Christ, (by grace ye are saved;)

Through the mercy of God, no one needs to remain dead and under sin's power. There is the promise of life—because God loves us. Love is one of the great attributes of God, and when this love is expressed toward humanity, it is called *grace*. God's mercy causes Him not to give us what we deserve, and His grace causes Him to give us wonderful things we do not deserve. All of this was made possible because of Christ's death on the cross. At Calvary, God displayed His utter hatred for sin, but also His great love for sinners.

The word *quickened* means "to be made alive, or brought back from death." Three times in the Gospels, Jesus raised people from the dead: the widow's son (Luke 7:11-17), Jairus' daughter (8:49-56), and Lazarus (John 11:41-46). In each case, He spoke life into their lifeless bodies through the power of the Holy Spirit operating in Him. His words were the *Word* of God. Hebrews 4:12 says, "For the word of God is living and active. Sharper than any double-edged sword, it penetrates even to dividing soul and spirit, joints and marrow; it judges the thoughts and attitudes of the heart" (*NIV*).

These physical resurrections are comparable to the spiritual resurrections that happen when a sinner hears the Word and believes. Jesus said, "He that heareth my word, and believeth on him that sent me, hath everlasting life, and shall not come into condemnation; but is passed from death unto life" (John 5:24). It is the Word in action that gives life. Every Christian has experienced resurrection power (Ephesians 1:19, 20).

B. The Believer Exalted (vv. 6, 7)

6. And hath raised us up together, and made us sit together in heavenly places in Christ Jesus:

7. That in the ages to come he might shew the exceeding riches of his grace in his kindness toward us through Christ Jesus.

We are not just raised from the dead to live here on earth. Because we are *in Christ*, we have been exalted to share His throne in heaven. Physically, we are still here on earth, but spiritually we are with Christ. Because of this, we know that our bodies will be raised from the dead, and we will spend eternity ruling and reigning with Christ. Not only that, our spiritual position gives us the power to control our actions in the physical realm. We can live victoriously! This is not of ourselves, but of the power of Christ residing in us through the Holy Spirit.

C. Saved by Grace (vv. 8, 9)

8. For by grace are ye saved through faith; and that not of yourselves: it is the gift of God:

9. Not of works, lest any man should boast.

Paul has taken his readers through a death valley (vv. 1-3), and then to the mountain heights of life in the Lord—from hell to heaven, bondage to freedom, despair to hope, wrath to glory, and death to life. Now, on top of the mountain, he reiterates the truth of what brought us there—God's grace. These two verses are the gospel in a nutshell.

Grace is the single source of salvation. Just as we saw in lesson 1 that the Holy Spirit is the conduit between the believer and the riches of Christ, so faith is the conduit for salvation between the sinner and God. Faith is the channel, but not the cause. God is the source. Salvation originates with Him.

Notice that the word *saved* is in the past tense. Our salvation was procured in the past through Christ's work on the cross. We can do nothing to earn salvation. Notice, too, that faith is a *gift of God*. Even our faith does not originate in ourselves, but comes from above. Thus, we cannot take pride in our position as a Christian. We can only humbly rejoice at what has been done for us.

D. Created in Christ (v. 10)

10. For we are his workmanship, created in Christ Jesus unto good works, which God hath before ordained that we should walk in them.

The Greek word for *workmanship* is *poiema,* from which we get the word *poem.* A poem is an artistic creation by a master of words. Thus, we are part of God's "new creation" (2 Corinthians 5:17, *NKJV*). However, He is not finished with us, but rather continues to work on us like clay, forming something special for eternity. His ultimate purpose is to "conform us to the likeness of His Son" (see Romans 8:29).

"Christ finished His work of redemption on the cross, but He arose from the dead and returned to heaven. There He carries on His unfinished work of perfecting His church" (Wiersbe). This is why it is so important to study the Word, meditate on it, and feed on it. The Word provides spiritual nourishment and it cleanses us. Through the operation of the Holy Spirit, we are gradually changed into the likeness of Christ.

The resurrection power that saves us and conforms us to Christ also instigates us toward good works. We are saved by grace through faith, but our faith is then demonstrated by our works. Jesus said, "Let your light so shine before men, that they may see your good works, and glorify your Father which is in heaven" (Matthew 5:16). Paul said we should "abound to every good work" (2 Corinthians 9:8) and be "fruitful in every good work" (Colossians 1:10). Hebrews 13:16 encourages us to do good works, "for with such sacrifices God is well pleased." In other words, our works are a spiritual sacrifice to the Lord. We cannot earn salvation by our good works, but we do our works as a result of salvation. They are evidence of a spiritual work taking place in us, and they witness to others.

III. MADE ONE IN CHRIST
(Ephesians 2:11-22)

A. The Greatest Peace Mission
(vv. 11-18)

(Ephesians 2:17, 18 is not included in the printed text.)

11. Wherefore remember, that ye being in time past Gentiles in the flesh, who are called Uncircumcision by that which is called the Circumcision in the flesh made by hands;
12. That at that time ye were without Christ, being aliens from the commonwealth of Israel, and strangers from the covenants of promise, having no hope, and without God in the world:
13. But now in Christ Jesus ye who sometimes were far off are made nigh by the blood of Christ.
14. For he is our peace, who hath made both one, and hath broken down the middle wall of partition between us;
15. Having abolished in his flesh the enmity, even the law of commandments contained in ordinances; for to make in himself of twain one new man, so making peace;
16. And that he might reconcile both unto God in one body by the cross, having slain the enmity thereby.

There have been thousands of peace treaties over the centuries, but none brought lasting peace. Most are nothing but temporary truces, giving one or both states more time to arm itself for war. This has been dramatically illustrated in the past few years. The ethnic factions in what used to be Yugoslavia have been at each other's throats for hundreds of years. Also, the Arab/Israeli conflict goes back to Old Testament times. We watch from day to day the efforts of the *peace process* in the Middle East—but we know this is nothing but wishful thinking.

The only lasting peace accord has been the one signed in blood by Jesus on the cross. Christ came to earth (into enemy territory) to set up a new covenant between God and humanity, and to establish peace between Jew and Gentile as well. We might say this was the greatest peace mission of all time.

All ethnic or racial pride is nothing but that—pride. Pride does nothing but separate people. The Jews ("the Circumcision") considered all non-Jews (Gentiles or "the Uncircumcision") as unclean. They saw themselves as pure, and as God's *elect*, because of their calling as a nation, their heritage, and their relentless adherence to religious ceremony. Paul here, however, points out that this is all folly. All, including the Jews, are unclean and need to be cleansed by Christ's blood. At the same time, everyone is invited to partake of the Lord's invitation and become part of one great body of believers. Being part of the body of Christ is the one thing we can be proud of—proud because He accepts even us as part of Himself.

Most of the believers at Ephesus were Gentiles. They knew that the Old Testament had been directed to the Jews. For centuries the Jews had looked down on them with a terrible attitude that God never intended. The fact that a Jew might carry the mark of the covenant (circumcision) was no proof that he was a true person of faith, in the same sense that just because someone comes to church today doesn't prove he or she is a Christian. Also, many denominations baptize infants and say that they are thus Christians. The rite of baptism itself is no proof of a relationship with Christ.

The Jews were never called out just so they could boast of being God's chosen people. They were called to bring the revelation of who God is to the rest of the world. Jesus the Messiah would come from a Jewish lineage. However, they became proud of the fact they were seed of Abraham who had a covenant with God. They elevated themselves above everyone else. At the same time, the Gentiles resented the Jews' holier-than-thou attitude. In fact, the Jews were generally despised because of their pride. Both groups were lost and hated each other, and both were alienated from God.

"The middle wall of partition" (v. 14) refers to the wall in the Temple which separated the court of the Gentiles from the court of the Jews. The wall had been destroyed by the once-for-all sacrifice of Jesus Christ, making the blessings of God equally accessible to both Jews and Gentiles.

B. No Longer Aliens (vv. 19-22)

(Ephesians 2:19-22 is not included in the printed text.)

In these verses Paul gives three ways of describing the new arrangement of peace that has been established: "fellowcitizens" of one nation, members of one family (the "household of God"), and joined together into a "holy temple."

1. *Fellowcitizens*—The new nation that God established is the church. Peter said the church is "a chosen people, a royal priesthood, a holy nation, a people belonging to God, that you may declare the praises of him who called you out of darkness into his wonderful light" (1 Peter 2:9, *NIV*). All believers, regardless of their background, nationality or race, belong to this holy nation. Their citizenship is in heaven.

2. *Household of God*—By grace through faith in Christ, we become part of God's family. God becomes our Father, and Jesus our brother. Paul said, "For this cause I bow my knees unto the Father of our Lord Jesus Christ, of whom the whole family in heaven and earth is named" (Ephesians 3:14, 15).

The family of God exists in two places—earth and heaven—those who are still alive on earth and those who have already gone to heaven. At some time in the future every knee will bow to Jesus, "in heaven and on earth and under the earth, and every tongue [will] confess that Jesus Christ is Lord, to the glory of God the Father" (Philippians 2:10, 11, *NIV*). None of God's family members will be under the earth. We are all part of one family in Christ.

3. *One temple*—In the Old Testament, God's presence dwelt in the Tabernacle until Israel sinned so grossly that the glory departed. His

next dwelling place was in the body of Jesus (see John 1:14). However, men took that body and nailed it to a cross. Now, through the Holy Spirit, God dwells in the church—the temple of God. This temple is not a building, but rather the hearts of those who trust Christ.

The foundation for the church was laid by the apostles and New Testament prophets. Jesus is the foundation (1 Corinthians 3:11) and chief cornerstone (Psalm 118:22; Isaiah 28:16). The cornerstone holds the entire building together. Jesus has united Jew and Gentile into one structure—the church. This temple is "fitly framed together" (Ephesians 2:21) so that every part has a role to play in the purposes of God.

GOLDEN TEXT HOMILY

"FOR BY GRACE ARE YE SAVED THROUGH FAITH; AND THAT NOT OF YOURSELVES: IT IS THE GIFT OF GOD" (Ephesians 2:8).

Some things are of man and some things are of God. The two must never be confused. Humanism attributes the works of God to man. Evolution theorizes there are no works of God in what we know as creation. Some people advocate a salvation by man's works. However, Ephesians 2:8 verifies that salvation is solely the work of God.

"By grace" (God's unmerited favor) "are ye saved" (not by yourself, but from yourself) "through faith" (that comes from God); "not of yourselves" (but of God); "it is the gift of God" (we did not, and could not earn it).

By rightly dividing the Scriptures, we find that they complement one another and never contradict one another. The entire Bible teaches that salvation comes from God alone.

• "*By grace*"—Romans 11:6: "And if by grace, then is it no more of works: otherwise grace is no more grace."

• "*Are ye saved*"—Acts 4:12: "Neither is there salvation in any other: for there is none other name [other than Jesus Christ] under heaven given among men, whereby we must be saved."

• "*Through faith*"—Romans 5:1: "Therefore being justified by faith, we have peace with God through our Lord Jesus Christ."

• "*Not of yourselves*"—Matthew 18:11: "The Son of man is come to save that which was lost."

• "*It is the gift of God*"—John 3:16: "God so loved the world, that he gave his only begotten Son, that whosoever believeth in him should not perish, but have everlasting life."

Salvation through Christ is not a work of the flesh or of the Law; rather it is God's greatest work toward mankind.—**Terry A. Beaver**

SENTENCE SERMONS

SALVATION IS the gift of God through Jesus Christ.
—Selected

JESUS LIVED that He might die, and died that we might live.
—Speaker's Sourcebook

GOD'S WRATH comes by measure; His mercy without measure.
—Selected

EVANGELISM APPLICATION

CHRISTIANS ARE CALLED TO PROCLAIM GOD'S TRANSFORMING GRACE TO SINNERS.

When Paul was shipwrecked on the island of Malta (Acts 28:1-10), the natives there were kind and helped the crew and passengers. When a deadly viper struck Paul, they expected him to die quickly, thinking he was receiving a just reward for some evil he had done. When he simply shook the reptile off and into the fire, showing no signs of injury, they suspected him to be a god. These were kind people, but they were unsaved pagans.

When Paul went to Publius, the chief official on the island, and prayed for his healing, the man was healed. Then the people brought all their sick to Paul, and all were healed. After staying there three months, Paul and the others finally put out to sea in another ship. The people were again kind to them and gave them supplies.

Kind as they were, the islanders were still pagans. Only those who accepted Christ were made alive. The rest were still dead in their sins. Their good works were appreciated, but this did not give them life. Only Christ gives life. Good deeds are simply that—good deeds. They don't change the heart and give life to the dead.

ILLUMINATING THE LESSON

Have you heard of the frog that fell into a large can of milk? For all its efforts, the frog could not get out of the can. There was nothing he could do but keep paddling. Eventually his sloshing about paid off, for a large pad of butter formed beneath him, from which he leaped out of the can to safety

The moral is that no matter what the circumstances, one should keep trying, and eventually success will be gained. There is a measure of truth here, for often we simply have to keep up our efforts against all odds before success is attained.

However, when it comes to salvation, there is nothing any of us could do to ever earn favor in God's sight. No saving pad of butter will ever form beneath us to give a launching pad, no matter how long or how hard we try to do good. The Old Testament is proof that a salvation of works is a failure. If one could achieve God's favor this way, eventually a new generation of self-righteous Pharisees would arise.

No, everyone is dead in their sins, no matter how great their efforts. It is only through God's grace that any are saved.

DAILY BIBLE READINGS

M. The Fall.
   Genesis 3:1-15
T. Sin Grieves God.
   Genesis 6:5-8
W. Blessing of Forgiveness.
   Psalm 32:1-11
T. Set Free by Jesus.
   Luke 8:26-39
F. A Changed Life.
   Luke 19:1-10
S. Testimony of Transformation.
   Acts 26:9-18

TRUTH SEARCH
Creatively Teaching the Word

STARTING ACTIVITY

Items needed: Index cards, pencils

Pass out an index card and a pencil to everyone. Each student should write a description of the kindest or most generous deed he or she has ever done. They should not put their names on the cards.

Collect the cards and read the various deeds.

Imagine that one person performed all of these kind deeds. Would that be enough to get him or her into heaven? Why or why not?

DISCUSSION QUESTIONS

Dead in Sin
(Ephesians 2:1-3)

1. What is a trespass? What is a sin?

2. In what sense is an unsaved person "dead"?

3. Describe "the course of this world" (v. 2).

4. Who is "the prince of the power of the air," and what does he do (v. 2)?

5. Describe the lives of lost people as depicted in verse 3.

Made Alive in Christ
(Ephesians 2:4-10)

1. How does verse 4 describe God, and how do His past, present and future actions prove His character (vv. 5-7)?

2. Why does Paul use the word *together* three times in verses 5 and 6?

3. Explain the statement "by grace you have been saved" (vv. 5, 8, *NKJV*). Why is this important?

4. Where does saving faith come from?

5. What is God's design for us (v. 10)?

Made One in Christ
(Ephesians 2:11-22)

1. What was the past condition of Gentile people (vv. 11, 12)?

2. What did the "wall of partition" (v. 14) separate, and how was it demolished (vv. 13-16)?

3. To whom did Christ bring the gospel (vv. 17, 18)?

4. Draw a picture of the building described in verses 19-22, labeling its various parts.

Unity and Edification

Study Text: Ephesians 4:1-16
Objective: To identify the basis of Christian unity and seek to build up the church.
Time: Around A.D. 61
Place: Written by Paul from a Roman prison
Golden Text: "With all lowliness and meekness, with longsuffering, forbearing one another in love; endeavoring to keep the unity of the Spirit in the bond of peace" (Ephesians 4:2, 3).
Central Truth: Christian unity edifies the church.
Evangelism Emphasis: Christian unity enhances evangelism.

PRINTED TEXT

Ephesians 4:1. I therefore, the prisoner of the Lord, beseech you that ye walk worthy of the vocation wherewith ye are called,

2. With all lowliness and meekness, with longsuffering, forbearing one another in love;

3. Endeavouring to keep the unity of the Spirit in the bond of peace.

4. There is one body, and one Spirit, even as ye are called in one hope of your calling;

5. One Lord, one faith, one baptism,

6. One God and Father of all, who is above all, and through all, and in you all.

7. But unto every one of us is given grace according to the measure of the gift of Christ.

8. Wherefore he saith, When he ascended up on high, he led captivity captive, and gave gifts unto men.

11. And he gave some, apostles; and some, prophets; and some, evangelists; and some, pastors and teachers;

12. For the perfecting of the saints, for the work of the ministry, for the edifying of the body of Christ:

13. Till we all come in the unity of the faith, and of the knowledge of the Son of God, unto a perfect man, unto the measure of the stature of the fulness of Christ:

14. That we henceforth be no more children, tossed to and fro, and carried about with every wind of doctrine, by the sleight of men, and cunning craftiness, whereby they lie in wait to deceive;

15. But speaking the truth in love, may grow up into him in all things, which is the head, even Christ:

16. From whom the whole body fitly joined together and compacted by that which every joint supplieth, according to the effectual working in the measure of every part, maketh increase of the body unto the edifying of itself in love.

LESSON OUTLINE

I. BASIS FOR UNITY
   A. From Doctrine to Duty
   B. Graces That Build Unity
   C. Grounds for Unity

II. SOURCE FOR MINISTRY
   A. Giftings for Unity
   B. Growth of Unity

III. PURPOSE OF MINISTRY
   A. Maturity, the Goal of Ministry
   B. Correction Without Offense

LESSON EXPOSITION

INTRODUCTION

In our last lesson we saw that the only peace accord that has ever lasted is the one Jesus signed with His own blood when He died on the cross. The peace that Jesus negotiated by dying for people's sins accomplished two things—peace between God and humanity, and peace between Jew and Gentile.

The Jews were never called God's chosen people just so they could boast of such. They were called to be the means of revelation of who God is to the rest of the world. But they became proud of the fact they were special in God's sight, and thus elevated themselves above everyone else. In fact, the Jews were despised by Gentiles simply because of their arrogance. The problem was that both groups were lost and alienated from God.

Paul told the Ephesians, "For Christ himself is our way of peace. He has made peace between us Jews and you Gentiles by making us all one family" (2:14, *TLB*). Jesus is the ultimate peacemaker. He didn't come just to hold a fragile truce in place. He came to revolutionize the way people think about each other. He showed that both Jews and Gentiles were doomed and far from God in their old

ways—the Jews in their futile efforts to maintain a righteousness by keeping laws and rituals, and the Gentiles by trying to worship so many idol gods.

Jesus was revolutionary because He showed no favoritism to anyone—He saw all as needing love, mercy and grace. Think of the story of the Good Samaritan (Luke 10:30-37), Christ's meeting with the Samaritan woman at the well (John 4), and the healing of the Roman centurion's servant (Matthew 8:5-13). Christ loved the Samaritans and Romans whom most Jews despised. The Jews who listened to Jesus regarded Him as a heretic—in the same way that many Southern whites regarded civil rights crusaders back in the 1960s. Jesus stepped over social taboos and prejudices to reach out to all people.

The only reason God ever made a difference between Jew and Gentile was so His purposes of salvation for all people could be accomplished. Once the plan of salvation and reconciliation was revealed through Jesus, being a Jew meant nothing. There was to be no more difference between peoples. All people are now candidates for God's grace. They are all created equal in His sight.

Obviously, however, the history of the last 2,000 years certainly doesn't show all people becoming one. There have been countless wars over this period—and the hatred between Jew and Gentile has probably been even more pronounced. Jews have become the most hated, most persecuted people of all time. Why? Because the peace that Jesus brings can only apply to those who receive Him and become part of the kingdom of God. The wall between Jew and Gentile has been demolished, but only for those who are in Christ.

Because of the peace Jesus brings, we as believers should be at peace with everyone else. However, peace must be pursued. We must make every effort "to keep the unity of the Spirit in the bond of peace" (Ephesians 4:3).

It is the peace of Christ, through the operation of the Holy Spirit, that breaks fetters, establishes harmony, and empowers various members of the body of Christ to work together in unity. He unctions us to send peace to others. It is not a peace that we naturally have, for people can hurt us. From the world's perspective we may have legitimate grounds to feel resentful and angry. However, if we send peace toward others instead of hatred, then the kingdom moves forward and we operate in harmony.

I. BASIS FOR UNITY
(Ephesians 4:1-6)

A. From Doctrine to Duty (v. 1)

1. I therefore, the prisoner of the Lord, beseech you that ye walk worthy of the vocation wherewith ye are called.

Paul's letters all have a balance between doctrine and daily application of doctrine. The first three chapters of Ephesians deal with our riches in Christ, the peace that Christ brings, and reconciliation between God and people, Jew and Gentile. Now, with chapter 4, Paul transitions from theology to practicality, from creed to conduct, from the Christian's wealth to his walk, from exposition to exhortation.

A body has to work in harmony or it doesn't function at all. Three words stand out in the first verse of this passage—*therefore, beseech* and *worthy.* The word *therefore* indicates Paul is at the transition point of his letter. Everything he is about to say will be based on what he has just postulated in doctrine. No one should even try to live the Christian life in ignorance but rather in knowledge; for

the more we know and understand of truth, the more logical it is to obey. Any Christian who is not interested in learning more of what the Bible teaches needs to check his or her spiritual well-being. The moment we think we know all we need to know is the moment we are in the most danger. Our beliefs determine our daily behavior.

The word *beseech* indicates urgency. Paul had not postulated doctrine just to show how much God had revealed to him. No, this was truth the people needed in order to live effective lives.

The third word, *worthy,* is translated from the Greek word *axios,* which means "to be of equal weight." From it the English word *axiom* is derived. "In an equation the axiom indicates doing something to each side of the equation so it remains true" (Hughes). Thus, Paul is saying that our lives should be lived equivalent to the blessings we have received. In other words, "Christ has done so much for me, I must give Him my all in return."

Walking worthy of the blessings we have received should be our natural response. How can we do this? By walking in unity. The entire idea of this lesson is unity of believers in Christ. God is building a body of believers—the temple. He has reconciled Jew and Gentile to Himself in Christ. In return, our responsibility is to strive for unity among ourselves, not just our small group but the entire church.

B. Graces That Build Unity (vv. 2, 3)

2. With all lowliness and meekness, with longsuffering, forbearing one another in love;

3. Endeavouring to keep the unity of the Spirit in the bond of peace.

Unity begins with character, and character is a combination of graces.

"Pride and self-promoting arrogance sow disunity, but a humble, gentle man or woman is like a caressing breeze" (Hughes). Seven Christian graces are listed in these two verses. There is no hint in Paul's words of self-condemnation. He simply shows that others should come first. He told the Romans, "Do not think of yourself more highly than you ought, but rather think of yourself with sober judgment, in accordance with the measure of faith God has given you" (Romans 12:3, NIV). The seven graces are as follows:

1. *Lowliness*—This is the same as humility. It means putting Christ first, others second, and oneself last.

2. *Meekness*—This is not weakness, but "power under control" (Wiersbe). Moses was a meek man. Numbers 12:3 says, "Now the man Moses was very meek, above all the men which were upon the face of the earth." Yet Moses led an entire nation. Jesus was "meek and lowly in heart" (Matthew 11:29), but twice He drove the money changers from the Temple.

3. *Long-suffering*—This means having a long fuse instead of a short one.

4. *Forbearing*—This means tolerance or mercy toward others. It cannot be experienced outside of the next grace, love.

5. *Love*—Paul said, "Love suffers long and is kind" (1 Corinthians 13:4, NKJV).

6. *Endeavouring*—This means striving to maintain unity in the face of opposition.

7. *Peace*—This is the inward peace that comes from knowing Christ. "The reason for war on the outside is war on the inside" (Wiersbe). If there is peace inside, it will be reflected in one's outward actions.

C. Grounds for Unity (vv. 4-6)

4. There is one body, and one Spirit, even as ye are called in one hope of your calling;

5. One Lord, one faith, one baptism,

6. One God and Father of all, who is above all, and through all, and in you all.

A typical question asked in a courtroom is, "On what grounds do you base your case?" Here, Paul lists the grounds we have for unity in the body of Christ. As said earlier, he spent the first three chapters of this letter giving sound Christian doctrine. Unity has to be based on sound principles, or it will fail. These principles come from that doctrine:

1. *One body*—This is the body of Christ, of which every believer is a member. We become members at conversion. The body universal is the model for the countless local bodies all over the world.

2. *One Spirit*—This is the Holy Spirit, who seals us at salvation and indwells us so that we belong to each other. He is the conduit between us and the blessings of Christ.

3. *One hope of your calling*—Our hope is the return of the Lord Jesus to take us to heaven for eternity.

4. *One Lord*—We all serve the same Lord, Jesus Christ. "There is no other name under heaven given to men by which we must be saved" (Acts 4:12, NIV).

5. *One faith*—There are fine points of difference from denomination to denomination, but all who are truly part of the body of Christ agree on certain basic principles. Paul wrote to Timothy, "The things you have heard me say in the presence of many witnesses entrust to reliable men who will also be qualified to teach others" (2 Timothy 2:2, NIV).

6. *One baptism*—This refers to the baptism, or sealing by the Holy Spirit, that places all believers into the body of Christ. Acts 2:4 speaks of the 120 being *filled* with the Holy Spirit. That infilling is one of empowerment for service.

7. *One God and Father of all*—Paul emphasized the role of God the Father, who is over all, and from whom everything originates.

Paul was concerned in all his letters that believers maintain unity, but also that they stay away from false doctrines. He did not suggest unity at any cost, for uniting with those of dangerous ideas would ultimately destroy unity. At the same time, he also knew that purity of doctrine would not necessarily produce unity. This is why he later in this chapter joins the two when he says "speaking the truth in love" (v. 15).

II. SOURCE FOR MINISTRY
(Ephesians 4:7, 8, 11, 12)

A. Giftings for Unity (vv. 7, 8, 11)

7. But unto every one of us is given grace according to the measure of the gift of Christ.

8. Wherefore he saith, When he ascended up on high, he led captivity captive, and gave gifts unto men.

11. And he gave some, apostles; and some, prophets; and some, evangelists; and some, pastors and teachers.

The word *grace* here means "gifting," or ability to perform some task in the Kingdom. In Romans 12:6, Paul said we have "gifts differing according to the grace that is given to us." His own apostleship came as a gift of God's grace (Ephesians 3). Every person in the body of Christ has received some enablement to carry out a duty that helps the entire body. This gift is to be used for the unity and edification of the body. While some have more abilities than others, each has been given something to be used for the good of the whole. Peter said, "Each one should use whatever gift he has received to serve others, faithfully administering God's grace in its various forms" (1 Peter 4:10, *NIV*).

"The gifts are given sovereignly by the ascended Christ in order to build up the church. Thus the body of Christ is to function like a machine in which every part is essential for getting a job done. But unlike a machine, the body of Christ should maintain itself and build every one of its members up so that they can do good works" (*The Nelson Study Bible*).

There are three lists of spiritual gifts in the New Testament: in 1 Corinthians 12:4-11, 27-31; Romans 12:3-8; and Ephesians 4:11. The lists are not identical, and thus there are many potential giftings. Paul does indicate that certain gifts are more important (from a leadership perspective) than others, but all believers are still needed for the body of the Lord to function properly.

For those who might say, "I must be less valuable, for I have a lesser gifting," we can point to the parable of the workers in the vineyard (Matthew 20). Though some were hired at the end of the day, all received the same wages. It is the Master's prerogative to give gifts where He so chooses. It is not ours to decide what gifts we want (as it was not the workers' place to determine their wages). Ours is to find our gifting, and then do it well.

In the present text, Paul enumerates gifted people God has placed in the church; namely, apostles, prophets, evangelists, pastors and teachers.

1. *Apostles*—An *apostle* is "one who is sent with a commission." The apostles were men who gave witness to the resurrection of Christ. They all saw Him alive again. These men laid the foundation of the church, as seen from Acts to the end of the New Testament. In a narrow sense, there are no more apostles. The foundation has already been laid.

2. *Prophets*—Old Testament prophets were frequently associated with telling events of the future. In a strict sense, however, prophets simply proclaim the will of God. In the early days

of the church, there were few copies of the Old Testament Scriptures, and the New Testament was only gradually being written. How did local assemblies understand God's will? Sometimes by believers who possessed the gift of prophecy—the ability to proclaim the truth of God's will for the people. Paul hinted at this when he said, "Though I have the gift of prophecy, and understand all mysteries, and all knowledge . . ." (1 Corinthians 13:2).

3. *Evangelists*—Evangelists are bearers of the good news of the gospel. Their mission is to witness and bring sinners to conversion. "The apostles and prophets laid the foundation of the church, and the evangelists built upon it by winning the lost to Christ" (Wiersbe).

4. *Pastors and teachers*—Pastors are shepherds of flocks, indicating leadership of local assemblies. Teachers explain the Word to the flock. Together, they nourish the sheep and keep them in good spiritual health.

B. Growth of Unity (v. 12)

12. For the perfecting of the saints, for the work of the ministry, for the edifying of the body of Christ.

There are three stages of growth shown in this verse, each building on the last. The gifted leaders mentioned in verse 11 are responsible to equip ("perfect") the members of the local body; the equipped saints then do the work of the ministry on a day-to-day basis. As a result, the entire body of Christ is built up (edified). Everyone is involved.

III. PURPOSE OF MINISTRY
(Ephesians 4:13-16)

A. Maturity, the Goal of Ministry
(vv. 13, 14)

13. Till we all come in the unity of the faith, and of the knowledge of the Son of God, unto a perfect man, unto the measure of the stature of the fulness of Christ:

14. That we henceforth be no more children, tossed to and fro, and carried about with every wind of doctrine, by the sleight of men, and cunning craftiness, whereby they lie in wait to deceive.

Children are vulnerable and easily victimized. This has been dramatically illustrated in recent years by the frequent abductions of children. Why are children targets for such a crime? Because they are gullible. They take people at face value without questioning motives. However, a church operating as it should will work to move from being babes in Christ to mature believers, "rightly dividing the word of truth" (2 Timothy 2:15).

Everyone utilizing their giftings and working together in harmony produces maturity of the body. Evidence of this is stability. Mature assemblies do not get tossed about by every religious fad that comes along. False teachers are unable to sway them.

B. Correction Without Offense
(vv. 15, 16)

15. But speaking the truth in love, may grow up into him in all things, which is the head, even Christ:

16. From whom the whole body fitly joined together and compacted by that which every joint supplieth, according to the effectual working in the measure of every part, maketh increase of the body unto the edifying of itself in love.

Where love exists, the Spirit is free to work. Correction can be made without the guilty party taking offense. Not only that, the body will increase in size. Churches grow where there is unity. What we see here is total cooperation among the body members. Each needs the other, and all recognize this need.

In recent years we have heard much about orphanages in Eastern Europe where babies were not properly cared for. These children did not develop well after adoption by American families simply because they had not received love as infants. So it is in the church. Christians cannot mature in isolation. We need each other. All are knitted together to become one body. That is what Christ calls for.

GOLDEN TEXT HOMILY

"WITH ALL LOWLINESS AND MEEKNESS, WITH LONGSUFFERING, FORBEARING ONE ANOTHER IN LOVE; ENDEAVORING TO KEEP THE UNITY OF THE SPIRIT IN THE BOND OF PEACE" (Ephesians 4:2, 3).

The apostle specified six virtues that believers should maintain in their daily lives: *lowliness*, *meekness*, *longsuffering*, *forbearance*, *love* and *peace*. The first two, lowliness and meekness, may be regarded as two ways of expressing the same quality. Jesus used the two terms together in Matthew 11:29 when He said, "I am meek and lowly in heart."

Meekness and lowliness of heart are primarily attitudes we as Christians show toward God. We recognize that before Him we are nothing, but through Him we become persons of worth. When we are lowly in heart and meek, we have a thankful sense of dependence upon God; we are not proud or conceited; our focus is not on ourselves but upon God.

Longsuffering and forbearance are attitudes we should have toward people. When we manifest these graces we will not be short-tempered, impatient and unfeeling toward others. These virtues are part of the fruit of the Spirit listed in Galatians 5:22, 23. The Spirit within us can produce godly patience and love.

Christians have a responsibility to seek and keep unity among themselves. The word *endeavouring* is too mild a word to express all that Paul was saying, for his admonition really was to "spare no effort toward keeping unity." Christians should do everything within their power to maintain unity in the body of Christ.

The Spirit within us is the basis of inner harmony which makes unity with others a possibility. The fruit of the Holy Spirit is peace, and peace creates unity.—**Selected**

SENTENCE SERMONS

CHRISTIAN UNITY edifies the church.
—Selected

AS THE PRESENCE OF THE KING makes the palace, so the presence of Christ makes the church.
—Benedict's Scrapbook

CHRISTIANS MAY NOT SEE eye to eye, but they can walk arm in arm.
—Alexander Maclaren

EVANGELISM APPLICATION

CHRISTIAN UNITY ENHANCES EVANGELISM.

At the end of World War II, it took time for the news of both Germany's and Japan's surrender to the Allies to reach every area. War continued in some places, people were killed, others persecuted, and general misery extended—even though peace had been achieved.

The work that Jesus did on the cross established peace between God and people, but that peace only applies to those who hear the news and accept the peace agreement. Thus, only believers can be part of the family of God—a people of peace. However, anyone who has lived very long as a Christian knows that maintaining peace among the brethren is not always easy. It takes work. Paul said to endeavor "to keep the unity of the Spirit through the bond of peace" (Ephesians 4:3, *NIV*).

We cannot establish peace, for that has already been done. Nor can we create unity. However, we can work to *keep* the unity that has already been given us.

Our first responsibility is to introduce individuals to the peace agreement Jesus bought with His own blood. Our second responsibility is to maintain such a unity among fellow believers that the world will desire to become members of the family of God.

ILLUMINATING THE LESSON

In 1997, through the orbiting Hubble space telescope, scientists discovered lone stars without a galaxy. These isolated stars drift more than 300,000 light years from the nearest galaxy.

"Somewhere along the way," wrote John Noble Wilford, "they wandered off or were tossed out of the galaxy of their birth, out into the cold, dark emptiness of intergalactic space" (*New York Times*).

Like these lone, nomadic stars, Christians can wander away from the warmth and unity of the church into the coldness of isolation. But this is never what God intends. Instead, He calls all Christians into the warmth of loving fellowship with one another, where they can shine together.

DAILY BIBLE READINGS

M. The Comfort of Forgiveness.
   Genesis 50:15-21
T. Forbearing One Another.
   1 Samuel 24:4-22
W. Blessing of Unity.
   Psalm 133:1-3
T. Seek Reconciliation.
   Matthew 18:15-20
F. Servant Leadership.
   Matthew 20:20-28
S. Jesus Prays for Unity.
   John 17:20-26

TRUTH SEARCH
Creatively Teaching the Word

DISCUSSION QUESTIONS
Basis for Unity
(Ephesians 4:1-6)
1. Why did Paul call himself "the prisoner of the Lord" (v. 1)?

2. What does it mean to "walk worthy" of the calling God has placed upon our lives?

3. According to verses 2 and 3, how must we live in order to "keep the unity of the Spirit"?

4. Why does Paul repeatedly use the word *one* in verses 4-6?

5. What point is made by the four uses of *all* in verse 6?

Source for Ministry
(Ephesians 4:7-12)
1. What is given to each child of God, and how is it apportioned (vv. 7, 8)?

2. Why does Christ have the authority to give gifts to the church (vv. 9, 10)?

3. Describe the different ministry offices listed in verse 11.

4. What are the spiritual leaders supposed to "perfect" (equip) the "saints" (Christians) to do, and why (v. 12)?

Purpose of Ministry
(Ephesians 4:13-16)
1. How are immature believers described in verse 14?

2. Name some of the current "winds of false doctrine" that are blowing today.

3. How are mature believers described in verse 13?

4. What does it mean to speak "the truth in love" (v. 15)? Why does the church need leaders who speak the truth in love?

5. Describe how a healthy church body functions (v. 16).

DEMONSTRATION

Divide the students into four groups, and have each group stand in a different corner of the room. Once they are in a corner, each group should talk about issues that could divide a church, and then settle on two issues they will name. Next, have each group name their two issues.

Just as the class is now separated into four groups, so churches sometimes allow differences to separate them. However, God wants us to function as one body, putting aside our petty differences and lifting up Jesus Christ.

Stand in the center of the room and read verses 4-6 aloud. Now have the four groups to come together as one group by walking to the center of the room and joining hands. Then pray together for unity to prevail in your class and in your church.

Advancement of the Gospel

Study Text: Philippians 1:12-30

Objective: To understand God will advance the gospel even through our difficulties and live worthy of Christ.

Time: A.D. 63

Place: Written from a Roman prison

Golden Text: "According to my earnest expectation and my hope, that in nothing I shall be ashamed, but that with all boldness, as always, so now also Christ shall be magnified in my body, whether it be by life, or by death" (Philippians 1:20).

Central Truth: The Christian's faith-filled response to difficulties advances the gospel.

Evangelism Emphasis: The Christian's faith-filled response to difficulties advances the gospel.

PRINTED TEXT

Philippians 1:12. But I would ye should understand, brethren, that the things which happened unto me have fallen out rather unto the furtherance of the gospel;

13. So that my bonds in Christ are manifest in all the palace, and in all other places;

14. And many of the brethren in the Lord, waxing confident by my bonds, are much more bold to speak the word without fear.

15. Some indeed preach Christ even of envy and strife; and some also of good will:

16. The one preach Christ of contention, not sincerely, supposing to add affliction to my bonds:

17. But the other of love, knowing that I am set for the defence of the gospel.

18. What then? notwithstanding, every way, whether in pretence, or in truth, Christ is preached; and I therein do rejoice, yea, and will rejoice.

19. For I know that this shall turn to my salvation through your prayer, and the supply of the Spirit of Jesus Christ,

20. According to my earnest expectation and my hope, that in nothing I shall be ashamed, but that with all boldness, as always, so now also Christ shall be magnified in my body, whether it be by life, or by death.

21. For to me to live is Christ, and to die is gain.

22. But if I live in the flesh, this is the fruit of my labour: yet what I shall choose I wot not.

23. For I am in a strait betwixt two, having a desire to depart, and to be with Christ; which is far better:

24. Nevertheless to abide in the flesh is more needful for you.

25. And having this confidence, I know that I shall abide and continue with you all for your furtherance and joy of faith;

26. That your rejoicing may be more abundant in Jesus Christ for me by my coming to you again.

27. Only let your conversation be as it becometh the gospel of Christ: that whether I come and see you, or else be absent, I may hear of your affairs, that ye stand fast in one spirit, with one mind striving together for the faith of the gospel;

28. And in nothing terrified by your adversaries: which is to them an evident token of perdition, but to you of salvation, and that of God.

LESSON OUTLINE

I. SPEAK BOLDLY OF CHRIST
  A. Paul's Imprisonment
  B. Paul's Patience
  C. Contrasting Motives
  D. No Matter the Motive
  E. Powerful Prayers
  F. Confident Expectation
II. HAVE CONFIDENCE IN CHRIST
  A. Unshaken Faith
  B. Fruitful Labor
  C. Advantage to the Philippians
  D. Spiritual Growth
III. LIVE WORTHY OF CHRIST
  A. Exhortation to Unity
  B. The Privilege of Suffering

LESSON EXPOSITION

INTRODUCTION

Some of the greatest writings of all time have taken place in the cells of dank, dark prisons. Imprisonment seems to focus one's mind on his or her deepest beliefs. Sometimes the imprisoned writer is there for religious or political reasons. In the case of Paul's first imprisonment, it was both.

The Jewish leaders in Jerusalem had brought false charges against Paul because he preached Jesus (whom they had crucified as a false messiah) and because they resented his desertion from Judaism. However, they also saw Paul's dedication to spreading Christianity as a threat to their own political position in Palestine. Though Rome was a stern overlord, local officials were still allowed some leverage in ruling over certain areas of life. So many people becoming Christians were eroding this arrangement; thus, much effort was spent in persecuting believers.

Stephen and James (brother of John) had both been martyred. To defend himself from the religious leaders' harassment, Paul used his Roman citizenship to get himself sent to Rome for trial. Of course, he also saw this as a way of carrying the gospel to the center of the known world.

Some have said that God let Paul go to prison so he would slow down long enough to write much-needed letters to various churches—letters that became a rich part of the Scriptures. Paul himself admitted that his incarceration served to advance the gospel (Philippians 1:12).

Usually imprisoned writers take potshots at their torturers or the political system opposing them. Paul had nothing negative to say about his situation. Instead, he focused on the Christ-centered life. The theme of this particular letter is pure joy, even though Paul had no idea what the outcome of his trial would be. This is highlighted by his words, "For I have learned, in whatsoever state I am, therewith to be content" (4:11).

The church at Philippi was founded in what is now northern Greece. While on his second missionary journey, and in response to a vision God gave him, Paul left Troas in the province of Asia (present day Turkey) and traveled to the city of Philippi in Macedonia. Philippi was a Roman military colony and a major crossroads on the Egnatian Way. It was an affluent city, and Paul's first convert there was Lydia (Acts 16:14), an upper-class businesswoman who sold an expensive dye—purple—that was as valuable as gold. This commodity was used as tender in international trade.

Paul's words to the Christians in this city show no condemnation for wealth or commerce. Likely, this was because the believers there were such a warm and generous congregation—people who had not let materialism overshadow their love for God. Besides, many of them were not affluent. The Philippian jailer (Acts 16:22-34) would have been middle-class, and the delivered demon-possessed girl would have been from the lower class (vv. 16-18). Paul's emphasis is on Christ. He had surrendered everything to Christ, and longed for his readers to experience the same level of fellowship and joy he had found.

To the believers at Ephesus, Paul emphasized their *riches in Christ*. Infinite spiritual blessings were theirs, and they could draw on untold wealth for their daily living. To the Philippians, however, he presented Christ clothed in humility. He pictured the human side of the Lord, His willingness to lay down His rights and take on the role of a servant. In Colossians, Paul showed Christ's power, glory, and lordship over creation. Paul tailored his words to fit the needs of believers in different situations.

Philippians was written nearly a decade after the church was established. The people there had learned of Paul's trial in Jerusalem and subsequent imprisonment in Rome. The news caused sympathy for him, and they sent funds to help in his situation. This was typical of the charitable attitude they had expressed from the founding of the church. Epaphroditus, the messenger from the church, had brought their gifts to Paul, and in turn had become seriously ill while in Rome. Paul considered his recovery an answer to prayer, and sent him back to Philippi with the letter (2:25-30).

Unlike many of Paul's writings, this letter was not written because of any conflict or problem. Its tone is one of affection and appreciation—much like an extended thank-you note. Throughout, Paul focuses on Christ Jesus as the very reason for living, and the believer's hope for eternal life. Still, he does address three minor problems at Philippi: (1) their frustration and discouragement over his imprisonment (1:12-26); (2) small seeds of friction and disunity between two women in the congregation (2:2-4; 4:2); (3) the constant threat of Judaizers infiltrating a false doctrine among them (3:1-3).

Still, what comes through most predominantly in Philippians are three simple themes: (1) joy in the midst of all circumstances; (2) Christian humility and service; (3) the surpassing value of knowing Christ.

I. SPEAK BOLDLY OF CHRIST
    (Philippians 1:12-20)

A. Paul's Imprisonment (v. 12)

12. But I would ye should understand, brethren, that the things which happened unto me have fallen out rather unto the furtherance of the gospel.

At least three years before the writing of this letter (about A.D. 58), Paul had returned from his third missionary journey and determined to go to Jerusalem, despite warnings and prophecies from friends (Acts 21:10-13). Thus, his arrest there was no surprise to him. He found himself before a hostile Sanhedrin Council. Noticing it was made up of Sadducees and Pharisees (two groups that hated each other), Paul announced he was a Pharisee himself and believed in the resurrection. This brought the reaction he hoped for. The Sadducees were materialistic and political, and held no hope of a future life. The Pharisees (who adamantly believed in a resurrection) immediately saw Paul in a more positive light. A dispute broke out between the two parties at the council and brought an impasse. To protect Paul's life from the squabble, he was put in a castle jail. There something extremely important happened: "And the night following the Lord stood by him, and said, Be of good cheer, Paul: for as thou hast testified of me in Jerusalem, so must thou bear witness also at Rome" (23:11).

Paul was moved to a prison in Caesarea and held there for two years, during which time he had opportunities to witness before both Felix and Festus, provincial Roman governors. After appealing to Caesar, he was on his way to Rome, only to be shipwrecked at Malta. Finally arriving in Rome, he was permitted to live in a private residence with a soldier guarding him. This allowed some freedom to have visitors and to visit Christians in the area, especially those in the church at Rome (to which he had written some 10 years earlier).

Paul had only been in Rome for three days before he called a meeting of the local Jewish leaders. His efforts to stay in touch with the Jews is indicative of the deep love and hope he had for the Jewish nation, despite all the hostility that had been expressed against him. These Jewish folk had heard nothing of the controversies surrounding Paul, and had heard only a little about Jesus himself. Consequently, for a whole day Paul preached about the kingdom of God and used proofs from the Old Testament Law and Prophets to verify his claims. Some of the Jews believed his message, while others did not. Despite Paul's love for his own people and desire to see them come to Christ, the majority of those he witnessed to refused his message. Consequently, he turned again to the Gentile world.

For two whole years (28:30) Paul lived and preached the gospel in Rome, giving a great witness. He carried out his ministry with confidence, despite his prisoner status. He had full tolerance from the Roman government, and the local Jews had no way to prevent him.

This brings us back to our text. Everything that had happened to Paul, though discomforting to him personally, still had the effect of further spreading the gospel. For that Paul was thankful and had no complaints about his present situation. He knew the Philippians were distressed over his incarceration, and he sought to show it in a positive light. He realized that his circumstances weren't as important as how he handled them.

B. Paul's Patience (vv. 13, 14)

13. So that my bonds in Christ are manifest in all the palace, and in all other places;

14. And many of the brethren in the Lord, waxing confident by my bonds, are much more bold to speak the word without fear.

Sometimes leaders are appalled that the work they leave behind in a place prospers in their absence. Insecurity makes them believe that their very presence is necessary. Not so with Paul. Behind his words is an implied exhortation for the Philippians to move forward with the gospel without undue dependence on his presence. They had sent Epaphroditus to brings gifts to him and check on his well-being. He assured his friends that his circumstances had not been detrimental, but rather advantageous to the gospel. Many people had come to his quarters to hear his message, and other Christian coworkers had come for exhortation from him. He was grateful that the Philippians were fretful over him, but the bad situation had turned into a good one. They should be encouraged in their own work because of this.

Paul had apparently recently been moved from his hired house (Acts 28:30) to a place closer to his trial location. All the palace guard were aware of his situation and that his imprisonment was purely for the cause of Christ. "During the first century, prisoners sent to Rome in cases of appeal were entrusted to the care of praetorian guards. As these guards were assigned in succession to Paul, it soon became clear to them that he was no ordinary captive" (*Zondervan NIV Bible Commentary*). These soldiers were elite and highly trained, and because they were one-by-one chained to Paul, they had no choice but to listen to him preach the gospel.

"Although Paul could not go to the world to preach, in this way God brought the world to Paul. In an ironic twist, they were the captives and Paul was free to preach" (*Nelson Study Bible*). Paul saw his imprisonment as part of the sovereign will of God for his life.

Paul was also encouraged because his situation had bolstered other Christians to speak out in Rome. "They drew their courage from Paul's example, laid their fears aside, and became more bold in proclaiming God's Word" (*Zondervan NIV Bible Commentary*).

C. Contrasting Motives (vv. 15-17)

15. Some indeed preach Christ even of envy and strife; and some also of good will:

16. The one preach Christ of contention, not sincerely, supposing to add affliction to my bonds:

17. But the other of love, knowing that I am set for the defence of the gospel.

It seems odd that some of those who were now preaching boldly did so from the wrong spirit. These were not heretics, as Paul often battled in other places, but rather people who were jealous of the attention Paul received. It appears they were determined to cause him trouble for the purpose of elevating themselves.

At the same time, there were those who were preaching out of goodwill feelings toward Paul. They thought highly of him and of the gospel, and were firmly dedicated to serving God. They saw Paul's sincerity and realized that what had happened to him was part of God's larger plan for reaching out to the people of Rome. The gospel had spread in just 30 years all the way from Judea to the Caesar in Rome, the controlling power of the entire known world.

Paul had the spiritual sense to discern the motives of all those preaching around him. Some preachers were self-seeking at his expense and were likely enjoying their newfound place of

prominence while he was incarcerated. These likely were men who had been highly esteemed in the church at Rome before Paul arrived. The great apostle's presence had overshadowed their own influence, and now they were battling back to win the people's favor. If this was their motive, it had certainly failed to sway Paul himself. He was simply happy that the gospel was being preached.

D. No Matter the Motive (v. 18)

18. What then? notwithstanding, every way, whether in pretence, or in truth, Christ is preached; and I therein do rejoice, yea, and will rejoice.

The conclusion was simple in Paul's mind. It didn't matter what motives those around him had in preaching—as long as the message was the right one. He could overlook any reflection they were intending on him. Seeing the gospel proclaimed was much more important than any personal grievances. Good news was still going out to a lost world.

E. Powerful Prayers (v. 19)

19. For I know that this shall turn to my salvation through your prayer, and the supply of the Spirit of Jesus Christ.

The word *salvation* means "deliverance." It was used in the New Testament to indicate physical healing, rescue from danger, justification, sanctification, and even glorification. Here, however, Paul used it to indicate personal empowerment for handling his circumstances. He knew that God would work through the difficult situation to get the charges against him dropped. The prayers of the believers in Philippi were key to this happening. The prayers of believers, in conjunction with the work of the Holy Spirit, bring results.

F. Confident Expectation (v. 20)

20. According to my earnest

expectation and my hope, that in nothing I shall be ashamed, but that with all boldness, as always, so now also Christ shall be magnified in my body, whether it be by life, or by death.

Paul's entire life centered on living for Christ and telling others about Him. Though others might lie and bring false charges against him, he wanted his own motives and actions to be pure and glorifying to Christ. The only judgment that concerned him was a heavenly one. His only request was that he maintain boldness and courage to always stand for Christ. In his mind, there was no difference between living and dying, as long as Christ was magnified before others.

II. HAVE CONFIDENCE IN CHRIST (Philippians 1:21-26)

A. Unshaken Faith (v. 21)

21. For to me to live is Christ, and to die is gain.

Though he was not asking to die, Paul saw death as a positive. In fact, he would experience gain, for then he would be with Christ permanently. He was simply saying, "It doesn't matter how things turn out. Nothing anyone can do to me can affect my future. My very reason for living is Christ, and He will determine when it is time for me to be with Him."

Death would be nothing but a doorway into Christ's presence. Also, if he were executed, this would serve to further advance the gospel. In retrospect, we see this to be true. Though Paul was released from this imprisonment, he was later arrested again and ultimately beheaded.

Because of Paul's firm stand, his writings, his witness, his evangelism and his death, Paul is viewed as one of the greatest Christian of all times. Christ made his life worth living, but He also made his death worth dying.

B. Fruitful Labor (vv. 22, 23)

22. But if I live in the flesh, this is the fruit of my labour: yet what I shall choose I wot not.

23. For I am in a strait betwixt two, having a desire to depart, and to be with Christ; which is far better.

There is an old song that says, *Que sera, sera*—"Whatever will be, will be." The attitude expressed in these words is one of fatalism. The individual has no influence over the outcome of life, and really doesn't care. He or she seems to be numb toward everything.

In contrast, Paul's words express absolutely no sign of fatalism. He was totally positive about his future, no matter what direction it might take. He simply didn't know which he would choose—life or death—if the option were left to him. If he continued to live, then he would resume his labor of carrying the gospel everywhere possible. This certainly had not been easy. He had undergone constant persecution and hardship, as well as emotional anguish. "Yet he looked on his apostolic ministry as a challenge to be grasped and as fruit to be harvested" (*Zondervan NIV Bible Commentary*). In his perplexity, Paul saw it best to leave his future purely in the Lord's hand.

C. Advantage to the Philippians (v. 24)

24. Nevertheless to abide in the flesh is more needful for you.

It's as if Paul had been in a daze pondering his future, when suddenly, he remembered that his constituents really needed him. By continuing to live he could be helpful to those he had won to Christ, specifically the Philippians. He certainly didn't want them to think he was anxious to leave them. He loved those he had ministered to, and was very willing to continue doing so on their behalf.

D. Spiritual Growth (vv. 25, 26)

25. And having this confidence, I

know that I shall abide and continue with you all for your furtherance and joy of faith;

26. That your rejoicing may be more abundant in Jesus Christ for me by my coming to you again.

If to continue his ministry was God's plan, then Paul wanted to see his friends grow in Christ. He wanted their joy deepened. He was not content that they should just be saved, but that they should grow in their knowledge of Christ and relationship with Him. If he lived, then seeing their maturity was to be his goal.

III. LIVE WORTHY OF CHRIST
(Philippians 1:27-30)

A. Exhortation to Unity (v. 27)

27. Only let your conversation be as it becometh the gospel of Christ: that whether I come and see you, or else be absent, I may hear of your affairs, that ye stand fast in one spirit, with one mind striving together for the faith of the gospel.

The phrase "Let your conversation be" implies a daily walk. Paul exhorted the Philippians to daily walk in one spirit and purpose, standing together as warriors in an army. They were to live as if they were aliens in a foreign country. They were representatives of Christ to the Roman world, and they should prove themselves to be positive ambassadors.

"Striving together" indicates teamwork. God never intended that Christians become spiritual hermits. Effective Christianity is best lived as a community, with all individuals loving and caring for each other.

"One spirit" means unity. Unity can only be achieved by the operation of the Holy Spirit. As we said in our last lesson, Christ had already brought us peace, and He has given us a unity of faith—yet we have to *keep* it (Ephesians 4:3). Paul saw the local church body as one that ministers to each other, grows together, and thereby experiences unity.

Warren Wiersbe tells of a freelance missionary visiting a pastor and asking for financial support. The pastor asked him what group he was associated with. The missionary replied, "I belong to the invisible church." He apparently had no ties to any denomination or missions outreach group. The pastor ultimately replied to him, "Well, here's some invisible money to help you minister to the invisible church!" (*Be Joyful*).

Being part of a local body and working together with others produces an outreach that cannot be achieved individually. It also provides a means of accountability.

B. The Privilege of Suffering
(vv. 28-30)

(Philippians 1:29, 30 is not included in the printed text.)

28. And in nothing terrified by your adversaries: which is to them an evident token of perdition, but to you of salvation, and that of God.

The privileges and benefits of the gospel come with certain responsibilities, one of which is suffering. The Philippians had watched 10 years earlier as Paul endured persecution in their own city, and had also heard of trials he had endured since then. Paul, however, turns this around and shows suffering as a tool God uses to accomplish His purposes. Suffering matures the believer, it removes those who only superficially believe, and it strengthens the faith of those who are looking for an example to follow.

SENTENCE SERMONS

THE CHRISTIAN'S FAITH-FILLED RESPONSE to difficulties advances the gospel.

—Selected

MEN MAY READ THE GOSPEL in cloth covers, but they can't get away from the gospel in shoe leather.

—Donald Gray Barnhouse

THE WORLD has many religions; it has but one gospel.

—**George Owen**

EVANGELISM APPLICATION

THE CHRISTIAN'S FAITH-FILLED RESPONSE TO DIFFICULTIES ADVANCES THE GOSPEL.

What is the one thing you live for? What makes you tick? Is it your career? Your family? Your hobbies? Your accomplishments? Your influence? Your standing in the public eye? Your legacy? Generally, these are the things most people feel the most passionate about.

Many statesmen and politicians, no matter how crafty and ruthless they might have been in their prime, usually begin to worry about how they will be remembered when they die. They begin to question what they had lived for, and whether the things they had most passionately pursued had any real value.

Thus, a better question to ask is this: What would I die for? What makes death worth dying? Paul knew the answer to this question. His only reason for living was Christ. He had perfect peace, and had no worries about legacy or accomplishments. All that mattered was that Christ be glorified in him.

If we can take on this same motivation, how much more will we actually accomplish for the Kingdom? If Christ is our passion, then everything we do will be a witness for Him.

ILLUMINATING THE LESSON

Are your motives always pure? Paul spoke to his Philippian readers about others who were preaching the gospel in Rome out of selfish ambition, and who were also spreading seeds of dissension against him personally. Yet he was happy that the gospel was at least going forth. In other words, they had the right message but wrong heart.

Can you look back and see that everything you have ever done in Christ's name was with the right motive? Or were there times when you hoped your efforts would bring you a better salary, a higher esteem among the people, an advancement to a larger ministry, or a more favorable position over some other brother or sister?

The fact is that none of us are totally pure in heart. We can do things out of our own selfishness without realizing such. However, as we look back, we often can see fruit, even when we were wrong. Thank God He didn't expose us for who we really were. At the same time, we should pray that we see ourselves properly, that we lay down selfish desires, that we only have pure intentions in everything we do for the Lord. The world is watching us with a critical eye. They can often see our motives, even when we don't. May the Lord purify us as we work for Him.

DAILY BIBLE READINGS

M. Bold Confrontation.
    1 Kings 18:21-40
T. Courageous Faith.
    Daniel 3:8-18
W. Bold Obedience.
    Amos 7:10-15
T. Bold Preaching.
    Acts 4:13-20
F. Anointed Preaching.
    Acts 7:51-60
S. Obligated to Preach.
    Romans 1:14-17

TRUTH SEARCH
Creatively Teaching the Word

DISCUSSION QUESTIONS

Speak Boldly of Christ
(Philippians 1:12-20)

1. What difficulties did Paul experience (vv. 12, 13)?

2. How was God using Paul's situation for His glory (vv. 13, 14)?

3. What different motives were leading people to preach about Jesus (vv. 15-17)?

4. Why did Paul rejoice (v. 18)?

5. What gave Paul hope (v. 19)?

6. What was Paul's passionate desire (v. 20)?

Have Confidence in Christ
(Philippians 1:21-26)

1. Explain Paul's statement in verse 21.

2. What two competing desires did Paul have (vv. 22, 23)?

3. What motivated Paul to continue his earthly ministry (vv. 24, 25)?

4. What did Paul anticipate would come from a future visit to the Philippian church?

Live Worthy of Christ
(Philippians 1:27-30)

1. How can a Christian's "conduct be worthy of the gospel of Christ" (v. 27, NKJV)?

2. What was Paul's desire for the Philippians' regarding their oneness (v. 27)?

3. What double meaning would it have for the Philippians to stand brave before their opponents (v. 28)?

4. What two opportunities had the Philippians been granted (v. 29)?

5. How would Paul's example be significant to these believers?

OBJECT LESSON

Items needed: Ball of yarn

Have the students stand in a circle along with you.

Name one trial you have experienced since becoming a Christian. Next, while holding one end of the yarn, toss the rest of it to someone across the circle from you. That person should name a trial he or she has experienced, and then toss the ball across the circle while holding a piece of it. Continue this back-and-forth pattern with students naming trials and then passing the yarn. If possible, give everyone a chance to participate.

We have created a tangled web of yarn, haven't we? Sometimes our lives appear as crisscrossed as this yarn, and there seems no pattern or purpose to it. However, if we will be faithful to God, He will work through our difficulties to supernaturally advance the gospel.

Have everyone drop the yarn they are holding; then have someone gather up the yarn and take it out of the room.

Just as we removed this yarn, there is coming a time when all trials and problems will end. In the meantime, let's trust God to work through our crises to bring Christ glory.

Imitating Christ

Study Text: Philippians 2:1-18

Objective: To discover that Christlike humility produces unity and determine to be like Him.

Time: A.D. 63

Place: Written from a Roman prison

Golden Text: "Let this mind be in you, which was also in Christ Jesus" (Philippians 2:5).

Central Truth: Christlikeness comes only through an intimate relationship with Him.

Evangelism Emphasis: Believers who are truly Christlike will draw others to Christ.

PRINTED TEXT

Philippians 2:1. If there be therefore any consolation in Christ, if any comfort of love, if any fellowship of the Spirit, if any bowels and mercies,

2. Fulfil ye my joy, that ye be likeminded, having the same love, being of one accord, of one mind.

3. Let nothing be done through strife or vainglory; but in lowliness of mind let each esteem other better than themselves.

4. Look not every man on his own things, but every man also on the things of others.

5. Let this mind be in you, which was also in Christ Jesus:

6. Who, being in the form of God, thought it not robbery to be equal with God:

7. But made himself of no reputation, and took upon him the form of a servant, and was made in the likeness of men:

8. And being found in fashion as a man, he humbled himself, and became obedient unto death, even the death of the cross.

9. Wherefore God also hath highly exalted him, and given him a name which is above every name:

10. That at the name of Jesus every knee should bow, of things in heaven, and things in earth, and things under the earth;

11. And that every tongue should confess that Jesus Christ is Lord, to the glory of God the Father.

12. Wherefore, my beloved, as ye have always obeyed, not as in my presence only, but now much more in my absence, work out your own salvation with fear and trembling.

13. For it is God which worketh in you both to will and to do of his good pleasure.

14. Do all things without murmurings and disputings:

15. That ye may be blameless and harmless, the sons of God, without rebuke, in the midst of a crooked and perverse nation, among whom ye shine as lights in the world;

16. Holding forth the word of life; that I may rejoice in the day of Christ, that I have not run in vain, neither laboured in vain.

17. Yea, and if I be offered upon the sacrifice and service of your faith, I joy, and rejoice with you all.

18. For the same cause also do ye joy, and rejoice with me.

LESSON OUTLINE

I. WALK IN UNITY AND HUMILITY
   A. Four Incentives
   B. Like-Mindedness
   C. Selfless Ambition
II. HAVE THE MIND OF CHRIST
   A. Nature of the Incarnation
   B. Exaltation of Christ
III. LET YOUR LIGHT SHINE
   A. Spiritual Growth
   B. God's Work in Us
   C. Shining as Lights
   D. Poured Out as an Offering

LESSON EXPOSITION

INTRODUCTION

The Philippian congregation had sent Epaphroditus to Rome with a financial gift to take care of Paul's needs while incarcerated. He was instructed to minister to the apostle during this visit, an arrangement indicating that this man must have had a servant's heart. In the process of helping Paul, however, he became very ill, possibly nearly dying.

When he was feeling better, Paul sent him back with this letter, but it seems that Paul had to defend Epaphroditus' conduct to the Philippian believers. He asked the church to receive him back with joy and love. He assured them that the man had labored well and that his sickness had been serious. He had given his time and services for the cause of Christ and should be honored for having done so.

Of all Paul's letters, he was most appreciative of the congregation at Philippi. He didn't have to deal with unsettling problems there. He simply encouraged them in Christ. He asked no sympathy for himself, and neither did he view himself in dire straits, though his trial was likely going on at the same time.

The golden text for this lesson is Philippians 2:5, but the theme is most exemplified in verse 8: "And being found in appearance as a man, he humbled himself and became obedient to death—even death on a cross!" (NIV). Jesus Christ was both fully man and fully God. He willingly stepped down from glory and humbled Himself to be a servant. Even though He never deserved to die, He allowed Himself to be crucified so that the sins of the world could be charged against Him. This was the ultimate picture of humility.

Because Christ so humbled Himself, we should walk in the same grace. The person of humble heart "regards himself as being not his own, but God's in Christ. He cannot exalt himself, for he knows that he has nothing of himself. The humble mind is thus at the root of all other graces and virtues. Self-exaltation spoils everything" (International Standard Bible Encyclopaedia).

The example of Christ's life of humility is the centerpiece of Paul's argument for unity among believers. Following after such a perfect model will produce lives of purity, selflessness and close interpersonal relationships. However, doing so is the opposite of what secular society preaches. Such was true in the first century and is even more pronounced today.

Contemporary society has duped most people into believing that the world owes them something. Everything is centered on "me, my needs, my pleasures." There is no sense of caring for anyone else.

In contrast, Jesus came to do the work His Father had assigned Him. "Being in very nature God," He took on "the very nature of a servant" (vv. 6, 7, NIV). Paul wanted the people of Philippi to know that humility and a servant's heart are strengths, not weaknesses. Jesus himself had said that the second greatest commandment is to love others.

I. WALK IN UNITY AND HUMILITY (Philippians 2:1-4)

A. Four Incentives (v. 1)

1. If there be therefore any consolation in Christ, if any comfort of love, if any fellowship of the Spirit, if any bowels and mercies.

Paul talked in the first chapter of this letter about external circumstances that battle against believers, things that produce suffering. However, the external problems were less a hindrance to unity than potential internal ones. He now turned his focus to attitudes within the body that destroy unity.

Paul could speak from experience. He had battled persecutions, beatings, shipwrecks, ostracism by the Jews, and a host of other problems, yet he had refused to let his attitude be affected. He also dealt with issues involving fellow Christian leaders. His disagreement with the Judaizers at the Jerusalem Council over the treatment of Gentile Christians (Acts 15; Galatians 2), his rift with Barnabas over John Mark (Acts 15:36-39), and his rebuke of Peter for slighting Gentile believers in Antioch (Galatians 2.11-21) all point to the fact that keeping unity within the ranks of the church is not easy. His use of the word *therefore* links his own struggles with the Philippians' struggles.

Paul uses four conditional clauses that begin with *if*, but these clauses are positive in nature. Each *if* actually means *since*, and is followed by a truth.

1. *Consolation*—This means encouragement that comes from being a part of the body of Christ, fully accepted and redeemed.

2. *Comfort of love*—The fact that Christ's love had pervaded them and caused them to love one another would give them a basis to build on.

3. *Fellowship of the Spirit*—These believers had heard the full gospel preached to them by Paul, which had included receiving the fullness of the Spirit. Thus, they knew what effect the Spirit had already produced in their lives. They were in fellowship with God.

4. *Bowels and mercies*—The *New International Version* translates these words as "tenderness and compassion." The work of the Lord in their hearts had produced these fruits. The Greek term for *mercy* means "compassionate desires that develop in response to a situation and that stimulate a person to meet recognized needs in that situation" (*Nelson Study Bible*).

B. Like-Mindedness (v. 2)

2. Fulfil ye my joy, that ye be likeminded, having the same love, being of one accord, of one mind.

Paul was already experiencing joy because of the Philippians, but he now set forth a fourfold appeal to bring him even greater joy—joy because of unity in the church. The word *likeminded* indicates a unity of spirit so that the entire community of believers expresses one soul and purpose. The next three phrases *same love, one accord, one mind*—are simply more ways of expressing the same idea, "harmony of thought and disposition" (*The Wycliffe Bible Commentary*). Paul's expressing the same thought in various ways indicates the importance of the subject.

C. Selfless Ambition (vv. 3, 4)

3. Let nothing be done through strife or vainglory; but in lowliness of mind let each esteem other better than themselves.

4. Look not every man on his own things, but every man also on the things of others.

Paul himself was a victim of selfish ambition, perpetrated by other preachers in Rome who were jealous of his influence. Although he had said earlier that he was pleased these men were at least preaching Christ and doctrinal truth (even though their motives were wrong), still he didn't condone such behavior. These men gloried in their successes, not in Christ. What a lesson for today when so many high-profile ministers have great numbers of followers because of the mass media. Praise and adulation from admiring constituents is hard for anyone to handle without some vanity arising. Paul insisted that humility be the order of the day—no matter how useful one had found himself in the Kingdom. The glory had to go to Jesus and no one else.

Putting others ahead of oneself was a stiff antidote to selfish behavior. "The self-centeredness that considers only one's rights, plans, and interests must be replaced by a broader outlook that includes the interests of one's fellow Christians" (*Zondervan NIV Bible Commentary*).

At the same time, Paul never advocated putting oneself down and groveling in lack of self-respect. What he called for was an honest evaluation of one's nature, calling, gifts and value to the community of believers. If one had more giftings, he or she should rejoice in using them for the glory of the Lord. The phrase "let each esteem" means that all Christians should see themselves properly in the fellowship, neither belittling nor elevating themselves.

The church at Philippi was apparently comprised of people from many backgrounds and nationalities, making unity difficult to maintain. The commonality among them was that Christ had come into their individual hearts. They needed to build on this unifying factor. Although there seems to have been no sign of friction, Paul encouraged the Philippians to safeguard against such, for their differences could be used by Satan in stirring prejudices and ill will.

II. HAVE THE MIND OF CHRIST (Philippians 2:5-11)

A. Nature of the Incarnation (vv. 5-8)

5. Let this mind be in you, which was also in Christ Jesus:

6. Who, being in the form of God, thought it not robbery to be equal with God:

7. But made himself of no reputation, and took upon him the form of a servant, and was made in the likeness of men:

8. And being found in fashion as a man, he humbled himself, and became obedient unto death, even the death of the cross.

The supreme example of humility is found in Christ. Reducing Himself from deity to mere man, and even allowing Himself to be killed on a cross, is the most severe humbling possible. One definition of the Hebrew word for *humility* is "to be brought low." Even this doesn't do justice to the journey Christ made. Words cannot describe such condescension.

This beautiful passage is regarded by many to have been an early Christian hymn that Paul incorporated into his letter (much in the same way we would quote poetry or hymn stanzas today). However, Paul himself was quite capable of eloquent words and poetic style (as seen in 1 Corinthians 13), so it is more likely that he simply overflowed with wonder at the lowliness Christ experienced.

These verses offer one of the most crystallized wordings of the entire gospel, much the same as John 3:16, 17. They fully describe the Incarnation—the Son of God, existing from eternity past, willingly laying aside His rights as God and becoming a man, with a human body and human nature, all for the purpose of reconciling humanity to God.

Several of the included phrases need to be examined individually for their truth and beauty:

1. *Let this mind be in you*—Right actions begin with right thinking. If we are to overcome our carnal nature, we have to take on a different way of reasoning. In Romans 12:2 Paul calls for a "renewing of your mind," using Christ as the example. We must decide to think as He thought, and then act accordingly. This is both an individual and corporate admonition. Bodies of believers must together think and act as one, that is, reflecting the very nature of Christ.

2. *Being in the form of God*—The word *being* is present tense, indicating a continuation of condition. The essential nature of Christ was not changed when He became man. Jesus has always been God, equal with the Father. This is reiterated with the phrase "equal with God." He simply let go of His divine privileges so He could take on manhood and bring redemption. His divine nature never changed, even as He wore the body of humanity.

3. *Made himself of no reputation*—If I were God and planned to lower myself to be a human, I would at least make myself an exalted and highly regarded individual. Not so with Jesus. He was born into an impoverished part of the world during extremely difficult times.

4. *Form of a servant*—This was the lowest social status, the total opposite of the term *Lord.* The God who created the universe chose to become like the smallest speck of dust.

5. *Likeness of men*—Jesus was all man, having all the aspects and natures of a man, yet sinless. He faced the same temptations, but totally overcame them.

6. *Found in fashion as a man*—This implies external characteristics. He did not simply appear out of nowhere on earth. He was born as a human baby, grew up in human circumstances, and had the actions and manners of a man.

7. *Humbled himself*—He was not forced to be a servant, but took on this role willingly. Having godly powers at His disposal, He could have made earthly life easy for Himself, but chose not to do so.

8. *Death of the cross*—Knowing He had come to die as a sacrifice, Jesus could have made His own death easier. Instead, Paul shows His humility in choosing the cruelest form of capital punishment—crucifixion. "The Romans reserved the agonizing death of crucifixion for slaves and foreigners, and the Jews viewed death on a cross as a curse from God" (*Nelson Study Bible*).

B. Exaltation of Christ (vv. 9-11)

9. Wherefore God also hath highly exalted him, and given him a name which is above every name:

10. That at the name of Jesus every knee should bow, of things in heaven, and things in earth, and things under the earth;

11. And that every tongue should confess that Jesus Christ is Lord, to the glory of God the Father.

When Jesus ascended back to glory (Acts 1:9), He was given the greatest hero welcome of all ages. He was elevated to the highest position in heaven and given a name above all other names. Everything He had laid down in coming to earth was restored—with much more added.

The prophet Daniel saw the Exaltation hundreds of years before the Lord's earthly ministry took place: "In my vision at night I looked, and there before me was one like a son of man, coming with the clouds of heaven. He approached the Ancient of Days and was led into his presence. He was given authority, glory and sovereign power; all peoples, nations and men of every language worshiped him. His dominion is an everlasting dominion that will not pass away, and his kingdom is one that will never be destroyed" (Daniel 7:13, 14, *NIV*). Those who watched Jesus' ascension in Acts 1:9 saw Jesus leave the earth. Daniel saw Him arrive in heaven.

The completion of Christ's exaltation hasn't yet occurred, for every knee hasn't yet bowed to Him. It will be at the Last Judgment that this finally occurs. Even those who are condemned to everlasting torment will recognize Jesus and bow to Him. Only those who have put their faith in Him during this life, however, will have an eternal relationship with the Lord.

III. LET YOUR LIGHT SHINE
(Philippians 2:12-18)

A. Spiritual Growth (v. 12)

12. Wherefore, my beloved, as ye have always obeyed, not as in my presence only, but now much more in my absence, work out your own salvation with fear and trembling.

Paul exhorted the Philippians to pursue Christ without any undue dependence upon him. It was obvious he could no longer be nearby to remind them of how they should live. He had given them an adequate foundation of the truth of God's commands. Their own relationships with Christ should now be strong enough to keep them on track. Every believer must strive to build his or her own relationship with the Lord, learning the truths of Scriptures and never depending on a cherished leader.

The word *ye* here is plural, indicating both the individual and the corporate body. To "work out" means to dig in, discover, find a treasure. "Thus salvation can be compared to a huge gift that needs to be unwrapped for one's thorough enjoyment" (*Nelson Study Bible*).

Paul was by no means deserting his friends. However, like an eagle teaches its growing chick to fly, he recognized the Philippians had to press in to Christ themselves. They could not build their relationships with Christ on Paul's coattails.

Note, too, that Paul doesn't speak of working *for* one's salvation. They already had received that—by grace through faith. They were simply to work out the nuances of their walk with Christ.

B. God's Work in Us (v. 13)

13. For it is God which worketh in you both to will and to do of his good pleasure.

Everything we have is a gift from God. Obviously He wants us to obey Him, so He works in our hearts even helping us to *want* to obey Him. He doesn't leave us alone in our struggles but comes alongside to encourage and help us. He builds *desire* within us and then gives us the *power* to carry out those desires.

At the same time, effort on our part is required. We cannot be passive. We have to take on a new mind, obey God's Word, seek direction through the Holy Spirit, and give ourselves sacrificially to the work of the Kingdom. As we put our hearts and lives into action, the Holy Spirit *unctions* us with the desire to further love and obey Christ.

C. Shining as Lights (vv. 14-16)

14. Do all things without murmurings and disputings:

15. That ye may be blameless and harmless, the sons of God, without rebuke, in the midst of a crooked and perverse nation, among whom ye shine as lights in the world;

16. Holding forth the word of life; that I may rejoice in the day of Christ, that I have not run in vain, neither laboured in vain.

Working together without complaining or disputing serves a twofold purpose. It builds unity and harmony, thus furthering the Kingdom. Also, it bears witness to the watching world.

A church that has conflicts among its members is a poor witness to the surrounding community. The "crooked and perverse" are looking for something pure and blameless. When they see a church working together in unity, they easily recognize the futility of their own sinfulness. Shining as *lights* pictures believers to be like bright stars shining in the sky on a dark night. Jesus said, "Ye are the light of the world" (Matthew 5:14). Christ is the true light, but we are to be reflections of that light.

D. Poured Out as an Offering
(vv. 17, 18)

17. Yea, and if I be offered upon the sacrifice and service of your faith, I joy, and rejoice with you all.
18. For the same cause also do ye joy, and rejoice with me.

Paul was content with himself, even if death was to be his sentence. Likely, his trial was going on during the same time this letter was written. There was no guarantee of his release, though he obviously felt his case would be dropped. He was ready for whatever came his way.

Knowing he was helping others to grow in Christ was payment for anything he was enduring. He uses the word *sacrifice*. This depicts someone who carries out public duties at personal risk and expense. Here it also means worship humbly offered up without complaint or reservation.

GOLDEN TEXT HOMILY

"LET THIS MIND BE IN YOU, WHICH WAS ALSO IN CHRIST JESUS" (Philippians 2:5).

To have Jesus' "mind" is to have His frame of mind, His priorities.

He lived to serve. Behold Him: thronged, no time to eat, very tired. He and the Twelve slip away from the crowd, grab their sleeping bags, and head across the lake. But the multitude outruns their boat—more than 5,000 of them! Moved with compassion, Jesus ministers all day long, and prepares supper for everybody! This was His "mind."

He was humble. He forewent the use of certain attributes, ate with publicans and sinners, touched lepers, washed self-important little men's feet—and gave His life a ransom! This was His "mind."

He put God's will first—even when it meant going to the Garden, the judgment hall, the cross, death, and hades. This was His "mind."

Both we and our circumstances are different—quite different; but the principle remains. Our lives must be governed by the "mind" of Christ.—**Selected**

SENTENCE SERMONS

CHRISTLIKENESS comes only through an intimate relationship with Him.

—Selected

ARE YOUR CONVERSATIONS and your facial expressions good advertisements for your faith?

—Selected

JESUS CHRIST didn't commit the gospel to an advertising agency; He commissioned disciples.

—Joe Bayly

THEY THAT KNOW GOD will be humble, and they that know themselves, cannot be proud.

—John Flavel

EVANGELISM APPLICATION

BELIEVERS WHO ARE TRULY CHRISTLIKE WILL DRAW OTHERS TO CHRIST.

Look for a moment at how Paul began his letter to the Philippians: "Paul and Timothy, bondservants of

Jesus Christ" (1:1, *NKJV*). *The Living Bible* rendition uses the word *slave* instead of *bondservant*. Basically, both mean the same.

Paul willingly had no life of his own, but was a slave to whatever Jesus called him to do and wherever He called him to go. Thus, sitting in a jail in Rome was no different than preaching in Corinth or Ephesus. In all situations he was simply serving his Master. This is the idea Paul expressed to the Philippians. They should serve Jesus with complete joy—in total servanthood—because they had been redeemed.

An excellent illustration of this same point can be drawn from the life of William Bright. In the beginning of their marriage, Bright and his wife, Vonette, were materialistic, self-centered people. However, when they met Jesus, their lives were changed completely: "He gave us a deep and abiding love for Himself and a deep desire to realize that living for Christ and serving Him was our major goal in life. Our Lord Jesus Christ, God the Son, Creator of more than one hundred billion galaxies, left His place of glory in heaven to become a slave for us" (Bill Bright and John N. Damoose, *Red Sky in the Morning*).

In response to what Christ had done for them, the Brights made a contract with the Lord. They chose to become slaves of Jesus. In 1951 they actually wrote out a contract declaring their slavery and formally surrendering everything to the Lord. Amazingly, it was less than 48 hours later that he received the vision for forming Campus Crusade for Christ, a ministry which excels and carries the gospel around the world through various means.

ILLUMINATING THE LESSON

Most of us have tried to make *deals* with the Lord at one time or another.

We say, "Lord, I'll go to such a place, if You will do such and such for me." Or, "I'll do this if You will meet my every need." Rarely are we willing to offer our obedience without some strings attached. The thought of giving up earthly comforts to go to remote corners of the earth might frighten us. We hear the stories of deprivation that missionaries have undergone and shudder that God might demand such service of us.

However, if we look at the example of Christ, everything takes on a new perspective. Paul said we should take on the mind of Christ. What is that mind? It is one that refused to hold to the slightest demand for personal comfort. Jesus left a place that we cannot even imagine—heaven. What He had to give up to come to earth is indescribable. Not only that, He chose not to be born into a wealthy family at a comfortable time in earth's history. There were no modern conveniences (What would we do without air-conditioning?), no means of quick travel or mass communication. No, He chose to come to earth at one of its darkest times, to a place that was considered the worst in the far-strung Roman Empire. There were no strings attached to His obedience.

Given His example, how dare we demand comforts and perks when we offer our meager services to the Lord!

DAILY BIBLE READINGS

M. Prefer One Another.
    Genesis 13:5-18
T. A Rebellious Attitude.
    1 Samuel 15:16-23
W. God Sees the Heart.
    1 Samuel 16:1-13
T. Salt and Light.
    Matthew 5:13-16
F. Christlike Love.
    Matthew 5:43-48
S. Walk in the Spirit.
    Galatians 5:22-26

TRUTH SEARCH
Creatively Teaching the Word

DISCUSSION QUESTIONS

**Walk in Unity and Humility
(Philippians 2:1-4)**

1. How did Paul say the Philippians could make his joy complete?

2. In verse 2, how many different phrases does Paul use to describe unity? Why?

3. According to verse 1, what should motivate Christians to be unified?

4. What problems can "strife or vainglory" (v. 3) cause in a church?

5. What should be the Christian's attitude toward himself and toward others (v. 3)?

6. How should the Christian live out this Christlike attitude (v. 4)?

**Have the Mind of Christ
(Philippians 2:5-11)**

1. What kind of "mind" did Jesus have?

2. Who was Jesus Christ (v. 6)?

3. What did God's Son become (v. 7)?

4. Explain the phrase "obedient unto death" (v. 8).

5. How and why did Jesus humble Himself?

6. Why is Jesus' name "above every name" (v. 9)?

7. Who will submit themselves unto Christ's lordship (vv. 10, 11)?

**Let Your Light Shine
(Philippians 2:12-16)**

1. What does it mean to "work out your own salvation," and why must it be done "with fear and trembling" (v. 12)?

2. How does God work in His children's lives (v. 13)?

3. How can believers shine Christ's light in a dark world (vv. 14, 15)?

4. What would it mean for the Philippians to "hold forth the word of life," and why would this cause Paul to rejoice (v. 16)?

OBJECT LESSON

Items needed: Four stars made out of poster board, marker

Draw each of the following symbols on a different star: dollar sign, light bulb, musical note, large smile, gift-wrapped box. Display the stars as you talk about them.

Think about some of the types of people we tend to honor and respect in the church: the wealthy (dollar sign), **the brilliant** (light bulb), **the musically talented** (note), **the outgoing** (smile), **and those with other outstanding talents** (gift).

While all of those qualities are a blessing to a church, Paul mentioned none of those when he urged the Philippian Christians to shine like stars. Let's name some of the characteristics Paul mentioned in today's text. Answers could include unity, love, humility, serving, harmless, blameless, selfless, obedient and Christlike.

As the traits are mentioned, write one or two on the back of each star. Then display all the stars, showing only the words. Pray together that these traits will shine through members of your class.

The Preeminence of Christ

Study Text: Colossians 1:1-29

Objective: To acknowledge and submit to the authority of the indwelling presence of Jesus Christ.

Time: Around A.D. 62

Place: Written from prison, probably in Rome

Golden Text: "[Christ] is the head of the body, the church: who is the beginning, the firstborn from the dead; that in all things he might have the preeminence" (Colossians 1:18).

Central Truth: Jesus Christ is preeminent over all creation.

Evangelism Emphasis: Christians must proclaim that reconciliation to God is made possible through the shed blood of Jesus Christ.

PRINTED TEXT

Colossians 1:15. Who is the image of the invisible God, the firstborn of every creature:

16. For by him were all things created, that are in heaven, and that are in earth, visible and invisible, whether they be thrones, or dominions, or principalities, or powers: all things were created by him, and for him:

17. And he is before all things, and by him all things consist.

18. And he is the head of the body, the church: who is the beginning, the firstborn from the dead; that in all things he might have the preeminence.

19. For it pleased the Father that in him should all fulness dwell;

20. And, having made peace through the blood of his cross, by him to reconcile all things unto himself; by him, I say, whether they be things in earth, or things in heaven.

21. And you, that were sometime alienated and enemies in your mind by wicked works, yet now hath he reconciled

22. In the body of his flesh through death, to present you holy and unblameable and unreproveable in his sight:

23. If ye continue in the faith grounded and settled, and be not moved away from the hope of the gospel, which ye have heard, and which was preached to every creature which is under heaven; whereof I Paul am made a minister;

24. Who now rejoice in my sufferings for you, and fill up that which is behind of the afflictions of Christ in my flesh for his body's sake, which is the church:

25. Whereof I am made a minister, according to the dispensation of God which is given to me for you, to fulfil the word of God;

26. Even the mystery which hath been hid from ages and from generations, but now is made manifest to his saints:

27. To whom God would make known what is the riches of the glory of this mystery among the Gentiles; which is Christ in you, the hope of glory:

28. Whom we preach, warning every man, and teaching every man in all wisdom; that we may present every man perfect in Christ Jesus:

29. Whereunto I also labour, striving according to his working, which worketh in me mightily.

LESSON OUTLINE

I. CHRIST REIGNS SUPREME
   A. Wonderful Benefits
   B. Firstborn Over All Creation
   C. Head of the Church
II. CHRIST BRINGS RECONCILIATION
   A. The Fullness of Christ
   B. All Things Reconciled
   C. Individual Reconciliation
   D. Individual Responsibility
III. OUR HOPE OF GLORY
   A. Suffering With Christ
   B. The Mystery Revealed
   C. Maturity in Christ

LESSON EXPOSITION

INTRODUCTION

The motivation for Paul writing to the Colossians was a visit by his friend Epaphras. Epaphras had apparently been the founder of the church at Colosse, himself having been one of Paul's converts during the apostle's two-year stay at Ephesus. He had traveled all the way to Rome, a tremendous journey for those times, to seek Paul's counsel in dealing with problems in his congregation.

Paul himself had never been to Colosse (which was 100 miles east of Ephesus), but had developed ties with the church, especially through the leadership of Epaphras. In the salutation of his letter he speaks of praying for the Colossians and giving thanks to God for their salvation. They were people near to his heart, though he did not know them personally.

Paul's house in Rome was apparently a busy place. Church leaders, a runaway slave (Onesimus), and fellow Christian workers visited regularly. For once the apostle was not preaching the gospel from place to place, but was settled in one location (although under house arrest and likely chained to a Roman soldier). He had time to deal with problems cropping up in the church, and to write letters to congregations. In a manner of speaking, his house became the center of the church, surpassing the importance of Jerusalem.

Colosse was a Roman city in Asia Minor at the base of Mount Cadmus in the Lycus River valley. It had been a prosperous industrial center in the past, but now was obviously in decline, much like the textile mill towns that dot the American South. The city was increasingly eclipsed by its neighbor, Laodicea. Secular history records there was a major earthquake near Colosse in A.D. 61, possibly the same year as the writing of this letter. Paul makes no mention of such, meaning it probably had not yet occurred, or word of it had not yet reached him.

For Epaphras to have made such a long journey to see Paul indicates the problems in Colosse were serious. A doctrinal heresy was creeping into the church. Possibly a strong enough foundation of truth had not been taught there, since Paul had not visited the area, but more probably it was simply the fact that Colosse was a cultural mix of peoples with every type of strange idea, each demanding to be heard. Greek Hellenism had its proponents—with a dualistic point of view that said things are either spiritual or material. There were Jews there who taught a strict adherence to laws and rituals. Finally, there were diverse pagans who brought occultism and mystical rites into the mix.

The result of all this was a syncretism of conflicting ideas slipping into the church, a hybridization of the gospel. This would later come to be known as Gnosticism, a heresy that plagued the church over the next century. Church fathers Irenaeus and Tertullian both argued against it.

Gnosticism can be summarized by answering three questions:

1. *What is God like?* Gnostics saw everything as either good or evil. The good was associated with the spiritual, or immaterial. Evil was anything material. To be spiritual, then, one had to have no contact with the material world. Thus, Christ had to have been a lower being (and not God himself), or only a spiritual character who never really became a man. By this thinking, human beings had a spark of the divine, but only through the release of the inner person from the physical body. Thus, bodily resurrection (as Christ had done) was impossible.

2. *How do people gain access to God?* In the Gnostic mind, God was far away from this universe and could only be approached "through a series of angelic intermediaries, each more distant and more spiritual than the other. If Christ were supernatural, he must have been of a lower order because he had contact with the world" (Lawrence O. Richards, *Illustrated Bible Handbook*).

3. *How should people live?* The Gnostics taught that man is body, soul and spirit, but since the body and the soul are part of his earthly existence, they are evil. The spirit is the only real substance, so the aim of salvation is to awaken the spirit by knowledge. Of course, this knowledge was available to only the select and well-informed. At the same time, since the spirit man was all that was good, many reasoned that it didn't matter how they lived. This was a form of libertinism. Still others tried to separate themselves entirely from life in order to avoid contamination by sin.

What Paul faced in Colosse was a quagmire of strange and conflicting philosophies—all far from the truth of the gospel. The result was that individuals customized their own worldview to satisfy their own background, ideas and prejudices.

Paul's intent in writing the letter was to make a solid stand for the truth that held no ambiguities: Jesus is preeminent; He is Lord; He rules over the world and is the Creator and Sustainer of the universe. Other religions may seem attractive, but they are nothing more than human ideas that are empty and worthless. The only way to God is through His Son, Jesus Christ.

Jesus is the *fullness* of God (Colossians 1:19) and the only source for living a life pleasing to God. Paul's claim had tremendous implications. Christianity is the only way! As he said, "I tell you this so that no one may deceive you by fine-sounding arguments" (2:4, *NIV*). This was bound to cause a stir. The same is true today. The world again is full of conflicting, foolish philosophies, all vying to be heard, all claiming to be truth, and all turning against anyone who says Jesus is the only way. Yet, nothing has changed. Jesus is still "the way, the truth, and the life" (John 14:6).

I. CHRIST REIGNS SUPREME
    (Colossians 1:1-18)

A. Wonderful Benefits (vv. 1-14)

(Colossians 1:1-14 is not included in the printed text.)

Paul sent a warm greeting to the people of Colosse, calling them faithful brothers and sisters in Christ (v. 2). He made it clear that he prayed for them and gave thanks for them coming to Christ. He spoke of their faith, love and hope as they looked forward to heaven, but left out the controversial word *knowledge* in his greeting. Having a special knowledge was one of the boasts of the heretical Gnostics, whom he would be exposing. He knew he had to do some heavy-handed corrective teaching, but did not want to hurt the people.

Though he had never been to Colosse, Paul began to pray for this congregation as soon as he heard about their faith in Christ. In verses 9 to 13, he elaborated on how he prayed

for them, while making this a prayer itself. He prayed they would . . .
- be filled with the knowledge of God's will
- gain wisdom and spiritual understanding
- live holy lives worthy of the Lord
- be fruitful in good works
- increase in the knowledge of God
- be strengthened spiritually
- develop the fruits of patience, long-suffering, and joyfulness
- have thankful hearts to the Father
- recognize they had been delivered from darkness
- understand they had been made citizens in the kingdom of God's Son.

All of this had been accomplished through the blood of Jesus, "in whom we have redemption" (v. 14). What a comprehensive prayer! Paul not only prayed for the Colossians, but listed the benefits all believers have in Christ (vv. 12-14):
- Sharing His inheritance
- Being rescued from Satan's kingdom
- Coming into Christ's eternal kingdom
- Being free from sin by His own blood

Paul wrote with an underlying philosophy—the best antidote to false doctrine is to know the truth. He was well aware of the conflicting doctrines taking hold in Colosse, but instead of attacking people, he laid the truth out before them in glorious fashion. He prefaced his prayer for the Colossians with the phrase "for this cause" (v. 9), showing that his petitions were based on the news of their wonderful experience in Christ. By virtue of their union with Christ, redemption and forgiveness from sin belonged to them.

B. Firstborn Over All Creation
(vv. 15-17)

15. Who is the image of the invisible God, the firstborn of every creature:

16. For by him were all things created, that are in heaven, and that are in earth, visible and invisible, whether they be thrones, or dominions, or principalities, or powers: all things were created by him, and for him:

17. And he is before all things, and by him all things consist.

If anyone wants to know what God is really like, then simply look at Jesus. Jesus brings the eternal God into an image that people can grasp. He is the visible image of the invisible God. When Paul speaks of Jesus here, he is not referring to His preincarnate existence, nor to the life Jesus lived as a man from Galilee. He is primarily speaking of the glorified Christ now in heaven. Also, by the word *image,* Paul is expressing that Jesus fully reveals the character of God.

Throughout the Old Testament there was a gradual and progressive revelation of God's nature to various people of faith by the names God called Himself—names such as *Jehovah-jireh* (The Lord Will Provide), *Jehovah-nissi* (The Lord Is My Banner), *Jehovah-shalom* (The Lord Is Peace), *Jehovah-shammah* (The Lord Is There), *Jehovah-sabaoth* (The Lord of Hosts), and many more. Most of these derived from the basic name, *Yahweh,* meaning simply "I Am Who I Am." When Moses asked God who he should tell the Israelites had sent him, God said, "Thus you shall say to the children of Israel, 'I AM has sent me to you'" (Exodus 3:14, *NKJV*). All of these names gave some sense of who God is, but in Jesus we see God's fullness revealed completely.

Does the phrase "firstborn of every creature" (Colossians 1:15) refer to priority in time or in rank? Certainly we can't say Christ was the first being

God created in time, for Jesus is eternal, He existed before the Creation, and by Him all things were made. He is God. *Firstborn* in Hebrew culture didn't necessarily mean birth order, but referred more to rank and privilege, or simply the idea of supremacy. The firstborn "was his father's representative and heir, and to him the management of the household was committed" (*Zondervan NIV Bible Commentary*). However, in one sense Jesus was firstborn in time. He was the "firstborn from the dead" (v. 18), that is, the first to experience eternal resurrection. Paul told the Corinthians, "But Christ has indeed been raised from the dead, the firstfruits of those who have fallen asleep" (1 Corinthians 15:20, *NIV*).

Verse 16 of the text was used as an early Christian hymn, and emphasizes the superiority of Christ over all things. He created everything, both material and immaterial. Not only that, all things were created for His purposes, and He is the One who sustains creation. This contradicted the teachings of the Gnostics who claimed that angelic beings created the earth, Jesus being only one of those beings.

C. Head of the Church (v. 18)

18. And he is the head of the body, the church: who is the beginning, the firstborn from the dead; that in all things he might have the preeminence.

The fact that Jesus was the first to rise from the grave and not die again proves His victory over death, and thus His lordship over the material world. To be the *head* of the church is to be its sovereign ruler, for the head rules over the rest of the body. The word *body* suggests three things about the church:

1. The church is a living organism—a living body directed by its head. The members of the body are all vitally joined together in one union.

2. The church is the living representation of Christ on this earth. Whatever Christ does on earth, He does through the church.

3. There is an intimacy within the body, and between the body and Christ. There is a literal union between Christ and His people, and among the people themselves. Christianity is meant to be lived as a community of believers, though each believer must have his own relationship with Christ.

II. CHRIST BRINGS RECONCILIATION (Colossians 1:19-23)

A. The Fullness of Christ (v. 19)

19. For it pleased the Father that in him should all fulness dwell.

Paul's opponents, the forerunners of the Gnostics, believed that the realm between heaven and earth is a giant chasm. The word *fullness* for them became their descriptive term to describe the many layers of spiritual powers existing between God and people. Christ was but one of the many spirits in the hierarchy.

Paul refuted their argument and used *fullness* to mean the complete embodiment of God in the person of Jesus. Christ is the only intercessor, and He fully embodies the entire nature of God. There is nothing lacking in Him; neither is there any need of anyone else.

The Gnostics believed that various spirit beings served as intermediaries between God and the world. Although they included Christ as one of these intermediaries, He represented only one aspect of God's nature. This left room for them to incorporate other deities and philosophies.

Gnosticism is alive and well today. People will tolerate the idea of Jesus being divine—but not exclusively divine. To say He is the only way to God immediately draws their fire. Like Paul, we should not be hesitant in speaking the truth. Jesus is the only way. We don't have to be offensive, but neither do we have to accept foolish notions and vain philosophies.

B. All Things Reconciled (v. 20)

20. And, having made peace through the blood of his cross, by him to reconcile all things unto himself; by him, I say, whether they be things in earth, or things in heaven.

God the Father was pleased with reconciling Himself with humanity through His Son Jesus. To *reconcile* means to "remove all disagreement and enmity." This does not mean, however, that all people are automatically reconciled against their wills. Anyone who rejects Christ is still the enemy of God. Unbelievers will suffer eternal separation from God. Jesus said, "Then they will go away to eternal punishment, but the righteous to eternal life" (Matthew 25:46, *NIV*). "Here the main idea is that all things eventually are to be decisively subdued to God's will and made to serve his purposes" (*Zondervan NIV Bible Commentary*).

C. Individual Reconciliation (v. 21)

21. And you, that were sometime alienated and enemies in your mind by wicked works, yet now hath he reconciled.

The previous verse shows the general work of Christ in reconciling humanity to God. Now Paul brings it to a personal level. It's one thing to say that God loves all people. It's quite another to recognize that He loves *me*. Paul shows that the cosmic reconciliation applied to every individual in Colosse. No one need feel alienated or an enemy of God. At the same time, no one could expect friendship with God unless he went through Jesus. God hates sin, and the only solution to sin is through the work of Christ on the cross.

D. Individual Responsibility (vv. 22, 23)

22. In the body of his flesh through death, to present you holy and unblameable and unreproveable in his sight:

23. If ye continue in the faith grounded and settled, and be not moved away from the hope of the gospel, which ye have heard, and which was preached to every creature which is under heaven; whereof I Paul am made a minister.

The false teachers confusing the people at Colosse claimed that redemption could only be accomplished through a spirit-being. They rejected the notion that Christ could be both human and divine. In their minds Jesus had been a spirit. He could not have had a fleshly body. Paul refuted them, saying Jesus was totally human (*body* and *flesh*), and that he experienced a human death.

The rubber meets the road in verse 23. The phrase "if ye continue" put responsibility on the backs of his readers. They each had to abandon the false ideas they had been exposed to, adhering fully to the truth. When the gospel was originally preached to them, it was preached with clarity by Epaphras. The gospel had brought about their conversion. Paul wanted them to return to what they had been taught, and not be confused by strange ideas that muddied the picture.

III. OUR HOPE OF GLORY (Colossians 1:24-29)

A. Suffering With Christ (vv. 24, 25)

24. Who now rejoice in my sufferings for you, and fill up that which is behind of the afflictions of Christ in my flesh for his body's sake, which is the church:

25. Whereof I am made a minister, according to the dispensation of God which is given to me for you, to fulfil the word of God.

Paul did not imply there was an insufficiency in the sacrifice Jesus made on the cross. Neither was he saying that his own personal discomforts and sacrificial life somehow elevated him to the level of coredeemer. He simply said that the sufferings Christians endure are the same ones Christ would be enduring if He were still in the world. Jesus told His disciples before His crucifixion, "If the world hates you, keep in mind that it hated me first. If you belonged to the world, it would love you as its own. As it is, you do not belong to the world, but I have chosen you out of the world. That is why the world hates you" (John 15:18, 19, *NIV*).

Paul viewed his own difficulties as something to be joyful over because he was able to share in the Lord's suffering.

B. The Mystery Revealed (vv. 26, 27)

26. Even the mystery which hath been hid from ages and from generations, but now is made manifest to his saints:

27. To whom God would make known what is the riches of the glory of this mystery among the Gentiles; which is Christ in you, the hope of glory.

Innate to fallen human nature is the desire to have some secret knowledge no one else has, to have some insight that the world longs for. The false teachers in Colosse smugly believed that the hidden plan of people reaching God was available only to the few "illumined" minds—mostly their own inner circle. Common people were not eligible for such privilege.

Paul made it clear, however, that the mysteries of the ages are revealed completely in Christ and are available to everyone. Paul himself was a steward of this revelation, but by no means saw himself as having exclusive rights. On the contrary, he wanted everyone to know the good news. The mystery is

that Christ now lives in the heart of anyone who believes on Him (Jew and Gentile alike). All believers are united in Him into one body—His church.

C. Maturity in Christ (vv. 28, 29)

28. Whom we preach, warning every man, and teaching every man in all wisdom; that we may present every man perfect in Christ Jesus:

29. Whereunto I also labour, striving according to his working, which worketh in me mightily.

We see here the reason for Paul's writing his letter to the Colossians. He was not content that they had received Christ as Savior. They must grow in their faith—and that could only be done by understanding the truth. By *perfect* Paul meant completeness or maturity in Christ. "Here the reference is probably to the coming of Christ, when every believer will experience the completion of Christ's work in him or her" (*Nelson Study Bible*).

Without Christ, people are doomed to eternal separation from God. Without proper doctrine and teaching, they are doomed to confusion and stunted spiritual growth. Paul wanted all people saved, but he also wanted them to understand the true meaning of what Christ was offering them. Paul worked agonizingly to help people grow in Christ, but through Christ's strength, not his own.

GOLDEN TEXT HOMILY

"[CHRIST] IS THE HEAD OF THE BODY, THE CHURCH: WHO IS THE BEGINNING, THE FIRSTBORN FROM THE DEAD; THAT IN ALL THINGS HE MIGHT HAVE THE PREEMINENCE" (Colossians 1:18).

In the fourth century the church found itself facing one of the greatest threats to orthodox Christian doctrine when a Libyan presbyter named Arius began teaching that Jesus was the first creation of God and that He, in turn, created everything else. Arius and his followers maintained that since Scripture refers to Jesus as "firstborn," He could not be coequal and coeternal with God the Father.

Through a letter-writing campaign, the teachings of a man named Athanasius, and a called council of bishops at Nicea in 325, Arianism was declared a heretical doctrine and Christianity was saved from one of its first major internal threats. Unfortunately, Arianism lives on (primarily through the Jehovah's Witnesses) and is peddled door-to-door to people who cannot offer a defense against it through lack of a proper knowledge.

Paul's use of the Greek word *prototokos* in Colossians 1:18, commonly translated "firstborn," does not mean Jesus was the first creation of the Father. Careful study shows that the term is consistently applied in the New Testament to refer to Jesus' superiority over creation.

Using a questionable translation of one word to establish a major doctrine, without considering what the Bible teaches about Christ (Genesis 1:26; Isaiah 9:6; John 1:1-3; 10:30; Philippians 2:5-9; Colossians 2:9; Revelation 1:8; 22:13-16), is a gross misapplication of sound Biblical study and an exercise in willing disobedience. Not withstanding the fact that Paul offered a defense against the misuse of *prototokos* in Colossians 1:19 by declaring that "God was pleased to have all his fullness dwell in him [Christ]" (*NIV*). *All* still means "all," and *fullness* still means "fullness," regardless of what Arian doctrine teaches.—**Richard Raines**

SENTENCE SERMONS

JESUS CHRIST is preeminent over all creation.
—Selected

THE PURPOSE OF LIFE is not to find your freedom, but your master.
—P.T. Forsyth

AS THOU WILT; what Thou wilt, when Thou wilt.
—Thomas à Kempis

EVANGELISM APPLICATION

CHRISTIANS MUST PROCLAIM THAT RECONCILIATION TO GOD IS MADE POSSIBLE THROUGH THE SHED BLOOD OF JESUS CHRIST.

The Bible is clear in speaking of the reality of angels. The writer of Hebrews says, "Are not all angels ministering spirits sent to serve those who will inherit salvation?" (Hebrews 1:14, *NIV*). He also says angels are superior to people by nature: "Thou madest him [man] a little lower than the angels" (2:7). Angels minister to us without our knowledge of them, and they often help us sense coming danger (Matthew 2:13). However, angels have nothing to do with our access to God.

In recent years we have seen strange ideas developing among New Age religionists where angels become guides to lead men and women through this life. Is this any different from what the ancient Gnostics taught? They believed that the chasm between God and man could only be transversed by means of angelic intermediaries. Paul clearly refuted such ideas.

Yes, there are times when angels minister to us, and they protect us from harm; however, our relationship is with Christ, not with some ethereal guide. We look to Christ, we study His Word, and rely totally on Him to carry us through the days of our lives. When we witness to others, we present them with Christ, not some strange spirit. It is Christ who will save them. It is Christ who will be their closest friend. It is Christ who shed His blood for them.

ILLUMINATING THE LESSON

Ye call Me Master and obey Me not,
Ye call Me Light and see Me not,
Ye call Me Way and follow Me not,
Ye call Me Life and desire Me not,
Ye call Me wise and acknowledge
Me not,
Ye call Me fair and love Me not,
Ye call Me rich and ask Me not,
Ye call Me eternal and seek Me not,
Ye call Me gracious and trust Me
not,
Ye call Me noble and serve Me not,
Ye call Me mighty and honor Me
not,
Ye call Me just and fear Me not,
If I condemn you, blame Me not.

—*Resource*

DAILY BIBLE READINGS

M. Messianic Reign.
    Psalm 2:1-12
T. King of Glory.
    Psalm 24:1-10
W. Messianic Vision.
    Isaiah 9:1-7
T. Dominion of Christ.
    Daniel 7:9-14
F. Savior of the World.
    John 3:14-21
S. Reconciliation Through Christ.
    Romans 5:1-11

TRUTH SEARCH
Creatively Teaching the Word

DISCUSSION QUESTIONS

Christ Reigns Supreme
(Colossians 1:12-18)

1. According to verse 12, why should Christians give thanks to the heavenly Father?

2. What is "the power of darkness," and how have Christians been "translated" out of it (v. 13)?

3. What does the word *redemption* mean, and how have Christians been redeemed (v. 14)?

4. What do the following verses reveal about Jesus Christ's identity and authority?

- 15:
- 16:
- 17:
- 18:

Christ Brings Reconciliation
(Colossians 1:19-23)

1. Explain "the fullness" that dwells in Jesus Christ (v. 19).

2. How did an instrument of torture (the cross) become an instrument of peace (v. 20)?

3. What alienates people from God (v. 21)?

4. How can reconciliation take place, and how does it change people (v. 22)?

5. What does it mean to "continue in the faith" (v. 23)?

Christ Gives Hope
(Colossians 1:24-29)

1. How could Paul find joy in his suffering (v. 24)?

2. How did Paul become a minister of the gospel (v. 25)?

3. What *mystery* did God reveal to His followers (vv. 26, 27)?

4. Explain the phrase "hope of glory" (v. 27).

5. What was the goal of Paul's preaching ministry (v. 28)?

6. How could Paul strive toward such a lofty goal (v. 29)?

ILLUSTRATION

Items needed: Marker board, marker

Have students name things created by God. Of course the list is endless. Write many of their answers on the board, filling it up except for a border around all four sides.

Next, draw the outline of a crown as the border, so that all the created things now appear to be on the crown.

Christ reigns supreme over all created things! Colossians 1:16, 17 declares, "All things were created by him and for him. He is before all things, and in him all things hold together" (*NIV*).

Worship Christ together for being Lord over all.

Practical Instructions for Living

Study Text: Colossians 3:1 through 4:6
Objective: To learn that being a Christian requires godliness and live according to God's Word.
Time: A.D. 62
Place: Written from a prison, probably in Rome
Golden Text: "Whatsoever ye do in word or deed, do all in the name of the Lord Jesus, giving thanks to God and the Father by him" (Colossians 3:17).
Central Truth: God's Word requires Christians to live godly.
Evangelism Emphasis: God's Word requires Christians to live godly as witnesses to the world.

PRINTED TEXT

Colossians 3:1. If ye then be risen with Christ, seek those things which are above, where Christ sitteth on the right hand of God.

2. Set your affection on things above, not on things on the earth.

3. For ye are dead, and your life is hid with Christ in God.

4. When Christ, who is our life, shall appear, then shall ye also appear with him in glory.

5. Mortify therefore your members which are upon the earth; fornication, uncleanness, inordinate affection, evil concupiscence, and covetousness, which is idolatry:

6. For which things' sake the wrath of God cometh on the children of disobedience:

7. In the which ye also walked some time, when ye lived in them.

8. But now ye also put off all these; anger, wrath, malice, blasphemy, filthy communication out of your mouth.

9. Lie not one to another, seeing that ye have put off the old man with his deeds;

10. And have put on the new man, which is renewed in knowledge after the image of him that created him:

11. Where there is neither Greek nor Jew, circumcision nor uncircumcision, Barbarian, Scythian, bond nor free: but Christ is all, and in all.

12. Put on therefore, as the elect of God, holy and beloved, bowels of mercies, kindness, humbleness of mind, meekness, longsuffering;

13. Forbearing one another, and forgiving one another, if any man have a quarrel against any: even as Christ forgave you, so also do ye.

14. And above all these things put on charity, which is the bond of perfectness.

18. Wives, submit yourselves unto your own husbands, as it is fit in the Lord.

19. Husbands, love your wives, and be not bitter against them.

20. Children, obey your parents in all things: for this is well pleasing unto the Lord.

21. Fathers, provoke not your children to anger, lest they be discouraged.

22. Servants, obey in all things your masters according to the flesh; not with eyeservice, as menpleasers; but in singleness of heart, fearing God:

23. And whatsoever ye do, do it heartily, as to the Lord, and not unto men;

24. Knowing that of the Lord ye shall receive the reward of the inheritance: for ye serve the Lord Christ.

DICTIONARY

inordinate affection—Colossians 3:5—lustful passion
evil concupiscence—Colossians 3:5—evil desire
Barbarian—Colossians 3:11—one who did not belong to the cultivated Greek race
Scythian (SITH-ih-un)—Colossians 3:11—the savage and uncivilized; the lowest type of barbarian slave

LESSON OUTLINE

I. PUT AWAY UNGODLINESS

  A. Heavenly Priorities

  B. Hidden in Christ

  C. Earthly Desires

  D. Truthfulness

  E. Old Versus New

II. ACT WITH GODLY LOVE

  A. The Elect of God

  B. Patience

  C. Love

  D. Peace and the Word

III. PRACTICE GODLINESS IN RELATIONSHIPS

  A. Husbands and Wives

  B. Children and Parents

  C. Servants and Masters

LESSON EXPOSITION

INTRODUCTION

Colossians 1 laid the theological underpinning for everything Paul would say to his readers. It might be labeled as "Christ, the Full Expression of God." Christ is preeminent; He is Lord of the universe. He rules as Creator and Sustainer of everything. In other words, Christianity is exclusive. It is not one of many religions containing truth, but the only way to God.

Having established that, Paul then, in chapter 2, turned his attention to something that deeply touched his own heart—pastoral concern for those he served. He had a tremendous burden for those his ministry had affected. Even though he had never met the Colossian congregation, nor their sister church at nearby Laodicea, he wrestled constantly in prayer for them. Those churches had been founded by his converts, and he felt responsibility toward them.

An alarming message had come to him that strange doctrines were invading these congregations. The false teachers at Colosse tried to convince the people they had to be initiated into some type of secret, superior knowledge, but Paul insisted they could understand everything necessary by simply knowing Christ. The Gnostics sought knowledge as their primary objective, but Paul wanted to show that true knowledge demonstrates itself in love and unity among the brethren. The Gnostics taught elitism, but Paul said every believer could have equal access to God.

The letter to the Colossians sounds a little different in wording from other Pauline epistles because the apostle used the very language of the Gnostics to challenge their ideas. Expressions such as "full assurance of understanding" and "mystery" (2:2), "treasures of wisdom and knowledge" (v. 3) were terms that sounded high and lofty, but actually had meanings his readers could understand—simply because they were fulfilled in Christ. Paul assured his readers they did not have to be intimidated by high-sounding arguments, but should remain steadfast in their faith in Christ.

Paul understood the pitfalls of not knowing correct doctrine. In the absence of sound teaching, aberrations of the truth will always rush into the vacuum. He hoped that his teaching in this letter would help them see the truth, so they could avoid vain human philosophies that paraded themselves as Christian teaching. Thus, chapter 2 is a breaking down, reiteration and explanation of what he had said in chapter 1. Christ is all that matters, and believers must walk in faith and fellowship with Him.

Paul used four terms in 2:7 to encourage the people in their walk: *rooted, built up, established* and *abounding. Rooted* means a complete action. The deeper the roots grow in Christ, the less likely one can be deceived. *Built up* has to do with construction. Believers are to build lives on a strong foundation that has been laid in Christ. That building becomes a habitation of the Holy Spirit. *Established* indicates the truth of the gospel that was laid by the apostles and faithful ministers who followed them. In the Colossians' case, this would have been Epaphras, who had been mentored by Paul. *Abounding* has to do with overflowing thanks to God for making the means of salvation available.

Paul then said that any philosophy of life that is not based on Christ is wrong, empty, carnal and destructive. The phrase "lest any man spoil you" (v. 8) does not imply *decay* in this situation, but rather to *plunder* or *rob*. "These false teachers would strip them of their faith and hope, as an invading army would rob a country of all that was valuable" (*Barnes' Notes*).

Paul could refute the Gnostics because he knew what they were teaching. His grounding in the Word of God gave him the ability to distinguish false doctrines when he saw them.

Today, we must have the same grounding. There is no way we can avoid the humanistic religions cropping up everywhere. We must educate our children (and ourselves) firmly in the Word of God so we will be able to distinguish truth from error.

Secular humanism is the manmade religion that threatens Christianity today. We should be just as much alarmed as Paul was in his writing to the Colossians. Humanism has invaded every area of secular education and government, and is obviously the guiding force for the news media and entertainment industries. Following is a brief overview of the tenets of humanism:

• All that exists is a matter of chance.

• Humanity is a product of the chance process called evolution.

• There is no revelation of God to man, because God doesn't exist.

• Knowledge comes through human discovery and reasoning.

• Human reasoning alone determines what is right or wrong.

• The human condition is improved through education and human wisdom.

• Moral standards are relative to the situation.

• Human fulfillment is the highest goal in life.

All of this is nothing more than Satan's lies that began in the Garden of Eden. There he convinced Eve that she would be like God if she ate of the forbidden fruit. Paul summed it up in Romans 1:25: "They exchanged the truth of God for a lie, and worshiped and served created things rather than the Creator—who is forever praised" (*NIV*).

Paul affirmed in verse 9-15 all that he had stated thus far: Jesus is God. He lived as a man bodily among humans. Since the power of God rests in Him, He overcomes all other powers. The symbol of belonging to Christ is not the physical mark of circumcision, but rather a circumcision of the heart, where the old carnal nature is cut away and a new spiritual nature is imparted. Baptism is the outward sign of this inward working.

In the rest of chapter 2, Paul taught that the Christian is freed from legal and ceremonial practices. Outward observances of man-made traditions may make people look holy but have no bearing on their heart condition. No human practice can add to what Christ did at the Cross. Christ's work is complete in God's eyes.

All of this sets up the present lesson. As in his other letters, Paul spent the first section setting forth doctrine. Now, in chapter 3, practical applications are made to what has been said.

I. PUT AWAY UNGODLINESS
(Colossians 3:1-11)

A. Heavenly Priorities (vv. 1, 2)

1. If ye then be risen with Christ, seek those things which are above, where Christ sitteth on the right hand of God.
2. Set your affection on things above, not on things on the earth.

Paul's first practical rule is to change one's focus of life. The distinction between the two spheres—things "above" and things "on the earth" can be easily misunderstood. While the Gnostics advocated a mystical spiritual journey by means of angelic intermediaries (of whom Jesus was considered only one of many), they still imposed a series of strange daily rituals and rules that set themselves apart from everyone else. Like the Pharisees, they prided themselves in their righteous living.

Paul, in contrast, said to focus on things above, that is, the eternal realities of heaven, yet discipline oneself in terms of daily human existence. The Christian isn't expected to withdraw from life, but just not be dictated by it. Some things on earth are evil, while others are harmless; but if the believer focuses on material goods, pleasure, power, the praise of others, and so on, he or she has lost focus of heavenly things.

B. Hidden in Christ (vv. 3, 4)

3. For ye are dead, and your life is hid with Christ in God.
4. When Christ, who is our life, shall appear, then shall ye also appear with him in glory.

To be *dead* here means to have abandoned searching for fulfillment in the present world. This doesn't mean we shouldn't find any joy and satisfaction in the normal routine of daily life, but we simply recognize that all things here are temporary. Because Christ literally died and was buried in a tomb, we also are dead—dead to sin, worldly pleasure, earthly ambition.

Christ is our treasure. Knowing Him and living for Him is all that's really important. "Christ is the life of your souls; and as he is hidden in the bosom of the Father, so are ye, who live through and in him" (*Adam Clarke's Commentary*).

When we make Christ *our life*, communion and fellowship with Him are our most important priorities. We live primarily by inner experience with Christ, but we look forward to that time when He *appears* in glory and all that is presently invisible will be made visible.

C. Earthly Desires (vv. 5-8)

5. Mortify therefore your members which are upon the earth; fornication, uncleanness, inordinate affection, evil concupiscence, and covetousness, which is idolatry:
6. For which things' sake the wrath of God cometh on the children of disobedience:
7. In the which ye also walked some time, when ye lived in them.
8. But now ye also put off all these; anger, wrath, malice, blasphemy, filthy communication out of your mouth.

If our focus is on communion with Christ, then that should express itself in how we handle our thoughts, actions, and relationships with other people. *Mortify* means to kill. We have to exterminate everything that bespeaks of our former lives. In verse 5 Paul identifies vices: *fornication* (sexual immorality); *uncleanness* (moral impurity); *inordinate affection* (lustful passion); *evil concupiscence* (evil desire); and *covetousness*, which he called "idolatry." In Old Testament times, idolatry was easily recognized—people bowing to images carved out of wood, reciting incantations and carrying out strange rites. The idolatry of covetousness rises up when things grab such a place in our hearts that we want them more than we want God. It also means we aren't willing to trust Him to supply our needs.

The heavy emphasis on sexual sins (v. 5) was due to the extremely immoral climate of Paul's day. In the heathen world, these things were not sins, and the early Christians were forced constantly to remind their converts of what a holy God expected of them in practical holiness.

The Colossian Christians had apparently come largely from the Gentile or heathen population. Because of this, these sins were of particular danger to them. But that life was now over and this separateness must be demonstrated by their conduct.

Paul was not content to call simply for separation from the old acts, but he also called for separation from the old attitudes. Verse 8 names five things that are to be thrust from the believer. Three have to do with human relationships: *anger* (habitual enmity), *wrath* (a more turbulent, explosive, more temporary manifestation), and *malice* (an attitude of ill-will toward another person, a wishing of harm for him). The other two have to do with human communication: *blasphemy* (slander or defamation, either of God or man) and *filthy communication* (obscene or abusive talk).

Every vice Paul speaks of in verses 5 and 8 falls under the category "works of the flesh," which he listed in Galatians 5:19-21. We cannot insulate ourselves so completely that we never face temptations. However, we must stop them before they destroy us. We make a conscious, daily (and even sometimes hourly) decision to starve such thoughts and instead turn to the Holy Spirit for power to overcome.

D. Truthfulness (v. 9a)

9a. Lie not one to another.

Lying does great damage. It hinders unity, tears human relationships apart, sets up useless suspicions, and wounds character (of both the liar and the object of his lies). The habitual liar is eventually caught in his own trap, simply because he hasn't a memory strong enough to keep track of all his falsehoods. From both practical and spiritual standpoints, the simple truth without embellishment is always the best path to take.

E. Old Versus New (vv. 9b-11)

9b. Seeing that ye have put off the old man with his deeds;
10. And have put on the new man, which is renewed in knowledge after the image of him that created him:
11. Where there is neither Greek nor Jew, circumcision nor uncircumcision, Barbarian, Scythian, bond nor free: but Christ is all, and in all.

These verses parallel Paul's statements in Romans 6 about being "dead to sin" but "alive unto God through Jesus Christ" (vv. 2, 11). What is the difference between the "old man" and the "new man"? Because of the command to "put on," the metaphor first refers to how one is clothed. The old man is dressed in old clothes—worn, dirty, soiled, rancid. These clothes are stripped away and new clothes are put on—clean, pure, fresh. Obviously, the admonition is to stay dressed as the new man.

Second, there is a difference in masters. The old man is still under the rule and ownership of Satan, while the new man has a new master, the Holy Spirit living within. The old man is the "unregenerate nature before conversion," while the new man is the "recently-put-on nature at regeneration" (*Jamieson, Fausset and Brown Commentary*).

Another way of viewing the difference between the two is in terms of character and ethics. The new man takes off the negative and puts on the positive. He takes off old, selfish, earthbound perspectives. He puts on new Christlike and selfless perspectives. The old man lives for self; the new man lives for others.

The new knowledge of the new man does away with the old divisions between people, whether these refer to ancestry ("Greek nor Jew"), or religious ceremony or custom ("circumcision nor uncircumcision"), or cultural level ("Barbarian, Scythian"), or social and economic standing ("bond nor free"). In Christ these divisions just do not exist, for He is the whole, and He is in all of the individuals from these different divisions who have come to new life in Him.

II. ACT WITH GODLY LOVE
(Colossians 3:12-17)

A. The Elect of God (v. 12)

12. Put on therefore, as the elect of God, holy and beloved, bowels of mercies, kindness, humbleness of mind, meekness, longsuffering.

Paul has already said to put on the new man. He now gives three reasons to do so. Christians are the "elect," that is, chosen of God; they are holy in God's sight; they are dearly loved by God. They now occupy the same favored position that Israel occupied under the old covenant. Before Christ there was no obligation for God to show mercy to those outside His covenant. Now all believers are fully embraced by the new covenant.

Paul next lists five virtues that characterize Christians: mercy, kindness, humility, meekness, and long-suffering (patience). These are qualities which, when active in a church, will enable it to function as the body of Christ. These characteristics are all manifestations of a loving spirit (v. 14).

B. Patience (v. 13)

13. Forbearing one another, and forgiving one another, if any man have a quarrel against any: even as Christ forgave you, so also do ye.

Paul describes patience as making allowances for others by remembering what God has done for us. We should willingly forgive the negative traits we see in others when we realize how God has forgiven us. The action words here are *forbear* (tolerate) and *forgive*.

C. Love (v. 14)

14. And above all these things put on charity, which is the bond of perfectness.

The Greek word for *charity* here is *agape*, or "godly love." All other virtues are merely expressions of this highest grace. Love is "larger than any one of them, indeed, larger than all of them combined" (*Zondervan NIV Bible Commentary*).

We might think of each virtue as an article of clothing. All but love are undergarments. Love is the outer garment, the beautiful gown a fine lady wears to a regal ball. Without love there is still a measure of nakedness, but with love, the lady is fully dressed and ready to be presented to the king.

D. Peace and the Word (vv. 15-17)

(Colossians 4:15-17 is not included in the printed text.)

Paul said to "let the peace of Christ rule in your hearts" (v. 15). The word *peace* means the inner satisfaction that comes from obedience to Christ. The word *rule* comes from the language of athletics, meaning "to act as umpire." Peace should be the umpire that referees the conflicting feelings and desires. Though we have put on the new man, the old carnal nature still fights for survival. We must constantly decide which to follow. The desire for the peace only Christ can give should be the decision maker.

Verse 16 says, "Let the word of Christ dwell in you richly." The "word of Christ" is the gospel message. Everything Paul taught the Colossians was based on right doctrines. Wrong doctrines and ideas lead to confusion, perhaps even death. The Christian life must be built on truth, not myth or superstition. Every believer should carefully study the Word to know what to believe. To *dwell* means to have the Christian message firmly implanted into our beings so it controls our thinking.

Doing everything "in the name of the Lord Jesus" (v. 17) is to do all as a representative of Him. We as Christians must reflect Christ at all times, with everything we do and say.

III. PRACTICE GODLINESS IN
RELATIONSHIPS
(Colossians 3:18—4:1)

In this passage Paul gives practical rules to follow in terms of day-to-day family relationships. They are divided into three categories.

A. Husbands and Wives (vv. 18, 19)

18. Wives, submit yourselves unto your own husbands, as it is fit in the Lord.
19. Husbands, love your wives, and be not bitter against them.

Paul here moves from the theoretical to the practical, from moral teaching to daily application. Christian virtues must first and foremost be lived out in the home. There should be no difference between the public person and the private one.

The word rendered *submit* here is a military term meaning "arrange oneself under." This is a willing surrender,

not a forced one. The wife, understanding her role in the marriage, is to defer authority to the husband. At the same time, the husband should never lord his position over the wife. He simply recognizes that God has appointed him to be head of the household.

B. Children and Parents (vv. 20, 21)

20. Children, obey your parents in all things: for this is well pleasing unto the Lord.
21. Fathers, provoke not your children to anger, lest they be discouraged.

The father's role in bringing up his children is that of training them for adulthood. The word *fathers* likely denotes a broader meaning of "parents" in this situation, for the mother is certainly involved in the process. Parents must be careful in administering discipline. "Don't aggravate them by nagging, deriding, or destroying their self-respect so that they quit trying" (*Life Application Study Bible*).

One way a child can be discouraged is to see inconsistency in the parent's actions. If Mom or Dad demands something of the children that he or she does not live up to, the child is left in confusion. The old adage "Don't do as I do, but do as I say" doesn't hold up to Biblical scrutiny.

C. Servants and Masters
(Colossians 3:22-25; 4:1)

(Colossians 3:25; 4:1 are not included in the printed text.)

22. Servants, obey in all things your masters according to the flesh; not with eyeservice, as menpleasers; but in singleness of heart, fearing God:
23. And whatsoever ye do, do it heartily, as to the Lord, and not unto men;
24. Knowing that of the Lord ye shall receive the reward of the inheritance: for ye serve the Lord Christ.

The entire question of slaves, servants and masters may seem remote and out of date to contemporary society, but still there is a principle that applies here. Paul admonishes every worker to do his best for his employer, no matter how menial the assigned task might be. Doing your best is a proper witness to what Christ has done for you.

We might ask why Paul and the other apostles didn't condemn slavery and demand its overthrow. We must remember that this institution was universally accepted in the ancient world. To have thrown all their efforts into changing culture would have robbed them of their role as heralds of the gospel. Remember, too, it was the principles of the gospel that eventually brought the impetus to do away with slavery.

While slaves owned no personal property, God promised them an eternal inheritance if they did their work as if Christ were their Master. However, dishonest service would result in judgment.

In Colossians 4:1, Paul commanded masters to treat their servants justly and equitably. This was countercultural, for slaves in the Roman Empire were not thought of as people and thus had no rights. But in Christ "there is no respect of persons" (3:25).

Christian employers and employees will be Christian in their treatment of each other if they are filled with the Spirit and the Word. The heart of every problem is the problem of the heart, and only God's Word and God's Spirit can transform people.

GOLDEN TEXT HOMILY

"WHATSOEVER YE DO IN WORD OR DEED, DO ALL IN THE NAME OF THE LORD JESUS, GIVING THANKS TO GOD AND THE FATHER BY HIM" (Colossians 3:17).

Doing all in the name of the Lord Jesus suggests that everything is hallowed to the Christian. Not just churchgoing or praying or singing, but even our eating and drinking.

Nothing is too small to be done in His name. A cup of cold water takes on a far greater significance when it is offered because of Him. God delights to use common things for His glory. Our living offering shall be our actions, our speech and our attitudes, reflecting His presence.

To do everything in His name is to do nothing unworthy of His name. Here is the great challenge for the child of God. Little debate is needed as to whether something is right or wrong. The simple test is whether it can be done so as to bring glory to Him. This rule is good in all places, under all circumstances, at all times, and for any age. It is the rule by which God tests the length and the breadth of our Christian commitment. The unconverted cannot relate to this text because it requires Christ to be first, last, and in all.

To do everything in His name is to do nothing in our own name. We accept responsibility for our actions but point always to Him whose ambassadors we are.

One of our former presidents said there were two people in the White House: Truman the President and Truman the man. The implication was that Truman the man could do what he pleased and the people had no reason to question it, while Truman the President must be responsible to the people for his actions and deeds. This is not true in the Christian religion. All we do represents Him whose ambassadors we are. Our private life and our public life speak one message.

Colossians 3:17 implies also that the Christian does all in God's strength. By what power do we witness? By whose strength do we endure? What secret supply is available to the Christian? "I can do all things through Christ which strengtheneth me" (Philippians 4:13) is the declaration of God's children everywhere. We have no power but His; but having His power we need none other.—**Selected**

SENTENCE SERMONS

GOD'S WORD requires Christians to live godly.

—Selected

NEVER THINK that Jesus commanded a trifle, nor dare to trifle with anything He has commanded.

—D.L. Moody

CHRISTIANITY IS EITHER relevant all the time or useless anytime.

—Richard Halverson

EVANGELISM APPLICATION

GOD'S WORD REQUIRES CHRISTIANS TO LIVE GODLY AS WITNESSES TO THE WORLD.

All of us are called to evangelism, no matter what type of job we have. Our conduct and character, whatever our occupation, are most important. Paul said, "Whatsoever ye do in word or deed, do all in the name of the Lord Jesus, giving thanks to God and the Father by him" (Colossians 3:17).

The Holy Spirit empowers the believer to live and to work as Christ would. Occupations of every kind carry the responsibility of ministry. Not all believers will be missionaries on a foreign field or pastors of churches. Some will be construction workers, maids, cooks, technicians, computer operators, and so on. These may seem to have only earthly value, but God sees value in our work. Doing a good job for a secular employer is a witness for Christ in itself. It brings attention to one's character and opens the door for sharing the gospel.

ILLUMINATING THE LESSON

Paul insisted that the Christian concentrate on eternal realities in heaven rather than on rituals and rules. At the same time, he said that normal conduct should reflect the change of heart Christ has brought. If Christ is Lord in us, then He is Lord over everything.

Yet, this is hard for us to see. John Ortberg said: "Too often people think about their 'spiritual lives' as just one more aspect of their existence, alongside and largely separate from their 'financial lives' or their 'vocational lives.' Periodically they may try to 'get their spiritual lives together' by praying more regularly or trying to master another spiritual discipline. It is the religious equivalent of going on a diet or trying to stick to a budget" (*The Life You've Always Wanted*).

The reality is that our spiritual lives are our entire lives. Our daily habits, attitudes, work ethics, treatment of others, and so on, make up who we are. The true measure of spiritual growth is whether or not we are growing in our love for God and for others.

Our prayer should be, "Lord, be Lord of everything in me."

DAILY BIBLE READINGS

M. Avoid Bad Company.
    Proverbs 1:10-19
T. Seek Wisdom.
    Proverbs 1:20-33
W. Be Just to Others.
    Proverbs 3:27-35
T. Do Not Judge.
    Matthew 7:1-5
F. Do Not Worry.
    Luke 12:22-34
S. Watch Over Your Heart.
    1 Timothy 6:11-20

TRUTH SEARCH
Creatively Teaching the Word

OPENING ACTIVITY

Parents are known for giving advice to their children—whether or not the kids are ready to listen. Let's name some of the practical advice our parents preached to us as we were growing up. (Wash your hands before mealtime; eat your vegetables; share your toys; don't try reading in the dark; and on and on).

While parental advice is not infallible, most of it is usually sound. Those who listen to their parents and obey are on a good path.

In today's lesson we get a lot of perfect practical advice from the Book of Colossians. Practicing it will bring us great reward.

DISCUSSION QUESTIONS

**Put Away Ungodliness
(Colossians 3:1-11)**

1. What does it mean to be "risen with Christ" (v. 1)?

2. How is it possible to obey the command in verse 2?

3. What does it mean to have "your life . . . hid with Christ in God" (v. 3)?

4. What do all the sins in verse 5 have in common? What does it mean to "mortify" those things?

5. What awaits the unrepentant "children of disobedience" (v. 6)?

6. What is similar about the sins listed in verses 8 and 9?

7. How is a Christian able to overcome carnal desires (v. 10)?

8. What people groups can receive Christ's righteousness (v. 11)?

**Act With Godly Love
(Colossians 3:12-17)**

1. Who are the "elect of God," and how must they live (vv. 12, 13)?

2. Why is love the most important Christian virtue, and what can it accomplish (v. 14)?

3. Why is it important for God's peace to "rule in your hearts" and in the body of Christ (v. 15)?

4. How are believers to minister to each other (v. 16)?

5. How is it possible to express thankfulness to God in whatever you say or do (v. 17)?

**Practice Godliness in Relationships
(Colossians 3:18—4:1)**

1. Summarize the instructions given to the following people:
- Wives
- Husbands
- Children
- Parents
- Servants
- Masters

2. As we serve others, what should our attitude be (vv. 22-24)?

Christian Character

Study Text: Philemon 1-25
Objective: To examine Paul's appeal to Philemon and act with integrity in dealing with others.
Time: A.D. 62
Place: Written from a Roman prison
Golden Text: "Having confidence in thy obedience I wrote unto thee, knowing that thou wilt also do more than I say" (Philemon 21).
Central Truth: Integrity ought to govern Christian character.
Evangelism Emphasis: Christians should always act with integrity as a witness to the lost.

PRINTED TEXT

Philemon 1:1 Paul, a prisoner of Jesus Christ, and Timothy our brother, unto Philemon our dearly beloved, and fellowlabourer,

2. And to our beloved Apphia, and Archippus our fellowsoldier, and to the church in thy house:

3. Grace to you, and peace, from God our Father and the Lord Jesus Christ.

4. I thank my God, making mention of thee always in my prayers,

5. Hearing of thy love and faith, which thou hast toward the Lord Jesus, and toward all saints;

6. That the communication of thy faith may become effectual by the acknowledging of every good thing which is in you in Christ Jesus.

7. For we have great joy and consolation in thy love, because the bowels of the saints are refreshed by thee, brother.

8. Wherefore, though I might be much bold in Christ to enjoin thee that which is convenient,

9. Yet for love's sake I rather beseech thee, being such an one as Paul the aged, and now also a prisoner of Jesus Christ.

10. I beseech thee for my son Onesimus, whom I have begotten in my bonds:

11. Which in time past was to thee unprofitable, but now profitable to thee and to me:

12. Whom I have sent again: thou therefore receive him, that is, mine own bowels:

13. Whom I would have retained with me, that in thy stead he might have ministered unto me in the bonds of the gospel:

14. But without thy mind would I do nothing; that thy benefit should not be as it were of necessity, but willingly.

15. For perhaps he therefore departed for a season, that thou shouldest receive him for ever;

16. Not now as a servant, but above a servant, a brother beloved, specially to me, but how much more unto thee, both in the flesh, and in the Lord?

17. If thou count me therefore a partner, receive him as myself.

18. If he hath wronged thee, or oweth thee ought, put that on mine account;

19. I Paul have written it with mine own hand, I will repay it: albeit I do not say to thee how thou owest unto me even thine own self besides.

DICTIONARY

Philemon (fye-LEE-mun)—Philemon 1—a Christian man living in Colosse whom Paul had won to Christ

Apphia (AF-ih-uh)—Philemon 2—the wife, or close relative, of Philemon

Archippus (ar-KIP-us)—Philemon 2—a Christian at Colosse known as a champion of the gospel; a close friend or perhaps son of Philemon

Onesimus (oh-NES-ih-mus)—Philemon 10—a runaway slave belonging to Philemon

---

LESSON OUTLINE

I. EXPRESS APPRECIATION

   A. Salutation

   B. The Basis for Reconciliation

   C. Communication of Faith

II. BE RESPECTFUL AND DISCREET

   A. Boldness Empowered by Love

   B. A Play on Words

   C. Service as a Brother

III. DO THE RIGHT THING

   A. Partners in Christ

   B. Paying Another's Debts

   C. Promise of a Visit

LESSON EXPOSITION

INTRODUCTION

At the time of Paul's _____ 'ng there were estimated to be _____ million slaves in the Rom_____ which were ho_____ and the othe_____ end slav_____ dimini_____ the _____

_____ely
_____even
Su _____

The adage "Choose your battles wisely" applies to Paul. There was no use fighting an ingrained institution. That would be left for later generations of believers. Instead, he preached love, generosity and fair treatment. He reminded slave masters that they themselves were slaves: "Masters, give unto your [slaves] that which is just and equal; knowing that ye also have a Master in heaven" (Colossians 4:1).

Paul preached complete obedience by slaves to their masters (Colossians 3:22-25; Ephesians 6:5-8), but here he was addressing Christian households. A slave should obey his master, whether good or bad, but if a Christian slave was given orders contrary to God's commands, he or she should not obey. For instance, a slave should never be willing to steal or kill. "The Christian's highest duty is to God, and all lesser duties must give way to this" (*Zondervan NIV Bible Commentary*).

This is the same standard a believer should use today in dealing with _____il disobedience. We are to obey the _____s that govern our societies except _____ they violate the law of God. At _____oint we have the right to dis-_____hough God doesn't guarantee _____t face the penalties for doing _____note that Paul was himself _____on when writing these letters. _____was there because of his obedience _____o Christ and not to people.

In today's lesson, Onesimus was a runaway slave who belonged to a Christian master—Philemon. It was some time after his escape that the slave himself became a believer. Under Roman law, any slave who ran from his or her master's household was subject to punishment, even the death penalty. This letter is Paul's appeal to Philemon that Onesimus no longer be viewed as a runaway, but rather received as a Christian brother who had seen the error of his past ways and now wanted to rectify it.

Paul made converts to the gospel from all walks of life—some poor and some wealthy. Philemon apparently was a successful merchant, trader, or other type of businessman. Like most affluent citizens of the Roman world, he owned slaves. It is unknown whether Onesimus had stolen from his master, had grown tired of living in bondage, or simply had taken advantage of Philemon's new faith in Christ—a faith which expressed itself in love and generosity. Whatever the case, Onesimus had made his way to Rome. Philemon had probably given up hope of him being captured and returned, and had written him off as a loss.

Paul's letter to Philemon is intensely personal, very carefully worded, and appeals to Philemon's sense of Christian love and responsibility. It contains a message of reconciliation as taught in another of Paul's letters, 2 Corinthians: "All things are of God, who hath reconciled us to himself by Jesus Christ, and hath given to us the ministry of reconciliation" (5:18).

I. EXPRESS APPRECIATION
(Philemon 1-7)

A. Salutation (vv. 1, 2)

1. Paul, a prisoner of Jesus Christ, and Timothy our brother, unto Philemon our dearly beloved, and fellowlabourer,
2. And to our beloved Apphia, and Archippus our fellowsoldier, and to the church in thy house.

The letter is addressed to three people, as well as the church congregation in Colosse, but it quickly becomes apparent this is a very personal correspondence with Philemon. Apphia likely was the wife of Philemon. Archippus, referred to as a "fellowsoldier," is mentioned at the end of the Colossian letter. Some suggest he may have been a converted Roman soldier who was a member of the Colossian church; others conjecture that he was Philemon's son, or even a local pastor.

Whatever his role, in the Colossian letter Paul asked Archippus to "complete the work you have received in the Lord" (4:17, *NIV*). What was this work? Probably to be an added mediator between Philemon and his slave. Both letters were delivered at the same time by Tychicus, accompanied by Onesimus. Likely, Paul did not want to send Onesimus back to his master without a representative to explain the situation. Paul did everything possible to make sure the Christian slave would be well received. Tychicus was one of Paul's beloved associates, and likely delivered the Ephesian letter while on this same journey. He had even been with Paul years earlier when the apostle made his last trip to Jerusalem.

House churches were typical in places where Paul had ministered. Several such groups likely made up the congregation at Colosse. Philemon was obviously a visible and prominent member, since his home was a meeting place. Church history records that it wasn't until the third century that separate buildings were mentioned as meeting places.

B. The Basis for Reconciliation
(vv. 3-5)

3. Grace to you, and peace, from God our Father and the Lord Jesus Christ.
4. I thank my God, making mention of thee always in my prayers,
5. Hearing of thy love and faith, which thou hast toward the Lord Jesus, and toward all saints.

We don't know what caused Onesimus to seek out Paul in Rome. Their meeting might even have been accidental. Both were likely living in a Greek-speaking section of the city. Possibly Onesimus came to Paul for financial help, or because of a guilty conscience over his escape. However they met, it proved to be providential. The slave decided to give his life to Christ and made himself available for service to the apostle. As he was being mentored in the faith, the guilt for having abandoned his master must have been discussed. By law, Paul was required to return the slave to his master, or at least report his whereabouts to local authorities.

How was Paul to handle such a situation? Very carefully and prayerfully. After all, there were many visitors coming and going at his house. Word would eventually get back to Philemon that his slave was now serving the apostle. Paul's letter is the epitome of Christian statesmanship.

Typical of letters of the time, Paul sent a warm greeting to Philemon. *Grace* and *peace* express the greatest good Paul could pray for his friend. He then spoke of reports he had received of Philemon's love and faith (possibly from Onesimus himself). It would be this love, plus the strength of their friendship, on which Paul would base his request for reconciliation.

C. Communication of Faith (vv. 6, 7)

6. That the communication of thy faith may become effectual by the acknowledging of every good thing which is in you in Christ Jesus.

7. For we have great joy and consolation in thy love, because the bowels of the saints are refreshed by thee, brother.

Here is the focus of Paul's prayers for Philemon—that Philemon's good works might make his sharing of his faith effectual. A person cannot effectively impart his faith to another if his

deeds are not consistent with his expressed beliefs. In a subtle way, Paul was praying that Philemon would not be hypocritical. He wanted Philemon to be as charitable toward Onesimus as he would be to a Christian of high social status.

Paul also wanted his friend to communicate his faith as a means of growing in that faith. The words we speak about Christ reinforce them in our hearts and help us mature. We gain more of Christ by giving Him to others.

Paul called Philemon his brother, which is the title of greatest spiritual esteem and relationship among Christians. Paul remarked about how Philemon had been the source of much blessing to the saints, their hearts being refreshed by his fellowship, his love, and his wise counsel.

II. BE RESPECTFUL AND DISCREET (Philemon 8-16)

A. Boldness Empowered by Love (vv. 8-10)

8. Wherefore, though I might be much bold in Christ to enjoin thee that which is convenient,

9. Yet for love's sake I rather beseech thee, being such an one as Paul the aged, and now also a prisoner of Jesus Christ.

10. I beseech thee for my son Onesimus, whom I have begotten in my bonds.

Paul was staking much on the value of his friendship with Philemon and the Christlike character he had seen in him. To understand the significance of what he was asking Philemon to do, we must understand slavery as it existed at that time. Owning slaves was as common as any employer-employee relationship today. There was nothing wrong seen in it. At the same time, though they might hate their personal status, most slaves generally accepted their lot in life.

Paul, while not showing his disapproval of the institution, still shed the light of the gospel on the subject. He was grounded in the Hebrew tradition of the Old Testament. According to the law of Moses, Jews could own slaves, but the time of servitude was limited to six years, and during that time there were certain rights guaranteed to the slave. Even if the slave was Gentile, the rules still applied. If a slave was unduly punished or injured by his master, the slave was to be set free. Slaves were not to be treated as chattel, but as persons of worth, even though their class was at the bottom of society.

In Jewish culture, slaves comprised only a small part of the population. Paul, however, had a much more cosmopolitan upbringing than most Jews, and even held Roman citizenship. He was well aware of both cultures. Roman landowners had many slaves, most of whom were treated like personal property. Though most treated their slaves civilly, many were cruel. There were no laws against masters treating their slaves harshly. "With slaves outnumbering citizens, controlling the slave population was an imperative to the Romans" (*Nelson Study Bible*).

Philemon was a Roman, a Gentile without godly conscience—but he had become a Christian. Paul pleaded to the fact that he had been transformed on the inside. No matter what the pervading culture might say, Paul hoped Philemon would receive the reformed slave with love. Instead of using his authority as an apostle, Paul appealed to Philemon as a brother in Christ. Paul called himself "aged" and a "prisoner of Jesus Christ," calling on Philemon to have respect for him as an older man and a believer in bonds.

The picture Paul painted in verse 10 is vivid. He called Onesimus "my son," meaning he had led him to faith in Christ. The Greek word here means "child." Paul asked Philemon not to see Onesimus as a wicked runaway, but rather as a child birthed by Paul, a spiritual son.

B. A Play on Words (vv. 11-14)

11. Which in time past was to thee unprofitable, but now profitable to thee and to me:

12. Whom I have sent again: thou therefore receive him, that is, mine own bowels:

13. Whom I would have retained with me, that in thy stead he might have ministered unto me in the bonds of the gospel:

14. But without thy mind would I do nothing; that thy benefit should not be as it were of necessity, but willingly.

Paul used a play on words here to emphasize a point. *Onesimus* means "useful," yet the runaway had been anything but useful to his master. However, the former unprofitable servant would now be profitable to his master. Paul admitted that he would have liked to have Onesimus stay with him (for he was of great help in the ministry), but certainly recognized Philemon's priority in the case. Neither did Paul want to pressure Philemon into sending the slave back to Rome to serve the apostle. The emphasis is on the fact that the slave had undergone a change, a transformation of heart. Paul hoped Philemon would see this and judge accordingly. "Paul had given Philemon several good reasons to forgive Onesimus, but here he returns to the foundation of his argument: Philemon's actions had to proceed from his own love" (*Nelson Study Bible*).

C. Service as a Brother (vv. 15, 16)

15. For perhaps he therefore departed for a season, that thou shouldest receive him for ever;

16. Not now as a servant, but above a servant, a brother beloved,

specially to me, but how much more unto thee, both in the flesh, and in the Lord?

Was there a hidden reason for Onesimus having run away and later returned? Perhaps God was working providentially on behalf of everyone involved so Philemon would now have not only a slave but a brother as well. What had apparently occurred out of evil had been turned to good. Onesimus had heard the message of salvation, had given his heart to Christ, and had been transformed into a new creation. Paul's appeal takes on a spiritual quality. Not only would he now be a good servant on a human level, but also a worker in the kingdom of God.

The principle given here extends far beyond a master/slave relationship. Christians must welcome back those who have made mistakes in the past. Too often one who has failed in some way is ostracized forever, or at least labeled as untrustworthy. God may forgive, but people don't readily do so. The wonderful thing about Christ is that He welcomes us with open arms when we repent—no matter how strong the transgression. The story of the Prodigal Son (Luke 15:11-32) bears this out. Paul's hope was that Philemon would treat Onesimus in the same way the father treated the prodigal, not the way the elder brother treated him.

III. DO THE RIGHT THING
(Philemon 17-25)

A. Partners in Christ (v. 17)

17. If thou count me therefore a partner, receive him as myself.

Paul used a business term, *partner*, to define his relationship with Philemon. However, the business he implied was that of propagating the gospel. They were "partners in Christ." Paul hoped the change that had been wrought in Onesimus would be seen by Philemon as a ben-

efit to their mutual goal—winning souls. He asked Philemon to give the slave the same welcome that he would give the aged and revered apostle.

B. Paying Another's Debts (vv. 18, 19)

18. If he hath wronged thee, or oweth thee ought, put that on mine account;

19. I Paul have written it with mine own hand, I will repay it: albeit I do not say to thee how thou owest unto me even thine own self besides.

There could have been one reason for Philemon to be hesitant about the slave's return—the possibility that Onesimus had stolen from his master. Paul used another business term, *account*, meaning "one's debt to another." Heartfelt repentance includes restitution, and although this is not necessarily indicated, Paul was prepared for such. He made it clear that he would repay any debts the slave might owe. This reminds us of the truth that Christ paid the debt for our sins with His own blood.

The fact that Paul signed the letter in his own handwriting indicates how personal the letter was, and that this was a legal document. It would obligate him, if necessary, to pay for anything Onesimus might have taken.

C. Promise of a Visit (vv. 20-25)

(Philemon 20-25 is not included in the printed text.)

Paul appears somewhat positive of the outcome of the case against him in Rome. He believed the charges would be dropped. He spoke of tentative plans to visit Philemon when the trial was over. At that time he would further discuss the qualities of Onesimus with his friend. He never demanded that Philemon free Onesimus from slavery, but did make a strong intuitive case. Also, he hinted that Onesimus be loaned to him for help in the ministry. He did not assault slavery directly, but showed that Christian ethics go far beyond human institutions.

There are major lessons learned from this beautiful story even though we do not know its outcome. First, we see that people should be given a second chance. The adage "Today is the first day of the rest of your life" should be applied to anyone repentant of his or her sins.

Second, we see God working behind the scenes to bring people—even slaves—to a relationship with Christ.

Third, we see the value of Paul taking the time to disciple Onesimus. He was not content to see just his salvation but his maturity as well.

Finally, we see that distance and time do not hinder God's work. Years may have passed between the slave's escape and his salvation, but God had a hand on his life during that time. We should not be discouraged when loved ones run from the gospel for years. Instead, we need to continue to pray for them.

GOLDEN TEXT HOMILY

"HAVING CONFIDENCE IN THY OBEDIENCE I WROTE UNTO THEE, KNOWING THAT THOU WILT ALSO DO MORE THAN I SAY" (Philemon 21).

In our fragmented society, confidence and trust in one another is becoming increasingly rare. We long for friends and colleagues in whom we can place our complete confidence. We need people with whom we can entrust our innermost thoughts, needs, hopes and dreams. We need faithful brothers and sisters in the Lord—people who will do even more than is required of them.

The apostle Paul expressed that kind of trust in Philemon. Paul was confident of Philemon's obedience to the Lord, and Paul believed Philemon would do even more than was required of him. Apparently Philemon had demonstrated his trustworthiness. Thus, Paul knew that Philemon was dependable.

Philemon's dependability is a great example for us. Our family, our church, our friends and our nation need us. Let us prove we can be trusted. Let us live so others can place their full confidence in us. Let us build a reputation for doing even more than is required of us.

Let us exhibit the fruit of the Holy Spirit, which includes faithfulness (Galatians 5:22, 23). Let us live in such a way that we will inspire confidence.—**Lee Roy Martin**

SENTENCE SERMONS

INTEGRITY ought to govern Christian character.
                                    —Selected

THE GOOD PERSON increases the value of every other person whom he influences in any way.
                                    —Anonymous

CHRISTIANS WHO MOVE THE WORLD are those who do not let the world move them.
                                    —Moody Monthly

EVANGELISM APPLICATION

CHRISTIANS SHOULD ALWAYS ACT WITH INTEGRITY AS A WITNESS TO THE LOST.

We never see in Scripture whether Paul's appeal for Onesimus worked or not. Not long after this time Paul was released from prison. Did he go to Colosse to check on his friends? We don't know. His travels between his first and second imprisonment are hard to trace.

Interestingly enough, however, the name *Onesimus* appears in church history in a letter written by Ignatius about A.D. 110. Ignatius had been arrested and was being taken to Rome for trial. This was during a period of persecution of the church. Along the journey, he wrote a letter to the Ephesus church and addressed it to the new bishop there—a man named Onesimus. Many believe this was the same person as the slave Paul defended in his letter to Philemon. Assuming Onesimus was a young man (perhaps in his 20s) at the time of his meeting Paul (about A.D. 61), this would have put him in his 60s or early 70s as bishop of Ephesus.

Whether this was the same man or not, the lesson is the same—when people repent, they need to be given a second chance. We never know what giants they may become in God's kingdom.

ILLUMINATING THE LESSON

Paul fully expected that the godly character he saw in Philemon would cause him to extend forgiveness to his runaway slave. Still, he used every means possible to make a convincing argument. He pleaded Onesimus' case with great care.

If it is hard for people to forgive those transgressing against them, how much harder is it for the person who committed the wrong to allow himself to be forgiven? We don't hear from Onesimus himself in the letter, but we can imagine a bowed head, a humble spirit, a broken heart. He had found forgiveness from Christ, but would his master forgive him and accept him as a fellow believer?

It is also hard for Christians to forgive themselves—no matter if their sin is against another or simply a failure to live up to Christian standards. We all have a tendency to feel far from God when we fail, no matter how often we pray for forgiveness. A quote from George Muller perhaps will clear our thinking: "Do not let the consciousness of your unworthiness keep you from believing what God has said concerning you. If you are a believer in the Lord Jesus, then this precious privilege of being in partnership with the Father and the Son is yours" (*The Autobiography of George Muller*).

DAILY BIBLE READINGS

M. Integrity Maintained.
   Genesis 39:7-12
T. Kindness Shown.
   Ruth 2:4-16
W. Obeying God.
   2 Chronicles 34:1-8
T. Submission to God's Will.
   Matthew 1:18-25
F. Bringing Others to Christ.
   John 1:35-51
S. Love One Another.
   1 John 4:7-21

TRUTH SEARCH
Creatively Teaching the Word

DISCUSSION QUESTIONS

Express Appreciation
(Philemon 1-7)

1. What did Paul call Philemon, and why (v. 1)?

2. Though apart, how was Paul ministering to Philemon (v. 4)?

3. Describe Philemon's reputation (v. 5).

4. How was Paul praying for Philemon (v. 6)?

5. How had Philemon brought joy to Paul (v. 7)?

Be Respectful and Discreet
(Philemon 8-16)

1. What did Paul have the right to do (v. 8)?

2. "Yet for love's sake" (v. 9), how did Paul approach Philemon (vv. 9, 14)?

3. Whom was Paul representing (v. 10), and how had this person changed (v. 11)?

4. Describe the relationship Paul had developed with Onesimus (vv. 12, 13).

5. What had caused the turn-around in Onesimus' life (vv. 15, 16)?

Do the Right Thing
(Philemon 17-25)

1. How did Paul want Philemon to treat Onesimus (v. 17)?

2. What offer did Paul make (v. 18)?

3. How was Philemon indebted to Paul (v. 19)?

4. What confidence did Paul have (vv. 20, 21)?

5. What hope did Paul have (v. 22)?

6. What did Paul wish for Philemon (vv. 3, 25)?

GROUP TALK

Items needed: Index cards, pencils

Have students break up into groups of two or three students each. Give each group an index card and a pencil.

Ask each group to write down three principles from the Book of Philemon that Christians can use in dealing with fellow believers. Then bring everyone back together and discuss the principles they found. Finally, pray that the Lord will help you and your students to put those principles into practice.

Confession and Repentance

Study Text: Psalms 30:1-12; 51:1-19

Objective: To recognize the need for self-examination and respond to God with a contrite heart.

Golden Text: "Create in me a clean heart, O God; and renew a right spirit within me" (Psalm 51:10).

Central Truth: God restores to spiritual vitality those who confess and repent of their sins.

Evangelism Emphasis: God saves those who confess and repent of their sins.

PRINTED TEXT

Psalm 51:1. Have mercy upon me, O God, according to thy lovingkindness: according unto the multitude of thy tender mercies blot out my transgressions.

2. Wash me thoroughly from mine iniquity, and cleanse me from my sin.

3. For I acknowledge my transgressions: and my sin is ever before me.

4. Against thee, thee only, have I sinned, and done this evil in thy sight: that thou mightest be justified when thou speakest, and be clear when thou judgest.

5. Behold, I was shapen in iniquity; and in sin did my mother conceive me.

6. Behold, thou desirest truth in the inward parts: and in the hidden part thou shalt make me to know wisdom.

7. Purge me with hyssop, and I shall be clean: wash me, and I shall be whiter than snow.

8. Make me to hear joy and gladness; that the bones which thou hast broken may rejoice.

9. Hide thy face from my sins, and blot out all mine iniquities.

10. Create in me a clean heart, O God; and renew a right spirit within me.

11. Cast me not away from thy presence; and take not thy holy spirit from me.

12. Restore unto me the joy of thy salvation; and uphold me with thy free spirit.

13. Then will I teach transgressors thy ways; and sinners shall be converted unto thee.

14. Deliver me from bloodguiltiness, O God, thou God of my salvation: and my tongue shall sing aloud of thy righteousness.

30:2. O Lord my God, I cried unto thee, and thou hast healed me.

3. O Lord, thou hast brought up my soul from the grave: thou hast kept me alive, that I should not go down to the pit.

4. Sing unto the Lord, O ye saints of his, and give thanks at the remembrance of his holiness.

5. For his anger endureth but a moment; in his favour is life: weeping may endure for a night, but joy cometh in the morning.

10. Hear, O Lord, and have mercy upon me: Lord, be thou my helper.

11. Thou hast turned for me my mourning into dancing: thou hast put off my sackcloth, and girded me with gladness;

12. To the end that my glory may sing praise to thee, and not be silent. O Lord my God, I will give thanks unto thee for ever.

LESSON OUTLINE

I. CONFESSION
    A. Cry for Compassion
    B. Honesty With God and Oneself
    C. Plea for Pardon and Purity

II. REPENTANCE
    A. A New Creation
    B. The Sacrifices of God
    C. Prayer for Prosperity

III. JOY OF RENEWAL
    A. Praise to the God Who Saves
    B. A Reflection of Repentance
    C. Results of a Changed Life

LESSON EXPOSITION

INTRODUCTION

Perhaps the most important picture we see in the Psalms is the path taken by a sin-sick soul back into fellowship with Almighty God. Such is the case in Psalm 51. It begins with a gut-wrenching plea to God from a position of absolute helplessness. We are taken into the depths of the soul to witness firsthand the spiritual desolation caused by sin. The gravity of that desolation weighs heavily on David as he pens the cry, "Have mercy on me, O God." Understanding how David dealt with his sin and how he found his way back to God will help us to know how we can enjoy the renewing power of the Holy Spirit. Confession and repentance bring the joy of renewal.

The familiar story of David's "fall from grace" can be found in 2 Samuel 11. A few introductory points will be helpful for understanding David's writing in Psalm 51.

Since ancient armies did not have the resources contemporary military forces enjoy, it was customary to postpone hostilities until winter was over. For this reason, springtime was the time when nations went to war. Also unlike contemporary militaries, the highest-ranking official in the land went with his troops. This was the case in the time of King David, approximately 1,000 years before Christ was born. Thus, 2 Samuel 11:1 is an important indicator of the spiritual condition of David even before his sin with Bathsheba: "In the spring, at the time when kings go off to war, David sent Joab . . ." (*NIV*). Because David was not fulfilling his responsibilities as king, he was already beginning a turn away from God.

Who knows exactly why David did not go to war? Perhaps he was tired, or maybe he was proud, or maybe he was simply lazy. Whatever the case, his decision to stay back marked the beginning of his moral decay. Once we become comfortable with simple sins, the larger, ugly ones come much easier.

David had the opportunity to walk away from the temptation. David may not have been able to avoid seeing Bathsheba or even being enticed by her beauty. However, the sin was conceived in his heart when he sent his servants to inquire about the woman (v. 3). Even the servants were shocked that David was embarking on this collision course with disaster.

David's plot to cover his sin was foiled because of the integrity of Bathsheba's husband, Uriah. First, David invited the warrior home from battle and offered him the honor of reporting the events of the battlefield. David contrived to honor the war hero by allowing him a visit with his wife. Of course, David wanted to create the opportunity to explain Bathsheba's pregnancy with Uriah's conjugal visit from the battlefield. The plot, however, was foiled because of the integrity of the Hittite. Uriah refused to allow himself the comfort of his own home and the pleasure of his wife. The integrity of Uriah is meant to be seen in sharp contrast to David. Uriah would not even sleep with his own wife under these circumstances, yet David slept with the wife of another!

When plan A failed, David contrived plan B: He would get Uriah drunk. Amazingly, even under the influence of alcohol, the fortitude of Uriah's character is further contrasted to David's. Uriah slept the second night where he slept the first night, at the entrance to the palace with the servants.

Finally, David resorted to his most heinous sin of all—having Uriah killed in battle so he could take Bathsheba as his wife. It is true that sin always takes us farther than we wanted to go, keeps us longer than we wanted to stay, and costs us more than we ever dreamed of paying. David sent Uriah back to the battlefield with his own letter of execution. Once again, the faithfulness of Uriah's service to David is contrasted with David's fractured relationship with God. Back at the front line, General Joab had to undergo a senseless maneuver and sacrifice the lives of many good men in order to stage Uriah's demise.

When David got word of his seasoned general's self-defeating strategy, he was furious—until he learned that Uriah had been killed. The avalanche of sin in David's life broke his relationship with God and replaced his zeal for God with an icy emptiness in his innermost being.

I. CONFESSION (Psalm 51:1-9)

A. Cry for Compassion (vv. 1, 2)

1. Have mercy upon me, O God, according to thy lovingkindness: according unto the multitude of thy tender mercies blot out my transgressions.

2. Wash me thoroughly from mine iniquity, and cleanse me from my sin.

The first step in coming to God is to cry out to Him. There must be a recognition of the absolute helplessness of our situation and an acute understanding of our need of God.

There can be no presumption that we have anything within ourselves that is going to make our situation better. That is exactly the humility with which David approached God in these verses.

Consider David's condition. He had just been through what may have been the most humiliating and taxing experience of his life. He had committed the two sins for which the Law carried no provision of forgiveness (adultery and murder)—death was the penalty for both. He was at the end of his rope. From this desperate situation he cried out in unmitigated, raw emotion. He knew he couldn't defend his actions. Past accomplishments meant nothing now. He threw himself at the feet of the Supreme Judge and pled for mercy.

David's cry for mercy was based on his understanding of God's unfailing love. A revelation of God's enduring compassion is reminiscent of the apostasy of the Israelites after they were rescued from Egyptian slavery. It had only been a few months since they left Egypt. Certainly many of them still nursed wounds inflicted by the cruel taskmasters. The scars from the vicious whippings were grisly reminders of the lives they had lived. Yet the people built an image of an idol god at the very foot of the Lord's mountain.

A brief look at the prophets' sermons against the sins of idolatry indicates how deeply this sin hurts God (see Jeremiah 2:2-13). The personal loss, betrayal and hurt that result from adultery are the images used to describe how idolatry makes God feel. And, after His people had cut Him so deeply by worshiping an object that could neither see their needs nor hear their prayers, we would expect God to have wiped them off the face of the earth. He certainly responded in judgment (Exodus 32:27-29), but immediately following the judgment, He passed before Moses with a revelation of such love that the words of S.T. Francis' hymn can be considered a vain expression: "O the deep, deep love of Jesus, vast, unmeasured, boundless, free, rolling as a mighty ocean in its fullness over me." Though hurt deeply by His people's sin, God revealed Himself to Moses as "the Lord, the Lord, the compassionate and gracious God, slow to anger, abounding in love and faithfulness" (Exodus 34:6, *NIV*).

B. Honesty With God and Oneself (vv. 3-6)

3. For I acknowledge my transgressions: and my sin is ever before me.

4. Against thee, thee only, have I sinned, and done this evil in thy sight: that thou mightest be justified when thou speakest, and be clear when thou judgest.

5. Behold, I was shapen in iniquity; and in sin did my mother conceive me.

6. Behold, thou desirest truth in the inward parts: and in the hidden part thou shalt make me to know wisdom.

David made the startling observation that he had sinned only against God. This seems strange since we would count his seduction of Bathsheba as a sin against her. And what about Uriah? Surely the most offended party should have been Uriah himself. No matter who is hurt by our actions, no matter the harm to others, sin is primarily an offense to God. It is exactly at this point that most people misunderstand what sin is all about. We think things are OK as long as we don't hurt anybody else.

On any given evening, one can watch half a dozen TV sitcoms where the morality of inclusion and self-expression is preached to the viewer. There is no right or wrong—only what seems right. David took the opposite

approach; he was honest enough with himself to own his guilt. He knew that God's judgment against him was righteous and true.

The problem of sin is not limited to the specific wrongs we commit. We are sinful from the time of birth. Since the disobedience of Adam, people have been estranged from God. Every person born has a nature that is warped because of that sin, as well as the sin the individual commits. In our spirit, there is a proclivity that draws us away from God. To forget we have this condition results in pride and complacency. David recognized this and acknowledged a problem far deeper than his recent actions.

C. Plea for Pardon and Purity (vv. 7-9)

7. Purge me with hyssop, and I shall be clean: wash me, and I shall be whiter than snow.

8. Make me to hear joy and gladness; that the bones which thou hast broken may rejoice.

9. Hide thy face from my sins, and blot out all mine iniquities.

When we come to a place where we grasp that even the best actions and motives which adorn us are nothing more than filthy rags, the natural thing for us to do is cry out for the pardon and cleansing only God can give. Hyssop is a small plant that often grows in the crevices in a wall. It has a consistency ideal for brushing on liquids. It was required by the Law to be used to apply blood and water in purification ceremonies (Exodus 12:22; Leviticus 14:4-6; Numbers 19). It was used to apply the blood of the lambs to the doorposts during the first Passover.

David knew that only the shedding of blood could cleanse sin. The Old Testament sacrificial system foreshadowed the ultimate sacrificial Lamb whose blood would atone for the sins of the world. Those to whom Christ's blood is applied lose every stain of guilt and stand justified before God. Nothing but the blood washes away sin and makes us whole. Nothing but the blood cleanses us to the depths of our being. The cleansing blood of Christ provides the means of restoration and renewal for our soul.

No matter how deep the stains, the application of the blood brings purity. But that purity does not come without travail. In Hebrew, there are several words for *wash*. The word used in Psalm 51:7 is almost exclusively used to mean the washing of clothes, typically from contact with a disease or other impurity. It is not the simple submersion of an object in water. It refers to "washing garments by beating them with a stick or pounding them on a flat rock submerged in water" (W.T. Purkiser, *Beacon Bible Commentary: Psalms*). The cleansing is thorough and complete (Malachi 3:2).

When God cleanses a person's heart, there is relief as if a great burden is being lifted. The greater a person's acknowledgment of their sinfulness, the greater will be their joy the moment the sin is taken away (Luke 7:47). David was well aware of the destructive effects his sin had upon him. The idea of crushed bones in verse 8 was an idiom for absolute destruction. At the same time, he knew the love of God would keep him. At such a low point in life, the only thing that can relieve the depression caused by sin is the hope that God will not hold you accountable for your sins and will not focus on the wrong you have done (cf. Isaiah 1:18). To have one's iniquities blotted out is to have the impurities whitewashed and covered completely.

James Boice uses the example of the ancient manuscripts called *palimpsests* to illustrate this point. *Palimpsests* are documents that have been written over. An older text was either flawed or outdated. The old writing would be rubbed off, the paper (papyrus) turned sideways, and the text rewritten. Boice states: "The books of our lives have been written upon with many sins and these stand as a terrible indictment against us. . . . But God can and will do something, if we ask Him. God will rub out the ancient writing, turn the pages sideways, and write over the newly prepared surface the message of His everlasting compassion through the work of Jesus Christ" (*Psalms, Vol. 2: Psalms 42—106*).

II. REPENTANCE (Psalm 51:10-19)

A. A New Creation (vv. 10-12)

10. Create in me a clean heart, O God; and renew a right spirit within me.

11. Cast me not away from thy presence; and take not thy holy spirit from me.

12. Restore unto me the joy of thy salvation; and uphold me with thy free spirit.

True repentance involves more than being sorry for our sins. It involves making a 180-degree turnaround and going in the opposite direction. Even this act, however, must be empowered by God. David realized he needed more than simply being cleansed. He needed spiritual heart surgery. His prayer for God to create in him a clean heart is exactly what the prophets had in mind when they declared God's intention to give His people a heart to know Him—a heart with absolute integrity, one upon which His law can be written directly (Jeremiah 24:7; 31:33; 32:39; Ezekiel 11:19).

The verb *create* is the same one used in Genesis 1:1 when God made the universe from nothing by speaking it into existence. What sinners need is not simply a cosmetic overhaul. Paul referred to this as becoming a new creation—"Therefore, if anyone is in

Christ, he is a new creation; the old has gone, the new has come!" (2 Corinthians 5:17, *NIV*). This is nothing short of a miracle and can only be accomplished by God himself.

David also prayed for a clean heart. In English, the word *heart* refers to the seat of the emotions. For example, we might say to someone, "I love you with all my heart." We mean that our deepest and most powerful emotions are involved in our heart. In Hebrew, the word used to make this point is *bowels* or *kidneys*. In Genesis 43:30, "Joseph made haste; for his bowels did yearn upon his brother: and he sought where to weep; and he entered into his chamber, and wept there."

The use of the word *heart* in Hebrew refers instead to the mind and will. This is important because often we make a commitment to serve God better. We promise to do more, give more and seek more. We know we need to try harder, but trying harder is not good enough. No one can serve God by a sheer act of the will. What we need is a change that goes to the center of our being. We need more than a change in our emotions; we need a change in our will to obey God. The second half of Psalm 51:10 says the same thing in a different way. We need a spirit that is upright and straightforward—one that will consistently do what is right.

The alternative to becoming a new creation would be to endure the curse of broken fellowship with God. This fear is expressed in verse 11. David prayed that God neither cast him away nor go away and leave him alone. It is the opposite of how David asked God to deal with his sin in verse 9. He wanted God to turn away from the sin but not to turn away from him. Elsewhere, David was overwhelmed by the amazing grace of God—"If you, O Lord, kept a record of sins, O Lord, who could stand? But with you there is forgiveness; therefore you are feared" (130:3, 4, *NIV*).

Only the renewing power of God can change our inner being and restore the joy of our salvation. The end of 51:12 takes up this idea in a request for a *willing spirit*. Although the King James Version translates this passage, "Uphold me with thy free spirit," the original is probably better rendered as, "Grant me a willing spirit, to sustain me" (*NIV*). Rather than the emphasis being on God's Spirit as in the King James Version, the request is really that God would change the heart, the soul, the will—to make it amenable to God's law. In other words, "I need a new desire. Help me to submit humbly to Your rule in my life with welcoming gladness."

B. The Sacrifices of God (vv. 13-17)

(Psalm 51:15-17 is not included in the printed text.)

13. Then will I teach transgressors thy ways; and sinners shall be converted unto thee.

14. Deliver me from bloodguiltiness, O God, thou God of my salvation: and my tongue shall sing aloud of thy righteousness.

When God does a work in a person's life, the natural response is to tell others what He has done. Nothing draws people to God as much as seeing how His love and power have changed the lives of those who believe in Him. No sermon, no song, no dramatic production holds as much sway as a life that has been redeemed. For example, when people see the one who was formerly addicted to drugs talking about freedom in Christ, they become compelled by the power of the truth of the Christian message. It is easier to throw intellectual objections at a philosophical system than to deny that someone who was totally hopeless has been redeemed. A person with an experience is never at disadvantage to a man with only an argument.

It is fair to say that a litmus test of God's work in an individual's life is the degree to which he or she wishes to tell others about it. If someone does not wish to talk about what Jesus has done, it may be appropriate to question whether that person has allowed Jesus to do anything at all.

The "bloodguiltiness" referred to in verse 14 is probably not solely related to the murder of Uriah. The idea of having blood on one's hands is commonly used to express guilt before God. Isaiah 1:15 records that God hides his eyes (cf. Psalm 51:9, 11) from people and refuses to listen to them if their hands are "full of blood." It is possible that this referred to blood of animals offered to idol gods, but more likely it is a general expression of extreme guilt.

Such a sense of guilt has a way of causing people to be silent. Think of people engaged in an argument. When one party cites incontrovertible evidence of the other's guilt, the guilty may become angry for being outdone, but he is speechless in the face of the truth. Only God can open our lips and give our sin-ridden hearts reason to sing. The only proper response for God's gracious salvation from our "bloodguilt" is praise and adoration (v. 15).

In verse 16 David was not saying that God no longer required sacrifices or burnt offerings. These things were part of the ritual of worship in David's time. David was saying that these things were pointless in themselves if they were not done in the true spirit of worship. Sacrifices were powerless without the believer's heart turning to the living God.

Thankfully, the sacrifice of God's ultimate sacrificial Lamb has made unnecessary the ritualistic observance of the Law. But we must not forget the human tendency to reduce true worship to a system of works. Doing so makes us feel self-important and self-righteous. Unfortunately, those who are full in this manner are the only ones who ever leave God's presence empty.

When God's people approach Him in an attitude of contrition and humility, He is pleased. He is not moved by ritualistic acts. To expect mechanical worship to affect Him only heightens our proclivity to think we can achieve our own salvation through our righteous works. The smallest attitude of self-reliance is offensive to God. A broken spirit is unassuming and humble. God never turns away those who approach Him with this attitude.

C. Prayer for Prosperity (vv. 18, 19)

(Psalm 51:18, 19 is not included in the printed text.)

David's prayer for the prosperity of Zion is especially interesting with regard to the historical background. We learned from 2 Samuel 11:1 that David's sin began with neglecting his duties as king. Being unfaithful to what God had called him to do had left him vulnerable to a pattern of sinfulness that escalated into the unthinkable. After dealing with the personal effects of his sin, surely David had to realize the negative implications his actions would have on his kingdom. Not only had he jeopardized his personal relationship with God, but he had placed the spirituality of an entire nation on the line. In essence, Psalm 51:18 is a request that God would undo what damage had been caused by the moral turpitude of David's failure.

When our priorities get put back into the proper perspective, we can enjoy worshiping God in the ways He has prescribed. Verse 19 declares that when God sends prosperity to His people, their ceremonial worship will be accepted. The renewal brought by God's Spirit will reinvest the religious system with its meaning, and the people who were doing perfunctory service will be infused with new life and purpose.

III. JOY OF RENEWAL
   (Psalm 30:1-12)

Psalm 30 is said to have been written or used at the dedication of a house or temple of David, though commentators disagree on which building was involved. Was it the house David built for himself on Mount Zion, the altar David built on a threshing floor after a divine plague struck Israel, or the site of the future Temple built by Solomon? Whatever the occasion, the message is the same: God renews and restores when people repent.

A. Praise to the God Who Saves
   (vv. 1-5)

(Psalm 30:1 is not included in the printed text.)

2. O Lord my God, I cried unto thee, and thou hast healed me.
3. O Lord, thou hast brought up my soul from the grave: thou hast kept me alive, that I should not go down to the pit.
4. Sing unto the Lord, O ye saints of his, and give thanks at the remembrance of his holiness.
5. For his anger endureth but a moment; in his favour is life: weeping may endure for a night, but joy cometh in the morning.

The psalmist declared He would "extol" God—putting God first in His thoughts and affections—because God had lifted him up and not let his foes rejoice over his near demise (v. 1). He had been "lifted up" as one who is rescued from a deep hole, and now he wanted to lift up the name of the Lord.

The words *pit* and *grave* in verse 3 mean the psalmist had nearly died, but the Lord spared him. "You healed me" and "You have kept me alive" (vv. 2, 3, *NKJV*), the writer said.

However, the psalmist was not satisfied in singing solo; instead, he cried out for all of God's people to sing His praises. Specifically, he urged the saints to "give thanks at the remembrance of his holiness" (v. 4). We, too, must never forget that our God is *holy*—"wholly other; there is none like Him"—and that He calls and enables us to lead pure lives.

While God in His perfection could justifiably condemn us all to instant death and eternal suffering for our failures, He is also a merciful God.

Adam Clarke commented, "When God afflicts, it is for our advantage, that we may be partakers of His holiness, and be not condemned with the world. If He be angry with us, it is but for a moment; but when we have recourse to Him, and seek His face, His favor is soon obtained, and there are lives in that favor—the life that now is, and the life that is to come. When weeping comes, it is only to lodge for the evening; but singing will surely come in the morning."

B. A Reflection of Repentance
   (vv. 6-10)

(Psalm 30:6-9 is not included in the printed text.)

10. Hear, O Lord, and have mercy upon me: Lord, be thou my helper.
The psalmist reflected on a time when he felt secure in his prosperity, assuming that the wealth and success he was enjoying was of his own doing, and that nothing could destroy it. When God withdrew His protective hand and let trouble enter the man's life, then he became freshly aware of just how dependent he was on God.

C. Results of a Changed Life
   (vv. 11, 12)

11. Thou hast turned for me my mourning into dancing: thou hast put off my sackcloth, and girded me with gladness;
12. To the end that my glory may sing praise to thee, and not be silent. O Lord my God, I will give thanks unto thee for ever.

The psalmist had been transformed and renewed. His days of self-reliance, which resulted in his wandering from the Lord, were over. He recognized that the place to remain was in the hollow of the Lord's hand. Like the returning Prodigal Son, there is nothing so sweet as the fellowship of the Father.

The writer now boasted in God and sang His praises. The Lord was faithful in changing his circumstances. The Lord came to his rescue, despite his sinful behavior. Because of the mercy of the Lord, the psalmist vowed to constantly give praise to Him.

GOLDEN TEXT HOMILY

"CREATE IN ME A CLEAN HEART, O GOD; AND RENEW A RIGHT SPIRIT WITHIN ME" (Psalm 51:10).

As I pondered the meaning of this text, an early winter announced its arrival by a heavy snow that fell overnight. In the morning the world seemed to have been reborn.

Gone was the muddy roadway and the ugly rubbish heap, for all was now covered by pristine, white snow, glistening in the sun under an azure sky.

Do we not wish sometimes that our life could be changed in a similar way—our mistakes covered, everything fresh and clean again? But despite our wishing, and often despite our desperate attempts to ward off the problems, the hurts and the mistakes, our life goes on.

David, king of Israel and the anointed of God, had fallen in sin. A weak moment? An evil design of a sinning heart? Whatever brought him into his sinful predicament, in this psalm he is calling to God for forgiveness and divine help for a fresh start. He calls for a creative initiative of God in his heart and pleads for a renewal of his spirit.

When our life has come into disharmony or when sin has ensnared us, we have but one way available for help. That is the way of repentance and confession, which leads into the presence of God. He who spoke the world into existence can restore peace to our heart, grant forgiveness for our sins, and give fresh joy to our spirit.

As dark as David's sin was, his repentance lighted a lamp in the dark that showed the way back to God. It is a way still open today for anyone who has fallen in sin and yearns to be restored to fellowship with God.—**Selected**

SENTENCE SERMONS

GOD RESTORES to spiritual vitality those who confess and repent of their sins.

—Selected

SLEEP WITH CLEAN HANDS—either kept clean all day by integrity or washed clean at night by repentance.

—John Donne

BY A CARPENTER mankind was made, and only by that same carpenter can mankind be remade.

—Desiderius Erasmus

EVANGELISM APPLICATION

GOD SAVES THOSE WHO CONFESS AND REPENT OF THEIR SINS.

Many lost souls have been driven from the church because of the misconception that God is angry at them. What God is really angry at is sin. He loves sinners and wants to see them repent and find redemption. Within the walls of the church, however, saints are often harder on sinners than God is. Of course, the only people condemned by Christ were those who fostered a religious spirit. To the sinner He typically responded, "Neither do I condemn thee" (John 8:11).

We are all guilty at one time or another and need forgiveness. There is a story of a prosecutor who came to visit a prison looking for a man to set free. The shocked inmate who was chosen wondered at his release. He told the prosecutor that there must be some mistake. "You see," he responded, "for the past seven years, I have been thinking about my crime and I know that I deserve to be here. I am guilty." The prosecutor answered, "I know. That is why you were set free. Everyone else I interviewed said he was innocent!"

ILLUMINATING THE LESSON

Repentance can only come when we recognize the horror of our sin. David was struck with conviction for his evil. He used three words in Psalm 51:1, 2 to describe his actions: *transgressions*, *iniquity* and *sin*. In each case he accepted responsibility for the actions.

Transgressions refers to stepping over a boundary we know better than to cross, such as going 75 mph in a 55 mph zone. *Iniquity* refers to the general idea of the distortion from which every person's soul suffers because of broken relationship with God. *Sin* conveys the idea of "missing the mark," like an arrow aimed at a bull's eye but missing the target altogether.

It is startling to see such a thorough recognition of personal sinfulness—especially at a time today when it is considered taboo to accept blame for anything. Yet God only hears cries for compassion that come from people who recognize their condition.

David reached this point and he longed to be clean. The pangs of his guilt had robbed him of the joy of the Lord. His estrangement from God had left a hole in his spirit. He was horrified by his own actions and desperately desired to have the devastating effects of his sin blotted out.

DAILY BIBLE READINGS

M. Humility and Confession.
2 Chronicles 7:11-16
T. A Cry for Help.
Psalm 38:18-22
W. Means to Restoration.
Joel 2:12-14
T. Preparation for Kingdom Living.
Matthew 3:1-6
F. Confess and Be Saved.
Romans 10:3-13
S. God Is Faithful to Forgive.
1 John 2:1-6

TRUTH SEARCH
Creatively Teaching the Word

DISCUSSION QUESTIONS

Confession
(Psalm 51:1-9)

1. In his cry for mercy, what aspects of God's character did David appeal to (v. 1)?

2. What did David ask God to do for him (vv. 1, 2)?

3. David had a man murdered and committed adultery with that man's wife, so why did he tell God, "Against You, You only, have I sinned" (v. 4, *NKJV*)?

4. Is David's statement in verse 5 true for all people? How do you know?

5. What does God desire (v. 6), and why?

6. In what sense had God broken David's bones (v. 8)?

7. What would bring David joy and happiness (vv. 7-9)?

Repentance
(Psalm 51:10-17)

1. What kind of spirit did David request, and why (v. 10)?

2. What did David ask God *not* to do (v. 11)?

3. In response to God's salvation, how did David pledge to . . .
- serve others (v. 13)?
- serve God (vv. 14, 15)?

4. What does God desire (vv. 16, 17)?

Joy of Renewal
(Psalm 30:1-12)

1. List three reasons David glorified God:
- v. 1:
- v. 2:
- v. 3:

2. How did David compare God's favor with His anger (v. 5)?

3. Where had David wrongly placed his security (v. 6), and what lesson did he learn (v. 7)?

4. How desperate was David's plea to the Lord (vv. 8-10)?

5. How did God restore David (v. 11), and why (v. 12)?

OBJECT LESSON

Items needed: Blank paper, scissors, small sack, marker

Display the paper.

Just as this paper is perfectly clean, some people pretend that sin has never entered their heart. However, all of us were born as sinners, and all of us have chosen to sin.

Write various sins on the paper. **The first step in dealing with sin is admitting we have sinned—confessing it to God.** Display the sins you have listed.

The second step is repenting of our sins. That means, through the grace and power of God's Spirit, to turn away from our sins to follow Christ. Turn the paper around to show the blank side. **Just as I turned this sign around, God wants to turn us around through repentance.**

Third is the joy of renewal in Jesus Christ. Begin cutting up the paper into tiny pieces, letting them fall into the bag.

With our sins forgiven and our lives made new, we can shout with David, "You have turned for me my mourning into dancing" (Psalm 30:11, *NKJV*).

Toss the confetti you just made into air.

Hearing and Obeying

Study Text: John 10:1-30; Romans 6:6-23; James 1:19-27
Objective: To know that God wants to guide His people and learn to follow Him.
Golden Text: "Be ye doers of the word, and not hearers only, deceiving your own selves" (James 1:22).
Central Truth: Christians who maintain a close relationship with Christ willingly hear and obey His voice.
Evangelism Emphasis: Christians who maintain a close relationship with God will love the lost.

PRINTED TEXT

John 10:4. And when he putteth forth his own sheep, he goeth before them, and the sheep follow him: for they know his voice.

5. And a stranger will they not follow, but will flee from him: for they know not the voice of strangers.

27. My sheep hear my voice, and I know them, and they follow me:

28. And I give unto them eternal life; and they shall never perish, neither shall any man pluck them out of my hand.

29. My Father, which gave them me, is greater than all; and no man is able to pluck them out of my Father's hand.

30. I and my Father are one.

James 1:22. But be ye doers of the word, and not hearers only, deceiving your own selves.

23. For if any be a hearer of the word, and not a doer, he is like unto a man beholding his natural face in a glass:

24. For he beholdeth himself, and goeth his way, and straightway forgetteth what manner of man he was.

25. But whoso looketh into the perfect law of liberty, and continueth therein, he being not a forgetful hearer, but a doer of the work, this man shall be blessed in his deed.

Romans 6:16. Know ye not, that to whom ye yield yourselves servants to obey, his servants ye are to whom ye obey; whether of sin unto death, or of obedience unto righteousness?

17. But God be thanked, that ye were the servants of sin, but ye have obeyed from the heart that form of doctrine which was delivered you.

18. Being then made free from sin, ye became the servants of righteousness.

19. I speak after the manner of men because of the infirmity of your flesh: for as ye have yielded your members servants to uncleanness and to iniquity unto iniquity; even so now yield your members servants to righteousness unto holiness.

20. For when ye were the servants of sin, ye were free from righteousness.

21. What fruit had ye then in those things whereof ye are now ashamed? for the end of those things is death.

22. But now being made free from sin, and become servants to God, ye have your fruit unto holiness, and the end everlasting life.

23. For the wages of sin is death; but the gift of God is eternal life through Jesus Christ our Lord.

LESSON OUTLINE

I. RECOGNIZE CHRIST'S VOICE
   A. Jesus, the True Shepherd
   B. False Shepherds
   C. The Shepherd Knows His Sheep
   D. Jesus and the Father Are One

II. OBEY GOD'S WORD
   A. Doers of the Word
   B. Forgetting One's Face
   C. The Perfect Law of Liberty

III. OBEDIENCE RESULTS IN RIGHTEOUSNESS
   A. Slaves to Sin or Obedience?
   B. Servants of Righteousness
   C. Righteousness Leads to Holiness

LESSON EXPOSITION

INTRODUCTION

We live in a church era today where the walls of denominational loyalty have crumbled. In one sense this is very good, for far too often the body of Christ has been fractured into sects and ideologies that identify with some specific Biblical truth or aspect of the gospel, but meanwhile see everyone else as having less of a grasp of the Word. Seldom have the various denominations fellowshipped together as the single body of Christ, but rather have eyed each other distrustfully. However, there has at least been general accountability within each denomination for what pastors, evangelists, and teachers preached and taught.

It's a different story now. We see a proliferation of parachurch ministries, independent congregations and preachers, resulting in little loyalty among the general church body to any broader governing authority. A sad by-product is that aberrations of the gospel can be expounded, and then people are led astray by those who are not true shepherds in the Kingdom. All we have to do is turn on some "Christian" television programs and we can see this demonstrated.

Thus it becomes imperative for the believer to have a listening ear for the voice of the Lord, so he or she can distinguish truth from deception. Also, if there are many conflicting false voices within the church leading believers astray, how many more are there out in the world enticing people into all manner of false religion and philosophy!

Three major Scripture passages are utilized in our lesson. The Lord's use of the shepherding metaphor in John 10 shows us the importance of believers hearing and following the true voice of the Lord. This discourse followed His confrontation in chapter 9 with Jewish leaders and Pharisees over His healing of a blind beggar.

Shepherds, sheep and sheepfolds were a common scene in Palestine. It was also common for several flocks to be sheltered together in a single large sheepfold. Even crowded together, sheep from the different flocks knew the voice of their own shepherd, and would respond to no other. Jesus was immediately showing that the religious leaders who had just excommunicated the beggar from the synagogue for believing on Him (after being healed) were themselves false shepherds. They certainly didn't care about the beggar, but resented his being healed. Jesus, the true Shepherd, went back and found the beggar and took him into the Kingdom (9:35-38).

Those in the audience listening to Jesus, though captivated by the shepherd metaphor, had no idea what Jesus meant. Christ's parables have to be spiritually discerned, and often their most obvious interpretation is not the most important one. This is especially true here.

To His specifically Jewish audience Jesus was saying that He came just as the Scriptures had predicted the Messiah would come. God the Father sent the Son to earth. If Christ the Shepherd spoke the truth, then those who really were sheep would hear His voice and follow. Believing Jews in Israel would recognize His voice. Jesus was contrasting Himself with the many false messiahs, as well as the Pharisees, showing He was the "legitimate heir of the chosen seed" (*Zondervan NIV Bible Commentary*, Vol. 2).

Calling the religious leaders thieves and robbers, Jesus showed they did not have the approval of God on them, nor did they have the good of the people at heart. The poor beggar who had just been healed was a good example of their thievery. These men were interested only in providing for themselves and protecting their territory. They were so threatened by Jesus' popularity that they ultimately murdered Him—all to protect their own interests.

Jesus is the true Shepherd who came to expose false shepherds. The motivating factor behind these false shepherds turns out to be Satan. He is the thief in John 10:10 who comes to steal, slaughter and destroy. Only the protective hand of the real Shepherd can keep this from happening. By going through Jesus as the door into the sheepfold, we can be protected from the Evil One. Here, within the protective borders of Christ's care, we can enjoy life in full.

Our second study passage is from James. Although our text picks up with James 1:22, the prior three verses set up the intent of the message James preached. In other words, to be Christians who hear and obey the Word, we should be "quick to listen, slow to speak and slow to become angry, for man's anger does not bring about the righteous life that God desires. Therefore, get rid of all moral filth and the evil that is so prevalent and humbly accept the word planted in you, which can save you" (1:19-21, *NIV*).

If we are too quick to talk and too slow to listen, we give others the mistaken idea that what we are saying is more important than what they have to say. Also, we hinder ourselves from hearing messages God meant for our hearts. Reversing the process keeps our hearts open for the Lord to teach us. This is especially important for those who are preachers, teachers and shepherds.

Our third passage is Paul's words to the Romans concerning slavery (Romans 6:16-23). Everyone is a slave to someone or something. We are slaves to whomever and whatever we commit our lives to. Therefore, we must choose carefully whom we will be committed to. When we wisely choose to obey the One who created us, we will see that such obedience leads to righteousness and to eternal life in heaven.

I.   RECOGNIZE CHRIST'S VOICE (John 10:4, 5, 27-30)

A. Jesus, the True Shepherd (v. 4)

4. And when he putteth forth his own sheep, he goeth before them, and the sheep follow him: for they know his voice.

To adequately understand our text, we must look back to the preceding three chapters of John's Gospel. In chapter 7, Jesus journeyed to Jerusalem for the Feast of Tabernacles. All the events between 7:10 and 10:21 occurred during this visit, which found Jesus in constant conflict with the Jewish leaders, chief priests, and Pharisees. To them He was a heretic. They were blinded to His identity. They connived to arrest Him. They tried to rebuff Him with theological arguments. They tried to trap Him with legal arguments by bringing a woman caught in adultery and insisting that He condemn her. Then they physically tried to stone Him.

Of course, Jesus was able to elude their phony arguments and escape their assaults unharmed, knowing it wasn't yet time for His sacrifice. The point, though, is that all those denying Him were the supposed shepherds of the people. They were the ones to whom the people looked for help in distinguishing the truth. The blind were certainly leading the blind.

Prior to using the shepherd analogy, Jesus had come across a blind man in chapter 9. Before healing him, Jesus said of Himself, "I am the light of the world" (v. 5). He accused the Pharisees because they claimed to have such spiritual insight, though blind themselves (v. 41). Their hard-headed unwillingness to see apparently caused Him to change to the shepherd metaphor.

John 10:1-30 is the Lord's discourse on being the Good Shepherd. He contrasted Himself with the false shepherds of the day. In many Old Testament passages the prophets also condemned the false shepherds of their day (see Isaiah 56:9-12; Jeremiah 23:1-4; Ezekiel 34; Zechariah 11). Paul later used this same imagery to admonish the church leaders in Ephesus: "Keep watch over yourselves and all the flock of which the Holy Spirit has made you overseers. Be shepherds of the church of God, which he bought with his own blood" (Acts 20:28, *NIV*).

Shepherding was a common occupation and provided a perfect metaphor for Jesus to use. Identifying leaders as shepherds and people as sheep was easy for everyone to understand. Here are some of the symbolic meanings:

• Jesus himself is the Good Shepherd.

• The true Jews who accepted Him were the sheep of His flock. In a broader sense, everyone who believes in Christ becomes one of His sheep.

• The sheepfold is the protective enclave (Judaism in the Old Testament and the church in the New Testament).

• The gate (or door) is Jesus. He is the means of entrance into the sheepfold. He is the way to life.

• The gatekeeper is God the Father.

Ezekiel 34 pictured this same scene and prophetically spoke of the true Shepherd (the Messiah) coming to provide secure shepherding and a safe sheepfold. In John 10:1-3 Jesus shows that every sheep must enter by the gate. Anyone entering otherwise is a thief or charlatan. The sheep must follow the Good Shepherd. Jesus rebuked anyone who tried to lead sheep without recognizing Him as the Shepherd. Those who do are acting so out of selfish ambition, inflated egos and evil intentions.

Not only does the Shepherd lead the sheep into the sheepfold, He also leads them out to pastures for feeding during the day. For all the many meanings that can be drawn from this analogy, the central theme is that real sheep will follow only the voice of the real shepherd. This is the message we today must hear.

B. False Shepherds (v. 5)

5. And a stranger will they not follow, but will flee from him: for they know not the voice of strangers.

To be qualified as Christ's sheep, we must attune our hearts and ears to His voice. There are so many illegitimate voices calling that Jesus would later say in the Olivet Discourse: "For there shall arise false Christs, and false prophets, and shall shew great signs and wonders; insomuch that, if it were possible, they shall deceive the very elect" (Matthew 24:24).

C. The Shepherd Knows His Sheep (vv. 27-29)

27. My sheep hear my voice, and I know them, and they follow me:

28. And I give unto them eternal life; and they shall never perish, neither shall any man pluck them out of my hand.

29. My Father, which gave them me, is greater than all; and no man is able to pluck them out of my Father's hand.

John 10:1-21 took place during the Feast of Tabernacles, while verses 22-39 occurred a couple months later during winter at the Feast of Dedication. Jesus was again in Jerusalem, and the Jewish leaders were still blind to recognize Him as Messiah. Here (vv. 27-29) Jesus describes the characteristics of His sheep:

- *They hear His voice.*
- *He knows them.* Paul said, "For those God foreknew he also predestined to be conformed to the likeness of his Son, that he might be the first-born among many brothers" (Romans 8:29, *NIV*).
- *They follow the Good Shepherd.*
- *They shall never perish.* Their eternal life has been secured by the Father's plan for the sacrifice of His Son to purchase their redemption.
- *Christians (sheep) are given to Jesus by the Father.*
- *The Father is more powerful than anyone who tries to steal the sheep.* No devil nor any person has the power to steal eternal life from the sheep. That loss can only happen when the sheep refuse to follow the Shepherd and reject Him.

During this confrontation the Jews demanded, "If thou be the Christ, tell us plainly" (v. 24). Most of the time Jesus answered their trapping questions obliquely. Here (vv. 25, 26) Jesus answered by pointing out that the issue was not His true identity (the Messiah), but their unwillingness to believe—no matter how He might answer them. They were so blinded by disbelief that they would not allow themselves to believe.

"Evidently they did not belong to Him, since they had not been willing to follow Him. They perceived that His shepherd teaching meant a new order, and they were not prepared to leave the Judaism they knew, to which they clung. Yet the new order offered blessing and security which they could not have known in their Pharisaism" (*Wycliffe Bible Commentary*).

D. Jesus and the Father Are One (v. 30)

30. I and my Father are one.

The sheep are as important to the Father as they are to the Son. The Father has a love for the sheep that is all-encompassing. Since He is greater than any other power, no one can steal the sheep from His protective hand. The conclusion, then, is that there is no separation or distinction between the Father and the Son. They are inseparable and are one entity. The word *one* used here is not masculine, but rather is neuter in gender, indicating a oneness of being.

When Christ says believers are in His hand (v. 28), He is also saying they are in His Father's hand (v. 29), for Christ and the Father are one.

II. OBEY GOD'S WORD (James 1:22-25)

A. Doers of the Word (v. 22)

22. But be ye doers of the word, and not hearers only, deceiving your own selves.

In verse 19 James admonished his readers to be slow to speak and more careful to listen. Talking too much reinforces ideas of our own (that just might be incorrect), as well as giving others the impression that we are more important than they are, and their words less valuable.

We should follow the example of Jesus. "His speaking tended to be marked by brevity. He asked questions. He listened. We should ask ourselves, 'Have I listened enough to know that what I've said was heard?'" (*Life Application Commentary*).

James then said that we should purge ourselves of all moral filthiness (v. 21). Someone has said that if we do something intentionally 21 times, then it becomes a habit. For example, if we catch our tongues before we speak 21 times or if we turn our heads from seeing certain images on television 21 times, then we are on the road to disciplining that temptation from our hearts. "We must be aware that allowing *any kind* of moral filth into our lives or homes, including filthy language or obscenity through videos and television, grieves the Spirit and violates God's holy standards for his people" (*Full Life Study Bible*).

We must get rid of bad habits and actions, much like we would take off dirty clothes. We also must receive the corrections and commands of the Lord with humble hearts, that is, be amenable to change in ourselves.

The Word of God is *planted* in us, but we must tend the soil of our hearts so it is fertile ground that will allow for good growth. That means being active and not passive in our hearing of the Word. Reading and studying the Word is not enough. We must do all that it says to do. Obedience is the fertilizer in the soil that makes us grow. Paul said, "For it is not those who hear the law who are righteous in God's sight, but it is those who obey the law who will be declared righteous" (Romans 2:13, *NIV*). Jesus called those blessed who "hear the word of God, and keep it" (Luke 11:28).

B. Forgetting One's Face (vv. 23, 24)

23. For if any be a hearer of the word, and not a doer, he is like unto a man beholding his natural face in a glass:

24. For he beholdeth himself, and goeth his way, and straightway forgetteth what manner of man he was.

A mirror is supposed to give us an accurate representation of who we are. As we study God's Word, we see a picture of ourselves—mostly the blemishes and faults that need to be corrected, but also the good things that have already been accomplished in us. However, in viewing ourselves through the mirror of the Word, we can make serious mistakes.

• *"Taking too quick a glance and missing a blemish.* This comes from reading the Word in a cursory manner, or not really studying it to let it become God's message to our hearts. The Word is always active, and God uses it to speak specific words to us. If we aren't reading and studying prayerfully and carefully, we will miss the message. Thus, the correction we need is overlooked.

• *"Forgetting what we see.* Do you remember the first time you were under conviction for your sins? What a terrible feeling of guilt, unworthiness and filth that was! Isaiah said, "Woe is me! for I am undone; because I am a man of unclean lips, and I dwell in the midst of a people of unclean lips: for mine eyes have seen the King, the Lord of hosts" (Isaiah 6:5). That conviction followed Isaiah the rest of his life and kept his heart malleable. However, some people sit under great preaching, their hearts gripped by conviction, yet they don't respond. These people go back to living their same sinful lives, forgetting what they experienced.

• *"Failing to obey.* As believers we can hear God's Word and let it convict our hearts regarding a certain habit, deed or command. However, if we don't immediately set about to heed the Word, we can become numb and disobedient. It is best to move quickly when God tells us what to do.

C. The Perfect Law of Liberty (v. 25)

25. But whoso looketh into the perfect law of liberty, and continueth therein, he being not a forgetful hearer, but a doer of the work, this man shall be blessed in his deed.

We all need boundaries in our lives. There is freedom and joy within God's boundaries because they give us protection. The psalmist said, "I will walk about in freedom, for I have sought out your precepts" (Psalm 119:45, *NIV*).

A perfect example of this is David Berkowicz. Convicted as a serial killer and arsonist in New York, David later miraculously came to Christ in prison. Recently he had a probation hearing. Recognizing that he still has to pay for the crimes he committed in the past, he asked that he never come up for a parole hearing again. He has given his life to serving other prisoners and sharing the gospel with them. He is certainly held within the bounds of the prison walls, as well as within the bounds of God's law. However, there is great liberty for him there.

The law of God gives us liberty. The righteous person is the one who looks at the law of God and obeys it. That person makes obedience his or her chosen lifestyle. The mirror of the Word reveals personal flaws so corrections can be made. "The Law gives freedom because it is only in obeying God's Law that true freedom can be found (cf. John 8:31, 32). Obeying our emotions and giving in to all our desires is true slavery. But in accepting God's will, we are truly free to be what God created us to be" (*Life Application Commentary*).

III. OBEDIENCE RESULTS IN RIGHTEOUSNESS (Romans 6:16-23)

A. Slaves to Sin or Obedience? (v. 16)

16. Know ye not, that to whom ye yield yourselves servants to obey, his servants ye are to whom ye obey; whether of sin unto death, or of obedience unto righteousness?

Paul gave Christians a solemn warning against the idea that believers can abuse grace by sinning willfully. If we give ourselves over to temptation, then we become a slave of the resulting sin. Then we lose the abiding presence of God in our lives. If not stopped, the sin will result in death.

Paul also indicates here that everyone is a slave to something or someone. If we choose sin as our master, we have no choice ultimately but to obey it. However, if we choose to commit ourselves as slaves to the Lord, then we will find righteousness as a by-product. The fact is, however, that we have to make a choice. Jesus said, "No one can serve two masters. Either he will hate the one and love the other, or he will be devoted to the one and despise the other. You cannot serve both God and Money" (Matthew 6:24, *NIV*). The word *money* here can mean anything of this world that displaces Christ in our lives.

B. Servants of Righteousness (vv. 17, 18)

17. But God be thanked, that ye were the servants of sin, but ye have obeyed from the heart that form of doctrine which was delivered you.

18. Being then made free from sin, ye became the servants of righteousness.

Paul praised his readers in Rome for choosing slavery to righteousness, but he also admonished them to stay on this course. Early-church believers were committed to following the teachings of the apostles. These teachings laid down standards of conduct and ethics—all based on what

Christ had taught. This is the *doctrine* Paul speaks of.

In his letters Paul frequently urged the people to remain true to the things he had taught while he was among them. For instance, he wrote to the Thessalonians, "Brethren, stand fast and hold the traditions which ye have been taught, whether by word, or our epistle" (2 Thessalonians 2:15). The obedience Paul urged was not a begrudged one, but rather obedience *from the heart.* He knew that a choice must be made—either slavery to sin or slavery to righteousness. If we are going to choose righteousness, then we should put our total beings behind that choice.

C. Righteousness Leads to Holiness (vv. 19-23)

19. I speak after the manner of men because of the infirmity of your flesh: for as ye have yielded your members servants to uncleanness and to iniquity unto iniquity; even so now yield your members servants to righteousness unto holiness.

20. For when ye were the servants of sin, ye were free from righteousness.

21. What fruit had ye then in those things whereof ye are now ashamed? for the end of those things is death.

22. But now being made free from sin, and become servants to God, ye have your fruit unto holiness, and the end everlasting life.

23. For the wages of sin is death; but the gift of God is eternal life through Jesus Christ our Lord.

The analogy of slavery was one Paul's readers could easily understand. There were far more slaves than citizens in the Roman Empire. Paul apologized rhetorically for borrowing so heavily on the Christians' former manner of life in sin to describe their new life in Christ. The kind of slavery experienced in sin is not at all similar to the kind of slavery experienced as a servant of Christ.

The work of the Lord in believers' hearts, no matter the social class, has a tendency to make them one together—all slaves together to righteousness, and all becoming more like Christ daily. The opposite is true when sin is the slave master. Such slavery leads to bondage—and ultimately death.

There is a certain paradox here. Though Christians have been set free from sin and do not have to obey its demands, we are nevertheless slaves instead to something else—righteousness. Freely we should give ourselves to serving our new Master, just as much as we were in bondage to our former master. The result of serving sin is death. The result of serving our new relationship with God is eternal life through Jesus Christ our Lord.

GOLDEN TEXT HOMILY

"BE YE DOERS OF THE WORD, AND NOT HEARERS ONLY, DECEIVING YOUR OWN SELVES" (James 1:22).

There are two sides to the Christian life—the "believing side" and the "behaving side." There are both creeds and deeds, experience and ethics, being and doing, the root and the fruit.

Some people separate these two. Some would make of Christianity a system of beliefs, right words, true creeds. Beliefs, words, creeds—these are essential. But they are not sufficient.

Others would make of Christianity a system of ethics, a program for social reform. They would have us all to be activists. Ethics, reform, activism—these, too, have their place. But when they are what they ought to be, they are the fruit of the Christlife within.

We need to hold firmly the truth that James puts before us. We need to be hearers of the Word. We need its light, its inspiration, its power to motivate. But we cannot stop with being hearers of the Word. We must be doers as well.

Like the wings of a bird in flight, the legs of a man who walks, hearing and doing go together. And "what God hath joined together, let not man put asunder" (see Matthew 19:6).— **Selected**

SENTENCE SERMONS

CHRISTIANS WHO MAINTAIN a close relationship with Christ willingly hear and obey His voice.

—Selected

ONLY HE WHO BELIEVES is obedient; only he who is obedient believes.

—Dietrich Bonhoeffer

A BIBLE IN HAND is worth two on the shelf.

—Selected

ILLUMINATING THE LESSON

When we give our lives to Christ, we give Him the absolute right to do whatever is necessary to discipline us back into the fold, should we ever stray. Backsliding, or wandering away from the protective care of the Shepherd, is a serious, life-threatening mistake to make. When one strays from the sheepfold, he puts himself at the mercy of the Enemy—and the Enemy is only out to steal and destroy. The writer of Hebrews said, "My son, do not make light of the Lord's discipline, and do not lose heart when he rebukes you, because

the Lord disciplines those he loves, and he punishes everyone he accepts as a son" (12:5, 6, *NIV*). Two verses later he said, "If you are not disciplined (and everyone undergoes discipline), then you are illegitimate children and not true sons" (v. 8, *NIV*).

Do you sometimes feel you are undergoing an overly tough trial in life? Rejoice, because the trials of believers are part of the discipline process—and it will certainly be for your ultimate good: "God disciplines us for our good, that we may share in his holiness. No discipline seems pleasant at the time, but painful. Later on, however, it produces a harvest of righteousness and peace for those who have been trained by it" (vv. 10, 11, *NIV*).

The Lord's hand may feel heavy, but He has your eternal good at heart. Rejoice that He cares enough to discipline His children.

DAILY BIBLE READINGS

M. Obey the Supreme
     Commandment.
     Deuteronomy 6:1-9
T.   Hearing God Produces Joy.
     Isaiah 51:7-11
W.   The Folly of Not Listening.
     Jeremiah 5:19-25
T.   To Love Is to Obey.
     John 14:23-26
F.   Obedience Leads to
     Righteousness.
     Romans 6:15-23
S.   Obedience Learned Through
     Suffering.
     Hebrews 5:5-10

TRUTH SEARCH
Creatively Teaching the Word

DISCUSSION QUESTIONS

Recognize Christ's Voice
(John 10:4, 5, 27-30)

1. Why do sheep follow their shepherd (v. 4)?

2. How does a sheep respond to a stranger (v. 5)? Why?

3. According to verse 27, how do Christians live?

4. Describe the security believers have in Christ (vv. 28-30).

Obey God's Word
(James 1:22-25)

1. How do some people deceive themselves (v. 22)?

2. Explain the illustration James uses in verses 23 and 24.

3. How does God want us to study His Word (v. 25)?

4. How can we have a blessed life (v. 25)?

Obedience Results in Righteousness
(Romans 6:16-23)

1. What makes someone a slave (v. 16)?

2. Identify the two types of spiritual slavery (v. 16). Can one be a slave to both masters?

3. How does someone move from slavery of sin to slavery of righteousness (vv. 17, 18)?

4. Describe the life of the person enslaved to sin (vv. 19-21).

5. Describe the life of the person enslaved to righteousness (vv. 19, 22).

6. Contrast the eternal results of both types of slavery (v. 23).

7. Why is the eternal result of sin called "wages" while the eternal result of righteousness is called a "gift" (v. 23)?

OBEDIENCE ILLUSTRATION

Arabian horses go through rigorous training in the deserts of the Middle East. The trainers require absolute obedience from the horses, and test them to see if they are completely trained.

The final test is almost beyond the endurance of any living thing. The trainer forces the horses to do without water for many days. Then he turns them loose, and of course they start running toward the water; but just as they get to the edge, ready to plunge in and drink, the trainer blows his whistle. The horses that have been completely trained and have learned perfect obedience will stop. They turn around and come pacing back to the trainer. They stand there quivering, wanting water, but they wait in perfect obedience. When the trainer is sure he has their obedience, he gives them a signal to go back to drink.

This may be severe, but when you are in the desert of Arabia and your life is entrusted to a horse, you better have a trained, obedient one. We must accept God's training and obey Him (*sermonillustrations.com*).

Renewal Through Spiritual Disciplines

Study Text: Matthew 6:5-13; 14:22, 23; Mark 1:35-39; Luke 6:12, 13; 22:39-41; Romans 15:4; 2 Timothy 2:15; 3:16, 17

Objective: To recognize the importance of spiritual disciplines and practice them for renewal.

Golden Text: "When he [Jesus] had sent the multitudes away, he went up into a mountain apart to pray: and when the evening was come, he was there alone" (Matthew 14:23).

Central Truth: Spiritual disciplines are ways of spending time with God for the purpose of renewal and transformation.

Evangelism Emphasis: A Christian's striving for Christlikeness is a powerful witness to an unsaved world.

PRINTED TEXT

Matthew 14:22. And straightway Jesus constrained his disciples to get into a ship, and to go before him unto the other side, while he sent the multitudes away.

23. And when he had sent the multitudes away, he went up into a mountain apart to pray: and when the evening was come, he was there alone.

Mark 1:35. And in the morning, rising up a great while before day, he went out, and departed into a solitary place, and there prayed.

Luke 22:39. And he came out, and went, as he was wont, to the mount of Olives; and his disciples also followed him.

40. And when he was at the place, he said unto them, Pray that ye enter not into temptation.

41. And he was withdrawn from them about a stone's cast, and kneeled down, and prayed.

Matthew 6:7. But when ye pray, use not vain repetitions, as the heathen do: for they think that they shall be heard for their much speaking.

8. Be not ye therefore like unto them: for your Father knoweth what things ye have need of, before ye ask him.

9. After this manner therefore pray ye: Our Father which art in heaven, Hallowed be thy name.

10. Thy kingdom come. Thy will be done in earth, as it is in heaven.

11. Give us this day our daily bread.

12. And forgive us our debts, as we forgive our debtors.

13. And lead us not into temptation, but deliver us from evil: For thine is the kingdom, and the power, and the glory, for ever. Amen.

Luke 6:12. And it came to pass in those days, that he went out into a mountain to pray, and continued all night in prayer to God.

13. And when it was day, he called unto him his disciples: and of them he chose twelve, whom also he named apostles.

Romans 15:4. For whatsoever things were written aforetime were written for our learning, that we through patience and comfort of the scriptures might have hope.

2 Timothy 2:15. Study to shew thyself approved unto God, a workman that needeth not to be ashamed, rightly dividing the word of truth.

3:16. All scripture is given by inspiration of God, and is profitable for doctrine, for reproof, for correction, for instruction in righteousness:

17. That the man of God may be perfect, throughly furnished unto all good works.

LESSON OUTLINE

I. SOLITUDE
   A. Seeking Spiritual Renewal
   B. Making Time for Solitude
   C. Practicing Solitude
   D. Having a Regular Place of Solitude

II. PRAYER
   A. Hypocritical Prayer
   B. Vain Prayer
   C. A Model Prayer
   D. Extended Times of Prayer

III. BIBLE STUDY
   A. God's Acts in the Past
   B. Approved and Disapproved Workers
   C. Study of Scripture

LESSON EXPOSITION

INTRODUCTION

Too often we look for revival as a catch-all outpouring of the Spirit brought on through a series of protracted church services. We are looking for instant gratification to our spiritual needs. Somehow we expect God to pour down His presence among us and change us without any regimented effort on our part. However, true revival comes when we practice spiritual discipline.

Paul said, "I beseech you therefore, brethren, by the mercies of God, that ye present your bodies a living sacrifice, holy, acceptable unto God, which is your reasonable service" (Romans 12:1). This speaks of daily self-controlled obedience to God's Word. "The purpose of spiritual disciplines is the total transformation of the person. They aim at replacing old destructive habits of thought with new life-giving habits" (Richard J. Foster, *Celebration of Discipline*, HarperCollins Publishers).

Our study will focus on three areas of discipline: *solitude, prayer* and *Bible study.*

Dietrich Bonhoeffer spoke of *solitude*: "Let him who cannot be alone beware of community. . . . Let him who is not in community beware of being alone. One who wants fellowship without solitude plunges into the void of words and feelings, and one who seeks solitude without fellowship perishes in the abyss of vanity, self-infatuation, and despair" (*Life Together*, HarperSan Francisco).

Prayer is the most central discipline for the spiritual life. It is the method God uses to transform us. If we are unwilling to be changed, we will quickly abandon prayer. However, if we really want God's will done in us, we will pray fervently and constantly.

The third discipline we will look at is *Bible study.* Many saints fail to grow spiritually because they refuse to develop healthy study habits. "They may sing with gusto, pray in the Spirit, live as obediently as they know, even receive divine visions and revelations, and yet the tenor of their lives remains unchanged. Why? Because they have never taken up one of the central ways that God uses to change us: study" (Foster).

If we check the lives of those who are confused and slow in spiritual growth, most often we will see it is because of ignorance of the Word. And this creates a bondage perpetuated from generation to generation. Children learn by what they see their parents doing. If we don't study the Scriptures, how will our children be motivated to do so? Our lack of study sets a horrible example of discipleship for those who come after us.

In contrast, those who do apply themselves to getting the Word into their hearts grasp what Paul said: "Be not conformed to this world: but be ye transformed by the renewing of your mind, that ye may prove what is that good, and acceptable, and perfect, will of God" (Romans 12:2).

Our primary purpose in life is to produce fruit that glorifies Christ. Jesus said, "I am the vine; ye are the branches: He that abideth in me, and I in him, the same bringeth forth much fruit: for without me ye can do nothing" (John 15:5). Staying connected to the Vine is the key to Christian lives. How do we stay connected? By maintaining spiritual disciplines.

I. SOLITUDE (Matthew 14:22, 23; Mark 1:35-39; Luke 22:39-41)

A. Seeking Spiritual Renewal (Matthew 14:22)

22. And straightway Jesus constrained his disciples to get into a ship, and to go before him unto the other side, while he sent the multitudes away.

Loneliness is a fearful state where we think no one cares; solitude is time wisely spent alone with the Lord. Jesus calls us to move from our loneliness to solitude. It is here we can hear Him speaking to our hearts.

Jesus was spiritually depleted at the time of our text. There had been little chance for Him to be alone with His Father. Looking back earlier in the chapter, we know He was grieving over the cruel execution of John the Baptist. He tried to escape the crowds not because of callousness to their needs, but because He craved private time to reflect, pray and be replenished. Verse 13 says, "When Jesus heard what had happened, he withdrew by boat privately to a solitary place" (NIV). Mark's rendition indicates that the 12 disciples were with Him (Mark 6:32). He likely had wanted them to see the value of time spent away from the crowds. That was not to be, however, for the multitudes soon found them.

In His fatigued state, Jesus still had compassion on the people, teaching and healing their sick. As evening approached, He even miraculously

fed them with just two fish and five loaves. All of this served, however, to further deplete Him and drive Him to seek escape.

The language of our text, using the imperative words *straightway* (immediately) and *constrained* (made or insisted), indicates how much Jesus yearned for a place of solitude. Not only that, He realized the disciples would much rather have enjoyed basking in the great miracle He had just performed. This would have added to their already prideful attitudes at being in His inner circle. Instead of basking, however, He directed them into a storm.

In directing the disciples to cross the Sea of Galilee without Him, Jesus finally had some time to Himself. The crowds, upon witnessing the spectacular miracle just performed, were so excited that they wanted to declare Jesus to be their king (John 6:14, 15), but not for the right motives. By getting away from the people, Jesus cooled their misplaced zeal and excitement.

B. Making Time for Solitude (v. 23)

23. And when he had sent the multitudes away, he went up into a mountain apart to pray: and when the evening was come, he was there alone.

After sending the disciples away and dispersing the crowd Himself, Jesus made His way up the mountain. The act of climbing had to be even further exhausting to His body. Was it necessary to have climbed the mountain? No, for "solitude is more a state of mind and heart than it is a place" (Foster). Still, there was something symbolic about climbing to a higher place in order to "see the forest and not just the trees." High above the lake, Jesus was able to watch the disciples as they faced the stiff wind. There is comfort for us here, for even as Jesus sent them into the storm He still had a watchful eye on them, making sure of their ultimate safety. Later that night He would come walking on the water to them.

C. Practicing Solitude (Mark 1:35-39)

(Mark 1:36-39 is not included in the printed text.)

35. And in the morning, rising up a great while before day, he went out, and departed into a solitary place, and there prayed.

Here again the surrounding verses reveal that Jesus was extremely busy preaching, teaching and healing. Also, He drove evil spirits out of many individuals. There is nothing more exhausting than ministry to extreme needs. If there is no spiritual refreshment during such intense ministry, spiritual resources are quickly depleted. In this situation we see that Jesus prayed. It wasn't just time alone in the Father's presence, but it was time spent asking for guidance and strength. Jesus had to be led by the Holy Spirit in all He did while on earth, and this was an early crucial time in His ministry.

The previous day of feverish ministry had been on a Sabbath. It was the following morning when He found time alone. This should be a pattern for anyone in church ministry. Sunday is a draining day. If time is not set aside on Monday for solitude and prayer, the new week will weaken a worker's spiritual condition. Finding solitude may sound impossible for those who have regular jobs during the week. However, whether alone or among people, the heart can still be a portable sanctuary.

Notice that it was "very early in the morning" (*NIV*) that Jesus slipped away to pray. Even though it wasn't long before the disciples went looking for Him, He had still broken away from the crowd to talk with His Father. By the time they found Him, He had replenished Himself and was ready for the challenges of the coming day (see vv. 36-39).

The tense of the verb *prayed* in verse 35 indicates a deliberate, concerted action. "Jesus' prayer life was successful because it was planned, private, and prolonged. He got up early enough, got far enough away, and stayed at it long enough" (*Nelson Study Bible*).

D. Having a Regular Place of Solitude (Luke 22:39-41)

39. And he came out, and went, as he was wont, to the mount of Olives; and his disciples also followed him.

40. And when he was at the place, he said unto them, Pray that ye enter not into temptation.

41. And he was withdrawn from them about a stone's cast, and kneeled down, and prayed.

Jesus was facing the ultimate test of His ministry—total sacrifice for the sins of humanity. Where did He go? The phrase "as he was wont," or "as usual" (*NIV*), tells us He had made a habit of going to a particular spot outside of Jerusalem. The Mount of Olives was just to the east of the city. On its southwestern slope was an olive grove called Gethsemane. This must have been a regular place of solitude for Jesus, for Judas knew where to find Him for betrayal.

Before Judas' arrival, Jesus left eight of the disciples at one spot in Gethsemane and took the three most intimate with Him to another location in the garden (see Mark 14:32, 33). This was the third time these three men had been given such opportunity. The first was at the raising of Jairus' daughter (Luke 8:41-56), the second at the Transfiguration (9:28-36). In each situation Jesus was dealing with death. We know that James would later be the first apostle martyred. Peter and John would prove to be the most prominent apostles (along with Paul) in the spread of the gospel, both suffering great persecution. Thus, these men were given special privilege.

Jesus moved a little further away to be by Himself. He knew what lay ahead for Him—that He would suffer humiliation, agony, abuse and death. He prayed three times that the "cup" would be removed (Matthew 26:39, 42, 44), and returned to the disciples three times, each time finding them sleeping. He desperately wanted their support, but they were ignorant of the impending horror He would go through. Luke tells us that an angel came and strengthened Him (22:43). It was this time of agonizing prayer alone that gave Him the determination to finish the work the Father had sent Him to do.

II. PRAYER (Matthew 6:5-13;
    Luke 6:12, 13)

A. Hypocritical Prayer (Matthew 6:5, 6)

(Matthew 6:5, 6 is not included in the printed text.)

A hypocrite is a person playing a role, that is, acting a part—looking for recognition. Many people think it makes them appear holy if they act religious in public. Flowery prayers were used by the religious leaders of Jesus' day as a means of getting attention. Jesus gave a clear warning here: Never pray, nor do anything else, to impress others. He didn't condemn praying in public, but simply the display of false piety.

A person who is truly interested in relationship with Christ will be drawn to private prayer. The prayer closet is any place one finds where he or she can regularly meet the Lord for fellowship. Here, the distractions of life can be forgotten and attention fully centered on the One who has the answers to all things.

B. Vain Prayer (vv. 7, 8)

7. But when ye pray, use not vain repetitions, as the heathen do:
for they think that they shall be heard for their much speaking.
8. Be not ye therefore like unto them: for your Father knoweth what things ye have need of, before ye ask him.

Pagan prayers often involved constant repetition of religious sayings and muttering the same phrase over and over. "Such action regards prayer as an effort to overcome God's unwillingness to respond by wearying him with words" (*Wycliffe Bible Commentary*). People who have a covenant relationship with God need not treat Him as an unwilling, hardhearted Lord. He wants to be spoken to as a Person who is interested in the needs of His people.

We should be careful not to let our prayer life become stale. It is easy to fall into the trap of praying for the same things over and over while our minds are elsewhere. Our words may sound pious, but real prayer doesn't begin until we are honestly expressing our thoughts, feelings, desires and needs to the Lord.

C. A Model Prayer (vv. 9-13)

9. After this manner therefore pray ye: Our Father which art in heaven, Hallowed be thy name.
10. Thy kingdom come. Thy will be done in earth, as it is in heaven.
11. Give us this day our daily bread.
12. And forgive us our debts, as we forgive our debtors.
13. And lead us not into temptation, but deliver us from evil: For thine is the kingdom, and the power, and the glory, for ever. Amen.

A more accurate title for the "Lord's Prayer" (vv. 9-13) would be the "Disciples' Prayer." It has been memorized by millions down through the centuries. However, Jesus never meant it to be a recitation, but rather a pattern to keep us from using vain repetitions. That pattern involves four parts—worship, petition, repentance and preservation.

The first step is to express concern for the sacred name of God and His kingdom. The phrase "Our Father which art in heaven" addresses God from a respectful yet intimate attitude. Pagans pray to mindless idols, while we have the privilege of addressing the Creator of the universe as our Father. The term *Father* evokes the image of One who provides for us, protects us, and gives us an identity as part of His family. Ours is a personal and intimate relationship.

The phrase "which art in heaven" shows that God reigns above and sees what is best for us. His domain is not confined to earthly influence alone.

The phrase "Hallowed be thy name" indicates a reverential attitude in approaching God. We exalt His name, character, holiness and authority.

After exalting His name, we pray that God establish His kingdom here, just like He rules in heaven. Jesus introduced the Kingdom through His earthly ministry, sacrificial death, and resurrection. The Kingdom is real right now within the hearts of people who accept Him. We pray and long for the day when it will be demonstrated to the entire world.

The second, third and fourth parts of the prayer deal with us as individuals. We have just seen that before we become self-focused, we should first honor God, that is, by making ourselves God-focused. Only then do we have the right to petition Him for our personal situations. The phrase "daily bread" encompasses much more than food. It indicates all those things that are required for a healthy life. The term *bread* is a reminder of how God fed the Israelites with manna in the wilderness.

After making ourselves God-focused, and after praying for our daily needs to be met, we next recognize our inherent sinfulness. The third part of the prayer is for forgiveness of sins. It is impossible to ask for

such, however, if we are harboring ill will toward someone else. We can't ask for forgiveness if we refuse to forgive.

The final part of the prayer is for preservation from evil. The previous part dealt with past sin. Now we ask for help to avoid future sin. James said, "When tempted, no one should say, 'God is tempting me.' For God cannot be tempted by evil, nor does he tempt anyone" (James 1:13, *NIV*). God is always working to refine us, and He does allow us to be tempted, but with every test He makes sure we have a way out (see 1 Corinthians 10:13). His testing is always for a purpose—to strengthen our character and make us more like Him.

D. Extended Times of Prayer
   (Luke 6:12, 13)

12. And it came to pass in those days, that he went out into a mountain to pray, and continued all night in prayer to God.
13. And when it was day, he called unto him his disciples: and of them he chose twelve, whom also he named apostles.

Prayer should always precede any important decision. As Jesus prepared to choose His closest disciples (men who would later be called *apostles*), He prayed all night for the Father's direction. Judging by their actions and attitudes during the three-year training period of Christ's ministry, one might think He had chosen foolishly. However, He was led by the Father's guidance in picking men with qualities that only needed to be unlocked by the Holy Spirit later operating in them. We know now just how wise His choices were.

This gives us hope when we are frustrated at our own weaknesses. Jesus took men who were as flawed as anyone and made great witnesses out of them. Jesus said once of the disciples, "You did not choose me, but I chose you and appointed you to go and bear fruit—fruit that will last" (John 15:16, *NIV*).

If Jesus took so much care as to pray long hours over His important decisions, how much more should we do the same thing!

III. BIBLE STUDY (Romans 15:4; 2 Timothy 2:15; 3:16, 17)

A. God's Acts in the Past (Romans 15:4)

4. For whatsoever things were written aforetime were written for our learning, that we through patience and comfort of the scriptures might have hope.

We gain hope from seeing how God worked for the benefit of His people in past times. This is the very reason He preserved His Word—that we might understand how to conform to His will and build a brighter future for ourselves. Study of the Word is the road map for the future. The more we know of what He has done already, the more we know *Him*—for we see what He desires of us.

Many Christians never grow because they never avail themselves to study. One typical excuse is "I hate to read." Even though they may be faithful to attend church, are involved in religious activities, and even have a regular prayer life, they still miss this basic means of hearing God speak. It is knowledge of the truth that sets people free. Jesus said, "If ye continue in my word, then are ye my disciples indeed; and ye shall know the truth, and the truth shall make you free" (John 8:31, 32). The word *free* means freedom from the bondage of sin. Study puts the Word in our hearts, and with that Word we are able to overcome temptation. Jesus quoted the Word to Satan when being tempted in the wilderness (Matthew 4). If He had to use the Word, how much more should we have it embedded in our hearts and minds!

Two key words stand out in our text: *patience* and *comfort*. As we study the lives of past saints recorded in the Word, we gain patience for the struggles we go through. We are encouraged by their example and receive comfort in the fact that God will see us through, just as He did them. Scripture gives the stories of people who pleased God, those who rebelled against Him, and others who failed but repented and learned from their failures. For virtually everything we could endure in this life, there has been someone in the recorded Word who has faced the same struggle. We can see there is great reason to have confidence in God.

B. Approved and Disapproved Workers (2 Timothy 2:15)

15. Study to shew thyself approved unto God, a workman that needeth not to be ashamed, rightly dividing the word of truth.

There are two kinds of Christian workers in this world—those who get the job done, and those who don't. The *ashamed* workman never seems to get things right even though he may be working hard. Contrastly, the *approved* workman builds on a solid foundation (v. 19). He is competent because he has studied, he knows right from wrong, and he handles the Word by having stored it in his heart. The term *rightly dividing* literally means "cutting straight." A contemporary rendition of this might be a "straight shooter."

Is study the same as meditation? No, for meditation is devotional in nature. Meditation relishes in the Word, while study analyzes it. Meditation relates back to our earlier point—solitude. Meditation is a reflective process, while study is a learning process. Study involves four steps:

1. *Repetition.* "Ingrained habits of thought can be formed by repetition alone, thus changing behavior" (Foster). No one fully learns a subject in one sitting. It takes reviewing constantly.

2. *Concentration.* This is the focusing of the mind on what is being studied. While the prayer closet is the best place for prayer, it is also the best place to study, away from distractions.

3. *Comprehension.* Many people think that to read the Bible through once or twice a year is study. However, if they don't understand what they are reading, little good has been accomplished. As Jesus said, it isn't truth alone that sets us free, but *knowledge of the truth* (John 8:32). Never before in history have there been so many available study tools as we have today. One only has to look for them.

4. *Reflection.* This is closely related to meditation. It is much like a cow "chewing the cud." We take what we have read, think on it, and search for ways to apply it to our hearts. "Reflection brings us to see things from God's perspective" (Foster).

Just studying the Word does not make a person a strong Christian. Accumulation of knowledge doesn't necessarily bring wisdom. Our study should be bathed in prayer and devotion. Only then can the Word we learn be fully applied to our lives.

C. Study of Scripture (3:16, 17)

16. All scripture is given by inspiration of God, and is profitable for doctrine, for reproof, for correction, for instruction in righteousness:

17. That the man of God may be perfect, throughly furnished unto all good works.

Scripture is the ultimate and primary place we should study. We live in an age when many excellent Christian books are written yearly, most of which expound some portion of Scripture. However, studying only books about the Bible gives opportunity for error, because the Word is being filtered through someone's opinion. When Paul said "all scripture," he referred primarily to the Old Testament, but also to the letters he had written. He was writing as an apostle of Jesus Christ. Even Peter verified that Paul's writings had the authority of Scripture (see 2 Peter 3:15, 16).

Scripture is valuable for four things: (1) *doctrine*—what we believe; (2) *reproof*—conviction of sins; (3) *correction*—setting something straight where there is confusion; (4) *instruction*—principles for training. The last one refers primarily to the process of training our children.

Only one of these, *doctrine*, has to do with knowledge. The other three involve training for change in us. Knowledge that doesn't change us is of no value. However, proper study of the Scriptures helps make believers *perfect* (complete), *throughly furnished* (thoroughly equipped) for whatever may come our way.

GOLDEN TEXT HOMILY

"WHEN HE [JESUS] HAD SENT THE MULTITUDES AWAY, HE WENT UP INTO A MOUNTAIN APART TO PRAY: AND WHEN THE EVENING WAS COME, HE WAS THERE ALONE" (Matthew 14:23).

I grew up in New York City. It is full of activity and teeming with people. For me, it was an energizing and fascinating place to live. I assumed that all there was to know and experience was to be found in the city. However, there were few places where one could really be alone and away from distractions.

An interesting phenomenon is that the lights of the city create a sort of canopy that effectively blocks out the night sky. Constellations and star clusters were to be seen only in the planetarium at the museum.

Then I came to Lee College in Cleveland, Tennessee. It was a dramatic change. Several of us students were out in the country one night and I was startled by the brilliance of the night sky. Without the lights of the city in the way, I could see it as never before. It was spectacular!

In Matthew 14:23 Jesus taught us by example the benefit of getting away from distractions to nurture our relationship with God. Jesus got alone to pray, and so must we.

Songwriter Charles Tindley, in his hymn "Nothing Between," wrote, "Nothing preventing the least of His favor. Keep the way clear! Let nothing between." When we "lay aside every weight, and the sin which so easily ensnares us," we can "run with endurance the race that is set before us" (Hebrews 12:1, *NKJV*). What a challenge; what a joy! May God help us to cultivate an uncluttered walk with Him.—**Benjamin Pérez**

SENTENCE SERMONS

SPIRITUAL DISCIPLINES are ways of spending time with God for the purpose of renewal and transformation.
—Selected

DEVELOP THE ART OF SOLITUDE and you will unearth the gift of serenity.
—William Ward

ONE OLD SAINT WAS ASKED, "Which is more important: reading God's Word or praying?" To which he replied, "Which is more important to a bird: the right wing or the left?"
—A.W. Tozer

EVANGELISM APPLICATION

A CHRISTIAN'S STRIVING FOR CHRISTLIKENESS IS A POWERFUL WITNESS TO AN UNSAVED WORLD.

When we practice a disciplined life, something happens as a by-product: We naturally reach out to others. People are touched by our witness. In our lesson we showed how Jesus condemned those who paraded their religiosity. However, when proper spiritual disciplines are in place in a humble heart, people are won to the Kingdom. Bearing fruit is not a tedious process. It is a natural outcome of being attached to the Vine. When we have the life-flow coming into us as branches, we cannot help but bear fruit. The spiritual disciplines give us the practical means of keeping that flow of life from the Vine into the branches viable and open.

DAILY BIBLE READINGS

M. Longing for God.
    Psalm 42:1-11
T. Righteousness Produces Quietness.
    Isaiah 32:14-20
W. Power Over Darkness.
    Mark 9:20-29
T. Praise the Triumphant King.
    Luke 19:37-40
F. Renewal Through the Holy Spirit.
    Titus 3:1-8
S. Draw Near to God.
    Hebrews 10:19-25

TRUTH SEARCH
Creatively Teaching the Word

DISCUSSION QUESTIONS

Solitude
(Matthew 14:22, 23; Mark 1:35-39; Luke 22:39-41)

1. What did Jesus do immediately after feeding the 5,000, and why (Matthew 14:22, 23)?

2. In Mark 1:35, when and why did Jesus get alone?

3. How did Jesus describe His purpose, and how did He carry it out in Galilee (vv. 38, 39)?

4. What was a custom of Jesus (Luke 22:39)? Why?

5. What did Jesus urge His disciples to do (v. 40)?

6. Why did Jesus get apart from His disciples (v. 41)?

Prayer
(Matthew 6:5-13; Luke 6:12, 13)

1. What is the reward for praying just to be seen (Matthew 6:5)?

2. What is the reward for sincere personal praying (v. 6)?

3. What is a vain way to pray (v. 7)?

4. Since God knows what we need before we pray (v. 8), why should we pray?

5. Based on the model Christ gave in Matthew 6:9-13, describe five aspects of Biblical prayer.

6. How can our relationship with other people affect our prayers (vv. 14, 15)?

7. In Luke 6, what is the connection between Jesus' actions in verse 12 and in verse 13?

Bible Study
(Romans 15:4; 2 Timothy 2:15; 3:16, 17)

1. How can the Scriptures help us (Romans 15:4)?

2. What does it mean to *correctly handle* ("rightly divide") the Word of God (2 Timothy 2:15), and why is this important?

3. What does "by inspiration of God" mean (3:16)?

4. Describe the various functions of Scripture (v. 16).

5. What can the study and application of Scripture accomplish in our lives (v. 17)?

SKIT

Items: Bible, cell phone, radio, newspaper, ball

To illustrate the need to find a place of solitude, have three volunteers help with the following skit.

One person (Seeker) will come forward, sit in a chair, and pretend to read a Bible. Seeker has a cell phone.

After 30 seconds, start playing the radio. Seeker still tries to read the Bible while swaying to the music. Thirty seconds later, have someone come forward with the ball and stand next to the chair, pleading for Seeker to come play. Seeker covers one ear with his hand while still swaying to the music and trying to read.

Next, the cell phone starts ringing and won't stop. Thirty seconds later, someone comes in with the newspaper, yelling, "Big news! Read all about it!" He tosses the paper onto Seeker's lap, yet continues to stand there yelling, "Read all about it!"

All the sounds should continue, getting louder and louder. After about 30 seconds, Seeker slowly stands, Bible in hand. Placing the phone and newspaper in your hand, he quietly leaves the room. All the noises continue for about a minute, then fade and finally stop as you come forward.

Talk about the importance of regularly spending time alone with God, even though the pressures of life may demand otherwise. We sometimes have to push everything else aside to focus on Him.

HEb, 13. 8   *Luke 2. 37 ANNa She, Pray.*

Renewal Through Praise

Study Text: Psalms 92:1-5; 100:1-5; 107:1, 2, 31, 32; 134:1-3; Hebrews 13:15, 16

Objective: To understand that praise is essential to renewal and exalt God with grateful hearts.

Golden Text: "By [Christ] therefore let us offer the sacrifice of praise to God continually . . . for with such sacrifices God is well pleased" (Hebrews 13:15, 16).

Central Truth: Praising God precedes and follows renewal.

Evangelism Emphasis: A Christian's life of praise is a witness to the lost.

PRINTED TEXT

Psalm 92:1. It is a good thing to give thanks unto the Lord, and to sing praises unto thy name, O most High:

2. To shew forth thy lovingkindness in the morning, and thy faithfulness every night,

3. Upon an instrument of ten strings, and upon the psaltery; upon the harp with a solemn sound.

4. For thou, Lord, hast made me glad through thy work: I will triumph in the works of thy hands.

5. O Lord, how great are thy works! and thy thoughts are very deep.

134:1. Behold, bless ye the Lord, all ye servants of the Lord, which by night stand in the house of the Lord.

2. Lift up your hands in the sanctuary, and bless the Lord.

3. The Lord that made heaven and earth bless thee out of Zion.

Hebrews 13:15. By him therefore let us offer the sacrifice of praise to God continually, that is, the fruit of our lips giving thanks to his name.

16. But to do good and to communicate forget not: for with such sacrifices God is well pleased.

Psalm 100:1. Make a joyful noise unto the Lord, all ye lands.

2. Serve the Lord with gladness: come before his presence with singing.

3. Know ye that the Lord he is God: it is he that hath made us, and not we ourselves; we are his people, and the sheep of his pasture.

4. Enter into his gates with thanksgiving, and into his courts with praise: be thankful unto him, and bless his name.

5. For the Lord is good; his mercy is everlasting; and his truth endureth to all generations.

107:1. O give thanks unto the Lord, for he is good: for his mercy endureth for ever.

2. Let the redeemed of the Lord say so, whom he hath redeemed from the hand of the enemy;

31. Oh that men would praise the Lord for his goodness, and for his wonderful works to the children of men!

32. Let them exalt him also in the congregation of the people, and praise him in the assembly of the elders.

LESSON OUTLINE

I. PRAISE AS SACRIFICE
   A. Corporate Sabbath Praise
   B. Worship Through the Night
   C. Continual Sacrifice of Praise

II. PRAISE AS RESPONSE
   A. Let the Whole Earth Praise God
   B. Serve With Gladness and Singing
   C. Enter With Thanksgiving and Praise

III. PRAISE AS GRATITUDE
   A. Praise for God's Enduring Mercy
   B. Praise for Redemption
   C. Praise for God's Great Works
   D. Testify to the Congregation

LESSON EXPOSITION

INTRODUCTION

One of the commands most frequently given to us in Scripture is to praise the Lord. This is not just for the Lord's sake (though He inhabits our praise), but for ours as well. If we will set our hearts toward praising Him in every situation, then we can expect revival. *To Live Victory*

I. PRAISE AS SACRIFICE
(Psalms 92:1-5; 134:1-3; Hebrews 13:15, 16)

A. Corporate Sabbath Praise
(Psalm 92:1-5)

1. It is a good thing to give thanks unto the Lord, and to sing praises unto thy name, O most High:
2. To shew forth thy lovingkindness in the morning, and thy faithfulness every night,
3. Upon an instrument of ten strings, and upon the psaltery; upon the harp with a solemn sound.
4. For thou, Lord, hast made me glad through thy work: I will triumph in the works of thy hands.

5. O Lord, how great are thy works! and thy thoughts are very deep.

This psalm expresses delight in Sabbath Day worship services at the Temple. Although very personal, it speaks of praise on a corporate level. Something wonderful occurs when the people of God get together and praise Him in a spirit of unity. The psalmist lists various instruments that were used in his day, and then proclaims the reason for praising God—because of His wonderful works.

Praising God pleases Him. "It is our duty, the rent, the tribute, we are to pay to our great Lord; we are unjust if we withhold it. It is our privilege that we are admitted to praise God, and have hope to be accepted in it" (*Matthew Henry*). No matter the circumstances we face, praising God recognizes that He is the authority, He is the controller, He is the One who vindicates us. His rule over earth is pure, never capricious, and His faithfulness toward His people is forever.

Titled "A Psalm or Song for the Sabbath Day," it was intended for Sabbath worship, in the same way that Psalm 81 was meant to be used at Passover. *Morning* and *night* comprise the entire day, alluding to the morning and night sacrifices that were made on the Sabbath Day at the Temple.

Throughout the last hundred or more years of evangelical Christianity, Sunday night services were an ingrained part of the church community. In recent times, however, the trend has been for believers to make Sunday evenings a time of family activity and bonding. While it is true that the pace of modern lifestyles has left little opportunity for parents and children to spend quality time together, one could make the argument from this psalm that God intended the Sabbath in its entirety to be time spent with Him. It is a sad commentary on our times to see that people don't want to be in the house of the Lord on Sunday evenings.

"The Sabbath is the day that God has hallowed, and that is to be consecrated to God by our turning away from the business pursuits of the working days (Isaiah 58:13) and applying ourselves to the praise and adoration of God, which is the most proper, blessed Sabbath employment" (Keil & Delitzsch). If we want to see revival in our day, we must be willing to give time to praising God corporately. Praise is good for God and for us.

The statement in verse 5, "O Lord, how great are thy works!" indicates that the worshiper is spending time meditating on the overwhelming great things God has done. Unless time is consciously allotted for such reflection, we soon take God for granted. We lose track of the prayers He has answered unless we stop to see that He did indeed answer our requests and has shown wonderful kindness to us. Most Christians are so busy begging God to take care of some current crisis that they fail to acknowledge His answers to their last petitions.

In looking back we see that many of our daunting quandaries and calamities proved to be trivial. But were they really trivial—or did God answer prayers concerning such? In taking the time to reflect on God's goodness, we see that He really does take care of us. Acknowledging His care is more than a courtesy. It blesses God for us to bless Him.

Praise and thanksgiving thus are basic necessities for the Christian life. We should make a regimen of thanking God in the mornings and evenings for salvation (through His Son Jesus Christ), for His guidance and care over us, and for His love and grace toward us.

B. Worship Through the Night
   (134:1-3)

1. Behold, bless ye the Lord, all ye servants of the Lord, which by night stand in the house of the Lord.

2. Lift up your hands in the sanctuary, and bless the Lord.

3. The Lord that made heaven and earth bless thee out of Zion.

This psalm addresses the value of those who are willing to worship and intercede in God's house throughout the night. It is one of the psalms used by pilgrims going up to Jerusalem for festivals (especially the Feast of Tabernacles), and was often sung at the close of the services at evening sacrifice. Here we see that the lifting of hands toward the Lord is an admirable act of worship. Such body language indicates an attitude of prayer and blessing toward the Lord.

The *servants of the Lord* were primarily the Levites. They were charged with tending the Lord's house, guarding the holy items in the Temple, making sure nothing was profaned or looted. They also made certain that the fires on the altar and the candlesticks never went out. To do such, some had to stay awake and alert through the night. It was also likely down through the centuries of Israel's history for devout worshipers to remain at the Temple praying through the night. Luke 2:37 describes such a person in the prophetess Anna: "She never left the temple but worshiped night and day, fasting and praying" (*NIV*).

"There is something favorable to devotion in the silence of the night; when the world sleeps; when we are alone with God; when it seems as if God would more particularly attend to our cry since the rest of the world is still, and does not (as it were) need His care. All this may be fancy; but the effect may be to make the mind more solemn, and better suited for devotion" (*Barnes' Notes*).

This psalm, though very short, has two parts. Verses 1 and 2 are an exhortation from the high priest directed to the priests and Levites who kept watch at night. They were to redeem the night hours in the Temple by blessing the Lord, not merely sitting by numbly. To "bless the Lord" is to speak of His good name, to proclaim the wonders He has done. The second part (v. 3) is a response by the night-keepers toward the high priest—a blessing of God on him.

The practice of all-night prayer meetings, given precedence by this psalm, is a lost art in our generation. Duncan Campbell, in describing the efforts that resulted in the Hebrides revival (1949-54), said, "We were in revival, and in revival time doesn't exist. Nobody was looking at the clock" ("When the Mountains Flowed Down"). For revival and renewal to take place, the body of Christ has to be willing to give its time, day and night, to praise, worship, petition and blessing of the Lord.

In the same message, Campbell described another night's protracted service: "The meeting lasted unto four o'clock in the morning, and I had not witnessed anything to compare with it at any other time during my ministry. Around midnight, a group of young people left a dance and crowded into the church. There were people who couldn't go to sleep because they were so gripped by God."

If we will make ourselves willing to forget the clock and give ourselves to prayer into the late hours, God will again meet us in mighty ways.

C. Continual Sacrifice of Praise (Hebrews 13:15, 16)

15. By him therefore let us offer the sacrifice of praise to God continually, that is, the fruit of our lips giving thanks to his name.

16. But to do good and to communicate forget not: for with such sacrifices God is well pleased.

In the Hebrew system of worship, sacrifices were offered at specified times. Because Christ offered Himself as the ultimate sacrifice, there is no need for any further blood to be shed.

The sacrifice for the Christian is constant praise and acknowledgment of Christ. Paul urged the Romans (as well as all believers) "to offer your bodies as living sacrifices, holy and pleasing to God—this is your spiritual act of worship" (Romans 12:1, *NIV*). First Peter 2:5 says that believers are "like living stones . . . being built into a spiritual house to be a holy priesthood, offering spiritual sacrifices acceptable to God through Jesus Christ" (*NIV*).

These praises should not just be a mental assent, but rather words spoken from our lips. Speaking forth praise puts action to what is felt in the heart. We should continually confess God's name in praise, both when we are alone and when others are in hearing distance.

Praise of God is extended to doing good toward others (Hebrews 13:16). To *communicate* means "to share." Acts of kindness—sharing our time, resources, testimonies and listening ears—are all spiritual sacrifices given in the name of Christ and for His glory. With such God is well pleased.

II. PRAISE AS RESPONSE (Psalm 100:1-5)

A. Let the Whole Earth Praise God (v. 1)

1. Make a joyful noise unto the Lord, all ye lands.

The Hebrew verb interpreted as "make" is a command. It is a charge for all to shout acclamation as they would when a new king ascends his throne. We see this when Solomon was anointed king by the priest Zadok. The trumpeters "blew the trumpet; and all the people said, God save king Solomon" (1 Kings 1:39).

This charge to make a joyful noise is not just to Israel, but to all the nations of the earth. Israel was the nation to whom God had revealed Himself, but their purpose for existence was to draw all other peoples into worship of Jehovah. The ancient

Jews never grasped this truth, although they did recognize that all nations of the earth were to be blessed by them in some way. Instead of seeing their holy purpose, the Jewish people saw themselves as exclusive, the elect, the special ones. They were special only in that they were to be the means of revelation of salvation to everyone. This, of course, came with the sacrifice and resurrection of Jesus.

B. Serve With Gladness and Singing (vv. 2, 3)

2. Serve the Lord with gladness: come before his presence with singing.
3. Know ye that the Lord he is God: it is he that hath made us, and not we ourselves; we are his people, and the sheep of his pasture.

One can be a subject under a king and serve dutifully, but the psalmist here calls for all to serve with absolute submission. David had to deal many times with citizens who bowed to him publicly, but secretly held rebellion against him in their hearts. True worshipers lay down any hesitations, resentments and reservations, giving themselves totally and humbly to their king with joyful abandon. Singing is an expression of that willing heart. "In song we remember that he created us and redeemed us, and that we are now his people and he is our shepherd" (*Full Life Study Bible*).

This joyous praise is freely offered because God is the source of highest joy. It is the joy of knowing that we who are as weak, defenseless, and helpless as sheep have been rescued and are being cared for by the Good Shepherd.

The psalmist acknowledges that humans are creations of the Lord. We did not create ourselves, neither are we the center of the world. If we try to set ourselves up on the throne of our heart, we will ultimately lose everything, including hope itself. We can fully enjoy life only as we realize that everything proceeds from God.

Simply put, there are three reasons given in verse 3 for praising God:
1. The Lord is God. He is the Creator and we are the creation.
2. He made us in His image and for His pleasure. We are not our own.
3. God shepherds His people. He is not aloof. Instead, He is active in our lives. Even when we feel nothing is happening, something is happening. He is always working in our behalf.

C. Enter With Thanksgiving and Praise (vv. 4, 5)

4. Enter into his gates with thanksgiving, and into his courts with praise: be thankful unto him, and bless his name.
5. For the Lord is good; his mercy is everlasting; and his truth endureth to all generations.

Though literally speaking of entering the physical Temple in Jerusalem for worship, still God's people are encouraged to recognize they can step into His manifest presence as they corporately worship. Certainly God is everywhere, but coming together entreats a more intense awareness of His presence. Recognizing that truth, we should always enter with a proper posture and heart. We should not come with gloom and doom, but rather with joyous praise and thanksgiving. Such an attitude recognizes that no matter what we might be facing, we know He has an answer.

God is not capricious. He is not for us at one time, and against us at another. He remains faithful forever. We can surely count on Him. Goodness is part of His very nature. "Mercy and compassion are modifications of his goodness; and as his nature is eternal, so his mercy, springing from his goodness, must be everlasting" (*Adam Clarke's Commentary*).

III. PRAISE AS GRATITUDE (Psalm 107:1, 2, 31, 32)

A. Praise for God's Enduring Mercy
(v. 1)

1. O give thanks unto the Lord, for he is good: for his mercy endureth for ever.

This psalm exhorts the redeemed of God to give thanks for deliverance from terrible situations. There are four types of troubles pointed out that come against His people: hunger and thirst (vv. 4-9); bondage (vv. 10-16); desperate illness (vv. 17-22); storms (vv. 23-32).

We can cry out to God today when these same perils come against us. Does God actually deliver us every time? No, for many faithful believers have suffered and died from all these causes. Did God hear the pleas of these people? Yes, but He also is sovereign, and sees a larger picture. We should always go to Him expecting positive answers, but willing to keep our faith intact if He doesn't do as we ask.

The answer to this dilemma can be found in Jesus' response to John the Baptist's cry from prison. Sitting alone in Herod's cell, John grew doubtful that Jesus was really the Messiah and sent a questioning message to Him. Jesus replied with a report of wonderful miracles taking place, but He added one peculiar line: "Blessed is the man who does not fall away on account of me" (Matthew 11:6, *NIV*). In other words, "Blessed is the person who believes and worships despite the fact that I may not answer his or her prayer, still embracing the reality of who I am without having to see deliverance."

The writer of Hebrews says, "Now faith is the substance of things hoped for, the evidence of things not seen" (11:1). Of course, this is the beginning of the great faith chapter of the Bible. Yet, none of the great heroes enumerated there saw the promises of God fulfilled in their lifetimes. No, they were trusting God for the future—for eternity. They gave thanks because God is good and His mercy endures forever. Thanksgiving for God's mercy should always be on the lips of the believer no matter whether prayers receive the desired answer or not.

B. Praise for Redemption (v. 2)

2. Let the redeemed of the Lord say so, whom he hath redeemed from the hand of the enemy.

This psalm was likely composed upon the return of the people from captivity in Babylon. It is a lesson in the Lord's mercy and kindness to His people. Again, as we mentioned in verse 1, God's redemption does not necessarily mean great ease and comfort. We only have to read of the difficult circumstances the returning pilgrims to Palestine faced to see that life was not a bed of roses. Still, God had done great. The people were preserved. He had been faithful, and would continue to be faithful. If God has shown Himself faithful, then we should let everyone know such by proclaiming His goodness to all who will listen.

C. Praise for God's Great Works
(v. 31)

31. Oh that men would praise the Lord for his goodness, and for his wonderful works to the children of men!

In this verse the psalmist cries out for people who have seen the deliverance of God (especially in the case of peril at sea—vv. 23-30) to acknowledge who it was that brought their deliverance. God frequently brings us to a place where we can do nothing for ourselves but cry out to Him. No human can help us. Only divine intervention will do. Too often, however, as soon as the deliverance has been accomplished, we forget who it was that answered our cries. We should regularly look back to see how God has delivered us, and give Him the appropriate credit and praise for His help.

D. Testify to the Congregation (v. 32)

32. Let them exalt him also in the congregation of the people, and praise him in the assembly of the elders.

God's rescuing us from peril deserves not only a heart of praise, but a mouth that speaks joyfully to the congregation. In many evangelical churches there used to be regular nights for "testimony services." Saints would stand and give public thanks to God for some wonderful work He had done recently in their lives. We need to hear testimonies in our worship today. We should acknowledge God's work "not merely in private, but in public. As His doings are public and conspicuous—as they pertain to all—people should acknowledge Him in their public capacity, or when assembled together" (*Barnes' Notes*).

GOLDEN TEXT HOMILY

"BY [CHRIST] THEREFORE LET US OFFER THE SACRIFICE OF PRAISE TO GOD CONTINUALLY . . . FOR WITH SUCH SACRIFICES GOD IS WELL PLEASED" (Hebrews 13:15, 16).

The *New International Version* renders verse 15: "Let us continually offer to God a sacrifice of praise—the fruit of lips that confess his name."

To confess the lovely name of Jesus is to live a life that pleases God. We are called upon to confess His name in both word and deed, in good times and in bad times. A sacrifice (offering) of praise is what God calls upon each born-again believer to give.

Our faith must be fixed upon Christ, who is "the same yesterday, and to day, and for ever" (v. 8). With our faith fixed in Him, we shall not be carried about by every strange doctrine that comes along. Instead, we will live a committed life which will bring praise, honor, and glory to God the Father who sent His Son into the world that we might have eternal life.

We are not to be ashamed of the death of Christ or His redemption by blood. Instead, we are to share the reproach that sinful people place upon Him and in so doing confess He is Lord. Even in this age of tolerance there are still times when we may be ostracized for our faith. Yes, there is a social ostracism that Christians must endure, even in our day. This is often the posture of the believer who refuses to compromise his faith in Christ.

To be shut out from the circle of evildoers is to be drawn near to God. A life set apart from sinful practices is one that lifts up the name of Jesus. Let us pursue the good life—the life that exalts the One who gave His life for us.

Let our prayer each day be this: "May the words of my mouth and the meditation of my heart be pleasing in your sight, O Lord, my Rock and my Redeemer" (Psalm 19:14, *NIV*).—**Selected**

SENTENCE SERMONS

PRAISING GOD precedes and follows renewal.

—Selected

TO WORSHIP means to recognize supreme worth.

—Harold Bonnell

WORSHIP IS AT THE HEART of the battle between God and Satan.

—Ron Owens

EVANGELISM APPLICATION

A CHRISTIAN'S LIFE OF PRAISE IS A WITNESS TO THE LOST.

Just prior to the writing of this lesson, a terrible hurricane was bearing down on the Gulf Coast of the United States. Classified as a category 4 storm, it was expected to wreak havoc on a large population of Southern states. On the night before its anticipated landfall, churches everywhere prayed that somehow God would stay the storm. People cried out for the Lord's mercy.

Amazingly, the next day that terrible storm fizzled out to nearly nothing, merely dumping large amounts of rain in Texas, Louisiana and Mississippi. Only minor damage was reported. Sadly, the media almost totally ignored the fact that God had intervened. Mostly, people just assumed this was a fluke of nature.

Often we miss the great things God has done for us. The fact that He answers our prayers before things happen often allows us the time to forget to thank Him. In our lesson we have seen that praise to God is always good. He deserves our thanksgiving because He is sovereign. He watches out for us. So much more evil and destruction could come our way, but He prevents it.

How will the world know if we don't publicly acknowledge what He has done? Our praise should be vocal to everyone, not only among other believers but among the general public as well. The testimony of His goodness, coupled with the work of the Holy Spirit in bringing conviction to people's hearts, will work toward bringing revival and renewal to a lost generation.

ILLUMINATING THE LESSON

Most of our lesson here on praising God deals with public praise and public worship services. David said, "I was glad when they said unto me, Let us go into the house of the Lord" (Psalm 122:1). At a time when many people, including Christians, are slack in their attendance to worship services, we should remind ourselves that God desires corporate worship. There are many reasons for churches to come together as a body:

• Together the body can be taught and led in worship by the shepherd.

• Together the body can hear how other believers are struggling, growing, and living out their faith. All are encouraged as they share one with another.

• Together the body can reflect on the needs of others around them.

• Together the body gets a message from the Lord, instead of the constant barrage of the secular culture in daily life.

• Together they can be still before the Lord and hear Him speak.

• Together they can raise their voices in unified praise.

• Together they can confess their sins and find forgiveness and acceptance.

God never intended that His people be islands unto themselves. We were meant for community. We should never forsake the visible church, but rather embrace the nurture, correction, and fellowship that it gives us.

DAILY BIBLE READINGS

M. Praise for Deliverance.
   Genesis 14:17-20
T. Praise With the Congregation.
   Psalm 22:19-24
W. A Fountain of Youth.
   Psalm 103:1-5
T. Example for Others.
   Matthew 5:13-16
F. Gratitude for Daily Renewal.
   2 Corinthians 5:6-17
S. Method of Renewing the Mind.
   Philippians 4:4-8

TRUTH SEARCH
Creatively Teaching the Word

DISCUSSION QUESTIONS
Praise as Sacrifice
(Psalms 92:1-5; 134:1-3; Hebrews 13:15, 16)

1. What is the significance of the name ascribed to the Lord in Psalm 92:1?

2. Why is the morning an especially good time to praise God for His love, and why is night the perfect time to worship Him for His faithfulness (vv. 2, 3)?

3. In verses 4 and 5, why did the psalmist say he would worship God?

4. What should we do for God (Psalm 134:1), and what will He do for us (v. 3)?

5. What is the significance of lifting up one's hands in worship (v. 2)?

6. In Hebrews 13:15, why is praising God called a sacrifice?

7. What other "sacrifices" bring glory to God (v. 16)?

Praise as Response
(Psalm 100:1-5)

1. Who should worship God (v. 1)?

2. What is a proper attitude in worship (v. 2)?

3. Why should we worship God (vv. 3, 5)?

4. How should we worship Him (v. 4)?

Praise as Gratitude
(Psalm 107:1, 2, 31, 32)

1. Why should we "give thanks unto the Lord" (v. 1)?

2. Why is God called a Redeemer, and why should this spur us to praise Him (v. 2)?

3. How does God prove His *goodness* ("unfailing love," v. 31)?

4. Name some of God's "wonderful works" (v. 31).

5. Why is it important to praise the Lord together "in the assembly of the people" (v. 32, *NIV*)?

ILLUSTRATED PRAISE

Items needed: Paper, pencils, markers

Distribute paper and writing tools to all the students. Ask them to draw simple illustrations expressing worship to God. If some choose to express their praise with written words instead of pictures, that's fine.

After a couple of minutes, let students break into small groups to display their praise illustrations. Or, if your class is small, let students take turns displaying their work to the entire group.

Finally, lead everyone in worshiping God together by lifting hands and speaking out praises.

Passion for Christ

Study Text: Philippians 3:1-21
Objective: To appreciate passion for Christ and desire to be like Him.
Time: A.D. 63
Place: Written from a Roman prison
Golden Text: "I count all things but loss for the excellency of the knowledge of Christ Jesus my Lord" (Philippians 3:8).
Central Truth: Knowing Christ reveals the true value of all other attachments.
Evangelism Emphasis: Believers who have a passion for Christ will obey the Great Commission.

PRINTED TEXT

Philippians 3:1. Finally, my brethren, rejoice in the Lord. To write the same things to you, to me indeed is not grievous, but for you it is safe.

2. Beware of dogs, beware of evil workers, beware of the concision.

3. For we are the circumcision, which worship God in the spirit, and rejoice in Christ Jesus, and have no confidence in the flesh.

4. Though I might also have confidence in the flesh. If any other man thinketh that he hath whereof he might trust in the flesh, I more:

5. Circumcised the eighth day, of the stock of Israel, of the tribe of Benjamin, an Hebrew of the Hebrews; as touching the law, a Pharisee;

6. Concerning zeal, persecuting the church; touching the righteousness which is in the law, blameless.

7. But what things were gain to me, those I counted loss for Christ.

8. Yea doubtless, and I count all things but loss for the excellency of the knowledge of Christ Jesus my Lord: for whom I have suffered the loss of all things, and do count them but dung, that I may win Christ,

9. And be found in him, not having mine own righteousness, which is of the law, but that which is through the faith of Christ, the righteousness which is of God by faith:

10. That I may know him, and the power of his resurrection, and the fellowship of his sufferings, being made conformable unto his death;

11. If by any means I might attain unto the resurrection of the dead.

12. Not as though I had already attained, either were already perfect: but I follow after, if that I may apprehend that for which also I am apprehended of Christ Jesus.

13. Brethren, I count not myself to have apprehended: but this one thing I do, forgetting those things which are behind, and reaching forth unto those things which are before,

14. I press toward the mark for the prize of the high calling of God in Christ Jesus.

20. For our conversation is in heaven; from whence also we look for the Saviour, the Lord Jesus Christ:

21. Who shall change our vile body, that it may be fashioned like unto his glorious body, according to the working whereby he is able even to subdue all things unto himself.

LESSON OUTLINE

I. REJECT ALL SUBSTITUTES
    A. Finally, Rejoice
    B. Beware of Those Who Distort the Truth
    C. Paul's Right to Boast
    D. Counted Loss for Christ

II. SEEK TO KNOW CHRIST
    A. Seek the Knowledge of Christ
    B. Seek the Righteousness of Christ
    C. Seek the Fellowship of His Sufferings
    D. Seek the Resurrection of the Dead

III. STRIVE TO BE LIKE CHRIST
    A. Winning the Race
    B. An Example to Follow
    C. Heavenly-Mindedness

LESSON EXPOSITION

INTRODUCTION

The church at Philippi was the first founded on European soil. While on his second missionary journey, and responding to a vision, Paul left Troas and traveled to Macedonia, when Philippi was located.

Philippi was a Roman military colony, the highest status a provincial city could attain. Citizens could own property and were exempt from poll and land taxes. This status gave them a confidence bordering on arrogance. They were not just a conquered people; they were a viable part of the empire. Many were affluent, and Paul's first convert there was Lydia (Acts 16:14), an upper-class businesswoman who sold purple, an expensive dye. To the believers living in this prosperous area, Paul's letter presented Jesus as one clothed in humility. He is both human and divine, gentle, and accessible to everyone. He willingly laid down His rights to take the role of a servant.

The church here had a mixture of people, primarily Gentile, but still with some Jews who tried to hold to old customs. The letter to them was written nearly a decade after the church was established. The people had learned of Paul's trial in Jerusalem, difficult times afterward, and subsequent imprisonment in Rome. The news caused sympathy for him, and they sent funds to help in his situation. This was typical of their charitable attitude. Epaphroditus, the messenger from the church, had brought their gifts to Paul, and in turn had become seriously ill while in Rome. Paul considered his recovery an answer to prayer (Philippians 2:25-27), and sent him back to Philippi with the letter.

Chapter 3 is the text for this particular lesson. Here Paul shows there is no greater joy than that of knowing the secret of life—that righteousness comes from God by faith in Christ. It isn't achieved by human effort, that is, keeping a set of legal codes and rituals. Salvation comes only by personal knowledge of Christ and daily relationship with Him. Knowing Christ is the only thing that can change the human condition. It is His resurrection power operating in the believer that produces a transformation of character and guarantees life after death.

Our text begins with the statement "Finally, my brethren, rejoice in the Lord" (3:1).

It's as if Paul was about to close his letter. Possibly he had taken a break from dictating to his scribe (Timothy, Luke, or one of his other associates) and had returned to finish—when suddenly, an inspiration from the Holy Spirit moved into another subject. Or, maybe he had just gotten his second wind. Whatever was going on in his heart, the exhortation to "rejoice in the Lord" was intended as a precedent to what was about to be said. His readers were to keep the joyful spirit he had already been speaking of, even though his next thoughts would deal with unpleasant and difficult matters.

Paul constantly dealt with Judaizer Christians who wanted Gentile converts to obey Jewish traditions and rituals, namely the ceremonial law of Moses. Most Jewish believers were so ingrained in the Law that they had a terrible time recognizing freedom in Christ. Paul was aware of Judaizers among the Philippian church and was taking steps to make sure Gentile believers didn't sacrifice their freedom to someone else's convictions.

I. REJECT ALL SUBSTITUTES (Philippians 3:1-7)

A. Finally, Rejoice (v. 1)

1. Finally, my brethren, rejoice in the Lord. To write the same things to you, to me indeed is not grievous, but for you it is safe.

The word *finally* would seem to indicate that Paul is about to end the letter. However, he more likely means *furthermore*. He changes subjects and warns his readers about false teachers. Interestingly, the Judaizers' determination to incorporate Jewish traditions as integral to Christianity had not yet become a serious threat to the Philippian church, but it was hounding other congregations. The entire letter of Galatians had been written to refute their maneuvering.

Rejoicing in the Lord would be a safeguard against anything the Judaizers might attempt. It would also keep true believers from despondency in the face of opposition. Nothing, no matter how grievous, should interfere with one's joy in the Lord. In fact, some form of the word *joy* occurs 12 times in the letter.

The Judaizers were guilty of attitudes of spiritual superiority. They sought to bring dissension and disunity through their grumbling. Maintaining joy at all times would help the Philippian Christians remain free from the Judaizers' nasty spirit. A complaining spirit and disunity don't harmonize with joy in Christ.

B. Beware of Those Who Distort the Truth (vv. 2, 3)

2. Beware of dogs, beware of evil workers, beware of the concision.

3. For we are the circumcision, which worship God in the spirit, and rejoice in Christ Jesus, and have no confidence in the flesh.

The gospel came first to the Jews, but God made it known they did not have a monopoly on the good news. The first seven chapters of Acts describe an early church made up of Jews and proselytes to Judaism. In Acts 8, the message spread to the Samaritans. An uproar began, however, with chapter 10 when Peter went to the Gentiles. Gentiles were becoming Christians without first becoming Jews. Paul further deepened the conflict when he was sent out especially to the Gentiles (13:1-3). Soon Jewish believers were following him everywhere to "correct" his teaching. Even after the Jerusalem Council settled the issue in Acts 15, the dissenters continued their fight. Trying to mix law and grace, these false teachers became known as Judaizers.

Paul describes them here with harsh terms, calling them *dogs* and *evil workers*. The word *concision* means "mutilation." Paul was saying that circumcision by itself was only a mutilation of the body and served no purpose. Real circumcision is one of the heart, or a spiritual circumcision (Colossians 2:11) where sin and evil are cut away. No religious act, ritual or practice can save a person. Only faith in Christ can remove sin.

There is nothing anyone can do in the flesh to improve on what Christ has already done by providing salvation by grace. Jesus said, "The Spirit gives life; the flesh counts for nothing" (John 6:63, *NIV*). "The Bible has nothing good to say about 'flesh,' and yet most people today depend entirely on what they themselves can do to please God" (Warren Wiersbe, *Be Joyful*).

C. Paul's Right to Boast (vv. 4-6)

4. Though I might also have confidence in the flesh. If any other man thinketh that he hath whereof he might trust in the flesh, I more:

5. Circumcised the eighth day, of the stock of Israel, of the tribe of Benjamin, an Hebrew of the Hebrews; as touching the law, a Pharisee;

6. Concerning zeal, persecuting the church; touching the righteousness which is in the law, blameless.

Paul could criticize the Judaizers because he had once walked in their shoes. He himself had tried, like them, to achieve righteousness by living the Law to the letter. He had attempted to earn salvation by doing good works. In fact, he could probably look at these people and point out all their shortcomings—for he had exceeded them all. As a young student he had sat at the feet of Gamaliel, the pinnacle of Jewish teachers. Paul had been seen in Jerusalem as the next great rabbi. His rising star was already bright on the horizon. Yet, he gave it all up to become a member of a band of "heretics" known as Christians.

Paul spent a moment reflecting on his heritage and exploits—not that he desired to go back there, but rather to show the futility of it all. He had been born into a pure Hebrew family, from the tribe of Benjamin. This in itself was a point of pride, for Benjamin had been one of Jacob's two favorite sons (the other being Joseph), both born to Rachel, Jacob's one true love. By Jewish standards, Paul was a blueblood. He had also been a Pharisee. Though we today associate the very word with hypocrisy, it was not so at that time. The Pharisees were seen as the top of the lot, the cream of society, culture and religion. In today's world,

Pharisee faces would show up on weekly news shows and magazine covers. Also, Paul had defended the Jewish faith. His persecution against Christians would have made him a national hero. Young Hebrews would have seen Paul (Saul at the time) as the one to emulate.

Saul of Tarsus would have been a righteous hero by standards of the Law, but Paul the apostle had found a different and far superior gauge for determining righteousness. Paul abandoned his "works of righteousness" and sought the "righteousness of Christ."

D. Counted Loss for Christ (v. 7)

7. But what things were gain to me, those I counted loss for Christ.

Paul had found a totally different life, one that made everything in the past obsolete and worthless. The fact that he called everything of his own attainment a *loss* by no means indicates any regret on his part. "When Paul met Christ, he realized how futile were his good works and how sinful were his claims of righteousness" (Wiersbe). Paul was a totally different man now, living with different goals and standards. His treasures of the past may have brought him earthly honor, but they did not nothing to gain heaven or the favor of God.

At the same time, Paul did not mean to dishonor nor disclaim his Jewish heritage. He valued his Jewishness, and now saw himself as a completed Jew. Neither did Paul give up a quest for righteousness. He simply recognized that he now lived for a higher standard than even the Pharisees lived for.

II. SEEK TO KNOW CHRIST (Philippians 3:8-11)

A. Seek the Knowledge of Christ (v. 8)

8. Yea doubtless, and I count all things but loss for the excellency of the knowledge of Christ Jesus my

Lord: for whom I have suffered the loss of all things, and do count them but dung, that I may win Christ.

Paul now had a new set of goals—all of them having to do with knowing Christ better and more intimately. His encounter with the risen Christ on the road to Damascus had not been a dream or a fluke. It had really happened. A total transformation had taken place in his soul. He was no longer the same person he once was. Everything was now staked on this relationship with Christ. The word *count* in the Greek means "to assess, to evaluate."

Most people take little time to evaluate what is really important. They are so caught up by the everyday details that they miss the larger picture. Not so with Paul. Sitting in a jail cell gave him time to reflect on what was truly worth living for. The *things* he had given up included an esteemed position in the Jewish religious hierarchy, a reputation for faithful obedience to the laws and traditions of his heritage, and an enviable record of defense of the religion of his forefathers. He knew that none of those things, as commendable as they were on a human level, could give him what really counted—favor with God. Only the knowledge of Christ could do that.

The Greek word for *knowledge* here "speaks of a personal, experiential, and progressive knowledge. The Judaizers might have their rituals and rules, but Paul (and all true believers) had a wonderful personal relationship and fellowship with Christ Jesus himself" (*Life Application Commentary Series*). When a ship is tossed on a stormy sea and in danger of sinking, the sailors on board have to decide what is important and what is not. As valuable as some things may seem, "they are willing to throw them all overboard in order to save themselves" (*Barnes' Notes*).

B. Seek the Righteousness of Christ (v. 9)

9. And be found in him, not having mine own righteousness, which is of the law, but that which is through the faith of Christ, the righteousness which is of God by faith.

From early on in Paul's life, his goal had been righteousness. He had sought it as a Pharisee, but this was a self-righteousness based on human effort alone. It had only left him with a sense of incompleteness, failure, and an awareness of impossible attainment. He looked at his former life and saw nothing but bankruptcy. He had invested in stocks that had no value whatsoever. However, in coming to Christ, he saw that God applied Christ's righteousness *to his own account.* His sins had been nailed to the cross with Christ. They would no longer hold him in slavery. The wealth of heaven had been deposited into an account with his name on it.

Paul's anger at the Judaizers was not a personal grudge. It was more a frustration at the fact that, like the Jews as a whole, they refused to abandon their human efforts at becoming righteous. Instead of receiving the gift of Christ, they were trying to achieve holiness on their own. And they could not see the futility of their labors.

C. Seek the Fellowship of His Sufferings (v. 10)

10. That I may know him, and the power of his resurrection, and the fellowship of his sufferings, being made conformable unto his death.

Paul's encounter with the risen Christ on the road to Damascus had been the end of an old life but the beginning of a new one. The gospel he had once fought against was now the treasured truth he was dedicated to advancing. The intensity he had given to persecuting Christ (by persecuting Christians) was now equally directed toward knowing Christ and making new disciples to the faith.

In his former life Paul had lived by rules; now he lived by fellowship. His former life was marked by intense loneliness; his new life was filled with intense companionship. Everything was accounted to the resurrection power of Jesus.

If Paul suffered, he made no complaint, for Jesus had suffered as well. Suffering only intensified his ability to relate to Jesus. It was a privilege to suffer for his Lord. He had gained far more than he had lost. There were no regrets. Everything of his old life was nothing but rubbish compared to what he now had.

D. Seek the Resurrection of the Dead (v. 11)

11. If by any means I might attain unto the resurrection of the dead.

Paul lived knowing there was a prize to be gained—resurrection from the dead and life eternal with Christ in heaven. Not only were attainments of this life garbage, they were temporary as well. There was no future in them.

Those who live for this life only are never going to be satisfied. Putting one's treasure in Christ is the only way to permanency. "The fact that Christ has risen from the dead, when fully believed, will produce a sure hope that we also shall be raised, and will animate us to bear trials for his sake, with the assurance that we shall be raised up as he was" (*Barnes' Notes*).

Resurrection from the dead and eternal life with Christ was the absolute goal of Paul's life. He understood that resurrection from the grave is the essence of what distinguishes the Christian faith from other religions. The motivating factor of his existence was to participate fully and gloriously in such an event.

The phrase "might attain" by no

means indicates doubt on Paul's part. This was rather a way of humbly showing his trust in what Christ had promised. Paul was not a doubter. He fully trusted that just as Jesus had been raised from the dead, so would he also.

The resurrection Paul speaks of here refers to the righteous dead arising when Jesus returns to the earth. Of course, most believers of Paul's day fully expected Christ to return for them before experiencing death. Was Paul aware that the Lord's return might be in some distant future? Certainly. He had already dealt with this issue in his first letter to the Thessalonians (see ch. 4). Many believers had already died, some of natural causes and others in martyrdom for the faith. Paul lived with a daily expectation that Christ could return at any moment, but also with the realization that death was a part of life. Either way, Christ's resurrection, and subsequently every believer's personal resurrection, ensured eternity.

III. STRIVE TO BE LIKE CHRIST (Philippians 3:12-21)

A. Winning the Race (vv. 12-16)

(Philippians 3:15, 16 is not included in the printed text.)

12. Not as though I had already attained, either were already perfect: but I follow after, if that I may apprehend that for which also I am apprehended of Christ Jesus.

13. Brethren, I count not myself to have apprehended: but this one thing I do, forgetting those things which are behind, and reaching forth unto those things which are before,

14. I press toward the mark for the prize of the high calling of God in Christ Jesus.

Thus far in this chapter of Philippians, Paul has given an autobiographical sketch of his life—before and after Christ changed him. Now, the tone of his words changes to that of winning a race. Yes, Christ had changed him and revolutionized his life. Still, there was a race to be won or lost.

In these verses we see Paul pressing toward the finish line. He knew he had lost valuable time in those years before his conversion. Those were years he could have given to spreading the gospel and making disciples. Still, he decided there was no merit in regretting what could have been. He forgot the past and concentrated on the future. Every effort had to be put forth to win the prize.

There is a paradox here, however. Paul was not talking about earning salvation. He just finished telling his readers that righteousness cannot be gained by keeping the Law. Righteousness is imputed to the individual when he or she accepts Christ as Savior. This is not a race to gain citizenship. It is a race to achieve the goals God has set for believers. Paul did not merely want to just barely make it into heaven. No, he wanted to achieve everything in this life that had been planned for him.

Paul knew there was a great responsibility to his calling. He had been sent to carry the gospel to the Gentile world. He had even been privileged to have the Lord appear to him personally in his conversion. There was a great race to be won. He knew every effort had to be expended to win that race. He wasn't afraid of losing his citizenship in heaven, but neither did he want to disappoint his Lord for not completing everything he had been sent to do.

Too many Christians walk about with a false satisfaction to their lives. This is because they compare themselves to others—usually those who don't appear as "righteous" as themselves. Paul knew better than to sink into such a folly. Certainly he could have "proved" himself righteous by comparison to others. However, no one else had the same call and responsibility. Paul knew he had not arrived, no matter how much he had accomplished or how many sufferings he had endured. He knew he had to fulfill the specific calling on his life.

B. An Example to Follow (vv. 17-19)

(Philippians 3:17-19 is not included in the printed text.)

While not bragging, Paul recognized that his new life could be followed as an example of dedication to Christ. In his old life he had been a great persecutor of believers, but since his Damascus-road experience, he had focused everything on becoming more and more like Christ. He challenged the Philippians to emulate the pattern of himself and others like him.

This should not be seen as egotism. The fact is, there was little written doctrine (the four Gospels were either not yet written or not yet in circulation) at this time; so people had only the words and examples of leaders to follow. Paul's own life was a practical guide.

Paul warned that many who proclaimed Christ bore no godly fruit. Their only fruit was earth-centered. He wept as he described this type of people. What were they like?

• They were captivated by the cares, concerns, and comforts of this life.

• They were living to satisfy their fleshly desires.

• They were heading toward destruction. Worse still, they seemed unaware of their own laxity.

Paul called these people "enemies of the cross of Christ" (v. 18). In contrast, true Christians live not for this life but for the glory of heaven. Real believers will always have heaven on their mind. At the same time, they will be the ones who do the most for the Kingdom while still here.

Mark Buchanan said, "People fixated on earth generally do not have this deep taproot of courage and conviction. Seldom do they stand down Pharaohs, Caesars, Stalins, with nothing but a stick in their hand or a cross on their back. Nor do they generally look after widows and orphans in distress or care for the dying or feed the hungry. This is left for the heavenly-minded to do" (*Things Unseen*, Multnomah Press).

C. Heavenly-Mindedness (vv. 20, 21)

20. For our conversation is in heaven; from whence also we look for the Saviour, the Lord Jesus Christ:

21. Who shall change our vile body, that it may be fashioned like unto his glorious body, according to the working whereby he is able even to subdue all things unto himself.

The word *conversation* in verse 20 means "citizenship." The hope of heaven creates a gravitational pull elsewhere, but we are at the same time anxious to carry others with us. It is only as we look forward to being changed from this body to a glorified one that we have the moral fortitude to work and fulfill our callings. Being heavenly-minded is "the best regimen for keeping our hearts whole, our minds clear. It allows us to enjoy earth's pleasures without debauchery. It allows us to endure life's agonies without despair" (Buchanan). With our eyes set on heaven we gain a wide-scope perspective on what is happening on earth. It enables us to distinguish the treasures from the trinkets of earth.

Paul rejoiced in spite of his circumstances (imprisonment, suffering, etc.) because he trusted God for the future. He allowed nothing to discourage him. People who don't understand the joy of Christ may rejoice when things are going well, but when the bottom falls out, so do they. They sink into depression, doubt and despair. True believers transcend above the circumstances, knowing that nothing on earth is permanent. Jesus helps them manage adversity without losing heart.

GOLDEN TEXT HOMILY

"I COUNT ALL THINGS BUT LOSS FOR THE EXCELLENCY OF THE KNOWLEDGE OF CHRIST JESUS MY LORD" (Philippians 3:8).

What language could express with greater contrast the goals of life before and after conversion? Paul saw every earth-related thing as subject to the laws of disintegration and decay. On the other hand, he saw that Christ gives life and hope.

Is there something which you cannot quite consent to give up for Christ? Then turn your thinking around, and consider the gain of having Christ himself as your own. Doing that intelligently, you will surely see that no one can afford to miss Christ.

Without Christ, all will be lost; with Christ, nothing of real value can be lost.—**Selected**

SENTENCE SERMONS

KNOWING CHRIST reveals the true value of all other attachments.
                                    —Selected

LOVE FOR THE LORD is not an ethereal, intellectual, dreamlike thing; it is the most intense, most vital, most passionate love of which the human heart is capable.

—Oswald Chambers

LOVE IS THE ONLY FIRE that is hot enough to melt the iron obstinacy of a creature's will.

—Alexander MacLaren

EVANGELISM APPLICATION

BELIEVERS WHO HAVE A PASSION FOR CHRIST WILL OBEY THE

GREAT COMMISSION.

We hear so much today about *specialization*. Every field of endeavor has many specialized areas. For instance, no one simply becomes a medical doctor anymore. Every physician has a specific concentration of expertise. And even that particular concentration is further broken down. One might be a brain surgeon, a thoracic surgeon, a spinal surgeon, and so on—all surgeons, but all very different in their training and proficiency. The areas are so narrowly defined that there is almost no overlap. A brain surgeon can do little for someone with a broken leg.

The same is somewhat true about our individual callings as Christian servants. Certainly we are all called to carry out the Great Commission as a whole. However, our giftings and talents are varied. We each have a race to win, a job to do. There are preachers, teachers, writers, administrators, singers, organizers, cooks, janitors, secretaries, and so on—all with different callings, but all who make up the body of Christ. None are called to run anyone else's race. Neither are we called to compare our calling to anyone else's. We are varied, but we are all valuable. We must run our individual race, not to earn salvation, but to fulfill all that Christ has planned for us to do.

ILLUMINATING THE LESSON

C.S. Lewis wrote: "If you read history, you will find that the Christians who did the most for the present world were just those who thought the most of the next. The apostles themselves, who set on foot the conversion of the Roman Empire, the great men who built up the Middle Ages, the English evangelicals who abolished the slave trade, all left their mark on earth, precisely because their minds were occupied with heaven. It is since Christians have largely ceased to think of the other world that they have become so ineffective in this" (*Mere Christianity*).

Paul filled his heart with heaven, even as he labored the most vigorously on this earth. To be of any real earthly good, one must be free from the fear of personal loss, or any other inclination toward earth. If we really want to see revival, we must set our eyes on heaven. When nothing else matters but heaven and pleasing Christ, then we are free of the ties of earth and can do the Lord's bidding without restraint. That is why Paul insisted that believers rejoice in every circumstance. Rejoice because earth is only temporary, but the joys of heaven are forever.

DAILY BIBLE READINGS

M. Value of Relationship With Christ.
Matthew 13:44-46

T. Obedience Leads to Knowledge.
John 15:9-15

W. Eternal Life.
John 17:1-5

T. Knowledge of Christ Is Wisdom.
1 Corinthians 1:18-21

F. Compelled by Love.
2 Corinthians 5:13-17

S. Imitate God: Love Like Christ.
Ephesians 5:1-10

TRUTH SEARCH
Creatively Teaching the Word

FOCUS ACTIVITY

Items needed: Marker board, markers

Write the following words on the board: *politics, sports, food, money, hobbies, work,* and *family.*

Look at the words I've written. What do they all have in common? Let students suggest answers.

These are some of the things people are passionate about. How can you tell if you have a passion for something?

At the top of the board write *Jesus Christ.*

Above all else, we should have a passion for Jesus Christ. Through Paul's example, we will discover what it means to love Christ above all else.

DISCUSSION QUESTIONS

Reject All Substitutes
(Philippians 3:1-7)

1. What does it mean to "rejoice in the Lord" (v. 1)?

2. Why was it *safe* (a safeguard) for Paul to pass on his teachings to the Philippians in written form (v. 1)?

3. Why did Paul use the terms "dogs" and "evil workers" to refer to those who insisted that Christians must be circumcised (v. 2)?

4. According to verse 3, who is "the circumcision"?

5. What does it mean to "have no confidence in the flesh" (v. 3)?

6. According to verses 4-6, what were the religious things in which Paul had once trusted?

7. How had Paul's world changed, and why (v. 7)?

Seek to Know Christ
(Philippians 3:8-11)

1. What was Paul now living for (v. 8)?

2. What was now *dung* (rubbish) to Paul, and why?

3. What are the differences between the two forms of righteousness discussed in verse 9?

4. What does it mean to "fellowship" with Christ "[in] his sufferings, being made conformable unto his death" (v. 10)?

5. How could Paul experience "the power of [Christ's] resurrection" in this life (v. 10)?

6. What was Paul's ultimate hope (v. 11)?

Strive to Be Like Christ
(Philippians 3:12-21)

1. What has Christ *apprehended* (taken hold of) for us, and how can we now take hold of it (v. 12)?

2. What did Paul strive to forget about, and why (v. 13)?

3. Describe the goal we must strive for (v. 14).

4. How should *perfect* (mature) believers live (vv. 15, 16)?

5. Whom should Christians follow as role models, and of whom should they be cautious of (vv. 17-19)?

6. Where is the Christian's citizenship ("conversation"), and what promises do Christians have concerning their future (vv. 20, 21)?

Jer. 19, 15
Gal. 6, 7